Perspectives on the American Community

SECOND EDITION

Perspectives on the American Community

A BOOK OF READINGS

Edited by ROLAND L. WARREN

BRANDEIS UNIVERSITY

RAND McNALLY & COMPANY

Chicago. New York. San Francisco. London

RAND McNALLY SOCIOLOGY SERIES

Edgar F. Borgatta, *Advisory Editor*

F H

Preface

A new edition of a widely accepted book of readings affords an opportunity to ponder the developments which have taken place in the community field in the years since the earlier edition. That first edition, published in 1966, began with the words:

> *In a way, this book of readings represents the record of a journey— a journey through the enormously rich and varied literature on the American community, a journey which the editor invites the reader to retrace with him by this means.*

Less than a decade has elapsed since those words were written. In the meantime, a tremendous resurgence has taken place in the interest which people take in their localities, in the nature of the actions which take place there, and in the nature of local decision-making processes. Paradoxically, this resurgence of interest in local communities has accompanied the increasing realization that what happens on the local scene is both induced and constrained by events taking place on the regional, national, and international level.

Somewhat less than half of the selections in this new edition were not included in the old one. In adding these, still others had to be removed, though with reluctance. The changes reflect not only the appearance of new and in part more sophisticated materials, but also the desire to add a section on alternative community forms. The sections on social change and on citizen action reflect the lively interest in these fields and the extensive publications which have appeared.

As in the original edition, many of the selections treat issues of intense current interest and controversy. But this book was not compiled simply to respond to current topics of interest or as a handbook for social change. Rather, it gathers together some of the more important attempts to conceptualize community life and some of the more generalizable analyses of community processes.

The more fateful the problem grows of how daily life is experienced where one lives and labors, the more important it becomes to seek a valid understanding of why things are as they are, so that we may go on to consider how they may become worthy of the best that is in us.

Both the earlier edition and the present edition of *Perspectives on the*

v

American Community were compiled during a period when the editor was the holder of a research scientist award from the National Institute of Mental Health, to which organization grateful acknowledgment is hereby expressed. For the typings and retypings, for the numerous letters to authors and publishers for permission to reprint, and for many other things, special thanks are due Mrs. Eleanor Fraser and Mrs. Anne Freeman, whose patience and persistence were admirable. Thanks are also due my wife, Margaret Hodges Warren, for her translation of the Bahrdt selection and for the preparation of the index.

ROLAND L. WARREN

October, 1972

Table of Contents

SECTION ONE

Basic Approaches to the Community

Introduction

Although there has been a rich succession of studies using the "city" or the "community" as their field of focus, it is still possible to raise the most fundamental questions: What is a city? What is a community? A number of circumstances contribute to the difficulties of definition and conceptualization.

First, even the most superficial consideration indicates the serious problems involved: the lack of a formally structured organization corresponding to the unit of study, the lack of clear geographic boundaries to delineate the locus of study, and especially the spilling over of social relationships beyond political boundaries.

Second, there are a number of different kinds of dimensions which all seem appropriate to the question of definition but which do not coincide as an aggregate: types of social relationships and behavior patterns, types and distributions of people and functions, means of sustenance, relationships to other population clusters, and so on through a long list. Depending on which dimensions are chosen as the crucial ones, different conceptions emerge.

The selections in Section One all speak to this question of fundamental conceptualization. They are not so much concerned with definitions as with a systematic examination of one or another fundamental aspect of the city or the community. In aggregate, they indicate some of the important ways of thinking about the community. They illustrate that there are many such ways, and suggest that no single way can be expected to account for all of the varied strands which make up their object of study.

Which way of thinking captures the essence of the social reality which we term the city? Max Weber had a stimulating answer: The city is essentially a settlement with a market. It is the market that characterizes urban life, rather than size, degree of impersonality, or other physical or social characteristics. Two things stand out about Weber's approach. It is a definition essentially in terms of social processes—the processes surrounding the exchange of goods and money in the market. And it is a definition which seeks the essence of the city in its historical origins. In his famous work *The City,* Weber did not so much explore the social consequences of the market in conditioning the nature of urban institutions, attitudes, and behavior patterns as he examined the various socio-historical contexts in which city life emerged.

Max Weber nowhere made a systematic analysis of the implications of the concept of the city as a market for the social and psychological aspects of urban life. Hans Paul Bahrdt, a German sociologist, has done so, and for this reason an excerpt from his book has been especially translated for this volume.

After considering Weber's approach, Bahrdt expands it with an analysis of public and private activity and their interrelationships. "A city is a settlement in which the total life and therefore the daily life as well show a tendency toward polarization, that is, either into a social aggregate of public activity or into one of private activity. . . . On the other hand, the areas of living which can be characterized as neither public nor private lose in importance."

Bahrdt's prototype of public activity is the market as described by Max Weber. From the psycho-social implications of the market as an "open system" of human interaction, Bahrdt derives his analysis of public activity.

He distinguishes such relationships from those which prevail in a closed system, "in which practically all social contacts are brought about by a tight, theoretically leakproof network of personal ties." In such a system, as in many rural villages, "a privatization is impossible, that is, a closing out of whole areas of life from the all-pervasive social connections." It is precisely in the city, with its public relationships approximating those of participants in a market, that the private sphere can be separated from the public. "The positive cultural contribution of the development of public life and activity consists in good measure in developing modes of communication which form a bridge across the social distance which exists and remains—and indeed should remain."

Although Bahrdt's theoretical approach is clearly in the Weberian tradition, his deftness and care in deriving social-psychological aspects of city life from a theory of the basic social relationships which prevail lends his work a strong affinity to that of Simmel.

One can approach the nature of city life from an examination of the differences in experience, attitude, and behavior which characterize urban life as differentiated from rural. This approach was taken by Georg Simmel, a German sociologist who had great influence on the development of sociological theory in Europe and America, and especially on the development of a theory of urbanism. His purpose was not so much to define the metropolis as to explore the relationship between the urban environment and the psychic experience of the inhabitants. Thus, his approach was mainly social-psychological. He showed how such characteristics as intensification of nervous stimulation, intellectuality, pecuniary evaluation, emphasis on a precise time schedule, a blasé attitude, individuality, division of labor, and casualness of contact are all interrelated in the life of the metropolis.

Although Simmel's paragraphs are tightly reasoned, they are also replete with rich and colorful images and penetrating observations. Thus, in indicating the tendency to evaluate things in monetary terms, he wrote, "All things float with equal specific gravity in the constantly moving stream of money." Speaking of reserve in connection with the multiplicity of casual contacts, he observed, "What appears in the metropolitan style of life directly as dissociation is in reality only one of its elemental forms of socialization."

Simmel was dispassionate in his analysis, asserting that "it is not our task either to accuse or to pardon, but only to understand." He pointed out that "today metropolitan man is 'free' in a spiritualized and refined sense, in contrast to the pettiness and prejudices which hem in the small-town man," but "it is obviously only the obverse of this freedom if, under certain circumstances, one nowhere feels as lonely and lost as in the metropolitan crowd."

The selection by Robert Ezra Park on "Human Ecology" may seem somewhat abstract and not sufficiently explicit to help capture substantial parts of the significant social aspects of the city. Based largely on Park's ecological conceptualization of city life, there developed over a period of two decades an intensive and exciting series of research investigations into the life of the great city of Chicago. This is of historical importance in the development or urban sociology. More than that, though, Park's ecological approach still has relevance as a valid way of conceiving the human community. Just as plants and animals occupying the same habitat come into competing but reciprocally meaningful relationships to each other and to the surrounding natural environment—relationships which constitute a "community" in that their activities quite inadvertently become intertwined in a "natural economy"—so also do the human inhabitants of a city. The nature of this interrelationship, associated especially with the division of labor, is in itself an important aspect of the urban scene. Park was particularly emphatic that although the concept "balance of nature" may be useful as a heuristic device at any particular moment of investigation, changes in the interrelationships of the habitants are taking place almost constantly, changes which can be examined using such basic ecological concepts as competition, dominance, and succession.

But beyond the economy of the biotic human community there is the cultural community. "In human as contrasted with animal societies, competition and the freedom of the individual is limited on every level above the biotic by custom and consensus."

It is precisely in this dynamic interplay between cultural values, controls, and behavior patterns and the ecological processes involving sustenance and the "natural economy" that the way opens for an ecology of urban community life. "Human ecology is, fundamentally, an attempt to investigate the processes by which the biotic balance and the social equilibrium (1) are maintained once they are achieved and (2) the processes by which, when the biotic balance and the social equilibrium are disturbed, the transition is made from one relatively stable order to another."

Norton E. Long, a political scientist, has contributed a colorful and imaginative perspective on the community by combining the ecological approach with the concept of local activities as a series of different, interrelated games. His use of the "game" analogy is not related directly to the recent developments in "game theory" as a method of calculation and decision-making. Rather, it is closer to the current theoretical formulation which sees the community as a social system, itself comprised of various subsystems, many of which have important ties to systems outside the locality. In such terms, Long seems to be saying that there are a number of identifiable social systems operating at the locality level, each with its own values, goals, norms, and behavior patterns. These systems stand in symbiotic relationship to one another and support each other in largely inadvertent ways. But Long is quite sufficiently explicit in his own terms: "The ecology of games in the local territorial system accomplishes unplanned but largely functional results. The games and their players mesh in their particular pursuits to bring about over-all results; the territorial system is fed and ordered. Its inhabitants are rational within limited areas and, pursuing the ends of these areas, accomplish socially functional ends."

Long is able, without belaboring his points, to integrate his line of discourse with major recent developments in ecological, power structure, and social system theory. Thus, although the text reads like an engaging article by an expert stylist and storyteller, his incisive remarks are interwoven with important theoretical considerations.

Principally, the analogy with a series of games and their players and rules provides a readily understandable means of getting at specific areas of community interest and acknowledging their interrelations, while escaping the need for saying everything at once.

Talcott Parsons has never written extensively on the local community. In the brief excerpt from the beginning of his essay on "The Principal Structures of Community," he lays out a rationale consistent with his general theory of action. It is interesting to note that he deliberately avoids taking the community as a discrete, organized entity—what he would call a collectivity. Rather, he raises the question of the locality aspect of every concrete social collectivity. He then goes on to examine the territorial and the personal aspects, the latter in terms of the concept of role. The subsequent development of his discourse is a tight, coherent piece which resists breaking or excerpting, but it is too long to reprint in this volume.

For our purposes, though, the few paragraphs quoted offer a significant approach to the community in their very avoidance of a consideration of a specific territorial entity, concentrating rather on social relationships which are associated with the locality aspects of various kinds of human collective-ities. Whether or not the specific formulation which Parsons gives this ap-proach is to be followed, it constitutes an important attempt to offer an alternative to the analysis of the community as a discrete territorial entity, a kind of conceptualization which is becoming increasingly difficult and less promising as the growing local ties to national organizations, the separation of residence from work, and the absence of clearly delineable geographic boundaries become more and more apparent in American society.

Rather than studying the community as a structure within which vari-ous types of social process occur, would it not be possible to study it in its dynamic aspects: not What is? but What happens? This is the approach of the interactional conception of the community, represented by the article by Harold F. Kaufman. Kaufman's article is particularly rich in citations from current literature on the community. Considering the community as the field or arena for a certain type of interaction, just one type among many, he distinguishes this field on the basis of six characteristics. These can be used to delineate the field of "community" interaction, as distinguished from other types of interactional fields, and they can also be employed to assess the extent to which a community field as such exists in a given locality. He also gives a five-phase model for the analysis of specific community actions.

The criticism which Kaufman levels at most community studies is typical of the viewpoint of the interactional approach: "Most so-called community context studies have been in the community but not of it. That is, they have used a locality as a basis of sampling but there has been no identification of the phenomena under study with the interactional com-munity."

The selection by Blaine E. Mercer examines communities from a struc-tural-functional point of view. It considers structure as "both persistence and an order of change," and therefore defines community function as having to do with "the processes which contribute to persistence and to change in the community or in the larger society of which the community is a part." The selection is a chapter from a book on the community, and Mercer has used it as the place for laying out his simple, but basic, con-ceptual approach. He views the community as "a dynamic, functioning system of the interrelationships of persons," and he emphasizes the functions which the community system performs on three different levels: those it performs for the surrounding larger society of which it is a part; the functional interrelations of people within the community itself; and the functions of the community in relation to its constituent groups and individuals. Mercer thus views the community as a social system of persistence and predictable change which at the same time is a subsystem of the larger society, itself an ordered relationship of persistence and change.

Robert A. Nisbet's selection, on the other hand, takes a more global view. The author is representative of a large group of students of the community who not only concern themselves with seeking to understand the structure and function of communities and the changes which are occurring in community life, but who are concerned about what they see. They admonish that the changes which are occurring are destructive of important aspects of human association, especially that association which occurs among people in a relatively enduring, face-to-face relationship. As more and more activities become oriented toward state and national organizations, many of them governmental, the questions which are left for purely local resolution are relatively less important. Having fewer things of importance in common, local people have a smaller basis for mutual association. The locality becomes largely irrelevant for the important issues of the day.

Nisbet points out that basic values of American culture can be inculcated only through meaningful face-to-face relationships. They cannot thrive "in a sociological vacuum." He criticizes the concept of individual freedom represented by the philosophers of the eighteenth century, pointing out that in reacting against nationalistic absolutism they formulated a philosophy of freedom which was essentially atomistic. Nisbet asserts that the term *social disorganization* is highly misleading when used to describe the larger developments which he portrays, for certainly just the opposite of social disorganization is occurring at the national level, with the growing power of national government and large-scale economic and voluntary associations. But at the community level, one is confronted with the evaporation of many vital relationships. It is necessary to seek deliberately for viable forms of community, for "neither moral values, nor fellowship, nor freedom can easily flourish apart from the existence of diverse communities each capable of enlisting the loyalties of its members."

In 1968, George A. Hillery, Jr., published his *Communal Organizations: A Study of Local Societies,* a work of profound importance for community theory. It brought into focus two ideas which had been largely neglected or left indefinite in the literature on communities. First was the idea that communities (he called them "vills," because of the ambiguity in the word community) differ from formal organizations in that the latter are oriented toward the attainment of a specific goal, and communities are not. The difference, he asserts, is one of kind, not merely of degree. Communities as such simply do not have goals at all, while formal organizations do. Vills are characterized by three principal components: space, families, and cooperation. Among vills, cities are differentiated from folk villages by the type of cooperation which prevails, the former being cooperation through contract, and the latter being generalized cooperation.

The second idea which Hillery developed systematically was that the distinction between goal-oriented and non-goal oriented organizations existed not only at the community level, but at levels both more inclusive and less inclusive than the community. Thus, to parallel the series of more inclusive formal organizations extending from the small formal organization to the state, he juxtaposed a series of *communal* or non-goal-oriented organizations extending from the family to the nation. Hence, vills are simply one form of communal organizations.

In the excerpt from his book presented here, Hillery sets forth a typology of organizations which includes these two dimensions as well as the dimension of institutionalization, or the extent to which organizations are structured by means of an extensive pattern of norms. These three dimensions form the basis for a systematic typology of human groups, in which communities, or vills, can be located in comparison with other types of human groups on all three dimensions.

1. The Nature of the City[1]

BY MAX WEBER

ECONOMIC CHARACTER OF THE CITY: MARKET SETTLEMENT

The many definitions of the city have only one element in common: namely that the city consists simply of a collection of one or more separate dwellings but is a relatively closed settlement. Customarily, though not exclusively, in cities the houses are built closely to each other, often, today, wall to wall. This massing of elements interpenetrates the everyday concept of the "city" which is thought of quantitatively as a large locality. In itself this is not imprecise for the city often represents a locality and dense settlement of dwellings forming a colony so extensive that personal reciprocal acquaintance of the inhabitants is lacking. However, if interpreted in this way only very large localities could qualify as cities; moreover it would be ambiguous, for various cultural factors determine the size at which "impersonality" tends to appear. Precisely this impersonality was absent in many historical localities possessing the legal character of cities. Even in contemporary Russia there are villages comprising many thousands of inhabitants which are, thus, larger than many old "cities" (for example, in the Polish colonial area of the German East) which had only a few hundred inhabitants. Both in terms of what it would include and what it would exclude size alone can hardly be sufficient to define the city.

Economically defined, the city is a settlement the inhabitants of which live primarily off trade and commerce rather than agriculture. However, it is not altogether proper to call all localities "cities" which are dominated by trade and commerce. This would include in the concept "city" colonies made up of family members and maintaining a single, practically hereditary trade establishment such as the "trade villages" of Asia and Russia. It is necessary to add a certain "versatility" of practiced trades to the character-

Reprinted with permission of the editors and The Free Press from *The City*, by Max Weber, translated and edited by Don Martindale and Gertrud Neuwirth, pp. 71–74. Copyright © 1958 by The Free Press, a Corporation. Footnotes have been renumbered.

[1] First published in *Archiv für Sozialwissenschaft und Sozialpolitik*, Vol. 47, p. 621 ff. (1921). Last edition: *Wirtschaft und Gesellschaft* (Tübingen: J. C. B. Mohr, 1956) Vol. 2, p. 735 ff.—All the notes in this translation are those of the editors.

istics of the city. However, this in itself does not appear suitable as the single distinguishing characteristic of the city either.

Economic versatility can be established in at least two ways: by the presence of a feudal estate or a market. The economic and political needs of a feudal or princely estate can encourage specialization in trade products in providing a demand for which work is performed and goods are bartered. However, even though the *oikos* of a lord or prince is as large as a city, a colony of artisans and small merchants bound to villein services is not customarily called a "city" even though historically a large proportion of important "cities" originated in such settlements.[2] In cities of such origin the products for a prince's court often remained a highly important, even chief, source of income for the settlers.

The other method of establishing economic versatility is more generally important for the "city"; this is the existence in the place of settlement of a regular rather than an occasional exchange of goods. The market becomes an essential component in the livelihood of the settlers. To be sure, not every "market" converted the locality in which it was found into a city. The periodic fairs and yearly foreign-trade markets at which traveling merchants met at fixed times to sell their goods in wholesale or retail lots to each other or to consumers often occurred in places which we would call "villages."

Thus, we wish to speak of a "city" only in cases where the local inhabitants satisfy an economically substantial part of their daily wants in the local market, and to an essential extent by products which the local population and that of the immediate hinterland produced for sale in the market or acquired in other ways. In the meaning employed here the "city" is a market place. The local market forms the economic center of the colony in which, due to the specialization in economic products, both the non-urban population and urbanites satisfy their wants for articles of trade and commerce. Wherever it appeared as a configuration different from the country it was normal for the city to be both a lordly or princely residence as well as a market place. It simultaneously possessed centers of both kinds, *oikos* and market and frequently in addition to the regular market it also served as periodic foreign markets of traveling merchants. In the meaning of the word here, the city is a "market settlement."

Often the existence of a market rests upon the concessions and guarantees of protection by a lord or prince. They were often interested in such things as a regular supply of foreign commercial articles and trade products, in tolls, in moneys for escorts and other protection fees, in market tariffs and

---

[2] For the place of the household or oikos-economy cf. Max Weber, *General Economic History*, trans. Frank H. Knight (Glencoe: The Free Press, 1950) pp. 48, 58, 124 ff., 131, 146, 162 and Johannes Hase Broek, *Griechische Wirtschaftsgeschichte* (Tübingen: J. C. B. Mohr, 1931) pp. 15, 24, 27, 29, 38, 46, 69, 284.

taxes from law suits. However, the lord or prince might also hope to profit from the local settlement of tradesmen and merchants capable of paying taxes and, as soon as the market settlement arose around the market, from land rents arising therefrom. Such opportunities were of especial importance to the lord or prince since they represented chances for monetary revenues and the increase in his treasure of precious metal.

However, the city could lack any attachment, physical or otherwise, to a lordly or princely residence. This was the case when it originated as a pure market settlement at a suitable intersection point (*Umschlageplatz*)[3] where the means of transportation were changed by virtue of concession to non-resident lords or princes or usurpation by the interested parties themselves. This could assume the form of concessions to entrepreneurs—permitting them to lay out a market and recruit settlers for it. Such capitalistic establishment of cities was especially frequent in medieval frontier areas, particularly in East, North, and Central Europe. Historically, though not as a rule, the practice has appeared throughout the world.

Without any attachment to the court of a prince or without princely concessions, the city could arise through the association of foreign invaders, naval warriors, or commercial settlers or, finally, native parties interested in the carrying trade. This occurred frequently in the early Middle Ages. The resultant city could be a pure market place. However, it is more usual to find large princely or patrimonial households and a market conjoined. In this case the eminent household as one contact point of the city could satisfy its want either primarily by means of a natural economy (that is by villein service or natural service or taxes placed upon the artisans and merchants dependent on it) or it could supply itself more or less secondarily by barter in the local market as that market's most important buyer. The more pronounced the latter relation the more distinct the market foundation of the city looms and the city ceases by degrees to be a mere appendaged market settlement alongside the *oikos*. Despite attachment to the large household it then became a market city. As a rule the quantitative expansion of the original princely city and its economic importance go hand in hand with an increase in the satisfaction of wants in the market by the princely household and other large urban households attached to that of the prince as courts of vassals or major officials.

[3] Charles H. Cooley's theory of transportation took the break in communication either physical or economic as the most critical of all factors for the formation of the city.

2. Public Activity and Private Activity as Basic Forms of City Association

BY HANS PAUL BAHRDT

MAX WEBER'S DEFINITION OF THE CITY

Perhaps the city planner might be able to dispense with theoretical considerations of a sociological nature and rely upon his sound good judgment if the intellectual world in which he lives were naive. But it is not. On all sides, as we have seen, he comes up against storehouses of intellectual analyses which often claim to be no more than matters of simple experience, while as a matter of fact they are of cultural-philosophic, social-scientific, or ideological origin.

If he is not to lose his way in this maze of judgments and prejudgments, then he needs, among other things, a sociological concept of the city.[1] Max Weber, the master formulator of sociological concepts, gave an economic definition at the beginning of his famous discussion of the city.[2] All settlements should be classified as cities in which "the resident population satisfies an economically important part of its daily needs in the local market, and to a large extent with products which have been produced or otherwise obtained for sale in the market by the residents and by the residents of the nearby countryside." Thus, an identifying characteristic of the city is the market. However, not every settlement which has a market is a city, but only those in which the daily economic life of the inhabitants is closely related to the market activity. Rural communities in which there is an annual market from time to time are not cities. The following also do not qualify as cities: the huge villages of the Ukraine or the princes' or bishops' great oikoses (large households). We can add a modern example: the large

Reprinted with permission of the author and publisher from Hans Paul Bahrdt, *Die moderne Grossstadt: Soziologische Überlegungen zum Städtebau* (Reinbek bei Hamburg: Rowohlt Taschenbuch Verlag GmbH, 1961), pp. 36–43, 61–62, translated by Margaret H. Warren.

[1] On the definition of the city: Article "Stadt," in *Hdwb. der Soz. Wiss.*, Bd. 9, Tübingen-Göttingen, 1956; W. Sombart, "Städtische Siedlung, Stadt," in *Hdwb. der Soziologie*, published by A. Vierkandt, Stuttgart, 1931. On the concept of the metropolis: E. Pfeil, *Grossstadtforschung*, Bremen-Horn, 1950, p. 13 ff.

[2] M. Weber, *Wirtschaft und Gesellschaft*, 2. Halbbd, 4. Auflage, Tübingen, 1956, p. 732. [See Selection 1 above.—R. L. W.]

camps of barracks, housing many thousands of soldiers on military installations, which are actually "large oikoses" too—these Max Weber would certainly not classify as cities.

What is accomplished by this definition? At first glance the sociologist is left unsatisfied. Does it not select only a single characteristic? Does not the economic interpretation of the concept lack precisely the decisive critical characteristics of the social structure?[3] It seems to us, however, that Max Weber has struck the right chord with his definition and has provided a fruitful starting point for further thought. He himself, however, did not draw the sociological conclusions in subsequent amplifications. These amplifications treated chiefly the differences between the cities of the orient, of the ancients, and of the Middle Ages. Of course we know that for Max Weber the market phenomenon always played an important role, namely as a source of social dynamics, for example as a hypothesis for the origin of social classes.[4]

THE MARKET AS THE EARLIEST FORM OF PUBLIC ACTIVITY

The market is a social phenomenon of a peculiar sort. It is a lasting institutionalized arrangement, in which repeatedly certain social contacts take place according to definite principles. It lacks, however, the formal structure of a social group as well as its quasi-subjectivity, which permits the identification of the individual with the group. To be sure, the individual in charge or the community of those taking part in the market process can determine the conditions under which the market operates. They can appoint a policing body to supervise the observance of the rules of the game. But it is the individual who must play the game; he enters into the market as an individual in order to buy or sell. This is the case even when the market is not "free," that is to say, when prices are manipulated by a market-controlling entrepreneur. So long as it is not irrevocably determined from whom a given amount of a certain product is to be bought, one can speak of a market.

The market is thus a form of distribution through trade wherein the traders are to a certain extent masters of their decisions; that is to say, they remain economic initiators, however small the area of their option may be. Herein lies a great difference from the large oikos.

For true trade, it is necessary to have at least the fiction of equivalence, from which the oikos' system of provision can and as a rule does differentiate itself completely. It is regulated according to a design which controls the whole oikos; in principle this design could also be derived from the

---

[3] Cf. the critique by R. König, *Grundformen der Gesellschaft: die Gemeinde,* Rowohlts deutsche Enzyklopädie, Bd. 79 (1958) p. 76.

[4] Max Weber, *op. cit.*, p. 531 ff.

decision of a democratic majority, as in an Israeli kibbutz. No matter how much freedom might be permitted the oikos members, they are not economic initiators in so far as they are provided for by the oikos economy.

From the partial freedom of the traders in the market there derives a further result: a partial choice of contact-making among all those who attend the market as buyers or sellers. The seller cries his wares to all that can hear him. The buyer goes from stand to stand. It is possible for direct contacts to be made between people who do not know one another, that is to say, where no one knows exactly how to classify the other.

Voluntary, fleeting social contacts conducted according to strict rules, made between individuals who are almost unknown to each other, and at the same time with the possibility of ignoring the social stratum to which these individuals otherwise belong, are not to be taken for granted. We find them also, to be sure, in archaic, strongly delineated social systems. Even primitive cultures, where it is not possible to speak of city formation, have markets. But here they are a great exception to the rule. The market is the earliest form of public activity in a sociological sense, and it assumes a special place in closed social structures which otherwise do not have a division of the social world into a public and a private sphere.

In the formation of a city in the sense of that described by Max Weber, where the daily economic life stands in constant relationship to the market, participation in public life is not just a festive exception but rather a daily form of social behavior for the mass of the inhabitants. This makes it possible and to a certain extent probable that other forms of public activity will develop, for example, public political activity.

DEVELOPMENT OF A PUBLIC AND A PRIVATE SPHERE OF ACTIVITY
AS CRITERION OF THE CITY

Our thesis is: A city is a settlement in which the total life and therefore the daily life as well show a tendency toward polarization, that is, either into a social aggregate of public activity or into one of private activity. There develop a public and a private sphere which stand in a close reciprocal relationship without loss of the polarity. On the other hand, the areas of living which can be characterized as neither public nor private lose in importance. The more clearly the polarity and the reciprocal relationship between public and private spheres are defined, the more "city-like," socio- logically speaking, is the life of a settlement. The less this is the case, the less strongly developed is the city character of a settlement.

Thus there exist fluid transitional stages between city and country which do not cause us conceptual difficulties. This is one advantage of our conceptual definition. A further advantage is that we can ignore legal characteristics in the definition. Certainly it is characteristic that settlements with such social characteristics achieve in the West a definite legal status and develop a legal system of their own; in the Orient, on the other hand, this was not usually the case although here, too, of course, there are cities.[5] Furthermore in the modern state one can speak of city laws or even of the law of a given city—as of "Lübische law" in the Middle Ages—in only a very limited sense.

The third advantage is that we are independent of quantitative characteristics. We were helped in this by the definition of Max Weber, which made it possible to deny city character in very large settlements and to grant to smaller settlements, though not exactly very tiny villages and hamlets, recognition as cities. This corresponds not only to the usual language usage, but obviously also to the fact: What matters is not the mere number of people living together, but the particular manner in which they relate to one another socially. Max Weber pointed to the daily dependence of the trading inhabitant upon the market, and thereby we defined a sociological criterion as well, not only an economic one.

As we now take a further step and assert in more general terms that polarity and reciprocal relationship between public and private spheres are criteria of city associational life, we have at hand categories which are useful for an urban community structure. Of course, for this we need still further theoretical consideration.

THE CONCEPT OF PUBLIC ACTIVITY

INCOMPLETE INTEGRATION

The market is not a closed social system in which all members are completely integrated. Not only are the persons who participate in the market not completely involved in market happenings; they stand at the same time in yet other social relationships which they have left and to which they will return and which are organized on principles different from the market. Neither is their behavior in the market fully determined by its order On the contrary the order of the market guarantees a certain voluntariness of contact-making of each with the other; or more exactly, of each individual with each other individual. A characteristic of the market is thus an incomplete integration, a freedom of social purpose for the individuals, who can choose with whom, in what manner, and for how long they keep up the contact for the purpose of trading. This incomplete integration is the negative precondition of public activity.

What can be observed in the market in the broadest sense—in a street of shops in a city suburb or in the business district of a large city—is charac-

[5] *Ibid.,* p. 744.

teristic also for broad areas of city life in general, in large restaurants, on the stage of sports arenas, in political gatherings, in public transportation: Everywhere it is, as a rule, not the exponents of groups, but single persons who make the contacts. The contacts made are generally evolved according to certain rules and then are generally broken again. Although they take place without friction, they are not binding. A great number of the contacts made serve the purpose of permitting each to go his own way undisturbed. Thirty passengers on a streetcar have thirty different destinations although they sit and stand in direct contact with one another, get out of each other's way when someone wants to get off, usually give directions politely when asked, and not infrequently demonstrate helpfulness to one another in getting on or off. Nevertheless they are in no sense integrated into a "social group" except perhaps in case of an accident or failure of electricial current. Here, as in other typical city situations, integration is incomplete. The various group memberships which apply for each individual remain suspended and are not joined together in an all-inclusive system. Indeed, the group affiliations are for the most part not at all recognizable. No mark of status is worn, no uniform, no feathered decorations and—except for the special case of student members of fighting fraternities—also no decorative scars which could indicate belonging to a special group; only mufti—middle-class clothing.

Such an incomplete integration typically does not exist in a "closed system." By this then we wish to indicate a social order in which practically all social contacts are brought about by a tight, theoretically leakproof network of personal ties. Contacts with persons of the wider social world represent links in a connecting chain of relationships which, on the one hand, determine the "how" of the contact, and on the other hand arrange the contact. To mention an example: In rural feudally-ordered relationships the inhabitant of the neighboring village meets a peasant as the second, non-inheriting son of Farmer X, who belongs to the people of Count Y, who in turn is related to his own overlord, Junker K, but is on the outs with him, etc. The contact-making exists on the one hand in that the unbroken system of relationships offers a contacting thread. It determines what the other person is supposed to be—he is never a completely unknown factor, one knows where to classify him. On the other hand the system of relationships in which one ranks the other always intrudes itself between the subjects, that is, it makes for an indirect meeting of the individuals. It hinders the individuals from meeting each other as individualities. Individuality remains hidden inside the characteristic appearance of the social group; the person does not lay this wrapping aside, and through it he is identified by the other person, who belongs to the same group or to the same negotiating system.

A meeting of people as individuals is possible, however, where integration is incomplete, i.e., where there is no all-inclusive unbroken network of intervening and negotiating connections, and where people meet constantly, enter into communication and stand in relationships to each other without the one being properly classified in a common social order for the other. This is, as has been stated, the case in the market and is characteristic as a whole for the life of the city.

Incomplete integration means, in many cases, the lack of mediating threads of prescribed and familiar connections. The contacts which occur are direct but also unmediated. In these, initially, social distance is noticeable, and this distance is not bridged because the fleeting nature of the contact hinders the development of intimacy.

The individual must adjust to the fact that his behavior is always dependent upon the reactions of people whose reactions he does not know and that he is observed by people who do not know him either. Nevertheless he must deal with these people, he cannot avoid them; he must communicate and negotiate with them. This cannot take place in the same manner as is customary in a closed system. Let us again imagine a walk through a city during the height of business hours. What a wealth of contacts, understanding by means of signs, and also brief verbal exchanges take place in a very short time between complete strangers about whom we know nothing and learn nothing. Let us contrast with this the progress of a farmer down the street to the public inn of an evening: He knows almost everyone he meets. He will exchange greetings, often a few words, because courtesy demands it. Through the social system of the village he has some sort of connection with everyone. But no special understanding or mutual consideration is necessary in order for him to get to the inn.

If the situation in which a person finds himself in incompletely integrated surroundings is to be controlled, there is required a stylization of behavior which ultimately brings about a modification of the social relationships. The social behavior must do justice to everyone in the unprotected atmosphere of a meeting with the unknown person—who will remain unknown in view of the fleeting nature of many of the contacts. In a certain sense he will make use of the prescribed social distance and, in some cases, accentuate and elaborate it. It is significant that in a city situation, in which distance must be artificially maintained, the subjects on which one may speak with a stranger are firmly and casuistically established, and this because in the city so many contacts must take place between people who are unacquainted. One may ask the time. A man may ask a light of another man who is smoking. One may also inquire for directions. But people from the country are immediately recognized because, at this opportunity, they also tell whom they plan to visit and why they do not know the way.

As a result of the carefully maintained social distance, only a small, random, abstract fraction of the personality becomes visible. If one does not wish to expose himself he will take care to conceal and keep private those things which are too personal for the openness of social contacts.

In a closed system a privatization is impossible, that is, a closing out of whole areas of life from the all-pervasive social connections; but it is possible in social surroundings which are not completely structured, which permit alternatives of social behavior in many areas, and thereby allow the individual to manipulate his social role or to develop social roles and to modify them according to the situation. Privatization is the negative precondition for the development of a private sphere—we will discuss this later.

On the other hand, social behavior must bridge over the given distance in incompletely integrated surroundings. It is taken for granted that constant contacts take place with little-known people, contacts which cannot be avoided, which are only indistinctly performed, and which must take shape and function immediately without a long warming-up period. So, when in a fleeting contact—for example in the traffic of the city streets—immediate communication and negotiation are to come into being, behavior must become clearer and more communicative than otherwise. In incompletely integrated social surroundings there arise, therefore, problems of communication which are foreign to closed systems. The positive cultural contribution of the development of public life and activity consists in good measure in developing modes of communication which form a bridge across the social distance which exists and remains—and indeed should remain.

*   *   *

The following things are so matter-of-course to us that we do not inquire about their specific origins, just as though they had existed at all times in societies with a developed culture: public life as an element of the civic state; the "republic of letters" as a public forum for scientific discussion; literary criticism to make openly available the discussions between the general public and the poets; museums and art exhibits as institutions for making works of art accessible to the public. Actually they are products of the democratization and at the same time of the urbanization of our society. They can be explained as a result of these processes, but also as a result of those cases where princes and aristocracy acted as initiators of cultural institutions and as founders of cities.

All of the following are typical phenomena of the enlargement of the private sphere and at the same time of the middle-class culture and manners: the intensification and the cultivation of family life or mode of living as a conscious shaping of the intimate material surroundings; the private possession of the tools of education and their mutual use by the smallest social group; intellectual exchange as a normal and integrating aspect of the living together of blood relatives; religious life within the family circle relatively independent of the church, as it is to be found, for example, in pietism and also to an especially marked degree in early Protestantism; the love-life of the individual; freedom of choice of a marriage partner, which in its ultimate stage of development does not even recognize the veto right of the parents.

The most characteristic example of the separation of public life and private life is probably the phenomenon of middle-class literary education. The bookcase in the living room makes available the world happenings of the present and the past. This making available is accomplished by means of "published" books. But the access to this world requires peace and quiet which only became available through the middle-class way of life, that is, through sheltering and cultivation of the private sphere for a greater number of people.

The attempt to bring all aspects of life into the separate areas of this alternating relationship between public and private activity is never fully realized. There always remain areas whose social structure can be characterized as neither private nor public. And of course, it takes a long time until this polarization depicted here permeates the social processes and produces these typical forms and symbols.

3. *The Metropolis and Mental Life*

BY GEORG SIMMEL

The deepest problems of modern life derive from the claim of the individual to preserve the autonomy and individuality of his existence in the face of overwhelming social forces, of historical heritage, of external culture, and of the technique of life. The fight with nature which primitive man has to wage for his *bodily* existence attains in this modern man its latest transformation. The eighteenth century called upon man to free himself of all the historical bonds in the state and in religion, in morals and in economics. Man's nature, originally good and common to all, should develop unhampered. In addition to more liberty, the nineteenth century demanded the functional specialization of man and his work; this specialization makes one individual incomparable to another, and each of them indispensable to the highest possible extent. However, this specialization makes each man the more directly dependent upon the supplementary activities of all others. Nietzsche sees the full development of the individual conditioned by the most ruthless struggle of individuals; socialism believes in the suppression of all competition for the same reason. Be that is it may, in all these positions the same basic motive is at work: the person resists to being leveled down and worn out by a social-technological mechanism. An inquiry into the inner meaning of specifically modern life and its products, into the soul of the cultural body, so to speak, must seek to solve the equation which structures like the metropolis set up between the individual and the super-individual contents of life. Such an inquiry must answer the question of how the personality accommodates itself in the adjustments to external forces. This will be my task today.

The psychological basis of the metropolitan type of individuality consists in the *intensification of nervous stimulation* which results from the swift and uninterrupted change of outer and inner stimuli. Man is a differentiating creature. His mind is stimulated by the difference between a momentary impression and the one which preceded it. Lasting impressions, impressions which differ only slightly from one another, impressions which take a regular and habitual course and show regular and habitual contrasts—all these use up, so to speak, less consciousness than does the rapid crowding of changing images, the sharp discontinuity in the grasp of a single glance, and the unexpectedness of onrushing impressions. These are the psychological conditions which the metropolis creates. With each crossing of the street, with the tempo and multiplicity of economic, occupational and social life, the city sets up a deep contrast with small town and rural life with reference to the sensory foundations of psychic life. The metropolis exacts from man as a discriminating creature a different amount of consciousness than does rural life. Here the rhythm of life and sensory mental imagery flows more slowly, more habitually, and more evenly. Precisely in this connection the sophisticated character of metropolitan psychic life becomes understandable—as over against small town life which rests more upon deeply felt and emotional relationships. These latter are rooted in the more unconscious layers of the psyche and grow most readily in the steady rhythm of uninterrupted habituations. The intellect, however, has its locus in the transparent, conscious, higher layers of the psyche; it is the most adaptable of our inner forces. In order to accommodate to change and to the contrast of phenomena, the intellect does not require any shocks and inner upheavals; it is only through such upheavals that the more conservative mind could accommodate to the metropolitan rhythm of events. Thus the metropolitan type of man—which, of course, exists in a thousand individual variants—develops an organ protecting him against the threatening currents and discrepancies of his external environment which would uproot him. He reacts with his head instead of his heart. In this an increased awareness assumes the psychic prerogative. Metropolitan life, thus, underlies a heightened awareness and a predominance of intelligence in metropolitan man. The reaction to metropolitan phenomena is shifted to that organ which is least sensitive and quite remote from the depth of the personality. Intellectuality is thus seen to preserve subjective life against the overwhelming power of metropolitan life, and intellectuality branches out in many directions and is integrated with numerous discrete phenomena.

The metropolis has always been the seat of the money economy. Here the multiplicity and concentration of economic exchange gives an importance to the means of exchange which the scantiness of rural commerce would not have allowed. Money economy and the dominance of the intellect are intrinsically connected. They share a matter-of-fact attitude in dealing with men and with things; and, in this attitude, a formal justice is often coupled with an inconsiderate hardness. The intellectually sophisticated person is indifferent to all genuine individuality, because relationships and reactions result from it which cannot be exhausted with logical operations. In the same manner, the individuality of phenomena is not commensurate with the pecuniary principle. Money is concerned only with what is common to all: it asks for the exchange value, it reduces all quality and individuality to the question: How much? All intimate emotional relations between persons are founded in their individuality, whereas in rational relations man is reckoned with like a number, like an element which is in itself indifferent. Only the objective measurable achievement is of interest. Thus metropolitan man reckons with his merchants and customers, his domestic servants and often even with persons with whom he is obliged to have social intercourse. These features of intellectuality contrast with the nature of the small circle in which the inevitable knowledge of individuality as inevitably produces a warmer tone of behavior, a behavior which is beyond a mere objective balancing of service and return. In the sphere of the economic psychology of the small group it is of importance that under primitive conditions production serves the customer who orders the good, so that the producer and the consumer are acquainted. The modern metropolis, however, is supplied almost entirely by production for the market, that is, for entirely unknown purchasers who never personally enter the producer's actual field of vision. Through this anonymity the interests of each party acquire an unmerciful matter-of-factness; and the intellectually calculating economic egoisms of both parties need not fear any deflection because of the imponderables of personal relationships. The money economy dominates the metropolis; it has displaced the last survivals of domestic production and the direct barter of goods; it minimizes from day to day, the amount of work ordered by customers. The matter-of-fact attitude is obviously so intimately interrelated with the money economy, which is dominant in the metropolis, that nobody can say whether the intellectualistic mentality first promoted the money economy or whether the latter determined the former. The metropolitan way of life is certainly the most fertile soil for this reciprocity, a point which I shall document merely by citing the dictum of the most eminent English constitutional historian: throughout the whole course of English history, London has never acted as England's heart but often as England's intellect and always as her moneybag!

In certain seemingly insignificant traits, which lie upon the surface of life, the same psychic currents characteristically unite. Modern mind has become more and more calculating. The calculative exactness of practical life which the money economy has brought about corresponds to the ideal of natural science: to transform the world into an arithmetic problem, to fix every part of the world by mathematical formulas. Only money economy has filled the days of so many people with weighing, calculating, with numerical determinations, with a reduction of qualitative values to quantitative ones. Through the calculative nature of money a new precision, a certainty in the definition of identities and differences, an unambiguousness in agreements and arrangements has been brought about in the relations of life-elements—just as externally this precision has been effected by the universal diffusion of pocket watches. However, the conditions of metropolitan life are at once cause and effect of this trait. The relationships and affairs of the typical metropolitan usually are so varied and complex that without the strictest punctuality in promises and services the whole structure would break down into an inextricable chaos. Above all, this necessity is brought about by the aggregation of so many people with such differentiated interests, who must integrate their relations and activities into a highly complex organism. If all clocks and watches in Berlin would suddenly go wrong in different ways, even if only by one hour, all economic life and communication of the city would be disrupted for a long time. In addition an apparently mere external factor: long distances, would make all waiting and broken appointments result in an ill-afforded waste of time. Thus, the technique of metropolitan life is unimaginable without the most punctual integration of all activities and mutual relations into a stable and impersonal time schedule. Here again the general conclusions of this entire task of reflection become obvious, namely, that from each point on the surface of existence—however closely attached to the surface alone—one may drop a sounding into the depth of the psyche so that all the most banal externalities of life finally are connected with the ultimate decisions concerning the meaning and style of life. Punctuality, calculability, exactness are forced upon life by the complexity and extension of metropolitan existence and are not only most intimately connected with its money economy and intellectualistic character. These traits must also color the contents of life and favor the exclusion of those irrational, instinctive, sovereign traits and impulses which aim at determining the mode of life from within, instead of receiving the general and precisely schematized form of life from without. Even though sovereign types of personality, characterized by irrational impulses, are by no means impossible in the city, they are, nevertheless, opposed to typical city life. The passionate hatred of men like Ruskin and Nietzsche for the metropolis is understandable in these terms. Their natures discovered the value of life alone in the unschematized existence which cannot be defined with precision for all alike. From the same source of this hatred of the metropolis surged their hatred of money economy and of the intellectualism of modern existence.

The same factors which have thus coalesced into the exactness and minute precision of the form of life have coalesced into a structure of the highest impersonality; on the other hand, they have promoted a highly personal subjectivity. There is perhaps no psychic phenomenon which has been so unconditionally reserved to the metropolis as has the blasé attitude.

The blasé attitude results first from the rapidly changing and closely compressed contrasting stimulations of the nerves. From this, the enhancement of metropolitan intellectuality, also, seems originally to stem. Therefore, stupid people who are not intellectually alive in the first place usually are not exactly blasé. A life in boundless pursuit of pleasure makes one blasé because it agitates the nerves to their strongest reactivity for such a long time that they finally cease to react at all. In the same way, through the rapidity and contradictoriness of their changes, more harmless impressions force such violent responses, tearing the nerves so brutally hither and thither that their last reserves of strength are spent; and if one remains in the same milieu they have no time to gather new strength. An incapacity thus emerges to react to new sensations with the appropriate energy. This constitutes that blasé attitude which, in fact, every metropolitan child shows when compared with children of quieter and less changeable milieus.

This physiological source of the metropolitan blasé attitude is joined by another source which flows from the money economy. The essence of the blasé attitude consists in the blunting of discrimination. This does not mean that the objects are not perceived, as is the case with the half-wit, but rather that the meaning and differing values of things, and thereby the things themselves, are experienced as insubstantial. They appear to the blasé person in an evenly flat and gray tone; no one object deserves preference over any other. This mood is the faithful subjective reflection of the completely internalized money economy. By being the equivalent to all the manifold things in one and the same way, money becomes the most frightful leveler. For money expresses all qualitative differences of things in terms of "how much?" Money, with all its colorlessness and indifference, becomes the common denominator of all values; irreparably it hollows out the core of things, their individuality, their specific value, and their incomparability. All things float with equal specific gravity in the constantly moving stream of money. All things lie on the same level and differ from one another only in the size of the area which they cover. In the individual case this coloration, or rather discoloration, of things through their money equivalence may be unnoticeably minute. However, through the relations of the rich to the objects to be had for money, perhaps even through the total character which the mentality of the contemporary public everywhere imparts to these objects, the exclusively pecuniary evaluation of objects has become quite considerable. The large cities, the main seats of the money exchange, bring the purchasability of things to the fore much more impressively than do smaller localities. That is why cities are also the genuine locale of the blasé attitude. In the blasé attitude the concentration of men and things stimulate the nervous system of the individual to its highest achievement so that it attains its peak. Through the mere quantitative intensification of the same conditioning factors this achievement is transformed into its op-posite and appears in the peculiar adjustment of the blasé attitude. In this phenomenon the nerves find in the refusal to react to their stimulation the last possibility of accommodating to the contents and forms of metro-politan life. The self-preservation of certain personalities is bought at the price of devaluating the whole objective world, a devaluation which in the end unavoidably drags one's own personality down into a feeling of the same worthlessness.

Whereas the subject of this form of existence has to come to terms with it entirely for himself, his self-preservation in the face of the large city demands from him a no less negative behavior of a social nature. This mental attitude of metropolitans toward one another we may designate, from a formal point of view, as reserve. If so many inner reactions were responses to the continuous external contacts with innumerable people as are those in the small town, where one knows almost everybody one meets and where one has a positive relation to almost everyone, one would be completely atomized internally and come to an unimaginable psychic state. Partly this psychological fact, partly the right to distrust which men have in the face of the touch-and-go elements of metropolitan life, necessitates our reserve. As a result of this reserve we frequently do not even know by sight those who have been our neighbors for years. And it is this reserve which in the eyes of the small-town people makes us appear to be cold and heartless. Indeed, if I do not deceive myself, the inner aspect of this outer reserve is not only indifference but, more often than we are aware, it is a slight aversion, a mutual strangeness and repulsion, which will break into hatred and fight at the moment of a closer contact, however caused. The whole inner organization of such an extensive communicative life rests upon an extremely varied hierarchy of sympathies, indifferences, and aver-sions of the briefest as well as of the most permanent nature. The sphere of indifference in this hierarchy is not as large as might appear on the sur-face. Our psychic activity still responds to almost every impression of some-body else with a somewhat distinct feeling. The unconscious, fluid and changing character of this impression seems to result in a state of indiffer-ence. Actually this indifference would be just as unnatural as the diffusion of indiscriminate mutual suggestion would be unbearable. From both these typical dangers of the metropolis, indifference and indiscriminate suggesti-bility, antipathy protects us. A latent antipathy and the preparatory stage of practical antagonism effect the distances and aversions without which this mode of life could not at all be led. The extent and the mixture of this style of life, the rhythm of its emergence and disappearance, the forms in which it is satisfied—all these, with the unifying motives in the narrower sense, form the inseparable whole of the metropolitan style of life. What appears in the metropolitan style of life directly as dissociation is in reality only one of its elemental forms of socialization.

This reserve with its overtone of hidden aversion appears in turn as the form or the cloak of a more general mental phenomenon of the metropolis: it grants to the individual a kind and an amount of personal freedom which has no analogy whatsoever under other conditions. The metropolis goes back to one of the large developmental tendencies of social life as such, to one of the few tendencies for which an approximately universal formula can be discovered. The earliest phase of social formations found in historical as well as in contemporary social structures is this: a relatively small circle firmly closed against neighboring, strange, or in some way antagonistic circles. However, this circle is closely coherent and allows its individual members only a narrow field for the development of unique qualities and free, self-responsible movements. Political and kinship groups, parties and religious associations begin in this way. The self-preservation of very young associations requires the establishment of strict boundaries and a centripetal unity. Therefore they cannot allow the individual freedom and unique inner and outer development. From this stage social development proceeds at once in two different, yet corresponding, directions. To the extent to which the group grows—numerically, spatially, in significance and in content of life—to the same degree the group's direct, inner unity loosens, and the rigidity of the original demarcation against others is softened through mutual relations and connections. At the same time, the individual gains freedom of movement, far beyond the first jealous delimitation. The individual also gains a specific individuality to which the division of labor in the enlarged group gives both occasion and necessity. The state and Christianity, guilds and political parties, and innumerable other groups have developed according to this formula, however much, of course, the special conditions and forces of the respective groups have modified the general scheme. This scheme seems to me distinctly recognizable also in the evolution of individuality within urban life. The small-town life in Antiquity and in the Middle Ages set barriers against movement and relations of the individual toward the outside, and it set up barriers against individual independence and differentiation within the individual self. These barriers were such that under them modern man could not have breathed. Even today a metropolitan man who is placed in a small town feels a restriction similar, at least, in kind. The smaller the circle which forms our milieu is, and the more restricted those relations to others are which dissolve the boundaries of the individual, the more anxiously the circle guards the achievements, the conduct of life, and the outlook of the individual, and the more readily a quantitative and qualitative specialization would break up the framework of the whole little circle.

The ancient *polis* in this respect seems to have had the very character of a small town. The constant threat to its existence at the hands of enemies from near and afar effected strict coherence in political and military respects, a supervision of the citizen by the citizen, a jealousy of the whole against the individual whose particular life was suppressed to such a degree that he could compensate only by acting as a despot in his own household. The tremendous agitation and excitement, the unique colorfulness of Athenian life, can perhaps be understood in terms of the fact that a people of incomparably individualized personalities struggled against the constant inner and outer pressure of a de-individualizing small town. This produced a tense atmosphere in which the weaker individuals were suppressed and those of stronger natures were incited to prove themselves in the most passionate manner. This is precisely why it was that there blossomed in Athens what must be called, without defining it exactly, "the general human character" in the intellectual development of our species. For we maintain factual as well as historical validity for the following connection: the most extensive and the most general contents and forms of life are most intimately connected with the most individual ones. They have a preparatory stage in common, that is, they find their enemy in narrow formations and groupings the maintenance of which places both of them into a state of defense against expanse and generality lying without and the freely moving individuality within. Just as in the feudal age, the "free" man was the one who derived his right merely from the narrow circle of a feudal association and was excluded from the larger social orbit—so today metropolitan man is "free" in a spiritualized and refined sense, in contrast to the pettiness and prejudices which hem in the small-town man. For the reciprocal reserve and indifference and the intellectual life conditions of large circles are never felt more strongly by the individual in their impact upon his independence than in the thickest crowd of the big city. This is because the bodily proximity and the narrowness of space makes the mental distance only the more visible. It is obviously only the obverse of this freedom if, under certain circumstances, one nowhere feels as lonely and lost as in the metropolitan crowd. For here as elsewhere it is by no means necessary that the freedom of man be reflected in his emotional life as comfort.

It is not only the immediate size of the area and the number of persons which, because of the universal historical correlation between the enlargement of the circle and the personal inner and outer freedom, has made the metropolis the locale of freedom. It is rather in transcending this visible expanse that any given city expands in a manner comparable to the way in which wealth develops; a certain amount of property increases in a quasi-automatical way in ever more rapid progression. As soon as a certain limit has been passed, the economic, personal, and intellectual relations of the citizenry, the sphere of intellectual predominance of the city over its hinter-land, grow as in geometrical progression. Every gain in dynamic extension becomes a step, not for an equal, but for a new and larger extension. From every thread spinning out of the city, ever new threads grow as if by them-selves, just as within the city the unearned increment of ground rent, through the mere increase in communication, brings the owner automatically increas-ing profits. At this point, the quantitative aspect of life is transformed directly into qualitative traits of character. The sphere of life of the small town is, in the main, self-contained and autarchic. For it is the decisive nature of the metropolis that its inner life overflows by waves into a far-flung national or international area. Weimar is not an example to the con-trary, since its significance was hinged upon individual personalities and died with them; whereas the metropolis is indeed characterized by its essential independence even from the most eminent individual personalities. This is the counterpart to the independence, and it is the price the indi-vidual pays for the independence, which he enjoys in the metropolis. The most significant characteristic of the metropolis is this functional extension beyond its physical boundaries. And this efficacy reacts in turn and gives weight, importance, and responsibility to metropolitan life. Man does not end with the limits of his body or the area comprising his immediate activity. Rather is the range of the person constituted by the sum of effects emanating from him temporarily and spatially. In the same way, a city consists of its total effects which extend beyond its immediate confines. Only this range is the city's actual extent in which its existence is expressed. This fact makes it obvious that individual freedom, the logical and historical complement of such extension, is not to be understood only in the negative sense of mere freedom of mobility and elimination of prejudices and petty philistinism. The essential point is that the particularity and incomparability, which ultimately every human being possesses, be somehow expressed in the working-out of a way of life. That we follow the laws of our own nature—and this after all is freedom—becomes obvious and convincing to ourselves and to others only if the expressions of this nature differ from the expressions of others. Only our unmistakability proves that our way of life has not been superimposed by others.

Cities are, first of all, seats of the highest economic division of labor. They produce thereby such extreme phenomena as in Paris the remunera-tive occupation of the *quatorzième*. They are persons who identify them-selves by signs on their residences and who are ready at the dinner hour in correct attire, so that they can be quickly called upon if a dinner party should consist of thirteen persons. In the measure of expansion, the city offers more and more the decisive conditions of the division of labor. It offers a circle which through its size can absorb a highly diverse variety of services. At the same time, the concentration of individuals and their struggle for customers compel the individual to specialize in a function from which he cannot be readily displaced by another. It is decisive that city life has transformed the struggle with nature for livelihood into an inter-human struggle for gain, which here is not granted by nature but by other men. For specialization does not flow only from the competition for gain but also from the underlying fact that the seller must always seek to call forth new and differentiated needs of the lured customer. In order to find a source of income which is not yet exhausted, and to find a function which cannot readily be displaced, it is necessary to specialize in one's services. This process promotes differentiation, refinement, and the enrichment of the public's needs, which obviously must lead to growing personal differences within this public.

All this forms the transition to the individualization of mental and psychic traits which the city occasions in proportion to its size. There is a whole series of obvious causes underlying this process. First, one must meet the difficulty of asserting his own personality within the dimensions of metropolitan life. Where the quantitative increase in importance and the expense of energy reach their limits, one seizes upon qualitative differentiation by playing upon its sensitivity for differences. Finally, man is tempted to adopt the most tendentious peculiarities, that is, the specifically metropolitan extravagances of mannerism, caprice, and preciousness. Now, the meaning of these extravagances does not at all lie in the contents of such behavior, but rather in its form of "being different," of standing out in a striking manner and thereby attracting attention. For many character types, ultimately the only means of saving for themselves some modicum of self-esteem and the sense of filling a position is indirect, through the awareness of others. In the same sense a seemingly insignificant factor is operating, the cumulative effects of which are, however, still noticeable. I refer to the brevity and scarcity of the inter-human contacts granted to the metropolitan man, as compared with social intercourse in the small town. The temptation to appear "to the point," to appear concentrated and strikingly characteristic, lies much closer to the individual in brief metropolitan contacts than in an atmosphere in which frequent and prolonged association assures the personality of an unambiguous image of himself in the eyes of the other.

The most profound reason, however, why the metropolis conduces to the urge for the most individual personal existence—no matter whether justified and successful—appears to me to be the following: the development of modern culture is characterized by the preponderance of what one may call the "objective spirit" over the "subjective spirit." This is to say, in language as well as in law, in the technique of production as well as in art, in science as well as in the objects of the domestic environment, there is embodied a sum of spirit. The individual in his intellectual development follows the growth of this spirit very imperfectly and at an ever increasing distance. If, for instance, we view the immense culture which for the last hundred years has been embodied in things and in knowledge, in institutions and in comforts, and if we compare all this with the cultural progress of the individual during the same period—at least in high status groups—a frightful disproportion in growth between the two becomes evident. Indeed, at some points we notice a retrogression in the culture of the individual with reference to spirituality, delicacy, and idealism. This descrepancy results essentially from the growing division of labor. For the division of labor demands from the individual an ever more one-sided accomplishment, and the greatest advance in a one-sided pursuit only too frequently means death to the personality of the individual. In any case, he can cope less and less with the overgrowth of objective culture. The individual is reduced to a negligible quantity, perhaps less in his consciousness than in his practice and in the totality of his obscure emotional states that are derived from this practice. The individual has become a mere cog in an enormous organization of things and powers which tear from his hands all progress, spirituality, and value in order to transform them from their subjective form into the form of a purely objective life. It needs merely to be pointed out that the metropolis is the genuine arena of this culture which outgrows all personal life. Here in buildings and educational institutions, in the wonders and comforts of space-conquering technology, in the formations of community life, and in the visible institutions of the state, is offered such an overwhelming fullness of crystalized and impersonalized spirit that the personality, so to speak, cannot maintain itself under its impact. On the one hand, life is made infinitely easy for the personality in that stimulations, interests, uses of time and consciousness are offered to it from all sides. They carry the person as if in a stream, and one needs hardly to swim for oneself. On the other hand, however, life is composed more and more of these impersonal contents and offerings which tend to displace the genuine personal colorations and incomparabilities. This results in the individual's summoning the utmost in uniqueness and particularization, in order to preserve his most personal core. He has to exaggerate this personal element in order to remain audible even to himself. The atrophy of individual culture through the hypertrophy of objective culture is one reason for the bitter hatred which the preachers of the most extreme individualism, above all Nietzsche, harbor against the metropolis. But it is, indeed, also a reason why these preachers are so passionately loved in the metropolis and why they appear to the metropolitan man as the prophets and saviors of his most unsatisfied yearnings.

If one asks for the historical position of these two forms of individualism which are nourished by the quantitative relation of the metropolis, namely, individual independence and the elaboration of individuality itself, then the metropolis assumes an entirely new rank order in the world history of the spirit. The eighteenth century found the individual in oppressive bonds which had become meaningless—bonds of a political, agrarian, guild, and religious character. They were restraints which, so to speak, forced upon man an unnatural form and outmoded, unjust inequalities. In this situation the cry for liberty and equality arose, the belief in the individual's full freedom of movement in all social and intellectual relationships. Freedom would at once permit the noble substance common to all to come to the fore, a substance which nature had deposited in every man and which society and history had only deformed. Besides this eighteenth-century ideal of liberalism, in the nineteenth century, through Goethe and Romanticism, on the one hand, and through the economic division of labor, on the other hand, another ideal arose: individuals liberated from historical bonds now wished to distinguish themselves from one another. The carrier of man's values is no longer the "general human being" in every individual, but rather man's qualitative uniqueness and irreplaceability. The external and internal history of our time takes its course within the struggle and in the changing entanglements of these two ways of defining the individual's role in the whole of society. It is the function of the metropolis to provide the arena for this struggle and its reconciliation. For the metropolis presents the peculiar conditions which are revealed to us as the opportunities and the stimuli for the development of both these ways of allocating roles to men. Therewith these conditions gain a unique place, pregnant with inestimable meanings for the development of psychic existence. The metropolis reveals itself as one of those great historical formations in which opposing streams which enclose life unfold, as well as join one another with equal right. However, in this process the currents of life, whether their individual phenomena touch us sympathetically or antipathetically, entirely transcend the sphere for which the judge's attitude is appropriate. Since such forces of life have grown into the roots and into the crown of the whole of the historical life in which we, in our fleeting existence, as a cell, belong only as a part, it is not our task either to accuse or to pardon, but only to understand.[1]

[1] The content of this lecture by its very nature does not derive from a citable literature. Argument and elaboration of its major cultural-historical ideas are contained in my *Philosophie des Geldes* [The Philosophy of Money; München and Leipzig: Duncker und Humblot, 1900].

4. Human Ecology

BY ROBERT EZRA PARK

I. THE WEB OF LIFE

Naturalists of the last century were greatly intrigued by their observation of the interrelations and co-ordinations, within the realm of animate nature, of the numerous, divergent, and widely scattered species. Their successors, the botanists and zoölogists of the present day, have turned their attention to more specific inquiries, and the "realm of nature," like the concept of evolution, has come to be for them a notion remote and speculative.

The "web of life," in which all living organisms, plants and animals alike, are bound together in a vast system of interlinked and interdependent lives, is nevertheless, as J. Arthur Thomson put it, "one of the fundamental biological concepts" and is "as characteristically Darwinian as the struggle for existence."[1]

Darwin's famous instance of the cats and the clover is the classic illustration of this interdependence. He found, he explains, that humblebees were almost indispensable to the fertilization of the heartsease, since other bees do not visit this flower. The same thing is true with some kinds of clover. Humblebees alone visit red clover, as other bees cannot reach the nectar. The inference is that if the humblebees became extinct or very rare in England, the heartsease and red clover would become very rare, or wholly disappear. However, the number of humblebees in any district depends in a great measure on the number of field mice, which destroy their combs and nests. It is estimated that more than two-thirds of them are thus destroyed all over England. Near villages and small towns the nests of humblebees are more numerous than elsewhere and this is attributed to the number of cats that destroy the mice.[2] Thus next year's crop of purple clover in certain parts of England depends on the number of humblebees in the district; the number of humblebees depends upon the number of field mice, the number of field mice upon the number and enterprise of the cats, and the

Reprinted with permission of The University of Chicago Press, publishers, from Robert Ezra Park, "Human Ecology," *American Journal of Sociology,* XLII, No. 1 (July, 1936), 1–15. Copyright 1936 by The University of Chicago.

[1] *The System of Animate Nature* (Gifford Lectures, 1915–16), II (New York, 1920), 58.

[2] J. Arthur Thomson, *Darwinism and Human Life* (New York, 1911), pp. 52–53.

number of cats—as someone has added—depends on the number of old maids and others in neighboring villages who keep cats.

These large food chains, as they are called, each link of which eats the other, have as their logical prototype the familiar nursery rhyme, "The House that Jack Built." You recall:

> *The cow with the crumpled horn,*
> *That tossed the dog,*
> *That worried the cat,*
> *That killed the rat,*
> *That ate the malt*
> *That lay in the house that Jack built.*

Darwin and the naturalists of his day were particularly interested in observing and recording these curious illustrations of the mutual adaptation and correlation of plants and animals because they seemed to throw light on the origin of the species. Both the species and their mutual interdependence, within a common habitat, seem to be a product of the same Darwinian struggle for existence.

It is interesting to note that it was the application to organic life of a sociological principle—the principle, namely, of "competitive co-operation"—that gave Darwin the first clue to the formulation of his theory of evolution.

"He projected on organic life," says Thomson, "a sociological idea," and "thus vindicated the relevancy and utility of a sociological idea within the biological realm."[3]

The active principle in the ordering and regulating of life within the realm of animate nature is, as Darwin described it, "the struggle for existence." By this means the numbers of living organisms are regulated, their distribution controlled, and the balance of nature maintained. Finally, it is by means of this elementary form of competition that the existing species, the survivors in the struggle, find their niches in the physical environment and in the existing correlation or division of labor between the different species. J. Arthur Thomson makes an impressive statement of the matter in his *System of Animate Nature*. He says:

> *The hosts of living organisms are not . . . isolated creatures, for every thread of life is intertwined with others in a complex web. . . . Flowers and insects are fitted to one another as hand to glove. Cats have to do with the plague in India as well as with the clover crop at home. . . .* Just as there is a correlation of organs in the body, so there is a correlation

[3] *Ibid.,* p. 72.

of organisms in the world of life. *When we learn something of the intricate give and take, supply and demand, action and reaction between plants and animals, between flowers and insects, between herbivores and carnivores, and between other conflicting yet correlated interests, we begin to get a glimpse of a vast self-regulating organization.*

These manifestations of a living, changing, but persistent order among competing organisms—organisms embodying "conflicting yet correlated interests"—seem to be the basis for the conception of a social order transcending the individual species, and of a society based on a biotic rather than a cultural basis, a conception later developed by the plant and animal ecologists.

In recent years the plant geographers have been the first to revive something of the earlier field naturalists' interest in the interrelations of species. Haeckel, in 1878, was the first to give to these studies a name, "ecology," and by so doing gave them the character of a distinct and separate science, a science which Thomson describes as "the new natural history."[4]

The interrelation and interdependence of the species are naturally more obvious and more intimate within the common habitat than elsewhere. Furthermore, as correlations have multiplied and competition has decreased, in consequence of mutual adaptations of the competing species, the habitat and habitants have tended to assume the character of a more or less completely closed system.

Within the limits of this system the individual units of the population are involved in a process of competitive co-operation, which has given to their interrelations the character of a natural economy. To such a habitat and its inhabitants—whether plant, animal, or human—the ecologists have applied the term "community."

The essential characteristics of a community, so conceived, are those of: (1) a population, territorially organized, (2) more or less completely rooted in the soil it occupies, (3) its individual units living in a relationship of mutual interdependence that is symbiotic rather than societal, in the sense in which that term applies to human beings.

These symbiotic societies are not merely unorganized assemblages of plants and animals which happen to live together in the same habitat. On the contrary, they are interrelated in the most complex manner. Every community has something of the character of an organic unit. It has a more or less definite structure and it has "a life history in which juvenile, adult

---

[4] "Ecology," says Elton, "corresponds to the older terms Natural History and Bionomics, but its methods are now accurate and precise." See article, "Ecology," *Encyclopaedia Britannica* (14th ed.).

and senile phases can be observed."[5] If it is an organism, it is one of the organs which are other organisms. It is, to use Spencer's phrase, a super-organism.

What more than anything else gives the symbiotic community the character of an organism is the fact that it possesses a mechanism (competition) for (1) regulating the numbers and (2) preserving the balance between the competing species of which it is composed. It is by maintaining this biotic balance that the community preserves its identity and integrity as an individual unit through the changes and the vicissitudes to which it is subject in the course of its progress from the earlier to the later phases of its existence.

II. THE BALANCE OF NATURE

The balance of nature, as plant and animal ecologists have conceived it, seems to be largely a question of numbers. When the pressure of population upon the natural resources of the habitat reaches a certain degree of intensity, something invariably happens. In the one case the population may swarm and relieve the pressure of population by migration. In another, where the disequilibrium between population and natural resources is the result of some change, sudden or gradual, in the conditions of life, the pre-existing correlation of the species may be totally destroyed.

Change may be brought about by a famine, an epidemic, or an invasion of the habitat by some alien species. Such an invasion may result in a rapid increase of the invading population and a sudden decline in the numbers if not the destruction of the original population. Change of some sort is continuous, although the rate and pace of change sometimes vary greatly. Charles Elton says:

The impression of anyone who has studied animal numbers in the field is that the "balance of nature" hardly exists, except in the minds of scientists. It seems that animal numbers are always tending to settle down into a smooth and harmonious working mechanism, but something always happens before this happy state is reached.[6]

Under ordinary circumstances, such minor fluctuations in the biotic balance as occur are mediated and absorbed without profoundly disturbing the existing equilibrium and routine of life. When, on the other hand, some sudden and catastrophic change occurs—it may be a war, a famine, or pestilence—it upsets the biotic balance, breaks "the cake of custom," and releases

[5] Edward J. Salisbury, "Plants," *Encyclopaedia Britannica* (14th ed.).
[6] "Animal Ecology," *ibid*.

energies up to that time held in check. A series of rapid and even violent changes may ensue which profoundly alter the existing organization of communal life and give a new direction to the future course of events.

The advent of the boll weevil in the southern cotton fields is a minor instance but illustrates the principle. The boll weevil crossed the Rio Grande at Brownsville in the summer of 1892. By 1894 the pest had spread to a dozen counties in Texas, bringing destruction to the cotton and great losses to the planters. From that point it advanced, with every recurring season, until by 1928 it had covered practically all the cotton producing area in the United States. Its progress took the form of a territorial succession. The consequences to agriculture were catastrophic but not wholly for the worse, since they served to give an impulse to changes in the organization of the industry long overdue. It also hastened the northward migration of the Negro tenant farmer.

The case of the boll weevil is typical. In this mobile modern world, where space and time have been measurably abolished, not men only but all the minor organisms (including the microbes) seem to be, as never before, in motion. Commerce, in progressively destroying the isolation upon which the ancient order of nature rested, has intensified the struggle for existence over an ever widening area of the habitable world. Out of this struggle a new equilibrium and a new system of animate nature, the new biotic basis of the new world-society, is emerging.

It is, as Elton remarks, the "fluctuation of numbers" and "the failure" from time to time "of the regulatory mechanism of animal increase" which ordinarily interrupts the established routine, and in so doing releases a new cycle of change. In regard to these fluctuations in numbers Elton says:

These failures of the regulating mechanism of animal increase—are they caused by (1) internal changes, after the manner of an alarm clock which suddenly goes off, or the boilers of an engine blowing up, or are they caused by some factors in the outer environment—weather, vegetation, or something like that?[7]

and he adds:

It appears that they are due to both but that the latter (external factor) is the more important of the two, and usually plays the leading rôle.

The conditions which affect and control the movements and numbers of populations are more complex in human societies than in plant and animal communities, but they exhibit extraordinary similarities.

[7] *Ibid.*

The boll weevil, moving out of its ancient habitat in the central Mexican plateau and into the virgin territory of the southern cotton plantations, incidentally multiplying its population to the limit of the territories and resources, is not unlike the Boers of Cape Colony, South Africa, trekking out into the high veldt of the central South African plateau and filling it, within a period of one hundred years, with a population of their own descendants.

Competition operates in the human (as it does in the plant and animal) community to bring about and restore the communal equilibrium, when, either by the advent of some intrusive factor from without or in the normal course of its life-history, that equilibrium is disturbed.

Thus every crisis that initiates a period of rapid change, during which competition is intensified, moves over finally into a period of more or less stable equilibrium and a new division of labor. In this manner competition is superseded by co-operation.

It is when, and to the extent that, competition declines that the kind of order which we call society may be said to exist. In short, society, from the ecological point of view, and in so far as it is a territorial unit, is just the area within which biotic competition has declined and the struggle for existence has assumed higher and more sublimated forms.

III. COMPETITION, DOMINANCE AND SUCCESSION

There are other and less obvious ways in which competition exercises control over the relations of individuals and species within the communal habitat. The two ecological principles, dominance and succession, which operate to establish and maintain such communal order as here described are functions of, and dependent upon, competition.

In every life-community there is always one or more dominant species. In a plant community this dominance is ordinarily the result of struggle among the different species for light. In a climate which supports a forest the dominant species will invariably be trees. On the prairie and steppes they will be grasses.

Light being the main necessity of plants, the dominant plant of a community is the tallest member, which can spread its green energy-trap above the heads of the others. What marginal exploitation there is to be done is an exploitation of the dimmer light below this canopy. So it comes about in every life-community on land, in the cornfield just as in the forest, that there are layers of vegetation, each adapted to exist in a lesser intensity of light than the one above. Usually there are but two or three such layers; in an oak-wood for example there will be a layer of moss, above this herbs or low bushes, and then nothing more to the leafy roof; in the wheat-field the dominating form is the wheat, with lower weeds among its stalks. But in tropical forests the whole space from floor to roof may be zoned and populated.[8]

But the principle of dominance operates in the human as well as in the plant and animal communities. The so-called natural or functional areas of a metropolitan community—for example, the slum, the rooming-house area, the central shopping section and the banking center—each and all owe their existence directly to the factor of dominance, and indirectly to competition.

The struggle of industries and commercial institutions for a strategic location determines in the long run the main outlines of the urban community. The distribution of population, as well as the location and limits of the residential areas which they occupy, are determined by another similar but subordinate system of forces.

The area of dominance in any community is usually the area of highest land values. Ordinarily there are in every large city two such positions of highest land value—one in the central shopping district, the other in the central banking area. From these points land values decline at first precipitantly and then more gradually toward the periphery of the urban community. It is these land values that determine the location of social institutions and business enterprises. Both the one and the other are bound up in a kind of territorial complex within which they are at once competing and interdependent units.

As the metropolitan community expands into the suburbs the pressure of professions, business enterprises, and social institutions of various sorts destined to serve the whole metropolitan region steadily increases the demand for space at the center. Thus not merely the growth of the suburban area, but any change in the method of transportation which makes the central business area of the city more accessible, tends to increase the pressure at the center. From thence this pressure is transmitted and diffused, as the profile of land values discloses, to every other part of the city.

Thus the principle of dominance, operating within the limits imposed by the terrain and other natural features of the location, tends to determine the general ecological pattern of the city and the functional relation of each of the different areas of the city to all others.

Dominance is, furthermore, in so far as it tends to stabilize either the biotic or the cultural community, indirectly responsible for the phenomenon of succession.

[8] H. G. Wells, Julian S. Huxley, and G. P. Wells, *The Science of Life* (New York, 1934), pp. 968–69.

The term "succession" is used by ecologists to describe and designate that orderly sequence of changes through which a biotic community passes in the course of its development from a primary and relatively unstable to a relatively permanent or climax stage. The main point is that not merely do the individual plants and animals within the communal habitat grow but the community itself, i.e., the system of relations between the species, is likewise involved in an orderly process of change and development.

The fact that, in the course of this development, the community moves through a series of more or less clearly defined stages is the fact that gives this development the serial character which the term "succession" suggests.

The explanation of the serial character of the changes involved in succession is the fact that at every stage in the process a more or less stable equilibrium is achieved, which in due course, and as a result of progressive changes in life-conditions, possibly due to growth and decay, the equilibrium achieved in the earlier stages is eventually undermined. In such case the energies previously held in balance will be released, competition will be intensified, and change will continue at a relatively rapid rate until a new equilibrium is achieved.

The climax phase of community development corresponds with the adult phase of an individual's life.

In the developing single organism, each phase is its own executioner, and itself brings a new phase into existence, as when the tadpole grows the thyroid gland which is destined to make the tadpole state pass away in favour of the miniature frog. And in the developing community of organisms, the same thing happens—each stage alters its own environment, for it changes and almost invariably enriches the soil in which it lives; and thus it eventually brings itself to an end, by making it possible for new kinds of plants with greater demands in the way of mineral salts or other riches of the soil to flourish there. Accordingly bigger and more exigent plants gradually supplant the early pioneers, until a final balance is reached, the ultimate possibility for that climate.[9]

The cultural community develops in comparable ways to that of the biotic, but the process is more complicated. Inventions, as well as sudden or catastrophic changes, seem to play a more important part in bringing about serial changes in the cultural than in the biotic community. But the principle involved seems to be substantially the same. In any case, all or most of the fundamental processes seem to be functionally related and dependent upon competition.

[9] *Ibid.*, pp. 977–78.

Competition, which on the biotic level functions to control and regulate the interrelations of organisms, tends to assume on the social level the form of conflict. The intimate relation between competition and conflict is indicated by the fact that wars frequently, if not always, have, or seem to have, their source and origin in economic competition which, in that case, assumes the more sublimated form of a struggle for power and prestige. The social function of war, on the other hand, seems to be to extend the area over which it is possible to maintain peace.

IV. BIOLOGICAL ECONOMICS

If population pressure, on the one hand, co-operates with changes in local and environmental conditions to disturb at once the biotic balance and social equilibrium, it tends at the same time to intensify competition. In so doing it functions, indirectly, to bring about a new, more minute and, at the same time, territorially extensive division of labor.

Under the influence of an intensified competition, and the increased activity which competition involves, every individual and every species, each for itself, tends to discover the particular niche in the physical and living environment where it can survive and flourish with the greatest possible expansiveness consistent with its necessary dependence upon its neighbors.

It is in this way that a territorial organization and a biological division of labor, within the communal habitat, is established and maintained. This explains, in part at least, the fact that the biotic community has been conceived at one time as a kind of superorganism and at another as a kind of economic organization for the exploitation of the natural resources of its habitat.

In their interesting survey, *The Science of Life,* H. G. Wells and his collaborators, Julian Huxley and G. P. Wells, have described ecology as "biological economics," and as such very largely concerned with "the balances and mutual pressures of species living in the same habitat."[10]

"Ecology," as they put it, is "an extension of Economics to the whole of life." On the other hand the science of economics as traditionally conceived, though it is a whole century older, is merely a branch of a more general science of ecology which includes man with all other living creatures. Under the circumstances what has been traditionally described as economics and conceived as restricted to human affairs, might very properly be described as Barrows some years ago described geography, namely as human ecology. It is in this sense that Wells and his collaborators would use the term.

[10] *Ibid.*

The science of economics, at first it was called Political Economy—is a whole century older than ecology. It was and is the science of social subsistence, of needs and their satisfactions, of work and wealth. It tries to elucidate the relations of producer, dealer, and consumer in the human community and show how the whole system carries on. Ecology broadens out this inquiry into a general study of the give and take, the effort, accumulation and consumption in every province of life. Economics, therefore, is merely Human Ecology, it is the narrow and special study of the ecology of the very extraordinary community in which we live. It might have been a better and brighter science if it had begun biologically.[11]

Since human ecology cannot be at the same time both geography and economics, one may adopt, as a working hypothesis, the notion that it is neither one nor the other but something independent of both. Even so the motives for identifying ecology with geography on the one hand, and economics on the other, are fairly obvious.

From the point of view of geography, the plant, animal, and human population, including their habitations and other evidence of man's occupation of the soil, are merely part of the landscape, of which the geographer is seeking a detailed description and picture.

On the other hand ecology (biologic economics), even when it involves some sort of unconscious co-operation and a natural, spontaneous, and non-rational division of labor, is something different from the economics of commerce; something quite apart from the bargaining of the market place. Commerce, as Simmel somewhere remarks, is one of the latest and most complicated of all the social relationships into which human beings have entered. Man is the only animal that trades and traffics.

Ecology, and human ecology, if it is not identical with economics on the distinctively human and cultural level, is, nevertheless, some thing more than and different from the static order which the human geographer discovers when he surveys the cultural landscape.

The community of the geographer is not, for one thing, like that of the ecologist, a closed system, and the web of communication which man has spread over the earth is something different from the "web of life" which binds living creatures all over the world in a vital nexus.

V. SYMBIOSIS AND SOCIETY

Human ecology, if it is neither economics on one hand nor geography on the other, but just ecology, differs nevertheless, in important respects from

[11] H. H. Barrows, "Geography as Human Ecology," *Annals Association American Geographers*, XIII (1923), 1–14. See H. G. Wells, *et al., op. cit.,* pp. 961–62.

plant and animal ecology. The interrelations of human beings and inter-actions of man and his habitat are comparable but not identical with inter-relations of other forms of life that live together and carry on a kind of "biological economy" within the limits of a common habitat.

For one thing man is not so immediately dependent upon his physical environment as other animals. As a result of the existing world-wide division of labor, man's relation to his physical environment has been mediated through the intervention of other men. The exchange of goods and services have co-operated to emancipate him from dependence upon his local habitat.

Furthermore man has, by means of inventions and technical devices of the most diverse sorts, enormously increased his capacity for reacting upon and remaking, not only his habitat but his world. Finally, man has erected upon the basis of the biotic community an institutional structure rooted in custom and tradition.

Structure, where it exists, tends to resist change, at least change coming from without; while it possibly facilitates the cumulation of change within.[12] In plant and animal communities structure is biologically determined, and so far as any division of labor exists at all it has a physiological and instinc-tive basis. The social insects afford a conspicuous example of this fact, and one interest in studying their habits, as Wheeler points out, is that they show the extent to which social organization can be developed on a purely physio-logical and instinctive basis, as is the case among human beings in the natural as distinguished from the institutional family.[13]

In a society of human beings, however, this communal structure is reinforced by custom and assumes an institutional character. In human as contrasted with animal societies, competition and the freedom of the indi-vidual is limited on every level above the biotic by custom and consensus.

The incidence of this more or less arbitrary control which custom and consensus imposes upon the natural social order complicates the social process but does not fundamentally alter it—or, if it does, the effects of biotic competition will still be manifest in the succeeding social order and the subsequent course of events.

The fact seems to be, then, that human society, as distinguished from plant and animal society, is organized on two levels, the biotic and the

[12] Here is, obviously another evidence of that organic character of the inter-relations of organisms in the biosphere to which J. Arthur Thomson and others have referred. It is an indication of the way in which competition mediates the influences from without by the adjustment and readjustment of relations within the community. In this case "within" coincides with the orbit of the competitive process, at least so far as the effects of that process are substantive and obvious. See Simmel's definition of society and the social group in time and space quoted in Park and Burgess, *Intro-duction to the Science of Sociology* (2d ed.), pp. 348–56.

[13] William Morton Wheeler, *Social Life among the Insects* (Lowell Institute Lectures, March, 1922), pp. 3–18.

cultural. There is a symbiotic society based on competition and a cultural society based on communication and consensus. As a matter of fact the two societies are merely different aspects of one society, which, in the vicissitudes and changes to which they are subject remain, nevertheless, in some sort of mutual dependence each upon the other. The cultural superstructure rests on the basis of the symbiotic substructure, and the emergent energies that manifest themselves on the biotic level in movements and actions reveal themselves on the higher social level in more subtle and sublimated forms.

However, the interrelations of human beings are more diverse and complicated than this dichotomy, symbiotic and cultural, indicates. This fact is attested by the divergent systems of human interrelations which have been the subject of the special social sciences. Thus human society, certainly in its mature and more rational expression, exhibits not merely an ecological, but an economic, a political, and a moral order. The social sciences include not merely human geography and ecology, but economics, political science, and cultural anthropology.

It is interesting also that these divergent social orders seem to arrange themselves in a kind of hierarchy. In fact they may be said to form a pyramid of which the ecological order constitutes the base and the moral order the apex. Upon each succeeding one of these levels, the ecological, economic, political, and moral, the individual finds himself more completely incorporated into and subordinated to the social order of which he is a part than upon the preceding.

Society is everywhere a control organization. Its function is to organize, integrate, and direct the energies resident in the individuals of which it is composed. One might, perhaps, say that the function of society was everywhere to restrict competition and by so doing bring about a more effective co-operation of the organic units of which society is composed.

Competition, on the biotic level, as we observe it in the plant and animal communities, seems to be relatively unrestricted. Society, so far as it exists, is anarchic and free. On the cultural level, this freedom of the individual to compete is restricted by conventions, understandings, and law. The individual is more free upon the economic level than upon the political, more free on the political than the moral.

As society matures control is extended and intensified and free commerce of individuals restricted, if not by law then by what Gilbert Murray refers to as "the normal expectation of mankind." The mores are merely what men, in a situation that is defined, have come to expect.

Human ecology, in so far as it is concerned with a social order that is based on competition rather than consensus, is identical, in principle at least, with plant and animal ecology. The problems with which plant and animal ecology have been traditionally concerned are fundamentally population problems. Society, as ecologists have conceived it, is a population settled and limited to its habitat. The ties that unite its individual units are those of a free and natural economy, based on a natural division of labor. Such a society is territorially organized and the ties which hold it together are physical and vital rather than customary and moral.

Human ecology has, however, to reckon with the fact that in human society competition is limited by custom and culture. The cultural super-structure imposes itself as an instrument of direction and control upon the biotic substructure.

Reduced to its elements the human community, so conceived, may be said to consist of a population and a culture, including in the term culture (1) a body of customs and beliefs and (2) a corresponding body of artifacts and technological devices.

To these three elements or factors—(1) population, (2) artifact (technological culture), (3) custom and beliefs (non-material culture)—into which the social complex resolves itself, one should, perhaps, add a fourth, namely, the natural resources of the habitat.

It is the interaction of these four factors—(1) population, (2) artifacts (technological culture), (3) custom and beliefs (non-material culture), and (4) the natural resources—that maintain at once the biotic balance and the social equilibrium, when and where they exist.

The changes in which ecology is interested are the movements of population and of artifacts (commodities) and changes in location and occupation—any sort of change, in fact, which affects an existing division of labor or the relation of the population to the soil.

Human ecology is, fundamentally, an attempt to investigate the processes by which the biotic balance and the social equilibrium (1) are maintained once they are achieved and (2) the processes by which, when the biotic balance and the social equilibrium are disturbed, the transition is made from one relatively stable order to another.

5. The Local Community as an Ecology of Games*

BY NORTON E. LONG

The local community whether viewed as a polity, an economy, or a society presents itself as an order in which expectations are met and functions performed. In some cases, as in a new, company-planned mining town, the order is the willed product of centralized control, but for the most part the order is the product of a history rather than the imposed effect of any central nervous system of the community. For historic reasons we readily conceive the massive task of feeding New York to be achieved through the unplanned, historically developed co-operation of thousands of actors largely unconscious of their collaboration to this individually unsought end. The efficiency of this system is attested to by the extraordinary difficulties of the War Production Board and Service of Supply in accomplishing similar logistical objectives through an explicit system of orders and directives. Insofar as conscious rationality plays a role, it is a function of the parts rather than the whole. Particular structures working for their own ends within the whole may provide their members with goals, strategies, and roles that support rational action. The results of the interaction of the rational strivings after particular ends are in part collectively functional if unplanned. All this is the well-worn doctrine of Adam Smith, though one need accept no more of the doctrine of beneficence than that an unplanned economy can function.

While such a view is accepted for the economy, it is generally rejected for the polity. Without a sovereign, Leviathan is generally supposed to disintegrate and fall apart. Even if Locke's more hopeful view of the naturalness of the social order is taken, the polity seems more of a contrived artifact than the economy. Furthermore, there is both the hangover of Austinian sovereignty and the Greek view of ethical primacy to make political institutions seem different in kind and ultimately inclusive in purpose and for

Reprinted with permission of the author and The University of Chicago Press, publishers, from Norton E. Long, "The Local Community as an Ecology of Games," *American Journal of Sociology*, LXIV (November, 1958), 251–261. Copyright © 1958 by the University of Chicago.

* This paper is largely based on a year of field study in the Boston Metropolitan area made possible by grants from the Stern Family Foundation and the Social Science Research Council. The opinions and conclusion expressed are those of the author alone.

this reason to give them an over-all social directive end. To see political institutions as the same kind of thing as other institutions in society rather than as different, superior, and inclusive (both in the sense of being sovereign and ethically more significant) is a form of relativistic pluralism that is difficult to entertain. At the local level, however, it is easier to look at the municipal government, its departments, and the agencies of state and national government as so many institutions, resembling banks, newspapers, trade unions, chambers of commerce, churches, etc., occupying a territorial field and interacting with one another. This interaction can be conceptualized as a system without reducing the interacting institutions and individuals to membership in any single comprehensive group. It is psychologically tempting to envision the local territorial system as a group with a governing "they." This is certainly an existential possibility and one to be investigated. However, frequently, it seems likely, systems are confused with groups, and our primitive need to explain thunder with a theology or a demonology results in the hypostatizing of an angelic or demonic hierarchy. The executive committee of the bourgeoisie and the power elite make the world more comfortable for modern social scientists as the Olympians did for the ancients. At least the latter-day hypothesis, being terrestrial, is in principle researchable, though in practice its metaphysical statement may render it equally immune to mundane inquiry.

Observation of certain local communities makes it appear that inclusive over-all organization for many general purposes is weak or non-existent. Much of what occurs seems to just happen with accidental trends becoming cumulative over time and producing results intended by nobody. A great deal of the communities' activities consist of undirected co-operation of particular social structures, each seeking particular goals and, in doing so, meshing with others. While much of this might be explained in Adam Smith's terms, much of it could not be explained with a rational, atomistic model of calculating individuals. For certain purposes the individual is a useful way of looking at people; for many others the role-playing member of a particular group is more helpful. Here we deal with the essence of predictability in social affairs. If we know the game being played is baseball and that X is a third baseman, by knowing his position and the game being played we can tell more about X's activities on the field than we could if we examined X as a psychologist or a psychiatrist. If such were not the case, X would belong in the mental ward rather than in a ball park. The behavior of X is not some disembodied rationality but, rather, behavior within an organized group activity that has goals, norms strategies, and roles that give the very field and ground for rationality. Baseball structures the situation.

It is the contention of this paper that the structured group activities that coexist in a particular territorial system can be looked at as games. These games provide the players with a set of goals that give them a sense of success or failure. They provide them determinate roles and calculable strategies and tactics. In addition, they provide the players with an elite and general public that is in varying degrees able to tell the score. There is a good deal of evidence to be found in common parlance that many participants in contemporary group structures regard their occupations as at least analogous to games. And, at least in the American culture, and not only since Eisenhower, the conception of being on a "team" has been fairly widespread.

Unfortunately, the effectiveness of the term "game" for the purposes of this paper is vitiated by, first, the general sense that games are trivial occupations and, second, by the pre-emption of the term for the application of a calculus of probability to choice or decision in a determinate game situation. Far from regarding games as trivial, the writer's position would be that man is both a game-playing and a game-creating animal, that his capacity to create and play games and take them deadly seriously is of the essence, and that it is through games or activities analogous to game-playing that he achieves a satisfactory sense of significance and a meaningful role.

While the calculability of the game situation is important, of equal or greater importance is the capacity of the game to provide a sense of purpose and a role. The organizations of society and polity produce satisfactions with both their products and their processes. The two are not unrelated, but, while the production of the product may in the larger sense enable players and onlookers to keep score, the satisfaction in the process is the satisfaction of playing the game and the sense in which any activity can be grasped as a game.

Looked at this way, in the territorial system there is a political game, a banking game, a contracting game, a newspaper game, a civic organization game, an ecclesiastical game, and many others. Within each game there is a well-established set of goals whose achievement indicates success or failure for the participants, a set of socialized roles making participant behavior highly predictable, a set of strategies and tactics handed down through experience and occasionally subject to improvement and change, an elite public whose approbation is appreciated, and, finally, a general public which has some appreciation for the standing of the players. Within the game the players can be rational in the varying degrees that the structure permits. At the very least, they know how to behave, and they know the score.

Individuals may play in a number of games, but, for the most part, their major preoccupation is with one, and their sense of major achievement is through success in one. Transfer from one game to another is, of course, possible, and the simultaneous playing of roles in two or more games is an important manner of linking separate games.

Sharing a common territorial field and collaborating for different and particular ends in the achievement of over-all social functions, the players in one game make use of the players in another and are, in turn, made use of by them. Thus the banker makes use of the newspaperman, the politician, the contractor, the ecclesiastic, the labor leader, the civic leader—all to further his success in the banking game—but, reciprocally, he is used to further the others' success in the newspaper, political, contracting, ecclesiastical, labor, and civic games. Each is a piece in the chess game of the other, sometimes a willing piece, but, to the extent that the games are different, with a different end in view.

Thus a particular highway grid may be the result of a bureaucratic department of public works game in which are combined, though separate, a professional highway engineer game with its purposes and critical elite onlookers; a departmental bureaucracy; a set of contending politicians seeking to use the highways for political capital, patronage, and the like; a banking game concerned with bonds, taxes, and the effect of the highways on real estate; newspapermen interested in headlines, scoops, and the effect of highways on the papers' circulation; contractors eager to make money by building roads; ecclesiastics concerned with the effect of highways on their parishes and on the fortunes of the contractors who support their churchly ambitions; labor leaders interested in union contracts and their status as community influentials with a right to be consulted; and civic leaders who must justify the contributions of their bureaus of municipal research or chambers of commerce to the social activity. Each game is in play in the complicated pulling and hauling of siting and constructing the highway grid. A wide variety of purposes is subserved by the activity, and no single overall directive authority controls it. However, the interrelation of the groups in constructing a highway has been developed over time, and there are general expectations as to the interaction. There are also generalized expectations as to how politicians, contractors, newspapermen, bankers, and the like will utilize the highway situation in playing their particular games. In fact, the knowledge that a banker will play like a banker and a newspaperman like a newspaperman is an important part of what makes the situation calculable and permits the players to estimate its possibilities for their own action in their particular game.

While it might seem that the engineers of the department of public works were the appropriate protagonists for the highway grid, as a general activity it presents opportunities and threats to a wide range of other players who see in the situation consequences and possibilities undreamed of by the engineers. Some general public expectation of the limits of the conduct of the players and of a desirable outcome does provide bounds to the scramble. This public expectation is, of course, made active through the interested solicitation of newspapers, politicians, civic leaders, and others who see in it material for accomplishing their particular purposes and whose structured roles in fact require the mobilization of broad publics. In a sense the group struggle that Arthur Bentley described in his *Process of Government* is a drama that local publics have been taught to view with a not uncritical taste. The instruction of this taste has been the vocation and business of some of the contending parties. The existence of some kind of over-all public puts general restraints on gamesmanship beyond the norms of the particular games. However, for the players these are to all intents as much a part of the "facts of life" of the game as the sun and the wind.

It is perhaps the existence of some kind of a general public, however rudimentary, that most clearly differentiates the local territorial system from a natural ecology. The five-acre woodlot in which the owls and the field mice, the oaks and the acorns, and other flora and fauna have evolved a balanced system has no public opinion, however rudimentary. The co-operation is an unconscious affair. For much of what goes on in the local territorial system co-operation is equally unconscious and perhaps, but for the occasional social scientist, unnoticed. This unconscious co-operation, however, like that of the five-acre woodlot, produces results. The ecology of games in the local territorial system accomplishes unplanned but largely functional results. The games and their players mesh in their particular pursuits to bring about over-all results; the territorial system is fed and ordered. Its inhabitants are rational within limited areas and, pursuing the ends of these areas, accomplish socially functional ends.

While the historical development of largely unconscious co-operation between the special games in the territorial system gets certain routine, over-all functions performed, the problem of novelty and break-down must be dealt with. Here it would seem that, as in the natural ecology, random adjustment and piecemeal innovation are the normal methods of response. The need or cramp in the system presents itself to the players of the games as an opportunity for them to exploit or a menace to be overcome. Thus a transportation crisis in, say, the threatened abandonment of commuter trains by a railroad will bring forth the players of a wide range of games who will see in the situation opportunity for gain or loss in the outcome. While over-all considerations will appear in the discussion, the frame of reference and the interpretation of the event will be largely determined by the game the interested parties are principally involved in. Thus a telephone executive who is president of the local chamber of commerce will be playing a civic association, general business game with concern for the principal dues-payers of the chamber but with a constant awareness of how his handling of this crisis will advance him in his particular league. The politicians, who might be expected to be protagonists of the general interest, may indeed be so, but the sphere of their activity and the glasses through which they see the problem will be determined in great part by the way they see the issue affecting their political game. The generality of this game is to a great extent that of the politician's calculus of votes and interests important to his and his side's success. To be sure, some of what Walter Lippmann has called "the public philosophy" affects both politicians and other game-players. This indicates the existence of roles and norms of a larger, vaguer game with a relevant audience that has some sense of cricket. This potentially mobilizable audience is not utterly without importance, but it provides no sure or adequate basis for support in the particular game that the politician or anyone else is playing. Instead of a set of norms to structure enduring role-playing, this audience provides a cross-pressure for momentary aberrancy from gamesmanship or constitutes just another hazard to be calculated in one's play.

In many cases the territorial system is impressive in the degree of intensity of its particular games, its banks, its newspapers, its downtown stores, its manufacturing companies, its contractors, its churches, its politicians, and its other differentiated, structured, goal-oriented activities. Games go on within the territory, occasionally extending beyond it, though centered in it. But, while the particular games show clarity of goals and intensity, few, if any, treat the territory as their proper object. The protagonists of things in particular are well organized and know what they are about; the protagonists of things in general are few, vague, and weak. Immense staff work will go into the development of a Lincoln Square project, but the twenty-two counties of metropolitan New York have few spokesmen for their over-all common interest and not enough staff work to give these spokesmen more substance than that required for a "do-gooding" newspaper editorial. The Port of New York Authority exhibits a disciplined self-interest and a vigorous drive along the lines of its developed historic role. However, the attitude of the Port Authority toward the general problems of the metropolitan area is scarcely different than that of any private corporation. It confines its corporate good citizenship to the contribution of funds for surveys and studies and avoids acceptance of broader responsibility. In fact, spokesmen for the Port vigorously reject the need for any superior level of structured representation of metropolitan interests. The common interest, if such there be, is to be realized through institutional interactions rather than through the self-conscious rationality of a determinate group charged with its formulation and attainment. Apart from the newspaper editorial, the occasional politician, and a few civic leaders the general business of the metropolitan area is scarcely anybody's business, and, except for a few, those who concern themselves with the general problems are pursuing hobbies and causes rather than their own business.

The lack of over-all institutions in the territorial system and the weakness of those that exist insure that co-ordination is largely ecological rather than a matter of conscious rational contriving. In the metropolitan area in most cases there are no over-all economic or social institutions. People are playing particular games, and their playgrounds are less or more than the metropolitan area. But even in a city where the municipal corporation provides an apparent over-all government, the appearance is deceptive. The politicians who hold the offices do not regard themselves as governors of the municipal territory but largely as mediators or players in a particular game that makes use of the other inhabitants. Their roles, as they conceive them, do not approach those of the directors of a TVA developing a territory. The ideology of local government is a highly limited affair in which the office-holders respond to demands and mediate conflicts. They play politics, and politics is vastly different from government if the latter is conceived as the rational, responsible ordering of the community. In part, this is due to the general belief that little government is necessary or that government is a congery of services only different from others because it is paid for by taxes and provided for by civil servants. In part, the separation of economics from politics eviscerates the formal theory of government of most of the substance of social action. Intervention in the really important economic order is by way of piecemeal exception and in deviation from the supposed norm of the separation of politics and economics. This ideal of separation has blocked the development of a theory of significant government action and reduced the politician to the role of registerer of pressure rather than responsible governor of a local political economy. The politics of the community becomes a different affair from its government, and its government is so structured as to provide the effective actors in it neither a sense of general responsibility nor the roles calling for such behavior.

The community vaguely senses that there ought to be a government. This is evidenced in the nomination by newspapers and others of particular individuals as members of a top leadership, a "they" who are periodically called upon to solve community problems and meet community crises. Significantly, the "they" usually are made up of people holding private, not public, office. The pluralism of the society has separated political, ecclesiastical, economic, and social hierarchies from one another so that the ancient union of lords spiritual and temporal is disrupted. In consequence, there is a marked distinction between the status of the holders of political office and the status of the "they" of the newspapers and the power elite of a C. Wright Mills or a Floyd Hunter. The politicians have the formal governmental office that might give them responsible governing roles. However, their lack of status makes it both absurd and presumptuous that they should take themselves so seriously. Who are they to act as lords of creation? Public expectation neither empowers nor demands that they should assume any such confident pose as top community leaders. The latter position is reserved for a rather varying group (in some communities well defined and clear-cut, in others vague and amorphous) of holders for the most part of positions of private power, economic, social, and ecclesiastical. This group, regarded as the top leadership of the community, and analogous to the top management of a corporation, provides both a sense that there are gods in the heavens whose will, if they exercise it, will take care of the community's problems and a set of demons whose misrule accounts for the evil in the world. The "they" fill an office left vacant by the dethronement of absolutism and aristocracy. Unlike the politicians in that "they" are only partially visible and of untested powers, the top leadership provides a convenient rationale for explaining what goes on or does not go on in the community. It is comforting to think that the executive committee of the bourgoisie is exploiting the community or that the beneficent social and economic leaders are wearying themselves and their digestions with civic luncheons in order to bring parking to a congested city.

Usually the question is raised as to whether *de facto* there is a set of informal power-holders running things. A related question is whether community folklore holds that there is, that there should be, and what these informal power-holders should do. Certainly, most newspapermen and other professional "inside dopesters" hold that there is a "they." In fact, these people operate largely as court chroniclers of the doings of the "they." The "they," because they are "they," are newsworthy and fit into a ready-made theory of social causation that is vulgarized widely. However, the same newspaperman who could knowingly open his "bird book" and give you a run-down on the local "Who's Who" would probably with equal and blasphemous candor tell you that "they" were not doing a thing about the city and that "they" were greatly to be blamed for sitting around talking instead of getting things done. Thus, as with most primitive tribes, the idols are both worshiped and beaten, at least verbally. Public and reporters alike are relieved to believe both that there is a "they" to make civic life explicable and also to be held responsible for what occurs. This belief in part creates the role of top leadership and demand that it somehow be filled. It seems likely that there is a social-psychological table of organization of a community that must be filled in order to remove anxieties. Gordon Childe has remarked that man seems to need as much to adjust to an unseen, socially created spiritual environment as to the matter-of-fact world of the senses.

The community needs to believe that there are spiritual fathers, bad or good, who can deal with the dark: in the Middle Ages the peasants combated a plague of locusts by a high Mass and a procession of the clergy who damned the grasshoppers with bell, book, and candle. The Hopi Indians do a rain dance to overcome a drought. The harassed citizens of the American city mobilize their influentials at a civic luncheon to perform the equivalent and exorcise slums, smog, or unemployment. We smile at the medievals and the Hopi, but our own practices may be equally magical. It is interesting to ask under what circumstances one resorts to DDT and irrigation and why. To some extent it is clear that the ancient and modern practice of civic magic ritual is functional—functional in the same sense as the medicinal placebo. Much of human illness is benign; if the sufferer will bide his time, it will pass. Much of civic ills also cure themselves if only people can be kept from tearing each other apart in the stress of their anxieties. The locusts and the drought will pass. They almost always have.

While ritual activities are tranquilizing anxieties, the process of experimentation and adaptation in the social ecology goes on. The piecemeal responses of the players and the games to the challenges presented by crises provide the social counterpart to the process of evolution and natural selection. However, unlike the random mutation of the animal kingdom, much of the behavior of the players responding within the perspectives of their games is self-conscious and rational, given their ends in view. It is from the over-all perspective of the unintended contribution of their actions to the forming of a new or the restoration of the old ecological balance of the social system that their actions appear almost as random and lacking in purposive plan as the adaptive behavior of the natural ecology.

Within the general area of unplanned, unconscious social process technological areas emerge that are so structured as to promote rational, goal-oriented behavior and meaningful experience rather than mere happenstance. In these areas group activity may result in cumulative knowledge and self-corrective behavior. Thus problem-solving in the field of public health and sanitation may be at a stage far removed from the older dependence on piecemeal adjustment and random functional innovation. In this sense there are areas in which society, as Julian Huxley suggests in his *The Meaning of Evolution,* has gone beyond evolution. However, these are as yet isolated areas in a world still swayed by magic and, for the most part, carried forward by the logic of unplanned, undirected historical process.

It is not surprising that the members of the "top leadership" of the territorial system should seem to be largely confined to ritual and ceremonial roles. "Top leadership" is usually conceived in terms of status position rather than specifiable roles in social action. The role of a top leader is ill defined and to a large degree unstructured. It is in most cases a secondary role derived from a primary role as corporation executive, wealthy man, powerful ecclesiastic, holder of high social position, and the like. The top-leadership role is derivative from the other and is in most cases a result rather than a cause of status. The primary job is bank president, or president of Standard Oil; as such, one is naturally picked, nominated, and recognized as a member of the top leadership. One seldom forgets that one's primary role, obligation, and source of rational conduct is in terms of one's business. In fact, while one is on the whole pleased at the recognition that member-ship in the top leadership implies—much as one's wife would be pleased to be included among the ten best-dressed women—he is somewhat concerned about just what the role requires in the expenditure of time and funds. Furthermore, one has a suspicion that he may not know how to dance and could make a fool of himself before known elite and unknown, more general publics. All things considered, however, it is probably a good thing for the business, the contacts are important, and the recognition will be helpful back home, in both senses. In any event, if one's committee service or whatever concrete activity "top leadership" implies proves wearing or unsatisfactory, or if it interferes with business, one can always withdraw.

A fair gauge of the significance of top-leadership roles is the time put into them by the players and the institutionalized support represented by staff. Again and again the interviewer is told that the president of such-and-such an organization is doing a terrific job and literally knocking himself out for such-and-such a program. On investigation a "terrific job" turns out to be a few telephone calls and, possibly, three luncheons a month. The standard of "terrific job" obviously varies widely from what would be re-quired in the business role.

In the matter of staffing, while the corporation, the church, and the government are often equipped in depth, the top-leadership job of port pro-motion may have little more than a secretary and an agile newspaperman equipped to ghost-write speeches for the boss. While there are cases where people in top-leadership positions make use of staff from their own busi-nesses and from the legal mill with which they do business, this seems largely confined to those top-leadership undertakings that have a direct connection with their business. In general, top-leadership roles seem to involve minor investments of time, staff, and money by territorial elites. The absence of staff and the emphasis on publicity limit the capacity of top leadership for sustained rational action.

Where top leaderships have become well staffed, the process seems as much or more the result of external pressures than of its own volition. Of all the functions of top leadership, that of welfare is best staffed. Much of this is the result of the pressure of the professional social worker to organize a concentration of economic and social power sufficient to permit him to do a job. It is true, of course, that the price of organizing top leadership and making it manageable by the social workers facilitated a reverse control of themselves—a control of whose galling nature Hunter gives evidence. An amusing sidelight on the organization of the "executive committee of the bourgeoisie" is the case of the Cleveland Fifty Club. This club, supposedly, is made up of the fifty most important men in Cleveland. Most middling and even upper executives long for the prestige recognition that membership confers. Reputedly, the Fifty Club was organized by Brooks Emery, while he was director of the Cleveland Council on World Affairs, to facilitate the taxation of business to support that organization. The lead time required to get the august members of the Fifty Club together and their incohesiveness have severely limited its possibilities as a power elite. Members who have tried to turn it to such a purpose report fairly consistent failure.

The example of the Cleveland Fifty Club, while somewhat extreme, points to the need on the part of certain activities in the territorial system for a top leadership under whose auspices they can function. A wide variety of civic undertakings need to organize top prestige support both to finance and to legitimate their activities. The staff man of a bureau of municipal research or the Red Feather Agency cannot proceed on his own; he must have the legitimatizing sponsorship of top influentials. His task may be self-assigned, his perception of the problem and its solution may be his own, but he cannot gain acceptance without mobilizing the influentials. For the success of his game he must assist in creating the game of top leadership. The staff man in the civic field is the typical protagonist of things in general—a kind of entrepreneur of ideas. He fulfills the same role in his area as the stock promoter of the twenties or the Zeckendorfs of urban redevelopment. Lacking both status and a confining organizational basis, he has a socially valuable mobility between the specialized games and hierarchies in the territorial system. His success in the negotiation of a port authority not only provides a plus for his taxpayers federation or his world trade council but may provide a secure and lucrative job for himself.

Civic staff men, ranging from chamber of commerce personnel to college professors and newspapermen, are in varying degrees interchangeable and provide an important network of communication. The staff men in the civic agencies play similar roles to the Cohens and Corcorans in Washington. In each case a set of telephone numbers provides special information and an effective lower-echelon interaction. Consensus among interested professionals at the lower level can result in action programs from below that are bucked up to the prestige level of legitimitization. As the Cohens and Corcorans played perhaps the most general and inclusive game in the Washington bureaucracy, so their counterparts in the local territorial system are engaged in the most general action game in their area. Just as the Cohens and Corcorans had to mobilize an effective concentration of top brass to move a program into the action stage, so their counterparts have to mobilize concentrations of power sufficient for their purposes on the local scene.

In this connection it is interesting to note that foundation grants are being used to hire displaced New Deal bureaucrats and college professors in an attempt to organize the influentials of metropolitan areas into self-conscious governing groups. Professional chamber of commerce executives, immobilized by their orthodox ideology, are aghast to see their members study under the planners and heretics from the dogmas of free-enterprise fundamentalism. The attempt to transform the metropolitan appearance of disorder into a tidy territory is a built-in predisposition for the self-consti-tuted staff of the embryonic top metropolitan management. The major disorder that has to be overcome before all others is the lack of order and organization among the "power elite." As in the case of the social workers, there is a thrust from below to organize a "power elite" as a necessary instru-ment to accomplish the purposes of civic staff men. This is in many ways nothing but a part of the general groping after a territorial government capable of dealing with a range of problems that the existing feudal disinte-gration of power cannot. The nomination of a top leadership by newspapers and public and the attempt to create such a leadership in fact by civic technicians are due to a recognition that there is a need for a leadership with the status, capacity, and role to attend to the general problems of the terri-tory and give substance to a public philosophy. This involves major changes in the script of the top-leadership game and the self-image of its participants. In fact, the insecurity and the situational limitations of their positions in cor-porations or other institutions that provide the primary roles for top leaders make it difficult to give more substance to what has been a secondary role. Many members of present top leaderships are genuinely reluctant, fearful, and even morally shocked at their positions' becoming that of a recognized territorial government. While there is a general supposition that power is almost instinctively craved, there seems considerable evidence that at least in many of our territorial cultures responsibility is not. Machiavellian *virtu* is an even scarcer commodity among the merchant princes of the present than among their Renaissance predecessors. In addition, the educational systems of school and business do not provide top leaders with the inspira-tion or the know-how to do more than raise funds and man committees. Politics is frequently regarded with the same disgust as military service by the ancient educated Chinese.

It is possible to translate a check pretty directly into effective power in a chamber of commerce or a welfare agency. However, to translate economic power into more general social or political power, there must be an organ-ized purchasable structure. Where such structures exist, they may be con-trolled or, as in the case of *condottieri,* gangsters, and politicians, their hire may be uncertain, and the hired force retains its independence. Where businessmen are unwilling or unable to organize their own political machines, they must pay those who do. Sometimes the paymaster rules; at other times he bargains with equals or superiors.

A major protagonist of things in general in the territorial system is the newspaper. Along with the welfare worker, museum director, civic technician, etc., the newspaper has an interest in terms of its broad reading public in agitating general issues and projects. As the chronicler of the great, both in its general news columns and in its special features devoted to society and business, it provides an organizing medium for elites in the territory and provides them with most of their information about things in general and not a little of inside tidbits about how individual elite members are doing. In a sense, the newspaper is the prime mover in setting the territorial agenda. It has a great part in determining what most people will be talking about, what most people will think the facts are, and what most people will regard as the way problems are to be dealt with. While the conventions of how a newspaper is to be run, and the compelling force of some events limit the complete freedom of a paper to select what events and what people its public will attend to, it has great leeway. However, the newspaper is a business and a specialized game even when its reporters are idealists and its publisher rejoices in the title "Mr. Cleveland." The paper does not accept the responsibility of a governing role in its territory. It is a power but only a partially responsible one. The span of attention of its audience and the conventions of what constitute a story give it a crusading role at most for particular projects. Nonetheless, to a large extent it sets the civic agenda.

The story is told of the mayor of a large eastern metropolis who, having visited the three capital cities of his constituents—Rome, Dublin, and Tel Aviv—had proceeded home via Paris and Le Havre. Since his staff had neglected to meet the boat before the press, he was badgered by reporters to say what he had learned on his trip. The unfortunate mayor could not say that he had been on a junket for a good time. Luckily, he remembered that in Paris they had been having an antinoise campaign. Off the hook at last, he told the press that he thought this campaign was a good thing. This gave the newsmen something to write about. The mayor hoped this was the end of it. But a major paper felt in need of a crusade to sponsor and began to harass the mayor about the start of the local antinoise campaign. Other newspapers took up the cry, and the mayor told his staff they were for it—there had to be an antinoise campaign. In short order, businessmen's committees, psychiatrists, and college professors were mobilized to press forward on a broad front the suppression of needless noise. In vindication of administrative rationality it appeared that an antinoise campaign was on a staff list of possibilities for the mayor's agenda but had been discarded by him as politically unfeasible.

The civic technicians and the newspapers have somewhat the same relationship as congressional committee staff and the press. Many members of congressional committee staffs complain bitterly that their professional consciences are seared by the insistent pressure to seek publicity. But they contend that their committee sponsors are only impressed with research that is newsworthy. Congressional committee members point out that committees that do not get publicity are likely to go out of business or funds. The civic agency head all too frequently communicates most effectively with his board through his success in getting newspaper publicity. Many a civic ghost-writer has found his top leader converted to the cause by reading the ghosted speech he delivered at the civic luncheon reported with photographs and editorials in the press. This is even the case where the story appears in the top leader's own paper. The need of the reporters for news and of the civic technicians for publicity brings the participants of these two games together. As in the case of the congressional committee, there is a tendency to equate accomplishment with publicity. For top influentials on civic boards the news clips are an important way of keeping score. This symbiotic relation of newsmen and civic staff helps explain the heavy emphasis on ritual luncheons, committees, and news releases. The nature of the newspapers' concern with a story about people and the working of marvels and miracles puts a heavy pressure for the kind of story that the press likes to carry. It is not surprising that civic staff men should begin to equate accomplishment with their score measured in newspaper victories or that they should succumb to the temptation to impress their sponsors with publicity, salting it to their taste by flattering newspaper tributes to the sponsors themselves. Despite the built-in incapacity of newspapers to exercise a serious governing responsibility in their territories, they are for the most part the only institutions with a long-term general territorial interest. In default of a territorial political party or other institution that accepts responsibility for the formulation of a general civic agenda the newspaper is the one game that by virtue of its public and its conventions partly fills the vacuum.

A final game that does in a significant way integrate all the games in the territorial system is the social game. Success in each of the games can in varying degrees be cashed in for social acceptance. The custodians of the symbols of top social standing provide goals that in a sense give all the individual games some common denominator of achievement. While the holders of top social prestige do not necessarily hold either top political or economic power, they do provide meaningful goals for the rest. One of the most serious criticisms of a Yankee aristocracy made by a Catholic bishop was that, in losing faith in their own social values, they were undermining the faith in the whole system of final clubs. It would be a cruel joke if, just as the hard-working upwardly mobile had worked their way to entrance, the progeny of the founders lost interest. The decay of the Union League Club in *By Love Possessed* is a tragedy for more than its members. A common game shared even by the excluded spectators gave a purpose that was functional in its time and must be replaced—hopefully, by a better one. A major motivation for seeking membership in and playing the top-leadership game is the value of the status it confers as a counter in the social game.

Neither the civic leadership game nor the social game makes the territorial ecology over into a structured government. They do, however, provide important ways of linking the individual games and make possible cooperative action on projects. Finally, the social game, in Ruth Benedict's sense, in a general way patterns the culture of the territorial ecology and gives all the players a set of vaguely shared aspirations and common goals.

6. *The Principal Structures of Community*

BY TALCOTT PARSONS

Contrary to a good deal of social science tradition, my attempt in this paper will be to treat community not as a type of concrete social unit, but as an *analytical* category. By the term "community" I would thus designate one "aspect" of *every* concrete social collectivity or structure. But by the same token, what I call its community aspect is only one of several cognate aspects of what I like to call a social system.

If, in the above respect, I take issue with much recent sociological tradition, in another, I would like to work directly from it. This is the way in which, particularly since MacIver's book *(Community: A Sociological Study),* emphasis has been placed on the relation of community to territorial location. I would thus give a tentative working definition of community as that aspect of the structure of social systems which is referable to the territorial location of persons (i.e., human individuals as organisms) and their activities. When I say "referable to" I do not mean determined exclusively or predominantly by, but rather observable and analyzable with reference to location as a focus of attention (and of course a *partial* determinant). In this respect the study of community structures comes close to what an important group of sociologists (centering in the University of Chicago and later, of Michigan) have called the "ecological approach" to the study of social phenomena. Though the territorial reference is central, it should also be pointed out that there is another term to the relation. The full formula, that is, comprises *persons acting in territorial locations,* and since the reference is to *social* relations, persons acting in relation to *other persons* in respect to the territorial locations of both parties. The *population,* then, is just as much a focus of the study of community as is the territorial location.

If the community aspect concerns population in relation to territorial location, then what are the important contexts in which this should be broken down? I would like to take a pluralistic view here and say that we should consider not one such context, but a number of them. The variables according to which these contexts should be discriminated, then, would be found on each side of the relational dyad, namely the territorial and the "personal." And since we are dealing with an aspect of social systems the relevant aspect of the personal category is *role,* which is the organizing and controlling matrix of the many physical *task* performances which make it up.

The main problems for analysis in this paper, then, are the questions of what role-categories of social structure are most directly relevant to the relations of persons to territorial locations; what in turn are the principal categories of *meaning* of territorial location to persons in roles, and how are all these related to each other? From this point of view a territorial location is always significant as a "place where" something socially significant has happened or may be expected to happen. As points of reference always *both* the place where the person of reference is or is to be located, *and* the place where the significant object to which his action is oriented is located, must be considered.

It is further important to note that the human being as a physical organism does not "stay put" in a given location, but moves about a great deal. Therefore you cannot say that a given individual is always in the same unit of community organization. Secondly, the individual person has not one, but a number of roles. Hence, apart from other types of movement, the appropriate unit of community *need* not be the same for any two of the different roles in which he is involved.

*   *   *

7. *Toward an Interactional Conception of Community*

BY HAROLD F. KAUFMAN

The growing concern of the general public and of opinion leaders for the development and preservation of the community as a social unit needs to be seen against the background of forces hastening its decline, namely, centralization, specialization, and the increase of impersonal relationships. Centralization is seen both in the massing of population and the pyramiding of power and leadership, culminating in the growth of the monolithic state.[1]

The search for community is not confined to the devotees of the rural way of life. The supporters of urban life, principally those concerned with the neighborhoods of the central city, are becoming increasingly concerned about the urban sprawl and the "anti-city" trends in metropolitan growth.[2] The many-sided community organization and community development movement of today, as seen especially by those involved, is a reaction to rapid community decline. Significant development programs are found in town and country communities and in urban neighborhoods, chiefly those in central cities.[3] Community development programs in the underdeveloped nations of the world are another very rapidly expanding area of work.

Reprinted with permission of the author and the University of North Carolina Press from Harold F. Kaufman, "Toward an Interactional Conception of Community," *Social Forces*, XXXVIII, No. 1 (October, 1959), 9–17.

[1] Robert Nisbet, *The Quest for Community* (New York: Oxford University Press, 1953). This writer considers one of the most important social facts in our world to be the growing concentration of power in the sovereign political state (p. viii). The state has taken up the vacuum created by the decline of the religious, kinship, and locality groups. The decline of "community has made ours an age of frustration, anxiety, disintegration, instability, breakdown, and collapse" (p. 7). [For a portrayal of some of Nisbet's views, see Selection 9 below.—R. L. W.] Cf. also Baker Brownell, *The Human Community* (New York: Harper & Brothers, 1950), p. 5. This writer states, "This public and private tendency toward indiscriminate centralization and mass control of life in fields of economics, corporative industry, technology, art, religion, politics, recreation, education, agriculture, and human affairs in general may well be a tendency toward death."

[2] William H. Whyte, Jr. *et al.*, *The Exploding Metropolis* (Garden City, N. Y.: Doubleday & Company, Inc., 1958). See especially chapter 1, "Are Cities Un-American?"

[3] Some streams of interest which have contributed to the present community development movement are community organization for social welfare, the community council movement, city planning, industrial and business promotion, and college research and service programs.

FOCUS OF PAPER

This interest in community change and development calls for theory and research focusing on dynamics and process. The purpose of this paper is to suggest some conceptual guidelines for the study of community from an interactional and process perspective. Following a short statement of some questions involved in definition, the conception of the community as an interactional field is presented. Basic elements of an interactional field are described and the distinctive features of the community arena are considered. The paper is concluded with a consideration of community design, the broad goals and focus of planned change.

DEFINING THE COMMUNITY

A sizable volume of research in recent years has been designated as work in community or closely allied fields.[4] A review of community research a decade ago classified research, on the basis of its central focus, into three categories: "ecological, structural, and typological."[5] A recent examination of definitions of community revealed that most students were "in basic agreement that community consists of persons in social interaction within a geographic area and having one or more additional common ties."[6]

Some consensus exists concerning at least three elements in the definition of community. One, community is a social unit of which space is an integral part; community is a place, a relatively small one. Two, community indicates a configuration as to way of life, both as to how people do things and what they want—their institutions and collective goals. A third notion is that of collective action. Persons in a community should not only be able to, but frequently do act together in the common concerns of life.[7]

Some students have observed that man is decidedly limited spatially in carrying on his daily activities.[8] This indicates that the community might

[4] Albert J. Reiss, Jr., *Review and Evaluation of Research on Community, A Working Memorandum Prepared for the Committee on the Social Science Research Council* (Nashville, Tenn.: Social Science Research Council, April 1954), pp. 3–4. Also Harold F. Kaufman *et al., Toward a Delineation of Community Research* (Social Science Research Center, Mississippi State College, Community Series No. 4, May 1954), p. 23 ff.

[5] A. B. Hollingshead, "Community Research: Development and Recent Conditions," *American Sociological Review,* 13 (April 1948).

[6] George A. Hillery, Jr., "Definitions of Community: Areas of Agreement," *Rural Sociology,* 20 (June 1955), p. 111.

[7] Dwight Sanderson and Robert A. Polson, *Rural Community Organization* (New York: John Wiley & Sons, Inc., 1939), pp. 49–50.

[8] "Community refers to the structure of relationships through which a localized population provides its daily requirements," Amos H. Hawley, *Human Ecology* (New York: Ronald Press, 1950), p. 180. Similarly, the "community arises through sharing

be defined as that area in which the great majority of people live and make a living. Because of greatly improved transportation, this area of daily living has greatly expanded. To see this vividly one need only visualize an American Indian village of several hundred persons which two centuries ago, might well have stood on the same site as a present day metropolis of several million. One would readily agree that to use the term community to apply to both situations leads to great generality; if the concept is not qualified by precise subclasses, it loses much if not all of its scientific usefulness.[9]

A difficulty in delineating the modern community in urban life is the separation of production from consumption and residence, a situation which did not exist in a predominantly agricultural society. When one looks for the locale of production in modern urban society, his attention is directed toward the metropolitan region or toward the relatively large trade center area. When one looks toward the community of residence, he sees at the urban level the suburb or the neighborhood of the central city, at the rural level the hamlet or the open country neighborhood.

In the search for a more precise definition of community there is not only the question of differentiating localities as to their size and complexity, but within any given locality there is the problem of distinguishing community phenomena from those which might be considered noncommunity. Specifically, does the community include the totality of the social life in an area—all family living and voluntary associations, political and economic organization? Most common usage at least leaves that inference. Community, from this point of view, is the local society in all its inclusiveness.

In this setting of the practical and theoretical problems just described, an attempt is made to formulate an interactional or process conception of community.

THE NOTION OF THE INTERACTIONAL FIELD

Community researchers are recognizing increasingly the need for analysis of community dynamics. This is seen in a growing number of studies with such emphasis.[10] The convergence of contributions from several research areas

a limited territorial space for residence and sustenance and functions to meet common needs generated in sharing this space by establishing characteristic forms of social action," Albert J. Reiss, Jr., "Sociological Study of Communities," *Frontiers of Community Research and Action* (a Symposium, May 8, 1958, Madison, University of Wisconsin [mimeographed]).

[9] Frank D. Alexander takes such a position in his "The Problem of Locality-Group Classification," *Rural Sociology*. 17 (September 1952), pp. 236–44.

[10] Jessie Bernard writes: "For the most part, the sociologists have been interested in the community structures which result from interaction rather than the interaction processes themselves. . . . It would seem . . . that the time may be ripe for a greater

would appear to be of value in developing the notion of the community as an interactional field. Several types of work may be noted. One is the conception of the community as a group. Perhaps the most quoted treatment is a paper entitled "The Community as a Social Group," written nearly two decades ago.[11] A second interest is the development of the notion of community action analysis,[12] while a third line of development is to be seen in studies of local leadership and power structure.[13]

A fourth area of studies which would appear to have a definite contribution to make in developing an interactional concept of community deals with the notions of field,[14] arena,[15] or situation.[16] The terms field and arena are used interchangeably in this paper. No implications of the terms, field and arena, as used in other contexts should be accepted here unless explicitly stated. That is, how much the conceptions of the "social situation," the "psychological field" or the "political arena" can contribute to the interactional notion of community as proposed here is yet to be determined.

The notion of the interactional field or arena presented here is a highly tentative one. It is much more an enumeration of elements of an interactional conception of community than a precise statement of their interrela-

---

emphasis on dynamic interaction in community studies and also, perhaps, for greater recognition of the community aspect of all interaction studies," in "Some Social-Psychological Aspects of Community Study: Some Areas Comparatively Neglected by American Sociologists," *British Journal of Sociology*, 2 (1951), pp. 12–30. As early as 1915 Robert Park in his paper, "The City," stated that studies of community should be "designed to furnish data that would throw light on the process of interaction."

[11] E. T. Hiller, "The Community as a Social Group," *American Sociological Review*, 6 (1941), pp. 189–202. This is one of the most referred to treatments of the subject. From a close study of this paper one may gain the notion that community as a group is a residual category. Henry Zentner describes Hiller's position to be that "the communal group may be regarded as that group which remains after all other types of groups and associations have been factored out of the total system of social organization constructed by the inhabitants of the locality," in "Logical Difficulties in Relating the Concepts Community, Society, and Institutions," *Alpha Kappa Deltan*. XXVIII, No. 1 (Winter 1958).

[12] This work is illustrated by the research at Michigan State University in their study, *Community Involvement: The Webs of Formal and Informal Ties That Make for Action*, Christopher Sower *et al.* (Glencoe, Illinois: The Free Press, 1957). Other publications by this group on this topic, as well as work by other individuals, are indicated below in the section on "The Community Action Process."

[13] See below for references.

[14] Kurt Lewin, *Field Theory in Social Science*, edited by Dorwin Cartwright (New York: Harper & Brothers, 1951). See also J. F. Brown, *Psychology and the Social Order* (New York: McGraw-Hill Book Company, 1936).

[15] Harold Lasswell and Abraham Kaplan, *Power and Society* (New Haven: Yale University Press, 1950), pp. 78–80.

[16] Leonard S. Cottrell, Jr., "The Analysis of Situational Fields in Social Psychology," *American Sociological Review*, 7 (1942) pp. 370–82.

tionships. Some guidelines, however, for further exploration are proposed. Although the concept is highly general, heuristic, and primarily of value in organizing concepts with more restricted reference, it is also amenable to graphic presentation and analogy. The interactional field probably has several dimensions, the limits and interrelation of which need to be determined.

The community field is not a Mother Hubbard which contains a number of other fields, but rather is to be seen as only one of the several interactional units in a local society. As discussed below, the relation of the community field to other fields such as the economic, the religious, the political, is a highly important concern.

Perhaps the notion of community arena or field can be made more comprehensible by the use of analogy. Keeping in mind the limitations of this method in scientific discussion, one may visualize the community field as a stage with the particular ethos of the local society determining the players and the plays. If the orientation is democratic and primary social contacts are dominant, many engage in script writing and acting and there are relatively few spectators. On the other hand, in situations where the population is relatively large, only a small proportion can occupy the stage at any one time. The same persons are likely to appear again and again, while the others either sit passively as spectators, or are carrying on their limited-interest shows on other stages, unmindful of the community drama.

In case the orientation is autocratic, as in a prison or to a lesser extent a totalitarian society, both the script and names of the cast are handed down from above; such orders may even state when the audience is to applaud.

Where the situation is one of status quo, little if any acting takes place and when it does it is the same old thing. Some, however, may look longingly toward the stage as they recall the pleasant experiences of years gone by.

The community field consists of an organization of actions carried on by persons working through various associations or groups. This organization of actions occupies the center of the community arena and is distinguished from other fields of action in a locality by a complex of characteristics or dimensions.[17] Providing a setting for community action and an integral part of the arena are patterns of demographic, ecological, and physical factors.

The community arena is by definition an integral part of the local society, or perhaps better stated, the locality agglomerate. The latter term is preferred because it has less implication with respect to the social organization and integration of the local area. Two highly significant types of relationships in studying the community field are the interplay of community actions and interactions (1) with the demographic, ecological, and physical

[17] Cf. the "interaction space approach and the social-group approach" in Albert J. Reiss, Jr., "The Sociological Study of Communities," *Rural Sociology*, 24 (1959), pp. 118–30.

setting and (2) with other interactional fields both in the given locality agglomerate and in the mass society.

ELEMENTS OF THE INTERACTIONAL MODEL

In order to make the notion of the community as an interactional arena as explicit as possible, ways of viewing action or units of interaction are described. This is done in this section, and in the following section those criteria which distinguish community activities from noncommunity activities are noted.

One unit of study at the interactional level is the action or interaction. The term action may be more appropriate when seen in a time sequence, the concept interaction when the relationship among persons is the major focus. At the observational level actions are called projects, programs, activities or events. Examples are planning and building the community hospital, operating the city park, and planning and carrying out the annual community homecoming. Three important analytical elements of any action, whether community or other, are (1) the persons involved, designated here as actors or participants, (2) the associations or groups through which the action takes place, and (3) the stages and phases of action through time.[18]

Although the values of community, the ends of community action may be discussed in a consideration of phases of action, they occupy such an important part in the conception of community presented here that the last section of this paper is devoted entirely to community design or patterns for the good community as defined by citizens, planners, and philosophers.

THE COMMUNITY PARTICIPANT

The community actor or participant may be identified by who he is and what he does. Who the participant is depends on his position in the structure of the local society. Among the characteristics of position are social rank, material possessions, age, and sex.[19]

In looking for what the community actor does, one investigates his behavior in organized groups and informal networks which are located in the locality. Formal indices of participation include memberships and officerships in voluntary organizations and positions held in agencies. An over-all

---

[18] Cf. James Green and Selz C. Mayo, "A Framework for Research in the Actions of Community Groups, *Social Forces,* 31 (1953), pp. 320–27; Christopher Sower *et al., op. cit.,* especially chap. 13; and Paul A. Miller, *Community Health Action* (East Lansing: Michigan State College Press, 1953), especially chap. 1.

[19] For an attempt to describe the characteristics of community leadership, see, for example, Paul A. Miller, *op. cit.,* chaps. 10–12; and Floyd Hunter, *Community Power Structure* (Chapel Hill: University of North Carolina Press, 1953), chap. 2.

index may be gained from a composite rating of one's fellow community members.[20] Definitive work at this point leads to a delineation of community positions and roles including their motivational and identification aspects.

The degree of involvement of a local population in the interactional community runs all the way from assuming a major role in policy making to no more than identification with the locality resulting from "residence and sustenance" activities. There, of course, would be in any population at any given time a greater or lesser number of visitors who would have little or no awareness of the community or involvement in it. It is likely that even in areas with the highest potential for community action, only a minority of the population is ever active at a given time.

Certainly a grouping of significant community participants are the leaders, "power elite" and/or "persons of influence." Who make decisions and influence community action? On what phases of a project do given persons appear? Is there a division of labor or do certain persons appear in every project? These and related questions are of concern in an analysis of community leadership—a central consideration in the interactional approach to community.[21]

COMMUNITY GROUPS

Sociologists have frequently designated the community a social group. The precise nature of this group, however, has seldom if ever been made clear.[22] Community, especially in the modern world, is seldom if ever expressed through only one association. To describe the community as a single group, one must either greatly oversimplify or make the conception highly abstract. An example of the former is to regard residence in an area as the essential criterion of community membership; an example of the latter is to describe the community as "that group which remains after all others have been factored out.[23]

A great variety of groups may at one time or another be involved in community action. They range from the coffee-break clique through the civic clubs to the more institutionalized groups such as the board of aldermen. In addition to groups in which primary contacts are dominant, publics such as that of the local newspaper are important. Only a few organizations, such as perhaps a community improvement association, are engaged entirely

[20] This may be either based on one's influence or one's prestige in the local society. As an example of the former, see Frank A. Steward, "A Sociometric Study of Influence in Southtown," *Sociometry*, 10 (1947), pp. 273–86; of the latter, Harold F. Kaufman, *Prestige Classes in a New York Rural Community* (Ithaca, N.Y.: Cornell University, Memoir 200, March 1944).

[21] For a recent critical discussion of selected studies on community leadership, see "The Sociology of Community Power: A Reassessment," *Social Forces*, 37 (March 1959), pp. 232–36.

[22] An exception is the work of Hiller, *op. cit.*

[23] *Ibid.*

in community activity. On the other hand, some never appear in the community field.

In a local society with relatively small population and simple organization, such as an open country neighborhood, associations engaging in community activity are relatively easy to recognize. An excellent example is the community club. In this one association all the families in the area may coordinate the several interests of their common life. By contrast, in a city a number of organized groups may be operating in each interest area. In this situation it is not only more difficult to identify the organized activities which lie in the community field, but it is especially so with respect to the informal networks.

At the associational level the community may be seen as a network of interrelated associations, formal and informal, whose major function is problem solving for the local society. In a changing society the community may be seen as a problem-solving process which provides needed adjustment for the local life. At any one time only a small proportion of the recognized associations in an area of any complexity would be involved in the community process. It is a research question to determine what associations and individuals are involved and how frequently and which ones remain outside or at the periphery of the community arena.

Discrete unrelated actions, no matter how great their individual contributions, do not make the interactional community. A degree of coordination, integration, and unity is essential. This is realized at the associational level through groups which coordinate and carry out community activity. At the cultural level, integration is effected through the widely shared values and objectives pertaining to the community field and, at the ecological level, through a "functional relation" of services.[24]

PHASES AND PROCESS OF COMMUNITY ACTION

The raw data for the study of community action are the sequences of observable events. The major problem in data collection is an adequate description of current happenings and a proper reconstruction of past ones, especially for informal and private activities. Phases or sequences of action have been observed by a number of writers.[25] Although based both on pre-

---

[24] Cf. Werner S. Landecker, "Types of Integration and Their Measurement," *American Journal of Sociology*, 56 (1951), pp. 332–40.

[25] One observer of community life suggested nearly four decades ago stages in the action process. See E. C. Lindeman, *The Community: An Introduction to the Study of Community Leadership and Organization* (New York: Association Press, 1921). To be noted is the similarity of this pattern of action to the problem-solving process as elaborated by John Dewey in his *How We Think* (1910). For a more recent treatment see James Green and Selz C. Mayo, *op. cit.*, Christopher Sower *et al., op. cit.*, and C. R. Hoffer and Walter Freeman, *Social Action Resulting from Industrial Development*, (Michigan State University Agricultural Experiment Station Special Bulletin 401, September 1955), especially pp. 24–32.

vious conceptualization and on refinements indicated from empirical studies, phases listed below are regarded as highly tentative. Five phases, two or more of which may be carried on concurrently, are suggested.

1. Rise of interest. Awareness of need and perhaps of general solution and the spreading of this consciousness.
2. The organization and maintenance of sponsorship. A major sponsor, a group or individual, can always be identified and frequently one or more auxiliary sponsors.
3. Goal setting and the determination of specific means for their realization. This is the decision and policy making phase.
4. Gaining and maintaining participation, especially of the rank and file. This is the public relations and recruitment phase.
5. Carrying out the activities which represent goal achievement.

Actions may be occasional, periodic, or continuous. Examples of these types are building a hospital, a fund drive, and a year-round educational program, respectively. It appears useful many times to regard actions as cyclical, with evaluation as the final phase. The second cycle might well be thought to begin with phase 2 above; that is, a reorganization of sponsorship and a renewal of interest. Many actions, of course, are abortive—they never complete the cycle. For example, many good intentions for community improvement never get beyond the "talk" stage.

What actors and associations are involved in each phase is a way in which three elements of action—persons, groups, and sequences—may be interrelated.[26]

For a short time span a dynamic analysis can be carried out with persons in interaction as the central focus. For longer time periods, however, other conceptions such as processes of change of groups and value patterns would appear more appropriate. What is needed is as precise an analysis of the community arena over generations as the above formulation suggests for a period of months and at the most a few years. Relevant are such notions as the life cycle of a community association and the natural history of the community both as an interactional arena and a locality agglomerate.[27]

[26] It may be contended that this model of community action is too rational, which is probably true. On the other hand, community development activity is defined by some as planned change. The above formulation focuses on the time dimension of an action project. Another important level is the degree to which an action promotes social cohesiveness or disorganization. Conflict as well as cooperation may appear in any of the phases listed above.

[27] Cf. J. H. Kolb and A. F. Wileden, *Making Rural Organizations Effective* (Agricultural Experiment Station, University of Wisconsin, Bulletin 403, 1928), and Dwight Sanderson, *The Rural Community* (Boston: Ginn & Company, 1932).

DISTINCTIVENESS OF THE COMMUNITY FIELD

The community field, like other interactional complexes, may be seen in terms of actors, associations, and process or phases of action, but what is its distinctiveness? How, especially in this complex world, does one find the community? Making explicit the criteria of community action which set off community from noncommunity activities is a crucial problem in interactional theory.

Six types of characteristics, dimensions, or criteria are suggested for differentiating community action from that not appropriate to the community field. Each dimension is to be seen as a necessary element of a complex, or pattern of characteristics. These criteria may be applied in distinguishing single actions as well as differentiating the community field as a whole from other interactional fields. The dimensions noted are (1) the degree of comprehensiveness of interests pursued and needs met, (2) the degree to which the action is identified with the locality, (3) relative number, status, and degree of involvement of local residents, (4) relative number and significance of local associations involved, (5) degree to which the action maintains or changes the local society, and (6) extent of organization of the action.[28]

RANGE OF INTERESTS

It is essential that an action be identified with the locality and that it either express a number of interests in the local life or be closely related to other actions which express such interests. If actions cover a wide range of interests of the local life, they will of necessity involve a number of significant participants and groups. An example of an activity which would rank very high in its community nature and would be considered at the center of the community field would be a well organized and productive community development program. An example of an action in a locality which has no local reference whatsoever would be a national convention with no local participants.[29]

By definition, the ends of the community development program are entirely oriented toward improving and increasing identification with the

[28] Cf. Willis A. Sutton, Jr. and Jiri Kolaja, The Concept of Community, unpublished paper. These writers suggest six dimensions of community action: (1) number of actors, (2) degree of structure, routine and emergent, (3) number of recipients of the action, (4) degree of awareness, (5) degree of local territorial orientation, and (6) degree of interrelationship of institutions.

[29] The present meeting of the Southern Sociological Society would also serve as a good illustration of a strictly noncommunity type of action. One must, however, distinguish between the activities of the visitors and that of the local residents in making the activities of the visitors possible.

locality. The program pursues a variety of interests, from economic development through the pursuit of religious goals. In this activity many significant community members and groups must be involved. The activity both makes changes in the local society and also, through its problem solving, tends toward equilibrium and stability. Much of the action process is organized, although many informal contacts would be involved.

IDENTIFICATION WITH LOCALITY

Many activities carried on in localities today have little or no reference to the locality, but instead are oriented toward the mass society.[30] An example of these two orientations would be the health fund drive, which is a part of community action when it is integrated in the community fund-raising campaign and in the community health council; but when carried on entirely from district or national headquarters, it is purely an activity of large-scale mass organization.[31]

Localities vary greatly as to the number of interests which are expressed through locally oriented actions. An important task of analysis is to discover the interplay between the specialized fields such as health, religion, and government, and the community arena.[32] Strong communities have actions locally oriented across the gamut of human interests, and these actions are coordinated through various associations and are integrated through a common ideology. On the other hand, many localities have at one time had many actions locally oriented and now have only a few, if any. A good example of the latter type locality is the rural neighborhood either in a marginal area with a rapidly declining population or the one located close to a rapidly growing urban center. In both cases the locality has lost many of its locally oriented actions (services) and thus has declined as an interactional unit.

In the study of any given locality the student of community interaction is interested in discovering whether the area is merely a "chunk of mass society" or whether it has a number of interrelated locally oriented associa-

---

[30] For a development of the community versus mass society orientations in the field of stratification, see Harold F. Kaufman, "An Approach to the Study of Urban Stratification,'" *American Sociological Review*, 17 (August 1952), pp. 430–37.

[31] The community chest campaign is a type of action common especially to larger localities. A few studies have been made which point up the fact that the so-called interactional component, effective organization of participants, is an extremely important factor in community action and that it is sometimes not appreciably affected by differences in the economic level and related factors. See, e.g., C. Arnold Anderson, "Community Chest Campaigns as an Index of Community Integration," *Social Forces*, 33 (October 1954), pp. 76–81.

[32] The same empirical problem of interrelationship is faced whether one uses the interactional perspective or some other, such as the social system. In the former case one might speak of the overlapping or intersecting of fields, whereas in the latter the concept, systemic linkage, has been used. See Charles P. Loomis, "Systemic Linkage of El Cerrito," *Rural Sociology*, 23 (March 1959), p. 54.

tions which are carrying out the common life. Most so-called community context studies have been in the community but not of it. That is, they have used a locality as a basis of sampling but there has been no identification of the phenomena under study with the interactional community.

DEGREE OF INVOLVEMENT

The number and significance of individuals and associations participating[33] are debatable criteria in community field definition. If the position is taken that for action to be highly community in character there must be a high level of participation on the part of both individuals and associations, then a bias is introduced favoring what is termed below the "participating community," and this of necessity limits the size of the population.

CHANGE AND STABILITY

As community action in the present-day world has a problem-solving orientation, it generally results in some change in institutional structure. Today the institutional base of the community field is always somewhat unstable.[34] In this fact are presented the dilemma and the challenge of community development. Although one of the greatest weaknesses of community programs is the lack of institutional and financial stability, to go too far in this direction means that programs cease to be agents of change and become guardians of existing conditions. When a program becomes too highly institutionalized, it may become solely the concern of a special group, and mass participation declines. This is easily seen in cases in which programs of widespread voluntary citizens' participation have after a time been handed over to some government bureau, with the rapid decline in citizen support and interest.

In the present world with many forces destroying locality group identity, much community action is oriented toward creating community. This makes of central importance in an interactional notion of community those value complexes and cultural themes which people want to realize in their localities. Community in the present-day world is always more a dream, an ideal, than a reality. These themes or community designs toward which community action may be oriented are considered briefly in the last section of this paper.

[33] The participants in community action may be classified as actors, those carrying on the action, and beneficiaries, those benefiting from it. The degree of involvement would range all the way from those who were providing the major leadership to individuals completely unaware of the activity. In between would be various degrees of participation in the activity itself and awareness of it but no direct involvement.

[34] In any age of the mass society or an agglomerate of publics, the community association and consequently its institutional form is frequently the first victim of competition and conflict among these publics.

THE INTERACTIONAL PERSPECTIVE IN RESEARCH

The relative usefulness of any perspective or framework of study is to be determined finally by the fruitful hypotheses developed. This paper has of necessity been more an enumeration of elements or components of the interactional perspective than it has been a precise and analytical presentation. Brief note should be made, however, of analytical designs possible within the interactional perspective. Before causal or sequential type of analysis can proceed far, indices must be developed of the various elements, e.g., extent and nature of participation or identification with locality. The physical, ecological and demographic factors would in most designs appear as independent variables.

At the present stage of development of community theory it is quite desirable that interplay among major perspectives take place. The ecological frame of reference has probably been worked on longer and is more fully developed than any other.[35] Recently formulations have been developed of what might be termed the social system perspective in community study.[36] Work of the anthropologists in the study of the small locality group is well known.[37]

Some contributions, realized and potential, of the interactional and process perspective should be made explicit. Three are noted here. One contribution is the emphasis on dynamics and change. The focus is on interaction through which forms of association and institutions change. The vagueness possible in process theory is avoided by making structure—community associations and actors—an integral part of the formulation.[38]

A second value is the scope and inductive nature of the perspective. Use is made of several levels of analysis. Although major focus is on interaction, institutional, demographic and ecological considerations are essential. The inductive emphasis in the perspective is seen in the concern for gather-

[35] See Hawley, *op. cit.*, and James A. Quinn, *Human Ecology* (New York: Prentice-Hall, Inc., 1950); Otis Dudley Duncan and Leo F. Schnore, "Cultural, Behavioral and Ecological Perspectives in the Study of Social Organization" [*The American Journal of Sociology*, 65 (1959), 132–46].

[36] Irwin T. Sanders, *The Community* (New York: Ronald Press, 1958), especially chaps. 11 and 18. Cf. also the position developed by Charles P. Loomis. See, e.g., Loomis and J. Allan Beegle, "Locality Systems," chapt. 2 in *Rural Sociology* (New York: Prentice-Hall, 1957).

[37] For some description of this work see J. H. Steward, *Area Research* (Social Science Research Center, Bulletin 63, 1950), pp. 20–53, and Robert Redfield, *The Little Community* (Chicago: University of Chicago Press, 1955).

[38] For a criticism of discussing process apart from structure, see Robert M. MacIver, *Social Causation* (New York: Ginn & Co., 1942), pp. 130–31. The notion of community arena or field as presented here focuses on structure and dynamics—order in change, people in interaction, groups in process.

ing data at a relatively low level of conceptualization, such as programs, projects, and participants.

The conception of arena or field presents a pluralistic and open system as contrasted to a monolithic explanation[39] and a closed logical system. It allows for convergence of various points of view, and carries the assumption that at this stage of development of community theory, it would be premature to attempt a neat systematization. What is needed is not closing the system, but rather the development of fruitful hypotheses that will help explain action and change regardless of where they might lead conceptually.

Third, the perspective developed here gives an opportunity for treatment of both descriptive and normative data in the same context. This aids in the orientation of research toward action, the importance of which is discussed below. With the increasing demand for research findings to support community organization and development, a combination of the descriptive and normative alone is justification for exploration of the conception of social field or arena.

COMMUNITY DESIGN

It is just as important a social fact to discover what people think community ought to be as it is to describe what community is. This is especially true in view of the fact that community action in the modern world is to a large extent problem solving and change oriented. It is directed more to the creating of new associations and institutional forms than to maintaining the existing ones. Thus special attention needs be given to the ends of community action, especially as discrete ends become integrated into meaningful themes or designs as to what constitutes the good community.

A legitimate and much needed task for the sociologist is to analyze those ends and goals which the average citizen as well as the leaders of thought and opinion regard as desirable and good. It is essential to carry out this analytical function for two reasons: (1) in order to complete the analysis of the action process and (2) to make interaction analysis highly relevant for community improvement and development programs.[40]

An analysis of the literature on community improvement and development reveals certain themes and designs or patterns for the good community. One investigator, focusing chiefly on overseas programs, sees two major recurring themes that sometimes are at cross purposes. The first emphasizes

[39] See Zentner, *op. cit.*, in his discussion of "Monolithic Versus Differentiated Theories of Community."

[40] Here, of course, is the problem of the relation of social norms to the research process. Needless to say, the sociologist in his study of normative society constantly has the problem of keeping his values explicit so they do not color his findings. An excellent treatment of this problem is to be found in Howard Becker's "Supreme Values and the Sociologist," *American Sociological Review*, 6 (April 1941), pp. 155–72.

the improvement of material conditions of life and measures success in terms of technical gains and economic growth. The second emphasizes the development of local groups which have skill in problem solving, strong identification with the locality, and a spirit of self-reliance.[41]

Another analyst has made explicit several "assumptions" or "ideological bases" on which community organization in American society rests. Some of those listed were local autonomy, folk wisdom, value of the group process, concern for the total life, and emphasis on "means as well as ends—the opposite of the totalitarian philosophy."[42]

In discussions of community design,[43] two somewhat distinctive and polar ideologies emerge. One may be characterized by the terms homogeneity, participation, and face-to-face contacts, the other by cosmopolitanism, anonymity, and mass contacts. There is a tremendous emphasis in the applied fields of adult education and social work in developing a participating community.[44] Perhaps one of the best examples of the homogeneous, participating community in the present world would be a relatively self-sufficient middle-class area outside of a central city. A good example of the cosmopolitan type of life would be found in the upper-class neighborhood in a central city. Proponents of cosmopolitan design decry the conformity and what one has termed the "sadness" of present-day suburbs.[45]

One may contend that the rush to the suburbs represents a return to community in an age of urban living. People are interested in nature and space and the integration of such services as school, church, and retail shops. If one's job is close by, it is even better. The separation of job from other aspects of living presents one of the major problems in present-day community organization and integration.

There is probably a place in present-day society for both the homogeneous and the cosmopolitan types of community. Also, within any given local society a balance needs to be maintained between what might be

[41] Melvin M. Tumin, "Some Requirements for Effective Community Development," *Community Development Review*, No. 11 (Washington, D. C., ICA, December 1958), pp. 1–40.

[42] Gordon W. Blackwell, "A Theoretical Framework for Sociological Research in Community Organization," *Social Forces*, 33 (October 1954), pp. 57–64.

[43] Other disciplines also have a contribution to make here. For a city planner's discussion of the "good community," see Percival and Paul Goodman, *Communities: Means of Livelihood and Ways of Life* (Chicago: University of Chicago Press, 1947).

[44] An example of this emphasis is to be found in Saul D. Alinsky's *Reveille for Radicals* (Chicago: University of Chicago Press, 1946). A somewhat opposing point of view is developed by Bernard Barber in "Participation and Mass Apathy in Associations," *Studies in Leadership*, A. W. Gouldner, ed. (New York: Harper & Bros., 1950).

[45] David Riesman, "The Suburban Sadness," Part IV in *The Suburban Community*, William M. Dobriner, ed. (New York: G. P. Putnam's Sons, 1958). See also William H. Whyte, Jr., *op. cit.*

termed processes of localization—those which focus on life within the locality and its distinctiveness—and the lateralization processes[46]—those which orient social life beyond the locality and tend to make the participants concerned members of various national publics.

IMPLICATIONS FOR ACTION

Community is the concern of both the scientist and the man of action; it is not only a phenomenon to be studied, but a place to live. An intensive search is going on at both levels. This paper is especially concerned with the development of theory which would support research that would contribute effectively to the growing community organization and development movement. The general notion of community as an interactional arena or field has been suggested and developed as a perspective.

The social value of community research may be measured by the extent to which it contributes to realizing the types of community that people desire. In this endeavor the sociologist has a continuing challenge to work with action leaders in developing and making explicit various alternative designs for the good community and suggesting conditions under which these goals may be realized.

[46] For the development of the concept lateralization, see Burt W. Aginsky, "The Fragmentation of the American Community," *Journal of Educational Sociology*, 26 (November 1952), pp. 125–33.

8. Community Functions

BY BLAINE E. MERCER

1. COMMUNITY STRUCTURE AND COMMUNITY FUNCTION

Social life is a process of interaction, and its essence is mutual awareness and the attempt of people to predict the behavior of others. When two or more persons become aware of the presence of the other or others and, consciously or unconsciously, predict their behavior, there exists a *social relationship,* one which denotes "the behavior of a plurality of actors in so far as, in its meaningful content, the action of each takes account of that of the others and is oriented in these terms."[1] Social relations are the province of the sociologist and, since they involve individual motivations, actions, and symbolic expressions, it is human behavior, broadly defined, which we study. We are concerned, to be sure, not only with the day-to-day activities of people living in communities, but with their myths, values, and institutions; but these can only be completely known through the study of the dynamic processes of social living.

The social life of any community is dynamic; so, too, is its structure. The structure of anything is a pattern of organization which persists in time. But all things in this world change. John Dewey used the analogy of the structure of a house when he wrote, "It is not something external to which the changes involved in building and using the house have to submit. It is rather an arrangement of changing events such that properties which change slowly, limit and direct a series of quick changes and give them an order which they do not otherwise possess. Structure is a constancy of means, of things used for consequences, not of things taken by themselves or absolutely."[2] Structure, then, can be conceived of as an ordering of change; and, in scientific analysis, whatever influences change is itself changed. There is no such thing as the "unmoved mover."[3]

[1] Weber, Max, *The Theory of Social and Economic Organization,* translated by A. M. Henderson and Talcott Parsons, Oxford University Press, New York, 1947, p. 118.
[2] Dewey, John *Intelligence in the Modern World,* edited by Joseph Ratner, The Modern Library, New York, 1939, p. 1053.
[3] *Ibid.,* p. 1054.

This does not imply that social change and social structure are synonymous, for there is, in the structure of social relationships, a tendency to persist. As Georg Simmel put it, "That destruction is easier than construction, is not unqualifiedly true of certain human relations, however indubitable it is otherwise."[4] The processes involved in the relationships of people may contribute to the persistence of the structure—even in instances in which there is a disappearance of conditions without which the relationship would not have been established.

An erotic relation, for instance, begun on the basis of physical beauty, may well survive the decline of this beauty and its change into ugliness. What has been said of states—that they are maintained only by the means by which they were founded—is only a very incomplete truth, and anything but an all-pervasive principle of sociation generally. Sociological connectedness, no matter what its origin, develops a self-preservation and autonomous existence of its form that are independent of its initially connecting motives. Without this inertia of existent sociations, society as a whole would constantly collapse, or change in an unimaginable fashion.[5]

If function is defined as the contribution made by an item to the continuity of a given structure, and if it is agreed that structure may be conceived of as both persistence and an order of change, then it would follow that community function must have something to do with the processes which contribute to persistence and to change in the community or in the larger society of which the community is a part. These functional processes—the social life of the people—are vitally important in the study of a community as of any society. They are the forces which render a community a system of action, which cement groups together, and which bring about the development and operation of those systems of behavior norms which we call institutions.

There are various ways of studying the community. The community may be regarded (1) as merely an aggregate of people living in a geographic area, in which case a census study may be the method of investigation; (2) as a pattern of control mechanisms exerted on the lives of individuals, calling, for example, for a legal study, or (3) as a functional entity, requiring studies based upon the analysis of the interactions of individuals.[6] While we shall not ignore entirely the first two approaches,

[4] Simmel, Georg, *The Sociology of Georg Simmel*, translated and edited by Kurt H. Wolff, The Free Press, Glencoe, Illinois, 1950, p. 380.
[5] *Ibid.*, pp. 380–81.
[6] Park, Robert Ezra, *Human Communities*, The Free Press, Glencoe, Illinois, 1953, p. 118. Park is referring to the study of the city.

we shall maintain throughout this book a basic interest in the community as a dynamic, functioning system of the interrelationships of persons. We shall study patterns of values according to which people, singly and as groups, regulate their behaviors; we shall study institutions and their organization into social systems which have their being in the context of ordinary life interest and everyday affairs. We shall study the arrangement of community members in social structures, and be concerned with patterns of persistence and change in these structures. Finally, the processes of social life, the functional interrelations of people who maintain the structure, will receive our attention.

Community functions may be analyzed from three points of view. The first is focused on the functional contributions of the community to a larger society of which it may be a part. (This cannot be applied to all communities, since not all of them are parts of any larger society.) The second is concerned with the functional interrelations of people within a given community. The third deals with the functions of the community as a whole to the structures of its constituent groups and individual personalities. We proceed to a brief discussion of each of these.

2. COMMUNITIES AND EXTERNAL FUNCTIONS

Most communities as units have *external* functions, that is, they contribute to the continuity and cohesion of the larger society. These external functions vary from one community to another, although it is possible to classify communities according to the type of function which predominates. Some communities, for example, broadly speaking, contribute primarily *things* and others primarily *services* to the larger society.

Communities whose functional emphasis is things include factory communities in which are made industrial products of whatever kind and agricultural communities which produce costly farm commodities. Service communities include, for example, university towns with their educational services and county seats and other governmental centers having control functions. These two general categories can be broken down into several subgroups according to the nature of the product or the service which is contributed. It is difficult to classify some communities in either of these categories, and, it must be emphasized, there is probably no community at all which exclusively contributes things *or* services, but not both. Some communities, however, emphasize one, rather than the other, and categorization is on the basis of this emphasis.

Communities whose basic function is to provide things which find their way into the larger society are clearly making a contribution to the continuity of the larger society. But that contribution is qualitatively different from the functions emphasized by the service community. In the former case, the contribution emphasizes the health, defense, physical comfort, and the socially determined psychological welfare. In the latter case, the contribution is especially related to the maintenance of the social system. Speaking broadly, this is because a larger proportion of the people of service communities tends to be especially concerned with ideas and values, which are the stuff of which the fabric of the social system is woven. The people of communities whose functional emphasis is on things are typically somewhat less involved in their daily lives with value systems, or at least tend to spend less time on them as subjects of thought and discussion; these communities are for this reason less likely to have direct and significant effect upon the social system of the larger society.

No community, as we have noted, contributes solely things or services, for it is difficult if not impossible to separate material things from the ideas which go with them (a basic criticism, by the way, of the old classification of culture items into *material* and *non-material*). But it is clear that in a great many communities, one or another contribution strongly predominates. A town dominated by one large factory making, say, chocolate products, certainly makes external functional contributions which are significantly different qualitatively from those made by another town dominated by a large university. The distinction is useful for the analysis and comparison of external functions of different communities. The situation is somewhat less clear in the case of internal functions.

3. COMMUNITIES AND INTERNAL FUNCTIONS

The contributions made externally by communities to the larger society are analogous to the contributions made by the institutions, groups, and individuals within it to a specific community. Therefore, what is said here can be referred back on a different plane of analysis to the external functions of communities.

Every community is in itself a society, held together by a social system of rules and values. It must provide, internally, for the maintenance of its population, that is for the satisfaction of the biological necessities of life, sustenance, the protection of its members from crippling or fatal injury, and the replacement of those members who die. There must be some rules for a division of functions among the population, for every community has work which must be done if it is to survive. The people of any community must possess a degree of group solidarity, including some motivation of contact between members and motivation of resistance to strangers within a framework of mutual tolerance of one another. Finally, there must be provided procedures for ensuring the perpetuation of the social system, the normative patterns regulating behavior, the rules and regulations, the values and goals. These procedures include socialization techniques for the transmission of the social heritage from generation to generation.[7]

Later in this book, we shall study status and role, social classes, the family, church, school, economic, and governmental associations, and such processes as conflict and competition. Our fundamental question will continue to be: What functional contribution does the subject of our analysis make to the continuity of structure or its ordered change of the community of which it is a part?

Not every institution, group, or culture item has necessarily a positive community function; some of them result in negative or disruptive contributions. Others produce no significant functional contributions whatever. We shall also note and describe these dysfunctional and nonfunctional aspects of community.

4. INDIVIDUAL AND GROUP FUNCTIONS

Social groups of smaller size than an entire community or society generally have structures or arrangements of members in terms of institutionalized behavior norms. Personalities, too, can be conceived of as structures of attitudes, habits, and values—in general, tendencies to react to certain stimuli in specific ways. The structures of small groups and individual personalities, as well as of entire communities, are dynamic and *tend* to change in predictable and ordered fashion. Communities, as wholes, make contributions to the structures of their constituent small groups and personalities. These community functions are contributions to sustenance, expression, self-identification and ego-satisfaction, and integration and cooperation.[8]

(1) *Contributions to sustenance.* As our definition indicates (see Chapter 2), no community is self-sufficient, but a person can live his entire life in his community. Human organisms and personalities are "fed" and sustained in communities. Material goods are obtained and consumed there, and education and the satisfactions necessary for the persistence of personality structure are gotten there. People *survive* in communities.

(2) *Contributions to expression.* Most persons receive satisfactions from various kinds of self-expression, and this expression, for the most part, takes place in their own communities. People interact with one another, learn values, inherit or acquire statuses and roles, and, to a large extent, obtain in their communities a sense of purposive living.

[7] Based on Kingsley Davis, *Human Society,* The Macmillan Company, New York, 1949, p. 30. . . .

[8] This classification of community functions is from Joyce O. Hertzler, *Society in Action,* The Dryden Press, New York, 1954, p. 190.

(3) *Contributions to self-identification and ego-satisfaction.* People identify themselves with their communities, take pride in them, and develop a sense of belonging with respect to them. One source of ethnocentrism is the individual's identification of himself and his destiny with his community.

(4) *Contributions to integration and cooperation of individuals and groups.* One focus of group life is the community. People develop there a "consciousness of kind" and an understanding of the function of human differences (as expressed through division of labor) in the creation and maintenance of social cohesion. The "sense of community" is a factor in orderly social life, and it is in communities that social controls are effected.

5. STRUCTURE, FUNCTION, AND CHANGE

Some writers have pointed out that the positive and identifiable external functions of communities in America seem to be on a decline. "Physical growth and the efficient specialization of functions may be, in terms of community values, disintegrative," Baker Brownell asserts.[9] At the present time, rural communities especially seem to be transferring many of their functions, even agricultural production, to larger centers, or abandoning them altogether. This is due to such factors as new marketing methods, educational concentrations such as school consolidation, rapid communication, the remarkable geographic mobility of the American people, and to their generally expanding horizon of interest and concern. Many American communities are undergoing rapid changes; they are growing larger, both in population and geographic size; their functional contributions to the whole society are becoming more diffuse and difficult of definition; and their people are becoming related to one another more nearly as members of secondary groups than as members of primary groups. This is another way of saying that our communities, broadly speaking, are taking on the urban characteristics we alluded to in the previous chapter and which we shall consider in detail later. . . . In certain other communities, such as residential suburbs, counter trends toward specialization in external functions can be observed.

While there may be what has been called "functional alienation," the removal of "operational control of a function from the community which it is supposed to serve,"[10] this does not necessarily mean that the community is in fact disintegrating. Such movements as school consolidation, the widening of trade, sport, recreation, and public information interests are not sure signs that the community is dissolving. It is true that, as community

---

[9] Brownell, Baker, *The Human Community,* Harper and Brothers, New York, 1950, p. 13.
[10] *Ibid.,* p. 15.

contacts widen outward in ever growing circles, community functions, both external and internal, may grow beyond the contact of many or most members of the local community. But neither is this development an indication that the community as a system of relationships is being completely disorganized or destroyed. Specialization of function, either by communities as wholes or by groups and individuals, may result in fragmentation and compartmentalization of social life to the extent that a person may interact with others only in specific situations, for example, at work *or* at play *or* at church, but not at work *and* at play *and* at church. But, again, this does not necessarily mean the destruction of community. What it does mean is that the old, isolated *gemeinschaft-like* rural community is being replaced with a newer contract-based urban type of community which, with modifications we will discuss later in this book, appears to be well on the road to becoming the typical American local community.

The American local community, in sum, is dynamic. Its structure should be viewed not only as persistence in the arrangement of people relative to one another, but also as an ordering of change. The processes which make up daily life in the community are the social processes which are functional or dysfunctional to the community structure. And, as the internal functions of institutions, persons, and groups are contributions to a pattern of community persistence and predictable change, so the functions of the community as a whole are contributions to the persistence and ordered change of the structure of the larger society of which it may be a part.

9. Moral Values and Community

BY ROBERT A. NISBET

The relationship between man, the community, and environment is one of the lasting themes to which every generation makes its contribution based upon knowledge and historical circumstances. To a large extent this relationship is dependent upon the system of authority and function which exists in society at large. During the Middle Ages, when centralized authority did not exist, local units tended to be strong and to enlist the loyalties of their members. The downfall of medieval communities came about in very large part as the result of centralization both of political authority and economy during the Renaissance and the Reformation. The basic problem of the community in the Western world is therefore to be seen in terms of what happened historically to the structure of power and function in the larger society. It is very difficult to maintain the eminence of the small, local units when the loyalties and actions of individuals are consolidated increasingly in the great power units represented by the nation states in the modern world.

But the problem of community is also a problem in values. Because of the widespread emphasis upon technique, mechanism, rationalization of authority, monopoly of economic activity, there has been a general disinclination in the social sciences and in modern planning to remain closely concerned with the problem of human values. Quite apart, however, from the ultimate origin of human values, we know that their nurture and transmission from generation to generation depends upon groups small enough to provide the medium of learning but possessed of sufficient significance to give them a meaningful role so far as the cultivation of values is concerned. Such values as love, honor, and loyalty do not, cannot, thrive in a sociological vacuum.

It is well known in the study of language that the meanings of words and sentences depend upon understandings which exist prior to the utterance of the words themselves. It is equally true that all formal statements of value contain and depend upon certain prejudgments which give formal judgments their roots of meaning and even possibility of communication.

Reprinted with permission of the author and publisher from Robert A. Nisbet, "Moral Values and Community," *International Review of Community Development*, No. 5 (1960), pp. 77–85.

Without some kind of agreement upon the unspoken but powerful prejudgments, all efforts to derive meaning from and to reach agreement about the
explicit judgments are fruitless. Most of the world's conflicts of faith and
action take their departure from lack of agreement about prejudgments
rather than from dissention about formal judgments; and these are never
within the reach of the language analyst. Finally, it is but an extension of the
foregoing to emphasize that the communities of assent on which the spoken
word depends, and the silent prejudgments which give meaning and efficacy
to formal judgments of value, are themselves reinforced and contained by
the more tangible communities of interest and behavior that compose a
social organization. No one of these three sets of elements is causative or
crucial. They exist as inseparable aspects of the one unified phenomenon.
Apart from residual values themselves, human associations can have no
more meaning than those which exist in the animal world. But apart from
communities of men, the values themselves will not long remain important
and meaningful to their human beings.

A wise philosopher, Susanne Langer has written:

*The mind, like all other organs, can draw its sustenance only from the
surrounding world; our metaphysical symbols must spring from reality. Such
adaptation always requires time, habit, tradition, and intimate knowledge
of a way of life. If, now, the field of our unconscious symbolic orientation is
suddenly plowed up by tremendous changes in the external world and in the
social order, we lose our hold, our convictions, and therewith our effectual
purposes. . . . All old symbols are gone, and thousands of average lives
offer no new materials to a creative imagination. This, rather than physical
want, is the starvation that threatens the modern worker, the tyranny of the
machine. The withdrawal of all natural means for expressing the unity of
personal life is the major cause of the distraction, irreligion, and unrest that
mark the proletariat of all countries.*[1]

It is not strange that in our century we should see so many evidences—
in practical behavior and also in philosophy and literature—of the kind of
dislocation of moral value to which Dr. Langer refers. The vast changes
in government, economy, and technology have had a striking impact upon
men's social relationships. In the 18th century the central problem taken by
philosophers was the problem of authority, and out of it came the theory
and jurisprudence of the modern nation state. In the 19th century the central
problem seemed to be economic, and in the works of the great economists of
the 19th century we see the outlines created of the industrial world to which
all of us, increasingly, belong. In the 20th century it is the moral-social prob-

[1] *Philosophy in a New Key*. London and New York, 1948, p. 235.

lem that has become uppermost. And it has become uppermost because of the profound changes which have taken place in state and economy.

What are the dislocations and deprivations which have driven so many, in this age of economic abundance and political welfare, to a quest for security and a general concern for community? They lie, I think, in the realm of the small primary personal relationships of society—the relationships that mediate directly between man and his larger world of economic, moral, and political and religious values. Our problem is concerned with all of these values and their greater or less acceptability to the individual. It is this that makes our problem also social. It is social in the exact sense that it pertains to the small areas of membership and association in which human values are made meaningful and compelling to human beings.

Behind the spreading sense of insecurity and alienation in western society, behind all of the popular as well as academic preoccupation with the problem of community, there is growing realization that the traditional primary relationships of men have become, in certain areas, functionally irrelevant to the larger institutions of society, and sometimes meaningless to the moral aspirations of individuals.

A great deal of the character of contemporary social action has come from the efforts of men to find in large scale organizations, especially political ones, those values of status and intellectual security which were formally acquired in church, family, and neighborhood. How else can we explain the success of such movements in the modern world as Communism, Nazism except as mass movements designed to confer upon the individual some sense of that community which has been lost under the impact of modern social changes. The horror and tragedy are that such political movements have been based upon, and dedicated to, force and terror.

Too often the problem of modern community is blurred under the phrase, "social disorganization." Such a term is made to cover too great a diversity of conditions. In any society as complex as ours it is unlikely however that all aspects are undergoing a similar change. Thus it can scarcely be said that the state, as a distinguishable relationship among human beings, is today undergoing disorganization, for in most countries, including western Europe and the United States the political relationship is being enhanced above all other forms. The contemporary state, with all its apparatus of bureaucracy, has become more powerful, more cohesive, and is endowed with more functions than at any time in its history.

Nor would it be sensible to speak of disorganization of the great impersonal relationships which we find in our society in the form of the large private and semi-public organizations of an educational, economic, and charitable nature. Large-scale labor organizations, political parties, welfare organizations, and business corporations show a continued and even increasing prosperity, at least when measured in terms of institutional significance. It may be true that these organizations do not offer the degree of individual identification that makes for a sense of social belonging but it would hardly be accurate to apply the word disorganization to these immense and influential organizations.

The problem of disorganization, if we are to use the term, must be located more precisely with respect to those types of relationship which have actually undergone dislocation. These, as I have indicated above, are the relationships of the smaller, inter-personal sort. It is worth remembering that when Durkheim first addressed himself to the problem of community in his *Division of Labor,* he did so in the optimistic belief that modern industrialism was creating a new and more viable form of solidarity than had ever been known in the history of the human race. This new form of solidarity, Durkheim said, was organic; organic in the sense it would be based upon division of labor, with each element of the system thereby made the more dependent upon all other elements. Durkheim distinguished this form of solidarity from the old and traditional form which he called mechanical. Mechanical solidarity, Durkheim defined, as that which exists when all human beings are pursuing identical functions.

It was Durkheim's bold argument that such difficulties and maladjustments as we now find in the society around us stem from the fact that organic solidarity has only incompletely and imperfectly come into existence. When the last evidences of mechanical solidarity are erased and when the new system based upon division of labor is functioning perfectly, all such maladjustments will disappear. Men will be drawn to one another not on the basis of ancient traditional interest but on the basis of felt, mutually perceived, functional interdependence.

Such was Durkheim's contention, but, as he himself came to realize after he finished the *Division of Labor* the argument could not really be sustained. Therefore we find Durkheim in his next great work, *Suicide,* proclaiming the need for the re-establishment of forms of association akin to those which existed successfully in the ages characterized by mechanical solidarity. Only these, he was forced to conclude, can rescue modern man from the loneliness and functional inadequacy that he finds in the industrial system around him. Thus, although Durkheim failed in the prime effort of his first great book, he set a problem that he came to answer brilliantly—but very differently, from what he had originally intended—that is, through human communities within industry and the state which would restore once again the sense of solidarity and inspire men with a deep devotion to moral purpose.

The great inadequacy of Durkheim was in failing, however, to search for those natural and autonomous communities of individuals which have developed somehow even within the great impersonal spaces of the modern state. Durkheim accepted the perspective of modern society as being almost unrelievedly impersonal, atomistic, and mechanical. It was for this reason that Durkheim argued the necessity of contriving and establishing from the ground up new forms of community life which would give the individual a sense of identification. This view corresponded, of course, with the view taken by many of the early sociologists in the United States and elsewhere, a view which saw the small primary groups becoming historically archaic and replaced by large "secondary" associations. The argument was that such primary groups as family, neighborhood, and local community are undergoing a process of disappearance, to be replaced by the greater associations of a secondary character based upon economic or educational or religious interest alone. But more careful study in recent decades reveals that even in the largest cities, primary groups of an autonomous and self perpetuating character are to be found.

I should like to refer in this connection to the fine study of the family in London done by Michael Young and Peter Willmott.[2] In this study it was discovered that, contrary to popular sociological belief, the extended family still has great relevance in the lives of many of the people in the lower class areas of London. Furthermore, when thousands of these individuals, under a program of planning, were removed from their slum areas and placed in model housing some distance away from the slums, considerable unhappiness was the consequence. Such unhappiness was the result of small families being separated from relatives on whom they had traditionally depended for a great deal of their human association. In short, well-intended but insufficiently prepared planning had taken modern sociology at its face value and assumed that only the small conjugal family was of any significance in the lives of individuals and that such families could safely thereby be removed.

I think this study of the family could undoubtedly be supplemented and reinforced by other studies of the kinds of small communities which exist, and which are all too frequently neglected by planning which takes the view that cities are merely collections of atomistic individuals.

Much thought is being given these days to the need for community centers, especially in the suburbs and in many of the "model" towns which are coming into existence in so many parts of the world. Such centers are considered as essential to the development of a community spirit. But I do not think there is very much hope for any one of these centers in the instilling of a sense of community purpose so long as they are regarded as mere adornments to the functions and loyalties which actually exist and are related to day to day lives. A community center will be important to individuals only insofar as it adapts itself to the activities and concerns which exist naturally among a people but which need only leadership and guidance to evoke their

---

[2] *Family and Kinship in East London.* London, 1957.

full manifestation. Such centers can hardly operate successfully in a social desert: that is an area inhabited simply by individuals impersonally united by economic or religious interests but not through the affiliations which actually give life and meaning to one's existence.

The old communities—tribe, clan, joint family, and guild—were held together to a very large extent by sacred, even religious, bonds. The towns of the Middle Ages, which are sometimes, perhaps uncritically, praised as ideal communities, sheltered the lives of their citizens by religious, civic, and economic associations, each of which aspired to be a kind of enlarged family, and was small enough to arouse deep personal loyalty. The reason why religion has figured so prominently in social history is that in any community a feeling of meaning, of shared purpose, is essential to the prosperity of the community. Religion, traditionally, has been the vessel in which most of the shared meanings and purposes of a deeper sort have been carried. But, it must be emphasized, religion is not indispensable so long as there is some other pattern of meanings and purposes which will do the same thing.

It may well be asked: why should we seek communities at all? Is it not sufficient, in an age of the welfare state that we should live simply and solely in terms of the great regulations, laws, and associations which this state provides? It is often said that today, for the first time in human history, the state has become a benevolent and protective association which is able to meet both the social and the physical demands of people formerly met by a plurality of smaller communities. To this we must say firmly, however, that the state which possesses the power to do things *for* people has also the power to do things to them. Freedom cannot be maintained in a monolithic society. Pluralism and diversity of experience are the essence of true freedom. Therefore even if the state were able to meet the basic problems of stability and security through its own efforts, we should have to reject it as the solution simply because of our concern for the problem of freedom.

However it is to be noted that the state does not even serve the security need. No large-scale association can really meet the psychic demand of individuals because, by its very nature, it is too large, too complex, too bureaucratized, and altogether too aloof from the residual meanings which human beings live by. The state can enlist popular enthusiasm, can conduct crusades, can mobilize in behalf of great "causes," such as wars, but as a regular and normal means of meeting human needs for recognition, fellowship, security, and membership, it is inadequate. The tragedy is that where the state is most successful in meeting the needs for recognition and security, it is most tyrannical and despotic, as the histories of Communist Russia and Nazi Germany have made clear. The only proper alternative to large-scale, mechanical political society are communities small in scale but solid in structure. They and they alone can be the beginning of social reconstruction because they respond, at the grass roots, to fundamental human desires: living together, working together, experiencing together, being together. Such communities can grow naturally and organically from the most elementary aspirations, they remain continuously flexible, and, by their very nature, they do not insist upon imposing and rigid organizations.

Not only for purposes of viable social planning, as contrasted with the mechanical type of planning, but also for purposes of motivation and general creativity, the contexts of informal association must be understood. These, we have learned full well, are indispensable to the nurture of vigorous and creative personality. They are also crucial to the preservation of political freedom.

When the basic principles of modern liberalism were being formulated by such men as Locke, Adam Smith, and Jefferson, the image of man that existed then in the philosophical mind was one constructed out of such abstract traits as reason, stability, security, and indestructible motivations toward freedom and order. Man alone was deemed to be inherently self-sufficing, equipped by nature with both the instinct and reason that could make him autonomous.

What we can now see with the advantage of hindsight was that the founders of liberalism were unconsciously abstracting certain moral and psychological attributes from a social organization and considering these as the timeless natural qualities of the individual, who was regarded as independent of the influences of any historically developed social organization. Those qualities were qualities actually inhering to a large extent in a set of institutions and groups, all of which were aspects of historical tradition. But, with the model of Newtonian mechanics before them, the moral philosophers insisted on reducing everything to human atoms in motion, to natural individuals driven by impulses and reason deemed to be innate in man.

Given this image of man as inherently self-sufficing, given the view of communities and groups as merely secondary, as shadows of the solid reality of man, it was inevitable that the strategy of freedom should have been based upon objectives of release and the emancipation of man from his fettering institutions.

A creative society would be one in which individuals were "emancipated" from all types of social relationship. A free society would be, similarly, one in which human beings were morally and socially, as well as politically, free from any kind of authorities and institutional functions. The ideal, insensibly, became one of a vast mass of individuals separated from one another in social terms, participating only through the impersonal mechanisms of the market and of the legal state.

Thus, in Bentham's terms the fundamental cement of society would be provided not through groups and close personal relationships, but through certain "natural" identifications of interest rising in almost equal part from man's instinctual nature and from his reason. "It is not strange," George E. Adams has written, "that the self discovery and self-consciousness of the individual should have steadily mounted higher as the environment of individuals more and more takes on the form of an impersonal, causal, and mechanical structure. For the mobility and freedom of the individual can be won only as he becomes detached from his world; his world becomes separated from him only when organized and defined in objective and impersonal terms."[3]

In strictly sociological terms, what this means is that the individual's community was becoming an ever more remote thing to him in the 19th century. Because of profound shifts in the structure of authority and functions of society, more and more men were being made small parts in a social machine ever larger, ever more impersonal, ever more regimented. With authority becoming more and more objectified and externalized, the consequences were deleterious to those primary forms of authority with which man had traditionally and subjectively identified himself for ages. These ceased to be important. Their moral virtues were transferred as it were to him, even as their historic authorities were being transferred to the state.

But what we have learned under the guidance of studies in modern social psychology is that the rationalist image of man is theoretically inadequate and practically intolerable. We have learned that man is not self-sufficing in social isolation, that his nature cannot be deduced simply from elements innate in the germ plasm, and that between man and such social groups as the family, local group, and interest associations there is an indispensable connection. No conception of individuality is adequate that does not take into consideration the many ties which normally bind the individual to others from birth to death.

Individuality cannot be understood except as the product of normatively oriented interaction with other persons. Whatever may lie neurologically in the human being, we know that a knowledge of man's actual behavior in society must take into consideration the whole stock of norms and cultural incentives which are the product of social history. The normative order in society is fundamental to all understanding of human nature. We do not see, think, react, or become stimulated except in terms of the socially inherited norms of human culture.

But the normative order is itself inseparable from the associative order. Culture does not exist autonomously; it is always set in the context of social relationships. Only thus do the ends and patterns of culture make themselves vivid and evocative to human beings. And we have learned that with the dislocation of the social relationships which immediately surround the human being there occurs also a disruption of his cultural or moral order. The intensity of personal incentive, whether in the context of therapy or day to

[3] *Idealism and the Modern Age.* New Haven, 1919, p. 35.

day life of the normal human being tends to fluctuate with the intensity of meaningful social relationships. This is what we have learned from studies of motivation in learning, from studies of character formation, and from observation of personal morale in all kinds of stress situations.

The philosophy of individualism, John Dewey wrote a generation ago,

ignores the fact that the mental and moral structure of individuals, the pattern of their desires and purposes, change with every great change in social constitution. Individuals who are not bound together in associations, whether domestic, economic, religious, political, artistic, or educational, are monstrosities. It is absurd to suppose that the ties which hold them together are merely external and do not react into mentality and character, producing the framework of personal disposition.[4]

So too with creativeness. Admittedly, it is the freedom of persons that is crucial. Great works of art or literature or science are not created by anonymous organizations. They are the concrete results of personal performance. But from the obvious centrality of the person in intellectual or cultural achievement it does [not] follow that such achievement is the sole consequence of innate individual forces nor that it is the result simply of processes of separation. To be sure there is in the achievement of any great work, whether it be a painting or a treatise in metaphysics, a relatively high degree of detachment in the minds of the creator. But we are still compelled to regard the important interdependences between the creator and his community.

Creation is individual, or at most the work of a small group, but much creative work would never have been done apart from such communities as the guilds, colleges, philosophical societies, monasteries, and institutes. In such organizations as these the informal, the spontaneous, and the autonomous types of relationship assume great importance. In them the creative process can move freely, tensions can be relaxed and inhibitions overcome. Sparks are thrown off by difference rubbing on difference in small compass. Imaginations are fired. Admittedly, small groups can be as deadly as large ones, but the important point is that, unlike more formal types of associations, small and informal groups are not likely to last for long when their purpose is dead and their fellowship flagging. They are not saved by by-laws or dues invested, when their true resources run out.

In conclusion, the search for viable forms of community must be a continuous one. All the resources of knowledge must be brought to bear on the problem. Neither moral values, nor fellowship, nor freedom can easily flourish apart from the existence of diverse communities each capable of enlisting the loyalties of its members.

[4] *Individualism Old and New.* New York, 1930, pp. 81–2.

10. A General Typology of Human Groups

BY GEORGE A. HILLERY, JR.

One of the most important taxonomic contributions which a comparison between vills and total institutions can make is a distinction between various kinds of organizations.* To see the distinction, we must relate each of these systems to some larger class of systems and thus consider them within a more general theory of social organization. For total institutions, the larger class of systems has been extensively developed as the theory of formal organizations. And although the lack of uniformity in community theory prevents such a similar identification for vills, we can reach such a goal by comparing vills with formal organizations.

The question now arises, what is the simplest and most extensive way of separating vills and formal organizations? Most apparent is the kind of goals for which the group members strive, as group members. The goals of formal organizations are sharp and recognizable: profit, or custody of dangerous people, or recreation, or education, or so on. The vill, on the other hand, has no goal, as a vill. It may be described, instead, as the consequence of cooperation among families in a given location. Of course, vills contain systems with specific goals, but these must be distinguished from any goals which would be pertinent to the vill as a whole. Also, vills may follow specific goals, such as occur in a community chest drive, but these goals are either temporary or they are peculiar to specific vills rather than being common to vills in general.

This distinction suggests that one way of classifying groups is in terms of whether the system as a whole possesses goals. Accordingly, groups may be viewed as being defined by specific goals, on the one hand, or merely being a result of following other goals. We are thus distinguishing between groups which come into existence because they are purposely

Reprinted with permission of the author and the University of Chicago Press from George A. Hillery, Jr., *Communal Organizations: A Study of Local Societies* (Chicago: The University of Chicago Press, 1968), pp. 145–52.
*[The term "vill," as used by Hillery, corresponds roughly to "local community." He defines vill as "a localized system integrated by means of families and cooperation." There are two types of vill, the folk village and the city. A total institution, however, is not a type of vill. It may be described as "a system in which a bureaucratic staff compels a localized collectivity to act for certain ends." Hillery places great stress on conceptual precision, and these key concepts are developed at length in his book.— R. L. W.]

created to do certain things, and groups which are seldom if ever specifically created but which evolve because other groups bring them into being. To express this distinction in another way, some groups are brought into being merely through the process of human living.

As important as this distinction is, it includes entirely too many unlike things. Crowds are not formal organizations, but in part they are defined in terms of specific goals (rioting crowd, lynch mob, spectator crowd, etc.) and, similarly, cliques and ethnic groups are not vills, but they need not give primacy to specific goals. Obviously, there must be further subdivision.

Two questions will show the nature of the needed division: (1) How are crowds different from formal organizations? (2) How are cliques different from vills? Note that the first pair of these groups is defined by specific goals, the second pair is not. Within each of these pairs, a further distinction may be drawn in terms of the degree of their institutionalization. One member of each pair is structured by means of an extensive pattern of norms—that is, it is institutionalized—whereas the other member of each pair is much less institutionalized.

On the basis of the reasoning thus far, a preliminary typology may be constructed as shown in Figure 2. There are numerous groups yet to be placed within this scheme, but there are several questions to be asked before the typology can serve as a working tool for future discussion.

The System Is:

	Defined by specific goals	Not defined by specific goals
Structured (institutionalized)	Formal organizations	Vills
Relatively unstructured (uninstitutionalized)	Crowds	Cliques

Norms:

FIGURE 2. PRELIMINARY TYPOLOGY OF HUMAN GROUPS

The first question concerns the manner in which one distinguishes systems with specific goals. Following Parsons,[1] we may describe a specific goal as having at least three characteristics: (1) the product of the goal

[1] Talcott Parsons, *Structure and Process in Modern Societies* (Glencoe, Ill.: The Free Press, 1960), pp. 17–18.

is identifiable, such as automobiles, academic degrees, etc; (2) the product can be used by another system—that is, the output of one system is an input for another system; and (3) the output is amenable to a contract, it can be bought and sold. An organization *has* specific goals if its members recognize the possession of specific goals and if its norms are so organized that they contribute to the attainment of those goals.

At this point, goals must be carefully distinguished from functions.[2] The latter may be defined as a contribution to the existence of a given system. The attainment of the goal is virtually always functional for such groups as formal organizations, of course, but there are other functions besides goal attainment, as well as dysfunctions.

In formal organizations, both the goals and the structures are intentionally (manifestly) functional for each other. The organization *may* achieve latent or unintended results, but the latent consequences cannot be so important that they prohibit the attainment of the manifest goals in the eyes of the members of the organization. For example, a latent dysfunction of prisons is that inmates are taught to be more efficient criminals. This dysfunction *impedes* the attainment of the manifest goal, that of custody, but it does not *prohibit* the attainment of that goal.

The situation is almost exactly reversed in structured systems without goals. Vills, for example, have no specific raison d'être. At least in the vills studied here, no specific goal they were created to attain is ever overtly stated. Indeed, none of them were purposely created to do what they do (at least within the memories of their inhabitants): to promote living and cooperation among a collection of families who reside in a given place.

One of the basic identifying features of such groups as vills and cliques, therefore, is the absence of specific "defining" goals, that is, those goals for which the system exists. In this sense, one might say that such systems are ends in themselves, though such a statement leaves too many questions unanswered, not the least of which is the number of people that must feel this way before the criterion applies. Further, there is little evidence on the point: all that we know is that people are ethnocentric about vills; but they are ethnocentric about other groups, too. Thus, in the absence of better data, we will say that the vill and similar types must be identified by a negative criterion: There are no specific goals which define the system, there is no specific goal to which the members give top priority or "primacy of orientation," in Parsons' terms.[3]

It is possible for vills to have specific goals, but only insofar as these goals are not intentionally harmful, that is, manifestly dysfunctional, to the goals

[2] Kingsley Davis, *Human Society* (New York: The Macmillan Co., 1949), pp. 124–25.
[3] *Op. cit.*

of living and cooperating together. Thus, the same condition prevails as in systems with specific goals, except that the presence of the goal varies. In one case, the system is a consequence of recognized goals without which the systems will not exist. In the other case, the system is a consequence of the goals of other systems and has no goals of its own.

The second question concerning the typology develops from the first: Is the distinction between the cells discrete or continuous? A first answer can be obtained by considering the distinction between institutionalized and relatively uninstitutionalized systems. Obviously, prisons are heavily institutionalized, whereas crowds are practically uninstitutionalized. But as one considers other types of systems, the distinction is not always so clear. The best example would be a political party. Its goal is the attainment of political power. In its infancy, it can hardly be called institutionalized—it may not even follow (may even oppose) the norms established for it by the larger society. As parties mature, however, they become institutionalized.

The same argument can be made for ethnic groups: Negroes widely scattered over a city are an ethnic group but not a vill. Gathered into a ghetto, they begin to assume some of the attributes of a vill. It is conceivable that either of two things could happen eventually: the ghetto will become institutionalized to such an extent that it matches the model of the vill, or it will expand in size sufficiently to the point where the city would, in effect, be a Negro city (and this again would be a vill).

Social systems, then, are regarded as *more or less* institutionalized rather than as either institutionalized or not. The same, however, does not hold true with reference to goals. There is hardly a continuum between systems with specific and those with no goals. A system either has goals or it does not, as of a given point in time. In fact, the very nature of groups defined by specific goals makes impossible any continuum between such groups and systems without such goals. Whenever a group becomes so organized that its existence depends on the continued striving for a specific goal, then that group, by its very nature, can no longer be said to be the same kind of a thing as a vill. It is possible for a group to be two things at once, as when a boys' gang (which has no specific goal) engages in a riot, but the distinction remains.

This possibility of a group having a "double identity" is brought about in part because groups change from cell to cell in the typology. Formal organizations can produce social movements which can establish vills (for example, "utopian" communities), vills can produce ethnic groups, etc. In fact, a basic principle of the typology is that *groups in any cell can produce types that appear in any other cell.* The number of types that can participate in this process seems endless: families operating a business concern, social movements operating hospitals, vills operating businesses, etc.

To the extent that the principle is valid, then one will expect "in-between" types.

The typology also has another dimension, a systematic variation which appears in each of the cells of the typology: the systems will be found to vary from those which include all of the other systems in its class to those which include none of the others. Thus, nations include vills which include neighborhoods, etc., but not vice versa (at least normally). Similarly, ethnic groups may include cliques, but not vice versa, and social movements may include crowds, but not vice versa. Formal organizations are more difficult to describe, because in order to classify them we must also consider the segment of society which benefits from the formal organization.[4] With this principle in mind, we may distinguish between organizations which serve the entire society, or commonweal organizations; those which serve some limited segment of it (either service organizations or business concerns); and those which serve only themselves (mutual benefit associations). This principle will be referred to as the principle of inclusiveness.

Thus, three principles or criteria have been identified which may be used in classifying human groups: The quality of working for a specific goal or of having no goal, the degree of institutionalization, and the degree of inclusiveness. The application of these three principles produces the categories found in Figure 3. The groups have been distributed within each

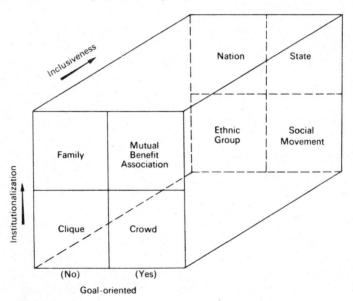

FIGURE 3. SCHEMATIC FOR A GENERAL TYPOLOGY OF HUMAN GROUPS

[4] Peter M. Blau and W. Richard Scott, *Formal Organizations: A Comparative Approach* (San Francisco: Chandler Publishing Co., 1962).

of the four cells of the preliminary typology according to the criteria of inclusiveness. Accordingly, at the upper end of each of the lists of groups are the most inclusive systems: nations, ethnic groups, social movements, and commonweal organizations (for example, states). At the lower end of each list are the most limited systems: families, cliques, crowds, and mutual-benefit associations.

The concepts of "formal" organizations and "informal" groups are of course well-established in the literature in the general sense in which they are used here (although unanimity has by no means been reached). The distinction between "group" and "organization" is intended merely to emphasize the greater complexity in organizations. "Expressive group"

A GENERAL TYPOLOGY OF HUMAN GROUPS

	The system has primacy of orientation to specific goals:		Inclusiveness relative to the smaller systems:
	Yes	No	
Institutionalized	(Formal Organizations) * Commonweal organiza- tions (e.g., police) Service organizations (e.g., hospitals) Business concerns Mutual-benefit associations	(Communal Organizations) Nations Vills Neighborhoods Families	Maximum Minimum
Relatively un- institutionalized †	(Expressive Groups) Social movements Crowds	(Informal Groups) Ethnic groups Cliques	Maximum Minimum

Principles: 1. Any group can be formed from any cell. 2. Some types in any cell can contain types in other cells.

* The typology for formal organizations is that of Blau and Scott, *op. cit.*, pp. 42 ff.
† As noted in the text, no group is ever completely uninstitutionalized. The distinction is relative.

is a term borrowed from Hawley.[5] It refers to forms of collective behavior. Hawley's general term appears preferable, especially since the term "collectivity" has recently been used to refer to groups in general.

The most troublesome name is that of "communal organization." "Community" has been used in so many contradictory ways as to render it almost useless for describing a specific system. "Communal organization"

[5] Amos Hawley, *Principles of Sociology* (Flushing, N.Y.: Data Guide, 1962).

is used because it connotes a range of specific things. "Communal" associates the term with a broad collection of related groups, and "organizations" gives the collection some specificity.

There are numerous groups which do not appear in the typology. Their absence is due, first, to the fact that their existence as social systems with a relatively distinct membership may be in question (for example, publics or social classes). Second, their distribution may be too limited to warrant including them in a general typology (for example, the Hindu caste). Or, third, they may be in-between types, such as city-states. Only those types are described which would most clearly be a product of the various forces that have been mentioned: goal attainment (or its lack), institutionalization, and inclusiveness. Human groupings are inherently things of change. The types we have described are thus not immutable objects. They are, rather, the product of innumerable social forces which may at times even be contradictory. As such, the types that have been described are only those coalescences of forces which emerge clearly.

SECTION TWO

Metropolis, City, Suburb, and Village

Introduction

In recent decades, changes in the structure and function of American communities have been characterized in large measure by a reduction in contrasts between urban and rural social organization and by a rapid growth of communities surrounding the central cities. Associated with these and other factors have been a number of different kinds of change which have tended to blur the contrast between the metropolis and the village or small city.

The small community's Main Street increasingly embraces types of activity which resemble "city ways." One need only mention the chain stores, branch banks, supermarkets, and parking meters to indicate the changed social relationships which underlie these tangible symbols of change. They symbolize changes in other aspects of village and small-city life as well.

But in numerous instances, Main Street itself has grown from its earlier status as a smalltown shopping center to become the "downtown" section of a growing city in its own right. Perhaps even more significant, Main Street has in many cases come clearly within the orbit of the nearest large city, becoming in a very real sense a suburb of that city.

Looked at from a different perspective, the development of large metropolitan complexes has come to characterize whole sections of the country, and although there may be some fields and woods and smaller communities within these large agglomerations, the network of their symbiotic interconnections grows ever stronger, and the character of their institutions changes.

Jean Gottmann examines the most dramatic instance of metropolitan agglomeration in this section's first selection. A vast Megalopolis, as he calls it, stretches from southern Maine to northern Virginia, containing a population of 37 million in 1960. Within it, the distinction between city and countryside has become blurred in a series of overlapping spheres of social organization centered in cities of different sizes. This huge agglomeration has come to serve many functions for the entire nation, acting, in many respects, as a center of activities for it. In this sense, it is conceived as the "Main Street" of the nation in the passage cited, which constitutes the first pages of Gottmann's book.

There is every reason to believe that other parts of the country will become more like Megalopolis rather than less so, according to Gottmann: hence, its importance as a harbinger of tomorrow. In outlining the book, he indicates some of the important dimensions for analysis of this newly developing "megalopolitan" complex, pointing out some of the problems which emerge, including those of increasingly dense concentrations of people, and he raises the question of whether such increasing concentration entails a high enough payoff to make up for its costs. But the drama of Megalopolis rests primarily on the fact that "on this scaffold swings the future." Within Megalopolis are being evolved some of the outlines of tomorrow's world. "Megalopolis stands indeed at the threshold of a new way of life, and upon solution of its problems will rest civilization's ability to survive."

Daniel J. Elazar raises the stimulating question: Are we a nation of cities? The major emphasis of his answer to that question is that the phrase "a nation of cities" gives a misleading impression of the nature of life in American society. He first gives figures to indicate the fallacy of the notion that most Americans live under conditions which are popularly perceived as characteristic of the city. But then he goes on to point out that most American city life is vastly different from the life that is found in a small number of large metropolises. The characteristics which Simmel associated with the metropolis simply do not prevail in most American cities, largely because they do not share the same cultural heritage as do such cities as Paris, Rome, or Hamburg. And even the northeastern Megalopolis described by Gottmann is vastly different for most of its inhabitants from the sidewalks of New York City. "Many of these American-style city dwellers," he points out, "live on plots of land that would look large to a Chinese or Indian farmer."

Three factors have had particular effect in shaping the pattern of life and land-use in American cities—agrarianism, metropolitanism, and nomadism. Americans have carried agrarian attitudes and life styles with them into the cities and have shaped city life accordingly. They have developed the metropolitan areas which include the large cities in a type of suburban life style which utilizes the city while preserving local small town autonomy. And they have developed patterns of nomadism within metropolitan areas which make personal identification with the central city much less pertinent to their life styles.

This article is an important antidote to simplistic assumptions about American urban life. Later statistics based on the 1970 census have done little to undermine the main outlines of Elazar's analysis.

Edward C. Banfield's book *The Unheavenly City: The Nature and Future of Our Urban Crisis* caused a great furor when it appeared in 1968, receiving strong support in some circles and scathing criticism in others. The book was characterized by great candor, somewhat unconventional diagnoses of many urban problems, and somewhat unconventional proposals for what government might do, if anything, to alleviate them. To its critics, the book seemed to offer a counsel of complacency by asserting that in general the seriousness of urban problems was exaggerated and by asserting that many proposed remedies were self-defeating.

In the excerpt given here, Banfield takes three mutually consistent positions. The first is his assertion that most governmental programs are directed at relatively superficial problems rather than at the important ones. Second, he asserts that programs such as the federal expressway program and the housing and urban renewal programs actually benefit the middle class rather than the poor. Then, in reference to the problems of rapid population growth, poverty, substandard housing, school dropouts, and police brutality, he asserts that, contrary to prevailing impressions, substantial improvement has occurred in every one. The problem is not the situation in each of these areas, but the rise in social expectations, which, if more rapid than the rate of real improvement, can make things seem worse while in actuality they are getting better.

The settlement of large areas around key central cities and the persistence of smaller municipal entities surrounding these cities have resulted in a proliferation of governmental units without a specific means for making governmental decisions at the level of the metropolitan area. The result has been a seeming choice between neglect of metropolitan-wide problems or the establishment of a metropolitan government. Oliver P. Williams and his associates made an intensive study of the situation with regard to Philadelphia and its surrounding suburbs. They diagnosed the situation in Philadelphia and elsewhere as reflecting "the basic dualism characteristic of metropolitan areas: the existence of specialization and the need for integrative mechanisms."

An important reason for the existence of areal specialization—that is, the use of land areas for different purposes and by different people—is that many people want it that way. They have moved to the suburbs precisely because—among other reasons—they wish to escape the inner city environment and the inner city problems. To have their present suburban governments consolidate with the city is the farthest thing from their minds.

The result, as this study points out, is that a process takes place in which metropolitan problems such as water and sewage disposal are handled piece-meal through setting up special purpose districts, thus proliferating the governmental maze but making it possible for the system of areal specialization to persist. The authors show the importance of discriminating between three kinds of metropolitan problems, which are surrounded by different sets of political dynamics: the problem of maintaining the system of areal specialization, the problem of unequal distribution of resources and services among the municipalities of the metropolitan area, and the problem of border relationships between contiguous municipalities.

As might be conjectured from its title, Bennett M. Berger's article on "The Myth of Suburbia" asserts that much current thinking about suburbia is based on myth rather than reality. But it does more than this. It examines why the myth persists despite clear evidence of its distorted description of suburban life, and goes on to examine at closer range the assertion that suburban society is essentially "middle-class" society. The oversimplified picture of suburbia as characterized by a homogeneous group of commuter families living in ranch houses, engaged in frenetic social activity, and obsessed with the pressure to "conform" dies hard, despite much evidence to the contrary, including that which Berger himself presented in his book *Working-class Suburb*. The myth survives largely because it performs certain functions for four different types of people. The criticism which many intellectuals (one of the four different types) level at the suburbs is largely of the middle class and, more precisely, of the upper-middle class. For, as Berger points out, the suburb is also inhabited by large numbers of lower-middle-class people, whose outlooks and behavior patterns are significantly different from those of the upper-middle class—more different, in fact, than the mere difference in income would suggest. Thus, Berger makes a strong case for questioning the practice of generalizing "about 'suburbia' on the basis of a few studies of selected suburbs whose representative character has yet to be demonstrated."

How much simpler things appeared to be in the days when one could be fairly confident about locating and delineating the small rural community, with its trade center and surrounding service area! Within the boundaries so drawn, people lived out the major roles of their lives, being thrown together in meaningful interaction on the basis of their common residence and identification with the locality. Building on an earlier tradition of community studies, Dwight Sanderson arrived at what was perhaps the classic formulation of the concept and major social characteristics of the rural community. He also was instrumental in perfecting a methodology for locating and delineating it in quite practical fashion. His procedure is presented here for two reasons. First, its simple method for delineating the community exemplifies, perhaps better than any other approach, the classic conception of the rural community as a largely self-contained unit with definite boundaries. Second, the very consideration of such a concept and method under today's conditions dramatizes the enormous changes which have taken place in recent decades, changes which have led to the increasing lack of relevance of this model of community living for most American communities. For better or worse, it becomes more and more meaningless to mark a series of mutually exclusive geometric figures on a map to purport to represent any meaningful units called communities. The structures of social interaction which are closely related to propinquity have become much more complex than that, and the prospects of their becoming simpler in the foreseeable future are virtually nonexistent.

11. Megalopolis: The Main Street of the Nation

BY JEAN GOTTMANN

The Northeastern seaboard of the United States is today the site of a remarkable development—an almost continuous stretch of urban and suburban areas from southern New Hampshire to northern Virginia and from the Atlantic shore to the Appalachian foothills. The processes of urbanization, rooted deep in the American past, have worked steadily here, endowing the region with unique ways of life and of land use. No other section of the United States has such a large concentration of population, with such a high average density, spread over such a large area. And no other section has a comparable role within the nation or a comparable importance in the world. Here has been developed a kind of supremacy, in politics, in economics, and possibly even in cultural activities, seldom before attained by an area of this size.

A VERY SPECIAL REGION: MEGALOPOLIS

This region has indeed a "personality" of its own, which for some three centuries past has been changing and evolving, constantly creating new problems for its inhabitants and exerting a deep influence on the general organization of society. The modern trends in its development and its present degree of crowding provide both examples and warnings for other less urbanized areas in America and abroad and call for a profound revision of many old concepts, such as the usually accepted distinctions between city and country. As a result new meanings must be given to some old terms, and some new terms must be created.

Great, then, is the importance and significance of this section of the United States and of the processes now at work within it. And yet it is difficult to single this area out from surrounding areas, for its limits cut across established historical divisions, such as New England and the Middle Atlantic states, and across political entities, since it includes some states entirely and others only partially. A special name is needed, therefore, to identify this special geographical area.

Reprinted with permission of the author and the Twentieth Century Fund from Jean Gottmann, *Megalopolis: The Urbanized Northeastern Seaboard of the United States.* © 1961 by The Twentieth Century Fund, New York, pp. 3–16.

This particular type of region is new, but it is the result of age-old processes, such as the growth of cities, the division of labor within a civilized society, the development of world resources. The name applied to it should, therefore, be new as a place name but old as a symbol of the long tradition of human aspirations and endeavor underlying the situations and problems now found here. Hence the choice of the term *Megalopolis,* used in this study.

Some two thousand years before the first European settlers landed on the shores of the James River, Massachusetts Bay, and Manhattan Island, a group of ancient people, planning a new city-state in the Peloponnesus in Greece, called it *Megalopolis,* for they dreamed of a great future for it and hoped it would become the largest of the Greek cities. Their hopes did not materialize. Megalopolis still appears on modern maps of the Peloponnesus but it is just a small town nestling in a small river basin. Through the centuries the word *Megalopolis* has been used in many senses by various people, and it has even found its way into Webster's dictionary, which defines it as "a very large city." Its use, however, has not become so common that it could not be applied in a new sense, as a geographical place name for the unique cluster of metropolitan areas of the Northeastern seaboard of the United States. There, if anywhere in our times, the dream of those ancient Greeks has come true.

AN URBANIZED AREA WITH A NEBULOUS STRUCTURE

As one follows the main highways or railroads between Boston and Washington, D.C., one hardly loses sight of built-up areas, tightly woven residential communities, or powerful concentrations of manufacturing plants. Flying this same route one discovers, on the other hand, that behind the ribbons of densely occupied land along the principal arteries of traffic, and in between the clusters of suburbs around the old urban centers, there still remain large areas covered with woods and brush alternating with some carefully cultivated patches of farmland. These green spaces, however, when inspected at closer range, appear stuffed with a loose but immense scattering of buildings, most of them residential but some of industrial character. That is, many of these sections that look rural actually function largely as suburbs in the orbit of some city's downtown. Even the farms, which occupy the larger tilled patches, are seldom worked by people whose only occupation and income are properly agricultural. And yet these farm areas produce large quantities of farm goods!

Thus the old distinctions between rural and urban do not apply here any more. Even a quick look at the vast area of Megalopolis reveals a revolution in land use. Most of the people living in the so-called rural areas, and still classified as "rural population" by recent censuses, have very little, if anything, to do with agriculture. In terms of their interests and work they are what used to be classified as "city folks," but their way of life and the landscapes around their residences do not fit the old meaning of urban.

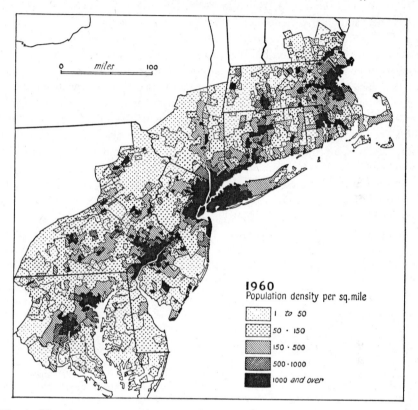

Fig. 1. The density of population according to the 1960 Census, by minor civil divisions. . . .

In this area, then, we must abandon the idea of the city as a tightly settled and organized unit in which people, activities, and riches are crowded into a very small area clearly separated from its nonurban surroundings. Every city in this region spreads out far and wide around its original nucleus; it grows amidst an irregularly colloidal mixture of rural and suburban landscapes; it melts on broad fronts with other mixtures, of somewhat similar though different texture, belonging to the suburban neighborhoods of other cities. Such coalescence can be observed, for example, along the main lines of traffic that link New York City and Philadelphia. Here there are many communities that might be classified as belonging to more than one orbit. It is hard to say whether they are suburbs, or "satellites," of Philadelphia or New York, Newark, New Brunswick, or Trenton. The latter three cities themselves have been reduced to the role of suburbs of New York City in many respects, although Trenton belongs also to the orbit of Philadelphia. (See Fig. 1, the distribution of population density.)

The "standard metropolitan areas,"[1] first used by the U.S. Bureau of the Census in 1950, have clarified this confused situation somewhat but not entirely. For example, the New York–Northeastern New Jersey standard metropolitan area cuts across political boundaries to reveal the relationships of this vast region to the core city of New York. And yet the mechanical application of the term "standard metropolitan area" has resulted in the establishment of separate areas for Trenton, which is closely tied to both Philadelphia and New York, and for Bridgeport, which is for many practical purposes part of the New York area. Similar problems can be found in other parts of Megalopolis.[2]

Thus an almost continuous system of deeply interwoven urban and suburban areas, with a total population of about 37 million people in 1960, has been erected along the Northeastern Atlantic seaboard. It straddles

[1] The U.S. Bureau of the Census defined a standard metropolitan area as "a county or group of contiguous counties which contains at least one city of 50,000 inhabitants or more. In addition to the county, or counties, containing such a city, or cities, contiguous counties are included in a standard metropolitan area if according to certain criteria they are essentially metropolitan in character and socially and economically integrated with the central city." In New England, "towns and cities, rather than counties, are the units used in defining standard metropolitan areas."

[2] For the 1960 Census the term "standard metropolitan area" was changed to "standard metropolitan statistical area." The definition was modified and a somewhat different set of criteria used which resulted in breaking down several of the formerly recognized larger metropolitan areas into smaller such units. The results thus achieved may be more precise in some respects but in the case of Megalopolis they may cause some confusion. The New York–Northeastern New Jersey standard metropolitan area of 1950 has been replaced by four standard metropolitan statistical areas: one for New York in New York State and three in New Jersey, those of Paterson-Clifton-Passaic, Jersey City, and Newark. The stricter definition of metropolitan integration of adjoining counties now excludes Somerset and Middlesex counties, formerly classified as metropolitan. As a result the percentage of the population of New Jersey residing in metropolitan areas fell from 89.9 in 1950 to 78.9 in 1960—a statistical trend surprising to those who know how much more metropolitan—or should we say Megalopolitan—the whole of New Jersey grew through the 1950's. To compensate for such an impression and for the separation between New York City and Northeastern New Jersey, a new term has been created and defined: "Standard Consolidated Areas," of which there were two (recognized for 1960) in the country: The New York–Northeastern New Jersey area (which included Somerset and Middlesex counties in New Jersey), and the Chicago-Northwestern Indiana area. The recognition of these broader areas was intended to stress "the special importance of even more inclusive metropolitan statistics" (see Executive Office of the President, Bureau of the Budget, *Standard Metropolitan Statistical Areas*, U. S. Government Printing Office, Washington, D.C., 1961). The metropolitan area of Philadelphia remained unchanged in both its Pennsylvania and New Jersey parts.

state boundaries, stretches across wide estuaries and bays, and encompasses many regional differences. In fact, the landscapes of Megalopolis offer such variety that the average observer may well doubt the unity of the region. And it may seem to him that the main urban nuclei of the seaboard are little related to one another. Six of its great cities would be great individual metropolises in their own right if they were located elsewhere. This region indeed reminds one of Aristotle's saying that cities such as Babylon had "the compass of a nation rather than a city."

MEGALOPOLIS—MAIN STREET AND CROSSROADS OF THE NATION

There are many other large metropolitan areas and even clusters of them in various parts of the United States, but none of them is yet comparable to Megalopolis in size of population, density of population, or density of activities, be these expressed in terms of transportation, communications, banking operations, or political conferences. Megalopolis provides the whole of America with so many essential services, of the sort a community used to obtain in its "downtown" section, that it may well deserve the nickname of "Main Street of the nation." And for three centuries it has performed this role, though the transcontinental march of settlement has developed along east-west axes perpendicular to this section of the Atlantic seaboard.

In recent times Megalopolis has had concentrated within it more of the Main Street type of functions than ever, and it does not yet seem prepared to relinquish any of them. Witness, for example, the impact of the Federal government in Washington, D.C., as it tightens up over many aspects of national life; the continued crowding of financial and managerial operations into Manhattan; New York's dominance of the national market for mass communication media, which resists all attempts at erosion; and the pre-eminent influence of the universities and cultural centers of Megalopolis on American thinking and policy-making. Megalopolis is also the country's chief facade toward the rest of the world. From it, as from the Main Street of a city, local people leave for distant travel, and to it arriving strangers come. For immigrants it has always served as the chief debarkation wharf. And just as passing visitors often see little of a city except a few blocks of its Main Street, so most foreign visitors see only a part of Megalopolis on their sojourns in the United States.

Just as a Main Street lives for and prospers because of the functions of the whole city, rather than because of any purely local advantages of its own, so is Megalopolis related to the whole United States and its rich resources. In general, Megalopolis itself was blessed only moderately by nature. It has no vast expanse of rich soils (there are some good soils but more poor ones), no special climatic advantages (its cyclonic climate is far from ideal), and no great mineral deposits (though there are some). In these respects it cannot compare with the generous natural potential of the Middle West or Texas or California. But it does excel in locational advantages—deep harbors of a drowned shoreline, on which its principal cities were early established, and a connecting-link relationship between the rich heart of the continent and the rest of the world. By hard work man has made the most of these locational resources, the most outstanding ones in an otherwise average natural endowment. As a result, early in its history Megalopolis became a dynamic hub of international relations, and it has maintained and constantly expanded that role to the present day. It is now the most active crossroads on earth, for people, ideas, and goods, extending its influence far beyond the national borders, and only as such a crossroads could it have achieved its present economic pre-eminence.

MEGALOPOLIS AS A LABORATORY OF URBAN GROWTH

Modern technology and social evolution provide increasing opportunity in urban pursuits on the one hand, and on the other steadily improving means of producing more agricultural goods with less manpower. The forces at work in our time, coupled with the growth in population, are, therefore, bound to channel a rising flow of people toward urban-type occupations and ways of life. As this tide reaches more and more cities they will burst out of old bounds to expand and scatter all over the landscape, taking new forms like those already observable throughout Megalopolis. This region serves thus as a laboratory in which we may study the new evolution reshaping both the meaning of our traditional vocabulary and the whole material structure of our way of life.

Tomorrow's society will be different from that in which we grew up, largely because it will be more urbanized. Nonagricultural ways of life will be followed by more and more people and will occupy much more space than they ever did, and such changes cannot develop without also deeply modifying agricultural life and production. So great are the consequences of the general evolution heralded by the present rise and complexity of Megalopolis that an analysis of this region's problems often gives one the feeling of looking at the dawn of a new stage in human civilization. The author has visited and studied various other regions of the world but has not experienced such a feeling anywhere else. Indeed, the area may be considered the cradle of a new order in the organization of inhabited space. This new order, however, is still far from orderly; here in its cradle it is all in flux and trouble, which does not facilitate the analyst's work. Nevertheless, a study of Megalopolis may shed some light on processes that are of great importance and interest.

A STUDY IN ENTANGLED RELATIONSHIPS

As the work of data-gathering and analysis progressed it became evident that the key to most of the questions involved in this study of Megalopolis lies in the interrelationships between the forces and processes at work within the area rather than in the trends of growth or the development of techniques. Thus the trend of population increase, easy to measure and perhaps to forecast approximately, provides less insight into the nature of the area than do the interrelations existing between the processes that caused the local population to grow, those that attracted certain kinds of people to Megalopolis, and those that supplied the swelling crowds with the means to live and work together there. Many of these processes are statistically measurable and some of them can be mapped, but the degree to which each of them stems from the others or determines them is a much more subtle matter, and is more basic to an understanding of what is going on and what can be done about it.

Most regional studies stay on the safer and more superficial grounds of statistical description and functional classifications. Had this report followed that pattern it would have been devoted mainly to summing up the abundant data available from the Censuses and other sources of general information about the various characteristics of Megalopolis. A description of natural conditions, such as topography, climate, hydrography, and vegetation, would have introduced a historical sketch to be followed by chapters on population, industries, trade, transportation and communications, the real estate market, other occupations and descriptions of the main cities and of the general features of "rural areas." Such a report would have concluded with a description of present problems and forecasts of the future presented by means of graphs, based on the assumption that the trends of the past twenty to fifty years will continue for the next twenty years.

A mere compilation of such data would probably be of service to some people but it could hardly help those who need further insight into and understanding of the basic problems of the area. By attempting to find out more about the deeper processes and their entanglements, one may hope to achieve a more fundamental kind of knowledge, which can be applied to another area or projected into the future more safely, though not always more easily. This is why the present report is organized along a somewhat less classical outline, its goal being a more reasoned discussion and an objective analysis. For such complicated phenomena as the social and economic processes at work in Megalopolis there are, of course, numerous and interlocking determining factors. The author has endeavored to search for *all* these factors, keeping in mind their multiplicity and entanglements and avoiding any arbitrary choices among them.

OUTLINE OF THIS REPORT

Part One [of Gottmann's book] presents a sketch of the *dynamics of urbanization* and attempts to show, in terms of the region's history, why things have come to be as they are and where they are. Although this section is largely descriptive it cannot avoid raising some new questions.

Part Two takes up what may be called the *"modern revolution in land use."* The new mixture of urban and rural must be dissected and each part related to the others in the newly developing system. Separation between place of work and place of residence creates within the area the system of daily "tidal" movements involved in commuting. Over these are superimposed other currents, some seasonal and some irregularly recurrent. These reflect relations between different parts of Megalopolis that stem from more complicated needs than the simple journey from home to work. These other needs grow more complicated and more general as average family income rises and both goods and activities that were once considered dispensable come to be regarded as necessary by large numbers of Megalopolitans. As Montesquieu observed two centuries ago, on the eve of the Industrial Revolution, "It is the nature of commerce to make the superfluous useful and the useful necessary." Perhaps it is not commerce but just human nature that produces this sequence. At any rate it has certainly been proven true of the consumption of goods, and now it seems to apply to the consumption of activities and space. The modern urban revolution, so apparent already in the affluent society of Megalopolis, devours time and space as well as food and industrial goods, and the fulfilling of these needs requires many types of movements.

These various tidal movements involve a reshaping of land use. Much agricultural land has been taken over by residential and industrial development. On the remaining farms a new specialized type of agriculture is developing, which requires less space than did the old system of farming. Woods have spread over much of the land abandoned by the farms, and this expansion of forests calls for new methods and concepts of forestry management, to provide for recreational and other suburban needs and for a better conservation of the landscape and of wildlife. Simultaneously the old city cores of "downtowns" are evolving toward decline or renewal, while uptowns, suburbs, and outer suburbia are becoming interlocked in a new and still constantly changing web of relationships. Regional integration is taking on forms unknown a generation or two ago, and the old system of local, state, and national authorities and jurisdictions, which has changed little, is poorly suited to present needs.

New *patterns of intense living* that have become normal in Megalopolis affect not only land use. They also exert a strong influence on the economic and social foundations of society, and Part Three endeavors to describe the problems thus created. The density of activities and of movement of all kinds is certainly the most extraordinary feature of Megalopolis, more characteristic even than the density of population and of skyscrapers. It has become a means of maintaining economic growth and stabilizing society; but how far can it go without destroying itself? For example, the growth of Megalopolis owes much to the automobile, but highway traffic jams are beginning to strangle city activities and to take the pleasure and efficiency out of driving a car. At the same time cars contribute to the ruination of other means of transportation, made more necessary than ever by the massive tidal currents of people and goods. The self-defeating effect of dense concentrations may be observed also in other fields than transportation. Many industries, for example, are now aiming at decentralization. The intense living of Megalopolis make a great deal of waste inescapable, waste of space and time as well as of materials. For a long time such waste may have seemed justifiable, for, paradoxically, the crowding that caused it brought higher economic yields. Now this crowding seems at times to defeat its own aims. Why and how does such intense living grow and threaten itself? Answers to these queries build up a general picture of a dynamic and prosperous society, obviously responsible for maintaining the growth of large-scale urbanization but responsible also for the problems the process creates and for finding the badly needed solutions.

It is easier to accept responsibility for solutions than to provide them. The many millions of people who find themselves *neighbors in Megalopolis,* even though they live in different states and hundreds of miles from one another, are barely becoming aware of the imperatives of such a "neighborhood." Part Four attempts to point them out. Responsible public opinion is becoming conscious of the problems involved, and the struggle to find solutions has started. It is especially difficult because no one problem can be tackled without affecting the others. Transportation, land use, water supply, cultural activities, use and development of resources, government and politics—all are interrelated.

Today it is essential that solutions be found to save this area from decay and to reassure the nation and the world about the kind of life modern urbanization trends presage for the future. Megalopolis has been built and often reshaped by its people. These people are now wealthier, better educated, and better endowed with technological means than ever. They ought to be able to find ways of avoiding decline of the area.

FOR THE BETTER OR FOR THE WORSE?

The preceding paragraph may seem to imply an unwarranted optimism about society's ability to control itself. True, history records a long list of brilliant civilizations that have sunk under the pressure of internal decay and external jealousy. We remember their names: Babylon, Corinth, Sparta, Athens, Rome, and many others. In the shadowy vistas of ancient times they vanished into the distance like shipwrecked ships loaded with ambition and precious cargo. Can such a fate be looming in the offing for Megalopolis? Modern urban sprawl is viewed by many as a threat to progress and general welfare. What is happening in Megalopolis today has been described as a pathological phenomenon, a sickness, a cancer. Such views are held by distinguished and respectable citizens of the area. One may well be alarmed by their invectives, all the more so as one does not have to go far away from Megalopolis to hear expressions of distrust and jealousy inspired by the amazing concentration of wealth and power in the great seaboard cities. Are people both in and out of this extraordinary region united in condemning it?

Urban growth in general has been discussed and condemned on moral grounds for a long time. Such debate is expectable and desirable, but on the whole history has shown the condemnation to be unjust, as can be seen by a brief review of some of the consequences of crowding.

Contrasts between rich and poor, for example, are especially striking in the crowded communities of cities. These may exist in rural areas too, but there they are diluted by scattering and veiled in greenery. The growth of urban pursuits (industries, trade, services) sharpens the contrasts by condensing them into a smaller area. Rich and poor live within short distances of one another and mix together in the streets in a way that often arouses righteous indignation. It seems brutally amoral to witness destitution neighboring on elegant sophistication, poverty mixing with prosperity. And yet, alas, a growing city's environment can hardly escape offering such sights. For many centuries there was an enormous difference between the advancement possible in trade and industry on the one hand and in farming on the other (though modern farm mechanization and subsidies to agriculture have substantially increased the profit possibilities of farming), and so to rise economically within the span of one lifetime has traditionally been easier in cities than in rural areas. The affluence of those who have so risen draws to the city large groups of humbler people, who come there to profit by the local abundance of money and the volume of spending and to serve the wealthier. In contrast to the more conservative "open" country, the "closed-in" city offers a more dynamic environment, socially and economically.

In cities, too, other vicious aspects of economic growth and social life have always been more evident than in the country. As urban development was accelerated by the Industrial Revolution, some of these vicious aspects became increasingly obvious. Slums and mobs grew worse than ever, making the urban landscape ethically and aesthetically shocking to those who cared about the people. From his sojourns in an industrializing western Europe, and especially from Paris during the French Revolution, Thomas Jefferson brought back impressions that reinforced his normal Virginian opposition to great cities and the development of manufactures or large-scale commerce. As slums and mobs became more general in European cities in the first half of the nineteenth century there arose more awareness about the classes of society and social injustice. There was more discussion of these matters, and the early Socialist doctrines were largely inspired by them. Then came the teachings of such philosophers as Fourier and Proudhon in France and Engels and Karl Marx in Germany, opposing great urban concentration as much as great concentration of capital. Engels' writings on the slums and working conditions in the then fast-developing British cities, such as Manchester, are well known. Because urban conditions of living and working were largely at the root of nineteenth-century Socialist doctrines, Karl Marx stressed that his theories applied much more to the industrialized countries of western Europe, which had accumulated large amounts of capital, than to the rural, little-urbanized countries to the east. Twentieth-century events have proved him wrong on this score, however, for communism has conquered the mainly rural countries, and the forms of socialism that developed in the more urban and capitalistic countries of the West have turned away from Marxism.

Crowding of population within a small area creates shortages of various resources, and most of the crowded people are bound to suffer in some ways because of the shortages. To alleviate them, to make crowding more bearable and the population happier, ways and means of constantly better distribution must be found. Otherwise no lasting growth can develop, and the whole enterprise will soon be doomed. From the struggle against such shortages have come some of mankind's most important advances. In the arid areas of the Middle East, for example; early civilization arose when people first congregated around the main springs and permanent rivers. As the settlement grew, the supply of both water and irrigable land became scarce. To insure survival of the people a proper distribution system had to be achieved, and rules and regulations had to be set up and accepted. Thus organized society, ruled by law, was born. Because authorities were needed to enforce law, political power arose, and people organized themselves to avoid more oppression than was necessary. Everywhere, the more crowded people have become in cities the more they have craved both security and freedom. Modern political life and its concepts of liberty, self-government, and democracy are the products of urban growth, the inheritance of cities in process of growth and development—places such as Jerusalem, Athens,

Rome, Bruges, Florence, Paris, London, to mention only those that have been most studied by historians. And the same places, or similar urban centers, have contributed most of our scientific and technological developments, either because people there were struggling to solve pressing problems or because urban societies make possible a leisurely enough elite, some of whose members can devote themselves to disinterested research and a search for a better understanding of the universe.

Thus urban crowding and the slums and mobs characteristic of it may be considered growing pains in the endless process of civilization.

In the same way, the picture of Megalopolis is not as dark as the outspoken pessimists and frequent protests would seem to paint it. Crowded within its limits is an extremely distinguished population. It is, *on the average,* the richest, best educated, best housed, and best serviced group of similar size (i.e., in the 25-to-40 million-people range) in the world. The area is still a focus of attraction for successful or adventurous people from all over America and beyond. It is true that many of its sections have seen pretty rural landscapes replaced by ugly industrial agglomerations or drab and monstrous residential developments; it is true that in many parts of Megalopolis the air is not clean any more, the noise is disturbing day and night, the water is not as pure as one would wish, and transportation at times becomes a nightmare. Many of these problems reflect the revolutionary change that has taken place as cities have burst out of their narrow bounds to scatter over the "open" countryside. In some ways this suburban sprawl may have alleviated a crowding that had threatened to become unbearable, for residential densities of population per square mile have decreased. But new problems have arisen because of the new densities of activities and of traffic in the central cities and because the formerly rural areas or small towns have been unprepared to cope with the new demands made upon their resources. New programs are needed to conserve the natural beauty of the landscape and to assure the health, prosperity, and freedom of the people. In spite of these problems, however, available statistics demonstrate that in Megalopolis the population is on the average healthier, the consumption of goods higher, and the opportunity for advancement greater than in any other region of comparable extent.

Thus the type of urban growth experienced here generates many contrasts, paradoxes, and apparently contradictory trends. It calls for debate and naturally excites passionate opinions for and against it. Are its results for the better or for the worse? It is not for our generation to moralize on the matter, but to strive to make the outcome be for the better, whatever obstacles may be in the way. Megalopolis stands indeed at the threshold of a new way of life, and upon solution of its problems will rest civilization's ability to survive. In the search for such solutions there will be found no easy keys to success, no "gimmicks" or "open-sesames." Solutions must be thought out, ironed out, and constantly revised in the light of all the knowledge that can be acquired by all concerned. It is the author's hope that this report, a systematic and sometimes critical analysis of the past and present of Megalopolis, will contribute to the gathering of such knowledge and to its distribution. At the same time, it will tell the story of an extraordinary region as its people have made it.

12. Are We a Nation of Cities?

BY DANIEL J. ELAZAR

It is generally agreed that the United States is now "a nation of cities "—
to use a phrase popularized by Lyndon B. Johnson—and that this has given
rise to a unique and dramatic "urban problem." When a proposition of this
kind receives general assent, however, it may be just the right moment to
look at it critically and skeptically.

The difficulty of understanding the "cities problem" in America is
heightened by the existence of numerous mythical assessments of urban
reality; particularly since the prevalent urban myths have given rise to
all sorts of mythical models for urban improvement. Perhaps the central myth
is the one that adheres to the very notion of "a nation of cities"—a notion
which conjures up a vision of nearly 200 million Americans living shoulder
to shoulder along crowded streets, seeking their pleasures in theatres or
poolrooms and suffering the pains of living under conditions of heavy congestion. The foundation of this central myth is the "fact" that over 70 percent of all Americans now live in urban places. This "fact," however, must
be considered in the context of the United States Census Bureau's definition
of "urban place": any settlement of 2,500 population or more. Only when
cities are thus defined, is the United States a nation of cities. But, of course,
a town of 2,500—or even 25,000—is not likely to conform to the foregoing
vision which most of us share when we speak of cities.

The 1960 population distribution by city size reveals that *58.3 percent
of the nation's total population lived in rural areas or in cities of under
50,000 people (which means approximately 15,000 families)*—and that only
9.8 percent lived in cities of over one million population. O˙ the more
than 6,000 legally constituted cities in the nation, only five have a population of over one million, and only 51 have populations of over 250,000.

Furthermore, while the rural population has continued its decline, *the
percentage of population in urban places of less than 50,000 has actually
increased by 50 percent since 1920. In the same period, the percentage of
the national population living in cities of over 500,000 barely increased at
all.* At least since 1920, the class of cities with the largest single segment

Reprinted with permission of the author and publisher from Daniel J. Elazar,
"Are We A Nation of Cities?" *The Public Interest,* No. 4 (Summer, 1966): 42–58.
Copyright © National Affairs, Inc., 1966.

of the nation's urban population (and it is also the fastest growing segment) has been that of the 10,000 to 50,000 group. Most Americans would agree that cities of that size hardly deserve to be considered cities at all, in common-sense usage.

Proponents of the current myths may argue that most small city growth has taken place within the nation's metropolitan areas. While they are technically correct, they are wrong to assume that "the metropolitan area" is just some kind of bigger city, lacking only a single government to formalize reality. The independent suburban townships and smaller cities exist for real reasons, not by historical accident. In fact, the larger the metropolitan area, the more likely the small cities within it are to value their autonomy and their separate identities. Moreover, while the rise of small cities originally created the contemporary metropolitan pattern, their continued growth—together with the stagnation of the central city—is now working to replace that pattern with one which dilutes the supposed "extended city" character of metropolitanism, replacing it with a pattern of extended urban settlement based on a whole ménage of cities of varying sizes and degrees of inter-relationship.

The non-urban character (in common-sense usage) of American urban settlement (in Census Bureau usage), even in metropolitan areas, is shown in the relatively low density of population in the "nation of cities." The accepted minimum measure of an urban environment is a population density of 1,000 or more per square mile; the measure of suburbanization is a population density of 500 per square mile. *Seventeen states do not have even one county—not a single county—with a population density of 500 per square mile.* Only five of the small Northeastern states have more than 30 per cent of their counties in the suburban-density category. Less than half the states—24 to be exact—have even one county with an urban-density of 1,000 or more. *Population density in the Northeastern "megalopolis" exceeds the suburbanization level only in the biggest cities.* Furthermore, three-fourths of all Standard Metropolitan Statistical Areas contain fewer than 500,000 people, *even when central cities and suburbs are combined.* This usually means that the central city population is less than 250,000, and may even be less than 100,000. In short, what is developing in the United States is the spread of a relatively low-density population engaged in urban economic pursuits; many of these American-style city dwellers actually live on plots of land that would look large to a Chinese or Indian farmer.

American urban living is further complicated by the vast difference in the life-styles of residents of American cities, depending on each city's size and location. It should not be difficult to visualize the differences between cities of 20,000 on the fringes of Boston and those of the same population in the heart of the Rockies, between a Philadelphia of two million people in the shadow of New York and a Denver of half a million which serves as the "capital" of a region that ranges five hundred or more miles in any direction. Yet the picture of urbanized America that is implicit in most contemporary discussion depicts all urbanized Americans as living in the same kind of environment and facing the same, or at least very similar, problems. Thus, the national news media convey pictures of traffic jams in New York and talk about the American city being crushed by the automobile. This may be as true of New Rochelle (pop. 77,000) as it is of Manhattan, but it is hardly true of Minneapolis or even Philadelphia, where rush-hour delays hardly add fifteen minutes to the total travel time of motorists who drive to the peripheries of the commuting belt. The media show pictures of miles of slum or small tract houses on both sides of the Hudson River and complain that the American urban population is miserably housed and has destroyed its open spaces. These may become problems in Atlanta or Los Angeles, but neither slums nor sprawl have hindered a very comfortable life style in either place as yet. The media show pictures of violent crime in the nation's capital and describe the American city as a place where people cannot go out on the streets after dark. While the crime rate is rising in most parts of the country, in Peoria or Indianapolis women still consider the streets sufficiently safe for evening movement. Whatever the national spread of traffic jams, water pollution, and violent crime—and these problems are certainly present nationwide—any well-traveled person can vouch for the differences in magnitude of all three from community to community and from region to region, differences which reflect different meanings of "urbanization" from place to place.

MYTHICAL PROBLEMS, MYTHICAL SOLUTIONS

On a slightly different plane, American cities are typified in the contemporary mythology as places where people wish to live anonymously, and where they make every effort to seek the variegated activities cities are supposed to offer. From this, one is led to draw a picture of an urbanized population that is also urbane, except insofar as its urbanity is frustrated by the "crisis of the city." Thus, according to the myth, we face a newly urbane population frustrated because it cannot easily get to the concert halls, the art museums, and the theaters; a population that is forced, against its will, to live in sprawling suburbs; forced to depend upon the family automobile; forced to maintain lawns, raise flowers, and rake leaves. The *Life* double-issue of December, 1965, devoted to "The City," provides the most recent comprehensive example of this myth, presented in its most universally accepted form.

An honest look at the evidence belies this whole picture for all but a small portion of the urban population, located in a few of the largest cities. Wherever the choice has been offered, Americans have worked to cultivate their identities among neighbors, whether through "togetherness" or through neighborhood associations; have sought activities that are by no means citified in character, whether through "Little Leagues" and "do it yourself activities" or through outdoor barbecues and camping; and have clearly sought the suburban conditions of living with lawns and automobiles—often within the great cities themselves. Philadelphia, for example, in the heart of the great eastern megalopolis, boasts that 70 percent of its dwellings are owner-occupied and that there are over 6 million trees within its limits—an average of three per person.

This composite of myths about American urban reality has led to the conclusion that our cities have failed us and that we face an urban crisis. This, in turn, has led to the development of certain models for urban improvement which are based on another set of myths, derived from the classic European stereotype of the city, either directly or as translated into modern terms by social scientists. The most obvious of these is the notion that fragmentation of governmental responses to the urban situation represents a frustration of the will of the people. This argument is used whether the critics of the present situation speak of fragmentation of programs or fragmentation of governmental jurisdictions. Their position is that "rational consolidation" of these programs and jurisdictions will solve the urban problem.

Below the surface of the "fragmentation" argument, however, lies a particular kind of commitment as to the direction in which the American city should develop. Most of those who articulate such solutions for urban problems start with the hidden assumption that there is a public interest in favor of the radical "citification" of the United States, i.e., that the people would like nothing better than to make their cities modern versions of Florence or Rome or Paris, and that they are frustrated in their efforts to do so by fragmentation, by tradition, or by the politicians.

But there is a great deal of evidence to indicate that most of the models of improvement proposed for the American city are nothing more than projections of the desires of certain articulate minorities in American society today. Whatever the dissatisfactions that stir the American people regarding the urbanized world in which they live, they are not the dissatisfactions pointed to by the spokesmen for "the city in crisis." Traffic jams and urban sprawl are not high on the agenda of complaints of the American people—because those are not great problems to most of the people who are defined as "urban dwellers" in the United States today. The blighting of old neighborhoods does not appear to concern the overwhelming majority of Americans, most of whom have never seen a slum. Governmental fragmentation has been ratified time and again when the issue has been presented to the voters; and, indeed, support for fragmentation of one kind or another is so great that the issue has rarely reached the stage of formal voting.

Whatever changes the American people seem to be seeking, they are not directed toward the enhancement of the facilities that lead to an urbane or citified life, but rather to the introduction into the city of qualities associated with the rural life—whether trees, cleaner air and water, larger parks, or new family-style dwellings to reduce the overall density of population. The most recent Gallup Poll on the subject, published in March, 1966, shows that only 22 percent of the American people desire to live in cities, while 49 percent would prefer to live in small towns or on farms, with the remainder (28 percent) opting for the suburbs, probably as a small-town surrogate. This attitude of wistful longing for the rural life is fully as prevalent among younger adults (ages 21–29) as among their elders. (In contrast, two out of three Negroes say they would live in a city or suburban area, if they could live anywhere they chose.) No doubt this response also reflects a mythology—but it is a mythology that must be considered when we seek to understand American attitudes toward the city. The historical record confirms this American desire to gain the economic benefits of urbanization while resisting the way of life usually associated with living in cities. It might be said that the American people persist in maintaining an implicit distinction between urbanization and citification, willingly accepting the former while seeking to avoid the latter.

THE THREE FACTORS AFFECTING AMERICAN CITIES

In understanding the reasons for the rejection of citification we can understand the real character of the American city and of the "American way of urbanization." *The American urban place is preeminently an "anti-city,"* implicitly developed to reflect a basic American life-style which has repeatedly emphasized agrarian elements from the days of the first colonists to our own. The underlying character of the American urban place is shaped by three basic phenomena: agrarianism, metropolitanism, and nomadism.

AGRARIANISM

Since the nation's founding, American values have been rooted in a vision of a commonwealth that supports and encourages the agrarian virtues of individual self-reliance and family solidarity, within a cooperating community of freeholding property-owners where class distinctions are minimal. This agrarian ideal has held the qualities of urbanity, sophistication, and cosmopolitanism to be seriously suspect, despite their undeniable attractiveness.

Nobody conversant with American history need be reminded of the rural roots of American civilization. Articulate Americans consistently viewed the rural life as the good life, or, indeed, the best life, where the vices inherent in man by virtue of Adam's fall would be least likely to flourish. Until the middle of the 19th century, this doctrinal position was reinforced by an agrarian economic system and a pattern of political organization that rested on individual agricultural freeholders. Furthermore, social equality—always a basic, if abstract, element in the American ideal system—found its closest approximation in the middle-class agricultural society of early America (at least in the North and West), a fact which was not lost upon those who seriously concerned themselves with the problems of creating the good society.

From an ideology which looked upon rural living (either in separated farms or in agricultural villages) as the best way to limit individual sin, the agrarian doctrine was translated into positive terms to become part of the world view of the 18th-century enlightenment. Thomas Jefferson, the best-known spokesman for positive agrarianism, articulated the new view as one which saw the agrarian life as the life best suited to bringing out the natural virtues of individual men and most likely to prevent the social evils always possible in society. The city was seen as the source of social corruption even more than individual corruption; the city was to be avoided as a source of inequality, class distinction, and social disorganization that could lead to tyranny in one form or another.

Both the positive and the negative views of "agrarian virtue" versus "urban corruption" became part of the mainstream of American thought, articulated by intellectuals from Thoreau to Frank Lloyd Wright, and made the basis of political movements from Jeffersonian Democracy, through Populism and the New Deal, to the "new conservatism" of the 1960's. The city was and continues to be viewed by many as a breeder of crime, corruption, social disorganization, and *anomie,* not really fit to be lived in, even when valuable for its economic utility. While it is now fashionable in many quarters to attack this kind of thinking as a ridiculously naive relic of the nation's unsophisticated past, there is at least enough probable truth in many of its conclusions to give those who do not otherwise wish to foster citification ample justification for their position. . . .

Even when the agrarian myth was in full flower, Americans had begun to flock to the cities, primarily to gain economic advantage; and the cities had become the pace-setters in American life. But, while they desired to gain economically and socially by exploiting the benefits of urban concentration, the new city-dwellers rejected the classically urban styles of living (as developed in Old World cities). Accepting the necessity and even the value of urbanization for certain purposes, in particular, economic ones. Americans, have characteristically tried to have their cake and eat it, too, by bringing the old agrarian ideals into the urban setting and by reinterpreting them through the establishment of a modified pattern of "rural"-style living within an urban context. The result has been the conversion of *urban* settlements into *metropolitan* ones, whose very expansiveness provides the physical means for combining something like rural and urban life-styles into a new pattern which better suits the American taste. It was hoped that this pattern would combine the advantages of an urban environment with the maintenance of the essence of the traditional American "agrarian" virtues and pleasures, to preserve as much as possible of what is conceived to be the traditional "American way of life."

As part of this effort, sets of institutions and symbolic actions have been developed, partially by design, which are meant to evoke rural and small-town America and its traditional way of life. Limited and fragmented local government is one of these. The creation of many smaller cities—the *bête noire* of most professional city-planners—in place of a single large metropolis reflects this desire for maintenance of the small community, both as an abstract principle and in order to control such crucial local functions as zoning and police, which in a direct or derivative sense embody the traditions of local control. We see this in the continued emphasis on political autonomy for suburban communities, and in their resistance to any efforts, real or imagined, to absorb them into the political sphere of the central city.

Moreover, in many parts of the nation there is a hesitancy among suburbanites to use government for local services, for fear that the addition of more local services will increase the urban character of the environment. Even in the fringe areas of cities, large numbers of people resist sidewalks because sidewalks represent "the city." Street lights are often frowned upon, sewer systems resisted, and the maintenance of the neighborhood school is an article of faith, all for the same reasons.

It is generally known by now that suburbia has become the equal of small-town America as the symbol of the country's "grass-roots" and as the fountainhead of what is distinctive about "the American way of life." This is so regardless of whether suburbia is praised or condemned for its role. (The Chicago *Tribune,* traditional champion of the agrarian virtues as it perceives them, now features suburban settings for its "rural virtue" cartoons.) The popular literature defending suburbia and that attacking it are both strongly reminiscent of the popular literature devoted to small-town America two to four generations ago. If some see virtue in the small community—whether it is typified by a predominantly small-town society or a predominantly suburban society—others see ignorance, provincialism, decadence, and even corruption in the same locale. If the latter speak loudly with words, the former are speaking louder with their feet.

Yet another manifestation of neo-agrarianism is the physical structure characteristic of American cities. The American city sharply separates its commercial and residential areas, creating a "town and country" pattern within its boundaries. Outside of its central core, it emphasizes low-density construction set along wide, easily accessible, tree-lined streets that fade into the countryside without sharp distinctions. At its best, the American urban place further reflects an effort to merge city and country through the development of large, unmanicured public parks which thrust the country into the city and which, in turn, merge into private lawns to further that penetration by creating an overall natural setting that is not subordinated to the buildings. Still another manifestation of Americans' agrarian outlook is the continued emphasis on home ownership, and the complex of activities and symbols which surround it. Owner-occupied, free-standing homes, each with its lawn and garden, represent a major voluntary expenditure of energy and resources in contemporary American society. Virtually every American urban area embodies these neo-agrarian features in some way. Outstanding examples in every section easily come to mind: the greater part of Connecticut in the Northeast, Miami and Nashville in the South, Cleveland and St. Paul in the Middle West, Denver and Seattle in the Far West, to name only a few of the largest and best. . . .

While urbanization and metropolitanization in other nations have led to the development of official policies to encourage high-density living, federal, state, and even local policies (other than the property tax) in the United States are heavily weighted in favor of the homeowner and low-density development. Mortgage guarantees, home financing funds, homestead exemptions, zoning regulations, and many other specific devices have been enacted into law to encourage widespread home ownership. The foundations for today's widespread home ownership were laid during the 1930's by the New Deal, as part of the New Dealers' over-all efforts to translate the ideals and values of traditional American agrarianism into terms appropriate to the new urban setting. The percentage of owner-occupied homes has been increasing rapidly since 1940, when only 43.6 percent of the nation's housing units were owner-occupied. By 1950, 55 percent were owner-occupied, a figure which rose to 61.9 percent by 1960. This figure compares well with the 64.4 percent of owner-occupied *farm* housing units in 1900.

The trend to owner-occupied housing has revived such symbolically rural occupations as gardening and "do-it-yourself" home maintenance. The public response to these activities—state and county fairs (not to mention home and garden shows) outdraw art galleries in annual attendance *even in the largest cities,* and the greater share of adult education courses deal with home-related activities—indicates that they are, in effect, an urban recrudescence of a significant "vernacular" cultural tradition long associated with rural and small-town life. The importance of this vernacular tradition in American life is generally overlooked in discussions of American culture since those who are generally deemed to be the custodians of the civilized arts in this country tend to be products of the more urbane traditions of Western civilization which originated in Europe.

Similarly, the impact that private maintenance of lawns and gardens has on the maintenance of the aesthetic qualities of American urban areas has generally been ignored by students of urbanization. In the days of "Great Society" beautification programs it would serve us well to recall that the private expenditure for lawn and garden maintenance far exceeds the public expenditures for parks, tree plantings, and similar efforts at urban beautification. It represents an important contribution to the "public good" that would be prohibitively expensive if charged against the public purse and sorely missed if eliminated.

The near-universal American concern with promoting home ownership as the solution to the problems of urbanization and metropolitanization is in itself a strong reflection of the strength of underlying agrarian ideals. Except for New York and Chicago, apartment living remains the domain of unmarried young adults, newly-married couples, and the retired. The recent spurt in apartment construction is apparently designed to meet the needs of those groups rather than to replace the single-family home. Curiously enough, much of the so-called apartment "boom" is a suburban phenomenon, one which is reinforcing the developing self-sufficiency of the suburbs by providing indigenous housing for those who are likely to live in apartments, thus helping to transform many suburbs from dormitories for the central city into smaller but self-sufficient cities (American-style) in their own right.

METROPOLITANISM

Excepting only the 19th-century factory towns, founded specifically to bring together enough population to serve industry, the American city was not created for its own sake or to be internally self-contained, but to serve as the center of a larger area—a hinterland tributary to it in some way. From the first, the American city was really part of a larger geographic entity rather than a self-centered community, even in its economic purposes. In contrast, the great cities of Europe, though each may be the metropolis of its particular country, have always offered their residents a self-contained way of life, one that is separated from that of the rest of the country in profound ways. In the United States, this is not true even of New York. The only American cities that even approach such a self-centered separation are San Francisco and New Orleans. In America, cities have thrived only by cultivating their hinterlands, whether it is New York serving as the nation's empire city, Minneapolis playing an imperial role in the Northwest, Pasadena serving the San Gabriel Valley in California, or Charlottesville serving its metropolitan region in central Virginia.

Metropolitanism of settlement, as well as metropolitanism of commerce, began with the very birth of cities in the United States. Urbanization and suburbanization went hand in hand. Even as the rate of urban growth began to accelerate after the War of 1812, a counter, almost anti-urban, trend began to develop alongside it. As fast as some Americans moved to the city, others who were able to do so moved out, while maintaining their ties with it. The process of suburbanization can be traced throughout the 19th century. After 1820, the nation's largest cities, such as New York, Boston, Philadelphia, Baltimore, and New Orleans, began to experience an out-migration to newly created suburban areas. Though most of these early suburbs were later annexed by their central cities, the suburbanization process continued after each set of annexations, gaining new impetus as new means of transportation were developed and made possible movement out of the city for people who worked in the city. First the railroad, then the electric trolley, and finally the automobile stimulated suburbanization past the "horse and buggy" stage.

By 1920, over half the nation lived in "urban places," and nearly a third lived in cities of over 100,000. However, no sooner did the big city become the apparent embodiment of the American style of life, than it began to be replaced by a less citified style in turn. *The upward trend in the growth of big cities came to an end during the depression,* then gave way to the development of medium- and smaller-size cities on the fringes of the big cities themselves. The decline of the big cities began when the problems of population density and congestion seriously cut into the possibilities for maintaining an agrarian-influenced life style within them. So long as city life was able to offer most of the amenities of rural-style living as well as the economic, social, and cultural advantages of the city to those who were in a position to determine the cities' growth, the expansion of cities as cities continued. Newly-settled suburbs and smaller cities were annexed to already large cities because their residents, or at least those who made the decisions locally, felt reasonably confident that their suburban style of life would be maintained, even within the city limits. When this became no longer possible, metropolitanism then became firmly fixed as suburbanization, with the semi-city becoming more important than the city as the locus of growth in area after area.

NOMADISM

This trend is additionally encouraged by the penchant toward nomadism which has always characterized Americans. With a population that is so highly mobile that one family in five moves every year, the older European notion of the city as a stable, self-perpetuating community could not apply in the New World. This penchant has been characteristic of Americans from the very first; *the actual percentage of families that have migrated from one state to another has not changed appreciably in the last century.* Consequently, the city, like every other local governmental subdivision, has become a politically defined entity populated to a great extent by different groups in every generation, with a relatively low level of continuity among groups from one generation to another.

This, in turn, significantly alters the meaning of moving from farm to city, and from central city to suburb, in the United States. In other countries, the great move from a fixed rural location to a fixed urban one has represented a major uprooting that is unique in the life experience of each family, perhaps for generations. In the United States the similar movement, for most people and their families, has been no more than one of a continual series that originally propelled European immigrants across the seas; then, as Americans, westward and into cities; and now from city to suburb or city to city.

The emergence of the "megalopolis" is a perfect reflection of the new nomadism. People escaping the cities of the Eastern seaboard, and now the cities of the interior and West Coast as well, settled first in the interstices between them wherever possible, first forming the traditional suburban circle and then a more or less continuous belt of urban-related settlement as the circles merged and overlapped. Now they have begun to move from place to place within each belt or its segments, preserving a nomadic way of life that is urban without being permanently attached to any particular city, or even to citified living. Traditionally these migrating Americans have been brought into the political realm as individuals through the possibilities of involvement in local communities, thus preventing them from becoming members of an anomic mass. . . .

In fact, the American urban place is a non-city because Americans wish it to be just that. Our age has been the first in history even to glimpse the possibility of having the economic advantages of the city while rejecting the previously inevitable conditions of citified living, and Americans apparently intend to take full advantage of the opportunity. If we wish to make a realistic approach to our real urban problems, we would be wise to begin with that fact of American life.

13. The Nature of the Urban Crisis

BY EDWARD C. BANFIELD

If some real disaster impends in the city, it is not because parking spaces are hard to find, because architecture is bad, because department store sales are declining, or even because taxes are rising. If there is a genuine crisis, it has to do with the essential welfare of individuals or with the good health of the society, not merely with comfort, convenience, amenity, and business advantage, important as these are. It is not necessary here to try to define "essential welfare" rigorously: it is enough to say that whatever may cause people to die before their time, to suffer serious impairment of their health or of their powers, to waste their lives, to be deeply unhappy or happy in a way that is less than human affects their essential welfare. It is harder to indicate in a sentence or two what is meant by the "good health" of the society. The ability of the society to maintain itself as a going concern is certainly a primary consideration; so is its free and democratic character. In the last analysis, however, the quality of a society must be judged by its tendency to produce desirable human types; the healthy society, then, is one that not only stays alive but also moves in the direction of giving greater scope and expression to what is distinctively human. In general, of course, what serves the essential welfare of individuals also promotes the good health of the society; there are occasions, however, when the two goals conflict. In such cases, the essential welfare of individuals must be sacrificed for the good health of the society. This happens on a very large scale when there is a war, but it may hap·pen at other times as well. The conditions about which we should be most concerned, therefore, are those that affect, or may affect, the good health of the society. If there is an urban crisis in any ultimate sense, it must be constituted of these conditions.

It is a good deal easier to say what matters are not serious (that is, do not affect either the essential welfare of individuals or the good health of the society) than it is to say what ones are. It is clear, however, that poverty, ignorance, and racial (and other) injustices are among the most important of the general conditions affecting the essential welfare of individuals. It is plausible, too, to suppose that these conditions have a very direct bearing

131

upon the good health of the society, although in this connection other factors that are much harder to guess about—for example, the nature and strength of the consensual bonds that hold the society together—may be much more important. To begin with, anyway, it seems reasonable to look in these general directions for what may be called the serious problems of the cities.

It is clear at the outset that serious problems directly affect only a rather small minority of the whole urban population. In the relatively new residential suburbs and in the better residential neighborhoods in the outlying parts of the central cities and in the older, larger, suburbs, the overwhelming majority of people are safely above the poverty line, have at least a high school education, and do not suffer from racial discrimination. For something like two-thirds of all city dwellers, the urban problems that touch them directly have to do with comfort, convenience, amenity, and business advantage. In the terminology used here, these are "important" problems but not "serious" ones. In a great many cases, these problems cannot even fairly be called important; a considerable part of the urban population—those who reside in the "nicer" suburbs—lives under material conditions that will be hard to improve upon.

The serious problems are to be found in all large cities and in most small ones. But they affect only parts of these cities (and only a minority of the city populations). In the central cities and the larger, older suburbs the affected parts are usually adjacent to the central business district and spreading out from it. If these inner districts, which probably comprise somewhere between 10 and 20 percent of the total area classified as urban by the Census, were suddenly to disappear, along with the people who live in them, there would be no serious urban problems worth talking about. If what really matters is the essential welfare of individuals and the good health of the society as opposed to comfort, convenience, amenity, and business advantage, then what we have is not an "urban problem" but an "inner-central-city-and-larger-older-suburb" one.

The serious problems of these places, it should be stressed, are in most instances not caused by the conditions of urban life as such and are less characteristic of the city than of small-town and farm areas. Poverty, ignorance, and racial injustice are more widespread outside the cities than inside them.

One problem that is both serious and unique to the large cities is the existence of huge enclaves of people (many, but not all of them, Negro) of low skill, low income, and low status. In his book *Dark Ghetto,* Kenneth B. Clark presents Census data showing that eight cities—New York, Los Angeles, Baltimore, Washington, Cleveland, St. Louis, New Orleans, and Chicago—contain a total of sixteen areas, all of at least 15,000 population and five of more than 100,000, that are exclusively (more than 94 percent)

Negro.[1] There are smaller Negro enclaves in many other cities, and there are large Puerto Rican and large Mexican ones in a few cities. Whether these places can properly be called ghettoes is open to some doubt, as will be explained later. However, there is no question but that they are largely cut off both physically and psychologically from the rest of the city. Whatever may be the effect of this separation on the essential welfare of the individual (and it is arguable that it is trivial), it is clear that the existence of huge enclaves of people who are in some degree alienated from it constitutes a kind of hazard not only to the present peace and safety but also to the long-run health of the society. The problems of individual welfare that these people present are no greater by virtue of the fact that they live together in huge enclaves rather than in isolation on farms, or in small neighborhoods in towns and cities (the problem of individual welfare *appears* greater when they live in huge enclaves, but that is because in this form it is too conspicuous to be ignored). The problem that they present to the good health of the society, on the other hand, is very different and vastly greater solely by virtue of the fact that they live in huge enclaves. Unlike those who live on farms and in small towns, disaffected people who live in huge enclaves may develop a collective consciousness and sense of identity. From many stand-points it is highly desirable that they do so. In the short run, however, they represent a threat to peace and order, and it must be admitted that even in the long run the accommodation that takes place may produce a politics that is less democratic, less mindful of individual rights, and less able to act effectively in the common interest than that which we have now.

This political danger in the presence of great concentrations of people who feel little attachment to the society has long been regarded by some as *the* serious problem of the cities—the one problem that might conceivably produce a disaster that would destroy the quality of the society. "The dark ghettoes," Dr. Clark has written, "now represent a nuclear stockpile which can annihilate the very foundations of America."[2] These words bring up-to-date apprehensions that were expressed by some of the Founding Fathers and that Tocqueville set forth in a famous passage of *Democracy in America:*

The United States has no metropolis, but it already contains several very large cities. Philadelphia reckoned 161,000 inhabitants, and New York 202,000, in the year 1830. The lower ranks which inhabit these cities constitute a rabble even more formidable than the populace of European towns.

[1] Kenneth B. Clark, *Dark Ghetto* (New York: Harper & Row, 1965), table, p. 25.
[2] Kenneth B. Clark, "The Wonder Is There Have Been So Few Riots," *New York Times Magazine,* September 5, 1965, p. 10.

They consist of freed blacks, in the first place, who are condemned by the laws and by public opinion to a hereditary state of misery and degradation. They also contain a multitude of Europeans who have been driven to the shores of the New World by their misfortunes or their misconduct; and they bring to the United States all our greatest vices, without any of those interests which counteract their baneful influence. As inhabitants of a country where they have no civil rights, they are ready to turn all the passions which agitate the community to their own advantage; thus, within the last few months, serious riots have broken out in Philadelphia and New York. Disturbances of this kind are unknown in the rest of the country, which is not alarmed by them, because the population of the cities has hitherto exercised neither power nor influence over the rural districts.

Nevertheless, I look upon the size of certain American cities, and especially on the nature of their population, as a real danger which threatens the future security of the democratic republics of the New World; and I venture to predict that they will perish from this circumstance, unless the government succeeds in creating an armed force which, while it remains under the control of the majority of the nation, will be independent of the town population and able to repress its excesses.[3]

Strange as it may seem, the mammoth government programs to aid the cities are directed mainly toward the problems of comfort, convenience, amenity, and business advantage. Insofar as they have any effect on the serious problems, it is, on the whole, to aggravate them.

Two programs account for approximately 90 percent of federal government expenditure for the improvement of the cities (as opposed to the maintenance of more or less routine functions). Neither is intended to deal with the serious problems. Both make them worse.

The improvement of transportation is one program. The urban portions of the national expressway system are expected to cost about $18 billion. Their main effect will be to enable suburbanites to move about the metropolitan area more conveniently, to open up some areas for business and residential expansion, and to bring a few more customers from the suburbs downtown to shop. These are all worthy objects when considered by themselves; in context, however, their justification is doubtful, for their principal effect will be to encourage—in effect to subsidize—further movement of industry, commerce, and relatively well-off residents (mostly white) from the inner city. This, of course, will make matters worse for the poor by reducing

[3] Alexis de Tocqueville, *Democracy in America*, trans. by Henry Reeve (New York: Knopf, 1945) I: 289–90.

the number of jobs for them and by making neighborhoods, schools, and other community facilities still more segregated. These injuries will be only partially offset by allowing a certain number of the inner-city poor to commute to jobs in the suburbs.

The huge expenditure being made for improvement of mass transit facilities (it may amount to $10 billion over a decade) may be justifiable for the contribution that it will make to comfort, convenience, and business advantage. It will not, however, make any contribution to the solution of the serious problems of the city. Even if every city had a subway as fancy as Moscow's, all these problems would remain.

The second great federal urban program concerns housing and renewal. Since the creation in 1934 of the Federal Housing Authority (FHA), the government has subsidized home building on a vast scale by insuring mortgages that are written on easy terms and, in the case of the Veterans Administration (VA), by guaranteeing mortgages. Most of the mortgages have been for the purchase of *new* homes. (This was partly because FHA wanted gilt-edged collateral behind the mortgages that it insured, but it was also because it shared the American predilection for newness.) It was cheaper to build on vacant land, but there was little such land left in the central cities and in their larger, older suburbs; therefore, most of the new homes were built in new suburbs. These were almost always zoned so as to exclude the relatively few Negroes and other "undesirables" who could afford to build new houses. In effect, then, the FHA and VA programs have subsidized the movement of the white middle class out of the central cities and older suburbs while at the same time penalizing investment in the rehabilitation of the run-down neighborhoods of these older cities. The poor—especially the Negro poor—have not received any direct benefit from these programs. (They have, however, received a very substantial unintended and indirect benefit, as will be explained later, because the departure of the white middle class has made more housing available to them.) After the appointment of Robert C. Weaver as head of the Housing and Home Finance Agency, FHA changed its regulations to encourage the rehabilitation of existing houses and neighborhoods. Very few such loans have been made, however.

Urban renewal has also turned out to be mainly for the advantage of the well-off—indeed, of the rich—and to do the poor more harm than good. The purpose of the federal housing program was declared by Congress to be "the realization as soon as feasible of the goal of a decent home and a suitable living environment for every American family." In practice, however, the principal objectives of the renewal program have been to attract the middle class back into the central city (as well as to slow its exodus out of the city) and to stabilize and restore the central business districts.[4] Unfortunately, these objectives can be served only at the expense of the poor. Hundreds of thousands of low-income people have been forced out of low-cost housing, by no means all of it substandard, in order to make way for luxury apartments, office buildings, hotels, civic centers, industrial parks, and the like. Insofar as renewal has involved the "conservative" or "rehabilitation" of residential areas, its effect has been to keep the poorest of the poor out of these neighborhoods—that is, to keep them in the highest-density slums. "At a cost of more than three billion dollars," sociologist Scott Greer wrote in 1965, "the Urban Renewal Agency (URA) has succeeded in materially reducing the supply of low-cost housing in American cities."[5]

The injury to the poor inflicted by renewal has not been offset by benefits to them in the form of public housing (that is, housing owned by public bodies and rented by them to families deemed eligible on income and other grounds). With the important exception of New York and the less important ones of some Southern cities, such housing is not a significant part of the total supply. Moreover, the poorest of the poor are usually, for one reason or another, ineligible for public housing.

Obviously, these government programs work at cross-purposes, one undoing (or trying to undo) what the other does (or tries to do). The expressway program and the FHA and VA mortgage insurance and guarantee programs in effect pay the middle-class white to leave the central city for the suburbs. At the same time, the urban renewal and mass transit programs pay him to stay in the central city or to move back to it.

In at least one respect, however, these government programs are consistent, they aim at problems of comfort, convenience, amenity, and business advantage, not at ones involving the essential welfare of individuals or the good health of the society. Indeed, on the contrary, they all sacrifice these latter, more important interests for the sake of the former, less important ones. In this the urban programs are no different from a great many other government programs. Price production programs in agriculture, Theodore Schultz has remarked, take up almost all the time of the Department of Agriculture, the agricultural committees of Congress, and the farm organizations, and exhaust the influence of farm people. But these programs, he says, "do not improve the schooling of farm children, they do not reduce the inequalities in personal distribution of wealth and income, they do not

---

[4] Cf. Robert C. Weaver, "Class, Race and Urban Renewal," *Land Economics,* 36 (August 1960): 235–51. On urban renewal in general, see James Q. Wilson, ed., *Urban Renewal: The Record and the Controversy* (Cambridge, Mass.: M.I.T. Press, 1966).

[5] Scott Greer, *Urban Renewal and American Cities* (Indianapolis: Bobbs-Merrill, 1965), p. 3.

remove the causes of poverty in agriculture, nor do they alleviate it. On the contrary, they worsen the personal distribution of income within agriculture."[6]

It is widely supposed that the serious problems of the cities are unprecedented both in kind and in magnitude. Between 1950 and 1960 there occurred the greatest population increase in the nation's history. At the same time, a considerable part of the white middle class moved to the newer suburbs, and its place in the central cities and older suburbs was taken by Negroes (and in New York by Puerto Ricans as well). These and other events—especially the civil rights revolution—are widely supposed to have changed completely the character of "the urban problem."

If the present situation is indeed radically different from previous ones, then we have nothing to go on in judging what is likely to happen next. At the very least, we face a crisis of uncertainty.

In a real sense, of course, *every* situation is unique. Even in making statistical probability judgments, one must decide on more or less subjective grounds whether it is reasonable to treat certain events as if they were the "same." The National Safety Council, for example, must decide whether cars, highways, and drivers this year are enough like those of past years to justify predicting future experience from past. From a logical standpoint, it is no more possible to decide this question in a purely objective way than it is to decide, for example, whether the composition of the urban population is now so different from what it was that nothing can be inferred from the past about the future. Karl and Alma Taeuber are both right and wrong when they write that we do not know enough about immigrant and Negro assimilation patterns to be able to compare the two and that "such evidence as we could compile indicates that it is more likely to be misleading than instructive to make such comparisons."[7] They are certainly right in saying that one can only guess whether the pattern of Negro assimilation will resemble that of the immigrant. But they are wrong to imply that we can avoid making guesses and still compare things that are not known to be alike in all respects except one. (What, after all, would be the point of comparing immigrant and Negro assimilation patterns if we knew that the only difference between the two was, say, skin color?) They are also wrong in suggesting that the evidence indicates anything about what is likely to be instructive. If there were enough evidence to indicate that, there would be enough to indicate what is likely to happen; indeed, a judgment as to what is likely

[6] Theodore W. Schultz, *Economic Crises in World Agriculture* (Ann Arbor: University of Michigan Press, 1965), p. 94.

[7] Karl E. and Alma F. Taeuber, "The Negro as an Immigrant Group: Recent Trends in Racial and Ethnic Segregation in Chicago," *American Journal of Sociology* 69 (January 1964): 382.

to be instructive is inseparable from one as to what is likely to happen. Strictly speaking, the Taeubers' statement expresses *their* guess as to what the evidence indicates.

The facts by no means compel one to take the view that the serious problems of the cities are unprecedented either in kind or in magnitude. That population growth in absolute numbers was greater in the decade 1950 to 1960 than ever before need not hold much significance from the present standpoint: American cities have frequently grown at fantastic rates (consider the growth of Chicago from a prairie village of 4,470 in 1840 to a metropolis of more than a million in fifty years). In any case, the population growth of the 1950's was not in the largest cities; most of them actually lost population in that decade. So far as numbers go, the migration of rural and small-town Negroes and Puerto Ricans to the large Northern cities in the 1950's was about equal to immigration from Italy in its peak decade. (In New York, Chicago, and many other cities in 1910, two out of every three schoolchildren were the sons and daughters of immigrants.) When one takes into account the vastly greater size and wealth of the cities now as compared to half a century or more ago, it is obvious that by the only relevant measure—namely, the number of immigrants relative to the capacity of the cities to provide for them and to absorb them—the movement in the 1950's from the South and from Puerto Rico was not large but small.

In many important respects, conditions in the large cities have been getting better. There is less poverty in the cities now than there has ever been. Housing, including that of the poor, is improving rapidly: one study predicts that substandard housing will have been eliminated by 1980.[8] In the last decade alone the improvement in housing has been marked. At the turn of the century only one child in fifteen went beyond elementary school; now most children finish high school. The treatment of racial and other minority groups is conspicuously better than it was. When, in 1964, a carefully drawn sample of Negroes was asked whether, in general, things were getting better or worse for Negroes in this country, approximately eight out of ten respondents said "better."[9]

If the situation is improving, why, it may be asked, is there so much talk of an urban crisis? The answer is that the improvements in performance, great as they have been, have not kept pace with rising expectations. In other words, although things have been getting better absolutely, they have been getting worse *relative to what we think they should be.* And this is because, as a people, we seem to act on the advice of the old jingle:

[8] William G. Grigsby, *Housing Markets and Public Policy* (Philadelphia: University of Pennsylvania Press, 1963), p. 322.
[9] Gary T. Marx, *Protest and Prejudice* (New York: Harper & Row, 1967), p. 6.

> Good, better, best,
> Never let it rest
> Until your good is better
> And your better best.

Consider the poverty problem, for example. Irving Kristol has pointed out that for nearly a century all studies, in all countries, have concluded that a third, a fourth, or a fifth of the nation in question is below the poverty line.[10] "Obviously," he remarks, "if one defines the poverty line as that which places one-fifth of the nation below it, then one-fifth of the nation will always be below the poverty line." The point is that even if everyone is better off there will be as much poverty as ever, provided that the line is redefined upward. Kristol notes that whereas in the depths of the Depression, F.D.R. found only one-third of the nation "ill-housed, ill-clad, ill-nourished," Leon Keyserling, a former head of the Council of Economic Advisers, in 1962 published a book called *Poverty and Deprivation in the U.S.—the Plight of Two-Fifths of a Nation.*

Much of the same thing has happened with respect to most urban problems. Police brutality, for example, would be a rather minor problem if we judged it by a fixed standard; it is a growing problem because we judge it by an ever more exacting standard. A generation ago the term meant hitting someone on the head with a nightstick. Now it often means something quite different:

> *What the Negro community is presently complaining about when it cries "police brutality" is the more subtle attack on personal dignity that manifests itself in unexplainable questionings and searches, in hostile and insolent attitudes toward groups of young Negroes on the street, or in cars, and in the use of disrespectful and sometimes racist language.*[11]

Following Kristol, one can say that if the "police brutality line" is defined as that which places one-fifth of all police behavior below it, then one-fifth of all police behavior will always be brutal.

The school dropout problem is an even more striking example. At the turn of the century, when almost everyone was a "dropout," the term and the "problem" did not exist. It was not until the 1960's, when for the first time a majority of boys and girls were graduating from high school and practically all had at least some high school training, that the "dropout

---

[10] Irving Kristol, "The Lower Fifth," *The New Leader,* February 17, 1964, pp. 9–10.

[11] Robert Blauner, "Whitewash Over Watts," *Trans-action* 3 (March–April 1966): 6.

problem" became acute. Then, although the dropout rate was still declining, various cities developed at least fifty-five separate programs to deal with the problem. Hundreds of articles on it were published in professional journals, the National Education Association established a special action project to deal with it, and the Commissioner of Education, the Secretary of Labor, and the President all made public statements on it.[12] Obviously, if one defines the "inadequate amount of schooling line" as that which places one-fifth of all boys and girls below it, then one-fifth of all boys and girls will always be receiving an inadequate amount of schooling.

Whatever our educational standards are today, Wayland writes, they will be higher tomorrow. He summarizes the received doctrine in these words:

Start the child in school earlier; keep him in school more and more months of the year; retain all who start to school for twelve to fourteen years; expect him to learn more and more during this period, in wider and wider areas of human experience, under the guidance of a teacher, who has had more and more training, and who is assisted by more and more specialists, who provide an ever-expanding range of services, with access to more and more detailed personal records, based on more and more carefully validated tests.[13]

To a large extent, then, our urban problems are like the mechanical rabbit at the racetrack, which is set to keep just ahead of the dogs no matter how fast they may run. Our performance is better and better, but because we set our standards and expectations to keep ahead of performance, the problems are never any nearer to solution. Indeed, if standards and expectations rise *faster* than performance, the problems may get (relatively) worse as they get (absolutely) better.

Some may say that since almost everything about the city can stand improvement (to put it mildly), this mechanical rabbit effect is a good thing in that it spurs us on to make constant progress. No doubt this is true to some extent. On the other hand, there is danger that we may mistake failure to progress as fast as we would like for failure to progress at all and, in panic, rush into ill-considered measures that will only make matters worse. After all, an "urban crisis" that results largely from rising standards and expectations is not the sort of crisis that, unless something drastic is

[12] Burton A. Weisbrod, "Preventing High-School Drop-outs," in Robert Dorfman, ed., *Measuring Benefits of Government Investments* (Washington, D. C.: The Brookings Institution, 1965), p. 118.

[13] Sloan R. Wayland, "Old Problems, New Faces, and New Standards," in A. Harry Passow, ed., *Education in Depressed Areas* (New York: Columbia University Teachers College, 1963), p. 67.

done, is bound to lead to disaster. To treat it as if it were might be a very serious mistake.

This danger is greatest in matters where our standards are unreasonably high. The effect of too-high standards cannot be to spur us on to reach the prescribed level of performance sooner than we otherwise would, for that level is by definition impossible of attainment. At the same time, these standards may cause us to adopt measures that are wasteful and injurious and, in the long run, to conclude from the inevitable failure of these measures that there is something fundamentally wrong with our society. Consider the school dropout problem, for example. The dropout rate can never be cut to zero: there will always be some boys and girls who simply do not have whatever it takes to finish high school. If we continue to make a great hue and cry about the dropout problem after we have reached the point where all those who can reasonably be expected to finish high school are doing so, we shall accomplish nothing constructive. Instead, we shall, at considerable cost to ourselves, injure the boys and girls who cannot finish (the propaganda against being a dropout both hurts the morale of such a youngster and reduces his or her job opportunities) while creating in ourselves and in others the impression that our society is morally or otherwise incapable of meeting its obligations.

In a certain sense, then, the urban crisis may be real. By treating a spurious crisis as if it were real, we may unwittingly make it so.

14. Suburban Differences and Metropolitan Policies

BY OLIVER P. WILLIAMS, HAROLD HERMAN, CHARLES S. LIEBMAN, AND THOMAS R. DYE

The term "metropolitan problem" has often been affixed to any situation requiring cooperation or interaction between adjacent units of government in urban areas. Problems are usually identified on a service basis, and there is hardly any governmental activity which has not been identified as constituting a metropolitan problem.[1] The advocacy of metropolitan government is, for some, based merely on the belief that almost every activity has an intergovernmental aspect.

Some writers have distinguished between *metropolitan problems* and *problems in a metropolitan area*.[2] This observation contains a very sound insight, but it lacks specificity. The following classification attempts to make explicit the crucial distinction between the two. The distinction is based on the recognition that the major characteristic of metropolitan areas is the coincidence of spatial specialization and autonomous local governing units. A metropolitan problem is one that, unlike other intergovernmental problems, results from this coincidence.

Problem One: Maintaining the System. If people want to work in one community, sleep in another, shop in a third, and play in a fourth; if high-status persons want to reside apart from those of low status; if smoky factories are to be separated from homes; in short, if spatial specialization is to exist within a metropolitan economy—then basic services necessary for the development of each subarea and means through which they may be accessible to one another, must be provided.

Transportation and communication are the primary avenues of maintaining accessibility. The latter is provided primarily through the private

Reprinted with permission of the authors and the University of Pennsylvania Press from Oliver P. Williams, Harold Herman, Charles S. Liebman, Thomas R. Dye, *Suburban Differences and Metropolitan Policies: A Philadelphia Story* (Philadelphia: University of Pennsylvania Press, 1965), pp. 299–312.

[1] In a recent national study, even the universal governmental function of personnel management has been given the metropolitan label. See: *Governmental Manpower for Tomorrow's Cities*, a report of the Municipal Manpower Commission (New York: McGraw Hill Book Co., 1962).

[2] Edward C. Banfield and Morton Grodzins, *Government and Housing in Metropolitan Areas* (New York: McGraw Hill Book Co., 1958).

sector of our economy, the former is shared by private and public management, with government playing an increasingly important role. But transportation is not the only service through which government makes the system feasible. Certain basic utilities, such as water and sewage disposal, are often requisites for urban development. If they cannot be locally provided, and if a larger service area is a technical or financial necessity for continued development, then autonomy in policy formulation must give way to integrated mechanisms if the component units are to survive. Thus we characterize as a truly metropolitan problem the *maintenance of services providing the supports necessary for the continued existence of areal specialization.*

Problem Two: Unequal Distribution of Resources and Services. In every metropolitan area, there are "have" and "have not" communities, with the core city often being the most advertised of the "have nots." Such disparities are largely a byproduct of the system of areal specialization. Of course there always have been, and probably always will be, differences in individual and community wealth. In a metropolitan context, such differences are aggravated by the efficiency with which the system of differentiation is maintained. Moreover, the multiplicity of local governing units, when imposed upon specialized populations, affects their ability to reconcile differences between groups. It is in this sense that we take exception to views such as that of Banfield and Grodzins who argue that housing is not a metropolitan problem. We agree that the structure of metropolitan government is not the *cause* of slums or blight; we agree that the mere existence of different housing standards does not constitute a problem; but we disagree with their belief that alterations in governmental structure will not alter housing policies. Such alteration can distribute the burden of housing costs over wider areas, it can impose higher minimum standards, it can organize leadership that is lacking in those areas where housing is poorest, it can attack the roots of the social and economic differences that segregate the poor and dictate their housing. It can do all this if one recognizes the extent to which urban differentiation affects the distribution of the supply of housing and the costs of remedying its inadequacies, and if one holds government responsible for producing change.

Our disagreement with Banfield and Grodzins is similar to that between the professionals and local politicians. As we have seen, some Suburbs may choose to deemphasize or do without some services. Although we did not specifically probe this question, we suspect that some working-class Suburbs would willingly forgo basic health services, for example, if commensurate tax savings would accrue. Thus the existence of different service standards reflect both differences in burdens associated with supplying financial support and differences in the preferences of specialized populations. Whether or not the local people approve of the differentials, disparities in services result. Professionals will identify such disparities as metropolitan problems when local officials and residents will not.

There is still another basis for labelling inequities in resources and services a metropolitan problem. When upper-middle-class suburbs draw off leadership, and, more particularly, wealth from the rest of the system, the remaining areas are impoverished thereby. As a result the cost and burden of providing services vary throughout the metropolitan area. The attainment of a recognized minimum standard becomes excessively costly to some communities and so an acceptable standard of service is not always provided throughout the area.

Thus we characterize as a metropolitan problem *the unequal distribution of resources and services that result from the process of specialization.*

Problem Three: Border Relationships. Contiguous units of government must engage in many reciprocal relations merely as a result of their proximity to one another. This is as true for rural as urban areas. The fleeing criminal crossing municipal boundaries is a clear example. Such fugitive pursuit problems are common to all governments; yet we frequently refer to this situation as metropolitan when it occurs in an urban environment, but not when it occurs in rural areas. River pollution evokes upstream-downstream conflicts regardless of whether the jurisdictions involved are urban or rural. Factories in rural areas may poison animals and plants with discharges of noxious fluids or fumes. That such discharges affect more than one political jurisdiction does not make the problem metropolitan.

The politics of mere propinquity does not constitute a truly metropolitan problem, since it is unrelated to the fundamental metropolitan characteristic—areal specialization. For this reason, cooperative demands that emanate simply from border relationships represent pseudo-metropolitan issues. Success in initiating and maintaining cooperation on matters such as fugitive-search systems, police-radio networks, common streets, minor utility exchanges, etc., should not be viewed as symbols of metropolitan fraternalism which are precursors of true union.

It should be added, however, that the density and greater activity of urban governments increases the number of border contacts between municipalities in metropolitan areas. While urbanism may thus generate a high level of municipal interaction, the qualitative nature of border policies is not thereby changed. These policies deal with problems that are distinct from those of system maintenance and resource and service inequities. Generally, border problems are easily solved until money is required. At that time, the nature of the problem changes, as questions of the proration of costs and obligations arise.

The three classes of problems described above are not mutually exclusive. It is difficult to conceive of any governmental policy or service without some overtones that would qualify it for inclusion in all three categories. Moreover, the importance of the three, and the degree to which they are popularly recognized at any one time, differ. Proposals offered as solutions to metropolitan problems are received and judged in accordance with how problems are perceived and what interest they evoke. A proposal for a joint sewer authority may at the same time be perceived as relating to (1) maintenance of the system (2) service and resource inequities or (3) a border problem of contiguous urbanized communities. How individual municipalities will react to the proposal is conditioned largely by what problem they view it as solving and what problems they feel may result from the proposal. Nevertheless, some policy areas tend to fall in one category more frequently than in another.

Transportation would undoubtedly head any list of policies related to the maintenance of the system of metropolitan specialization. While some integrated means of planning and managing transportation systems are increasingly being employed, their consequences are such as to profoundly influence the manner in which communities specialize their relationships to other communities and area-wide distributions of wealth. Thus while municipalities depend upon a more-or-less integrated transportation system for their accessibility to complementary municipalities, it is with the greatest reluctance that they relinquished control over transportation policy. But they have relinquished it.

In nearly every metropolitan area, state highway departments have always supplied a modicum of coordination over the highway network. In the Philadelphia area, transportation planning and operation is sufficiently recognized as metropolitan in character that the county and state governments have assumed jurisdiction over it. The creation of a regional transportation-planning agency sustained mostly by federal funds, and the signing of intercounty and interstate agreements on transit development reflect recognition of the essential integrative role of transportation. Municipal activity is becoming confined to lobbying before these higher units of government.

Water and sewage disposal systems are second only to transportation in providing support to the metropolitan system. It has been possible to secure cooperation from very diverse Suburbs for the provision of both these utilities. Cooperative arrangements between Philadelphia and the Suburbs are also common. Indeed, the only firm cooperative arrangements involving financial obligations between the Suburbs and the central city have concerned transportation, sewage disposal, or water.

In considering metropolitan problems which result from inequities, it must be recognized that the seeking of specialized areas by home-owners or businesses is the very cause of the "problem." To attempt to redress inequities on a voluntary basis is largely unrealistic. Wealth-sharing plans have never achieved great popularity among those who enjoy favored positions. Furthermore, in most areas, resolving inequities is not essential to maintaining the system. The fact that older industrial centers may, in the process of social segregation, end up with indigent populations for whom they cannot provide is, if of any interest to Main Line residents, perhaps welcomed by them. The very existence of inequities testifies to the success of specialization. Redistributions of resources and services are the most difficult area in which to achieve metropolitan agreement, in part because they are closely related to social inequalities.

The redistribution achieved by the state's school-subsidy program is the result of pressures applied from the outside. Hard-pressed Suburbs can find many other hard-pressed districts with which to ally in the state legislature, and the resulting redistribution encompasses not only metropolitan areas but the entire state. Service inequities peculiar to urban areas have found less favorable reception in state capitols; hence grants-in-aid for municipal services are a rarity in comparison with school grants.

THE BASIC CONFLICT OF METROPOLITAN GOVERNMENT

The question of structuring metropolitan government reflects the basic dualism characteristic of metropolitan areas: the existence of specialization and the need for integrative mechanisms. Most metropolitan proposals are caught between these centrifugal and centripetal elements of the system. The fact that one cannot have specialization without integration does not furnish a basis for agreement. It only assures that questions touching on these two facets of the system will continually be raised and not permanently ignored. Thus the metropolis furnishes an inexhaustible political agenda for discussion by political leaders, political scientists, and urbanists.

The underlying normative question implicit in any proposal for structuring government in a metropolitan area is whether the proposed government is designed to maintain or to modify the system. In the past, those who have advocated consolidation as the ultimate "solution to the metropolitan problem" have, in effect, sought a comprehensive modification of the existing system of areal specialization. So, too, have some of the "Garden City" planners, who, although they would not consolidate, would decentralize the metropolis into economically though not socially, specialized subareas. On the other hand, the narrowly designed, single-purpose special district or authority and the intermunicipal contract concepts have been conceived so as to have as small a disturbing effect on the status quo as possible.

Of the two extreme suggestions for structuring government in metropolitan areas, proposals closer to the latter have been most successful.

Metropolitan politics in the United States, as well as in Philadelphia, have never really encompassed a radical revamping of the metropolis as a system of specialization. Why should it? It is unrealistic to expect citizens to acquiesce voluntarily in giving up the prized values of urban differentiation. Thus, while the general-purpose, consolidated metropolitan government has had little acceptance, the special-purpose government has been used frequently. The criticism directed toward this latter development has been that we are in danger of assembling such a complex of special-purpose governments that the problem of policy coordination will be intensified rather than reduced. Such fears are well grounded.

Frequently, the quest for a solution to metropolitan problems is a quest for a governmental structure as politically acceptable as the special district and yet as comprehensive as consolidation. Such solutions do not exist. Moreover, the quest is perhaps misguided. While centralization or decentralization do affect such questions as economy, efficiency, and speed of action, the true test of the adequacy of a metropolitan governmental system is whether it can so structure the political process of negotiation and compromise as to deal effectively and adequately with metropolitan problems.

In the absence of a local political arena in which the demands for integrative services and the claims for greater equities can be arbitrated, such issues are often taken to the state capital and increasingly to Washington. The integrative demands take the form of requests for special regional agencies. Redressing inequities occurs through grants-in-aid. To achieve either goal, parties in the metropolitan area must gain allies or at least still opposition from parties outside the immediate region. The strategy with regard to the state capitol or Washington is much the same—the use of political party organizations to form a coalition of urban interests with their nominally affiliated partisan colleagues from non-urban territories. While the procedure varies from state to state, most of the essential metropolitan decisions are made outside the metropolitan area.

In part, this locus for decision-making is an outgrowth of the legal foundations upon which our federal system rests. In part, it is the inevitable outcome of the search for outside coalitions that has been fostered by the inability to gain consensus within the area.

PROSPECTS FOR METROPOLITAN GOVERNMENT

Metropolitan problems are not being overlooked entirely. Yet there are cogent arguments to suggest that the most effective and perhaps the only way to handle these problems adequately is to create *one* forum within the area to which *all* problems can be brought for negotiation and compromise —in short to create *one metropolitan government*. But to posit metropolitan government as a desirable goal and to view it as attainable are separate matters. Our analysis offers little encouragement to those who are working for metropolitan government. Our outlook is pessimistic, not because of the record of failures, but because of the underlying bases for the failure of metropolitan government proposals.

The attainment of metropolitan government is unlikely either through direct approaches or through the expansion of single-purpose agencies into general-purpose units. Single-purpose metropolitan agencies, whether special districts or new county departments, tend to concentrate on those activities that supply the integrative supports for subarea specialization. These are the services most widely recognized as essential to the well-being of the entire area and each of its parts. It is unrealistic to expect officials and supporters of such programs to endanger their agencies by expanding operations to include issues over which there is less agreement. Although county and regional planners often speak as if they would like to have it, would there be county planning agencies if it were seriously proposed that they be given zoning authority?

The creation of single-purpose agencies to provide integrative supports has an additional and even more important effect on the prospects for metropolitan government. By isolating these services in separate agencies, the political incentives for a general forum are removed; for the "piecemeal" approach to governing the metropolis first siphons off those issues for which there is little choice but cooperation between have and have nots, suburbs and core cities. Left are those problems for which there is the least incentive to negotiate and the least amount of flexibility in bargaining—those which most divide the metropolis. Will the stimulus for metropolitan government come from these?

Most metropolitan areas have developed governmental mechanisms for providing some integrative services. In so doing, the thornier problems of regional agreement on minimum service standards and equitable distributions of costs have been left in the cold. Denied the ability to attach their issues to the bargaining around integrative services, those who are concerned with problems of resource and service inequities have little leverage in their favor. No metropolitan area is likely to obtain voluntary cooperation among all its municipalities in pooling resources to furnish hospital care for the indigent. Such an issue will not even be accepted as a "legitimate" metropolitan responsibility. Dozens of other unevenly distributed services will be similarly dismissed. These questions cannot be raised as metropolitan problems if there is no metropolitan government to appeal to. There can be no metropolitan government if those activities which bind the region are handled on an item by item basis.

A pattern of government for metropolitan areas is emerging. Those services which maintain the system are increasingly being supplied by area-wide agencies of one type or another. Problems of inequities are ignored or shunted to the state and federal level. Border incidents are left to an inter-municipal ambassadorial system.

Thus ways are found to handle metropolitan problems. They are often slow, uneven, awkward, uncoordinated and incomplete, but there are ways. The case for a metropolitan government is not based on the lack of alter-natives, but in the belief that the alternatives do not work well enough. Does the pattern of government we have described provide a process of negotiation and compromise that deals effectively and adequately with metropolitan problems?

The question may be moot; for by now we may have built in so many provisional remedies that it may be too late to try to restructure the process. In most major metropolitan areas, regional organizations which are not limited to single purposes, but which also have no operating responsibility are being superimposed on the pattern of metropolitan government. The RCEO in Philadelphia, the MRC in New York, the COG in Washington, the ABAG in San Francisco, are examples of general-purpose metropolitan forums. Most are straining to keep going. Not the least of their difficulties is finding an agenda with which to occupy themselves; for existing single-purpose agencies have skimmed off those issues for which there is agreement on the necessity for regional action. The new metropolitan councils do not promise to alter the emerging governmental pattern. In those jurisdictions where activities necessary to maintenance of the system have not yet been organized, the councils may fix their agenda on one or more such issues and sponsor or become themselves single-purpose agencies. Elsewhere they will become fraternal, no-purpose organizations.

A change in the pattern of government coming from within the metro-politan area is hard to imagine. An alternative is the vision of pressure from outside the region producing change, and the possibility of federal and/or state action seems the more probable. Federal programs in urban areas have, for some time, been stressing regional planning and cooperation. Indeed, federal stimulus can be blamed for some of the single-purpose agencies that now exist. If the federal government can tie its programs together, a more comprehensive approach to metropolitan areas might be reflected in local reorganization of thought and action. An even greater "if" in the prospects for change is the actions of state governments. As yet, state governments have been reticent to use grants as enticements toward regional compromises. Will the stimulus to change federal and state policy be forthcoming?

An even greater "if" in the metropolitan future is the impact of tech-nological change. So important is this "if" that it may remove the conditions relevant to discussion of metropolitan government. Earlier, we described the automobile's effect on the structure of the metropolis. There is every reason to believe that new technology will have even more radical effects. Already there are indications that transportation and communication technology are reshaping the urban structure into a new mold. The automobile ended the rail-centered form. The perfected auto and improved communications may be ending the early automotive form. Improved highways and truck transport are enabling industrial plants to sever their connections with metropolitan centers. Increased automation will undoubtedly affect both the process of production and the nature and location of labor markets. Air transport and closed circuit television have already diminished the need for proximity in communications and supervision.

We do not wish to draw a picture of a completely automated society in which each person manipulates electronic impulses from a cell that can be located anywhere. Nevertheless, one should recognize that we are entering an era in which a new type of national system whose economic, social, and political consequences have yet to be felt, is being superimposed on the metropolitan system.

New forms of specialization are beginning to emerge. We already have national recreation and retirement towns, socially graded and related to the entire nation. More important, specific industrial activities that promise to represent a greater proportion of total economic activity in the future are already showing their independence from the urban complex. Some large research institutions can locate practically anywhere that their prized employees want to live.

The new interstate highway system raises the prospect of industrial centers scattered in small or large clusters around the intersections of major routes. The increased household and industrial appetite for space encourages a new form of development utilizing low-cost land in order to maintain a reasonable balance of land to total development costs. Conceivably, new widely scattered employment centers may separate into high- and low-wage places fostering a new form of areal specialization.

While we might speculate further on the specific possibilities of a new urban form, it would serve little useful purpose to do so here. We must emphasize, however, that there is no present indication that technology will be a servant helping to reknit the urban society into an integrated unit. Instead all the forces of technology are encouraging and enabling further areal specialization. Future technology will enable high- and low-social-status communities to have even greater physical distances between them. Whether this in fact happens will depend upon national policies affecting the distribution of income and opportunities as well as on compromise in metropolitan and regional bargaining agencies. But those who are concerned about metropolitan government as a form of local control over local problems should not look to technology for any comfort. It we confine our discussion to present conditions and technology, then we must reiterate that the governing of the metropolitan area is a matter of living with differences. The premise for action can never be leveling those differences, but only one of trading advantages or disadvantages.

15. The Myth of Suburbia

BY BENNETT M. BERGER

In recent years a veritable myth of suburbia has developed in the United States. I am not referring to the physical facts of large-scale population movement to the suburbs: these are beyond dispute. But the social and cultural "revolution" that suburban life supposedly represents is far from being an established fact. Nevertheless, newspapers and magazines repeatedly characterize suburbia as "a new way of life," and one recent textbook refers to the rise of suburbia as "one of the major social changes of the twentieth century."

To urban sociologists, "suburbs" is an ecological term, distinguishing these settlements from cities, rural villages, and other kinds of communities. "Suburbia," on the other hand, is a cultural term, intended to connote a way of life, or, rather, the intent of those who use it is to connote a way of life. The ubiquity of the term in current discourse suggests that its meaning is well on the way to standardization—that what it is supposed to connote is widely enough accepted and implicitly enough shared to permit free use of the term with a reasonable amount of certainty that it will convey the image or images it extends. Over the last dozen years, these images have coalesced into a full blown myth, complete with its articles of faith, its sacred symbols, its rituals, its promise for the future, and its resolution of ultimate questions. The details of the myth are rife in many popular magazines as well as in more highbrow periodicals and books; and although the details should be familiar to almost everyone interested in contemporary cultural trends, it may be well to summarize them briefly.

THE ELEMENTS OF THE MYTH

Approaching the myth of suburbia from the outside, one is immediately struck by rows of new "ranch-type" houses either identical in design or with minor variations built into a basic plan, winding streets, neat lawns, two-car garages, infant trees, and bicycles and tricycles lining the sidewalks. Nearby is the modern ranch-type school and the even more modern shopping center dominated by the department store branch or the giant supermarket, itself

Reprinted with permission of the author and publisher from Bennett M. Berger, "The Myth of Suburbia," *Journal of Social Issues,* XVII, No. 1 (1961), 38–49.

flanked by a pastel-dotted expanse of parking lot. Beneath the television antenna and behind the modestly but charmingly landscaped entrance to the tract home resides the suburbanite and his family. I should say *"temporarily* resides" because perhaps the most prominent element of the myth is that residence in a tract suburb is temporary; suburbia is a "transient center" because its breadwinners are upwardly mobile, and live there only until a promotion or a company transfer permits or requires something more opulent in the way of a home. The suburbanites are upwardly mobile because they are predominantly young (most commentators seem to agree that they are almost all between 25 and 35), well educated, and have a promising place in some organizational hierarchy—promising because of a continuing expansion of the economy and with no serious slowdown in sight. They are engineers, middle-management men, young lawyers, salesmen, insurance agents, teachers, civil service bureaucrats—groups sometimes designated as Organization Men, and sometimes as "the new middle class." Most such occupations require some college education, so it comes as no surprise to hear and read that the suburbanites are well educated. Their wives too seem well educated; their reported conversation, their patois, and especially their apparently avid interest in theories of child development all suggest exposure to higher education.

According to the myth, a new kind of hyperactive social life has developed in suburbia. Not only is informal visiting or "neighboring" said to be rife, but a lively organizational life also goes on. Clubs, associations, and organizations allegedly exist for almost every conceivable hobby, interest, or preoccupation. An equally active participation in local civic affairs is encouraged by the absence of an older generation who, in other communities, would normally be the leaders.

This rich social and civic life is fostered by the homogeneity of the suburbanites; they are in the same age range, have similar jobs and incomes; their children are around the same age, their problems of housing and furnishing are similar. In short, a large number of similar interests and preoccupations promotes their solidarity. This very solidarity and homogeneity, on top of the physical uniformities of the suburb itself, is often perceived as the source of the problem of "conformity" in suburbia; aloofness or detachment is frowned upon. The "involvement of everyone in everyone else's life" submits one to the constant scrutiny of the community, and everything from an unclipped lawn to an unclipped head of hair may be cause for invidious comment. On the other hand, the uniformity and homogeneity make suburbia classless, or one-class (variously designated as middle or upper-middle class). For those interlopers who arrive in the suburbs bearing the unmistakable marks of a more deprived upbringing, suburbia is said to serve as a kind of "second melting pot" in which those who are on the way up learn to take on the appropriate folkways of the milieu to which they aspire.

During the day, suburbia is almost wholly given over to the business of child rearing. Manless during the day, suburbia is a female society in which the young mothers, well-educated and without the interference of tradition (represented by doting grandparents), can rear their children according to the best modern methods. "In the absence of older people, the top authorities on child guidance (in suburbia) are two books: Spock's *Infant Care,* and Gesell's *The First Five Years of Life.* You hear frequent references to them."

The widely commented upon "return to religion" is said to be most visible in suburbia. Clergymen are swamped, not only with their religious duties but with problems of marriage counseling and other family problems as well. The revivified religious life in suburbia is not merely a matter of the increasing size of Sunday congregations, for the church is not only a house of worship but a local civic institution also. As such it benefits from the generally active civic life of the suburbanites.

Part of the myth of suburbia is the image of suburbanites as commuters. Much has been deduced about suburbia from the fact of commuting. For father, commuting means an extra hour or two away from the family—with debilitating effects upon the relationship between father and children. Sometimes this means that Dad leaves for work before the children are up and comes home after they are put to bed. Naturally, these extra hours put a greater burden upon the mother, and has implications for the relationship between husband and wife.

The commuter returns in the morning to the place where he was bred, for the residents of suburbia are apparently former city people who "escaped" to the suburbs. By moving to suburbia, however, the erstwhile Democrat from the "urban ward"[1] becomes the suburban Republican. The voting shift has been commented on or worried about at length; there seems to be something about suburbia that makes Republicans out of people who were Democrats while they lived in the city. But the political life of suburbia is characterized not only by the voting shift, but by the vigor with which it is carried on. Political *activity* takes its place beside other civic and organizational activity, intense and spirited.

THE SOURCES OF THE MYTH

This brief characterization is intended neither as ethnography nor as caricature, but it does not, I think, misrepresent the image of suburbia that has

---

[1] William Whyte has a way of making the phrase "urban ward" resound with connotations of poverty, deprivation, soot, and brick—as if "urban ward" were a synonym for "slum."

come to dominate the minds of most Americans, including intellectuals. Immediately, however, a perplexing question arises: why should a group of tract houses, mass produced and quickly thrown up on the outskirts of a large city, apparently generate so unique and distinctive a way of life? What is the logic that links tract living with suburbia as a way of life?

If suburban homes were all within a limited price range, then one might expect them to be occupied by families of similar income, and this might account for some of the homogeneity of the neighborhood ethos. But suburban developments are themselves quite heterogeneous. The term "suburbia" has not only been used to refer to tract housing developments as low as $8,000 per unit and as high as $65,000 per unit, but also to rental developments whose occupants do not think of themselves as homeowners. The same term has been used to cover old rural towns (such as those in the Westchester–Fairfield County complex around New York City) which, because of the expansion of the city and improvements in transportation, have only gradually become suburban in character. It has been applied also to gradually developing residential neighborhoods on the edges of the city itself. The ecological nature of the suburbs cannot justify so undifferentiated an image as that of "suburbia."

If we limit the image of suburbia to the mass produced tract developments, we might regard the fact of commuting as the link between suburban residence and "suburbanism as a way of life." Clearly, the demands of daily commuting create certain common conditions which might go far to explain some of the ostensible uniformities of suburban living. But certainly commuting is not a unique feature of suburban living; many suburbanites are not commuters; many urban residents are. It may be true that the occupations of most suburbanites presently require a daily trip to and from the central business district of the city, but it is likely to be decreasingly true with the passage of time. For the pioneers to the suburban residential frontier have been followed not only by masses of retail trade outlets, but by industry also. Modern mass production technology has made obsolete many two- and three-story plants in urban areas. Today's modern factories are vast one-story operations which require wide expanses of land, which are either unavailable or too expensive in the city itself. With the passage of time, "industrial parks" will increasingly dot suburban areas, and the proportions of suburbanites commuting to the city each day will decrease.

If the occupations of most suburbanites were similar in their demands, then this might help account for the development of a generic way of life in suburbs. And, indeed, if suburbia were populated largely by Organization men and their families, then one could understand more readily the style of life that is ascribed to it. Or, lacking this, if Organization men, as Whyte puts it, give the prevailing *tone* to life in suburbia, then one could more readily understand the prevalence of his model in the writing on suburbia. But there is no real reason to believe that the Organization man dominates the suburbs. Perhaps the typical Organization man is a suburbanite. But it is one thing to assert this and quite another thing to assert that the typical tract suburb is populated by Organization men and their families or dominated by an Organization way of life.

Clearly then one suburb (or *kind* of suburb) is likely to differ from another not only in terms of the cost of its homes, the income of its residents, their occupations and commuting patterns, but also in terms of its educational levels, the character of the region, the size of the suburb, the social and geographical origin of its residents, and countless more indices—all of which, presumably, may be expected to lead to differences in "way of life."

But we not only have good reason to expect suburbs to *differ* markedly from one another; we have reason to expect striking *similarities* between life in urban residential neighborhoods and tract suburbs of a similar social cast. In large cities many men "commute" to work, that is, take subways, buses, or other forms of public transportation to their jobs which may be over on the other side of town. There are thousands of blocks in American cities with rows of identical or similar houses in them within a limited rental or price range, and presumably occupied by families in a similar income bracket. The same fears for massification and conformity were felt regarding these urban neighborhoods as are now felt for the mass produced suburbs. Certainly, urban neighborhoods have always had a class character and a "way of life" associated with them. Certainly, too, the whole image of the problem of "conformity" in suburbia closely parallels the older image of the tyranny of gossip in the American small town.

In continually referring to "the myth of suburbia" I do not mean to imply that the reports on the culture of suburban life have been falsified; and it would be a mistake to interpret the tone of my remarks as a debunking one. *I mean only to say that the reports of suburbia we have had so far have been extremely selective.* They are based for the most part, upon life in Levittown, N.Y., Park Forest, Ill., Lakewood, near Los Angeles, and, most recently (the best study so far) a fashionable suburb of Toronto, Canada. The studies that have given rise to the myth of suburbia have been studies of *white collar suburbs* of large cities. If the phrase "middle class suburb" or "white collar suburb" strikes the eye as redundant, it is testimony to the efficacy of the myth. Large tracts of suburban housing, in many respects indistinguishable from those in Levittown and Park Forest have gone up and are continuing to go up all over the country, not only near large cities, but near middle sized and small ones as well. In many of these tracts, the homes fall within the 12,000 to 16,000 dollar price range, a range well within the purchasing abilities of large numbers of semi-skilled and skilled factory workers in unionized heavy industry. Many of these working class people are migrating to these new suburbs—which are not immediately and visibly characterizable as "working class," but which, to all intents and purposes, look from the outside like the fulfillment of the "promise of America" symbolized in the myth. Even more of them will be migrating to new suburbs as increasing numbers of factories move out of the city to the hinterlands. Many of these people are either rural-bred, or urban-working class bred, with relatively little education, and innocent of white collar status or aspiration. And where this is true, as it is in many low-price tracts, then one may expect sharp differences between their social and cultural life and that of their more sophisticated counterparts in white collar suburbs.

This should be no surprise; indeed, the fact that it should have to be asserted at all is still further testimony to the vitality of the myth I have been describing. My own research among auto workers in a new, predominantly "working class" suburb in California demonstrates how far removed their style of life is from that suggested by the myth of suburbia. The group I interviewed still vote 81% Democratic; there has been no "return to religion" among them—more than half of the people I spoke to said they went to church rarely or not at all. On the whole, they have no great hopes of getting ahead in their jobs, and an enormous majority regard their new suburban homes not as a temporary resting place, but as paradise permanently gained. Of the group I interviewed, 70% belonged to not a single club, organization, or association (with the exception of the union), and their mutual visiting or "neighboring" was quite rare except if relatives lived nearby. The details of the findings are available in another place (Berger, 1960); let me summarize then by saying that the group of auto workers I interviewed has, for the most part, maintained its working class attitudes and style of life intact in the context of the bright new suburb.

THE FUNCTIONS OF THE MYTH

Similar conditions probably prevail in many of the less expensive suburbs; in any case, semi skilled "working class" suburbs probably constitute a substantial segment of the reality of suburban life. Why, then, is the myth still so potent in our popular culture? Suburbia today is a public issue— something to talk about, everywhere from the pages of learned journals to best sellers, from academic halls to smoke-filled political rooms, from the pulpits of local churches to Hollywood production lots.[2]

[2] In the movie version of the novel *No Down Payment*, ostensibly a fictional account of life in the new suburbia, Hollywood makes a pointed comment on social stratification. The sequence of violence, rape, and accidental death is set in motion by the only important character in the story who is not a white-collar man: the rural

One source of the peculiar susceptibility of "suburbia" to the manufacture of myth is the fact that a large supply of visible symbols are ready at hand. Picture windows, patios and barbecues, power lawn mowers, the problems of commuting, and the armies of children manning their mechanized vehicles down the sidewalks, are only secondarily facts; primarily they are symbols whose function is to evoke an image of a way of life for the non-suburban public. These symbols of suburbia can be fitted neatly into the total pattern of the "spirit" of this "age." Suburbia is the locus of gadgetry, shopping centers, and "station wagon culture"; its grass grows greener, its chrome shines brighter, its lines are clean and new and modern. Suburbia is America in its drip-dry Sunday clothes, standing before the bar of history fulfilled, waiting for its judgment. But like Mr. Dooley's court, which kept its eyes on the election returns, the "judgments of history" are also affected by contemporary ideological currents, and the myth of suburbia is enabled to flourish precisely because it fits into the general outlook of at least four otherwise divergent schools of opinion whose function it is to shape the "judgment of history."

To realtor–chamber of commerce defenders of the American Way of Life suburbia represents the fulfillment of the American middle-class dream; it is identified with the continuing possibility of upward mobility, with expanding opportunities in middle-class occupations, with rising standards of living and real incomes, and the gadgeted good life as it is represented in the full-color ads in the mass circulation magazines.

To a somewhat less sanguine group, for example, architects, city planners, estheticians, and designers, suburbia represents a dreary blight on the American landscape, the epitome of American standardization and vulgarization, with its row upon monotonous row of mass produced cheerfulness masquerading as homes, whole agglomerations or "scatterations" of them masquerading as communities. To these eyes, the new tract suburbs of today are the urban slums of tomorrow.

Third, the myth of suburbia seems important to sociologists and other students of contemporary social and cultural trends. David Riesman says of the authors of *Crestwood Heights* that they, "collide, like Whyte, with a problem their predecessors only brushed against, for they are writing about *us*, about the professional upper middle class and its businessmen allies. . . . They are writing, as they are almost too aware, about themselves, their

---

Tennessee-bred service station manager. Frustrated at being denied the job of police chief (because of his lack of education), he drinks himself into a stupor, rapes his upper-middle-class, college-educated neighbor, and then is accidentally killed (symbolically enough) under the wheels of his new Ford. The film closes with his blonde, nymphomaniacal widow leaving the suburb for good on a Sunday morning, while the white-collar people are seen leaving the Protestant church (denomination ambiguous) with looks of quiet illumination on their faces.

friends, their 'type.' " There are, obviously, personal pleasures in profession-ally studying people who are much like oneself; more important, the myth of suburbia conceptualizes for sociologists a microcosm in which some of the apparently major social and cultural trends of our time (other-direction, social mobility, neoconservatism, status anxiety, etc.) flow together, and may be conveniently studied.

Finally, for a group consisting largely of left-wing and formerly left-wing critics of American society, the myth of suburbia provides an up-to-date polemical vocabulary. "Suburb" and "suburban" have replaced the now embarrassingly obsolete "bourgeois" as a packaged rebuke to the whole tenor of American life. What used to be condemned as "bourgeois style," "bourgeois values," and "bourgeois hypocrisy," are now simply designated as "suburban."

But while the myth of suburbia is useful to each of these four groups, it cannot be written off simply as "ruling class propaganda," or as an at-tempt to see only the sunny side of things, or, for that matter, as an attempt to see only the darker side of things—or even as a furtive attempt to peer into a mirror. Too many responsible intellectuals, while uncritically accepting the *myth* of suburbia are nevertheless extremely critical of what they "see" in it.

But precisely *what* is it that they see that they are critical of? Is it conformity? status anxiety? chrome? tail fins? gadgetry? gray flannel suits? No doubt, these are symbols powerful enough to evoke images of an enemy. But the nature of this "enemy" remains peculiarly elusive. Surely, there is nothing specifically "suburban" about conformity, status anxiety and the rest; nor is there anything necessarily diabolical about mass-produced do-mestic comfort and conservatively cut clothes. It is extraordinary that, with the single exception of William H. Whyte's attempt to trace the "web of friendship" on the basis of the physical structure of the Park Forest "courts," no one, to my knowledge, has come to grips with the problem of defining what is specifically *suburban* about suburbia. Instead, most writers are reduced to the use of hackneyed stereotypes not of suburbia, but of the upper middle class. When most commentators say "suburbia," they really mean "middle class."

The sources of this way of life, however, lie far deeper than mere resi-dence in a suburb. These sources have been much discussed in recent years, most notably perhaps, by Mills, Riesman, Fromm, and Galbraith. They go beyond suburbs to questions of wealth, social status, and corporate organiza-tion. Even Whyte's famous discussion of suburbia (upon which so much of the myth is founded) was undertaken in the context of his larger discussion of the Organization Man, a social type created by the structure of corporate opportunity in the United States—something a good deal more profound than the folkways of suburbanites. Seen in this light, suburbia may be nothing but a scapegoat; by blaming "it" for the consequences of our commitment to chrome idols, we achieve ritual purity without really threatening anything or anyone—except perhaps the poor suburbanites, who can't understand why they're always being satirized.

But heaping abuse on suburbia instead of on the classic targets of American social criticism ("success," individual and corporate greed, corruption in high and low places, illegitimate power, etc.) has its advantages for the not-quite-completely-critical intellectual. His critical stance places him comfortably in the great tradition of American social criticism, and at the same time his targets render him respectable and harmless—because, after all, the critique of suburbia is essentially a "cultural" critique; unlike a political or economic one, it threatens no entrenched interests, and contains no direct implications for agitation or concerned action. Indeed, it may be, as Edward Shils has suggested, that a "cultural" critique is all that is possible today from a left-wing point of view; the American economy and political process stand up fairly well under international comparisons, but American "culture" is fair game for anyone.

Despite the epithets that identify suburbia as the citadel of standardization and vulgarization and conformity, suburbia is also testimony to the fact that Americans are living better than ever before. What needs emphasis is that this is true not only for the traditionally comfortable white collar classes but for the blue collar, frayed collar, and turned collar classes also. Even families in urban slums are likely to be paying upward of $85 a month in rent these days, and for this or only slightly more, they can "buy" a new tract home in the suburbs. There is an irony, therefore, in the venom that left-wing critics inject into their discussions of suburbia because the criticism of suburbia tends to become a criticism of industrialization, "rationality," and "progress," and thus brings these critics quite close to the classic conservatives, whose critique of industrialization was also made in terms of its cultural consequences. It is almost as if left-wing critics feared the seduction of the working class by pie—not in the sky, not even on the table, but right in the freezer.

WHAT MIDDLE CLASS?

The "achievement" of suburbia by the working class is a *collective* achievement made possible by prosperity and the labor movement. As such, it does not constitute evidence of individual social mobility. In a prosperous society there occurs not only individual mobility between strata in a relatively stable hierarchy; the entire hierarchy is pushed up by prolonged widespread prosperity, and rearranged by changes in the distribution of occupations and income. The function of a system of social stratification is to maintain viable, hierarchical distinctions between different categories of people, and when symbols which formerly distinguished rank no longer can, because they have become available to all, we should expect a change in the symbolic aspects of social stratification—if, that is, symbols are to retain the power to make distinctions.

It is perhaps for this reason that in recent years there has been such a relative de-emphasis on economic criteria of stratification in favor of the distinctly cultural ones—that is, those having to do with style of life. For in a society in which even a semi-skilled factory worker can earn $5000 a year, own two cars, a ranch house, and a TV set, it should perhaps be no surprise that groups with higher prestige (but perhaps without considerably greater income) should defend themselves against the potential threat posed by widespread material abundance to their "prestige" by designating such economic possessions "vulgar" and by asserting the indispensability of a certain style of life—that is, something that cannot be immediately purchased with no down payment. Like universities, which respond to the clamor for higher education by tightening their entrance requirements, prestige groups respond to the clamor by money for prestige by tightening *their* entrance requirements. This has been common enough among aristocratic groups for a long time; money and possessions have rarely been sufficient to admit one to the select circles of old wealth; and the increasingly sharp symbolic distinction between the upper middle class and the lower middle class (not only distinctions of income) suggest that something similar may be occurring on lower levels of society.

Whereas at one time in recent history, the phrase "middle class" evoked images of Sinclair Lewis, Main Street, *The Saturday Evening Post* families of smiling faces around brown-turkeyed dinner tables, and a concern with "respectability," today the phrase is just as likely to evoke images of cocktail parties, country clubs, other-directedness, *The Atlantic Monthly,* Van Gogh prints in wide, deep mats, and a hypersensitivity to considerations of status. Sociologists recognize this ambiguity by designating the style suggested by the former series of images as "lower" middle class, and the style suggested by the latter series of images as "upper" middle class, and tend to think the issue has been clarified. But the real problem implicit in the terminological need to break the middle class into an upper and a lower stratum is too complex to be solved by a simple linguistic device. The problem is not only one of drawing a line between two contemporary "middle class" styles of life; the immense difference between the life styles of the lower middle class and that of the upper middle class also involves an historical dimension.

Nineteenth century America was a middle class society in the sense that its typical (if not its statistically modal) individuals were shoestring entrepreneurs, and the covers of *The Saturday Evening Post* are a testimony to their former hegemony and to the continuing power of the myth they created. Today, we designate the style of those who follow the lead of the "old" middle class, as "lower" middle class in order to make room for the style of the burgeoning "new" middle class, which we designate as "upper" middle class because this latter style is a tailored, truncated version of an older upper class model emphasizing "taste" and "grace," and made possible —even necessary—by the bright vistas looming before the increasing numbers of college educated people with a promising place in our burgeoning bureaucratic hierarchies. We have no clear images of American "working class style" precisely because the lowest positions on our socio-economic ladder were traditionally occupied by the most recent groups of European immigrants, each of which, as they arrived, pushed earlier groups of immigrants up. Our images of working class life, consequently, are dominated by ethnic motifs. But with the end of mass immigration from Europe, it is possible that an indigenous urban working class culture may develop in the United States in the near future. In its visible manifestations, however, this style is likely to approximate the style of the "old" middle class, for with the gradual disappearance of shopkeepers as a significant stratum in American economic life, the organized, well-paid, industrial workers have apparently taken over the style of the "old" middle class, *without,* however, inheriting the mantle of social mobility. In short, the lowest native stratum of substantial size in the American industrial order today (excluding Negroes, New York's Puerto Ricans, and marginal workers) probably lives in the style we call "lower middle class."

It is only in this sense that America can be called a middle class society and, to be sure, a substantial minority of the people I interviewed identified themselves as "middle class." But our society approves of this usage as synonomous with "homeowner," or "respectable standard of living," and the myth of suburbia itself may reinforce the propensity to identify oneself with "America" because America is increasingly characterized in the mass media as a "middle class society" and the new suburbs are submitted as strong evidence of this. "Anybody with a steady job and income is middle class," one of my respondents told me, and certainly this is true if we conceive of lower middle class people as upper middle class people with slightly lower incomes. For although it is true that these suburbanites I studied do have only slightly lower incomes than a young insurance salesman or a junior engineer, it illumines nothing to call them middle class because their style (whether it be designated as lower middle class or working class) is a *terminal* one; they live in the present, mostly in the solid, respectable style their income permits, but mobility is something that is possible only for their children. With a house in the suburbs, two cars, a TV set, a wife and two children, and many "major" and "minor" kitchen appliances, one respondent, explaining why he didn't want to be foreman, said, "I'm a working man; I don't like to be sitting down or walking up and down all the time." Another, explaining why he quit being a foreman after six months, said, "I got nothing against guys in white shirts, but I just ain't cut out for work like that." These are the statements of working class (or, if one insists, lower middle class) men, who, because of prosperity and the labor movement have been able to achieve a material standard of living never before possible on any large scale for manual workers. But the element of social mobility is missing; aspiration and anticipation as well as "status anxiety" and "conformity" are things for educated people with a fluid position in an organizational hierarchy, and it is this which makes suburban domesticity in a $12,000 house a *final* fulfillment.

Nothing I have said about suburbs gives us the right to doubt the truth of what many observers have said about places like Park Forest and Levittown. I do, however, question the right of others to generalize about "suburbia" on the basis of a few studies of selected suburbs whose representative character has yet to be demonstrated. It is remarkable how, despite the efflorescence of the mass produced suburbs in post World War II America, references to "suburbia" more often than not cite the examples of Park Forest and Levittown—as if these two communities could represent a nationwide phenomenon that has occurred at all but the very lowest income levels and among most occupational classifications. If "suburbia" is anything at all unique, we'll never know it until we have a lot more information about a lot more suburbs than we now, unfortunately, have.

REFERENCE

BERGER, BENNETT M. *Working-class Suburb*. Berkeley and Los Angeles: University of California Press, 1960.

16. Locating the Rural Community

BY DWIGHT SANDERSON

*   *   *

Altho the real community is a relationship, a "form of association," it is necessary to recognize that, because farm people have to have certain services which can be obtained only at centers where there is a sufficient patronage to support them, they inevitably associate themselves more or less definitely with one or more village centers. The area within which this association occurs between farms and village forms the geographical basis of the rural community.

Thus, while recognizing the psychological and sociological aspects of the rural community, for practical purposes one wishes to locate the areas within which these common associations exist. One may, then, define the geographical basis of the rural community, as *a rural area within which the people have a common center of interest, usually a village, and within which they have a sense of common obligations and responsibilities.* The rural community is the smallest geographical unit of organized association of the chief human activities.

Professor C. J. Galpin,[1] formerly in charge of The Division of Farm Population and Rural Life of the United States Department of Agriculture, originated a method of determining the community area. He starts from the business center and marks on a map the most distant farm homes which do most of their business at that center. This information is obtained from the village merchants and is then checked by personal inquiry from the people on the edge or boundary of the community. The same procedure is followed with the surrounding communities. When this information is mapped, usually the trade areas overlap those of adjoining communities. People near the common boundary of two communities possibly trade more or less at both centers. This overlapping territory has been termed the *neutral zone.* The same method of mapping is used also to determine the areas served by the

Reprinted from Dwight Sanderson, *Locating the Rural Community,* Cornell Extension Bulletin 413 (Ithaca: New York State College of Agriculture at Cornell University, 1939), pp. 6–8, 11–12. The footnote has been renumbered.

[1] The social anatomy of an agricultural community. By C. J. Galpin, Agricultural Experiment Station of the University of Wisconsin. Research Bulletin 34, 1915; and, Rural Life, Century Company, New York, 1918.

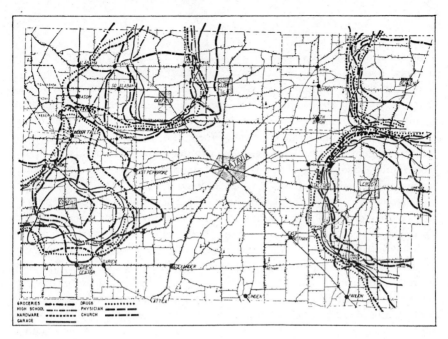

Figure 1. Seven representative service areas of Leroy, Oakfield, Bergen, and Corfu, Genesee County.

village church, the school, the bank, the milk station, the grange, and like institutions. The boundaries of these areas do not coincide, as may be seen in figure 1, which shows several of these areas for the rural communities in Genesee County, New York. However, when the service areas of the chief institutions of the adjacent communities are so located, it will be found that a composite of their boundaries will give a fairly clear line of demarcation between the areas serviced by the respective centers. A line which divides adjacent community areas so that most of the families either side of this line go most frequently to the center of which it is the boundary, or whose chief interests are at that center, will be the boundary of the respective communities. Thus, from the standpoint of location, a community is the local area tributary to the center of the common interests of its people.

In determining the boundaries of the community area it will be well to study the land-use maps of those counties for which they have been published. . . . Small communities with a large proportion of marginal land have declined and will probably become parts of larger communities that have enough good farm land to give an economic basis for the support of their institutions. The location of the community centers that will be most important in the future and of the boundaries of their areas, will be determined very largely by the geography of the different classes of land.

THE COMMUNITY CENTER

The community "center" is essential to the individuality of any community. It need not necessarily be at the geographical center of the community; indeed in many communities it is not; tho in an open, level country it will tend to approximate the center. The community center, in this sense, is that point in the community where the interests and activities of its people focus. Dr. Galpin uses the business center, where the people trade, as the base point, or community center, from which to determine the boundaries of the community. Usually a village is the community center, altho exceptional communities may have more than one village.

However, in some small communities, particularly in the older parts of the country or in hilly or mountainous regions, the trade or business center is not always the same as the center of the chief social activities of the people, and hence may not be the community center. Not infrequently a church, a school, and possibly a grange or lodge hall close together may form the nucleus of an open-country community which does its business at a railroad-station village some distance away, possibly over a range of hills. Some of these small open-country communities seem to have no real center, for the store, the church, and the school may be at some distance from each other in different parts of the community; but if these, or other, institutions draw their constituency from practically the same area, then the community boundary may be determined by a composite of the boundaries of the areas of these institutions.

The term *community center,* as here used should be distinguished from the *community-center idea,* which refers to a building, whether it be a community house, a school, a church, or a grange hall, as a community center. Such a building in which the activities of the community are largely centered may be a community center in a very real sense, but usually these activities will be divided between church, school, grange hall, and the like. No one of them can then be a center for the whole community, but taken together they constitute the center in which the chief interests of the community focus. Every community must necessarily have a more or less well-defined community center; it may or may not have some one building in which the chief activities of the community have their headquarters. But if such buildings exist, they may well be called *community houses* or *social centers.*

In the larger rural communities, the village where most of the people trade and where their children go to high school is the community center. It is these larger rural communities which will be important in the social organization of the country in the future and to whose location one needs to give attention.

MAPPING THE RURAL COMMUNITY

To locate the rural community, it is necessary to draw its boundaries on a map. For this a map of the area and adjoining areas showing the roads is needed.

*   *   *

To map the community, first determine the "community center" . . . and the centers of the surrounding communities, and mark each of these on the map.

Next determine the trade, or business, area of the community. Ask the leading merchants to locate on each of the roads radiating from the community center their regular customers who are farthest from the center on each road. On the map make a mark at each of the houses so located; then connect these points by straight lines. This will give the approximate trade area of the community. It will be found that the trade areas for groceries, hardware, and clothing differ considerably in size and shape.

In the same way locate on the map the areas of the different churches, of the high school or consolidated school, the bank, and of the grange and lodges, and draw their boundaries. Draw the boundary line of each area with a different color or use a different kind of line, as shown in figure 1. Use the same color or kind of line for the boundaries of the trade areas, church areas, or school areas, respectively, of each community. Usually these areas will be sufficient to determine the community area, altho it may be desirable to locate the area from which farm produce is drawn to this center.

After having determined the principal areas for each of the surrounding communities, it will now be possible to draw a boundary line for the community, which will be a composite of the boundary lines of the various areas previously located, and which will include all homes whose major interests are clearly connected with this community. The community boundary line should be a heavy black line, which will stand out from the other area boundaries.

The interest and the value of the map will be increased by mapping the state and hard-surfaced highways, with heavier lines than the unimproved dirt roads. In mapping the various areas of the community, it will be desirable to have each farm house marked by a dot, and each school or church in the open country with a uniform symbol. If the map is large enough, it will be well to number the farm homes, and make a list of the families corresponding to these numbers. . . .

This method of determining the social and economic area of the community brings out many points of value concerning the area served by its

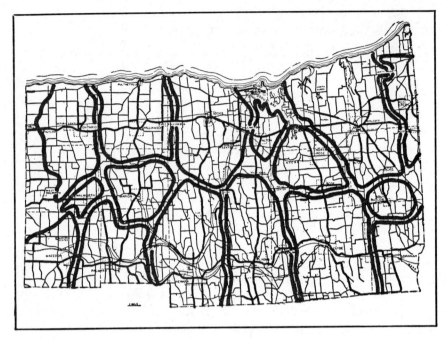

Figure 2. Composite service areas of Wayne County.

different institutions and agencies. However, a simpler method, which is sufficiently accurate for most purposes, is to mark each farm home toward the edge of the community with a colored dot or symbol indicating the village which its members visit most frequently and with which it is most closely identified. A boundary line can then be drawn around the area within which a majority of the families patronize the village center for economic and social services more frequently than any other. In most cases this is a quicker and more practicable method than that discussed in the preceding paragraphs.

It will now be necessary to pursue the same process in locating the areas for each of the surrounding communities, for it will be found that many of the areas overlap and will be claimed by two, or sometimes three, communities. In such areas, it is best to see the people living in this "neutral zone," and to learn from them to which center they go most frequently or at which center are their chief interests. Not infrequently families between two communities trade at one center and go to church or school at another. It may not be possible to make one boundary that will separate the two communities, and the boundary of each should be so drawn as to include those homes which clearly belong to it, leaving a strip of neutral territory between them.

*   *   *

SECTION THREE

The Community's Vertical and Horizontal Patterns

Introduction

Two sets of relationships are particularly central in understanding the various parts or units of the local community. One kind of relationship is the ties which such units—be they churches, business establishments, governmental offices, or voluntary associations—have to organizations outside of the community. In many cases these relationships are strong, and the location of the unit in the community seems almost coincidental, as in the case of a military base. The major decisions regarding the unit are made outside the community, perhaps thousands of miles away; the principal activities of the unit may have little special relevance to the community in which it is geographically located. Its whole focus of orientation may be elsewhere. Yet it is located within the community's confines, and certain symbiotic interrelationships with the local community may be clearly apparent, as well as other types of significant relationships and behavior.

Although few community units are oriented outward to the extent of a military base, nevertheless they all have some relationships to various organizations in the surrounding society, relationships which may be marked in some cases, extremely weak in others. This set of relationships of various community units to social systems outside the community may be described as the community's *vertical pattern*.[1]

But there is another set of important relationships: those of various units such as churches, schools, governmental offices, and business establishments within the community to each other. Indeed, the presence and interrelationship of such institutions are widely considered one of the principal characteristics of the community, as distinguished from other social groupings such as formal organizations or small groups. These relationships of community units to each other constitute the community's *horizontal pattern*.[2]

One of the important developments of this century is the strengthening of the vertical pattern of American communities. This has proceeded to such an extent that many students ask whether the local community can persist as a viable group, able to withstand the locally disintegrative tendencies associated with this strengthening of the outside ties of local units. Some even question whether one should not already concede that the community, in any meaning which would emphasize a vital interrelation of local units, is rapidly disappearing as a significant social group.

[1] See Roland L. Warren, *The Community in America* 2d ed. (Chicago: Rand McNally & Company, 1972), Chapter 8.
[2] See *ibid.*, Chapter 9.

The selections in this section all represent some aspect or aspects of this dual relationship of local units to extracommunity systems, and of local units to each other.

The days of "oh"ing and "ah"ing about the discovery of the unequal distribution of power over decision-making in American communities are long since past. Sophisticates now take for granted the type of situation first revealed systematically by Floyd Hunter in his *Community Power Structure,* first published in 1953, which pointed to concentration of decision-making power on major civic issues in the hands of a relatively small number of leaders who were not necessarily the occupants of formal positions of leadership. Hunter's work precipitated a rash of power structure studies which confirmed this unequal distribution of power but offered somewhat contradictory findings in the details of the way power is distributed and used.

One source of perplexity was the question as to what type of community situation was conducive to a concentrated or monolithic power structure, and what type was conducive to a dispersed or pluralistic power structure.

John Walton made a series of studies of the work which has been done to date in this field. The excerpt included here attempts to summarize and make theoretically intelligible the findings regarding power structure configurations. He concluded that the aggregate findings indicated that a number of variables thought at one time or another to be associated with the type of local power structure actually are not. These include region, population size, population composition, industrialization, economic diversity, and type of local government.

On the other hand, a number of variables were found to be positively associated with a pluralistic or competitive power structure. These included the presence of absentee-owned corporations, a competitive political party structure, adequate economic resources, and a satellite status. What these things have in common, he asserts, is that they reflect "an interdependence of the community and extra-community centers of power." Such "vertical" orientation of local institutions affords additional sources of resources and sanctions and induces changes in the local normative order which in turn are conducive to the emergence of competing centers of power.

Not only organizations, but also individuals can be considered in their relationship to extra-community systems, on the one hand, and to other individuals within the community, on the other. The selection from Robert K. Merton's study of "influentials" in Rovere discusses this relationship. The selection is part of a much larger report of his findings. In a section which precedes the present excerpt, Merton explains that it was only inadvertently, or "serendipitously," that the important contrast in the orientation of two types of influentials was found.

The distinction is between the localite and the cosmopolitan. The localite is oriented toward the local community as his primary focus of reference. "Devoting little thought or energy to the Great Society, he is preoccupied with local problems, to the virtual exclusion of the national and international scene." The cosmopolitan, though maintaining a modicum of relations within the community, "is also oriented significantly to the world outside Rovere, and regards himself as an integral part of that world. He resides in Rovere but lives in the Great Society. If the local type is parochial, the cosmopolitan is ecumenical." In the excerpt reprinted here, Merton explores the difference between these two types with regard to the strength or weakness of their roots in the community, the nature and number of their personal relationships in the community, the types of voluntary associations in which they participate and the nature of their participation, and the nature of the interpersonal influence which they exercise.

Merton is careful to note the smallness of the sample on which his generalizations are based, as well as the preliminary nature of his inquiry. Nevertheless, his initial conceptualization has proved useful as a frame of reference and as a basis for subsequent research. It has indicated the importance, on the individual as well as on the organizational level, of considering relationships within the community and relationships across community lines, as these affect community participation.

In *Small Town and Mass Society,* Arthur J. Vidich and Joseph Bensman give special attention to the relationship of the small New York community which they studied to institutions and systems in the "mass society." The selection included here deals with several aspects of this relationship. It points out how certain people through their connections with outside organizations constitute channels through which ideas, customs, and usages flow into the locality. A wide variety of organizational and personal channels provide "bridges" to the larger society and "gate-keeper roles" with regard to it, roles from which persons having special access to one system or another in the larger society derive local power.

At the same time, local government on both the village and the town levels constitutes a medium for the possible integration of community organizations, goals, and activities. Although the actual legal scope of local governmental authority is fairly limited, the village and town officials do not even make use of what authority does exist for the pursuing of common activities on the local level. There results a "political paralysis," which in turn leads to a reliance on experts, a dependence on initiative and financing from larger governmental units, and an abdication of local governmental responsibility to nongovernmental initiative and organization. The village board operates according to a tacit principle of "unanimity," which often stifles action, with the consequence that "in any situation which suggests that differences of opinion exist, action is postponed or delayed to a subsequent meeting or indefinitely."

Voluminous research has documented the existence of a system of social stratification according to which people are assigned informally to different positions in the social system. Various studies have indicated numerous dimensions, such as occupational prestige, ethnic grouping, style of life, opportunity structure, and amount of education, which are associated with such stratificational differences.

Bernard Barber, in the selection included here, maintains that there are, among other kinds of stratification variables, three distinct types of social ranking, "each with its independent functions and each with its own range of variation." These are: social-class position, family status, and local-community status. In other words, individuals or families are ranked on each of these three dimensions, and one cannot be sure that a given ranking in one will imply the same ranking in another. Social-class position is most usually associated with "occupational role," a type of relationship, one might observe, that constitutes a meaningful basis for relating the individual to the larger society. Family status, on the other hand, is dependent on the local evaluation of "the way in which component members perform their functions *vis-à-vis* one another," and the "kinds of good or bad contributions that the several members of the nuclear family unit make to their neighborhoods, their local communities, and the national society considered as a community." Finally, "where local community and larger society diverge, as they certainly do in modern industrial society, and as they do also even in many of the non-industrial societies we know about, individuals and families will be evaluated by two different standards, one for the contributions made to the local community, a second for contributions to the larger society." The former are involved in local-community status.

As an example of the independence of these variables, Barber points out that in many suburban communities, newcomers with high social-class position may have relatively lower local-community status than "old-timers" who have been in the community longer and, despite lower social-class position, have a higher local-community status because of their more extensive participation in community-oriented activities. "Indeed, in many cases, it is the occupational roles and social class position of the middle- and upper-class commuters which take them out of the local community and make it hard for them to serve the local community's special needs."

The next selection is also more a contribution to the study of the community than a substantive report of findings. Irwin T. Sanders, who over a period of decades has been engaged in conducting community studies, outlines a relatively brief method for conducting community studies for specific purposes. For various reasons, governmental agencies or business organizations or voluntary associations are concerned with gathering data about the social organization of a particular community for quite practical purposes. In this article, Sanders gives a practical procedure, which he himself has tried out on numerous occasions, for such a reconnaissance study of a particular community. Four or five workers can carry out such a study in less than a week's time, even in communities as large as a hundred thousand or so. The description of the kinds of data which are gathered and the way they are analyzed is suggestive both of the practical importance of community structure and function and of the way in which the necessary information can be obtained.

During the past two decades, extensive studies have been conducted on community power structure and decision-making processes. In an article earlier in this section, Walton seeks to account for the presence in some communities of a monolithic power structure and in others of a pluralistic, or competitive power structure. Other studies have provided findings which help answer a further question: What difference does it make whether the decision-making process is confined to relatively few individuals or is diffused more widely? For example, which type of power configuration is more conducive to the developing of new programs for community betterment?

In the selection from one of their research reports, Michael Aiken and Robert R. Alford examine the different responses to this question which have been given by various investigators of the subject. On the basis of their own data as well as that of others, they point to the inadequacy of five specific theoretical explanations which have gained wide circulation in the literature. They report on their own studies of the relationship between city characteristics and "innovation" such as is exemplified in the development of housing, urban renewal, and anti-poverty programs. They conclude that a small number of variables help account for differences in city performance on such indicators of innovation. These include the city's age, its population size, percent of foreign stock, and one or more measures of "need."

But what are the dynamics of the process which leads to such local programs? What are the intermediate variables between such city characteristics and the development of new programs? The authors conclude that such innovations are more frequently attained "in decentralized, heterogeneous, and probably fragmented community systems." They then seek to explain this in terms of the interorganizational structure which such cities exhibit.

17. Differential Patterns of Community Power Structure

BY JOHN WALTON

In the relatively brief period since its inception, the study of community power structure has attracted a wide range of enthusiasts. Researchers of diverse backgrounds have found their particular interests coalesce around the assumption that local leadership processes are of central importance to the explanation of community action. The research implications of this approach have been explored in a variety of areas including urban renewal, social welfare, health and hospital services, community conflict, and ethnic relations.[1] Though often divided on issues of how the leadership process is organized and the extent to which power is effectively exercised, investigators are in agreement concerning the viability of research problems suggested by the approach.

In addition to these fertile substantive applications, much has been done to develop the research methods of power structure studies.[2] The con-

Reprinted with permission of the author and the Chandler Publishing Company from Terry N. Clark, ed., *Community Structure and Decision-Making: Comparative Analyses* (San Francisco: Chandler Publishing Company, 1968), pp. 441–54.

[1] See, for example, Amos Hawley, "Community Power and Urban Renewal Success," [*American Journal of Sociology* 68, no. 4 (January 1964)]; Warner Bloomberg and Morris Sunshine, *Suburban Power Structures and Public Education: A Study of Values, Influence and Tax Effort* (Syracuse: Syracuse University Press); Ralph B. Kimbrough, *Political Power and Educational Decision Making* (Chicago: Rand McNally & Co., 1964); Irving A. Fowler, "Local Industrial Structure, Economic Power and Community Welfare," *Social Problems*, 6 (Summer, 1958), 41–51; Ivan Belknap and John Steinle, *The Community and Its Hospitals* (Syracuse: Syracuse University Press, 1963); Floyd Hunter, Ruth Connor Schaffer, and Cecil G. Sheps, *Community Organization: Action and Inaction* (Chapel Hill: University of North Carolina Press, 1956); James S. Coleman, *Community Conflict* (New York: The Free Press, 1957); William A. Gamson, "Rancorous Conflict in Community Politics," *American Sociological Review*, 31 (February, 1966), 71–81; James McKee, "Community Power and Strategies in Race Relations," *Social Problems*, 6 (Winter, 1958–59), 41–51.

[2] L. Vaughn Blankenship, "Community Power and Decision Making: A Comparative Evaluation of Measurement Techniques," *Social Forces*, XLIII December, 1964), 207–216; William V. D'Antonio and Eugene Erickson, "The Reputational Technique as a Measure of Community Power: An Evaluation Based on Comparative and Longitudinal Studies," *American Sociological Review*, 27 (June, 1962), 362–376; Linton C. Freeman, *et al.*, "Locating Leaders in Local Communities: A Comparison of Some Alternative Approaches," *American Sociological Review*, 28 (October, 1963), 791–798.

flict which prevailed a few years ago between proponents of rival methods seems to have subsided with the recognition that different methods tap different dimensions of the total power scene. Investigators now appear to agree on the need for methodologically balanced, comparative, and longitudinal studies. This trend is manifest in several notable works that have appeared recently.[3]

In spite of these convergences, however, there has been almost no progress in one vital respect: the development of theoretical explanations of the reported findings. Elaborate documentation of the atheoretical character of the field hardly seems necessary. One has only to peruse a portion of the literature to discover that the principal issues are almost entirely concerned with method and conflicting interpretations of how broadly power is distributed. Only rarely are some of the initial steps in theorizing represented by conceptual considerations and the development of propositional inventories.[4]

The purpose of this paper is to develop a theoretical explanation of how power is distributed in local communities, and to consider briefly how various power arrangements may account for different forms of community action. The analysis incorporates earlier theoretical discussions of the community and a systematic review of the power structure literature. Anticipating the conclusions for a moment, it will be argued that as communities become increasingly interdependent with extracommunity institutions, changes in the local normative order ensue producing more competitive power arrangements.

Starting with a review of previous research, the argument moves on to consider the adequacy of certain theoretical approaches and, finally, to develop the propositions concerning power structure and community action.

FINDINGS OF PREVIOUS RESEARCH

In an earlier paper the findings of thirty-three power structure studies dealing with fifty-five communities were analyzed in order to determine the relationship between a number of substantive and methodological variables and

[3] Robert Presthus, *Men at the Top: A Study in Community Power* (New York: Oxford University Press, 1964); Robert E. Agger, Daniel Goldrich, and Bert E. Swanson, *The Rulers and the Ruled: Political Power and Impotence in American Communities* (New York: John Wiley & Sons, 1964); William V. D'Antonio and William H. Form, *Influentials in Two Border Cities: A Study in Community Decision-Making* (Notre Dame: University of Notre Dame, Press, 1965).

[4] For some efforts in this direction see Agger, *et al., ibid.;* Presthus, *ibid.;* M. Herbert Danzger, "Community Power Structure: Problems and Continuities," *American Sociological Review,* 24 (October, 1964), 707–717; Terry N. Clark, "Community or Communities?," in Terry N. Clark, ed., *op. cit.*

the dependent variable type of power structure.[5] Subsequently that analysis was replicated using a somewhat larger number of studies.[6] The selection of studies was intended to be exhaustive of the published literature in social science devoted specifically to the study of community power structure. By dealing with the published literature some unpublished studies were excluded, especially dissertations. Confining the analysis to the social science literature excluded journalistic reports. Finally, the criterion that the research be specifically concerned with community power excluded a number of community studies dealing with stratification, local government, and related aspects of social and political life. These criteria were employed in a screening of the literature, and the resulting list of studies was checked against several lengthy bibliographies to insure its inclusiveness. Thus the studies are regarded as a universe, defined by the above criteria, rather than a sample.

Each study was reviewed and, when sufficient information was available, coded in terms of a number of self-explanatory independent variables (for example, region, population size, industrialization, economic diversity, and the like). Similarly, the type of power structure identified in each report was coded in terms of four categories: (1) pyramidal—a monolithic, monopolistic, or single cohesive leadership group; (2) factional—at least two durable factions that compete for advantage; (3) coalitional—leadership varies with issues and is made up of fluid coalitions of interested persons and groups; (4) amorphous—the absence of any persistent pattern of leadership or power exercised on the local level.

Table 1 indicates those few associations which were found to be significant or meaningful.[7]

In contrast to these positive findings, a large number of variables, including region, population size, population composition, industrialization, economic diversity, and type of local government, were *not* found to be related to type of power structure.

Taking these results as a summary of the present status of research, it appears that no firm generalizations are suggested. The findings fail to conform to any neat pattern such as an association between competitive power structures and greater complexity of local social and economic organization. The inadequacies of such an explanation are underscored by the negative

[5] John Walton, "Substance and Artifact: The Current Status of Research on Community Power Structure," *American Journal of Sociology,* 71 (January, 1966), 430–438.

[6] John Walton, "A Systematic Survey of Community Power Research" in Michael T. Aiken and Paul E. Mott, *The Structure of Community Power: Readings* (in press).

[7] A complete summary of the findings, positive and negative, is to be found in Walton, *ibid.*

TABLE 1.[a] COMMUNITY CHARACTERISTICS AND COMMUNITY POWER STRUCTURE[b,c]

	Pyramidal	Factional, Coalitional and Amorphous	Total
Absentee Ownership			
Present	2	18	20
Absent	12	9	21
Total	14	27	41
	$Q = -.85$ $.01 > p > .001$		
Economic Resources[d]			
Adequate	9	17	26
Inadequate	6	5	11
Total	15	22	37
	$Q = -.39$ $.30 > p > .20$		
Type of City[e]			
Independent	14	22	36
Satellite	2	10	12
Total	16	32	48
	$Q = -.52$ $.20 > p > .10$		
Party Competition			
Competitive	0	10	10
Noncompetitive	10	12	22
Total	10	22	32
	$Q = -1.0$ $.02 > p > .01$		
Change in Power Structure			
Dispersion	2	17	19
Concentration	0	0	0
No Change	3	4	7
Oscillation	2	1	3
Decline Locally	1	2	3
Total	8	24	32

[a] The cell entries in the table represent communities, rather than studies, since a single study often dealt with two or more towns.

[b] The variable power structure was originally coded in terms of four categories. The categories are collapsed here to avoid small N's and to provide a contrast between more and less concentrated power arrangements.

[c] The N's in each of the subtables vary because the studies coded do not uniformly provide data on each variable.

[d] Operational definitions of the following three variables are indicated by the type of information coded under each category. Adequate economic resources—includes towns with a reportedly prosperous business community, low rates of poverty, and unemployment; inadequate economically—underdeveloped with high rates of poverty and unemployment. Independent city—includes central cities of metropolitan areas and independent manufacturing, commercial or agricultural centers; satellite city—suburb or town dominated by a nearby city. Partly competition—the existence of two or more local parties (or affiliates in formally non-partisan cities) which regularly contend for public office; noncompetitive—a one party town.

[e] When the zero-order level findings on economic resources and type of city are examined controlling for research method, a factor associated with type of power structure identified, the differences here do not persist. The findings are reported here because they are suggestive and because the low quality of the data may be obscuring significant associations. That is, the lower the quality of the data, the more difficult it is to demonstrate statistically significant relationships and the more likely it is that such relationships may be obscured. That is, in the present context I have gone beyond a strict interpretation of the earlier findings in an attempt to draw some meaningful generalizations.

findings. The evidence may, however, be suggestive of some less obvious explanation. In order to explore that possibility some implicitly theoretical positions in the area of community power and a major theoretical work on American communities will be examined, considering, in both cases, how they square with the above findings and how they might inform the present analysis.

THEORETICAL APPROACHES

In one of the first attempts to bring some order out of the confusion of results, Rogers developed a series of propositions concerning community political systems.[8] His dependent variable, type of political system, was made up of the categories monolithic and pluralistic. In stating the relationship between these and a number of characteristics of community social structure, Rogers hypothesized that the following would be associated with a pluralistic system: a high degree of industrialization, a large population, a socially heterogeneous population, a polity differentiated from the kinship and economic systems, a local government of extensive scope, two or more political parties and the unionization, or other political and economic organization, of working class groups. The underlying theme in this series of propositions, what has been referred to as the implicit theory, centers on the effects of industrialization, and attendant processes of urbanization and bureaucratization, the outcome of these being structural differentiation which contributes to a pluralistic power situation. The approach is, of course, central to contemporary social science whether stated in terms of *gemeinschaft* and *gesellschaft* or any other of a variety of polar types.

Hawley has presented a somewhat more specific approach.[9] Here power is defined as a system property whose distribution can be measured by the ability to mobilize resources and personnel. In any total system, such as a community, this ability lies in the various component sub-systems and is exercised through their managerial functions. Hence, operationally, the greater the number of managerial personnel, the greater the concentration of power. It is is granted that success in a collective action requires the mobilization of resources and personnel, and that this ability is greatest where power is most highly concentrated, then it follows that the greater the concentration of power in a community the greater the *probability* of success in any collective action. In a recent paper, inspired in part by the Hawley piece, Butler

---

[8] David Rogers, "Community Political Systems: A Framework and Hypotheses for Comparative Studies," in Bert E. Swanson, ed., *Current Trends in Comparative Community Studies* (Kansas City: Community Studies Inc., 1962). A similar but more comprehensive formulation is Terry N. Clark, "Power and Community Structure: Who Governs, Where, and When?" *The Sociological Quarterly,* Summer, 1967.

[9] Hawley, *op. cit.*

and Pope have suggested another measure of power concentration—the number of profile or key industries and the concentration of managerial functions within these.[10]

It should be noted that the Hawley and Butler and Pope papers are concerned chiefly with community action; for each the premise is that more concentrated power situations are conducive to concerted action. Unlike Rogers they are not trying to explain patterns of power distribution but, rather, employ these to explain community action. Nevertheless, they are pertinent here because they imply a theoretical position involving the saliency of managerial functions in the determination of community power structures.

How do these explanatory schemes square with the findings culled from the existing literature? Considering first the hypotheses formulated by Rogers, the evidence runs counter to his notions of the effects of industrialization, population size, and population heterogeneity. On the positive side, his proposition about political parties, though not entirely equivalent to party competition, is supported. Unfortunately, no data are available on the remaining three propositions. What evidence exists, however, indicates that Roger's propositions do not fare very well within the present context, though they may have greater predictive power in a cross cultural or historical perspective. For our purposes the implication is that the theoretical approach implicit in these propositions is in need of revision. Perhaps it will be necessary to abandon the simplified notion of a unilinear relationship between the growing complexity of industrial society and more pluralistic local power arrangements, in favor of a more limited, yet more discriminating explanation.[11]

The evidence presented previously is not directly relevant to the Hawley and Butler and Pope approaches since these attempt to explain community action. If, however, it is assumed with these authors that concentrated power structures are associated with community action, and then the antecedent link in their chain of reasoning is examined, it is found that those community characteristics allegedly conducive to power concentration (ones engendering a large number of managerial functions)—industrialization, economic diversity, proportion of absentee ownership, and economic resources—are either unrelated or associated with the less concentrated power structures in the data. This fact can hardly be taken as a refutation of the positions presented. What it does indicate is that the number of managerial functions appears to be a poor indicator of type of power structure (though it may indicate the number of potentially powerful people in community action).

[10] Edgar W. Butler and Hallowell Pope, "Community Power Structures, Industrialization and Public Welfare Programs," paper read at the 61st annual meetings of the American Sociological Association, Miami Beach, Florida, August, 1966.

[11] This conclusion applies to similar propositional inventories based on the "evolutionary" or "continuum" notion. See, for example, Delbert C. Miller and William H. Form, *Industry, Labor and Community* (New York: Harper, 1960).

In short, the analysis thus far demonstrates the need for theoretical statements which are both more explicit and account better for the available data.

Warren's analysis of *The Community in America*[12] provides a pertinent general framework for dealing theoretically with the specific questions of power structure. Warren's central thesis is that American communities are undergoing a drastic transformation of their entire structure and function; "(this) 'great change' in community living includes the increasing orientation of local community units toward extracommunity systems of which they are a part, with a decline in community cohesion and autonomy."[13] Although Warren analyzes these changes along seven fundamental dimensions of community life, a summary statement indicates their relevance for present purposes:

In the first place, they signalize the increasing and strengthening of the external ties which bind the local community to the larger society. In the process, various parts of the community—its educational system, its recreation, its economic units, its governmental functions, its religious units, its health and welfare agencies, and its voluntary associations—have become increasingly oriented toward district, state, regional, or national offices and less and less oriented toward each other.

In the second place, as local community units have become more closely tied in with state and national systems, much of the decision-making prerogative concerning the structure and function of these units has been transferred to the headquarters or district offices of the systems themselves, thus leaving a narrower and narrower scope of functions over which local units, responsible to the local community, exercise autonomous power.[14]

On the basis of these observations concerning the "great change" and with the simultaneous recognition that communities (that is, 'combinations of social units and systems which perform the major functions having locality reference') do persist as meaningful units, Warren finds useful a distinction between the *horizontal* and *vertical axes* of community organization. The vertical axis refers to connections between community organizations and extracommunity centers, and the horizontal axis refers to connections between community organizations. The "great change" involves an increase in the former type of connections often at the cost of the latter.

In what follows several propositions will be developed which relate War-

---

[12] Roland L. Warren, *The Community in America* (Chicago: Rand McNally & Co., 1963) and "Toward a Reformulation of Community Theory," *Human Organization,* 15 (Summer, 1962), 8–11.

[13] *Ibid., The Community in America,* p. 53.

[14] *Ibid.,* p. 5.

ren's approach specifically to the question of how power is distributed on the local level. His concept of a vertical axis of community organization has particular importance for this analysis.

AN EXPLANATION OF DIFFERENTIAL PATTERNS
OF COMMUNITY POWER STRUCTURE

Power is defined here as *the capacity to mobilize resources for the accomplishment of intended effects with recourse to some type of sanction(s) to encourage compliance.*[15] This definition includes the elements of both potential and actualized power in that capacity for mobilizing resources refers to potential while the application of sanctions refers to actualized power. *Capacity* also implies a distinction from *right* such that *authority* is not confused with the definition. Following Lasswell and Kaplan, the threat of sanctions, positive or negative, distinguishes *influence* from power—influence refers only to the capacity to mobilize resources.

Power structure is defined as *the characteristic pattern within a social organization whereby resources are mobilized and sanctions employed in ways that affect the organization as a whole.*

For the sake of simplicity competitive and monopolistic power structures will be dealt with here.[16] Monopolistic power structures characterize social organizations in which the capacity for mobilizing resources and recourse to sanctions are the exclusive property of a group with similar interests. In competitive situations the capacity for mobilizing resources and recourse to sanctions are possessed by two or more groups with different interests.

The basic assumption of the theoretical statement to be developed here

[15] This definition derives from a number of discussions of the concept of power. Some of the most relevant writings include Bertrand Russell, *Power: A New Social Analysis* (New York: Barnes and Noble, 1962); Max Weber, *The Theory of Social and Economic Organization,* trans., A. M. Henderson and Talcott Parsons (New York: Oxford University Press, 1947); Talcott Parsons, "On the Concept of Political Power," *Proceedings of the American Philosophical Society,* 107 (June, 1963), 232–262; Harold Lasswell and Abraham Kaplan, *Power and Society: A Framework for Political Inquiry* (New Haven: Yale University Press, 1950).

[16] This is not meant to imply that such a dichotomy is the most useful framework, though it tends to preoccupy the literature, for example, Presthus *op. cit.,* D'Antonio and Form, *op. cit.* Etzioni has offered four types of control structure based on the means of control available to various positions within an organization; see *A Comparative Analysis of Complex Organizations* (New York: The Free Press, 1961). Agger, *et al.,* characterize power structures with two variables, "distribution of power" and "convergence of leadership ideology," and a resulting four-fold table. Construing the second variable as an indicator of leadership cohesiveness, the formulation provides an important distinction between truly competitive systems and cases where power is shared among a number of groups but similarity of interests unites them in a monopolistic power arrangement. Many controversies in the field stem from a failure to make this distinction.

is that a monopoly of power produces a situation in which consensus is the most important factor underlying the use of power. This consensus may, but need not, imply agreement on values and objectives. What it does imply is agreement concerning the capabilities of those holding power to realize their own intentions over a wide range of community relevant issues. In such a monopolistic situation expectations concerning the norms prescribed by the existing power arrangement tend to be widely recognized. That is, the limits of allowable (non-sanctionable) deviance and opposition are narrow and clear. As a result of these congruent expectations, potential rather than manifest power is more commonly the mechanism by which compliance is encouraged; overt conflict and coercion are relatively infrequent occurrences because compliance can be realized without them. Merriam captured the sense of this assumption when he wrote "Power is not strongest when it uses violence, but weakest."[17]

By contrast, in competitive situations the exercise of power moves from a reliance on consensus to more overt applications of sanctions. This becomes necessary to the extent that competing groups become capable of restricting the scope of each other's sanctions. Claims to power must be supported by effective action. Greater normative diversity, with attendant diversity in expectations, characterizes this situation. Such circumstances result in a greater incidence of conflict stemming from the fact that those who would exercise power are required to make evident their claim through the use of sanctions.

It should be added that each of these circumstances contains elements of the other. Monopolistic power arrangements do, at times, generate divergent norms and expectations just as they occasionally have recourse to overt applications of coercion. More important, the role of consensual expectations and potential power are critical to all forms of social organization and can be observed in many of the transactions carried on in competitive power settings. In this connection conflict is probably most characteristic of those transitional periods in which power is becoming more or less diffused since it is at this point that the normative order is most uncertain and expectations least clear.[18] In the event that this transition is one from monopolistic to competitive is may culminate in a new set of rules defining community power arrangements which, while more conducive to conflict than the monopolistic situation, produces less conflict than the transitional phase.

Because at first glance this assumption may appear to be a truism, its

---

[17] In a more elaborate statement Merriam writes "In most communities the use of force is relatively uncommon in proportion to the number of regulations, and the success of the organization is not measured by the amount of violence in specific cases but by the extent to which violence is avoided and other substitutes discovered." Charles E. Merriam, *Political Power,* Collier Books edition (New York: The Macmillan Company, 1964), p. 36.

[18] Although the present concern is with community conflict, this argument closely parallels Durkheim's thesis on suicide and changes in the normative order.

nontrivial character will be demonstrated. Presthus' study of two New York communities which differed on a pluralist-elitist continuum is valuable here. Discussing the more elitist of the two Presthus reasons:

> *In Riverview sharper class and economic differences and resulting disparities in expectations, values and consensus seem to have placed a premium on more centralized, imperative leadership. As organizational theory and studies of group behavior suggest, social support, shared values, and common expectations make possible the minimization of overt power and authority. When community consensus is limited, leaders tend to function in a more unilateral manner.*[19]

Here the minimization of overt power and authority is equated with a more pluralistic (competitive) power situation. The present argument agrees with the prior notion that common expectations result in a minimization of overt power (and conflict), but this is taken to be characteristic of a monopolistic situation. Thus, when community consensus is limited the leadership process tends to be more competitive.[20]

Obviously the relationship identified in my assumption may operate in either direction; changes in the competitiveness of the power situation can produce changes in norms and expectations and, similarly, changes in norms and expectations can lead to changes in power arrangements. This approach is concerned with developing an explanation of the change in power structures, that is, in the latter direction of the causal complex.

This section has reasoned that normative expectations bear a particular relationship to power structure and that conflict can be taken as an indicator of that relationship.[21] In what follows an attempt will be made to elaborate the connection between normative expectations and types of power structure in terms of the data drawn from existing community studies.

Returning to the data in Table 1, the question of how the ideas presented would account for the findings can now be raised. It will be recalled that the data indicate a relationship between competitive power structures and the presence of absentee-owned corporations, competitive party politics,

[19] Presthus, *ibid.*, p. 427.

[20] A more precise treatment of this relationship would specify types of conflict and how these are associated with various power arrangements. For example, monopolistic power structures may suppress dissent and conflict, they may manage it within innocuous limits or they may engender revolutionary conflict. Competitive power structures, on the other hand, may encourage conflict which results in a stalemate or in effective argument and nonrevolutionary change.

[21] James S. Coleman, *Community Conflict* (New York: The Free Press, 1957) accords with this point by arguing that whenever the pattern of control is so complete that certain elements can see no way of moving into a position of power, there may be sporadic conflict but no organized opposition (nor, presumably, regular conflict).

adequate economic resources, and satellite status. Further, in those communities where change was studied, the trend was in the direction of a greater dispersion of power. Do these findings suggest some underlying explanation?

Upon closer examination the evidence does point to an explanation. Each of the variables associated with competitive power structures reflects the interdependence of the community and extra-community centers of power or increased emphasis on the vertical axis. For example, a high proportion of absentee-owned industry suggests that many community relevant decisions are controlled by the personnel and interests of national corporate bodies whose influence may stem from either a deliberate intervention in local affairs or from the more characteristic aloofness to local responsibility.[22] Similarly competitive political parties may often reflect the involvement of county, state and national party organizations in a struggle for control of local constituencies.[23] While it could be reasonably argued that inadequate economic resources result in substantial intervention and control by state and federal agencies which extend aid to local bodies, the position taken here is that communities with more adequate economic resources maintain a greater number of interdependent ties to extracommunity institutions such as suppliers, markets, investors, and other economic units. Finally, in the case of type of city, the connection is apparent. Suburban municipalities and smaller towns which form satellites of large urban centers are interdependent in a variety of economic and political activities including municipal services, jobs, consumer behavior, and the like. If, at points, the relationship between each of these variables and community interdependence is not unambiguous, the position taken here is enhanced by the pattern they suggest when taken together.

Drawing together all that has been said up to this point, the proposition which seems to account best for the findings can be stated as follows; *to the extent that the local community becomes increasingly interdependent with respect to extra-community institutions (or develops along its vertical axis) the structure of local leadership becomes more competitive.*[24]

---

[22] For studies documenting this see Robert O. Schulze, "The Bifurcation of Power in a Satellite City" in Morris Janowitz, ed., *Community Political Systems* (Glencoe: The Free Press, 1961), 19–80; Roland J. Pellegrin and Charles H. Coates, "Absentee-owned Corporations and Community Power Structure," *American Journal of Sociology*, 61 (March, 1956), 413–419.

[23] On this point there is little evidence pro or con and I present it only as a plausible hypothesis.

[24] It should be noted that the inferences about change are drawn primarily from cross sectional data and thus run the risk of incorrectly inferring trends. Given the nature of available data there is no alternative other than recommending future longitudinal studies following the lead of Agger, *et al.* and D'Antonio and Form, *op. cit.* Other studies which attempt to replicate earlier work include Delbert C. Miller, "Decision-Making Cliques in Community Power Structures: A Comparative Study of

Theoretically this proposition derives from the more general statement concerning norms and power arrangements. That is, the mechanism by which interdependence, or increasing relevance of the vertical axis of community organization, affects the distribution of community power is the disruption of the local normative order associated with the existing power structure. Development along the vertical axis involves the introduction of new interests and new institutional relationships implying new definitions of the community, and these have the effect of disrupting consensual normative expectations.

In addition to a differentiation of allegiances, these changes include the introduction of new *resources* and *sanctions* into the community. Local organizations with vertical ties to extracommunity institutions frequently share in the capital and human resources of the larger entity making it possible for them to sustain a broader scope of activities than would otherwise be the case. For example, absentee-owned corporations may receive funds and skilled personnel for a desired expansion of local operations making them more important as local tax contributors, employers and suppliers. Such resources carry with them potential sanctions. In the above example some of these would include the threat to locate elsewhere,[25] threat of cut-backs or other actions having an adverse effect on the local economy, support or nonsupport in local elections. What has been said here of absentee-owned corporations could also be said, though perhaps in less dramatic ways, of other vertical community organizations. The point to be emphasized is that these organizations introduce new sources of power into the local picture and, being interdependent, they also have stakes in the local decision-making process which occasionally must be defended. The greater the number of community organizations with vertical ties, the more frequent and the more inclusive are contests surrounding the decision-making process.

In summary, the theoretical statement advanced here states that the introduction of organizations with vertical ties produces a greater interdependence between community and extracommunity centers of power. This interdependence brings changes in the local normative order, as well as new resources and sanctions, creating circumstances conducive to the emergence

---

an American and an English City," *American Journal of Sociology*, 64 (November, 1958), 299–310; David A. Booth and Charles R. Adrian, "Power Structure and Community Change: A Replication Study of Community A," *Midwest Journal of Political Science*, VI (August 1962), 277–296; Donald A. Clelland and William H. Form, "Economic Dominants and Community Power: A Comparative Analysis," *American Journal of Sociology*, 69 (March, 1964), 511–521; M. Kent Jennings, *Community Influentials: The Elites of Atlanta* (New York: The Free Press, 1964).

[25] For a discussion of this ploy and other sanctions available to economic institutions see Arnold Rose, *The Power Structure: Political Processes in American Society*, (New York: Oxford University Press, 1967), Chapter 3.

of competing power centers. Accordingly, variables which reflect the inter-dependence of the community and the "carrying society"—absentee owner-ship, party competition, adequate economic resources and satellite status—are associated with competitive power structures; whereas those variables which reflect only intracommunity change—economic diversity, population increase, etc.—are not so associated.[26]

---

[26] The point to be emphasized here is that greater complexity and specialization are not necessarily conducive to the changes under consideration, but only insofar as these developments produce greater interdependence. At some point, of course, complexity and specialization do necessitate greater interdependence but it would seem that this is not always the case at every level of community development. We would expect that some of these variables are confounded such that increasing size, for example, will be related to competitive power structures at that point in a community's development when size and interdependence vary together. According to this argument such an association would be spurious. This may be the case though the available data are too crude and provide too few observations to allow an unequivocal solution.

18. Local and Cosmopolitan Influentials

BY ROBERT K. MERTON

The terms "local" and "cosmopolitan"[1] do not refer, of course, to the regions in which interpersonal influence is exercised. Both types of influentials are effective almost exclusively within the local community. Rovere has few residents who command a following outside that community.[2]

The chief criterion for distinguishing the two is found in their *orientation* toward Rovere. The localite largely confines his interests to this community. Rovere is essentially his world. Devoting little thought or energy to the Great Society, he is preoccupied with local problems, to the virtual exclusion of the national and international scene. He is, strictly speaking, parochial.

Contrariwise with the cosmopolitan type. He has some interest in Rovere

Reprinted by permission of the author and Harper & Row, Publishers, from "Patterns of Influence: A Study of Interpersonal Influence and of Communications Behavior in a Local Community," by Robert K. Merton, in *Communications Research 1948–1949*, ed. Paul F. Lazarsfeld and Frank N. Stanton, pp. 189–202. Copyright 1949 by Harper & Brothers. Footnotes have been renumbered and those added in the version of the article printed in the author's *Social Theory and Social Structure* (Glencoe, Ill.: The Free Press, 1957), have been included.

[1] Upon identification of the two types of influentials, these terms were adopted from Carle C. Zimmerman, who uses them as translations of Toennies' well-known distinction between *Gemeinschaft* (localistic) and *Gesellschaft* (cosmopolitan). The sociologically informed reader will recognize essentially the same distinction, though with different terminologies, in the writings of Simmel, Cooley, Weber, Durkheim, among many others. Although these terms have commonly been used to refer to types of social organization and of social relationships, they are here applied to empirical materials on types of influential persons. Cf. Ferdinand Toennies, *Fundamental Concepts of Sociology* (New York, 1940), a translation by C. P. Loomis of his classic book, *Gemeinschaft und Gesellschaft,* and more importantly, a later article bearing the same title. See also Carle C. Zimmerman, *The Changing Community,* (New York and London: Harper & Brothers, 1938), especially 80 ff. For a compact summary of similar concepts in the sociological literature, see Leopold von Wiese and Howard Becker, *Systematic Sociology* (New York: John Wiley & Sons, 1932), especially 223–226n.

[2] The concept of influentials has been taken up in a study of the influence-structure of a suburb which houses men of national reputation and influence. As the authors say, "It is hardly surprising then that the personal characteristics of these 'influentials' differ from those of the lower-ranking cosmopolitan influential in Rovere." Kenneth P. Adler and Davis Bobrow, "Interest and influence in foreign affairs," *Public Opinion Quarterly*, 1956, 20, 89–101. See also Floyd Hunter, *Power Structure: A Study of Decision-Makers* (Chapel Hill: University of North Carolina Press, 1953).

and must of course maintain a minimum of relations within the community since he, too, exerts influence there. But he is also oriented significantly to the world outside Rovere, and regards himself as an integral part of that world. He resides in Rovere but lives in the Great Society. If the local type is parochial, the cosmopolitan is ecumenical.

Of the thirty influentials interviewed at length, fourteen were independently assessed by three analysts[3] as "cosmopolitan" on the basis of case-materials exhibiting their orientation toward the Rovere community, and sixteen, as "local."

These orientations found characteristic expression in a variety of contexts. For example, influentials were launched upon a statement of their outlook by the quasi-projective question: "Do you worry much about the news?" (This was the autumn of 1943, when "the news" was, for most, equivalent to news about the war.) The responses, typically quite lengthy, readily lent themselves to classification in terms of the chief foci of interest of the influentials. One set of comments was focused on problems of a national and international order. They expressed concern with the difficulties which would attend the emergence of a stable postwar world; they talked at length about the problems of building an international organization to secure the peace; and the like. The second set of comments referred to the war news almost wholly in terms of what it implied for interviewees personally or for their associates in Rovere. They seized upon a question about "the news" as an occasion for reviewing the immediate flow of problems which the war had introduced into the town.

Classifying influentials into these two categories, we find that twelve of the fourteen[4] cosmopolitans typically replied within the framework of international and national problems, whereas only four of the sixteen locals spoke in this vein. Each type of influential singled out distinctively different elements from the flow of events. A vaguely formulated question enabled each to project his basic orientations into his replies.

[3] This complete coincidence of assessments is scarcely to be expected in a larger sample. But the cosmopolitan and local syndromes were so clearly defined for this handful of cases, that there was little doubt concerning the "diagnoses." A full-fledged investigation would evolve more formal criteria, along the lines implied in the following discussion, and would, accordingly, evolve an intermediate type which approaches neither the local nor the cosmopolitan pole.

[4] It should be repeated that the figures cited at this point, as throughout the study, should not be taken as representative of a parent population. They are cited only to illustrate the heuristic purpose they served in suggesting clues to the operation of diverse patterns of interpersonal influence. As is so often the fact with quantitative summaries of case-studies, these figures do not confirm interpretations, but merely suggest interpretations. The tentative interpretations in turn provide a point of departure for designing quantitative studies based upon adequate samples, as in Katz and Lazarsfeld [Elihu Katz and P. F. Lazarsfeld, *Personal Influence* (Glencoe: The Free Press, 1955)].

All other differences between the local and cosmopolitan influentials seem to stem from their difference in basic orientation.[5] The group profiles indicate the tendency of local influentials to be devoted to localism: they are more likely to have lived in Rovere for a long period, are profoundly interested in meeting many townspeople, do not wish to move from the town, are more likely to be interested in local politics, etc. Such items, which suggest great disparity between the two types of influentials, are our main concern in the following sections. There we will find the difference in basic orientation is bound up with a variety of other differences: (1) in the structures of social relations in which each type is implicated; (2) in the roads they have traveled to their present positions in the influence-structure; (3) in the utilization of their present status for the exercise of interpersonal influence; and (4) in their communications behavior.

STRUCTURES OF SOCIAL RELATIONS

ROOTS IN THE COMMUNITY

Local and cosmopolitan influentials differ rather markedly in their attachment to Rovere. The local influentials are great local patriots and the thought of leaving Rovere seems seldom to come in mind. As one of them gropingly expressed it:

Rovere is the greatest town in the world. It has something that is nowhere else in the world, though I can't quite say what it is.

When asked directly if they had "ever thought of leaving Rovere," thirteen of the sixteen local influentials replied emphatically that they would never consider it, and the other three expressed a strong preference to remain, although they believed they would leave under certain conditions. None felt that they would be equally satisfied with life in any other community. Not so with the cosmopolitans. Only three of these claim to be wedded to Rovere for life. Four express their present willingness to live elsewhere, and the remaining seven would be willing to leave under certain conditions. Cosmopolitans' responses such as these do not turn up at all among the locals:

I've been on the verge of leaving for other jobs several times.

I am only waiting for my son to take over my practice, before I go out to California.

[5] Nothing is said here of the objective *determinants* of these differences in orientation. To ascertain these determinants is an additional and distinctly important task, not essayed in the present study.

These basic differences in attitude toward Rovere are linked with the different runs of experience of local and cosmopolitan influentials. The cosmopolitans have been more mobile. The locals were typically born in Rovere or in its immediate vicinity. Whereas 14 of the 16 locals have lived in Rovere for over twenty-five years, this is true for fewer than half of the cosmopolitans. The cosmopolitans are typically recent arrivals who have lived in a succession of communities in different parts of the country.

Nor does this appear to be a result of differences in the age-composition of the local and cosmopolitan groups. True, the cosmopolitans are more likely to be younger than the local influentials. But for those over forty-five, the cosmopolitans seem to be comparative newcomers and the locals Rovere-born-and-bred.

From the case-materials, we can infer the bases of the marked attachment to Rovere characteristic of the local influentials. In the process of making their mark, these influentials have become thoroughly *adapted to the community* and dubious of the possibility of doing as well elsewhere. From the vantage point of his seventy years, a local judge reports his sense of full incorporation in the community:

I wouldn't think of leaving Rovere. The people here are very good, very responsive. They like me and I'm grateful to God for the feeling that the people in Rovere trust me and look up to me as their guide and leader.

Thus, the strong sense of identification with Rovere among local influentials is linked with their typically local origins and career patterns in this community. Economically and sentimentally, they are deeply rooted in Rovere.

So far as attachment to Rovere is concerned, the cosmopolitans differ from the locals in virtually every respect. Not only are they relative newcomers; they do not feel themselves rooted in the town. Having characteristically lived elsewhere, they feel that Rovere, "a pleasant enough town," is only one of many. They are also aware, through actual experience, that they can advance their careers in other communities. They do not, consequently, look upon Rovere as comprising the outermost limits of a secure and satisfactory existence. Their wider range of experience has modified their orientation toward their present community.

SOCIABILITY: NETWORKS OF PERSONAL RELATIONS

In the course of the interview, influentials were given an occasion to voice their attitudes toward "knowing many people" in the community. Attitudes differed sharply between the two types. Thirteen of the sixteen local influentials in contrast to four of the fourteen cosmopolitans expressed marked interest in establishing frequent contacts with many people.

This difference becomes more instructive when examined in qualitative terms. The local influential is typically concerned with knowing *as many* people as possible. He is a quantitativist in the sphere of social contacts. Numbers count. In the words of an influential police officer (who thus echoes the sentiments of another "local," the Mayor) :

> *I have lots of friends in Rovere, if I do say so myself. I like to know everybody. If I stand on a corner, I can speak to 500 people in two hours. Knowing people helps when a promotion comes up, for instance. Everybody mentions you for the job. Influential people who know you talk to other people. Jack Flye (the Mayor) said to me one day, "Bill," he said, "you have more friends in town than I do. I wish I had all the friends you have that you don't even know of." It made me feel good. . . .*

This typical attitude fits into what we know of the local type of influential. What is more, it suggests that the career-function of personal contacts and personal relations is recognized by local influentials themselves. Nor is this concern with personal contact merely a consequence of the occupations of local influentials. Businessmen, professionals, and local government officials among them all join in the same paeans on the desirability of many and varied contacts. A bank president recapitulates the same story in terms of his experience and outlook:

> *I have always been glad to meet people. . . . It really started when I became a teller. The teller is the most important position in a bank as far as meeting people goes. As teller, you must meet everyone. You learn to know everybody by his first name. You don't have the same opportunity again to meet people. Right now we have a teller who is very capable but two or three people have come to me complaining about him. He is unfriendly with them. I told him, you've got to have a kind word for everyone. It's a personal and a business matter.*

This keynote brings out the decisive interest of local influentials in all manner of personal contacts which enable them to establish themselves when they need political, business, or other support. Influentials in this group act on the explicit assumption that they can be locally prominent and influential by lining up enough people who know them and are hence willing to help them as well as be helped by them.

The cosmopolitan influentials, on the other hand, have notably little interest in meeting *as many* people as possible.[6] They are more selective in their choice of friends and acquaintances. They typically stress the importance of confining themselves to friends with whom "they can really talk," with whom they can "exchange ideas." If the local influentials are quantitativists, the cosmopolitans are qualitativists in this regard. It is not *how many* people they know but the *kind of people* they know that counts.[7]

The contrast with the prevailing attitudes of local influentials is brought out in these remarks by cosmopolitan influentials:

I don't care to know people unless there is something to the person.

I am not interested in quantity. I like to know about other people; it broadens your own education. I enjoy meeting people with knowledge and standing. Masses of humanity I don't go into. I like to meet people of equal mentality, learning and experience.

Just as with the local influentials, so here the basic attitude cuts across occupational and educational lines. Professional men among the cosmopolitans, for example, do not emphasize the importance of a wide and extensive acquaintanceship, if one is to build up a practice. In contrast to a "local" attorney who speaks of the "advantage to me to know as many people as possible," a "cosmopolitan" attorney waxes poetic and exclusive all in one, saying:

I have never gone out and sought people. I have no pleasure in just going around and calling. As Polonius advised Laertes,

> *"Those friends thou hast, and their adoption tried,*
> *Grapple them to thy soul with hoops of steel,*
> *But do not dull the palm with entertainment*
> *Of each new-hatch'd unfledged comrade. . . ."*

In a later section of this study, we shall see that these diverse orientations of locals and cosmopolitans toward personal relations can be inter-

---

[6] This was interestingly confirmed in the following fashion. Our informants were confronted with a random list of names of Rovere residents and were asked to identify each. Local influentials recognized more names than any other group of informants, and cosmopolitans, in turn, knew more persons than the non-influential informants.

[7] In this pilot study, we have confined ourselves to the expression of attitudes toward personal contacts and relations. A detailed inquiry would examine the quantum and quality of *actual* personal relations characteristic of the local and cosmopolitan influentials.

preted as a function of their distinctive modes of achieving influence. At the moment, it is sufficient to note that locals seek to enter into manifold networks of personal relations, whereas the cosmopolitans, *on the same status level,* explicitly limit the range of these relations.

PARTICIPATION IN VOLUNTARY ORGANIZATIONS

In considering the sociability of locals and cosmopolitans, we examined their attitudes toward informal, personal relationships. But what of their roles in the more formal agencies for social contact: the voluntary organizations?

As might be anticipated, both types of influentials are affiliated with more organizations than rank-and-file members of the population. Cosmopolitan influentials belong to an average of eight organizations per individual, and the local influentials, to an average of six. This suggests the possibility that cosmopolitans make greater use of organizational channels to influence than of personal contacts, whereas locals, on the whole, operate contrariwise.

But as with sociability, so with organizations: the more instructive facts are qualitative rather than quantitative. It is not so much that the cosmopolitans belong to *more* organizations than the locals. Should a rigorous inquiry bear out this impression, it would still not locate the strategic organizational differences between the two. It is, rather, that they belong to different types of organizations. And once again, these differences reinforce what we have learned about the two kinds of influentials.

The local influentials evidently crowd into those organizations which are largely designed for "making contacts," for establishing personal ties. Thus, they are found largely in the secret societies (Masons), fraternal organizations (Elks), and local service clubs—the Rotary, Lions, and the Kiwanis, the most powerful organization of this type in Rovere. Their participation appears to be less a matter of furthering the nominal objectives of these organizations than of using them as *contact centers.* In the forthright words of one local influential, a businessman:

> *I get to know people through the service clubs; Kiwanis, Rotary, Lions. I now belong only to the Kiwanis. Kiwanis is different from any other service club. You have to be asked to join. They pick you out first, check you first. Quite a few influential people are there and I get to meet them at lunch every week.*

The cosmopolitans, on the other hand, tend to belong to those organizations in which they can exercise their special skills and knowledge. They are found in professional societies and in hobby groups. At the time of the inquiry, in 1943, they were more often involved in Civilian Defense organizations where again they were presumably more concerned with furthering the objectives of the organization than with establishing personal ties.

Much the same contrast appears in the array of public offices held by the two types of influentials. Seven of each type hold some public office, although the locals have an average somewhat under one office. The primary difference is in the *type* of office held. The locals tend to hold political posts—street commissioner, mayor, township board, etc.— ordinarily obtained through political and personal relationships. The cosmopolitans, on the other hand, more often appear in public positions which involve not merely political operations but the utilization of special skills and knowledge (*e.g.,* Board of Health, Housing Committee, Board of Education).

From all this we can set out the hypothesis that participation in voluntary associations[8] has somewhat different functions for cosmopolitan and local influentials. Cosmopolitans are concerned with associations primarily because of the activities of these organizations. They are means for extending or exhibiting their skills and knowledge. Locals are primarily interested in associations not for their activities, but because these provide a means for extending personal relationships. The basic orientations of locals and cosmopolitan influentials are thus diversely expressed in organizational behavior as in other respects.

AVENUES TO INTERPERSONAL INFLUENCE

The foregoing differences in attachment to Rovere, sociability, and organizational behavior help direct us to the different avenues to influence traveled by the locals and the cosmopolitans. And in mapping these avenues we shall fill in the background needed to interpret the differences in communications behavior characteristic of the two types of influentials.

The locals have largely grown up in and with the town. For the most part, they have gone to school there, leaving only temporarily for their college and professional studies. They held their first jobs in Rovere and earned their first dollars from Rovere people. When they came to work out their career-pattern, Rovere was obviously the place in which to do so. It was the only town with which they were thoroughly familiar, in which they knew the ins and outs of politics, business, and social life. It was the only community which they knew and, equally important,

---

[8] For types and functions of participation in such organizations, see Bernard Barber, "Participation and mass apathy in associations," in Alvin W. Gouldner, (ed.) *Studies in Leadership* (New York: Harper & Brothers, 1950), 477–504.

which knew them. Here they had developed numerous personal rela, tionships.

And this leads to the decisive attribute of the local influentials' path to success: far more than with the cosmopolitans, *their influence rests on an elaborate network of personal relationships.* In a formula which at once simplifies and highlights the essential fact, we can say: *the influence of local influentials rests not so much on what they know but on whom they know.*

Thus, the concern of the local influential with personal relations is in part the product and in part the instrument of his particular type of influence. The "local boy who makes good," it seems, is likely to make it through good personal relations. Since he is involved in personal relations long before he has entered seriously upon his career, it is the path of less resistance for him to continue to rely upon these relations as far as possible in his later career.

With the cosmopolitan influential, all this changes. Typically a newcomer to the community, he does not and cannot utilize personal ties as his chief claim to attention. He usually comes into the town fully equipped with the prestige and skills associated with his business or profession and his "wordly" experience. He begins his climb in the prestige-structure at a relatively high level. It is the prestige of his previous achievements and previously acquired skills which make him eligible for a place in the local influence-structure. Personal relations are much more the product than the instrumentality of his influence.

These differences in the location of career-patterns have some interesting consequences for the problems confronting the two types of influentials. First of all, there is some evidence, though far from conclusive, that the rise of the locals to influentiality is slow compared with that of the cosmopolitans. Dr. A, a minister, cosmopolitan, and reader of newsmagazines, remarked upon the ease with which he had made his mark locally:

The advantage of being a minister is that you don't have to *prove yourself. You are immediately accepted and received in all homes, including the best ones. [Emphasis supplied]*

However sanguine this observation may be, it reflects the essential point that the newcomer who has "arrived" in the outside world, sooner takes his place among those with some measure of influence in the local community. In contrast, the local influentials *do* "have to prove" themselves. Thus, the local bank president who required some forty years to rise from his job as messenger boy, speaks feelingly of the slow, long road on which "I worked my way up."

The age-composition of the local and cosmopolitan influentials is also a straw in the wind with regard to the rate of rise to influence. All but two of the sixteen locals are over forty-five years of age, whereas fewer than two-thirds of the cosmopolitans are in this older age group.

Not only may the rate of ascent to influence be slower for the local than for the cosmopolitan, but the ascent involves some special difficulties deriving from the local's personal relations. It appears that these relations may hinder as well as help the local boy to "make good." He must overcome the obstacle of being intimately known to the community when he was "just a kid." He must somehow enable others to recognize his consistent change in status. Most importantly, people to whom he was once subordinate must be brought to the point of now recognizing him as, in some sense, superordinate. Recognition of this problem is not new. Kipling follows Matthew 13 in observing that "prophets have honour all over the Earth, except in the village where they were born." The problem of ascent in the influence-structure for the home-town individual may be precisely located in sociological terms: the revamping of attitudes toward the mobile individual and the remaking of relations with him. The pre-existent structure of personal relations for a time thus restrains the ascent of the local influential. Only when he has broken through these established conceptions of him, will others accept the reversal of roles entailed in the rise of the local man to influence. A Rovere attorney, numbered among the local influentials, described the pattern concisely:

When I first opened up, people knew me so well in town that they treated me as if I still were a kid. It was hard to overcome. But after I took interest in various public and civic affairs, and became chairman of the Democratic organization and ran for the State legislature—knowing full well I wouldn't be elected—they started to take me seriously.

The cosmopolitan does not face the necessity for breaking down local preconceptions of himself before it is possible to have his status as an influential "taken seriously." As we have seen, his credentials are found in the prestige and authority of his attainments elsewhere. He thus manifests less interest in a wide range of personal contacts for two reasons. First, his influence stems from prestige rather than from reciprocities with others in the community. Secondly, the problem of disengaging himself from obsolete images of him as "a boy" does not exist for him, and consequently does not focus his attention upon personal relations as it does for the local influential.

The separate roads to influence traveled by the locals and cosmopolitans thus help account for their diverging orientations toward the local community, with all that these orientations entail.

SOCIAL STATUS IN ACTION: INTERPERSONAL INFLUENCE

At this point, it may occur to the reader that the distinction between the local and cosmopolitan influentials is merely a reflection of differences in education or occupation. This does not appear to be the case.

It is true that the cosmopolitans among our interviewees have received more formal education than the locals. All but one of the cosmopolitans as compared with half of the locals are at least graduates of high school. It is also true that half of the locals are in "big business," as gauged by Rovere standards, whereas only two of the fourteen cosmopolitans fall in this group; and furthermore, that half of the cosmopolitan influentials are professional people as compared with fewer than a third of the locals.

But these differences in occupational or educational status do not appear to determine the diverse types of influentials. When we compare the behavior and orientations of professionals among the locals and cosmopolitans, their characteristic differences persist, even though they have the same types of occupation and have received the same type of education. Educational and occupational differences may *contribute* to the differences between the two types of influentials but they are not the *source* of these differences. Even as a professional, the local influential is more of a businessman and politician in his behavior and outlook than is the cosmopolitan. He utilizes personal relationships as an avenue to influence conspicuously more than does his cosmopolitan counterpart. In short, *it is the pattern of utilizing social status and not the formal contours of the status itself which is decisive.*[9]

While occupational status may be a major support for the cosmopolitan's rise to influence, it is merely an adjunct for the local. Whereas all five of the local professionals actively pursue local politics, the cosmopolitan professionals practically ignore organized political activity in Rovere. (Their offices tend to be honorary appointments.) Far from occupation serving to explain the differences between them, it appears that the same occupation has a different role in interpersonal influence

[9] The importance of actively seeking influence is evident from an analysis of "the upward mobile type," set forth in the monograph upon which this report is based. See also Granville Hicks, *Small Town* (New York: The Macmillan Co., 1946), 154, who describes a man who is evidently a local influential in these terms: "He is a typical politician, a born manipulator, a man who worships influence, *works hard to acquire it,* and does his best to convince other people that he has it." (Italics supplied).

according to whether it is pursued by a local or a cosmopolitan. This bears out our earlier impression that "objective attributes" (education, occupation, etc.) do not suffice as indices of people exercising interpersonal influence.

The influential businessman, who among our small number of interviewees is found almost exclusively among the locals, typically utilizes his personal relations to enhance his influence. It is altogether likely that a larger sample would include businessmen who are cosmopolitan influentials and whose behavior differs significantly in this respect. Thus, Mr. H., regarded as exerting great influence in Rovere, illustrates the cosmopolitan big-business type. He arrived in Rovere as a top executive in a local manufacturing plant. He has established few personal ties. But he is sought out for advice precisely because he has "been around" and has the aura of a man familiar with the outside world of affairs. His influence rests upon an imputed expertness rather than upon sympathetic understanding of others.

This adds another dimension to the distinction between the two types of influential. It appears that the cosmopolitan influential has a following because *he knows;* the local influential, because *he understands.* The one is sought out for his specialized skills and experience; the other, for his intimate appreciation of intangible but affectively significant details. The two patterns are reflected in prevalent conceptions of the difference between "the extremely competent but impersonal medical specialist" and the "old family doctor." Or again, it is not unlike the difference between the "impersonal social welfare worker" and the "friendly precinct captain," which we have considered in Chapter I. It is not merely that the local political captain provides food-baskets and jobs, legal and extra-legal advice, that he sets to rights minor scrapes with the law, helps the bright poor boy to a political scholarship in a local college, looks after the bereaved—that he helps in a whole series of crises when a fellow needs a friend, and, above all, a friend who "knows the score" and can do something about it. It is not merely that he provides aid which gives him interpersonal influence. It is *the manner in which the aid is provided.* After all, specialized agencies do exist for dispensing this assistance. Welfare agencies, settlement houses, legal aid clinics, hospital clinics, public relief departments—these and many other organizations are available. But in contrast to the professional techniques of the welfare worker which often represent in the mind of the recipient the cold, bureaucratic dispensation of limited aid following upon detailed investigation are the unprofessional techniques of the precinct captain who asks no questions, exacts no compliance with legal rules of eligibility and does not "snoop" into private affairs. The precinct captain is a prototype of the "local" influential.

Interpersonal influence stemming from specialized expertness typically involves some social distance between the advice-giver and the advice-seeker, whereas influence stemming from sympathetic understanding typically entails close personal relations. The first is the pattern of the cosmopolitan influential; the second, of the local influential. Thus, the operation of these patterns of influence gives a clue to the distinctive orientations of the two types of influentials.[10]

[10] All this still leaves open the problem of working out the patterns of social interaction and of influence-relations *between* local and cosmopolitan influentials. This problem has been explored in a current study of high schools in relation to the value-structure of the environing community, a study by Paul F. Lazarsfeld in collaboration with Richard Christie, Frank A. Pinner, Arnold Rogow, Louis Schneider and Arthur Brodbeck.

In the course of this study, Frank A. Pinner found that school boards and school superintendents evidently varied in their orientation: some were distinctly "local," others "cosmopolitan" in orientation. Nor is this, it appears, simply a matter of historical "accident." Pinner suggests that communities of different types tend to elect people of differing orientation to the high school board. This, in turn, creates special circumstances affecting the interaction of the school board and the school superintendent, depending on the primary orientation of both. The orientations of school boards are also, it seems, linked up with the degree of control exercised over educational policies. The influentials in one community "being profoundly interested in local affairs, were bound to subject all community functions to constant scrutiny and to accept or reject policies as they seemed to be in agreement with or contradictory to commonly accepted standards [in the local community]. By the same token, the [other] district was a 'loosely' organized area in more than the sheer geographical sense. Interest in local affairs was not equally shared by those who, in view of their social and economic position, were capable of exerting some influence. As a result, the policies controlling the operation of the high school need not represent the consensus of the influential groups in the community; rather, a large number of potentially influential people could, by default, leave the running of high school affairs to some group of citizens who happened to take an interest in high school affairs.

"Degrees of 'looseness' and 'tightness' of a community structure are perhaps best measured in terms of the administration's opportunity for maneuvering."

The study of the *interaction* between groups having differing composition in terms of local and cosmopolitan influentials represents a definite advance upon the ideas set forth in this paper. The concept of "tight" and "loose" community structures, as connected with the prevailingly local or cosmopolitan orientations of those in strategically placed positions represents another advance. It is of more than passing interest that this conception of "loose" and "tight" social structures has been independently *developed* by those engaged in the afore-mentioned study and, at a far remove, by Bryce F. Ryan and Murray A. Straus, "The integration of Sinhalese Society," *Research Studies of the State College of Washington*, 1954, 22, 179–227, esp. 198 ff and 219 ff. It is important to emphasize that these conceptions are being *developed* in the course of systematic empirical inquiry; else one becomes the professional adumbrationist who makes it his business to show that there is literally nothing new under the sun, by the simple expedient of excising all that is new and reducing it only to the old. It is only in this limited sense that one will find the "same" central idea of "rigid" and "flexible" social structures in the writings of that man of innumerable seminal ideas, Georg Simmel. See his essay, translated a half-century ago by Albion W. Small and published in the *American Journal of Sociology* during its early and impoverished years when American sociologists of intellectual taste were compelled to draw upon the intellectual capital of European sociologists:

There is reason to believe that further inquiry will find differing proportions of local and cosmopolitan influentials in different types of community structures. At least this implication can be provisionally drawn from the ongoing studies of technological and social change in a Pennsylvania city during the past fifty years being conducted by Dorothy S. Thomas, Thomas C. Cochran and their colleagues.[11] Their detailed historical and sociological analysis yields the finding that the city comprised two distinct types of population: "fairly permanent residents, many of whom had been born there, and a migrating group that continually came and went." On the basis of crude statistics of turnover of population in other American cities, the investigators conclude further that this condition is fairly widespread. It may well be that the first, more nearly permanent group includes the local type of influential and the second, relatively transient group, the cosmopolitan. Diverse types of communities presumably have differing proportions of the two kinds of population and of the two kinds of influentials.

Other recent studies have found more directly that the proportions and social situations of the two types of influentials vary as the social structure of the community varies. Eisenstadt reports, for example, that a traditional Yemenite community almost entirely lacks the cosmopolitan type, whereas both cosmopolitans and locals play their distinctive roles in several other communities under observation.[12] On the basis of Stouf-

---

"The persistence of social groups," *American Journal of Sociology*, 1898, 3, 662–698; 829–836; 1898, 4, 35–50. The most compact formulation of the ideas in question is this one: "The group may be preserved (1) by conserving with the utmost tenacity its firmness and rigidity of form, so that the group may meet approaching dangers with substantial resistance, and may preserve the relation of its elements through all change of external conditions; (2) by the highest possible variability of its form, so that adaptation of form may be quickly accomplished in response to change of external conditions, so that the form of the group may adjust itself to any demand of circumstance." (831)

Evidently, the more it changes, the less it is the same thing. The re-emerging concepts of loose and tight social structures resemble the Simmelian observations; they are nevertheless significantly different in their implications.

[11] As reported by Thomas C. Cochran, "History and the social sciences," in *Relazioni del X Congresso Internazionale di Scienze Storiche* (Rome, 4–11 September 1955), I, 481–504, at 487–88 on the basis of Sidney Goldstein, *Patterns of Internal Migration in Norristown, Pennsylvania, 1900–1950*, 2 volumes (Ph.D. thesis, multigraphed), University of Pennsylvania, 1953.

[12] S. N. Eisenstadt, "Communication systems and social structure: an exploratory comparative study," *Public Opinion Quarterly*, 1955, 19, 154–167. A study of a small Southern town reports that the two types of influentials cannot be distinguished there; the present suggestion holds that, with the accumulation of research, it is no longer enough to report the presence or absence of the types of influentials. Rather, it is sociologically pertinent to search out the attributes of the social structure which make for varying proportions of these identifiable types of influentials. See A. Alexander Fanelli, "A typology of community leadership based on influence and interaction within the leader subsystem," *Social Forces*, 1956, 34, 332–338.

fer's study of civil liberties, David Riesman suggests ways in which the roles of local and cosmopolitan influentials may differ in different social structures. Cosmopolitans who take on positions of formal leadership in the community, he suggests, may be obliged to become middlemen of tolerance, as they are caught between the upper millstone of the tolerant elite and the nether one of the intolerant majority, and thus become shaped into being less tolerant than their former associates and more so than their constituency. As a result of differing structural context, also, cosmopolitans among the community leaders, themselves more "tolerant" of civil liberties than others, may be in more vulnerable situations in the South than in the East and West. For Stouffer has found that among all but the college-educated, Southerners are far less tolerant of civil liberties than Northerners of like education; "This means," Riesman points out, "that the college graduate in the South is, in these respects, quite sharply cut off from the rest of the community, including even those with some college attendance, for although education is everywhere associated with tolerance, the gradations are much less steep in the North. Moreover, much the same is true in the South for metropolitan communities against smaller cities, though in this dimension there are substantial differences in the East as well.[13]

From this evidence which is only now being accumulated, it would seem that the emergence of the two types of influentials depends upon characteristic forms of environing social structure with their distinctive functional requirements.

* * *

[13] Samuel A. Stouffer, *Communism, Conformity, and Civil Liberties* (New York: Doubleday & Company, 1955) provides the findings under review by David Riesman in his article, "Orbits of tolerance, interviewers, and elites," *Public Opinion Quarterly,* 1956, 20, 49–73.

19. Small Town in Mass Society

BY ARTHUR J. VIDICH AND JOSEPH BENSMAN

Springdale is connected with the mass society in a variety of different forms. The cumulative effect of these various connections makes possible the continuous transmission of outside policies, programs and trends into the community, even though the effects of the transmission and the transmitting agents themselves are not always seen. Outside influences can be transmitted directly by a socially visible agent such as the extension specialist who lives in the community for the purpose of acting upon it. Outside interests and influences can also be expressed indirectly through members of the community: policies and programs of relatively invisible outside interests are transmitted by *heads* of local branches of state and national organizations, by *heads* of local businesses dependent on outside resources and by *heads* of churches attached to larger organizations. In some instances the community is affected by the consequences of decisions made by business and government which are made with specific reference to the community, i.e., the decision to build a state road through the community or the decision to close down a factory. Plans and decisions that refer directly to the community are made from a distance by invisible agents and institutions. Perhaps most important are the mass decisions of business and government which are transmitted to the rural scene by the consequences of changes in prices, costs and communications. These affect the town even though they are not explicitly directed at it, and they comprise the invisible social chain reactions of decisions that are made in centers of power in government, business and industry. The invisible social chain reactions emanating from the outside no doubt alter the life of the community more seriously than the action of visible agents such as the extension specialist.

These types of transmission do not represent mutually exclusive channels, but rather exist in complex interrelationship with each other. They merely suggest the major ways in which the community is influenced by dynamics which occur in the institutions of mass society. How these combined dynamics in their various combinations affect the fabric of life in

Springdale can be seen by examining the way in which cultural importations and economic and political connections shape the character of community life. In their net effect they influence the psychological dimensions of the community.

CULTURAL IMPORTATIONS FROM MASS SOCIETY

The external agents of cultural diffusion range from specific observable individuals placed in the local community by outside institutions to the impact of mass media of communications and successive waves of migration. The consequence of these modes of diffusion lies in the effect which they have on local styles of living.

FORMAL IMPORTING ORGANIZATIONS

The adult extension program of the land grant college is mediated at the local level by the county agent and the home demonstration agent who respectively are concerned with farming methods and production, and patterns of homemaking and family life. These agents carry out their program through the Farm and Home Bureau organizations. In Springdale township these agencies have a membership of 300–400 adults. The county agent is primarily concerned with introducing modern methods of farm production and operation and with fostering political consciousness among the farmers. As a type of executive secretary to the local Farm Bureau whose officers are local farmers, the agent acts as an advisor in planning the organization's program, which includes such items as production and marketing problems, parity price problems and taxation problems.

The organizational structure of the Home Bureau parallels the Farm Bureau. From skills and techniques and personnel available at the extension center, local programs consist, for example, of furniture refinishing or aluminum working as well as discussions on such topics as child-rearing, nutrition, penal institutions and interior design. The Home Bureau extension specialist trains a local woman in information and techniques which are reported back to the local club. This program, geared as it is to modern home-making, child-rearing and the feminine role, has the effect of introducing new styles and standards of taste and consumption for the membership.

Other institutional connectors similar to the above in organizational structure account for the introduction of still other social values and social definitions. The 4-H Club, the Future Farmers of America and the Boy and Girl Scouts, as well as the Masons, Odd Fellows, American Legion, Grange and other local branches of national organizations and their auxiliaries, relate the Springdaler to the larger society through the social meanings and styles of activity defined in the programs, procedures and rituals of the national headquarters. State and national conventions, but not office holding, of these as well as church organizations directly link individuals to the outside. In effect these arrangements regularize and institutionalize the communication and organizational nexus between the small town and the point of origin of new ideas and values.

New cultural standards are also imported by agents who are not permanent residents of the town or who have only a transient relationship with it. These include the teachers at the central school, many of whom view their jobs as a temporary interlude in a progression of experience which will lead to a position in a city system. The other agents of contact are a wide variety of salesmen and "experts" who have a regular or irregular contact with business, government and private organizations. From the surrounding urban centers and the regional sales offices of farm implement and automobile manufacturers and nationally branded products, modern methods of merchandizing and business practice are introduced. Experts in civil defense, evangelism, fire-fighting, gardening, charity drives, traffic control and youth recreation introduce new techniques and programs to the local community. This great variety and diversity of semi-permanent and changing contacts in their cumulative effect act as a perpetual blood transfusion to local society. The net effect that these agents have as transmitters of life styles depends in a measure on their position and prestige in the community. The differential effect of these cultural contacts is treated below.

THE UBIQUITY OF MASS MEDIA

Social diffusion through the symbols and pictorial images of the mass media of communications has permeated the community, reducing the local paper to reporting of social items and local news already known by everyone. Few individuals read only the local weekly paper; the majority subscribe to dailies published in surrounding cities and in large metropolitan areas. This press, itself part of larger newspaper combines, presents an image of the passing scene in its news and nationally syndicated features to which the population of an entire region is exposed.

The mass culture and mass advertising of television and radio reach Springdale in all their variety. Television, particularly, is significant in its impact because for the first time the higher art forms such as ballet, opera and plays are visible to a broad rural audience. National events such as party conventions, inaugurations and investigative hearings are visible now to an audience which was previously far removed from the national centers of action and drama. . . . The state department of education syllabus defines minimum standards and content for subject matter instruction. Courses of Sunday School instruction are available for all age levels, and each faith secures its material from its own national religious press. In each of these major institutional areas the standards and *content* of instruction are defined in sources available only in standardized form.

THE IMMIGRANT AS CULTURAL CARRIER

Specific individuals are carriers of cultural diffusion, and the volume and extent of migration in and out of the community suggests the degree and intimacy of its contact with the mass society. In a community which is regarded as stable and relatively unchanging by its own inhabitants, only 25 percent of its population was born locally. Another 25 percent has moved into the community since 1946 and 55 percent are new to the community since 1920. Moreover, of the 45 percent who have moved to the community since 1932, more than 30 percent have lived for a year or longer in cities with populations in excess of 25,000; 7 percent in cities with populations in excess of one-half million.

*   *   *

The cumulative consequences of these channels of diffusion and the quantity and quality of the "material" diffused denies the existence of a culture indigenous to the small town. In almost all aspects of culture, even to speech forms, and including technology, literature, fashions and fads, as well as patterns of consumption, to mention a few, the small town tends to reflect the contemporary mass society.

Basically, an historically indigenous local culture does not seem to exist. The cultural imports of each decade and generation and the successive waves of migration associated with each combine to produce a local culture consisting of layers or segments of the mass culture of successive historical eras. In the small town the remaining elements of the gay-ninety culture are juxtaposed against the modern central school. The newer cultural importations frequently come in conflict with the older importations of other eras. The conflict between "spurious" and "genuine" culture appears to be a conflict between two different ages of "spurious" culture.

THE ECONOMIC NEXUS:
OCCUPATIONAL GATEKEEPERS TO THE MASS SOCIETY

Simply because individuals pursue given occupations, their interconnections with mass society follow given patterns. They may be direct employees of specific organizations of the mass society; they may be the objects and targets of the programs of mass organizations; they may be trained by and in great institutions or their skills may be utilized only in urban areas. Because of these occupational characteristics they are specially qualified, accessible and available as transmitters of specific organizational and cultural contacts and contents.

*   *   *

THE PROFESSIONALS

A number of institutional representatives who are residents of the town receive their position in the community by virtue of their connections with outside agencies. Their position in the community is secured in part by the institution to which they are connected and by the evaluation of the role they are imputed to have in the agency which they locally represent.

The group of individuals who possess a borrowed prestige based on their external affiliations fall largely in the professional category. They are individuals who uniformly possess a college education. Among their ranks are included lawyers, ministers, doctors, teachers, engineers, and a variety of field representatives of state and federal agencies who settle in the community for occupational purposes. All of these individuals, except one or two, have migrated to the community as adults. In addition to the prestige which they are accorded by virtue of being "educated," their overwhelming characteristic as a group lies in the influence which they have in mediating between the town and the larger society. They possess the knowledge and techniques necessary for connecting the small town to the intricate organization of the mass bureaucratic society. They possess "contacts" with outside agencies and their role requires an ability to understand "official" documents and forms, and to write appropriate letters to appropriate bureaus. Thus, for example, the lawyer is counsel to political bodies as well as to free associations and other local organizations, in which capacities he gains an extensive and intimate knowledge of affairs of the town and thereby acquires a position of influence. In like manner the technical knowledge of state educational regulations and policies possessed by the high-school principal is indispensable to the locally constituted school board.

*   *   *

Moreover, this professional group as a whole, including the relatively transient teaching staff, are felt to have access to styles of taste and consumption which are considered different from those available to the rest of the community. As a result these institutional connectors are considered outside the ordinary realm of prestige assignments and social stratification. That is, their social position in the community is not guaranteed by conforming to standards which are indigenous to the community but, rather, by imputed conformance to "alien" or "exotic" standards of urban life.

As a result of this dual position, individuals in this group, especially those who have come from or have resided for some time outside the community, are able to influence styles of consumption and thought in the community. They do this in three main areas of activity: in organizational activities, community projects and social fashions. They have been prime movers in setting up a formal program of youth recreation and in vigorously participating in and supporting local cultural activities such as plays, recitals and educational talks. In the P.T.A. they constitute the block favoring those modern methods and programs which bring the outside world to the small town—talks by foreign university students, race relations discussions and socio-dramas in dating and parent-child relationships. Ideas for the development of a community center and adult education programs emanate from and are supported by them. In terms of dress styles and personal adornment as well as home furnishings and styles of party giving, this group is in the forefront of innovation.

This innovating group of middle-class newcomers is supported by a group of college-educated locals who act as a bridge between the new standards and local society. In supporting these new standards, the local group absorbs some of the resentment which is directed at the innovating group by both the farmers and merchants.

It must be noted that the professionals' psychological orientation to accentuate the "elite" cultural values of mass society is more than merely a product of their residence, education or background in the mass society. The limitations on economic success and the limited professional opportunities in the community mean that the drive toward success through work and investment is not fully available to them. The possession of alien cultural standards makes it possible for the professionals to reject the success drive by accepting meaningful standards alternative to those available to the rest of the community; they distinguish themselves in the community by their identification with external values.

BUSINESSMEN

For storekeepers, filling station operators, appliance dealers, automobile and farm equipment dealers and feed mill operators, the external world is a source of supply for the goods and commodities which they sell on the local market. Their position in relation to their source of supply and the overall condition of the national economy determines the level of their business activity, ceilings on their potential income, and hence indirectly their style of life.

* * *

INDUSTRIAL WORKERS

Industrial workers represent a curious gap in the relationship of the rural community to mass society. Individuals who live in Springdale but work outside on products which are geared to a national market are not understandable to other members of the community because the rural community lacks the perceptual apparatus necessary to understand industry and the industrial process. The industrial worker lives in the community, but the occupational basis of his existence is not subject to the social pigeon-holing by others necessary to making judgments and assessments of him.

* * *

FARMERS

As noted earlier, there are two classes of farmers, the rational and the traditional. A major difference between them is the way they organize their production in relation to the mass market and government regulations.

Those who gear themselves to the mass market address themselves to favorably pegged prices, subsidies and quotas. As a consequence when prices and regulations are favorable they accept the favorable environment as a condition for their operations. They invest and expand, work hard and are successful. Their success stimulates confidence and buoyancy and produces an expansionist psychology.

In a peculiar way the traditional farmers who as a group do not gear themselves to the mass market do this specifically because of their relations with the mass market. As older farmers they have learned from the depression that they can be economically vulnerable, and they have learned that they can survive in the community by being immune to the market. The depression experience was so bitter for them that they have learned nothing since. Thus it happens that at the time of the study they were still living in the market of the early Thirties.

* * *

THE POLITICAL SURRENDER TO MASS SOCIETY

Local political institutions consist of a village board, a town board and local committees of the Republican and Democratic parties. The jurisdiction of the village board includes powers of control and regulation over a variety of community facilities and services—street lighting, water supply, fire protection, village roads, street signs and parks. To carry out the functions empowered to it, it possesses the power of taxation. The town board is concerned chiefly with fire protection, the construction and maintenance of roads; through its participation on the county board of supervisors, it participates in programs connected with welfare, penal and other county services.

However, at almost every point in this seemingly broad base of political domain the village and town boards adjust their action to either the regulations and laws defined by state and federal agencies which claim parallel functions on a statewide or nationwide basis or to the fact that outside agencies have the power to withhold subsidies to local political institutions.

Local assessment scales and tax rates are oriented to state equalization formulas which partially provide the standardized basis on which subsidies are dispersed by the state. State highway construction and development programs largely present local political agencies with the alternative of either accepting or rejecting proposed road plans and programs formulated by the state highway department.

The village board, more than the town board, is dependent on its own taxable resources (taxes account for almost half its revenues) and best illustrates the major dimensions of local political action. The village board in Springdale accepts few of the powers given to it. Instead, its orients its action to the facilities and subsidies controlled and dispensed by other agencies and, by virtue of this, forfeits its own political power. Solutions to the problem of fire protection are found in agreements with regionally organized fire districts. In matters pertaining to road signs and street signs action typically takes the form of petitioning state agencies to fulfill desired goals "without cost to the taxpayer." On roads built and maintained by the state there is no recourse but to accept the state traffic bureau's standards of safety. A problem such as snow removel is solved by dealing directly with the foreman of the state highway maintenance crew through personal contacts: "If you treat him right, you can get him to come in and clear the village roads." In other areas of power where there are no parallel state agencies, such as for garbage collection or parks, the village board abdicates its responsibility.

As a consequence of this pattern of dependence, many important decisions are made for Springdale by outside agencies. Decisions which are made locally tend to consist of approving the requirements of administrative or state laws. In short the program and policies of local political bodies are determined largely by acceptance of grants-in-aid offered them—i.e., in order to get the subsidy specific types of decisions must be made—and by facilities and services made available to them by outside sources.

Psychologically this dependence leads to an habituation to outside control to the point where the town and village governments find it hard to act even where they have the power. Legal jurisdictions have been supplanted by psychological jurisdictions to such an extent that local political action is almost exclusively oriented to and predicated on seeking favors, subsidies and special treatment from outside agencies. The narrowing of legal jurisdictions by psychologically imposed limits leads to an inability to cope with local problems if outside resources are not available.

Power in local political affairs, then, tends to be based on accessibility to sources of decision in larger institutions. Frequently this accessibility consists merely of the knowledge of the source, or it may mean a personal contact, or an ability to correspond to get necessary information. Under these circumstances, power in the political arena is delegated to those with contacts in and knowledge of the outer world and to those who are experts in formal communication with impersonal bureaucratic offices. These are, on the individual level, the lawyer and, on an institutional level, the political party. The lawyer gains his paramountcy through technical knowledge and personalized non-party contacts up the political hierarchy with other lawyers. He is the mediator between the local party and the party hierarchy, and transforms his personalized contacts into political indispensability in the local community. His access to outside sources of power determines his power and predominance in the local community.

* * *

PUBLIC INTERESTS AND POLITICAL PARALYSIS

The village board and the Republican committee do not represent all the community views. There exist other groups who would be interested in "desirable" social expenditures, who lament the do-nothing attitude of the village board, and who would be interested in a revision of assessment evaluations. Residents of Back Street, as well as residents of several other streets, constitute an interest group who want paved roads and street lights. More recent migrants from cities (particularly professionals and industrial workers) would like recreational facilities and swimming instruction for their children and a community building as a center for social activities. The village as a whole is interested in snow removal and a garbage and trash removal service. The entire community is interested in better fire protection (replacement of obsolete equipment) and increased water pressure in the kitchen spigots. Individual businessmen and home owners have grieved to the board for a reassessment of their property "to bring it in line with other assessments." A large but unorganized group of individuals is interested in bringing industry to the community. No action was taken on any of these measures in the years preceding and during the field work of the study.

These desires for improvement, change and increased expenditures are held by individuals who have no stake in or control over the village board and who are beyond the purview of party politics—they do not vote and only when they have a special cause or a special complaint or request do they attend meetings of the village board. Their efforts to secure the action they desire remain at the level of private complaining or of occasional attendance at a board meeting as individuals who represent themselves or a specialized organization with a specialized request. The most frequent complaint of local citizens, including board members themselves, concerns alleged inequities in the assessment structure of taxable property. In the entire history of the community, assessments have not been reviewed and great differences exist in assessments of equivalent properties.

*   *   *

The paralysis of the board in not being able to cope with this and other problems reflects an underlying paralysis of organized political action in the village at large, except for individual efforts among those groups which desire action. The groups and the individuals who want political action lack the tradition, the specialization and the organization to make their views felt. The complexity of organizing political support; the necessity for historical, legal and technological knowledge in defining an issue clearly; the lack of knowledge of procedure; the lack of time—all these factors lead to inaction and a complaining but dissatisfied acceptance of the "business as usual" ideology of the village board.

*   *   *

THE CONSEQUENCES OF POLITICAL PARALYSIS

RELIANCE ON EXPERTS

. . . The legal counsel acts and is regarded as a source of information and as an authority not only on legal questions but also on general matters of procedure, precedent and history. When he speaks he is listened to with attention and his suggestions and recommendations are ordinarily accepted without question.

In addition to the board's reliance upon the technical skill of its counsel, it is frequently unable to act without the expert advice of outside experts. When it comes to erecting street signs, for example, the board must deal directly with a sergeant in the state traffic bureau who is familiar with the type of sign required and the regulations about its placement. In matters of youth recreation, the board was advised by a state representative with respect to its legal part in the administration of the program. The reliance of the board on outside experts is seen most clearly, however, in the fact that a large part of its business is conducted by correspondence with state agencies. In this process the village counsel who possesses the necessary skills is the connecting link to the outside agency and it is through him as he acts on the village board that the reliance of the board on experts is demonstrated most clearly.

THE SOCIAL BASIS OF UNANIMITY

The dominating influence of Flint on the board does not deny the possibility of conflict among the members. Beneath the public unanimity of the board, there exist small but important differences of interest between board members. For one, who lives on a street without light, there exists a potential impulse to secure street lighting in needed places. Another who is superintendent of the fire district is more inclined than the others to spend money on fire equipment. The clerk who owns no business property and is not a voting member of the board would be favorably disposed to a reassessment program. The mayor tends to be more "economy-minded" than some of the trustees. Each participant on the board has a pet interest which serves as a potential basis for conflict. Yet this conflict is never openly apparent and the principle of unanimity of decision is never broken. When board business touches on issues of potential conflict, each board member brings up for subliminal assessment the position of other members on the issue in question—i.e., who would be apt to oppose the measure and with what intensity—and avoids further mention of the topic.

Since the board member has neither skill nor knowledge nor a constituency to support him, he lacks confidence in his own opinion and his own cause. Instead of pushing an idea, he retreats to more familiar territory, the espousal of "economy-mindedness" on which he knows all members agree. When an issue comes up on which the positions of all board members are not known—when some new problem presents itself, for instance—a long process of discussion, during which board members frequently contradict themselves, ensues. This discussion, which appears so strange to the outsider, takes place for the purpose of finding a common ground on which all can agree and in which no opinion stands out. In this way no member irrevocably commits himself on an issue and, hence, does not alienate himself from the other members of the board with whom he must deal from month to month and in his daily living on a "friendly" basis. These dynamics explain the lengthy and poorly directed discussion which occupies the time of the board and provide a partial explanation for the phenomenon of unanimity.

In addition, however, there is always the danger that, should an issue come into the open, conflicting parties will appeal to outside individuals or groups or to the more important figures in the machine. Public sentiment could easily be mobilized around the issues of assessments, street lighting and snow removal. There is the ever-present possibility that an issue can be taken directly to the leaders of the machine since the link between the board and the machine is intimate.

As a consequence of these dynamics, in any situation which suggests that differences of opinion exist, action is postponed or delayed to a subsequent meeting or indefinitely. Between meetings, interested parties are consulted, board members meet and talk informally and some type of "understanding" is reached before the next meeting. If the item at issue is small (where to place a street light), several important individuals in the neighborhood are talked to, and opinion is sounded in other neighborhoods which do not have street lights. If the issue is large (such as a several thousand dollar bank loan, to repair a broken water main—the issue being how good a job is to be done), Howard Jones is consulted directly. In many cases this activity between meetings settles the issue so that it comes up for perfunctory approval at a subsequent meeting; or, if a *modus vivendi* cannot be worked out, nothing further is heard of the issue.

In the ordinary conduct of business in this manner, potential issues and conflicts never become visible at a public level. Undisciplined appeals to outside groups which would threaten the monopoly of power of the controlling group do not occur. The board, especially the trustees who alone possess the voting privilege, openly state that they do not want "to stir up trouble." Since the board members themselves carry responsibility for their actions, they do not take action until the appropriate individuals are consulted and until it is apparent that responsibility is diffused into unanimity. There is the continuous effort to seek the formula by which unanimity can be achieved. Until unanimity is reached, there is a tacit agreement to discuss the proposal and to postpone the decision until the time comes when either by wearing down, time limitations or accident a formula is found. The formula itself takes many forms. Typically it is indefinite postponement. Frequently it is arrived at by "doing what we did last year or ten years ago." Sometimes it is reached by taking "the 'only' legal course open to us according to the law of the state." In no instance is a formula based on a recognition of conflicting interests which require balancing.

DEPENDENCE ON EXTRA-LEGAL BODIES

As a consequence of this structure of decision making, the village board is not usually in a position to act when pressing action is required. When special problems arise which require non-traditional solutions or quick decisions and quick action, extra-legal bodies take over the functions of village government and meet the problem by extra-legal, quasi-legal or private means.

* * *

POLITICAL CEREMONIES AND POLITICAL PARTICIPATION

The pattern of village politics can be summarized in terms of an analysis of the meaning of the political ceremony. The political ceremony consists of the endless and indecisive talk which occurs in formal meetings of the village board. The formal meeting itself is a social ritual in which discussion serves the purpose of avoiding decision making.

*   *   *

As a further result of these dynamics all opposition groups in the village are, and can only be, organized around a single issue at any one time. All such groups in the past have been temporary and the machine has survived, even though in the process a number of local programs have been accomplished which otherwise might never have happened.

It is in this, perhaps minimal, way that outside interest groups are represented and that to some degree a democratic process is carried out. For, no matter what their own interests may be and no matter how reluctantly they aquiesce, the village board and the political machine, in order to maintain political control, must find some method of accommodating these pressures which, if avoided, would result in their loss of control. The reluctant acceptance of these issues and the programs which they entail constitute the foundations of democracy in the rural village.

20. Family Status, Local-Community Status, and Social Stratification: Three Types of Social Ranking*

BY BERNARD BARBER

*   *   *

In addition to providing conceptual clarification in the field of social stratification, this paper has another purpose. In recent American sociology there has been some bias against acknowledging that family status and local-community status are independent and continuing aspects of social behavior. This bias, which has been losing ground, fortunately, in the face of recent empirical research and theoretical reformulation which will be presently examined, may be easier to abandon in the light of the analysis and evidence we are presenting here. This paper, then, seeks to make a contribution to the sociological study of the family and the local community, as well as of social stratification.

I. SOCIAL CLASS POSITION

A brief account of social class position as a variable provides us with a baseline for discriminating our other two variables and for establishing the independent variability of all three.[1] Social class position is the relative place in a hierarchy of such positions that an individual and his immediately associated family of wife and dependent children have as a result of the differential evaluation that people in society make of the relatively full-time, functionally significant role that he occupies. In our type of society these roles are called "occupational" roles; but since they are often

Reprinted with permission of the author and publisher from Bernard Barber, "Family Status, Local-Community Status, and Social Stratification: Three Types of Social Ranking," *Pacific Sociological Review*, IV, No. 1, (Spring, 1961), 3–10. Footnotes have been renumbered.

  * This paper was originally delivered, in full, as a University Lecture at the University of Michigan, May, 1960. In briefer form it was presented at the 1960 Annual Meetings of the American Sociological Association.

  [1] A more comprehensive and detailed account can be found in [Bernard Barber, *Social Stratification* (New York: Harcourt, Brace, 1957)] esp. Chs. 1 and 2.

not so named in other types of societies, it is necessary to point to the fact that in all types of societies it is these relatively full-time, functionally significant roles that are the criteria of evaluation for social class position. Men in society treat one another and themselves as worthy of more and less respect *partly* because of their relative location in the hierarchy of these roles. By a man's social class position, thus, we mean the relative amount of respect of this kind that he gets and feels he deserves. Both the structure of functionally significant roles into which a society is differentiated and the process of evaluation of these roles have their essential parts to play in every society. So also, therefore, does the resultant of their interaction, the hierarchy of social class positions, have its part to play.

What we have just said defines the independent nature and functions of the hierarchy of social class positions in society. Fortunately, there is no need to rest with definitions. Sociological research during the last fifteen years has provided empirical evidence, using social surveys, of the existence of social class hierarchies in this sense in a variety of contemporary societies, for example, the United States, Great Britain, Germany, France, Japan, Russia, and the Philippines.[2] And the evidence for a variety of other and non-contemporary societies, though not so satisfactory as that provided by social surveys, is quite convincing that social class hierarchies exist in all times and places.[3]

Given the confusion and controversy that exists in the field of "social stratification" as it is broadly defined, it is useful to make explicit certain qualifications about what is and is not intended by insisting that social class position is *one* independently variable aspect of social reality. Social class position is not in principle any more, or any less, weighty a determinant of social behavior than such other variables as influence (authority or power) position, or income position, or ethnic or racial membership, or family status, or local-community status, or any one of the other aspects of social reality to which the concept of "social stratification" has been vaguely attached. The relative importance of one or another of these variables, or of several conjointly in different multivariate patterns, in determining specific concrete behavior must be established by research. But the fruitfulness of such research presupposes the kind of conceptual

---

[2] Among other sources, see: National Opinion Research Center, "Jobs and Occupations: A Popular Evaluation," *Public Opinion News:* 9(1947), pp. 3–13; Alex Inkeles and Peter H. Rossi, "National Comparisons of Occupational Prestige," *American Journal of Sociology,* 61 (January, 1956), pp. 329–339; J. Clyde Mitchell and A. L. Epstein, "Occupational Prestige and Social Status Among Urban Africans in Northern Rhodesia," *Africa,* 29 (January, 1959), pp. 22–39; and, Edward A. Tiryakian, "The Prestige Evaluation of Occupations in the Under-Developed Country: The Philippines," *American Journal of Sociology,* 63 (January, 1958), pp. 390–99.

[3] For this evidence see Barber, *op. cit.,* esp. Chs. 4–8.

clarification we have in view here. It is a striking testimony to the effect of preconceived ideas (that is, of social theory and social ideology) upon men's behavior that university professors themselves, for whom differential evaluation of their performance as scholars and scientists means so much, should in some case minimize and even deny the importance of differential evaluation of functionally significant roles as one principle of explanation of social behavior. To start with, then, we shall accept, on analytic and empirical grounds, the independence of social class position as one significant aspect of social reality.

II. FAMILY STATUS

A nuclear family is a more or less identifiable and solidary group, consisting of husband-father, wife-mother, and dependent children, which performs essential functions both for all its component members and for the larger society and the local community of which it is a part. A family unit's performance with regard to these several functions is constantly being evaluated as better or worse than the performance of other family units. One criterion for this evaluation is, as we have just seen, the relatively full-time, functionally significant role of the adult male member of the family; and it is this criterion that establishes what we have called the "social class position" of the family. But there are other, independently variable criteria of evaluation of family units; and it is the evaluational resultants of these other criteria that require a separate name and that we shall call "family status." What are these other criteria? There is, first of all, the criterion of the way in which the component members perform their functions *vis-à-vis* one another. What we colloquially call "a good family" is one which is more highly evaluated because it contains a "good" husband or a "good" father or a "good" wife or a "good' mother or a "good" son or a "good" daughter or a "good" brother or a "good" sister. Contrariwise, we call a family "bad," or evaluate it less highly than another because one or more of its component role-functions is being performed less well. Common-sense, or what Rose has called "natural sociology," does in fact evaluate nuclear family units in the light of their relative performance of these internal family functions. So too ought scientific sociology, therefore, have a concept to refer to these evaluations. Perhaps we ought to attribute some sociological wisdom to those organizations that choose "The Father of the Year" or "The Mother of the Year," instead of dismissing these designations as "mere sentiment" or "mere commercialism."

A second criterion of relative "family status" consists of the kinds of good or bad contributions that the several members of the nuclear family unit make to their neighborhoods, their local communities, and the national society considered as a community. Thus, "a good family" is one in which the several component members, each according to his different capacities, behave in an orderly and helpful way in the immediate neighborhood; serve the needs of the local community through its schools, voluntary associations, and government; and contribute to the nation's welfare through service in its voluntary associations, its government, and its armed forces in time of war. Again, contrariwise, "a bad family" is one which is notably delinquent in one or more of these respects.

So far we have been describing the criteria by which nuclear families are evaluated and given a relative "family status" for what they do in the present. But functional activities in the near and even more distant past also are a criterion of "family status" in the present. This is because families are often perduring groups, with a social identity or solidarity that extends through time across the generations in a lineage of descent. As a result, the contemporary nuclear family is identified with, sometimes even when it is not solidary with, other nuclear groups going back directly and indirectly through the traceable lines of descent. As a result of this identification by self or others, the contemporary family is judged by a third criterion, the relative "family status" of the several units in its lineage. The influence of lineage identification on present "family status" is evident when we hear someone say, "They're not much, but they are Roosevelts," or, "You'd never know their grandfather was a Kallikak."

American sociologists have, of course, acknowledged the reality of what we have defined as "family status" for other kinds of society than our own, especially for what have been called "familistic" societies but in general also for "non-industrial" and "primitive" and "non-literate" societies. But the existence of "family status" in its own right in our society is not often enough explicitly recognized and investigated. Indeed, we seem to distort in both directions, to exaggerate the importance of family and the persistence of lineages in other societies and to be blind to their theoretical implications in our own.[4] Nevertheless, despite strong pressures against recognizing "family status" and lineages in our society, pressures, first, from our values of independence and individual responsibility, and, second, from the structural advantages of the residentially isolated nuclear family for geographical and social mobility, the lineage as an identifiable and solidary family unit still occurs. Sentiments of attachment to the laterally and lineally extended family, emotional and symbolic identification with it, persist and are recognized as legitimate by

---

[4] For historical evidence on the fragility of noble family lineages in earlier periods of European society, see Barber, *op. cit.,* pp. 360, 425–426.

the members of our society. The time seems ripe for a reconsideration of "family status" by sociologists.

One set of conditions in which the importance of "family status" in American society has had to be recognized as a social fact has been in the study of what is too inclusively called "social class" in old, established local communities such as Yankee City, Old City, Philadelphia, and Springdale.[5] The existence of lineages and variable "family status" in these communities forced itself upon the attention of the researchers. Or, perhaps, in some cases, the communities were chosen just because established high-status families could be found there. Warner says, for example, ". . . it seemed wise to choose a community with a social organization which had developed over a long period of time under the domination of a single group with a coherent tradition."[6] Yet none of these studies clearly distinguishes what we have defined as "social class position" from what we have defined as "family status," nor did they pay attention to the consequences of the independent variability of these two elements. This failure is all the more striking in view of the fact, which we shall document below, that these studies often included, but only in passing, the data on which the two variables and their mutual independence can be established.

As might be expected from the fact that he came to Yankee City from doing his classic study of kinship relations among the Australian Murngin, Warner came closest to seeing the independence of "family status." "The extended kinship relations of all groups in the community," he says, "were sampled in great detail, and charts were made. . . . These charts clearly demonstrate that kinship in our own society, far from being the moribund type of relationship of which many have accused it, is a vital structure which organizes much of the lives of the members of the community and gives them a firm place in the total society."[7] Davis, Gardner, and Gardner also referred to the importance of "family status" in Old City and Old County. "Upper-upper class reverence for ancestral generations, however, does not generally extend indefinitely into the past. . . . They do not concern themselves with tracing their ancestry to Old Virginia, New Orleans, or France, but are content that certain individuals in their lineal kind-groups were the original wealthy planters, and so

[5] See W. L. Warner and P. S. Lunt, *The Social Life of a Modern Community,* New Haven: Yale University Press, 1941; Allison Davis, B. B. Gardner, and M. R. Gardner, *Deep South,* Chicago: University of Chicago Press, 1941; E. D. Baltzell, *Philadelphia Gentlemen,* Glencoe, Ill.: Free Press, 1958; and, Arthur J. Vidich, and J. Bensman, *Small Town in Mass Society,* Princeton: Princeton University Press, 1958.

[6] *Op. cit.,* p. 5.

[7] *Op. cit.,* p. 60. See also, pp. 82, 86, 93, 98, 100, 102.

'the aristocracy' in the local community. As an explanation of this attitude, it is probably significant that, for the most part, their ancestors, before they appeared on the local scene, had little claim to wealth or high social position."[8] In the Old City, "family status" sometimes even created distinctions within the nuclear family. "A partner who has no kin relation at all with an 'old family' is subordinated to one who has."[9] And further, "The upper-class child . . . is first and foremost a member of a lineal-kin group, and as such he 'belongs' to *all* his forebears. . . ."[10]

Baltzell, in his study of Philadelphia, states clearly how relative a matter "family status" is, with fine distinctions being made within that group of families that is acknowledged to be high generally. ". . . the Proper Philadelphia world," he says, "includes such patrician families of old wealth as the Morrises, Ingersolls, and Hopkinsons, as well as Wideners, Kents, and Dorrances of more recent money. This is a somewhat democratic use of these terms, at least as far as many 'old families' in the city are concerned. Within the fashionable and sometimes snobbish world of Proper Philadelphia, for example, there are, of course, a few 'old families' who consider themselves and are reverently so considered by many others, to be 'first families' . . . subtle gradations . . . (thus exist)."[11]

The significance of the extended family and of resulting differences in "family status" has had to be recognized elsewhere than in studies of the older local communities. In its investigation of nepotism in the top ranks of American business, for example, *Fortune Magazine* has commented, "Blood ties are still very important in the U.S. business—and the whole subject is a touchy one."[12] Nor is the extended family in some form a fact only in the upper classes. Sussman has recently summarized the findings of studies in Detroit, New Orleans, Kansas City, and New Haven, and has presented evidence from a study of his own in Cleveland, all showing that there is considerable mutual identification and solidarity among laterally and lineally related nuclear families in the middle and lower classes in American society.[13] Litwak also, in a study of white, middle-class Protestant families, has provided evidence on the visits they make and on the "emotional succor" and economic support given one

[8] *Op. cit.,* p. 84.
[9] *Ibid.,* p. 91.
[10] *Ibid.,* p. 95.
[11] *Op. cit.,* p. 162. See also, pp. 78, 166. On "old families" in Springdale, a small farming town in upstate New York, see Vidich and Bensman, *op. cit.,* pp. 66–67.
[12] March, 1957.
[13] Marvin B. Sussman, "The Isolated Nuclear Family: Fact or Fiction," *Social Problems,* 6 (Spring, 1959), pp. 333–340. For evidence of a similar kind for contemporary urban England, see Michael Young and Peter Willmott, *Family & Kinship in East London.* Glencoe, Ill.: Free Press, 1957.

another by the nuclear families making up the "equalitarian coalition" that, he suggests, now constitutes the "modified extended family."[14]

There are other bits of evidence for the importance of extended family groups and "family status" in American society. The prejudices for and against ethnic and racial groups, for example, can usefully be taken as only the most extreme extension of the phenomenon of differentially evaluating members of what are seen as kin-related groups and aggregations. And much of the "snobbism" of country clubs, social clubs, fraternities, and *Social Registers* is an exercise in what is considered by some members of our society to be an illegitimate, by others a legitimate recognition of differential "family status." In his discussion of the influence of "family status" on membership in Philadelphia's prestigious men's social clubs, Baltzell quotes Crane Brinton, who has said that the social club "may perhaps be regarded as taking the place of those extensions of the family, such as the clan and brotherhood, which have disappeared from advanced societies."[15] To show the way in which "family status" determines what social clubs call "legacies," Baltzell says, ". . . every year a small group of younger men in their twenties and thirties, invariably relatives of present members, are taken into the club. . . . One might meet among the old-family members of the Philadelphia Club (the city's most distinguished) some charming and congenial wastrels. . . ."[16] It is the presence of these incompetents, these men of actual lower-class position, that especially clearly shows the effects of "family status." However, this factor is also working for the competent, but early-chosen sons of club members, who are admitted earlier than men of equal competence and class position but lower "family status." We are obviously dealing with a separate and independent social variable, one that has a measurable effect upon the way in which people in American society treat one another.

Now let us turn directly to the evidence for the independent variability of social class position and "family status." As a first illustration, consider the following news item in which family prestige is relatively much higher than social class position for the individual whose birth is being reported.

---

[14] Eugene Litwak, *Primary Group Instruments for Social Control in Industrialized Society: The Extended Family and the Neighborhood,* Unpublished Doctoral Dissertation, Columbia University, 1958. Condensed versions of this dissertation can be found in Litwak, "Occupational Mobility and Extended Family Cohesion," *American Sociological Review,* 25 (February, 1960), pp. 9–21, and Litwak, "The Use of Extended Family Groups in the Achievement of Social Goals: Some Policy Implications," *Social Problems,* 7 (Winter, 1959–1960), pp. 177–187.

[15] *Op. cit.,* p. 335.

[16] *Ibid.,* p. 348.

SITTING BULL IS BORN

Los Angeles, Dec. 1 (AP)—Sitting Bull V was born at the Los Angeles Medical Center Hospital yesterday. His great-great-grandfather defeated and destroyed the forces of Gen. George Armstrong Custer at the Battle of the Little Big Horn in 1876. His parents are Vincent (Sitting Bull IV) and Frances Cadotte. His father, a disabled veteran of the 101st Airborne Division, was injured in a jump in Korea and now is a mail clerk at the Hughes Aircraft Plant.[17]

For more systematic evidence, however, we have to turn again to the studies of old American cities and towns. Describing what he calls the "upper-upper class" families in Yankee City, which are those families whose ancestors for three or more generations had been in that city's upper class, Warner says: "In these brief family histories there is a wide range in wealth and occupation. . . The Z's and Y's are the only very wealthy families; the X's are fairly well-to-do; and the others have but a modest income."[18] In short, what these families have in common is not their own similar and present social class position but the similar and past high "family status" of their ancestors. Some of these members of what Warner calls "upper-upper class" seem to be of an upper social class position, others of a middling social class position. High "family status," not high social class position, seems to be the defining characteristic of the "upper-upper class" in Yankee City. This supposition is supported further by the fact that at least some of those whom Warner places in the "lower-upper class" have as high a social class position as the highest of those placed among the "upper-uppers," but do not share the high "family status" of the latter in Yankee City's local community. The members of the Starr family, for example, who are placed in the "lower-upper class," and who are described in the greatest detail of all the families in the several profiles, as if the fact of their family inferiority needed to be driven home, seem to be in the same social class position as any member of the "upper-uppers." The Starrs, however, are not from an old prestigious family in Yankee City but have just risen into the topmost position in its social class hierarchy. Moreover, Mr. Starr's parents, though dead and buried in a local lower-class cemetery, are identifiable past members of the Yankee City community. Hence, Mr. Starr's visible "family status" is low, though his social class position is high. In Yankee City, at least as Warner describes it, "family status" seems to be more weighty a determinant of behavior in

[17] *New York Times*, Dec. 2, 1957.
[18] *Op. cit.*, p. 98.

some situations than is social class. Why this should so be is an interesting problem which is not analyzed, because the fact of the independent variability of social class position and "family status" is not theoretically formulated, its sources examined, and its consequences traced out.

The persistence of at least self-defined high "family status" in a group of families of declining social class position in the rural community of Springdale is reported by Vidich and Bensman. "This is not the 'upper class' of Springdale," they say. "It is a group of about ten families who are a vestige of a former business and commercial elite which fifty or seventy-five years ago was an upper class. . . . Their ancestors are remembered as the founders of both the community and its respected institutions . . . The home is the repository of family heirlooms, antique furniture and the family Bible, which records the genealogical connections of illustrious ancestors."[19] The case of Springdale illustrates how their ancestors' outstanding service to the local community contributes to the present high "family status" of these families that have been declining in the social hierarchy.

Perhaps the clearest evidence, however, on the lack of a one-to-one relationship between "family status" and social class position is provided by Baltzell's study of Philadelphians who were listed in the 1940 *Social Register*, an indicator of high "family status," and the 1940 *Who's Who,* an indicator of high social class position. Of the 770 Philadelphians who were in *Who's Who* and thus probably of upper-middle to upper class position, only 226, or 29 per cent, were also listed in the *Social Register*.[20] Clearly many people of high social position did not also have high "family status," as one might expect in a society with much social class mobility. Perhaps the best proof of exclusion of families of high social class position from the *Social Register* on the basis of their low "family status" is the fact that only one Jewish family was listed, although there were in Philadelphia not only many upper-class Jews but some Jewish families which had been distinguished and in the upper classes for as many generations as some of the listed non-Jewish families. In addition to his Philadelphia data, Baltzell also compiled national statistics from *Who's Who* and the *Social Registers* on the independent variability of social class position and "family status." He found that of the 12,530 residents of those twelve metropolitan areas in which *Social Registers* arc published who were listed in *Who's Who,*

[19] *Op. cit.,* pp. 66–67. For a study of the independent variability of "family status" and social class position in a rural backwater in England, a study which suggests the strains that result from this inconsistency, see W. M. Williams, *The Sociology of an English Village: Gosforth,* London: Routledge and Kegan Paul, 1956, pp. 83–84.
[20] *Op. cit.,* pp. 8ff.

only 2,879, or 23 per cent, were also listed in one of the twelve *Social Registers.*[21]

III. LOCAL-COMMUNITY STATUS

We turn now to the examination of the special functions and independence of our third variable, "local-community status." Where a society is so small that the local community and the total society are coterminous, the evaluations made of individuals and their families will, of course, be the same in both. But where local community and larger society diverge, as they certainly do in modern industrial society, and as they do also even in many of the non-industrial societies we know about, individuals and families will be evaluated by two different standards, one for the contributions made to the local community, a second for contributions to the larger society. Each of these two collectivities has problems and functions of its own, and each values individuals and families in the light of its own special needs. The problems of each local community—its economic security and growth, its services to the young, its attractiveness as a place to realize one's interests and values, its conflicts and harmony, its continuity of tradition and change—are different from those of the larger society, though always related, of course. Individuals and families who serve the local community welfare more and less well earn a correspondingly higher or lower "local-community status."[22]

The brief and not exhaustive list of local community problems just presented has had to be put in abstract form because of the nearly endless variety in which such problems concretely present themselves. Perhaps we can get a better sense of the concreteness and reality of these local community problems by recalling the Lynds' description of the contributions made by the "X" family to Middletown.[23] The "X" family, reports the Lynds, give "increasingly large public benefactions"; they have a "long list of philanthropies." "Half a dozen other family names in Middletown are associated with the city's industrial development, but none of them so com-

[21] *Ibid.,* p. 29.

[22] An excellent recent survey and critique of the study of the local community in American sociology—Harold F. Kaufman, "Toward an Interactional Conception of Community," *Social Forces,* 38 (October, 1959), pp. 8–17—would seem to indicate, by its lack of reference to local community status, that this is an area of analysis and investigation neglected by sociologists of the community. For a classical analysis and empirical investigation showing that local communities exist and face their own special problems even within the great metropolis, in this case Chicago, see Morris Janowitz, *The Community Press in an Urban Setting,* Glencoe, Ill.: Free Press, 1952.

[23] Robert S. and Helen M. Lynd, *Middletown in Transition,* New York: Harcourt, Brace, 1937, Ch. III.

pletely *symbolizes the city's achievements.*"[24] They are "men who never spared themselves in business or civic affairs." "The X family sincerely regards itself as unusually scrupulous in looking out for its workers." "A member of the X family is president of Middletown's school board." "Both the Y.M.C.A. and the Y.W.C.A. buildings are X philanthropies." And finally, to become really concrete: "Among the family's other contributions . . . extensive gymnasium at the college and the college Arts Building—with its handsome auditorium for public lectures and recitals . . . the donation of the ground and the equipping of the spacious local airport; the rejuvenation of the local county fair . . . the donation of an entire city block containing an old mansion as headquarters for the American Legion; an important contribution toward . . . a large field house and athletic field for high-school sports; a city golf course . . . the development of the city's park system. . . A number of local churches . . . have been helped in their building programs by X generosity. . . . "[25]

One good indicator of the existence of "local-community status" is the distinction commonly made by members of a local community between "old-timers" (those who have identified with and served the community) and "new-comers" (those who have not yet helped the community deal with its special problems). The Lynds refer to "this cleavage according to length of residence" and also to its relativity, since some people who had been in Middletown for ten years were still considered "new people" by those who had served the community longer.[26] This folk distinction, which is nonetheless sociologically significant, between "old-timers" and "new-comers" also turns up in survey research studies of social stratification when the respondents are freely allowed to suggest their own views in response to the question "What different kinds of people would you say live around here?"[27] Two recent English studies provide comparative evidence for the importance of length of membership for local-community status. In the rural community of Gosforth, says Williams, the newcomer "is, and always will be, an 'offcomer' and as such is thought to be of lower status than any of the natives in the same class. . . . Estimates of the time one is required to live in the parish before being 'accepted' vary from twenty to forty-five years."[28] And in the East London Borough of Bethnal Green, Young and Willmot describe the "sense of community, that is, a feeling

[24] Emphasis inserted.

[25] Since the Lynds stress the moral significance of the control over Middletown's life which these benefactions give the "X" family, it should be explicitly stated that this is an important problem not of primary concern here. The "X" family's activities are used only to illustrate the wide variety of services that individuals and families can perform for a local community.

[26] Robert S. and Helen M. Lynd, *Middletown,* New York: Harcourt Brace, 1929, p. 480, fn. 3.

[27] See Barber, *op. cit.,* p. 194.

[28] *Op. cit.,* p. 106.

of solidarity between people who occupy the common territory, which springs from the fact that people and their families have lived there a long time."[29] And finally, to take an example from a quite different type of society, Bellah reports that in Tokugawa Japan, "There was another axis of status distinction depending on the length of family residence in the village, the old 'original' families having the highest status."[30]

Although the terms, "old-timers" and "new-comers" would seem to say so, it is not length of residence for its own sake which this folk idiom is singling out. That it is, rather, commitment and service to the local community, opportunities for which are, of course, partly dependent on the length of time spent in the community and on the point in time of the community's history at which the individual or his family arrived, is clearly brought out in Merton, West, and Jahoda's study of a planned housing community, Craftown.[31] In Craftown, these researchers tell us, among the members of the community themselves, "pioneers are distinguished from those who came afterwards . . . in status." The "pioneers" are not just those who came sooner than the "new-comers." They are those who came earlier and who also served the community in its "time of troubles." The "pioneers" were those who had established and manned all the essential services of Craftown in the early days, when it had none to start with: the township committee, the cooperative store, the volunteer police and fire departments, the nursery and child care center, and a variety of other organizations devoted to the needs of the local community. It was no wonder that they had a deeper commitment to Craftown, a greater intention to stay there permanently, and a higher local-community status, than the "newcomers." As Merton and his colleagues put it, "the pioneers telling of how they won over numerous difficulties for the common good are in effect validating their right to distinctive status."

"Local-community status," then, is an independent aspect of social reality with its own functions and range of variability. And this variability, as we have already suggested, is independent of the variability of social class positions; the two are not in a one-to-one relationship. Unfortunately, our evidence here is unsystematic and scanty, more so than with regard to the relationship between "family status" and social class position, though still sufficient to bear out the analysis. We may start again with some evidence from the Lynds' study of Middletown. In their first report, on Middletown in the 1920's, the Lynds pointed out that two upper-class families varied considerably in their local-community status. "The most prized citizens in Middletown," they said, "are the millionaire philanthro-

[29] *Op. cit.,* p. 89.

[30] R. N. Bellah, *Tokugawa Religion,* Glencoe, Ill.: Free Press, 1957, p. 42.

[31] R. K. Merton, P. S. West, and M. Jahoda, *Patterns of Social Life,* unpublished ms., esp. Ch. IV, "The Meanings of Craftown for Pioneers and Newcomers."

pists, [the "X" family] . . . Another family of large wealth but small interest in Middletown has little place in the activities or affections of the city."[32] And in the second report, the "Y" family is said to be still "as inconspicuous in Middletown as the X family is conspicuous. A prominent citizen . . . characterizes them as follows: '. . . they have no civic pride whatever. They . . . are all for themselves and contribute to Middletown only what they are forced by circumstances to give . . . they lead a narrow life, aloof from the local scene here . . . still have a feeling they don't quite belong here.' "[33] The "Y" family, for reasons which are not specified, seem only to "live there."[34] Even if it is a minority type, however, the "Y" family type deserves study.

Baltzell also refers to examples of the "Y" family type, "the new executive elite in Huntington Valley" who do not aspire to high "local-community status" in Philadelphia.[35] This is the situation, of just "living there," in which many middle- and upper-class commuters find themselves in some of the older local suburban communities of all our metropolitan areas. In these communities the lower-middle class "natives" or "old-timers" have a higher "local-community status" than the middle- and upper-class "new-comer" commuters because, unlike the latter, they are proud of the local community, serve as its legislators and officials, its voluntary firemen, its library trustees, and in other roles essential to and valued in the local community. Indeed, in many cases, it is the occupational roles and social class position of the middle- and upper-class commuters which take them out of the local community and make it hard for them to serve the local community's special needs. In Merton's terms, putting matters of influence aside, they are "cosmopolitans" whose world is chiefly elsewhere, in contrast to the lower-middle class "locals," whose occupational roles and social involvement are both located in the immediate local community.[36] Thus, in this situation, social class position and "local-community status" have an inverse correlation.[37]

[32] *Op. cit.,* 1929, p. 481, fn. 4.

[33] *Op. cit.,* 1937, p. 91.

[34] The "Y" family may be less typical among business families than the "X" family. F. X. Sutton and his colleagues have suggested, in their study of the American businessman's ideology, that "the political localism of the business creed . . . corresponds to the fact that businessmen have higher status locally than nationally. . . . Businessmen have relatively more prestige as individuals within a local community than in the nation at large. . . ." Sutton, *et al., The American Business Creed,* Cambridge, Mass.: Harvard University Press, 1956, pp. 377ff.

[35] *Op. cit.,* p. 214.

[36] R. K. Merton, "Patterns of Influence: Local and Cosmopolitan Influentials," in his *Social Theory and Social Structure,* rev. ed., Glencoe, Ill.: Free Press, 1957. [See Selection 18 above.—R. L. W.]

[37] In his study of a small, mid-western, liberal arts college as a local community, Gouldner found that the "locals" on the faculty were more "popular" (had higher local-community status?) than the "cosmopolitans." Like the suburban commuter as

One last bit of evidence for the independence of social class position and "local-community status." Recent studies of the influence structure of American and other local communities have shown that there is not one, but several different patterns of influence-structure in these communities. Moreover, they have shown that in one of these patterns, the middle- and even lower-middle class "old-timers" have more local influence, and presumably also a higher "local-community status" as a result, than the upper-class "new-comers" who have been sent to the local community to manage the local branch factory of some national corporation but who purposely refrain from participating in the problems of the place where they define themselves as "transients."[38] Social class position and "local-community status" and its associated influence patterns seem to be neither in principle nor in practice positively correlated.

CONCLUSION

In this paper, through theoretical analysis and empirical evidence, I have tried to show the independent functions of, and the absence of one-to-one relationships among three variables—social class position, family status, and local-community status—that are often lumped together in theories and researches on "social stratification." My purpose has been to suggest a better set of concepts for understanding the behavorial reality of American and other societies. Behind this immediate purpose lies a general conviction about present theory and research in social stratification. The conviction is that this specialized branch of sociology has contributed much to our knowledge in the recent past but is now turning into a dead-end with its crude and omnibus conceptions of "social stratification" and "social class." For an understanding of the multivariate reality that is concealed by our crude concepts, we need both conceptual refinement and research based on operationally specific indicators of the several variables this refinement will reveal to us.

---

opposed to the "old-timer," the "cosmopolitan" as opposed to the "local" on a college or university faculty only "lives there." See A. W. Gouldner, "Cosmopolitans and Locals: Toward an Analysis of Latent Social Roles," *Administrative Science Quarterly*, 2 (Dec., 1957), pp. 281–306, and 2 (March, 1958), pp. 444–480.

[38] For critical reassessments of this field, which are in part based on their own empirical research, see: Peter Rossi, "Community Decision-making," *Administrative Science Quarterly*, I (March, 1957), pp. 415–43; and, Nelson W. Polsby, "The Sociology of Community Power: A Reassessment," *Social Forces*, 37 (March, 1959), pp. 232–236. Among the empirical researches most relevant to the point being made here are: Robert O. Schulze and Leonard U. Blumberg, "The Determination of Local Power Elites," *American Journal of Sociology*, LXIII (November, 1957), pp. 290–96; Robert O. Schulze, "The Role of Economic Dominants in Community Power Structure," *American Sociological Review*, 23 (February, 1958), pp. 3–9; and, Nelson W. Polsby, "Three Problems in the Analysis of Community Power," *American Sociological Review*, 24 (December, 1959), pp. 796–803.

21. The Community Social Profile

BY IRWIN T. SANDERS

Sociologists, who for a long time have been subjecting the community to intensive study, are frequently asked by action-oriented professional persons to assist in the preparation of the studies they undertake or to review the results they have obtained. Such assistance, which includes the careful analysis of all available statistical data, must go beyond these figures to community characteristics not already quantified. What is called for in many cases is a short-run, easily administered method which, though lacking in completeness of detail, nevertheless is accurate as far as it goes and at the same time penetrating enough to be helpful in program planning. This is a report of one such method which, through a clearly-formulated reconnaissance, makes possible the preparation of a community social profile essentially sociological in content. Its utility has been tested over a twenty-year period in states as widely diverse as New York, Alabama, Kentucky, and Massachusetts.

THE FEATURES OF THE METHOD

THE RESEARCH TEAM

In any short-cut approach there must be relatively little waste motion. Thus research assistants must already have some skill in interviewing, some knowledge of how the data are to be processed, and some understanding of the community as a sociological concept. The tasks confronting such a research team are the interviewing of from 25 to 40 people in a local community, pulling together pertinent statistical support, and collecting available maps, documents, and newspapers which have some bearing upon the community situation. It is important to stress that this is essentially a sociological and not a social action undertaking. Its purpose is to describe competently and economically the chief social traits of the community; it is not designed to train the untrained citizen in community survey techniques.

Where possible, four or five people are formed into a team in preference to the more extended labors of a lesser number. This builds more cross-

Reprinted with permission of the author and the American Sociological Association from Irwin T. Sanders, "The Community Social Profile," *American Sociological Review*, XXV, No. 1 (February, 1960), 75–77.

checking into the operation because more trained people are reacting to the community and interacting with each other. Ordinarily, each interviewer averages from two to three interviews per day, that is, ten to fifteen man-days in the cases of communities where 30 interviews suffice. Four or five workers can carry out the necessary data collection in less than a week's time.

DATA COLLECTION

As already indicated, the chief schedule is one designed for administration to community leaders who, as experience has shown, have more knowledge about the community since they are accustomed to think of problems in a broader context than those whose major interests center almost exclusively around their jobs and their own homesteads. Experience also shows that, far from presenting a united and closed front, these leaders reveal in their responses the existence of the major groupings and social divisions one must investigate.

The "Community Leader Schedule" has undergone some modifications through the years but it remains essentially open-ended. It calls for data about the informant, social organizations and their leaders, and the "institutional" areas of church, school, economy, recreation, and local government. It asks what the informant likes best about the community and what he considers to be its chief problems, about social issues over the past five years, and major changes underway; and it asks the informant to list eight people whom he considers to be important community leaders and to give the reasons for their selection. Many of these questions, such as the one requesting the listing of community leaders, are carefully phrased and presented to each informant in a standardized way. But usually the main purpose of the questions is to prompt the informant to talk about his community with respect to certain topics set forth on the schedule. When these comments are fully recorded it turns out that what some people have called a "deceptively simple" schedule has elicited a wealth of valuable information.

But who are these key leaders to be interviewed? How are they determined? Before beginning a community study an effort is made to identify some of them, with whom appointments are arranged by telephone. When this is not possible the first three or four schedules are "wasted," that is, people are contacted who occupy positions which would seem to give them some knowledge of the community and who, in addition to answering other questions, are asked to name the eight most important leaders.[1] After two or three interviews the tabulation of the names mentioned may be initiated and

[1] This approach may be compared with the approaches followed by Floyd Hunter, Delbert C. Miller, Peter H. Rossi, Robert O. Schulze, and others who have studied "power structure," "influentials," "economic dominants," and other types of local elites.

subsequently interviews held with the "most frequently mentioned." Communities vary, of course, in the extent to which the leadership is concentrated and the frequency with which the same people are mentioned. Nevertheless the leadership structure begins to emerge quite clearly after only a few interviews with well-informed citizens. In some studies, even of cities of 100,000 inhabitants, twenty interviews cover all of the leaders mentioned as many as three times, illustrated by the actual distribution for such a city shown in Table 1.

TABLE 1. FREQUENCY DISTRIBUTION OF MENTIONS AS KEY COMMUNITY LEADERS, NEW BEDFORD, MASSACHUSETTS, 1958

No. Times Listed (Out of 23 Possibilities)	No. Persons Listed This No. of Times	Total Mentions (Column 1 × Column 2)
18	1	18
16	1	16
15	1	15
12	1	12
11	1	11
10	1	10
8	2	16
5	6	30
4	2	8
3	4	12
2	8	16
1	34	34
	62 people	198 mentions

It is assumed that completing the total universe of those named as leaders, which is the crucial aspect of this method, would not have changed the rank order materially, nor would it have brought to light more than five or six other individuals not previously named. Long before all of those listed have been interviewed one is able to predict many of the answers an informant will give, but the interviewing is continued in the hope that exceptions to the rule will be uncovered and thus reveal facets of community life that might not otherwise emerge. The team members find little difficulty in deciding where to "cut-off" the interviewing for they agree that they have gone well beyond the point of diminishing returns.

The leaders, however, do not necessarily represent all of the important social divisions which have been identified in the community. In this case, interviews are conducted with the spokesmen for these other groupings, starting with those suggested by the community leaders when they were asked to describe the community's significant social divisions. The interviews with these subleaders seek to determine how the divisions they represent fit into the overall community framework and only incidentally delve into the psychological problems of those involved.

Another aspect of the collection of data deals with contradictions in perceptions on the part of the informants. It is assumed from the beginning that these differential perceptions will be encountered, but it is expected that in some measure they will be consistent with socio-economic characteristics and other social traits uncovered. When these perceptions run counter to previous experience or to theoretical expectations further interviewing is required to account for the variation. In such cases, some leader already interviewed who has demonstrated a capacity to analyze such matters objectively may be revisited and asked to clear up the seeming difficulty.

The interview materials are checked with data collected from other sources. These include local histories, promotional literature prepared by the Chamber of Commerce, surveys and studies in such applied fields as health and education, statistical series of various kinds, and local newspapers. All of this material not only serves to cross-check what informants say but provides a depth of detail which proves most useful in preparing the community profile.

ANALYSIS AND PREPARATION OF THE SOCIAL PROFILE

As soon as the field work has been completed the research team meets to decide on those social traits[2] which require stress if a useful picture of the community is to be obtained. This selection is necessary on two counts: description of all traits would not be in order even if there were data available since the purpose of the social profile is to highlight rather than to catalog the characteristics of the community; there are some traits not central to the inquiry about which the team believes that insufficient data have been collected for an adequate treatment. Both the research team and the reader need to keep in mind what can be stated with confidence and what should be set forth as mere conjecture.

By using practically the same schedule in every community almost the same ground is covered in each study, permitting some comparability between communities. This very comparability allows the selection of a special combination of traits for a particular community as the pattern best describing its social features. This is why Tables of Contents of social profiles will read differently. Yet these variations grow out of what is essentially a comparative approach.

The traits to be described form the working outline in terms of which the analysis of the data proceeds. The data relating to each trait are excerpted on cards so that the person writing up that section will have before him all pertinent comments. Different team members are assigned different topics

[2] These traits include those that sociologists would conventionally look into: social divisions and other evidences of stratification; institutional behavior (religion, local government, economy, education, family, recreation); major organizations and their interaction; evidences of major current changes; leadership structure; issues or major community problems as defined locally; indications of competing or conflicting value systems.

in keeping with their training and with the types of informants they had encountered as the interviewing appointments were made.

Needless to say, any differences in points of view among the team members about a particular trait are ironed out by re-examination of the data, by a telephone call to some competent local informant, or by another field trip to the community. In preparing the study budget provision is always made for a final "clean-up trip" when the report itself is nearing completion. But such a trip is seldom necessary if the methods outlined above have been carefully followed.

UTILITY AND APPLICATION OF THE APPROACH

This approach, of course, has a serious limitation: it is idiosyncratic, being designed to gather information about one community to serve some particular purpose. Those who engage in several successive studies of this sort gain a general understanding of community structure and processes although the methods used are not designed to demonstrate its validity. Therefore this approach does not have the cumulative value that other types of research may possess.[3] Granting this limitation, it in no way reduces the utility of a well-executed reconnaissance report for those professionally interested in local social action programs.

In New England recently some of its possible applications have proven very interesting. An industrial firm wanted to know which of two New England towns was a better location for a new industrial facility on the basis of social traits alone. Another concern was interested in the connection between the controversy over industrial zoning and the general community traits; a third wished to learn whether or not a given community was a place to which engineers would be attracted.[4] In each of these cases the point was accepted that the easiest way to answer the central question was to use the reconnaissance method described here. Only after the overall social profile had been completed could a special "peel-off" report be prepared concerning the specific questions which had initiated the larger study. This same approach is adapted for use by local health departments, planning boards, school boards, library boards, and United Community Services, the representatives of which see their groups' activities in a new perspective when confronted with the overall picture provided by the community social profile.

[3] Samuel A. Stouffer is directing a project, in which the present writer is also engaged, designed to break through the idiosyncratic limitation of this approach. Through the use of special schedules and pre-determined types of informants, an effort is being made to standardize information gained about cleavages, issues, and key leadership structure so that many communities can be studied simultaneously and generalizations can be derived. Field tests of the instruments are still underway.

[4] These queries and the resulting studies have been channeled through the Community Analysis Division of Associates for International Research, Inc., a private applied social science research company located in Cambridge, Massachusetts, of which the writer has been serving as part-time Research Director.

22. Comparative Urban Research and Community Decision-Making[*]

BY MICHAEL AIKEN AND ROBERT R. ALFORD

Research on urban politics, community power structure, and local decision-making exhibits a diverse and checkered pattern of development in the literature in political science and sociology in the United States in the past two decades. Starting with the publication in 1953 of Floyd Hunter's *Community Power Structure,* sociologists and political scientists have conducted research about politics and decision-making in numerous American communities.

In retrospect, these studies of community power constituted a sterile debate over the appropriate methodology (reputational, decision-making, positional) and the correct generalizations about the decision-making process in American communities—elitist or pluralistic—and produced little real understanding of systematic variations in the decision-making capability, and the consequences of varying power and decision-making arrangements for local citizens. In addition, most studies of community power were case studies of single communities, although there were some occasional comparative studies of either community power (Barth, 1961; Agger, et al., 1964; D'Antonio, et al., 1961; D'Antonio and Form, 1965; Miller, 1958a and 1958b), community performance (Williams and Adrian, 1963), or the formal political structure (Kammerer, et al., 1963) that included from two to eight communities. But the unrepresentativeness of these studies in terms of such factors as city size and regional location (most were done within a

Reprinted with permission of the authors and publisher from Michael Aiken and Robert R. Alford, "Comparative Urban Research and Community Decision-Making," *The New Atlantis* 1, no. 2 (Winter, 1970): 85–110.

[*] This research was supported in part by funds granted to the Institute for Research on Poverty, University of Wisconsin, pursuant to provisions of the Economic Opportunity Act of 1964. We were aided greatly in this research by Louis S. Katz, Chief, Statistics Branch, and Robert S. Kenison, Attorney Advisor, both of the Housing Assistance Administration, Department of Housing and Urban Development. Neither is responsible for errors of fact or interpretation, however. We are also grateful to the Institute for Research on Poverty for its research and administrative support, and to Elizabeth Balcer, Janet Jensen, and Ann Wallace for their competent and vital research assistance.

single state or geographical region) limited the possible insights into the regularities of patterns of community decision-processes and performances.

There are at least two critical questions from this literature on community politics and decision-making that remain to be answered. The first is that of *consequences*. That is, what difference does it make for community outputs if many actors or few actors, if only business elites or if multiple elites, are actively involved in formulating policies for local government? Second, what are the *intervening processes* of community decision-making that account for variations in such outputs? The dominant values in a local community, the degree to which power is concentrated, the centralization and efficiency of the formal structure of government, and the degree of community integration have each been proposed as explanations of the variations in the capacity of local communities. . . .

We have gathered a considerable amount of data from a variety of sources on each of the 1,654 incorporated urban places of size 10,000 or more in the United States in 1960, although most of our analysis on community decision-making, innovation, and policy outputs has been limited to the subset of 676 cities that had a population size of 25,000 or more in 1960. We also have data on SMSA's, counties, and states regarded as possibly important elements of the environment within which cities function. None of these data are reported in this paper, however.

In this paper we shall summarize our findings about three types of policy outputs: public housing, urban renewal, and the War on Poverty reported in more detail elsewhere (Cf., Aiken and Alford, 1969, 1970a, 1970b). In earlier discussions of these findings we have characterized such policy outputs as various aspects of community innovation: 1) the incidence of innovation in these policy areas, 2) the speed of innovation in each of these policy areas, and 3) the level of output or performance of the innovative activity. In each of the three papers examining these decision-outcomes, we found that there were extremely high interrelationships among these three indicators of innovation within each policy area, and various community attributes were similarly related to each of the three aspects of innovation. Therefore, in this summary of our findings, we shall only include one measure of output in public housing, urban renewal, and the War on Poverty. The reader should bear in mind, however, that if either of the other two aspects of community innovation in public housing, urban renewal, or the War on Poverty were substituted, the results and conclusions would be the same as those included here. These measures are described below.

The strategy employed here has also been used by a number of researchers in sociology and political science to study such community decision outcomes as fluoridation (Crain, Katz, and Rosenthal, 1969; Pinard, 1963), urban renewal (Hawley, 1963; Straits, 1965; Wolfinger and Field, 1966;

Crain and Rosenthal, 1967), desegregation (Crain and Rosenthal, 1967; Dye, 1968), municipal expenditures (Linebery and Fowler, 1967) and other referenda (Wilson and Banfield, 1964). In each case the researchers used some community attribute, or set of attributes, to infer the intervening process. Nowhere have these various explanations of community decision-making dynamics been brought together and critically compared with respect to a common body of data. These five theories are:

1) *Political Culture:* Cities dominated by groups with "public regarding values" are hypothesized to be more innovative with respect to policies benefitting the community as a whole than cities dominated by groups with "private-regarding values." (Banfield and Wilson, 1963; Wilson and Banfield, 1964).

2) *Concentration or Diffusion of Community Power:* There are three aspects of this argument: concentration of systemic power (Hawley, 1963), diffusion of power through mass citizen participation (Crain and Rosenthal, 1967), and centralization of elite power (Clark, 1968a). In each case the hypothesis is the same, namely, the greater the concentration of power, the greater the degree of innovation. Conversely, the greater the diffusion of power, the lower the degree of innovation.

3) *Centralization of Formal Political Structure:* Cities with centralized administrative arrangements and a strong mayor, that is, cities with city manager or partisan mayor-council governmental structures are hypothesized to be more innovative (Crain, Katz, and Rosenthal, 1969).

4) *Community Differentiation and Continuity:* Older and larger cities have been hypothesized to be more bureaucratic, and consequently less receptive to policy innovations, suggesting that younger and smaller cities should exhibit higher policy innovation (Dye, 1968).

5) *Community Integration:* Cities in which community integration breaks down or is extremely low have a lower probability of innovation or other collective actions. Consequently, community innovation should be highest in integrated communities (Coleman, 1957; Pinard, 1963).

We have listed these five explanations separately and shall discuss them in greater detail below because it is possible to conceive of them as five independent theories of community innovation and policy outputs. We turn now to a description of the three output measures, some discussion of sources of data used in this paper, and a description of the methodology employed here.

DATA AND METHODS

An understanding of our findings presumes some knowledge about the various policy outputs included in this study: public housing, urban renewal, and the War on Poverty. . . . The policy outputs included here have certain characteristics in common. First, each requires some degree of initiative by the local community. In the federal system of the United States, local communities have a high degree of local autonomy relative to some European nations such as, for example, France or Spain. Unless some local agency takes some initiative and a favorable decision is rendered locally, a community cannot enter these programs. Only two of the programs discussed here—public housing and urban renewal—required approval by the local governing body, however. A second characteristic of these policy outputs is that there is an organization in the local community—a "community decision organization" (Warren, 1967a and 1967b)—that has been specifically created to coordinate and oversee the program. Third, most funds involved come from outside the community, from the federal government, although in each case some local money has to be provided. Fourth, none of these decisions typically involved mass participation by citizens. The decisions are made, in almost all cases, by representative organizations—the community decisions organization, the municipal government, and the city council—although community citizens and groups may be utilized at critical junctures to support or perhaps oppose a decision. The decision-making dynamics of these policy areas may not be found in other types of decision such as school bonds or other referenda. . . .

We do not have space here to include the results of a wide variety of multivariate analyses which have been performed on the data in an attempt to isolate the variables which independently explain the most variance. Suffice it to say that the age of a city, its population size, the per cent of foreign stock, and one or more of the need measures, including the nonwhite composition, most consistently explain more variance in these three community innovations than any of the other characteristics. Most of these variables are significantly related to the dependent variables, even after multivariate controls have been applied. The amount of variance explained by most other variables is small, and need alone explains little of the variance in these measures of outputs. The reader is referred to other papers which present these data and their analysis in greater detail (Aiken and Alford, 1969, 1970a, and 1970b). . . .

AN ALTERNATIVE EXPLANATION

Let us start negatively by reviewing the rejected explanations. The global properties of political ethos, decentralization, and integration seemed to fare most poorly. That is, characterizations of the city as a whole, those which cannot be reduced to properties of groups and organizations, seem both to use concepts most removed from the available data and be supported most inadequately by them. If anything, the data seem to point in the direction of communities with high outputs having characteristics exactly opposite

of centralization and integration. Cities that appear to be most heterogeneous, differentiated, and decentralized—as indicated by ethnicity, a large
working class, nonwhite composition, size and the qualitative data on centralization in the works of Clark (1968) and Aiken (1970)—are most likely
to have high policy outputs. An alternative theory of community policy outputs—at least for such programs as urban renewal, low-rent housing, the
War on Poverty, and model cities—must begin with the proposition that
successful performance in such programs is more frequently attained in
decentralized, heterogeneous, and probably fragmented community systems.

Our tentative alternative explanation is that community outputs of the
kind examined here must involve a two-level analysis. First, an explication
of the kinds of community attributes which create the conditions for the
development of certain types, number, and qualities or organizations that
are critical for innovations of the type under discussion here, and, second,
the kinds of attributes of organizations and their environments—or organization sets to use the term of William Evan (1966)—that facilitate the
speed of implementation and subsequent performances of the innovation.
To some extent these levels are the same thing examined from two points
of view.

With respect to the first, three kinds of concepts seem to be most important: the quality and stability of interorganizational ties, the accumulation of experience and information in a community system (continuity),
and structural differentiation. Interorganizational networks are conceived as
properties of community systems that are developed historically through the
experience of organizational units and their leaders with each other. If the
population of a community is relatively stable, these interorganizational networks are not likely to be disrupted by the continuous influx of new citizens
and organizations, and thus there is the greater potential for increasing their
capacity for coordination over time.

The degree of historical continuity in a community structure—especially
as it affects interorganizational networks—may also influence innovation
and subsequent performance. Presumably older cities have had a longer time
for existing organizations to have worked out patterns of interactions, al-
liances, factions, or coalitions. In such communities, the state of knowledge
in the community system about the orientations, needs, and probable reactions to varying proposals for community action is likely to be quite high,
thus increasing the probability of developing a sufficiently high level of
coordination in order to implement successfully a community innovation.

The degree of structural differentiation and complexity of a community
may also influence policy outputs for two reasons. First, larger cities are
likely to have more organizations devoted to specific kinds of decision-areas—
i.e., more likely to have a redevelopment agency, a housing agency, a com-

munity action agency, a city development agency for model cities, welfare councils, and other community decision organizations. Such organizations are likely to have larger, more specialized, and more professionalized staffs to provide the technical, administrative, and political knowledge required to innovate successfully not only within their organizations, but also innovations requiring the activation of interorganizational relationships and establishment of critical coalitions. Secondly, it is precisely in the larger, more structurally differentiated communities that coalitions that can implement an innovation will be easiest to establish. If we assume that all organizational units in a community do not have to be mobilized in a decision such as urban renewal, but rather that only a limited number of organizational units can suffice to bring about a decision, then it follows that in large, highly differentiated communities a lower proportion of organizations will participate in such decisions, and that there will be wider latitude in selecting organizations for these critical coalitions. The more highly differentiated or specialized a community system, the higher the proportion of decisions that are likely to be made by subsystems and the less likely the entire system will be activated.

We thus suggest that these three properties of communities—structural differentiation, the accumulation of experience and information, and the stability and extensiveness of interorganizational networks—may contribute to the capacity of a community to generate policy outputs. While we have no direct measures of these properties and while these suggestions are only inferential, such imagery about the factors involved does appear to be consistent with our findings about the characteristics of communities that exhibit the greatest quantity of policy outputs.

Let us turn to concepts and hypotheses suitable for the second perspective, that of characteristics of organizational structures and their interorganizational field. Community systems can be viewed as interorganizational fields in which the basic interacting units are *centers of power*. A center of power can be defined as an organization which possesses a high degree of autonomy, resources, and cohesion. The linking mechanisms among centers of power in a community we call *interfaces*, although it should be pointed out that interfaces are more than the current set of interorganizational relationships in the community, and more importantly include the historical accumulation of knowledge and experience among various centers of power. This accumulation of knowledge and experience is, of course, at one level a property of the entire community system, and community systems could conceivably be differentiated according to the state and nature of interfaces. An *issue arena* is defined as the organization set of centers of power which must be or are activated on a given issue in order to effectuate a decision (Evan, 1966). The "issue arena" involved in most innovations will require the participation of only a few of the organizations that exist in the community system. In one sense, this proposition is simply a spelling out of what is meant by "structural differentiation" or "functional specialization."

One could hypothesize that the greater the number of centers of power in a community and the pervasive and encompassing are the interfaces in the community system, the higher the probability that a community innovation in a given issue arena will occur. The reasoning has been partially alluded to before. The more choice among units in the system—centers of power—and the greater the state of information about organizational actors, the higher the probability that a coalition sufficient to make a decision will take place.

In addition, the extent to which the interorganizational field is "turbulent" may also influence policy outputs (Terreberry, 1968). Where many people are moving out of a community, the existing historically developed network of organizational relationships may be relatively undisturbed, except insofar as the fact of migration out indicates an economic or perhaps political crisis which existing institutions cannot handle. Conversely, where many people are moving in, bringing with them different ideas about the appropriate functions of local government, and perhaps creating demands for new services, newly established organizations may be severely limited since they are less likely to have established organizational networks available to them which can aid in achieving an adequate level of coordination.

One aspect of this increased capacity to coordinate over time will be the emergence of specialized centers of power—"community decision organizations"—whose function it is to initiate special types of innovation, mobilize support for them, and either carry out the activities required by the decision or else organize and supervise those agencies charged with such activities (Warren, 1967a, 1967b). And, of course, the characteristics of these organizations such as extensive interorganizational ties (Aiken and Hage, 1968; Thompson, 1965), professionalism of staff, degree of internal differentiation, or number of resources available, to name only a few, will also be critical to understand the quality and quantity of policy outputs. Community action agencies, housing authorities, welfare councils, and health departments are examples of such organizations.

The community decision organization, then, becomes a special type of center of power whose mission it is to supervise the planning, coordination, and delivery of a community function or activity. There is a very high likelihood that the professional staffs of such organizations will generate future innovations. For example, Walter describes how professionals such as the city manager and head of the local housing authority were primarily responsible for innovations in urban renewal, public housing, and a new city hall in Arcadia (Walter, 1962). However, it is entirely possible that the community conditions that lead to the introduction of an innovation in a given activity—structural differentiation and historical continuity in the inter-organizational field—may not be the factors that are most conducive to high levels of performance by such organizations. Once the innovation has been introduced, as James Vanecko of the National Opinion Research Center has suggested in a personal communication, community decision organizations may seek to establish autonomy within their issue arenas: relatively tight relationships with cooperating organizations and an exclusive mandate from other community decision organizations. Communities with high levels of output performance may well be those in which relatively autonomous issue arenas have emerged. Such autonomy cannot be complete because certain critical community decision organizations—such as the city government—play a part in a multiplicity of issue arenas.

REFERENCES

Agger, Robert, Daniel Goldrich and Bert E. Swanson. 1964. *The Rulers and the Ruled.* New York: Wiley.

Aiken, Michael. 1970. "The Distribution of Community Power: Structural Bases and Social Consequences." In Michael Aiken and Paul E. Mott (eds.), *The Structure of Community Power.* New York: Random House.

Aiken, Michael, and Robert R. Alford. 1969. "Community Structure and the War on Poverty." Unpublished manuscript.

————. 1970a. "Community Structure and Innovation: The Case of Urban Renewal," *American Sociological Review* 35 (August): 655–665.

————. 1970b. "Community Structure and Innovation: The Case of Public Housing," *American Political Science Review* 641 (September): 843–864.

Aiken, Michael, and Jerald Hage. 1968. "Organizational Interdependence and Intraorganizational Structure." *American Sociological Review* 33 (December): 912–930.

Banfield, Edward C., and James Q. Wilson. 1963. *City Politics.* Cambridge: Harvard University Press.

Barth, Ernest A. T. 1961. "Community Influence Systems: Structure and Change." *Social Forces* 40 (October): 58–63.

Clark, Terry N. 1968. "Community Structure, Decision-Making, Budget Expenditures, and Urban Renewal in 51 American Communities." *American Sociological Review* 33 (August): 576–593.

Clark, Terry N., et al. 1968. "Discipline, Method, Community Structure and Decision-Making: the Role and Limitations of the Sociology of Knowledge." *American Sociologist* 3 (August): 214–217.

Coleman, James S. 1957. *Community Conflict.* New York: Free Press.

Crain, Robert L., and Donald B. Rosenthal. 1967. "Community Status as a Dimension of Local Decision-Making." *American Sociological Review* 32 (December) : 970–984.

D'Antonio, William V., and William H. Form. 1965. *Influentials in Two Border Cities: A Study in Community Decision-Making.* South Bend, Ind.: University of Notre Dame Press.

D'Antonio, William V., William H. Form, Charles P. Loomis, and Eugene C. Erickson. 1961. "Institutional and Occupational Representation in Eleven Community Influence Systems." *American Sociological Review* 26 (June) : 440–446.

Dye, Thomas R. 1968. "Urban School Segregation: A Comparative Analysis." *Urban Affairs Quarterly* 4 (December) : 141–165.

Evan, William M. 1966. "The Organization Set: Toward a Theory of Interorganizational Relations." In James D. Thompson (ed.), *Approaches to Organizational Design.* Pittsburgh: University of Pittsburgh Press.

Hawley, Amos H. 1963. "Community Power Structure and Urban Renewal Success." *American Journal of Sociology* 68 (January) : 422–431.

Kammerer, Gladys M., Charles D. Farris, John M. DeGrove, and Alfred B. Clubok. 1963. *The Urban Political Community: Profiles in Town Politics.* Boston: Houghton Mifflin.

Lineberry, Robert L., and Edmund P. Fowler. 1967. "Reformism and Public Policies in American Cities." *American Political Science Review* 61 (September) : 701–716.

Miller, Delbert C. 1958a. "Industry and Community Power Structure: A Comparative Study of an American and an English City." *American Sociological Review* 23 (February) : 9–15.

————. 1958b. "Decision-Making Cliques in Community Power Structures: A Comparative Study of an American and an English City." *American Journal of Sociology* 64 (November) : 299–309.

Pinard, Maurice. 1963. "Structural Attachments and Political Support in Urban Politics: The Case of Fluoridation Referendums." *American Journal of Sociology* 68 (March) : 513–526.

Straits, Bruce C. 1965. "Community Adoption and Implementation of Urban Renewal." *American Journal of Sociology* 71 (July) : 77–82.

Terreberry, Shirley. 1968. "The Evolution of Organizational Environments." *Administrative Science Quarterly* 12 (March) : 590–613.

Thompson, Victor A. 1965. "Bureaucracy and Innovation." *Administrative Science Quarterly* 10 (June) : 1–20.

Walter, Benjamin. 1962. "Political Decision-Making in Arcadia." In F. Stuart Chapin, Jr., and Shirley F. Weiss (eds.), *Urban Growth Dynamics.* New York: Wiley.

Warren, Roland L. 1967a. "Interaction of Community Decision Organizations: Some Basic Concepts and Needed Research." *Social Service Review* 41 (September) : 261–270.

————. 1967b. "The Interorganizational Field as a Focus for Investigation." *Administrative Science Quarterly* 12 (December) : 396–419.

Williams, Oliver P., and Charles R. Adrian. 1963. *Four Cities: A Study in Comparative Policy Making*. Philadelphia: University of Pennsylvania Press.

Wilson, James Q., and Edward C. Banfield. 1964. "Public-Regardingness as a Value Premise in Voting Behavior." *American Political Science Review* 58 (December) : 876–887.

Wolfinger, Raymond E., and John Osgood Field. 1966. "Political Ethos and the Structure of City Government." *American Political Science Review* 60 (June) : 308–326.

SECTION FOUR

Social Change at the Community Level

Introduction

One of the most interesting aspects of social behavior in American communities is the attempt, through concerted action, to bring about change. Many changes occur within communities on the basis of unplanned modifications in the structure of the population, the gradual growth or decline of industries, the constant competition for land use, the gradual development or infusion of new ideas or usages and discarding of old ones. But some kinds of change are deliberately brought about. The development of a new pattern of health services or of a program of low-cost housing, the adoption of a new plan of land use, the mounting of a campaign for industrial expansion, a concerted attempt to reduce juvenile delinquency or poverty— all are examples. How is it possible to organize efforts for community change, and what are some of the conditions of effectiveness of such efforts?

But to begin with, how is social change in the community to be considered? Actions are taking place constantly, of course, and many of these involve changed patterns of interaction, however large or small, important or insignificant, these may be. Events are reported daily in the newspapers which undoubtedly involve changes in some aspect of the community. Is each of these events to be considered a social change, or a series of them? Or is social change of yet a different nature, having to do with gradual modifications, none of which attracts sufficient attention to be reported as news? How is social change in the community to be defined?

These questions are addressed in a selection from a chapter of the book by Lowry Nelson, Charles E. Ramsey, and Coolie Verner, *Community Structure and Change*. Social change, they have pointed out, is related both to social problems and to the process of community development. It is related to social problems in the sense that some of the changes which occur are looked upon as social problems by the people of the community; in turn, some of the actions which they take with regard to these problems may themselves constitute social change. The organized deliberate actions which are taken in communities in order to cope with some problem or to effect some change are often denoted by the term *community development*. Thus, purposive social change is one of the types which must be considered.

Yet most social change is unplanned. Nelson and his associates assert that in order to constitute such social change, an event or process must "alter

246

the form of human relations and structures." They classify such changes as long-term trends, the transfer of a function from one social unit to another, or a shift in a fundamental aspect of one or more of the dimensions of the community.

Change may occur on the level of the total community, or it may occur at the level of the community's relationship to other area-bound social units, the "pancommunity level." A third level involves change within the elements and dimensions of community structure. Still a fourth level is in the relation of a component of the community such as the family or the school to other components.

One of the dynamic processes frequently in operation at the community level is controversy. Typically, such controversy centers on specific issues, the resolution of which occasions a contest between those taking opposing sides. Numerous studies of controversies in communities have been recorded and analyzed. Most often, however, these are reported as single episodes without an attempt being made to group a number of them for comparative study in order to make general statements about such uniformities as may be observable. In a brilliant work, James S. Coleman gathered together for systematic analysis the reports of a large number of such controversies. Using these as data, he developed a theory of the general nature and dynamics of such episodes of controversy.

The selection presented here is devoted to analyzing the dynamics of the process of controversy. Put in another way, it seeks to illuminate the factors which operate to move a controversy along from one stage to another, usually toward greater intensity. For one thing, the controversial issue itself often is redefined, frequently in the direction of expanding the area of controversy. Specific differences become generalized into larger, more inclusive ones. At the same time, disagreement on the issues becomes transformed into antagonism toward the opposite side. During the process, changes in the social organization of the community occur, as individuals and organizations gradually range themselves on one side or the other of the controversy. It becomes difficult to remain uncommitted. Partisan organizations emerge, as do new leaders. These latter often do not have a strong sense of identification with the community and the sense of constraint which such identification implies. Word-of-mouth communication, often in the form of unverified rumors, helps to intensify the controversy. The actions of each side become the stimulus for more decisive action by the other, and thus the process gathers momentum as it goes along. Coleman notes a relationship which might be called a "Gresham's Law of Conflict," in that often the harmful and dangerous elements drive out the more moderate groups who might otherwise keep the conflict within bounds. In a subsequent chapter, Coleman deals with a different set of processes, those which operate to keep the controversy in bounds and to resolve it.

Two types of planning activity have arisen in recent decades, each with a more or less clearly delineated area of urban problems within which planning and action are carried forward, each with a specialized profession responsible for such planning activities. One is the general area often referred to as the planning of health and welfare services, or "social planning"; the other deals with the physical aspects of the community, especially its land-use patterns, or "physical planning." Although they are obviously interrelated, it is only recently that patterns of close intercommunication on matters of common interest have been developing between these planning areas and planning professions, and it is still widely conceded on both sides that only a beginning has been made. In the meantime, rapid changes are occurring in the practice of both professions, in accommodation to changed urban conditions.

The change in social planning for urban communities is clearly expounded in the excerpt from a paper by Robert Morris and Martin Rein. In an earlier section which is not included here, Morris and Rein point out that social planning in urban communities, through the traditional community welfare councils, has in the past been characterized by a federated structure, a rational utopian point of view, the major goal of coordination, and the strategy of consensus.

The newer approaches to urban social planning are found in "the new urban planning agencies, mobilizations for youth, the community mental health centers, the public health department, the new rehabilitation concepts in public welfare." These and other approaches tend to be partisan rather than federated, to be derived from nonlocal rather than local sources, to be public rather than voluntary, to be concerned with political skills more than with consensus-forming skills, and to have change, rather than coordination, as a goal. The authors explore some of the implications of these new planning agencies, including the question of how, if at all, their diverse efforts are to be coordinated. They suggest that if such coordination is to take place in any concerted way, it is likely to occur through the political process and "the Mayor's office" rather than in the form of some type of voluntary superagency which would seek—probably in vain—to coordinate the work of these extremely strong new planning agencies with their strong public, rather than voluntary, components. In any event, the problem of dealing with their interrelationships will "call upon the skills and knowledge of all the social sciences—sociology and psychology, with which we [in the social planning profession] are familiar, political science and political economy, with which we are unfamiliar."

Paradoxically, the selection by Robert R. Mayer is not even specifically addressed to community phenomena. It somewhat abstractly explores different system models, pointing out the differences in their implications for social planners. The pertinence of the selection, of course, is that social system models have been found useful in analyzing complex community phenomena, particularly those in large metropolitan areas.

Mayer's terminology for the different types of systems is somewhat imposing: microcollectivity, complex macrosystem, exchange system, interorganizational field, and ecological system. Each type, as he shows, is structured somewhat differently and is held together by its own particular type of "glue." Some of the important aspects of these different system models are the structuring of leadership and authority, the extent of consensus on values and on norms, the various relations of system, sub-system, and unit, and the degree of collectivity orientation.

In seeking to bring about change in communities, planners are confronted with highly complex phenomena whose interrelationships are not fully understood. Mayer's lucid analysis, though difficult, provides a kit of analytical tools with which their interrelationships can be more carefully investigated and more adequately understood.

Community development as a method of bringing about social change rose to prominence in the years following World War II, and continues as a leading strategy. There are different versions of its rationale, but most of them assume that the local community is or can become a significant social group, that the people of the community have many common interests which they unfortunately do not always realize and further because of lack of communication or faulty communication, and that in a quite dispassionate fashion, a community development worker can assist the people of a community to communicate with each other, to seek their common interests, to remove elements of diversity, to set goals, establish procedures for accomplishing them, implement their plans, and evaluate their experience.

Almost all these assumptions can be challenged. And indeed, much recent history, particularly of intergroup strife in urban communities, seems either to invalidate them or at least to make them appear remote and somewhat irrelevant to the important issues of social change which so often pit group against group.

Hans B. C. Spiegel, one of the leading experts on citizen participation, raised five such challenges in an address before the Community Development Society. He does not, like some other critics, attack community development as an ineffectual method. Rather, he attempts to allay some misconceptions about community development in order to make the method more consonant with current social realities, particularly the social realities of large cities.

Stephen M. Rose traced the development and change of the Community Action Program which was part of the more inclusive anti-poverty program. He showed that of three major methods of diagnosing poverty—the "culture of poverty" approach, the "dysfunctional social system" approach, and the "dysfunctional economic system" approach—the Presidential Task Force which planned the program was clear and explicit regarding the importance of the dysfunctional social system approach. In order to combat poverty effectively, the poor would need to be organized, they would have to have a greater share of power in decision-making, and there would have to be changes in the institutional structure which produces and sustains poverty.

The method through which such changes were to be brought about was that of collaborative planning among existing social agencies, with a greater voice for the needs and wishes of the poor to be assured through their direct participation in the collaborative effort.

Yet in his analysis of the Community Action Programs of twenty cities, done in connection with the Brandeis study of Community Representation in Community Action Programs, Rose found less than 3 percent of the projects were in any way designed to organize the poor, to transfer power, or to bring about institutional change. The overwhelming bulk of projects were to offer "services" to the poor, largely by the very agencies whose previous failures to eradicate poverty were the occasion for the new program.

Rose points out that the method of change was hardly pertinent to the change objectives. The method resulted in the control of the new program by the existing local agencies, a circumstance which virtually assured little significant change. He indicates, parenthetically, that while local community autonomy is allegedly decreasing in the face of increasing control from more inclusive systems, the ability of local institutions to thwart the purpose of federal programs testifies to continued local hegemony.

In an important book (*The Structure of Scientific Revolutions,* Chicago: University of Chicago Press, 1962, 1970), Thomas S. Kuhn asserts that natural science does not develop in incremental fashion, but rather through a series of "revolutions" in which one scientific paradigm, or unifying principle, supplants another. Such paradigms help explain certain problem areas; but since no explanation is capable of accounting for all the data in equally satisfactory fashion, alternative explanations or paradigms arise which themselves are fragmentary.

Although Kuhn confined his analysis to the natural sciences, Warren, in the final selection of this section, applies it likewise to the area of social problems. Here, as Valentine, Rose, and others had pointed out, there are alternative "paradigms" for explaining poverty and for addressing it as a social problem. The paradigm which explains poverty in terms of individual deficiency quite understandably takes as its intervention strategy a program of social services to remedy the deficiencies in those who are poor. The main point of the selection quoted here is that the definition of poverty in terms of individual deficiency and the seeking of a remedy in terms of expanded and better coordinated social services are in turn related to a supporting belief-value system, the specific rationales of the community decision organizations involved, their legitimation and power within the community, the characteristics of the interorganizational field within which they interact, and the nature of social research and evaluation. These components comprise an institutionalized thought structure with components of beliefs, organizational structures, technical practices, and social power. The operation of this institutionalized thought structure helps make understandable a number of findings from a nine-city study of the development of Model Cities programs. As an analytical framework, it also provides perspective assessing programs of social change through coordination of agencies and citizen participation.

23. Social Change and the Community

BY LOWRY NELSON,
CHARLES E. RAMSEY, AND COOLIE VERNER

Most of the problems of man involve social change in one way or another. In the first place, almost any kind of change produces problems if for no other reason than that it represents a deviation from that to which one is accustomed. It should be obvious by now, however, that the nature of social structure is such that a change in one dimension or element is likely to produce change in another. The resulting problems are likely to extend beyond that of mere deviation from the usual. A second relationship exists between social change and social problems.[1] When man faces problems, he adjusts his relations to ameliorate them. This adjustment in his relations is also, in fact, social change. Because of the nature of social structure, it will produce changes in relations which he did not intend or even anticipate. It is easily seen that this interaction is a continuing one, since one problem will produce changes which in turn create more problems and so on.

DIFFICULTIES IN UNDERSTANDING CHANGE

The fact of change does not need elaboration, but the understanding of it, its prediction and control, is not so easy. There are at least three difficulties in understanding it. First, change is coterminous with structure, for in any but the rare, ideal-type, traditional (sacred) society, most dimensions and elements are changing and all are capable of it. Therefore, the difficulties of understanding the total structure of the community may be multiplied many times over those involved in understanding or describing a particular structure at a given time. A second difficulty arises from the fact that there are many types of change, and the generalizations which are valid for one type do not hold for another. A third difficulty comes from the lack of knowledge based upon rigorous research. Before change can be understood, it is necessary to have a base line from which to measure it; that is, it is first necessary to understand structure at the beginning point

Reprinted with permission of the authors and The Macmillan Company from *Community Structure and Change,* by Lowry Nelson, Charles E. Ramsey, and Coolie Verner, pp. 391–97. Copyright © The Macmillan Company 1960.

[1] Don Martindale and Elio D. Monachesi, *Elements of Sociology,* Harper and Brothers, New York, 1951, Part iv; and Edward H. Spicer, editor, *Human Problems in Technological Change,* Russell Sage Foundation, New York, 1952.

from which change is to be measured. That this is difficult to accomplish is never denied by those who have begun to grasp the subtle nature of the power structure,[2] the dualism in the value system,[3] the shifting and ill-defined obligations of the family to the community,[4] and the elusive pressures exerted on the community from mass society.[5]

INTEREST IN CHANGE IS BOTH SCIENTIFIC AND PRACTICAL

Despite the difficulties mentioned above, change must be taken into consideration, whether the interest in the community be scientific or practical. From the scientific point of view, it is only half of the picture to describe and analyze structure at a given time. Indeed, it may be less than half since only through understanding the changes occurring over a course of time can prediction and scientific control be realized. From the practical point of view, change is of major interest because of its relationship to social problems. Community development is intimately bound up with this relationship. Because of its importance to both scientific and practical interest, change in elements and dimensions has been considered an integral part of the analysis throughout this book. It is now important to regard social change as a separate form.

THE NATURE OF SOCIAL CHANGE

The definition of change presupposes the definition of structure, but it is important to distinguish it from process. In a sense all human relations and structures are processual, in that they form and exist through time. Cooperation is obviously a process, but it is not social change. The assignment of status develops through time, and it operates in any concrete way only as men relate themselves to one another differentially. The elements of the community are also processual. The family's functions have concrete meaning only so far as, in day-to-day living, the remainder of the community can depend upon the family to socialize the next generation, to participate in community affairs, and to propagate the race.

CHANGE AND PROCESS

The first relation between process and change, then, is a logical one. Change is one of the social processes in that it is one form that human

---

[2] Floyd Hunter, *Community Power Structure,* University of North Carolina Press, Chapel Hill, 1953.

[3] Robert S. Lynd, *Knowledge for What?* Princeton University Press, New Jersey, 1939.

[4] William F. Ogburn and Meyer F. Nimkoff, *Technology and the Changing Family,* Houghton-Mifflin Company, Boston, 1955.

[5] Arthur J. Vidich and Joseph Bensman, *Small Town in Mass Society,* Princeton University Press, Princeton, New Jersey, 1958.

relations take through time. However, sociologists in the main have considered process in a very narrow sense. They have referred chiefly to four and sometimes five as if these were the only processes. These have been cooperation, conflict, competition, and accommodation.[6] Sometimes assimilation is added. Some theorists add many other processes, although there is no general agreement regarding them. Accommodation and assimilation are by their nature social change, and the other processes may be results or causes of change. To have meaning, change must involve more than this narrow concept of process. It must alter the form of human relations and structures, such as moving from competition to conflict, or from competition to cooperation.

In a given community situation, however, competition may exist quietly for years and suddenly flare up into conflict. After a period of time, the fires may die down and the old relation may be restored. Similarly, codes of conduct, such as rules of dress, may change for a while. Fundamentally, women's dress in American society remains much the same, but length and other minor features vary from time to time. It is desirable at present to exclude these fluctuations from the analysis, since the generalizations which are valid for social change are not applicable to many of these short-term cycles.

However, it is impossible at present to ascertain in all cases when a given sequence of behavior patterns is change and when it is some other type of process; when it is change and when fluctuation. More research is needed to show exactly what conditions are necessary for given generalizations. Nevertheless, much insight into social change can be gained without a precise definition. At least some of the criteria of social change can be observed and recorded.

TYPES OF SOCIAL CHANGE

The first type is the long-term trend. It can be seen clearly that the level of living in American communities has been steadily increasing since the beginnings of American society.[7] This trend has been reversed on occasion only slightly and only temporarily. A second type of social change is the apparently permanent transfer of a function from one social unit

[6] Robert E. Park and Ernest W. Burgess, *Introduction to the Science of Sociology,* University of Chicago Press, Chicago, 1921, Chapters 8–11; Louis Wirth, *The Ghetto,* University of Chicago Press, Chicago, 1928; Pitirim Sorokin, *Contemporary Sociological Theories,* Harper and Brothers, New York, 1928, Chapter 6; Lowry Nelson, *Rural Sociology,* American Book Company, New York, 1955, Chapters 8–10: and T. Lynn Smith, *The Sociology of Rural Life,* Harper and Brothers, New York, 1947, Part iv.
[7] Margaret Jarman Hagood, *Farm-operator Family Level of Living Indexes for Counties of the United States 1930, 1940, 1945, and 1950,* United States Department of Agriculture, Bureau of Agricultural Economics, Washington, D. C., 1952.

to another. The family has surrendered the function of producer to the economic institution. This change came about slowly and is relatively permanent. A third phenomenon which may be considered social change is the shift in a fundamental aspect of one or more of the dimensions of the community. By "fundamental" here is meant those aspects which are least amenable to fluctuation. For example, the mores and folkways do not fluctuate and therefore the shift in one of these fundamental codes of conduct always is relatively permanent. Likewise, an occupation may increase or decrease in influence. There might be a question as to whether this is social change or merely fluctuation, but if authority is given less importance for a long period of time in determining status, then social change has occurred. The status of the doctor in income, prestige, authority, and so on has risen from negative sanctions to one of the highest status positions in the community. This is likely to remain the case for a long time and probably represents social change. The soldier in American society was low in status before World War I, high during World War I, low again from 1919 until about 1940-1941, and then high again. The generalizations of social change probably do not apply to the status of the soldier during these periods, but they may be valid for the change in status of the physician.

The common factor in distinguishing change from mere fluctuation thus far is the length of time over which the change persists. However, man is not concerned with such long-range changes in his decision-making. Problems are problems today, and the man who views consequences of alternative solutions for ten to twenty years ahead is indeed far-sighted and rare. It follows that short, as well as longer, terms must be considered. How, then, can an immediate shift in human relations be viewed as social change? Perhaps the best criterion is some basis upon which it can be predicted whether this shift will persist or will return to yesterday's form. The nature of social structure gives a clue. If a given shift is tied up with many other dimensions and elements it may be expected to remain for a longer time. For the immediate situation, therefore, generalizations about social change may apply if a shift in one aspect involves shifts in other dimensions and elements of community structure.

THE PROBLEM OF SOCIAL CHANGE

Social change may be viewed several ways within the frame of reference of the present treatise. One meaningful view is the negative one of preventing change in one part of the community structure from producing problems in other elements or dimensions. Thus when, say, the family breaks down in its function, it produces problems for the legal, educational, and economic institutions in performing their functions. The response to the problem of socialization may then take several forms. The legal institution may deviate from its established procedure in the function of assuring order and justice. It may do away with trial by jury, right to defense counsel, and so on. The educational institution may extend its functions to include instilling respect for life and property. The economic institution may support the expenses of playgrounds and recreational directors. The religious institution, always functioning to instill basic mores and folkways, may intensify its efforts not only in its basic functions but also in extending them to include recreational programs which give direction to leisure-time activities for youth. Thus the gap between expectations from the family and achievement of those expectations is closed and the main problem at the moment may be ameliorated. However, the solution pictured here involves a higher budget, more personnel, activity in an area where experience is lacking, and closer ties among the institutions of the community. It may be seen, then, that change is produced throughout the elements of the community by virtue of what happens in one element.

Social change may also be viewed as an effort to meet problems, while at the same time maintaining a clearly understood agreement on function. Is it really the role of the school to socialize the child? There is disagreement on this point. Is it really the obligation of the economic institution to support playgrounds and recreational directors through direct contributions rather than through taxes? These are all points of contention and indicate the confusion which exists when patterns of behavior deviate from those expected and when long-established understandings are broken down.

In summary, social change is the modification of structure to maintain stability and consistency.[8] Social problems must be solved in anticipation of new problems which may be created by their solution.

WHAT IS IT THAT CHANGES?

There are four levels of structure which may change. The first and most important level is the total community. Change here is always slow and may occur only over many generations. In the course of time, a community may shift from a sacred-folk to a secular-prescribed structure.[9] Such change will occur in a short time only when it is in response to some disaster or some tremendously important event. The location of a very large plant near a relatively small community in which most codes of conduct are largely unwritten, where the status system is based mainly upon personal characteristics, and where the relations among the institutions are clearly understood by everyone, may change within two or three years

[8] Kingsley Davis, *Human Society*, The Macmillan Company, New York, 1948, Chapter 22.

[9] For example, see Howard Becker, *Through Values to Social Interpretation*, Duke University Press, Durham, North Carolina, 1950, Chapter 5.

to a buzzing confusion of anonymity, written laws, a status system based on position rather than acquaintance, and tremendous pressure on institutions to attain even partial success in fulfilling functions.

A second important point where change occurs is at the pan-community level. Since the community is made up of relations between other area-bound social units, like the school district and the township, the relations between it and nearby communities, as well as with the Great Society, will change as schools are consolidated or voting districts are altered. If a sufficient number of these changes are made, a small community may be swallowed up by a larger one, but ordinarily it will only surrender some of its functions. In addition, it is important to observe that the operation of mass communication as well as legislation enacted by state or federal governments will tend to remove from the local community many unique features it possesses. The local units become homogenized in the mass.

A third level of change is in dimensions and elements of community structure. It has been seen that dimensions are community-wide and thus may usually be expected to produce changes in more of the remainder of the community than would elements. However, both of them change within themselves and cause other social changes as well. The value system may change from being homogeneous to being heterogeneous; or from use of unwritten codes to written ones. The stratification system may change from being personality-based to one based on position. The relations between the family and the school may change from apathy to close cooperation. The relations between the church and the school may change from independent operation to closer ties and reinforcement in functions through released time for religious instruction.

The fourth level where change may occur is in a component, such as the family or the organization of the school itself. These changes in substructures become important to understanding the community only when they imply changes in function. For example, the working mother represents a change in family structure, but this implies at least two changes in community elements. The increase in the labor force is assured and the breakdown in the socialization function is threatened. In the first case, the relationship between the family and the economic institution is involved, and in the second case, that between the family and the total community. Change in the structure of the family is not community change as such, as was the case with changes in elements and dimensions, but may be significant in producing community-wide change. . . .

24. The Dynamics of Community Controversy

BY JAMES S. COLEMAN

The most striking fact about the development and growth of community controversies is the similarity they exhibit despite diverse underlying sources and different kinds of precipitating incidents. Once the controversies have begun, they resemble each other remarkably. Were it not for these similarities, Machiavelli could never have written his guide to warfare, and none of the other numerous works on conflict, dispute, and controversy would have been possible.[1] It is the peculiarity of social controversy that it sets in motion its own dynamics; these tend to carry it forward in a path which bears little relation to its beginnings. An examination of these dynamics will occupy the attention of this chapter.

One caution is necessary: we do not mean to suggest that nothing can be done about community controversy once it begins. To the contrary, the dynamics of controversy *can* be interrupted and diverted—either by conscious action or by existing conditions in the community. As a result, although the same dynamic tendencies of controversy are found in every case, the actual development in particular cases may differ widely. In the discussion below, the unrestrained dynamic tendencies will be discussed . . .

CHANGES IN ISSUES

The issues which provide the initial basis of response in a controversy undergo great transformations as the controversy develops. Three fundamental transformations appear to take place.

SPECIFIC TO GENERAL

First, specific issues give way to *general* ones. In Scarsdale, the school's critics began by attacking books in the school library; soon they

[1] The one man who emphasized particularly the possibility of abstracting principles of conflict from particular situations of conflict is Georg Simmel, who wrote several essays on the subject. Unfortunately, Simmel never got around to writing a comprehensive theory of conflict, though he did set down a number of insights into particular aspects. See Simmel (1955). Lewis Coser has brought together the best of Simmel's insights and elaborated on them (Coser, 1956).

focused on the whole educational philosophy. In Mason City, Iowa, where a city-manager plan was abandoned, the campaign against the plan started with a letter to the newspaper from a local carpenter complaining that the creek overflowed into his home. This soon snowballed, gathering other specific complaints, and then gave way to the general charge that the council and manager were dominated by local business interests and had no concern for the workingman.

Most of the controversies examined show a similar pattern. (Even those that do not are helpful, for they suggest just why the pattern *does* exist in so many cases. Political controversies, for example, exhibit the pattern much less than do disputes based primarily on differing values or economic interests. The Athens, Tennessee, political fight began with the same basic issue it ended with—political control of the community (Key, 1950). Other political struggles in which there is little popular involvement show a similar restriction to the initial issue.)

It seems that movement from specific to general issues occurs whenever there are deep cleavages of values or interests in the community which require a spark to set them off—usually a specific incident representing only a small part of the underlying difference. In contrast, those disputes which appear not to be generated by deep cleavages running through the community as a whole, but are rather power struggles within the community, do not show the shift from specific to general. To be sure, they may come to involve the entire community, but no profound fundamental difference comes out.

This first shift in the nature of the issues, then, uncovers the fundamental differences which set the stage for a precipitating incident in the first place.

NEW AND DIFFERENT ISSUES

Another frequent change in the issues of the dispute is the emergence of quite *new and different* issues, unrelated to the original ones. In the Pasadena school controversy, the initial issue was an increased school budget and a consequent increased tax rate. This soon became only one issue of many; ideological issues concerning "progressive education," and other issues, specific as well as general, arose. In another case, a controversy which began as a personal power struggle between a school superintendent and a principal shifted to a conflict involving general educational principles when the community as a whole entered in (Warner et al., 1949, p. 201-204). A study of the adoption of the city-manager plan in fifty cities (Stone, Price, and Stone, 1940, p. 34-38) shows that in one group of cities, designated by the authors "machine-ridden," the controversy grew to include ethnic, religious, political, and ideological differences. Political campaigns generally, in fact, show this tendency: issues multiply rapidly as the campaign increases in intensity.

There are two different sources for this diversification of issues. One is in a sense "involuntary"; issues which could not have been raised before the controversy spring suddenly to the fore as relationships between groups and individuals change. We see how this operates in an argument between two people, e.g., in the common phrases used to introduce new issues: "I hesitated to mention this before but now . . ." or, "While I'm at it, I might as well say this too. . . ." As long as functioning relations exist between individuals or groups, there are strong inhibitions upon introducing any issue which might impair the functioning. In a sense the stable relation suppresses topics which might upset it. But once the stability of the relation *is* upset, the suppressed topics can come to the surface uninhibitedly. We suggest that exactly the same mechanisms are at work in the community as a whole; networks of relations, however complex, act in the same fashion.

But in many other cases, illustrated best by political disputes, the diversification of issues is more a purposive move on the part of the antagonists, and serves quite a different function: to solidify opinion and bring in new participants by providing new bases of response. Again, this is evident in the two-person argument: each antagonist brings to bear all the *different* arguments he can to rationalize his position to himself and to convince his opponent. Just the same thing occurs in community conflict: each side attempts to increase solidarity and win new adherents from the still uncommitted neutrals by introducing as many diverse issues as will benefit its cause. Both these functions—increasing solidarity among present members, and gaining new members—are vital; the first aids in the important task of "girding for action" by disposing of all doubts and hesitancies; the second gains allies, always an important aim in community conflict.

The issues introduced must be very special ones with little potential for disrupting the group that initiates them. They are almost always "one-sided" in the sense that they provide a basis for response only in one direction, and they gain their value by monopolizing the attention of community members. In controversies where a challenge is offered to an incumbent administration, the issue of "maladministration" is, typically, a one-sided issue; the administration can only offer defense and hope that attention soon shifts elsewhere. In school controversies, the issue of Communist subversion in the schools is one-sided; as long as it occupies the attention of the community, it is to the advantage of school critics. In contrast, the issue "progressive education *vs.* traditional education" offers no differential advantage to either side (unless, of course, progressive education can be identified by its opponents as "Communistic") until one group can prove to the majority of the community that one approach is better from all points of view. Analysis of the different functions of different kinds of issues can be found in Berel-son, Lazarsfeld, and McPhee (1954), and in Coleman (1955, p. 253).

DISAGREEMENT TO ANTAGONISM

A third change in the nature of issues as a controversy develops is the shift from *disagreement* to *antagonism*. A dispute which began dispassion-ately, in a disagreement over issues, is characterized suddenly by personal slander, by rumor, by the focusing of direct hostility. This is one of the most important aspects in the self-generation of conflict: Once set in motion, hostility can sustain conflict unaided by disagreement about particular issues. The original issues may be settled, yet the controversy continues unabated. The antagonistic relationship has become direct: it no longer draws suste-nance from an outside element—an issue. As in an argument between friends, a discussion which begins with *disagreement* on a point in question often ends with each *disliking* the other.[2] The dynamics which account for the shift from disagreement to antagonism are two: "involuntary," and deliber-ate. Simmel explains the involuntary process by saying that it is "expedient" and "appropriate" to hate one's opponent just as it is "appropriate" to like someone who agrees with you (1955, p. 34). But perhaps there is a stronger explanation: we associate with every person we know certain beliefs, inter-ests, traits, attributes, etc. So long as we disagree with only one or a few of his beliefs, we are "divided" in our feelings toward him. He is not wholly black or white in our eyes. But when we quarrel, the process of argument itself generates new issues; we disagree with more and more of our oppo-nent's beliefs. Since these beliefs constitute *him* in our eyes, rather than isolated aspects of him, his image grows blacker. Our hostility is directed toward him personally. Thus the two processes—the first leading from a single issue to new and different ones, and the second leading from dis-agreement to direct antagonism—fit together perfectly and help carry the controversy along its course.[3] Once direct antagonism is felt toward an opponent, one is led to make public attacks on him.

Perhaps it would be fruitful to set down a little more precisely the

---

[2] Conversely, a relationship which begins with two people *agreeing* in tastes and interests often ends with both *liking one another*. For a discussion of the process through which this occurs, see Merton and Lazarsfeld (1954).

Georg Simmel notes the formal similarities between relations of positive and nega-tive attachments, contrasting these with the *absence* of relationship. He suggests that the psychological processes generating antagonism are just as fundamental as those generating liking. Simmel also notes the difference between a negative relationship based on disagreement over an outside object, and one which needs no such object, but is directly antagonistic. See Simmel (1955, p. 34, 36, passim), and Coser (1956).

[3] It should be emphasized that these suggestions for processes are highly tentative; systematic research into the psychological dynamics involved in these changing rela-tions would contribute greatly to our knowledge about the development of controversy.

"involuntary" processes which we suggest operate to shift issues from one disagreement to a multitude, ultimately to antagonism. In a diagram it might look something like this:

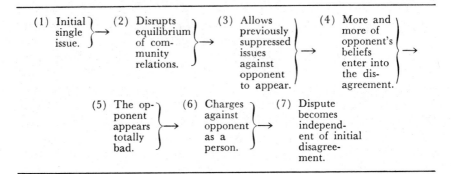

Men have a strong need (discussed in detail in the final chapter) for *consistency*. If I disagree violently with someone, then it becomes psychologically more comfortable to see him as totally black rather than gray.[4] This drive for consistency may provide the fuel for the generalization processes in Steps 3 and 4 above.

Apart from these "involuntary" or "natural" processes, the use of personal charges by the antagonists is a common device to bypass disagreement and go directly to antagonism. Sometimes consciously, often unconsciously, the opposing nuclei attempt to reach new people through this means, drawing more and more of the community to their side by creating personal hostility to the opponent.[5, 6] In political disputes the degeneration to personal charges is particularly frequent. V. O. Key notes that in the

[4] One might speculate that this tendency would be stronger among those who tend to personalize easily; they move more quickly perhaps from specific disagreement to hostility toward the opponent as a whole. Feuds among hill people (who are highly "person-oriented"), for example, seem to bear this out. Thus the course of controversy may vary greatly in two communities, simply as a result of differences in "person-orientation."

[5] The general process by which new people respond to such appeals is discussed more fully later under the heading "Social relations as a basis of response."

[6] Whether or not persons previously neutral can be brought into the controversy seems to depend greatly upon the time at which they are confronted with the alternative. If the antagonists are too involved too early they are viewed with puzzlement and distaste and detachment by neutrals. The situation is much the same as confronts a man arriving sober in the middle of a drunken party: he cannot join in because these people are "too far gone" for him to experience the events of the party as they do. The similarity between an orgy of community controversy and a drunken orgy is more than superficial in this and other respects. People collectively "forget themselves" in ways they may be ashamed of later. One of the major questions of community conflict concerns the processes through which this "forgetting" occurs.

South, state political campaigns are often marked by candidates' personal attacks on each other. He suggests that such attacks grow in the absence of "real" issues (1950, pp. 194–200). This seems reasonable since the use of personal attacks may be an attempt to incite antagonism in cases where there is not enough disagreement for the natural processes of conflict to operate. In other words, the attacks constitute an attempt to stimulate controversy artificially—a "short-cut"—by bypassing a stage in the process which might otherwise let the conflict falter. Such actions would seem to occur only when community leaders need to gain the support of an otherwise apathetic community which has no real issues dividing it.

In another group of controversies, focused around certain value differences, the shift to personal attacks is sometimes immediate, and seems to be a result of real disagreement and incipient antagonism. School controversies often begin with personal charges against teachers or principals of moral impropriety, or more frequently in recent days, subversion. Why is it that personal attacks in these instances succeed in creating immediate hostility within the community, while other kinds of personal attacks are viewed with disfavor by the community, that is, until the late, intense stages of controversy when all inhibiting norms and constraints are forgotten? The reason may be this: When a personal accusation refers to behavior viewed as extremely illegitimate by community members it outweighs the norm against personal attacks. Presumably the community members put themselves in the place of the attacker and say, in effect, "If I knew these things to be true, would I feel right about speaking out publicly?" When the charges concern sexual immorality or political subversion, many persons can answer "yes" to such a question;[7] thus they feel unconcerned about making the kind of attacks that they would ordinarily never allow except in the heat of dispute.[8] These attacks, in turn, quickly create the heat that might be otherwise slow in coming.

Changes in content and character of issues constitutes only one kind of change going on in the development of a controversy; at the same time, the whole structure of organizations and associations in the community is undergoing change as well. The nature of these changes is examined below.

[7] It is a matter of the relative strengths of different values: some, like those against immorality and subversion, override the values against personal slander. If we knew the relative strength of certain social values among various segments of the population, we would be far better able to judge the course of controversy ranged around a certain issue. But we lack even methods for measurement.

[8] In contrast to "putting oneself in the place of the attacker," those who hold civil liberties to be of great importance evidently put themselves in the place of the attacked, and ask themselves how it would feel to be unjustly charged in this fashion. It appears that the *variations in relative values* between these two groups cause them to identify with opposing parties in a case of such charges. Thus they are immediately brought in on one side or the other in such a dispute.

CHANGES IN THE SOCIAL ORGANIZATION OF THE COMMUNITY

POLARIZATION OF SOCIAL RELATIONS

As controversy develops associations flourish *within* each group, but wither *between* persons on opposing sides. People break off long-standing relationships, stop speaking to former friends who have been drawn to the opposition, but proliferate their associations with fellow-partisans. Again, this is part of the process of stripping for action: getting rid of all social encumbrances which impede the action necessary to win the conflict. Polarization is perhaps less pronounced in short-term conflicts, and in those in which the issues cut across existing organizational ties and informal relations. But in all conflicts, it tends to alter the social geography of the community to separate it into two clusters, breaking apart along the line of least attachment. . . .

THE FORMATION OF PARTISAN ORGANIZATIONS

In many types of community conflict, there are no existing organizations to form the nuclei of the two sides. But as the controversy develops, organizations form. In a recent controversy in Cincinnati over the left-wing political history of the city planning director (Hessler, 1953), supporters of the director and of the councilman who hired him formed a "Committee of 150 for Political Morality." This Committee used considerable sophistication in the selection of a name and in their whole campaign. Rather than remain on the defensive, and let the opposition blanket the community with charges of subversion, this Committee invoked an equally strong value—of morality in politics—and took the offensive against the use of personal attack by their opponents. This technique constitutes a way in which controversy can be held on a relatively high plane: by invoking community norms against smears, using these very norms as an issue of controversy. If the norm is strong, it may keep the controversy "within bounds."

In general, as a dispute intensifies the partisans form *ad hoc* groups, which have numerous functions while the controversy lasts: they serve as communication centers, as communication becomes more and more important within each side and attenuates between groups; they serve as centers for planning and organizing partisan meetings and other activities; and especially they can meet quickly—in a situation where speed is of utmost importance—any threat or challenge posed by the opposition.

The most common variation upon this theme is the union; in industrial disputes, the union is a defense organization *already* in existence; in a real controversy, it takes on all the aspects of the usual partisan organizations: secrecy, spirited meetings, pamphleteering, fund-raising.[9]

THE EMERGENCE OF NEW LEADERS

As partisan organizations are formed and a real nucleus develops around each of the opposing centers, new leaders tend to take over the dispute; often they are men who have not been community leaders in the past, men who face none of the constraints of maintaining a previous community position, and feel none of the cross-pressures felt by members of community organizations. In addition, these leaders rarely have real identification with the community. In the literature they often emerge as marginal men who have never held a position of leadership before. A study of the fight against city-manager plans pictures the leaders of the opposition as men personally frustrated and maladjusted (Stene and Floro, 1953, p. 21–39). The current desegregation fights have produced numerous such leaders, often young, one a former convict, usually from the outside. (*Life,* 1954; *Southern School News,* 1956.)

The new leaders, at any rate, are seldom moderates; the situation itself calls for extremists. And such men have not been conditioned, through experience in handling past community problems, to the prevailing norms concerning tactics of dispute.

One counter-tendency appears in the development of these organizations and the emergence of their leaders. In certain conflicts, e.g., in Cincinnati, one side will be composed primarily of community leaders, men of prestige and responsibility in the community. Though such groups carry on the functions of a partisan organization, they act not to lower the level of controversy, but to *maintain* or raise it. As did the Committee of 150 (and the ADA in Norwalk, Connecticut, and other groups in other controversies), they attempt to invoke the community's norms against personal attacks and unrestrained conflict. Sometimes (as in Cincinnati) they are successful, sometimes not.

In the face of all the pressures toward increasing intensity and freedom from normal constraint this last development is puzzling. The source of the reversal seems to be this: in certain controversies (particularly those having to do with the accusation of subversion), one side derives much of its strength from personal attacks and derogation, that is, from techniques which, were they not legitimated by patriotism or sex codes or similar strong values, would be outlawed by the community. Thus, to the degree that such methods are permitted, the attackers gain; and to the degree that community norms are upheld against these methods, the advantage is to the attacked. The more the attacked side can invoke the norms defining legitimate controversy, the more likely it is to win.

[9] See Pope's (1942) graphic account of union operations in Gastonia, North Carolina, and Jones's (1941) discussion of union activity in Akron.

Invocation of community constraints is almost the sole force *generated by the conflict itself* which acts in a restraining direction. It is a very special force, and which appears to operate *only* under the conditions discussed above. Even so, it represents one means by which some controversies may be contained within bounds of normal community decision-making.

COMMUNITY ORGANIZATIONS AS THE CONTROVERSY DEVELOPS

As conflict develops, the community's organizations tend to be drawn in, just as individual members are. It may be the American Legion, the P.T.A., the church, the local businessmen's association; if its members are drawn into the controversy, or if it can lend useful support, the organization will be under pressure from one or both sides to enter the controversy. This varies, of course, with the nature of the organization and the nature of the dispute.

At the same time there are often strong pressures, both within the organization and without, to remain neutral. From within: if its members hold opposing sentiments, then their disharmony forces the organization itself to remain neutral. And from without: the organization must maintain a public position in the community which might be endangered by taking sides in a partisan battle threatening to split the community.

Examples of internal and external constraints on community organizations and leaders are not hard to find. In the Denver school controversy a few years ago, the County P.T.A. felt constrained to dissociate itself publicly from the criticisms of the school system made by their retiring president (Martin, 1951). In Hastings, New York, the positions were reversed: the school administration and teachers remained neutral while a battle raged over the P.T.A. election (McPhee, 1954). Similarly, in the strike in Gastonia, North Carolina, local ministers felt constrained not to take a public position (Pope, 1942, p. 283). If they had done so, the course of the strike might have been quite different as religious matters entered in explicitly. In some fights over the city-manager plan, businessmen's associations tried to keep out because the plan was already under attack for its alliance with business interests (Stene and Floro, 1953, p. 60); and in at least one fluoridation controversy, doctors and dentists were reluctant to actively support the fluoridation plan, singly or as a group, because of possible community disfavor affecting business (Mausner, 1955).[10] In another case, union leaders

---

[10] There is some evidence that men in certain occupations are more sensitive than others to public opinion and thus less willing to commit themselves to either side and less able to hold on to a position of principle. On the Pasadena school board, the two members most sensitive to the mass mood were a retail merchant and an undertaker (both, it should be noted, like doctors and dentists, have a retail product to sell) (Hurlburd, 1950, p. 31 ff.). This and other evidence leads to the hypothesis that persons who have a clientele or set of retail customers in town cannot generally be trusted to stand up against a majority though they believe in the cause. Or even more generally, it seems that such men cannot *start* a controversy, since the initiator is

who had originally helped elect a school board could not bring their organizations to support a superintendent the board had appointed when he was accused of "progressivism" and favoritism to ethnic minorities. Their own members were too strongly split on the issue (McKee, 1953, p. 244). Ministers who were in favor of allowing Negro children to use the community house were influenced by the beliefs of influential members of their churches not to take a stand (The Inquiry, 1929, pp. 58–59). Even in Scarsdale, which was united behind its school board, the Town Club incurred disfavor with a minority of its members, who supported the school's critics, for taking as strong a stand as it did.

In sum, both community organizations and community leaders are faced with constraints when a dispute arises; the formation of a combat group to carry on the controversy and the emergence of a previous unknown as the combat leader are in part results of the immobility of responsible organizations and leaders. Both the new leader and the new organization are freed from some of the usual shackles of community norms and internal cross-pressures which make pre-existing organizations and leaders tend to soften the dispute.

The immobility of organizations resulting from a lack of internal (or sometimes external) consensus is one element which varies according to the kind of issue involved. This is best exemplified by different issues in national politics: when the issue is an economic one, e.g., Taft-Hartley legislation, groups mobilize on each side of the economic fence; labor unions and allied organizations vs. the National Association of Manufacturers, trade associations, and businesses themselves. When the issue has to do with tariffs, the composition of each side is different,[11] but there is still a mobilization of organizations on both sides. Sometimes the issue cuts directly across the organizations and institutions in society, thus immobilizing them, e.g., "McCarthyism," which blossomed such a short time ago. Labor unions never opposed McCarthy—their members were split. The Democratic party never opposed him—its constituency was split. Few of the powerful institutions in the country had enough internal consensus to oppose McCarthy. As it was, he drew his followers from all walks of life and from all levels of society. The cross-pressures resulting from lack of internal group consensus were reinforced by external pressures against opposing McCarthy, for all the values of patriotism were invoked by his forces. Almost the only organizations with neither internal nor external pressure against taking sides were

---

always in a minority; neither can they continue against the initiator once he has gained the majority.

[11] Sometimes labor unions and trade associations find themselves on the same side of the fence. The issue over an increase in watch tariffs saw the watchmakers' union and the manufacturers on the same side: both opposed a principle laid down by a tariff commission headed by the president of a steel company.

the professionally patriotic groups like the American Legion and the DAR. If the issue had not immobilized labor unions and the Democratic party then opposition to McCarthy would have been much more effective.[12]

THE INCREASING USE OF WORD-OF-MOUTH COMMUNICATION

As the controversy proceeds, the formal media of communication—radio, television, and newspapers—become less and less able to tell people *as much* as they want to know about the controversy, or the *kinds of things* they want to know. These media are simply not flexible enough to fill the insatiable need for news which develops as people become more and more involved. At the same time, the media are restricted by normative and legal constraints against carrying the kind of rumor which abounds as controversy proceeds. Word-of-mouth communication gradually fills the gaps, both in volume and in content, left by the mass media. Street-corner discussion amplifies, elaborates, and usually distorts the news that it picks up from the papers or the radio. This interpersonal communication offers no restraints against slander and personal charges; rather, it helps make the rhetoric of controversy consistent with the intensity.

SUMMARY

Several characteristic events carry the controversy toward its climax. The most important changes in *issues* are: (a) from specific disagreements to more general ones, (b) elaboration into new and different disagreements, and (c) a final shift from disagreement to direct antagonism. The changes in the *social organization* of the community are as follows: the polarization of social relations as the controversy intensifies, as the participants cut off relations with those who are not on their side, and elaborate relations with those who are; the formation of partisan organizations and the emergence of new, often extremist partisan leaders to wage the war more efficiently; and the mobilization of existing community organizations on one side or the other. Finally, as the pace quickens and the issues become personal, word-of-mouth communication replaces the more formal media. It now remains to examine some of the reciprocal causations constituting the "vicious circles" or "runaway processes" so evident in conflict. These should give somewhat more insight into the mechanisms responsible for the growth of conflict.

RECIPROCAL CAUSATION AND THE DEVELOPING DISPUTE

The inner dynamics of controversy derive from a number of mutually reinforcing relations; one element is enhanced by another, and, in turn,

---

[12] Interestingly, what is at one time an aid is at another time a hindrance: a movement with little organizational opposition also has little organizational support, and finds it difficult to become institutionalized without a coup.

enhances the first, creating an endless spiral.[13] Some of the most important relations depend heavily upon this reciprocal reinforcement; if one or more of these cycles can be *broken,* then a disagreement already on the way to real conflict can be diverted into normal channels.

MUTUAL REINFORCEMENT OF RESPONSE

Relations between people contain a built-in reciprocity. I smile at you; if you smile back, I speak to you; you respond, and a relationship has begun. At each step, my reaction is contingent upon yours, and yours, in turn, contingent upon mine.[14] If you fail to smile, but scowl instead, I may say a harsh word; you respond in kind, and another chain of mutual reinforcement builds up—this time toward antagonism. It is such chains which constitute not only the fundamental character of interpersonal relations, but also the fundamental cycle of mutual effects in controversy. Breaking that cycle requires much effort. The admonition to "turn the other cheek" is not easily obeyed.

The direct reinforcement of response, however, is but one—the most obvious—of the mutually reinforcing relations which constitute the dynamics of controversy. Others, more tenuous, are more easily broken.

THE MUTUAL EFFECTS OF SOCIAL AND PSYCHOLOGICAL POLARIZATION

As participants in a dispute become psychologically "consistent," shedding doubts and hesitancies, they shun friends who are uncommitted, and elaborate their associations with those who feel the way they do. In effect, the psychological polarization leads to social polarization. The latter, in turn, leads to mutual reinforcement of opinions, that is, to further psychological polarization. One agrees more and more with his associates (and disagrees more and more with those he *doesn't* talk to), and comes to associate more and more with those who agree with him. Increasingly, his opponents' position seems preposterous—and, in fact, it *is* preposterous, as is his own; neither position feeds on anything but reinforcing opinions.

The outcome, of course, is the division of the community into two socially and attitudinally separate camps, each convinced it is absolutely right. The lengths to which this continually reinforcing cycle will go in any particular case depends on the characteristics of the people and the com-

[13] The dynamics of controversy is a topic for the theoretician in sociology: it comes as close as any area of social life to constituting a closed system, in which all the effects are from variables within the system. When a theory of controversy does exist, the sets of mutually reinforcing relations like those examined in this section will constitute the heart of the theory.

[14] Talcott Parsons (1951, p. 36) who studies this characteristic of interpersonal relations in detail, speaks of it as the "double-contingency of interpersonal relations." Parsons has a full discussion of this aspect of relations between persons.

munity involved. . . . It is these characteristics which provide one "handle" for reducing the intensity of community conflict.

POLARIZATION AND INTENSITY: WITHIN THE INDIVIDUAL AND WITHIN EACH SIDE

As the participants become psychologically polarized, all their attitudes mutually reinforcing, the *intensity* of their feeling increases. One of the consequences is that inconsistencies within the individual are driven out; thus he becomes even more psychologically polarized, in turn developing a greater intensity.

This chain of mutual enforcement lies completely *within* the individual. But there is an analogous chain of reinforcement on the social level. As social polarization occurs (that is, the proliferation of associations among those who feel one way, and the attenuation of association between those who feel differently), one's statements meet more and more with a positive response; one is more and more free to express the full intensity of his feeling. The "atmosphere" of the group is open for the kind of intensity of feeling that previously had to remain unexpressed. This atmosphere of intensity, in turn, further refines the group; it becomes intolerable that anyone who believes differently maintain association within the group.

These are examples of reciprocal causation in community conflict, as they appear in the literature of these controversies. They constitute the chains which carry controversy from beginning to end as long as they remain unbroken, but which also provide the means of softening the conflict if methods can be found to break them. It is important to note that these reciprocal relations, once set in motion by outside forces, become independent of them and continue on their own. The one continuing force at work is the drive of each side to win, which sets in motion the processes described above; it carries the conflict forward "under its own steam," so to speak. But reciprocal relations also affect the initial drive, amplifying it, changing it; no longer is it simply a drive to win, but an urge to ruin the opponents, strip them of their power, in effect, annihilate them. This shift in goals, itself a part of a final chain of reciprocal causation, drives these processes onward with ever more intensity.

GRESHAM'S LAW OF CONFLICT

The processes may be said to create a "Gresham's Law of Conflict": the harmful and dangerous elements drive out those which would keep the conflict within bounds. Reckless, unrestrained leaders head the attack; combat organizations arise to replace the milder, more constrained pre-existing organizations; derogatory and scurrilous charges replace dispassionate issues; antagonism replaces disagreement, and a drive to ruin the opponent takes the place of the initial will to win. In other words, all the forces put into effect by the initiation of conflict act to drive out the conciliatory elements, replace them with those better equipped for combat.

In only one kind of case—exemplified best by the Cincinnati fight in which one side formed the "Committee of 150 for Political Morality"—"Gresham's Law of Conflict" did not hold. As we have said, it was to the *advantage* of that side—not altruism—to invoke against the opponents the community norms which ordinarily regulate a disagreement.

Yet a rather insistent question remains to be answered: if all these forces work in the direction of increasing intensity, how is it that community conflicts stop short of annihilation? After all, community conflicts *are* inhibited, yet the processes above give no indication how. Forces *do* exist which can counteract these processes and bring the dispute into orderly channels—forces which are for the most part products of pre-existing community characteristics, and may be thought of here as constituting a third side in the struggle.[15] Primarily this "third force" preserves the community from division and acts as a "governor" to keep all controversies below a certain intensity.

In part the variations in these forces in the community are responsible for the wide variation in the intensity of community conflicts. Thus, a conflict which reaches extreme proportions in one community would be easily guided into quieter channels in another.

Certain attributes of the community's leadership, techniques which are used—or not used—at crucial points to guide the dispute into more reasonable channels, also affect the development of conflict. These methods, along with the pre-existing community attributes, constitute the means by which a disagreement which threatens to disrupt the community can be kept within bounds. . . .

REFERENCES

Berelson, Bernard, Lazarsfeld, Paul F. and McPhee, William. *Voting*. Chicago: University of Chicago Press, 1954.

Coleman, James. "Political Cleavage within the International Typographical Union." Unpublished Ph.D. dissertation, Columbia University, 1955.

Coser, Lewis. *The Functions of Social Conflict*. Glencoe: The Free Press, 1956.

Hessler, William H. "It Didn't Work in Cincinnati," *The Reporter*, IX, (December 22, 1953), 13–17.

Hurlburd, David. *This Happened in Pasadena*. New York: Macmillan, 1950.

---

[15] This is not to say that some of these forces are not *within* the partisans themselves. Insofar as this is true, it leads to one of the important mechanisms by which conflict can be restrained.

Jones, Alfred W. *Life, Liberty, and Property*. Philadelphia: Lippincott, 1941.

Key, V. O. Jr. *Southern Politics*. New York: Knopf, 1950.

"Outsider Stirs Up Small Town Trouble," *Life*, XXXVII (October 11, 1954), 45–46.

Martin, Lawrence. "Denver, Colorado," *Saturday Review*, ("The Public School Crisis"), XXXIV, September 8, 1951, 6–20.

Mausner, Bernard and Judith. "A Study of the Anti-Scientific Attitude," *Scientific American*, CXCII (February, 1955), 35–39.

McKee, James B. "Organized Labor and Community Decision-making: A Study in the Sociology of Power." Unpublished Ph.D. dissertation, University of Wisconsin, 1953.

McPhee, William. "Community Controversies Affecting Personal Liberties and Institutional Freedoms in Education." Unpublished memorandum, Columbia University, Bureau of Applied Social Research, July, 1954.

Merton, Robert K. and Lazarsfeld, Paul F. "Friendship as a Social Process," in *Freedom and Control in Modern Society*, Monroe Berger, Theodore Abel, and Charles Page, (eds.), New York: Van Nostrand, 1954.

Parsons, Talcott. *The Social System*. Glencoe: The Free Press, 1951.

Pope, Liston, *Millhands and Preachers*. New Haven: Yale University Press, 1942.

Simmel, Georg. *Conflict and the Web of Intergroup Affiliations*. Glencoe: The Free Press, 1955.

Southern School News, III (October, 1956), p. 15.

Stene, Edwin K. and Floro, George K. *Abandonment of the Manager Plan*. Lawrence, Kansas: University of Kansas, 1953.

Stone, Harold S., Price, Don K., and Stone, Kathryn H. *City Manager Government in the United States*. Chicago: Public Administration Service, 1940.

The Inquiry, *Community Conflict*. New York, 1929.

Warner, W. Lloyd and Associates. *Democracy in Jonesville*. New York: Harper, 1949.

25. Emerging Patterns in Community Planning

BY ROBERT MORRIS AND MARTIN REIN

*   *   *

The discovery that social problems persist has troubled us because we had been lulled into complacency by welfare expansion and by overconfidence in the tempo of our great technical achievements. Advances in the medical sciences have only brought us to a confrontation of even more intractable chronic diseases for which we have no medical solution and for which we need a combination of social and medical approaches. Appropriate care of the large volume of long-term illness requires a great expansion of manpower and of physical resources. Important discoveries in psychiatry have not noticeably diminished the incidence of mental illness, although they have permitted us to consider new methods of treatment. Unfortunately, the treatment of mental illness outside institutional walls encounters the gross hazards provided by the new environment just described. The handling of delinquency and all forms of antisocial deviant behavior, such as illegitimacy, drug addiction, and so on, must be dealt with in a community in which multiple standards exist side by side without synthesis or apparent coherence. Poor housing cannot be resolved solely by the construction of new buildings because these new structures must somehow be related to the racial relationships which characterize our urban centers. Solutions through public assistance and vast public programs are not sufficient in themselves because they fail to take into account the enlarged aspirations of diverse social and economic groups, the raised plateau of expectation about what is a minimum standard for social existence.

These problems, or the new understanding about the dimensions of old problems, along with the new centers of influence in community life, have not been adequately articulated with the previously developed welfare planning structures for health and welfare. As a result, old planning structures have been increasingly criticized, and both new structures and new approaches to welfare planning are increasingly being experimented with.

Reprinted with permission of the authors and publisher from Robert Morris and Martin Rein, "Emerging Patterns in Community Planning," *Social Work Practice, 1963* (New York: Columbia University Press, 1963), pp. 165–76. Footnotes have been renumbered.

The new forms for planning and the new planning practices can be reviewed by comparison with the federated structure, the rational utopian view, the goal of coordination, and the strategy of consensus which characterized our past.

These new forms can also be understood in light of the changed community circumstances which we have just been discussing. If our past history led naturally and logically to the development of a certain approach to planning, it may be equally true that the new community life will lead equally to its own appropriate forms of planning.

What are these new approaches to planning? They are the new urban planning agencies, the mobilizations for youth, the community mental health centers, the public health department, the new rehabilitation concepts in public welfare. A comparison between these approaches and those of the traditional community-wide welfare planning council has been blurred because each of them uses the term "comprehensive community planning" with equal ease.

In some fifteen or twenty major cities urban renewal planning has stimulated the development of new organizations committed to the human and social aspects of urban renewal. These organizations are rooted in the necessities for the actual rebuilding of our core cities. They are equally committed to a comprehensive view of the needs of the human beings who are affected by this renewal. As a result, they turn to the schools, the family welfare agencies, the settlement houses, the hospitals, and seek to engage all of them in program development directly associated with the problems of family relocation and physical rebuilding.

Community mental health centers are committed to the development of positive mental health and adequate care of the mentally ill. They seek to encompass in this effort our schools, our family welfare agencies, our settlement houses, our general hospitals and our mental hospitals. In similar fashion, our youth development efforts, best characterized by Mobilization for Youth in New York City, are concerned with juvenile delinquency and the lack of opportunity for deprived youth. They seek to involve the school system, family welfare agencies, public welfare agencies, settlement houses, industry, and labor unions in the problems of youth opportunity as a major attack on delinquency.

Public welfare agencies are attacking the problem of dependency with a broadened concept of rehabilitation. They seek to engage the interest of schools, family welfare agencies, settlement houses, rehabilitation centers, hospitals, and industry with the view to overcoming the conditions which lead to dependency and opening up opportunities for families now on public assistance.

What we see is that a number of key social problems—mental and physical illness, deviant behavior or delinquency, financial dependency, and poor housing—are each viewed as a central organizing theme for comprehensive community planning. Each subject identifies a community of agencies and interests demanding its own action. Each grouping has the character of a community and each of them is approaching the same resources for its purposes.

This proliferation of planning centers has been decried and has met with harsh criticism on the grounds that it destroys the essential unity of comprehensive community planning. What critics of this evolution have not taken into account is the generating source for these multiple developments, namely, the changed community. The stable community has been replaced by a community of great complexity with many special interests. Each of these special interests is sufficiently complex in itself to justify a perception of itself as a community with many subelements. The fact that these specialized communities are paralleled by other specialized communities is a matter of no great concern to any of them because the requirements of their own community demand all their energies. Thus one interpretation would be that the total community concept has been paralleled by, if not eclipsed by, the rise of multiple special communities. These new welfare planning approaches are characterized by the following elements: they are partisan rather than federated; their influences are derived from nonlocal rather than local sources; they are likely to be public rather than voluntary; they are concerned with political skills more than they are with consensus-forming skills; and their goal is change in the community structure rather than coordination of available resources.

The new planning structures are essentially partisan in character. Their policy-making leadership consists primarily of like-minded persons with a definite image of the change they seek to promote and the objectives toward which they are striving. They seek to modify their environment so that it becomes consistent with their aims and objectives. Cooperation is desired, but primarily around their focal concerns. This contrasts with the federated approach in which the federated planning organization seldom if ever seeks to impose its image upon its cooperating organizations.

The base for much of the specialized interest planning is found outside the local community. The origin of stimulation of ideas is mainly located outside the local community—in the Ford Foundation, the national health agencies, the Federal Urban Renewal Program, the President's Committee on Juvenile Delinquency and Youth Crime, and the Hill-Burton Hospital Construction Program, to mention but a few. At the same time, funds are gathered (from local citizens, it is true) at national centers, especially through taxation, and redirected into local communities through national channels, such as the U.S. Department of Health, Education, and Welfare, the Housing and Home Finance Agency, and others. These channels are often fixed by congressional action which governs the funding of new programs.

The magnitude of change envisioned by some of the new planning organizations is so great that it has not yet been grasped by voluntary welfare agencies. As a result, public and governmental structures are either the centers for this planning or they become the dominant partners. Public health departments or state rehabilitation commissions are likely to be the generating source of planning in the field of physical health; state departments of mental hygiene, community health clinics, and community mental health boards, in the field of mental health; the Department of Public Welfare, in the field of dependency; the mayor's office or an urban renewal agency or department of public housing, in urban renewal.

Where the initiative is not vested chiefly in public programs, new organizations are created which bring public and voluntary organizations together into a new alignment, illustrated by agencies established to deal with the social consequence of urban renewal—Action for Community Development, in Boston; Community Progress, Inc., in New Haven; Philadelphia's Council for Community Advancement. Public organizations and city government are likely to be the principal partners in these new organizations. Thus the redevelopment authority, the schools, and the health or mental health departments enlarge their functions and assume responsibilities for community-wide planning (albeit along the axis of their special interest) previously considered the domain of the comprehensive voluntary welfare council.

The goals of the new planning organizations can also be contrasted with those of past planning bodies. They are concerned with new ways in which to alter the environment out of which social problems emerge. They are thus engaged in the pursuit of defined objectives, the achievement of which can be measured. They are less satisfied with coordination of available resources and seek in some more fundamental fashion to change the conditions which give rise to these problems. They seek to develop and enlarge rather than to integrate. Thus the problems of delinquency are attacked through the schools and employers. The schools provide a base for reaching all youth and their function is enlarged to provide, not only minimum education, but also appropriate educational facilities for all youth commensurate with the requirements of the society into which they are going to move. The schools may even become centers for much broadened character-building activities since they are more widely based than that of the smaller units of settlement houses.

The approach is not primarily one of motivating youth to desire a better life (an approach based upon the assumption that the problem rests within the individual), but rather one of opening up jobs in industry, on the assumption that the problem lies in the character of economic opportunity available. In the field of mental health, the community clinics are not exclusively concerned with assisting mentally ill individuals to adapt to the harsh realities of a competitive world; they turn to the development of supporting attitudes on the part of large segments of the community or to a major improvement in community receptivity of the mentally ill or handicapped. As part of the planning stimulated by the U.S. Department of Health, Education, and Welfare, the Federal Government is now employing workers who have a history of mental illness, a significant departure from previous policies.

In the health field there is no longer satisfaction with motivating individual patients to seek medical care through health education. Attention is now being directed to the organization of medical care to assure comprehensive and continuing health services. Many of the deficiencies in our health picture are viewed as inherent in the way in which we have organized the use of physicians, social workers, nurses, and so on, rather than as due to lack of information on the part of patients, necessitating devices to motivate potential consumers to use health services. The current assumption calls for unification of home care services, expansion of social insurances and group practices, and development of inclusive outpatient services; the former assumption demanding guidance, therapy, and education of the individual.

As is common with any form of social innovation, new problems are encountered as we seek to resolve old ones. It is perhaps readily evident that in the new situation, unclear and changing as it is, two problems can now be identified. The several planning approaches, each organized around a special interest, are necessarily in competition for limited funds and personnel. There is no definite allocation of funds and other resources for a balanced plan of action.

There is also in any community competition for the interest and help of citizens. The mental health organizations, the health agencies, the youth organizations, the urban renewal groups, are all endeavoring to attract the wholehearted interest of supporting citizens. The schools seek to develop parent-teachers associations with enlarged responsibilities; urban renewal agencies want to develop local block organizations; welfare councils try to organize neighborhood planning councils; settlement houses encourage the formation of tenant groups. In the abstract, it would appear that each of these organizations is appealing to the same citizen reservoir. In fact, they may be appealing to different citizen constituencies, but this remains to be determined by further analysis and study. It is not yet clear whether the central pool of community leadership with a comprehensive community view survives today and is the object of search by each of these special interest planning groups; or whether there are fragmented leadership centers, each attracted to one of the special groups mentioned above.

The present situation is still too new and too fluid to permit any final conclusions. However, one trite issue is clearly presented. Shall we strive for a new reintegration of these multiple planning centers into a comprehensive community planning organization consistent with our past tradition? Or shall we accept the existence over an indefinite period of time of multiple planning centers which must be in parallel competition? The first approach has been forecast by Zimbalist and Pippert;[1] the second has been developed most lucidly by Banfield and Dahl.[2]

Since our communities are now not only more complex, but also include a greater diversity of powerful influences and special interests, the question may reasonably be asked whether a reintegration into comprehensive community approaches can take place at any level other than government—or within government at any level other than regional, state, or Federal. If we seriously believe that reintegration can take place within the voluntary concepts of the past, we need to visualize a voluntary association capable of embracing the powerful economic, ethnic, and sectarian interests which dominate in our urban centers. It is unclear whether any community can delegate so much authority and influence to any voluntary organization based upon past patterns. If this is to be the route followed, new voluntary structures not now envisioned will have to be fashioned.

This position is not widely promoted today. Commenting on the exhaustion of nineteenth-century ideology by 1950, Bell observes that "few 'classic' liberals insist that the state should play no role in the economy, and few serious conservatives, at least in England and on the continent, believe that the welfare state is 'the road to serfdom.' "[3]

If the development of such potentially reintegrative planning is to center within our basic democratic governmental framework, we are also confronted with new and complex problems. Social problems will not defer to existing political boundaries. The need for regional planning and for embracing larger and larger units of government presents us with an ideological dilemma. Social workers favor self-determination and the control by the local citizen of his own destiny, while the increasing importance of state and Federal intervention to constrain local choices is apparent. The nonlocal center where resources for planning and service are abundant has become the chief locus for social innovation. Yet fiscal partnership between the locality and these larger units of government of necessity limits the autonomy of a local community.

The issue of centralized planning—an increasing reality in social work practice—will need to be squarely faced if we are to free ourselves from our

---

[1] Sidney E. Zimbalist and Walter W. Pippert, "The New Level of Integration in Community Welfare Services," *Social Work*, V, No. 2 (1960), 29–34.

[2] Edward C. Banfield, *Political Influence* (New York: Free Press of Glencoe, 1961); Robert A. Dahl and C. E. Lindblom, *Politics, Economics and Welfare* (New York: Harper and Brothers, 1957).

[3] Daniel Bell, *The End of Ideology* (New York: Collier Books, 1961), p. 402.

ideological distortions of social reality. We have seen the growth of planning responsibilities in public health, public welfare, and urban renewal organizations. Much of this development to date has been located in executive departments, and our sense of community comprehensiveness has frequently been outraged because we have observed that the competition between public departments is frequently as sharp and severe as that which once characterized relationships between voluntary agencies.

This has necessarily raised the question of whether there is any provision in our political framework for coping with this type of competition—a mechanism comparable to the voluntary welfare council in its dealing with voluntary agency competitiveness. It can be suggested that a mechanism does exist in our political environment, namely, the central executive office of government found at all levels. In several municipalities the mayor's office has begun to assume the kind of integrative responsibility over executive departments which has traditionally been carried by voluntary welfare councils over voluntary agencies. In these communities the mayor has brought together his Commissioner of Welfare, Commissioner of Health, and Director of Housing or Urban Renewal and in his own cabinet sought to integrate their approaches to fundamental social problems in the municipality. This integration has been challenged as being essentially unstable or dictatorial. It is argued with equal vigor that the basis for our democratic process permits the total citizenry of every jurisdiction to exercise its wishes by frequent elections; the acts of the mayor or of the executive officer in pooling the efforts of his own executive department heads are therefore subject to the constant review of the electorate. It is possible that the conception of the voluntary welfare council, representative of the public interest, has sufficient vitality to be extended to government.

Similarly, there has been in recent years an attempt to use the governor's office to bring about an integration of executive departments at the state level. California has brought together for more effective planning the departments of public health, mental health, and public welfare. In Pennsylvania, there has recently been advanced a proposal for a council on human resources to encompass these interests in the executive branch. In some less populous states, departments of public welfare and health have already been merged into one executive branch. In certain very populous states, such as New York, the governor's office has established interdepartmental committees with strong staffing responsible directly to the governor.

At the Federal level, this development is not so clearly discernible, although the organization of the Department of Health, Education, and Welfare itself a few years ago was a major step in the attempt to bring together the executive interests in public health, mental health, welfare, and education in one manageable administrative unit. This trend may not continue, for there has been persistent talk of a separate cabinet post for health which would suggest the strength of counterinfluences which derive from the special interests previously discussed.

It is also possible to envision a continuation of the present competitive situation between various centers for planning with each one focused on a special interest. Political scientists frequently seem to agree that the essence of democracy is the freest competition between special interests. In this view, special interests are neither evil nor undesirable but are the best assurance that the great variety of human needs will be ultimately served by the fullest expression of differences free to compete with each other. This theory has been advanced by authors as diverse as Sills, Banfield, Dahl, and Truman.[4]

The period in which we are living is obviously difficult and exciting. The outcome is uncertain, and there is ample room to argue for either of the preceding approaches. However, whichever we choose, one consequence for professional practice in community organization seems inevitable. Social work's concern with community planning needs to develop skills, not only in the traditional enabling processes, but equally in the political processes, in an understanding of conflict, and in negotiation, bargaining, and diverse strategies which can be utilized to reconcile differences.

Political knowledge and skill to achieve one's ends have often been considered by social workers to be unprofessional. We have somehow believed that strong advocacy of a particular point of view and the development of techniques to achieve those ends violate our professional commitment to the democratic process. We have generally ignored the fact that other professions, such as the law, have been built largely around the adversary principle, which assumes a conflict of interest. Professional expression is guided by ethical and legal limits in the promotion of client interests.

The question for us is whether our commitment to professional neutrality and noninvolvement is to continue to sustain our professional practice. If it is, it can be predicted that our contribution to modern life will lie largely in the coordinative realm—coordinative among organizations that share common interests. The requirements of the new community demand skill in advocating special points of view and in living with other professionals who advocate competing points of view. Thus social workers may be concerned with planning in health, youth development, or housing and each worker may be a respected member of the profession. Each may seek to engage the support, interest, or collaboration of the other. Each may succeed or fail in varying degrees and still be professionally reliable.

On the other hand, if we choose to seek a new level of reintegration so

---

[4] Banfield, *op. cit.;* Dahl, *op. cit.;* David Truman, *The Governmental Process* (New York: Alfred A. Knopf, 1951); and David L. Sills, *The Volunteers: Means and Ends in a [National] Organization* (Glencoe, Ill.: Free Press, 1957).

that we can recapture the over-all community view, we cannot avoid the development of political skills which are essential to bring together into agreement the competing interest groups which characterize the public scene. It is our view that this reintegration will probably take place at the public level in a form consistent with our heritage of political democracy. If this integration does take place at the government level, it will have certain similarities to the integration at the welfare council level in that consensus will have to be developed among a variety of interests, and this will then draw upon the community organization skills with which we have become so familiar. In one sense, we will be concerned with coordination and consensus simply on a wider field, and it could be argued that our practice will not differ much from that of the past.

However, this type of integration will differ substantially from the one we have known in one significant respect. The voluntary welfare councils have succeeded because they have concentrated on bringing together groups of leaders, trustees, and organizations with a largely common foundation of interest and association. The voluntary council has been able to screen out those likely to produce major conflict divisiveness, and to concentrate attention upon those who accept the standards and patterns expected by the voluntary council.[5] However, if we are to have community planning in the executive branch of government, the dynamism of our political processes makes it impossible to be so self-limiting. Therefore, the new forms of planning will of necessity have to deal with potentially and actually conflicting areas of interest in each community. The challenge which will be placed upon community organizers then will be how to deal with openly conflicting interests and how to bring them together in a general community approach. This type of conflict handling will call upon the skills and knowledge of all the social sciences—sociology and psychology, with which we are familiar, political science and political economy, with which we are unfamiliar.

[5] See Martin Rein, "Organization for Social Innovation," National Conference on Social Welfare, 1963.

26. Social System Models for Planners

BY ROBERT R. MAYER

PURPOSE OF THIS INQUIRY

This paper sets forth, in simple and concise terms, five distinct models of social systems which are derived from the literature, and relates these models to actual phenomena with which planners deal. This task is essentially definitional rather than explanatory. I will not deal here with the dynamics of such systems, with planned change, or with control of social systems. My primary objective is to clarify this very complex subject. Once distinctive models have been established it will be possible to take up such issues.

I will distinguish five types of social systems: (1) a microcollectivity, (2) a complex macrosystem, (3) an exchange system, (4) an interorganizational field (which can be characterized by two subtypes—the coalition and the federation), and (5) an ecological system. . . .

Social system models will be analyzed examining the work of four principal authors: Parsons, whose central ideas revolve around social systems which are collectivities; Ramsoy, whose writings focus on complex macrosystems; Blau, whose major interest is in systems based on exchange processes; and Warren, who provides a variation on Blau at the interorganizational level. Three elements of the different models are emphasized: (1) The level of the system, that is, macro- or micro-; (2) the structure of each model, that is, how are the elements of the system arranged relative to each other; and (3) the integrative mechanisms peculiar to the model, or "the glue" which holds the system together (integrative mechanisms refer to shared goals, shared values, reciprocity, and common resources). In addition, we shall look at examples of social behavior to which these models can be applied in the real world.

Before proceeding, it is necessary to define certain basic terms which underpin this discussion.

1. *Social system.*—By social system is meant any patterned social interaction or interdependency which persists over time. This definition is very

Reprinted with permission of the author and publisher from Robert R. Mayer, "Social System Models for Planners," *Journal of the American Institute of Planners* 38, no. 3 (May, 1972): 130–139.

loose and incorporates a wide range of social behavior from a friendship clique, to urban street life, to national society.[1]

2. *A microsystem.*—As defined by Blau, a microsystem is a social system in which the constituent elements are individuals or, more technically speaking, role incumbents (1964, pp. 12–32).

3. *Macrosystem.*—In contrast a macrosystem is a social system in which the constituent elements are social systems, referred to in this context as subsystems (Blau, 1964, pp. 12–32).

There is a tendency to think of macrosystems as large social systems and microsystems as small ones, in which case the only distinction rests on the question, "How big is big?" There are however some subtle and more substantive differences inherent in this dichotomous way of looking at social systems. As Blau points out, in a microsystem, composed as it is of individuals as constituent elements, personal attraction is an important integrative mechanism, whereas in a macrosystem, value consensus is necessary to provide the basis for indirect exchange. In addition, a macrosystem is characterized by an interplay between processes within subsystems and processes between subsystems. Finally, macrosystems develop enduring institutions which persist beyond the life of individual members.

Ramsoy refers to a similar distinction in his discussion of the problem of levels in social system analysis. Any social system can be thought of as containing smaller social systems, or as being contained by a larger social system. He calls the former an *inclusive system* and the latter a *subsystem*. These terms are useful in analyzing the relationship between different system levels. In this sense they are relational terms and not intrinsic terms. They should not be considered synonymous with macrosystem and microsystem because although all inclusive systems are necessarily macrosystems, not all subsystems are microsystems.

With these conceptual tools in hand let us now examine the various social system models.

A PARSONIAN MODEL: THE MICROCOLLECTIVITY

The first model is based on the work of Parsons and is contained in a planning model developed by Mayer (1972). Because my ultimate interest is in planning models and not basic theoretical schemes, I will focus on this translation of Parsons rather than on the model developed by Parsons himself.

[1] I agree with Ramsoy that "social system" is the central concept in sociology. To use more traditional criteria of boundary maintenance and value consensus ignores a considerable amount of behavior which has systemic properties (for example, urban street life), and a whole range of institutionalized conflict which has become a fact of life. To Ramsoy the single criterion of "double contingency" is sufficient.

The basic elements of this model are individual actors rather than groups of actors or systems. Parsons refers to the object of his analysis as the orientation of individual actors in a system of action (1951, pp. 3ff). In this sense the model is a microsystem. This assertion may puzzle many students of Parsons, since Parson's goal is to develop a theory of society. In much of Parson's work, however, the building blocks of the social system are social roles, and society is treated essentially as an aggregation of roles or of institutions (functional clusters of roles).[2]

One should not confuse the actor with the individual as a biopsychological being. An individual participates in many systems, but a role exists only as part of a particular system of action. The expected patterns of behavior or roles which people play in the context of a particular group are the elements of a microcollectivity. (See figure 1.)

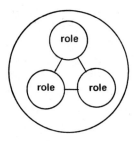

FIGURE 1. MICROCOLLECTIVITY

The structure of a microcollectivity is the arrangement among the particular roles and their accompanying statuses which comprise the system. Roles refer to the expected patterns of behavior which different actors perform. Statuses refer to the rights and obligations accompanying those roles. The structure, therefore, may be thought of as a division of labor and a distribution of rewards and duties among elements of the system. Such a structure can be highly differentiated or relatively undifferentiated; it can be hierarchical or lateral. Most systems, however, tend to some degree of hierarchy, in the sense that not everybody can be a leader.

The unique means by which this system is integrated is through shared goals and values. A collectivity exists because people have a common objective which is usually reinforced by a common set of values. The central thesis of Parsons' work is that value consensus is essential for system integration.

Examples of social behavior which conform to this model are common-

---

[2] Parsons does develop a macromodel of social systems in his analysis of the functional prerequisites of society, but this model is highly abstract and not clearly related to the one discussed here. See Lopreato (1971), and Gouldner (1970).

place. The classroom, friendship groups, and the nuclear family are classic examples of microcollectivities. A department or division of a bureaucracy may be treated as such a system, as may a work group in a factory, the governing board of an agency such as a planning commission, or the administration of an agency. Spatially defined units such as rooming houses or neighborhoods may become microcollectivities when inhabited by persons of common ethnicity or subculture. Client groups, as they become organized, are an increasingly important form of microcollectivity. It is interesting to note that this model, which is the oldest and most traditional of the models presented here, is currently having a revival among adherents of the New Left. The "communes" springing up around the country as precursors of a new social order are precise examples of microcollectivities (Roberts, 1971).

RAMSOY: THE COMPLEX MACROSYSTEM

Ramsoy's principal interest is in inclusive systems, which contain social systems that can be analyzed on two levels simultaneously. Ramsoy deals with macrosystems because the constituent elements of his inclusive system are social systems which are treated as subsystems.

In discussing the nature of social systems, Ramsoy shows why Parsons' collectivity is only one of several important models of social behavior. There are a variety of situations in which shared goals are not characteristic (for example, a buyer-seller relationship), and indeed in which conflicting goals may be the essence of the relationship (for example, a football game). Thus Ramsoy introduces the notion of the noncollectivity or the nonsolidary social system.

Thus we must distinguish between two distinctly different models of macrosystems presented by Ramsoy. The first model conforms to the definitions of a collectivity in that the system is characterized by having an inclusive goal, that is, a goal shared by all subsystems, and shared values. We may call this model a macrocollectivity. In such systems, argues Ramsoy, one of the subsystems always emerges as a leadership subsystem. This position is conferred on that subsystem which most adequately reflects the inclusive goals. Presumably, the norms of such a system reinforce allegiance to inclusive goals and legitimate the power exercised by the leadership subsystem. (See figure 2.)

Role and status define the structure of a microcollectivity, but what constitutes the structure of a macrocollectivity? Ramsoy points to several structural characteristics of the inclusive system, principally (1) the number of subsystems and degree of differentiation among them, (2) the presence of a leadership subsystem and the amount of power accruing to it, and (3) the distribution of power among subsystems. These characteristics are roughly analogous to the structural characteristics of microcollectivities. The

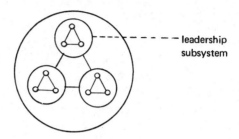

FIGURE 2. MACROCOLLECTIVITY

bureaucracy, long the dominant model of organizational behavior, is the classic example of a macrocollectivity.

Ramsoy distinguishes his alternate model on the basis of integrative mechanisms. The distinction rests on what Ramsoy refers to as "the problematic relationship" between subsystems and inclusive systems. In some inclusive systems the constituent elements are collectivities which pursue conflicting goals. Such systems are held together by institutionalized means of conflict resolution. In this sense the inclusive system can not be thought of as a collectivity. Ramsoy considers this situation the extreme case of the complex system. Following this line of reasoning I will call this model the "complex macrosystem." (See figure 3.)

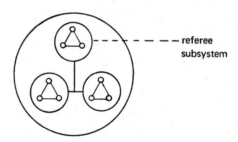

FIGURE 3. COMPLEX MACROSYSTEM

For example, in the case of a football game, both teams, collectivities, pursue conflicting goals, namely to win. But the inclusive system has a subsystem, referees, whose function it is to control the contest. Also, the inclusive system has certain norms to which subsystems subscribe that establish the ground rules by which the contest is waged. These norms or shared values prohibit conflict, in the sense of one party seeking to destroy the other, and reinforce acceptance of the outcome of the contest on the part of all subsystems. Thus, a complex macrosystem consists of two or more collectivities which have conflicting goals, but which share limiting values that are enforced by a referee subsystem.

An example of a complex macrosystem more relevant for social policy is the unionized factory. Such a system can be thought of as including two competing subsystems, the union and the management. The union seeks to maximize wages, the management seeks to maximize profits. Yet the system hangs together and certain outcomes are achieved. Contest is built into this system by a parallel hierarchical organization representing labor and management, from the shop foreman and steward up to the plant manager and union president. There are certain mechanisms for resolving conflict, such as arbitration and the use of contracts. When none of these mechanisms work, the unionized factory breaks up into two conflicting collectivities and there is a walkout or strike.

This example is important in an era when social conflict has become a continuous fact of life. Planners need to learn how to design social systems in which conflict is a normal process and is managed without destroying inclusive goals.

It might be argued that a factory is really a macrocollectivity. It has an inclusive goal of producing certain goods, a division of labor among various departments of the plant to achieve that common goal, and norms which support management's right to make decisions about product design and marketing. This conflicting view illustrates the danger of treating social system constructs as real objects rather than as analytical tools. A factory is neither a macrocollectivity nor a complex macrosystem: sometimes it functions as the former and other times it functions as the latter. It is in the interests of management to create the atmosphere of a collectivity. It is in the interests of union leadership to "polarize" the factory and to reinforce conflicting goals.

BLAU: THE EXCHANGE SYSTEM

The work of Peter Blau contrasts clearly with previous models of social systems (1964). Blau's thesis is that models which emphasize common goals and value consensus ignore an important basis of systemic behavior, namely, exchange processes and the distribution of power.

Blau's model, by his own admission, applies primarily to systems in which the constituent elements are individuals and which are based on voluntary association. The model cannot depict systems in which interaction is coerced or controlled by forces extraneous to the individual, such as prisons or kinship groups. An exchange system consists of individuals who are mutually attracted to each other by the expectation of an exchange of rewards. In the model's simplest form the classical example is the relationship between friends.

The structure of this system is undifferentiated; it consists of actors who at the outset are equal in terms of status or power and differentiated only in the sense that each has something the other needs. Yet Blau recognizes that such systems rarely remain undifferentiated. He notes that often one party in the exchange process has a reward for which the other party cannot reciprocate. Under such circumstances, the emptyhanded party has three choices: he can try to force the other party into giving up his reward; he can shop around for other sources of the reward; or he can try to live without the reward. If none of these alternatives is acceptable, the emptyhanded party must give up his autonomy or subordinate himself to the wishes of the other, thereby rewarding the other with power over himself. Under these conditions a system can be said to be differentiated on the basis of power—certain parties control resources or rewards needed by other parties and are able to extract compliance in return for those rewards. (See figure 4.)

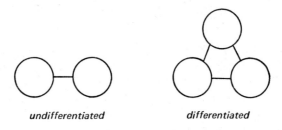

undifferentiated   differentiated

FIGURE 4. EXCHANGE SYSTEM

The integrative mechanism for the exchange system is the most unique feature of this model. Mutually satisfying rewards, and not common goals or values, are the basis for holding together this system of social relationships. Even in its more differentiated state, the relationship between the person in power and those over whom he exercises power has important exchange elements. If the demands set forth by the powerholder are reasonable in the eyes of the subordinates in relation to the rewards given then subordinates attribute legitimacy to the powerholder, compliance is reinforced, and the system is held together. If, on the other hand, the powerholder's demands are considered unreasonable in relation to the rewards given, the subordinates feel exploited. If this feeling of exploitation is widely shared, it provides the basis for opposition movements which threaten the integration of the system.

In its differentiated form, Blau's model of an exchange system looks very much like a large scale organization such as a bureaucracy; that is, the model is appropriate for the same set of phenomena to which the collectivity has been applied. The significant difference, of course, is that systemic behavior has been explained without reference to common goals or value consensus.

For this reason, Blau's exchange model is useful in explaining aspects of orga-nizations left unaccounted for by the collectivity model. Value consensus and shared goals are not the only means by which systems of social relationships are held together, as anybody who has been a bureaucrat or an administrator is quick to recognize. An office holder who consistently relies on the preroga-tives of his office or on moral authority to secure the compliance of subor-dinates soon discovers the tenuousness of his regime. Although some degree of value consensus is necessary if exchange processes are to be sustained, the exchange model suggests that such consensus is a function of the exchange and not a prerequisite.

The exchange model is uniquely suited to the social arrangements that take place outside normative systems, or to deviant subsystems within norma-tive inclusive systems. For example, in a study of relationships between police and criminals, Walsh discovered that some criminals negotiate a role of "stool pigeon" with the police in order to avoid arrest (1971). This ar-rangement is useful to the police in that it provides a source of information necessary for the surveillance of more serious crime. It is useful to the "stool pigeon" in that it guarantees him protection against arrest while carrying out his illegal activities. Thus in what may be thought of as an inclusive sys-tem structured by norms, deviant subsystems may be induced by exchange processes.

Exchange processes have much to do with the politics of planning. Most planners complain that the fruit of their labor ends up gathering dust on bureaucratic shelves. This fate results in large part because plans are usually drawn up based on goals assumed to be in the "public interest" and to have widespread commitment. These assumptions imply a collectivity which hardly exists in most American cities today. Although there may always be a need for plans which excite the imagination, action plans are made of differ-ent stuff. The exchange model suggests that in the absence of shared goals and values plans should be more in the nature of negotiated commitments to act on the part of relevant parties (contracts if you will).

The exchange model suggests a new approach in dealing with crime and deviancy: that crime and social deviancy are manifestations of the lack of value consensus among significant elements of urban populations. Rather than seeking conformity through programs of correction and rehabilitation, a more feasible approach might be to bargain with such groups around trade-offs that can be used to contain the antisocial aspects of such behavior, thus reducing the necessity for the very expensive procedures of apprehension and institutionalization. Such an approach has already been demonstrated by Shapiro (1966).

Finally, in situations of social conflict, common in much of urban life, the exchange model is the only basis for achieving solutions short of coercion.

The resort to force can be detrimental to the system which practices coercion, as well as to the coerced.

WARREN: THE INTERORGANIZATIONAL FIELD

In his work on the interorganizational field, Warren has developed a set of system models that is particularly relevant to planning at the local community level (1967). In many respects, Warren's models are the counterpart at the macro level of Blau's exchange system.

Warren's basic interest is in explaining how "community decisions" are made, how large scale public programs get launched and maintained over time. Warren has turned away from his earlier view of the community as a collectivity (1963), and has come to view the community as a field or environment in which a number of quasi-independent major organizations operate in pursuit of their view of the public interest. These major organizations, which Warren calls Community Decision-making Organizations (CDO's), have been legitimated through the allocation of resources, either official or voluntary, to operate within a given domain to satisfy the public interest or a public need.

The elements in the interorganizational field are formal organizations (systems); for example, the housing authority, the urban renewal authority, the board of education, the health department, the welfare department, as well as a host of voluntary health, welfare, and youth agencies. In spite of their official responsibility to local or state government or to major funding sources such as the United Fund, these organizations, according to Warren, operate largely independently of any centralized authority or control due to their discretionary power over large resources. Once the annual budgets have been approved, such agencies are active on a day to day basis in "running the community," in essence, with little accountability to some more inclusive system. Furthermore, they are not passive with respect to budget allocations —they initiate plans and lobby for expansion of domain or resources.

The basic factor which forces the elements of the interorganizational field to take cognizance of each other, and thus gives the field systemic quality, is the dependence of the elements on a common resource base, be it public monies, clientele, or legitimation. Because such elements do not necessarily interact and are not subordinate to a common authority or point of control, this system in its extreme form can be said to be an ecological system (Dunn, 1971, pp. 199f). It is the most elementary form of systemic life.

However, as Warren points out, there does emerge from time to time a degree of organization in the interorganizational field, an arrangement among elements which persists over time. Warren refers to such arrangements as "inclusive contexts." Following my analysis they can be thought of as alternative structures in the interorganizational field as a social system.

Warren identifies four such possibilities. However, two of them, the *social choice* and *unitary* contexts, form the outer boundaries of the interorganizational field and actually duplicate two of the other five models discussed here. The middle two alternatives, the *coalitional* and the *federative,* are more unique to the interorganizational field. However, I will discuss all four alternatives.

Warren calls the first structure a *social choice context.* It is the most elementary form of the interorganizational field; no concerted decision-making takes place among the elements. Warren uses Banfield's lucid definition:

A social choice . . . *is the accidental by-product of the actions of two or more actors—"interested parties," they will be called—who have no common intention and who make their selections competitively or without regard to each other. In a social choice process, each actor seeks to attain his own end; the aggregate of all action—the situation produced by all actions together—constitutes an outcome for the group, but it is an outcome which no one has planned as a "solution" to a "problem." It is a "resultant" rather than a "solution"* (1961, pp. 326–327).

One may question calling such a state of affairs a social system. However, it does satisfy Ramsoy's basic criterion, that of double contingency. To the extent that resources are limited, the choices of one actor will constrain the choices of another actor in the same field. A market in which various buyers or sellers influence each other even though there is no concerted decision among either group has this nature. I prefer to call this state of affairs an ecological system because such a term is more descriptive of the phenomenon involved, and because it links the discussion to a larger body of literature which is reasonably well established. I will therefore discuss this alternative more extensively as a separate model.

The structure involving the simplest form of concerted behavior in the interorganizational field is the *coalition.* The coalition emerges when two or more parties discover that they have more to gain by collaboration on a given issue than by pursuing independent courses of action. However, as Warren points out, the decision to collaborate is confined to a specific issue, and therefore the coalition is a transitory structure—as soon as the issue is resolved the structure disappears. Furthermore, the coalition involves no centralization of power or authority. All matters taken up by the coalition must be agreed to by all participating parties. There is no area over which the coalition is given authority to act unilaterally, and it is given no resources, such as a central office or staff, with which to function independently of its members. (See figure 5.)

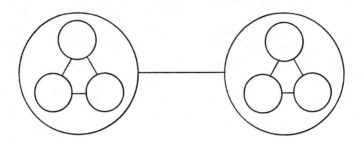

FIGURE 5. INTERORGANIZATIONAL FIELD—THE COALITIONAL CONTEXT

The best examples of coalitions are found in the political arena. Coalitions are formed to lobby for some special legislation which enhances the common interest or to influence some budgetary process. For example, health agencies may coalesce to prevent legislative actions which might inhibit their freedom in fund raising. Coalitions can be thought of as incipient structures of a high order; that is, they will either develop into a more differentiated form, the *federative* or *unitary* structure, or dissolve.

The third structure which emerges from Warren's discussion of the interorganizational field is the *federation*. This is the first differentiated structure with some hierarchical, centralized authority. The federation is a group of elements or organizations which have assigned some limited functions to a centralized body. In Ramsoy's terms, it is an inclusive system with a leadership subsystem. In more vivid terms, it is a coalition which has taken on an office, a telephone number, and an executive secretary. The distinguishing feature of a federation is its centralized authority (with accompanying resources), for it gives the federation a continuing interest in inclusive decision-making. Once such an authority is established, it is possible for the federation headquarters to initiate action, "to wheel and deal" for increased power over the constituent members. Formally, however, the federation is a consensus system in that any actions proposed by the federation must be ratified by its individual members. The federation is not a unitary system, a collectivity, because member organizations are recognized to have individual goals to pursue and the right to unilateral action in those areas not delegated to the federation. (See figure 6.)

The integrating mechanism of the federation, therefore, is its centralized resource or leadership subsystem, which pursues inclusive goals and tries to maximize the domain of the federation and maintain its existence.

There are many examples of federations at the community level: councils of churches, chambers of commerce, united funds, or community chests. The increasing awareness that urban problems cross city boundaries has led

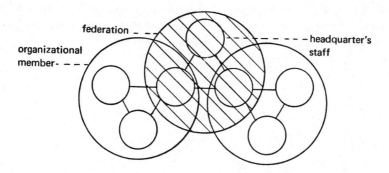

FIGURE 6. INTERORGANIZATIONAL FIELD—THE FEDERATIVE CONTEXT

to the creation of numerous councils of government or metropolitan planning commissions. A common complaint heard by the staff of most such structures is that they rarely overcome the local autonomy of constituent municipalities. This comment reflects a desire of the leadership subsystem to convert the structure into something beyond a federation. The metropolitan service districts, which are unitary systems, are the alternative.

The final structure offered by Warren is the *unitary context*. A unitary context is characterized by the pressure of a common goal, a leadership subsystem to which elements ascribe authority, and an orientation on the part of constituent elements to pursue common goals in preference to their own goals. Here we have returned to the Parsonian collectivity. In this sense Warren's unitary structure is the outer limit of the interorganizational field. It characterizes the state of affairs when the interorganizational field evolves from a system of units whose only integrating mechanism is shared resources into a collectivity. The unitary system has both the moral authority and the centralized power to enforce concerted decisions. I will treat Warren's unitary structure as synonymous with the macrocollectivity discussed by Ramsoy.

THE ECOLOGICAL SYSTEM

The ecological system as a model for social behavior is anticipated by Warren's social choice context of the interorganizational field. As such, its constituent elements are organizations or systems, making the model a macrosystem. However, it can also be thought of as a microsystem, as in Parsons' reference to the market as the best example of an ecological system.

The characteristic structure of an ecological system assumes equality among the individual elements; that is, no one element has prescribed power or authority over another. This characteristic is referred to by Dunn as the absence of any direct or formal management control over system components

(1971, pp. 199f). However, the counterpart of a stratification of elements may emerge. Some may achieve dominance by virtue of their greater influence over the common resources which are the basis of the ecological system (Duncan and Schnore, 1959). (See figure 7.)

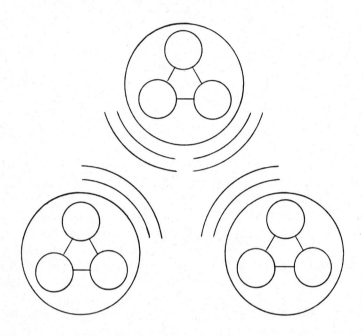

FIGURE 7. ECOLOGICAL SYSTEM

The ecological system is characterized by interdependence among its parts rather than by interaction. The integrating mechanism for such a system is a common resource base. Without such a base, the elements would be completely independent and their behavior would not be characterized as systemic. When the sharing of this common resource base is mutually beneficial, the interdependence is said to be symbiotic. One should not assume, however, that an ecological system is necessarily harmonious. Because of its dependence on common resources, which must be assumed to be limited, the ecological system may be characterized by partial conflict.[3]

The only way of influencing such a system, as Warren points out, is by controlling the allocation of resources or restricting the domain of activity of the elements. This process can be seen in the budgetary sessions of legislatures which review appropriations for different operating departments of govern-

[3] This point is made by Litwak and Hylton (1962) with respect to interorganizational behavior.

ment or in budget hearings for member agencies of a united fund. An aroused public opinion will often lead to legislation which restricts or expands the domain in which a CDO can legitimately operate. Consequently, budgetary decisions and public relations campaigns become important tools in dealing with such systems.

In actual practice there is no perfect ecological system. In the background there is always some latent, more inclusive system which can impose its goals and norms. For example, accepted forms of behavior between buyer and seller in a Mexican market differ markedly from those operating in an American market. At the national level, the government may set ground rules for the ecological system, as in the case of legislation governing fair trade or labor disputes. At the local community level, as Warren observes, the mayor often acts as a *deus ex machina* to resolve conflicts between competing organizations which threaten goals of the wider community (1967, p. 413). And Long notes that a newspaper often serves to arouse "the public," which then demands action (1958, pp. 259f). These interventions reflect the fact that parties external to the partial conflict of an ecological system may experience disutilities which stimulate them to act as an inclusive system and to force some collective goals on that ecological system.

Examples of such a system model are numerous. Much of urban social life is characterized by ecological relationships. At the simplest level (microsystem), Jane Jacobs has analyzed city street life in terms of the interdependency or symbiotic relationship between different types of street users (1961). City planners have considerable impact on patterns of city street life through their manipulations of land use. Dense urban neighborhoods are usually good examples of ecological systems, although they have often been treated mistakenly as collectivities. Suttles describes the symbiotic relationships between ethnic groups in Chicago's Westside (1968); and Gans claims that the Bohemians and the Italians in Boston's West End constitute an ecological system although they never mix socially, their compatible life styles allow them to share common space (1962, p. 15).

A cynic would say that most public organizations behave as though they were elements of an ecological system. The health or medical care field is a particularly good example. Specialized health serving agencies each seek legitimacy and resources to pursue their particular activities and carefully avoid any concerted action lest one agency lose public support or resources to another. Historically, the medical care system has operated as a market, a pattern which thwarts present efforts at comprehensive health planning. A similar state of affairs characterizes youth agencies; every year Boy Scout groups, Boys' Clubs, YMCA's, and similar agencies compete for youths to serve.

In summary, it should be noted that the figures depicting ecological systems and exchange systems lack any containing circles, in contrast to figures depicting models based on a collectivity. This difference reflects the fact that collectivities, unlike ecological or exchange systems, are bound together by common goals or values. This quality is expressed through boundary maintenance which determines who shall and shall not participate in the system, and through the power and authority granted the inclusive system to enforce collective interests. The exchange and ecological models take on all comers who wish to interact or who share some common resource. The system has no inherent power or authority which can hold it together. Reciprocity dictates the system's persistence.

UTILITY FOR PLANNERS

Social system models are useful to planners in two ways: they are instructive in how to achieve desired goals (the planning process), and they indicate appropriate goals around which to develop a plan (planning substance).

If planners are concerned with action, then the ability to distinguish between different types of social systems is instrumental in achieving the planner's objectives. For example, appeals to "the public interest" or to moral authority are relevant only in a collectivity. In such a system, the planner can have influence by aligning himself with the leadership set.

In an exchange system, on the other hand, exhortations of a value nature and appeals to common interests are wasted. The planner in such a system needs to be a negotiator, skillful in the art of finding trade-offs and assessing their relative values. The failure within the Model Cities Program to distinguish this difference in circumstances has been well documented by Warren (1969). The alternative is to invoke some more inclusive system which can establish ground rules that govern the exchanges or can impose solutions on the contesting parties.

In an ecological system, the planner must deal with the resource base which sustains the system if he is to have any influence. This implies that a more inclusive system exists or can be brought into existence which has some control over these resources.

Knowledge of the various social system models can also help the planner identify relevant goals or objectives. To the extent that a given condition can be identified with certain systems, the nature of the system may become an object of change. For example, the collectivity has the greatest degree of control over its members. It is also more stable and durable than exchange or ecological systems. To the extent that these qualities are desirable, the planner will strive to create conditions favorable to a collectivity. On the other hand, exchange systems are more responsive to change, and ecological systems probably foster the most individual freedom.

To the extent that these conditions are goals of the planner, he will try to convert existing systems into ecological or exchange systems.

The key factor in using system models seems to be the integrative mechanisms. If a plan is to have an impact on a system, either for purposes of adaptation or change, it must deal with the mechanism which holds the system together.

In using social system models, planners should be aware of certain inherent limitations. (1) As with any theoretical construct, there is always the problem of *reification*. Social systems are not real facts, they are convenient ways of looking at real facts to identify useful relationships. (2) There is an inherent *variability* in the social behavior depicted as social systems, so that a model may fit more or less well at any given point in time. (3) There is a *restricted determinancy* about social system models in the sense that they do not completely account for social behavior. They must be melded with theories of individual systems (psychological and physiological) and physical systems (economic and natural environmental). (4) A given social system has a built-in tendency toward *equilibrium,* or more appropriately self-preservation. This is often interpreted as a tendency to preserve the status quo, to define change as internal adjustment to maintain basic system states. In any event, the study of social systems is not inherently a conservative enterprise because an understanding of the forces working for stability can be used to good advantage in planning intentional change of social systems.[4]

QUESTIONS FOR FURTHER STUDY

When distinctive systems are identified, at least two major directions for further study present themselves. One is to identify the change processes inherent in these models. The second is to identify the implications of each system for the achievement of social goals such as maximization of individual freedom or creativity, conflict resolution, or system adaptability to changing environmental conditions.

With regard to change processes, each author gives some explanation of how his system changes. Indeed in almost every case, the model's proponent anticipates the alternative models in terms of states of development in his own model. In this sense, the array of models can be thought of as a range on a continuum of states which any social system may assume. For example, small microcollectivities may combine and form a macrocollectivity. Or in Blau's terms, a system, like an amoeba, may divide into two conflicting groups, one splintering off and starting a new system. Or in Warren's terms, a social choice context may convert into a coalition, which in turn may

[4] For a further discussion of these practical limitations, see Mayer (1972).

change into a federation, which eventually may become a unitary system. Identifying these change processes and how they may be brought about intentionally will be of considerable help to planning theory.

With regard to the achievement of social goals, a given system may be more favorable to some goals than to others. For example, it can be argued that nonnormative, egalitarian systems based on exchange processes (for example, a research center), are favorable to high levels of innovation. Similarly, current proposals to give clients the resources to purchase social services in the private market presumably will make the delivery of public services more responsive to client needs. However, as can be seen in the case of international relations, exchange systems are particularly poor at containing conflict which may adversely affect not only the parties involved but innocent bystanders as well. Unitary systems or some type of collectivity may be better suited to the achievement of social order. It is important, therefore, to understand fully each system model's implications for social goals.

REFERENCES

Banfield, E. C. (1961) *Political Influence* (New York: The Free Press).

Blau, P. M. (1964) *Exchange and Power in Social Life* (New York: John Wiley and Sons, Inc.).

Cloward, R. A. and L. E. Ohlin (1960) *Delinquency and Opportunity* (New York: The Free Press).

Duncan, O. D. and L. F. Schnore (1959) "Cultural, Behavioral, and Ecological Perspectives in the Study of Social Organizations," *American Journal of Sociology,* 65 (September): 132–146.

Dunn, E. S., Jr. (1971) *Economic and Social Development* (Baltimore: The Johns Hopkins Press).

Gans, H. (1962) *The Urban Villagers* (New York: The Free Press).

Gouldner, A. W. (1970) *The Coming Crisis of Western Sociology* (New York: Basic Books, Inc.).

Jacobs, J. (1961) *The Death and Life of Great American Cities* (New York: Random House, Inc.).

Litwak, E. and L. F. Hylton (1962) "Interorganizational Analysis: A Hypothesis on Coordinating Agencies," *Administrative Science Quarterly,* 6 (March): 395–420.

Long, N. E. (1958) "The Local Community as an Ecology of Games," *American Journal of Sociology,* 64 (November): 251–261.

Lopreato, J. (1971) "The Concept of Equilibrium: Sociological Tantalizer." Pp. 309–343 in H. Turk and R. L. Simpson, eds., *Institutions and Social*

Exchange: The Sociologies of Talcott Parsons and George C. Homans (New York: Bobbs-Merrill).

Mayer, R. R. (1972) *Social Planning and Social Change* (Englewood Cliffs, N. J.: Prentice-Hall, Inc.).

Parsons, T. (1951) *The Social System* (New York: The Free Press).

Ramsoy, O. (1963) *Social Groups as System and Subsystem* (New York: The Free Press).

Roberts, R. E. (1971) *The New Communes* (Englewood Cliffs, N. J.: Prentice-Hall, Inc.).

Shapiro, J. H. (1966) "Single-Room Occupancy: Community of the Alone," *Social Work,* 11 (October): 24–34.

Suttles, G. D. (1968) *The Social Order of the Slum* (Chicago: University of Chicago Press).

Walsh, J. L. (1971) "Cops and 'Stool Pigeons,' Professional Striving and Discretionary Justice in Two European Settings" (paper presented at the 66th Annual Meeting of the American Sociological Association, Denver, Colorado, 31 August 1971).

Warren, R. L. (1969) "Model Cities First Round: Politics, Planning, and Participation," *Journal of the American Institute of Planners,* 35 (July): 245–252.

Warren, R. L. (1967) "The Interorganizational Field as a Focus of Investigation," *Administrative Science Quarterly,* 12 (December): 396–419.

Warren, R. L. (1963) *The Community in America* (Chicago: Rand McNally).

27. Changing Assumptions About Community Change

BY HANS B. C. SPIEGEL

There are few things that inhibit community change more than the un-wavering dedication of good men to worn-out assumptions. Many of us in community development have been working on the basis of old assumptions that aren't really "wrong" as much as they have become conceptually thread-bare and applicable to a limited range of situations in the field. I want to examine a few of these assumptions and suggest ways in which they might be reformulated.

This is a good time to challenge old assumptions. During the past decade some strong, time-honored, and proud assumptions have fallen by the wayside—assumptions about religion, sex, and education, just to men-tion a few of the subjects in which fundamental questioning has been going on. And perhaps most amazing of all, as a nation we are about to challenge the assumption that the Republic can only survive if it administers a crush-ing military defeat upon its enemies. Many of us in universities have had one of the most sacred assumptions knocked out from under us, or at least seriously pummeled; namely, that only we on the faculty can decide whom to admit to our institutions and determine what should be taught and learned and how and when. Student discontent and minority group move-ments have triggered major challenges to academic assumptions.

This paper deals with five assumptions that have become, I believe, conventional wisdom within the field of community development.

The first assumption deals with the nature of the community; namely, that "the community" represents a single and identifiable unit for whose total development I can work.

The second assumption is about the institutional motivation of com-munity development workers, namely, "to give service" to the community.

The third assumption concerns one of the hoped-for goals of com-munity development; namely, to strive for incremental improvements of local institutions and processes.

The fourth assumption focuses on the political posture of the community development worker; an assumption that his role is essentially apolitical.

Reprinted with permission of the author and publisher from Hans B. C. Spiegel, "Changing Assumptions about Community Change," *Journal of Community Develop-ment Society* 2, no. 2 (Fall, 1971): 5–15.

The fifth assumption deals with professional identity; an assumption that there is one identifiable and codifiable process called "community development."

The assumptions above may sound innocent and noncontroversial. While not rejecting them out of hand, some serious doubts need to be raised about them.

1. The first assumption concerns the community development worker's perception of the nature of the community, and specifically that we can speak of "the community" or "the neighborhood" and that we can work for the total development of such an entity.

A study now drawing to an end examined the efforts of an urban community organization to involve an entire neighborhood in planning a multi-purpose health center. The area is multi-ethnic and otherwise heterogeneous: lower and middle-income whites, blacks, Puerto Ricans, an elderly population, some Haitians, Dominicans and other Carribeans. The organization tried hard to involve these segments of the community by hiring an inter-racial staff, calling small and large meetings, employing indigenous personnel, providing babysitting services to residents to encourage attendance at gatherings, multilingual announcements, involvement of political leadership, etc. The board of the organization, which was middle-class white dominated, was partially successful in changing the composition of the board.

Despite all these efforts, full, vibrant and broad-based participation did not result. Planning was done, but the in-put of minority groups was minimal. It was concluded that planning for this neighborhood as one entity was not functional, at least not during the initial phases. The more prominent sub-communities would have to get themselves together first, it was reasoned. It was recommended that multiple-unit planning be initiated instead. It was hypothesized that a single grant of say $50,000 being made to one over-arching community organization is probably not as useful as five separate grants of $10,000 each to a black group, a Puerto Rican group, the traditional white middle-class group, an organization representing the elderly and one probably representing the interests of youth. These groupings of people would have to figure out their own agendas first and gain some organizational strength before they could successfully engage in subsequent deliberations and negotiations.

This recommendation for multiple planning units within one heterogeneous neighborhood or community is based on the assumption that "the community" is not a unitary "single, living organism," but contains often competing groups and interests that have to be recognized as such. Only after such recognition can community sub-groupings identify and actively work for superordinate planning goals.

The more traditional assumption of "the community" is, of course, much more comforting. Yet, as Roland Warren points out,

A good case could be made for asserting that there is no thing out there to correspond to the term "community"—or, at best, that what is out there is, in the vernacular, a can of worms. Yet planners and community organizers—and at times sociologists—seem to find little difficulty in speaking of the community interest, of planning for the community, of securing community participation, of implementing community goals. Is it not essentially fallacious to convert this can of worms into a unit by the mere verbal magic of calling it a community, and then to treat the word itself as though it represented some virtually tangible thing that has interests, has goals, resists this, supports that, has needs, is planned for, and so on? [1]

Where do these considerations leave me as a community development worker?

They leave me still very much concerned about the condition of the total community and its development. But in heterogeneous urban situations at least, it can be argued that developing the total community is a subsequent step to helping underrepresented and relatively powerless subgroups of the community gain confidence, strength, leadership, and a recognition of where their own interests lie. At this stage, I am far less concerned about helping "an entire community increase its problem-solving capacity" or "developing the whole community." Once the functional subgroupings of a neighborhood have gotten "their thing together" I believe that they can negotiate the various tradeoffs and accommodations, even—Heaven forbid!—without my supposed expertise at third party intervention. Again Warren is instructive on this point. (When he speaks of "planners" he might well have included "and other community developers.")

. . . the planner's role must be redefined by substituting a model of the planning process in which any individual planner is not a consultant to the entire planning system, but to one of the parties thereto. In Model Cities, as in other programs, there are many planners, many conflicting points of view, many mutually incompatible claims to representing the community interest. These incompatibilities are sifted and reconciled, and a modus vivendi is developed not through the detached deliberations of some body of professional arbiters of the community's welfare, but in a hard struggle with high stakes in a process that is essentially—for want of a better word—political. The process is much more adequately captured by actor analysis than by system analysis, much more validly conceived as a struggle of parties than as the behavior of some unified whole [2].

A host of issues are raised by this emphasis, not upon the traditional geographical sub-units of a community or neighborhood, such as blocks, census tracts, or areas, but upon socioeconomic-racial interest groupings. One of those issues surely concerns neighborhood government, which has recently gained visibility. Is the geographical neighborhood the most functional unit for such decentralization? Another issue deals with the ethical questions of this form of functional separation: once we have helped build up the separate segments of a community will we have unwittingly aided the creation of rigid Apartheid?

These issues are real. But they should not prevent us from exploring the community development implications of looking at the community or neighborhood as a multiple entity needing to be enhanced as such.

2. Most community development institutions are dedicated to "serving the community," but underlying the assumption of institutional service may well be a measure of paternalism and arrogance.

Particularly when colleges serve communities, it's pretty clear who serves whom—who receives services and who donates them. We must be concerned about the unintentional message that sometimes parades behind the "service" concept such as "we've got information, skills, and knowledge which you out there need and we, in grandiose altruism, are willing to contribute to you." Community groups are increasingly suspicious of this form of service—at least urban minority groups appear to be.

Why could we not substitute trade-off relationship for the former "service" emphasis? Rather than giving service on a one-way basis we might try to effectuate an exchange where both parties give and receive.

Why could not a university go to a community group and, instead of offering extension courses, technical assistance, scholarships, etc. without any return commitment from the community, trade them off for, say, information for a research study, a roster of available community personnel for potential employment at the college, or even in return for some actual goods and services? The nature and provisions of this exchange relationship might be documented in an actual contract. I have indicated elsewhere[3] just what some of the items might be that community and college groups could trade off. It is important to emphasize, however, that "service to the community" has too often been a one-way street in which the community was tacitly prevented from making a reciprocal contribution to the college. Such reciprocity is at the very core of a non-altruistic trade-off; it cannot easily succeed when one party is intent on donating "community service."

3. The third assumption to be challenged deals with the magnitude of change the community worker is trying to achieve—specifically, with the goal of bringing about incremental changes in local institutions and conditions.

We've all been told that whatever we do, we should do well; through hard work and through perserverance in our positions be they ever so humble, we help bring about a better world. Translated into the framework of the community development worker this might read as follows: "Engage in institutional excellence. Work hard to develop your program in your own locality and the CD world will beat a path to your door. Create the bright and shining examples of CD excellence. Be a frontiersman in your own niche and if enough of us are similar frontiersmen, step by step, little victory by little victory the community development way will win. Keep your eye on the feasible, manageable goals. Don't overreach. Don't try to wholesale your wares, stick to the retailing trade, right next to the consumer-citizen."

The goals of community developers, I believe, must reach further than that. As professionals we must no longer be satisfied with aiming for small incremental changes and leaving the more fundamental and basic changes to other more activist-oriented forces and powers in our communities.

Let me give a personal example of what I mean. Presently I am involved in a small, but exciting store-front museum in one of New York's worst slums. With virtually no funds at all—the actual cash flow for 1970 was an incredible $2500—this operation has gained community acceptance, has active Puerto Rican participants, has indigenous leadership, has found sources of local and metropolitan support, has won Mayor Lindsay's Better Blocks award. In short, by most criteria it can probably be labelled a success. Affiliation with the project gives me considerable satisfaction and a welcome ego-boost for having had a small part in creating a shining new institution.

And yet, the impact of this endeavor on fundamental changes within this community is limited. We are not basically addressing ourselves to some of the painful issues of housing, poverty, and health. Nor is there any likelihood that in the forseeable future this particular group will engage in such activities.

Compare this effort with a change in my university that appears to have deep and lasting impact on formerly undertrained citizens of New York City—Open Admissions. All high school graduates in New York City are eligible for entry into the university system and cannot be flunked out for at least one year. This change to my mind represents an educational quantum jump. It forces a number of secondary and tertiary community changes in its wake. It impacts employment, politics, welfare, and a host of other aspects of the life of the city. The change instituted by the city's Board of Higher Education may well be an example of what Paul Ylvisaker described as social jujitsu: the application of minimal pressures to achieve the greatest social change.

I am not decrying the relatively small, incremental change. In a sense, all change proceeds by incremental steps. We can't all take giant quantum jumps—these fundamental, systemic changes are usually the result of smaller efforts that help create the time and place where the larger change becomes possible. Federal laws in civil rights, for example, could hardly have been enacted and enforced had it not been for innumerable smaller struggles in specific cities and towns, in the courts, in the Armed Forces, and on the streets.

Nevertheless, the goals of a community development worker should not stop where his institutional job description ends. His professional goal is not the limited and incremental change his employer seeks. Perhaps some of us have been too parochial in our work—too easily satisfied, for example, with the limited goal of helping one specific institution initiate a minor change in procedure.

If professional people working in community development were more daring we might raise our sights and work actively for quantum jumps such as the following:

—*Federal legislation to assist the development and capitalization of Community Development Corporations* [4]. *There are close to one thousand Community Action Agencies in the country—1000 CDCs might have an even greater impact.*
—*Additional federal legislation that will substantially assist in the creation of New Towns throughout the nation* [5]—*both new-towns-in-old-cities* [6], *and the more traditional European model of new towns in metropolitan areas or even in underpopulated areas. Our own country's new towns policies are considerably behind those of England and Scandinavia.*
—*There has been much talk and even some small projects concerning the introduction of Urban Agents into urban areas* [7]. *Colleges and universities could play a crucial function in directing this effort; 10,000 well trained urban generalists could make a tremendous difference in community development efforts.*

It will be noted that these few examples all deal with federal legislation and federal funding directly or indirectly. Many quantum jumps in community development can be accomplished only with massive federal support. If community development workers want to realize some of these measures they must (a) think through these issues with their many implications and fashion a strategy for approaching Washington, (b) form coalitions with other professional and interest groups that have similar legislative objectives as those of the Community Development Society, and (c) lobby and work for the enactment of such programs.

All this Washington emphasis brings us to the fourth assumption.

4. This assumption deals with the supposedly apolitical role of the community development worker. It seems that some of us are tempted to view our CD agency or college as a non-political jolly green giant here to serve all, a friend to all, an enemy to none, dispensing unquestioned truth, and, of course, loved by all.

That may correspond to your school or agency, but if I'm honest about my own experiences, that's not my school. If we define politics in the Laswell sense as who gets what when, then my program in urban affairs is inherently political. Some group gets more services than others and gets it more frequently. The empirical evidence is rather impressive of who is organized and gets served in our society. Curtis and Zurcher in a recent summary article claim that despite the war on poverty and numerous programs, the poor still are underorganized and don't know about the services available to them. They quote one study that "found that less than nine percent of a lower and working-class Black sample had good information about available vocational rehabilitation programs" [8]. The agricultural extension services have also been criticized for unintentionally serving those farmers who appeared to be more "industrious and cooperative" [9]. Some housing experts used to say, tongue in cheek, that governmental programs best serve the housing stock that represents "the cream of the crap," that is, those dwellings that are bad, but relatively salvageable. Studies that are now emerging concerning the war on poverty indicate that the most upwardly mobile of the poor were more involved, took greater part, and gained more benefits from its program [10].

There is, of course, a difference between narrow partisan politics and some of the broader public policy issues considered here. But I must confess that I have been more prone to err on the side of Monroe Doctrine-like avoiding political entanglements than to risk personal and professional involvement in a political issue of deep potential impact to community development.

The community development worker who wishes to fashion a political role for himself would probably have to stress three aspects of his work: (a) He has to examine what community groups he works with, (b) He has to examine the mode in which he works with these groups and (c) He has an obligation, as already mentioned, to try and impact national policy. Just a brief word about these three roles.

(a) The choice of what segment of CD to work with is, of course, far more difficult than saying. "I used to work with the better-off people, and now I will work with the poor." As most CD workers know full well, powerful barriers intrude themselves before a successful working relationship with a traditionally underserved population can be hammered out, among which are issues of credibility, trust, race, and even semantics.

"Maximum feasible manipulation" is how a large city's citizen group characterized the actions of the local model cities organization [11]—an organization that presumably had its share of urban CD workers on its payroll. The act of deciding which segment of the population will receive which CD assistance is not only highly political, it is also highly hazardous for the worker full of good intentions but short on skills.

(b) The mode of working with community groups may have to include more advocacy for a traditionally powerless group than impeccable neutrality in the local decision-making arena. It may be countered that a number of community development agencies prohibit advocacy, and that some CD workers can afford to be more openly partisan than others. Granted. But again, advocacy can and does occur in formal and informal guises, on the job and off. I believe we can take a lead from other professionals in other disciplines who, having felt penned-in while on the job have decided to use their professional skills to help a powerless group. I have in mind such organizations as Planners for Equal Opportunity, the so-called "advocacy planners;" the Medical Committee for Human Rights; and the "neighborhood lawyers." Again, such advocacy, whether part of one's professional or citizen role, challenges the role description of the community worker as catalyst. "How much of advocacy is a good thing for who and under what circumstances?" might be a fascinating topic for a long and intense discussion at another time.

(c) Trying to impact national policy may involve directly influencing legislation. Consider one additional example: There exists in this country at present a shameful manpower disequilibrium. On the one hand every mayor in the cities needs skilled warm bodies who can operate as block-level workers, urban agents, program expediters, etc. There is considerable dialogue about instituting little city halls and neighborhood governments. What model cities agency hasn't cried for more personnel? On the other hand, there is an amazingly large manpower pool of persons who, often with relatively little training, could successfully perform in this urban arena. There are returned Peace Corps volunteers, VISTA volunteers, former clergymen, other career-change persons, many of whom are from minority groups. There are students and early retirees. Somehow the manpower need and the manpower supply must be brought together. Eventually we must look to Washington to be the honest broker and funder of such an endeavor. It seems to me our professional association for community development workers could help speed the day of this occurrence.

5. The last assumption to be examined deals with the professional identity of a community development worker. I would hate to be the person designated to decide who should be called a CD worker and who not. The task reminds me of a story supposedly connected with the recent U.S. ping

pong team visit to mainland China. It appears that a Jewish member of the U.S. team wanted to attend synagogue. Upon arriving at the door, a Chinese gentleman said that he must be in the wrong place. Our ping pong player stood his ground protesting, "But I, too, am Jewish!" whereupon the gentleman in the doorway apologetically observed, "But you don't *look* Jewish."

There used to be a time when we thought we could tell a CD worker when we saw one. It is no longer so easy. The field is getting crowded. Besides the old stand-bys from the extension services and the technical assistance personnel, there are:

anti-poverty warriors
urban planners
Alinksy types
more typical community organization types
social workers
Community Action Program trainers
church-sponsored urban action centers
Model Cities groups
the National Association for Community Development with its unfortunate acronym
Title I people
community college outreach personnel
community health workers

Many of them have never heard of Dick Poston, Fred Wale, the Biddles or T. R. Batten. Nonetheless, they can justly lay claim to representing a piece of the CD turf. And it is to the great credit of the Community Development Society for having drawn an inclusive, rather than exclusive circle around the field. The Society, I think, has recognized the need to be flexible as it attempts to professionalize community development.

The time may well be here to empirically examine the various approaches currently being utilized under the rubric of domestic community development. The various models intrigue me. I for one would like to know more about the assumptions underlying the different approaches to CD, the personnel operative in each, the results that each produces, and the training methodologies employed by each. Part of this task has already been attempted. Much needs still to be accomplished.

May I submit one final caveat: While we challenge our old assumptions, let's not entirely discard them. My five assumptions still hold true under many conditions. Let's not throw the baby out with the bath water. It is useful to consult Forrester's Law—named after the MIT engineering professor—that holds "that in complicated situations efforts to improve things often tend to make them worse, sometimes much worse, on occasion calamitous"[12]. It may be immodest to say so, but most of us have done some pretty creative things with and for communities and we should not quit these efforts in a rash of self-doubt. There has never been a time when community development workers have been more needed than right now. We can't say to our communities, "Hold everything while I take time off to reevaluate my assumptions!"

But, at the same time and by the same token, community development workers cannot postpone the critical task of penetrating the manifest and latent assumptions made about their field of endeavor.

REFERENCES

1. Warren, Roland L., *Truth, Love, and Social Change* (Chicago, Rand McNally & Co., 1971), p. 129.
2. Ibid., p. 136.
3. Spiegel, Hans B. C. "College Relating to Community: Service to Symbiosis," *Junior College Journal,* Vol. 41, No. 1 August—September 1970, and Spiegel, Hans B. C. and Victor G. Alicea, "The Trade-Off Strategy in Community Research," *Social Science Quarterly,* Vol. 50, No. 3, Dec. 1969.
4. See *CDCs New Hope for the Inner City,* Report of the Twentieth Century Fund Task Force on Community Development Corporations (New York: The Twentieth Century Fund, 1971).
5. See *New Towns: Laboratories for Democracy,* Report of the Twentieth Century Fund Task Force on Governance of New Towns (New York: The Twentieth Century Fund, 1971).
6. Harvey S. Perloff, "New Towns Intown," *Journal of the American Institute of Planners,* Vol. 33, No. 3, May 1966.
7. I doubt whether there is any university community development program that is currently exclusively rural in context. By whatever name we call them, urban agents are, in fact, working in the field. And yet, "urban agents" or "urban extension workers" attached to universities are relatively few in number and have not yet had the opportunities to bring into reality the fond hopes of the 1961 Pittsburgh conference to "make a tremendous contribution to the revitalization of the American city." *A Plan of Operations for Neighborhood Urban Extension,* ACTION-Housing, Inc., Pittsburgh, 1963, p. 3.
8. Curtis, Russell L. and Louis A. Zurcher, Jr., "Voluntary Associations and the Social Integration of the Poor," *Social Problems,* Vol. 18, No. 3, Winter 1971, p. 343.
9. Summary by Vincent Matthews, *Citizen Participation: An Analytical Study of the Literature,* Community Relations Service, Department of Justice, 1968, p. 39.

10. Marshall, Dale Rogers, "Public Participation and the Politics of Poverty," in Peter Orleans and William R. Ellis, Jr., editors, *Race, Change, and Urban Society* (Beverly Hills: Sage Publications, 1971).
11. North City Area Wide Council as told to Sherry Arnstein, "Maximum Feasible Manipulation," *City,* Vol. 4, No. 3, October-November 1970.
12. Schwartz, Harry, "Forrester's Law," *The New York Times,* June 14, 1971. Professor Forrester is perhaps best known in community development circles for his book *Urban Dynamics* (Cambridge: MIT Press, 1969) in which he challenges much of the conventional wisdom of the field.

28. The Transformation of Community Action

BY STEPHEN M. ROSE

It is ironic that organizations, which are said to abhor uncertainty, exist in an uncertain context, the interorganizational field in the local community and in the broader society. To understand the transformation of the Community Action Program (CAP) as it moved from the planning phase at the national level to the operational phase at the local level, we must devote attention to the context in which Community Action Programs were to be run. Remember that the CAP planners did not focus on this issue as a critical one in their planning. Rather, they assumed that the organizations which have come to proliferate in American community life and to perform the necessary functions of communities voluntarily would become involved in the anti-poverty effort. They further believed that these organizations would modify their practices and policies to conform with the Community Action Program in its problem definition and social action strategy. These basic assumptions appear unwarranted in view of available evidence, and the failure of the social action strategy calling for institutional change through voluntary, internal reformulation of problems can be traced to this oversight.

The uncertainty forced upon any local organization (or national organization) in American communities comes from the absence of any overall, authoritative structure. Warren describes this complex situation:

communities are made up of numerous formal structures (city government, industries, labor unions, private agencies, for example) and interaction patterns rather than being constituted as a single organizational unit with comprehensive power and decision-making authority[1]

Warren developed an interest in the operations of large community organizations after analyzing American communities and their increasing reliance on formal organizations to perform the functions necessary for communal living. Through time, these organizations were sanctioned to operate in specified spheres of activity on behalf of the community. Warren concluded that

Reprinted with permission of the author and publisher from Stephen M. Rose, *The Betrayal of the Poor: The Transformation of Community Action* (Cambridge, Mass.: Schenkman Publishing Company, 1972), pp. 162–175.

[1] Warren, Roland L., "The Interorganizational Field as a Focus of Investigation," *Administrative Science Quarterly*, Vol. 12 No. 3 (December 1967), p. 401.

the interorganizational field at the local level consisted of an increasing number of city-wide or metropolitan level organizations, each of which was legitimated or given approval to carry out planning and/or programming in a particular sphere of community activities. In most cases, these organizations received a significant proportion of their funds from the Federal government, which also had varying influence over their program development activities. Interaction between these organizations seems inevitable because of a scarcity of either input or output resources. Thompson makes note of this fact of organization life, describing how organizations are necessarily involved with their environments in acquiring the input resources required by their technologies and in dispensing their products or services among an unpredictable output constituency.[2]

Norton Long has developed a similar concept of organizational interaction at the community level. In his view, the local community approximates an "ecology of games," interaction is unplanned, yet largely functional. Long sees the community as a natural system which "is the product of a history rather than the imposed effect of any central nervous system of the community."[3]

In line with this view of the community, Long asserts that there is no dominant power source capable of directed social planning and change. Long emphasizes this point:

The bases of power are not only split within the city, the splits are multiplied by the multiplicity of jurisdictions and the lack of any centripetal metropolitan institutions. The answer to the question "Who Governs?" . . . is quite literally nobody. The system after a fashion runs. Nobody runs it.[4]

In this unstructured and fluctuating environment, organizations must attempt to conduct their operations and negotiate settlements. The crucial issue to be resolved with other organizations is the domain, or functional relationship of any organization to its environment. Thompson defines a domain as claims which an organization stakes out for itself in terms of (1) problem area covered, (2) population served, and (3) services offered.[5]

The process of establishing a domain is a political one, requiring the establishment of dependencies (for input resources such as finances, staff, and legitimation) and the development of an explanatory mechanism to or-

[2] Thompson, James D., *Organizations in Action*, (New York: McGraw-Hill, 1967), p. 20.

[3] Long, Norton E., "The Local Community as an Ecology of Games," in Norton E. Long, ed., *The Polity*, (Chicago: Rand McNally and Company, 1962), p. 139.

[4] Long, Norton E., "Community Decision-Making," in *Community Leadership and Decision-Making*, University of Iowa Extension Bulletin, No. 842, p. 6.

[5] Thompson, *Organizations in Action*, p. 26.

ganize the personnel around the negotiated domain. The establishment of a viable domain engages the organization with the local ecological order or, in Thompson's words, the local "domain consensus," "a set of expectations both for members of an organization and for others with whom they interact, about what the organization will and will not do."[6]

The entrance onto the stage of a new organization, with the dynamics of the territorial stage at work, appears as a crisis for existing organizations and for the domain consensus negotiated over time. Long notes that along with an awareness of organizational boundaries within the system is a pattern of interaction and rules about the players of the game, the roles held by each party, and the mode of communication.

When a new organization brings with it an unclear set of domain expectations, regulations insisting on new participants in the local game, and undetermined methods of organizational interaction, the domain consensus within the community is unsettled. This was clearly the case with the Community Action Program. The CAP carried its own rhetoric of institutional change, comprehensive programming, and participation of the poor in the local agency structure, which it had attacked as being a partial cause of the problems the CAP sought to eliminate. The comprehensive thrust of the anti-poverty effort involved itself immediately in the domain concerns of every service system.

The rhetoric about institutional change created uncertainty beyond geographic or output constituency concerns as organizations responded to threats to their technologies (or services offered). And the new rules involving participation aroused further concern over the relationship between the organization and its control over output elements. Thus, from the beginning, the Community Action Program threatened all three components of an organization's domain—the services offered, the legitimation to operate in a protected problem area, and the population served. Long has developed a prescription for organizational action in response to such threats to their survival: "The need or cramp in the system presents itself to the players of the games as an opportunity for them to exploit or a menace to be overcome."[7]

The planners of the Community Action Program provided the local organizations with both an opportunity and a menace. The opportunity was clearly to increase their independence from local financial constraints by capturing the newly available Federal funds. The menace was the constraints and impositions on organizational autonomy which had previously been negotiated with other organizations—the domain consensus.

Thus, the creation of a community action agency posed two great threats: on one level, a challenge to the individual organization's domain;

[6] *Ibid*, p. 28.
[7] Long, "The Local Community as an Ecology of Games," p. 144.

on another level, an impending change in the local territorial system or domain consensus. Because of these conditions, and the circumstances of unplanned interaction between the various segments of community activity (service systems or, in Long's terminology, games), the situation could have been very uncertain. The potential for change in such circumstances was great, because organizational rationality could not function in such an open or unstable environment. Rationality can only exist in circumstances where organizations can control relevant variables and respond in fixed patterns to previously calculable contingencies. Neither of these controls existed in the problem definition and institutional change strategy of the Community Action Program planners. The possibility of achieving the goal of institutional change was enhanced by creating flux or turbulence in the interorganizational field and forcing the organizations into confronting uncertainty in unreliable ways.

But such change in the interorganizational context was not to occur. The organizational model designed by the CAP planners, stipulating the involvement of existing service systems, created an organizational framework which reduced uncertainty by channeling the decisions required to create the new agencies through the filtering device of coordinated planning. By including the interorganizational field within the organizational structure of the new community action agency, the Community Action Program planners provided the opportunity to recreate the local domain consensus or reinforce it with Federal funds. . . .

We have also noted the degree to which the interorganizational field was involved in creating the new agency and in developing its original program proposals. The purpose of the local interorganizational collaboration, as the data on program allocation and program strategy makes clear, was to preserve the domain consensus in the face of the newcomer's threat. Recall that approximately 80 percent of the programs developed through the local community action agency and approximately 80 percent of all Community Action Program funds were delegated to existing organizations. Further, almost 98 percent of the funds were spent on programs which came from an explanatory model contradicting the original planners' framework.

We can understand the capacity of the interorganizational field to dominate the decision-making of the new agencies by investigating the role of the "initiators and developers" of any new organization. Christopher Sower, *et al.*[8] found that the two crucial determinants of any action on social problems were: the constituencies represented by the initiators and the relationship of the proposed action to existing definitions of community welfare. According to Sower and his associates, furthermore,

[8] Sower, Christopher; Holland, John; Tiedke, Kenneth; and Freeman, Walter, *Community Involvement*, (Glencoe: The Free Press, 1957).

It is through a convergence of interest arising out of values, beliefs, and relationships of the larger community that a group is formed which is concerned with the initiation of a specific action. Until such a formation takes place, action exists only in the minds of individuals. The establishment of such an initiating set leads to the development of a common frame of reference from which concrete action flows.[9]

We can take the common frame of reference to which Sower and his associates refer as the domain consensus worked out by the initiators and developers. The boundaries established for the new action are confined to the problem definition determined by this group and to the allocation of resources among those authorized to operate programs stemming from the agreed upon definition. This process of definition and legitimation removes uncertainty from the interorganizational field, decreasing the turbulence created by the threat of institutional change.

We have seen that the various service systems in the community either were convened by the Mayor or constituted themselves as the local "initiating set." . . . The greater the involvement of the interorganizational field, the lower the level of autonomy of the community action agency. Related to community action agency autonomy was social action strategy (and through implication, definition of the problem)—the greater the autonomy of the community action agency, or the lower the involvement of the interorganizational field in the initiation set, the greater the likelihood of a program based on a strategy other than individual or cultural change.

The experience of the Community Action Program has demonstrated that the power to influence a program's outcome is largely determined by the actions of the initiation set in creating and developing the local action arena or in establishing the domain for the new organization within the interorganizational field. This phenomenon was obvious in the data from the twenty cities in this study. This locus of power raises critical question about capacity of existing institutions to legislate and plan local social change or to predict the outcome of a local program based on a Federal design. Investing power and authority in the existing service systems to involve themselves in their own reform seemed eventually to contradict the institutional change strategy. Reform did not come forth, as uncertainty was reduced by the regulations governing the structure of the community action agency. The actors powerful enough to join the group of initiators and developers of the new organizations turned out to be the primary beneficiaries of its resources.

At the time of the establishment of the community action agency, the relevant actors in the environment were the power holders previously legiti-

[9] *Ibid,* p. 68.

mated to perform negotiated services in the community. The dependencies created by these organizations resulted in a community action agency which generally reinforced the domain consensus which they had previously worked out over time. The evolution of the organization was predetermined by the originating commitments made by the initiators and developers in their own interests. The involvement of these groups was required, and the results were predictable. In overlooking the organizational reality, the planners created the demise of their own grand scheme.

The social base of the community action agency, the initiators and the developers of the organization, was further represented in the decision-making structure of the organization through membership on the board of directors. This inclusion within the input constituency . . . of the community action agency prevented the scope of conflict from spreading to new actors and confined it to the competitive yet cooperative interaction of established organizations.[10] The collaboration of these competing organizations indicated that the competition would emerge within an overall framework of cooperation, or mutual adjustment between the organizations involved. The effect of the domination of the input constituency of the community action agency by existing service systems was to create a quasi-closed system in which the previous forms of competition over resources were maintained.

Relative power was maintained in proportion to the security of each organization's domain. Thus, the principal beneficiary, the organization with the highest degree of domain autonomy, was the Board of Education; the second beneficiary, the voluntary social service agencies. Interference in this process by the Office of Economic Opportunity could be marginal at best. Constraints—on the composition of the local agencies' boards of directors— were compromised by the organizational need to allocate funds authorized by the Congress, and by political pressure from the local governments when the political equilibrium (the domain consensus) was threatened in fact as well as in theory.

The role of the Federal and Regional offices in initial and later problem definition and selection of programs is an area of vital interest for further research. For present purposes, we need only note that while local autonomy is allegedly disappearing from American community life, the Community Action Program experience serves as testimony to the continued hegemony of local institutions in the face of threats from the vertical system to reform them through rationally planned social change.

While it is beyond the scope of this study to engage in an extensive theoretical discussion of the potential for planned social change, a brief departure from the analysis of the Community Action Program is merited by the

[10]Schattschneider, E. E., *The Semi-Sovereign People,* (New York: Holt, Rinehart, and Winston, 1960).

questions raised in the CAP experience. Despite documented efforts which demonstrate that centrally planned, comprehensive social change is more a facet of the planners' training and orientation than empirically documented examination would merit,[11] the planners' insistence on its validity is maintained. Thus, coordination of existing service systems has developed out of the Community Council era, to be included in the Ford Foundation, President's Committee, Community Action, and now the Model Cities programs. The evidence from this study indicates that such collaboration between existing agencies serves to thwart reform and innovation rather than sponsor them.

Planners seem unable to reconcile rationality with political reality. As Thompson points out, planning is based upon certain rational assumptions about the context of American communities. Planning proceeds as if these communities were closed systems wherein contingencies as well as identifiable variables were fully known and controllable. Yet James Wilson clearly indicates that the power necessary to maintain such control, quite aside from the requisite knowledge regarding all contingencies, is unavailable in our social system.[12]

Why then are these myths perpetuated and allowed to remain the basis for American social policies? Why did such astute thinkers as the Community Action Program planners succumb to these myths at the cost of their planned strategy for bringing about institutional change? While the author does not presume to answer these complex questions adequately, he will offer a partial suggestion.

The ontological foundations of social planners seem rooted in a pluralistic assumption about the distribution of power in American society. Communities are said to be governed by interest groups which have legitimated domains of primary concern, but which can still be brought together in a rational manner to act in the "public interest" which overrides their specific concerns. Because of the total distribution of power among these easily identifiable sources, planning becomes a rational process of bringing these powerful actors together around a point of mutual concern and persuading them of the import and rationality of the planners' strategy. The theory assumes

[11] See, for example, Banfield, Edward C., *Political Influence,* (Glencoe: The Free Press, 1961); Meyerson, Martin and Banfield, Edward C., *Politics, Planning and the Public Interest,* (Glencoe: The Free Press, 1955); Selznick, Philip, *TVA and the Grass Roots,* (Berkeley: University of California Press, 1953); Marris, Peter and Rein, Martin, *The Dilemmas of Social Reform,* (New York: Atherton Press, 1967); Eckstein, Harry, *The English Health Service* (Cambridge: Harvard University Press, 1964); Thernstrom, Stephen, *Poverty, Planning, and Politics in the New Boston: The Origins of ABCD,* (New York: Basic Books, Inc., 1969).

[12] Wilson, James Q., "An Overview of Planned Change," in Robert Morris, ed., *Centrally Planned Change,* (New York: National Association of Social Workers, 1964).

that they will act accordingly on the changes or infringements on institutional prerogatives that are implied. The pluralistic sources of power are not only considered rational, but even altruistic. The planning process becomes, therefore, primarily a technological matter, bringing needed resources to bear on identified social needs. This notion comes from Robert Agger and his associates:

> *Pluralists take the position, specifically or implicitly, that . . . major decisional options are not shaped by a ruling elite so much as they are by "technical" factors which, assuming there is a desire for "functional rationality," would lead rational men to similar choice situations or decisional outcomes, regardless of socio-economic class or official position.*[13]

The vital ontological issue posed by these men is related to the assumption that men are rational. For the pluralists further believe that *a* best course of action exists and that it can be reached by technically or scientifically derived agreement.

The foundation of such beliefs is rooted in an ideology pervasive in this society which serves to bring about a "consensus" within the population where none in fact exists.[14] The façade of consensus is required to maintain the present form of economic and political structure which benefits the few at the expense of the vast majority. Ideology, in Mannheim's sense, prevents this fact from becoming widely known by providing a definition of reality which legitimates the existing power arrangements. Pluralism is one such definition that has substantial credibility because it appears to offer the opportunity to acquire influence and to wield power to those who really have neither. It promises to represent those who are not actually represented in the mythological competition said to characterize American society.

The influence of this ideology on rationality becomes clear when we examine its influence on planners. For them, the dictates of pluralism are unquestioned. The assumption of an altruistic rationality among the institutions of the social structure also exists a priori. Thus, even for the Community Action Program planners, who addressed the condition of powerlessness, the concept they generated was based upon a pluralistic rather than a class-based model of conflict. They wanted to create for the poor a competitive rather than a conflict oriented base of social power. Their strategy called for the organizations of the poor to take their place at the negotiating

---

[13] Agger, Robert E.; Goldrich, Daniel; and Swanson, Bert E., *The Rulers and the Ruled*, (New York: John Wiley and Sons, 1964), p. 76.

[14] Horowitz, Irving L., "A Formalization of the Sociology of Knowledge," in Irving L. Horowitz, ed., *Professing Sociology: Studies in the Life Cycle of a Social Science*, (Chicago: Aldine Publishing Company, 1968), p. 68.

table of rational, altruistic organizations in working out the reforms the existing institutions would have to undergo in responding to what was clearly the "public interest." The power of an ideology, blatant in these circumstances, is captured by Irving Horowitz:

> *By expanding our definition of the function of ideology to make room not only for justification (Marx) and rationalization (Weber), but also for the role of ideology in organizing and institutionalizing social drives, one can more readily understand the binding force of an ideological complex upon a social structure.*[15]

As an operational arm of the ideological complex, planning becomes the technology for extending social control throughout all sectors of society. When planning deals with social problems it functions to control those causing the "problems"—as defined by the institutions of the society. Planning thus serves to allocate the defined deviants to the legitimated management or control institutions. In this study, the educational systems and social service systems were the social control agencies which received the benefits of the Community Action Programs.

Using this unusual format to return to the transformation of the Community Action Program, we see the problem definition constructed by the planners as a counter-ideological posture. It charged the existing institutional order with failure to respond to the needs of the poor, and asserted that this failure was the result of powerlessness—the poor lacked the power to pressure the organizations. The Community Action Program planners' definition of the problem also departed from the traditional therapeutic concept or personal deviation orientation of the institutional structure.

The convergence of the institutions' desire for continuity in the existing order and their interest in the individual or subcultural deviation approach to social problems is understandable. With the onus of responsibility for change on the individual or his peers, the management or control institution —as part of the social structure—is guaranteed a superior power position in relation to its clientele. This conceptual position functions to maintain the existing power arrangements and allocation of resources.

The Community Action Program planners' view modified slightly the problem definition, and in doing so it can be characterized as a "liberal-humanitarian" version of utopian thought. Their thinking was utopian in that it suggested a counter-ideological definition of reality based on contemporary social conditions, but it also neglected aspects of political reality in its organizational strategy and is classified accordingly. The Community Ac-

[15] *Ibid*, p. 73.

tion planners' adherence in their organizational strategy to the ideological explanation of social change can be explained by C. Van Nieuwenhuijze's statement: "Faith makes the rational system watertight."[16]

The Community Action Program in its transformation shows the convergence of power, perception and program. The power position held by the organization employing the planner serves as a determinant of his perception of the problem. As this perception becomes operationalized through the planning process, programs coming from it are created. The covert function of these programs is to reinforce the power position of the organization.

We can impute this power-maintaining circle of power, perception, and program to the Community Action Program experience to understand the action of the local organizations in their almost universal adoption of the Culture of Poverty ideal type, in the construction of programs based upon an Individual and Cultural Change strategy, and in the perpetuation of poverty in America. We must relegate the belief that reform of the existing institutional order can be rationally planned, or that significant change can be effected from within the organizational structure of power, to the level of ideology and to the purpose of social control.

[16] Van Nieuwenhuijze, C. A. O., *Society as Process,* (The Hague: Mouton and Company, 1962), p. 114.

29. The Sociology of Knowledge and the Problems of the Inner Cities[1]

BY ROLAND L. WARREN

This paper examines the social structuring of knowledge concerned with the problems of the inner cities, particularly involving low-income residents in deteriorated neighborhoods. The analysis emerged from a series of perplexing problems encountered in a study of the participation of a number of community decision organizations in the Model Cities programs of nine cities. In the course of addressing these theoretical problems, relationships among various aspects of an institutionalized thought structure became apparent. Considered together, these aspects constitute an interlocking mutually supporting cognitive ordering of the "poverty problem" which is reflected not only in a knowledge and belief system but in the social structure of the interactional field of those organizations which are legitimated to address the problem. The bulk of this article analyzes the interrelationship between thought system and social structure in this segment of society.

As is well known, the examination of the relationship between knowledge and social structure raises the question as to whether the pointing out of such relationships invalidates the substantive aspects of the knowledge itself. In this, we take the epistemologically conservative position (or actually, non-position), asserting, with Znaniecki that the sociologist "is not entitled to make any judgments concerning the validity of any systems of knowledge except sociological systems."[2] Hence, the observation that a certain idea serves to perform a "function" in relation to some system or group is not to challenge its validity, any more than the *argumentum ad hominem* constitutes a logically acceptable refutation of a debated idea.

The "ordering" of experience into a conceptual framework related to the social position of the observer is approached by Kuhn in a special way

Reprinted with permission of the publisher from Roland L. Warren, "The Sociology of Knowledge and the Problems of the Inner Cities," *Social Science Quarterly* 52, no. 3 (December, 1971): 468–485.

[1] The author's work is supported by a research scientist award (No. K3-MH-21,-869) from the National Institute of Mental Health. The research project on which this paper is based was supported by a grant from the National Institute of Mental Health. Special thanks are due Stephen M. Rose, who acted as stimulus for this paper and as critic of earlier drafts.

[2] Florian Znaniecki, *The Social Role of the Man of Knowledge* (New York: Columbia University Press, 1940), p. 5.

which is particularly relevant to the present analysis. His central concept is that of the scientific paradigm. He explains his use of the concept of paradigms:

> *By choosing it, I mean to suggest that some accepted examples of actual scientific practice—examples which include law, theory, application, and instrumentation together—provide models from which spring particular coherent traditions of scientific research. These are the traditions which the historian describes under such rubrics as "Ptolemaic astronomy" (or "Copernican"), "Aristotelian dynamics" (or "Newtonian"), "corpuscular optics" (or "wave optics"), and so on.*[3]

Although Kuhn does not deal with the sociology of knowledge (in terms of the social-relational aspects of scientific knowledge), his analysis is highly relevant to it, and compatible with it. For he maintains that contrary to widely-held impressions, scientific knowledge does not advance through gradual accumulation of new knowledge and correction of previous error marked by particularly important discoveries. Rather, these important discoveries tend to mark discontinuities in the historical process; for a discovery is not merely a new addition to knowledge but characteristically brings with it a new definition of research problems and has reverberations throughout fairly large areas of scientific knowledge. Data which were formerly thought important are now regarded as inconsequential; problems which were recognized as unexplained but relatively unimportant now become critical. A new set of ways of conceptualizing, of relating data to each other, of ways of defining problems, of research techniques, usually accompanies such "scientific revolutions." These he defines simply as the supplanting of one scientific paradigm by another. He indicates that paradigm development is a symptom of the maturity of a science, and expresses doubt as to the status of the social sciences, saying that "it remains an open question what parts of social science have yet acquired such paradigms at all. History suggests that the road to a firm research consensus is extraordinarily arduous."[4]

The importance of Kuhn's analysis for the present paper lies in his emphasizing the characteristic discontinuities in scientific knowledge which exist between paradigms, and his explanation of the way in which the acceptance or rejection of an alternative paradigm involves a whole interrelated series of theoretical statements, problem formulations, testing methods, and data analyses. Once the structured paradigm is accepted, "normal science" can be pursued. It proceeds by "extending the knowledge of those facts that the paradigm displays as particularly revealing, by increasing the

---

[3] Thomas S. Kuhn, *The Structure of Scientific Revolutions* (2nd ed.; Chicago: University of Chicago Press, 1970), p. 10.
[4] *Ibid.*, p. 15.

extent of the match between those facts and the paradigm's predictions, and by further articulation of the paradigm itself."[5] He characterizes these procedures as "mopping-up operations" and asserts that such activities "engage most scientists throughout their careers."[6]

We need only add here that according to Kuhn such operations often lead to the uncovering of "anomalies," data which are not readily assimilable by the paradigm. As such anomalies increase, a crisis is reached which is accompanied on the one hand by increasing doubt in the adequacy of the paradigm and on the other by the emergence of one or more alternative paradigms which purport to account better for the anomalies. With the supplanting of the original paradigm by one of these new contenders, a scientific revolution has been effected.

In incorporating Kuhn's concept of the paradigm into the sociology of knowledge and applying it to the social structuring of the problems of the inner cities, we will make special use of his notion that a paradigm brings with it not only an "explanation" of a problem, but also a "reformulation" of the problem in conjunction with the explanation, a redefinition of what orders of data bear significantly on the problem, what orders of data are more or less irrelevant to it, and what methods of research validation are called for.

All of the above characteristics are present in the diagnosis of the social problems associated with poverty in the inner cities, and hence this complex of ideas will be referred to in this paper as the "diagnostic paradigm."

THE INTERORGANIZATIONAL STUDY PROJECT

The research project on which this paper is based was addressed primarily to theory, as distinguished from practice. Its goals were to provide exploratory generalizations regarding the behavior of a purposive sample of community decision organizations, to test a number of hypotheses concerning their interorganizational behavior, and to explore the nature of the interorganizational field in which this interaction occurs.

Community decision organizations are defined as organizations which are legitimated to make decisions on behalf of the community in a specified sector of interests.[7] Six such organizations were chosen for study, in nine different cities. The six organizations are: public school system, urban re-

[5] *Ibid.*, p. 24.

[6] *Ibid.*

[7] For an elaboration of the concept of community decision organizations, see Roland L. Warren, "The Interaction of Community Decision Organizations: Some Basic Concepts and Needed Research," *Social Service Review*, 41 (Sept., 1967), and "The Interorganizational Field as a Focus of Investigation," *Administrative Science Quarterly*, 12 (Dec., 1967). Both these articles are contained in the author's *Truth, Love, and Social Change—and Other Essays on Community Change* (Chicago: Rand McNally & Co., 1971).

newal agency, health and welfare council, community action agency (poverty program), model cities agency, and mental health planning agency. The cities were chosen as a purposive sample. Seven are middle-range cities with populations of 250,000 to 750,000, chosen to represent a broad distribution on 13 different variables, including such "hard" variables as "per capita income" and "percent nonwhite" and such "soft" variables as "degree of commitment to citizen participation in the Model Cities planning grant application." These cities are: Oakland, Denver, San Antonio, Columbus, Atlanta, Newark, and Boston. In addition, Detroit was chosen as a city of much larger population than the others, and Manchester, N.H. as a smaller city.

Field research associates were in these cities on a half-time basis for a period of 26 months from July 1968 through August 1970, gathering data in the form of schedules, questionnaires, structured interviews, and documents, as well as through observation at various meetings.

It was decided to give special emphasis to the Model Cities program, (all these cities were deliberately chosen from the "first round" of Model Cities), since it was anticipated that this program by its very nature would generate interaction among these sample organizations. Extensive data were gathered regarding certain organizational variables as well as a number of interaction variables, at first before the Model Cities program, then during its planning stage, and again during the early part of the implementation stage.

Among the several variables of the study, three were given special attention and included in a number of preliminary hypotheses. These were: interaction on a cooperation/contest scale; agency responsiveness to the needs and wishes of slum area residents; and innovativeness in administration, program, or interaction patterns. Each of these concepts required painstaking conceptual clarification and became somewhat transformed in the process of clarification and operationalization, as will be indicated later. It was partly in relation to this transforming process that some of the interconnections between knowledge and social structure became apparent.

We turn now to a consideration of the component parts of the institutionalized thought structure referred to earlier.

THE DIAGNOSTIC PARADIGM

By diagnostic paradigm is meant that paradigm which carries the "explanation" for why certain people are poor or disadvantaged, and in so doing implies the way poverty will be conceptualized as a problem, what strategies will be utilized to deal with it, what technologies will be required, and what aspects of the total situation surrounding poverty will be singled out as highly significant, and what aspects will be left as unimportant or irrelevant.

Two alternative paradigms are available for diagnosing poverty as a basis for conceptualization, strategy, and technology. Although both are fairly familiar in the poverty literature, one is clearly preferred when it comes to the moment of strategy choice. These two paradigms can be called, respectively, the approach based on "individual deficiency," and the "dysfunctional social structure" approach. The one paradigm takes as its point of orientation the particular situation of the individual-in-poverty, emphasizing that his poverty, as well as other attendant problems, is associated with his inability to function adequately within the accepted norms of American society. We call this Diagnostic Paradigm I. The other paradigm takes as its point of orientation the aspects of the social system which purportedly produce poverty as a system-output. We call this Diagnostic Paradigm II. Looked at from the standpoint of action orientation, Diagnostic Paradigm I indicates the need for a change in the individual, while Diagnostic Paradigm II indicates the need for a change in the social structure. We need not burden the reader by repeating the contents of these two positions which are widely familiar. A recent work by Rose gives a lucid and systematic resumé of the two positions, in relation to a study of the anti-poverty program.[8]

The sophisticated reader may ask, "*Must* we choose? Isn't it perfectly plausible to consider poverty as an integral property of the social structure while at the same time acknowledging that on a different level, individual people may experience serious social handicaps because of their poverty, and may need individual help to overcome these deficiencies?" The logical answer would seem to be an unqualified affirmative. But the sociological answer must be more equivocal. For in actual practice, just as Kuhn indicates for the natural sciences, the choice of either paradigm presumes a different conceptual framework, steers attention to different variables, poses problems of a different order, and suggests different methods of approach to solve these problems.

Hence, there are at present two competing diagnostic paradigms, each of which calls attention to different components of the problems, each of which can be granted "face" validity. But as will be shown, only one of these diagnostic paradigms, the approach based on individual deficiency, is part of an institutionalized thought structure.

THE INTERVENTION STRATEGY

The intervention strategy associated with Diagnostic Paradigm I is that of "providing services," broadly speaking, to a disadvantaged population. By

[8] Stephen M. Rose, *Community Action Programs: The Relationship between Initial Conception of the Poverty Problem, Derived Intervention Strategy, and Program Implementation*, Doctoral Diss., Florence Heller Graduate School for Advanced Studies in Social Welfare, Brandeis University, 1970. Published in 1972 by Schenkman Publishing Co., Cambridge, with the title *The Betrayal of the Poor: The Transformation of Community Action*. [See preceding selection in this book.]

such means, they will be restored, equipped, rehabilitated, and helped to become more nearly adequate to cope as self-sustaining, norm-abiding members of the larger society. As this occurs, they will take positions in the social structure which are provided for all who have "normal" competence to perform as members of society.

Diagnostic Paradigm I thus leads to an array of services, broadly considered, which permeate the institutional structure. In education, these are illustrated by special classes for slow learners, remedial reading courses, special education courses, and an array of other remedial approaches. As regards the economy, there are the manpower training programs, including the more widespread programs designed to instill regular and acceptable work habits, dress and speech habits, and vocational training, as well as the programs to help minority group members learn how to become individual entrepreneurs—"black capitalists." In the political area, inarticulate groups are taught that the pluralistic democratic system of government leaves room for all groups to represent their interests and win the support of a majority. Hence, they must be taught the value of voting, and something about the official decision-making processes and the way citizens can influence them. In the area of family life, they are helped through casework and counseling to become more adequate as family members, to play their family roles more responsibly and more effectively. In the area of associational activity, they are helped through "social group work" to learn to participate more effectively in formal and informal groups. Many of the poor get into trouble with the law. Consequently, protective services are designed to assure that children will not be abused nor come under immoral home influences. Children or adults who have committed law violations are afforded probation services in lieu of being held in custody. For those who are incarcerated, there is a parole system to ease the transition to law-abiding behavior after release. Since health problems are often associated with inability to function adequately, special social services are afforded to the sick and their families. Finally (although this list does not exhaust the service field), many of the above deficiencies or handicaps are associated with personality difficulties which require the services of psychological counseling, psychotherapy, or casework, or some mixture thereof.

This partial list serves to illustrate the extent to which the "social services" strategy permeates the spectrum of problems associated with various parts of the institutional structure. There are one or more services to correspond to almost every type of deficiency in institutional participation.

Accepting the paradigm and implied social services strategy, then, what are the normal "mopping up" problems within the human services field, impeding progress toward solving the poverty problem?

These "mopping up" problems are subsumable under the rubric of "improving service delivery systems." Various factors are thought to impede the optimal application and utilization of the social services described above, with the result that they are and continue to be ineffective in their impact on poor people.

A major problem area is recognized to inhere in the agencies themselves. This is the widely acknowledged tendency for middle-class professional people to prefer to serve middle-class clients and patients, people with whom they feel comfortable, people who make "good patients," people who, whether or not they are poor, don't act that way. The middle-class "knows" how to manipulate the system, how to get its share, and so service programs as programs are systematically deflected to the more advantaged groups and do not reach those for whom they were intended.

In summary: within Diagnostic Paradigm I and its attendant service strategy, the professional "problems" lie in the structure of service delivery systems, and "progress" lies in their improvement. The Model Cities program represented an intervention strategy to solve these problems as a means of more effectively attacking poverty.

SUPPORTING BELIEF-VALUE SYSTEM

We shall here discuss briefly certain relevant aspects of the belief-value system of the larger American society, of which the community decision organizations, along with more numerous direct-service agencies, are a part and from which they derive support.

The first aspect of the relevant belief-value system of American society is closely related to Diagnostic Paradigm I. American society, though hardly perfect, is *essentially sound in its institutional composition*. The social problems which attend it, including slums and poverty, are caused either by temporary periods of malfunctioning which are only transitory (business depressions or readjustments), by wickedness (dishonest politicians, occasional fraud and malfeasance among industrial leaders, and organized criminals), and by a residual problem-population comprising individuals who will not or cannot cope with the demands made for norm-abiding performance in various segments of the institutional structure.

Although such problems are serious, progress in solving them is being achieved. The two most important dynamics in such progress can be subsumed under the rubrics of democratic pluralism and science.

Democratic pluralism is a political and governmental system in which an equitable structure of governmental decision-making, administration, and adjudication prevails and in which these governmental channels are appropriately responsive to the needs, wishes, and rights of the electorate. If a group is unorganized it is its own fault, for all citizens have the right to organize and press their interests.

The second major dynamic of progress is *science*. As science advances, not only is a basis provided for improved physical well-being, but various professions are able to draw on scientific knowledge to help solve the so-called human problems attendant upon technological progress.

Another dynamic of progress, perhaps less basic than the first two, is *organizational reform*. Problems of bureaucracy and unresponsiveness must be acknowledged. But there is a constant process of organizational reform taking place which inevitably improves organizational performance. The constant clamor for organizational improvement is reflected in most any professional journal in the various service fields mentioned earlier.

A final aspect of the belief-value system can be called the *principle of inducements*. In many cases, an agency must be given an inducement—often in the form of a financial grant—to "make it worth its while" to take on some new responsibility, function, program, or clientele group.

This selection of aspects of the supporting belief-value system is not exhaustive, but it includes some of the more relevant and important components: the basic soundness of the American institutional structure, democratic pluralism, science, organizational reform, and the principle of inducements. These major beliefs from the larger society sustain Diagnostic Paradigm I and the social services strategy. They also support the technical and administrative rationales of the community decision organizations engaged with problems of the inner cities.

TECHNICAL AND ADMINISTRATIVE RATIONALES

Direct service is based on a professional-client relationship. The professional has as the basis for his performance a practice theory presumably derived from "science." Although the professional may be "permissive" and "non-directive," he is this way because of his own professional conviction, and not because of an accountability to the client to be so. The professional person is responsible for serving the client, but is not directly accountable to the client.

Whether or not they provide such direct services, community decision organizations such as the six in this study are by definition legitimated to make decisions on behalf of the community in their respective sectors of interest. In this function they are concerned with the planning and coordination of the direct services which are administered by them or by others. This function can be conceptualized as the concerting of decisions at the community level. By concerted decision-making is meant a process through which the decisions of a plurality of actors which would otherwise be made independently are made in direct relation to one another.[9] The objective of

---

[9] For an elaboration of the concept, see Roland L. Warren, "Concerted Decision-making in the Community," in *The Social Welfare Forum, 1965* (New York: Columbia University Press, 1965). It is also included in *Truth, Love, and Social Change.*

such concerted decision-making is to optimize the benefits derived from the actions based on those decisions.

In the interorganizational field of community decision organizations, concerted decision-making is usually called "planning" or "coordination of agency efforts." The principles of comprehensiveness and coordination are widely accepted as axiomatic.

Comprehensiveness constitutes a constant justification for striving toward a "full" battery of services, which in turn becomes a rationale for proliferation of varieties of service and expansion of agency budgets. But it is important in that it creates a need for "coordination." New and improved techniques such as psychological tests, teaching machines, and closed circuit television—to use the educational field as one example—constantly push out the borders of what constitutes "comprehensiveness." Operational coordination is facilitated by data banks and other data control systems assuring that service recipients will be referred to the proper facilities at the proper time. Allocational coordination is facilitated not only by advanced data control systems, but also by systems analysis, PPBS, costs-benefits analysis, and a number of other new and complex technologies.

LEGITIMATION AND POWER

Legitimation is here taken to mean the acknowledged right of an organization to operate in a particular field. By definition, community decision organizations are legitimated to carry on decision-making activities in their respective fields of interest. The rationale for such legitimation has already been considered. American society has a certain residual problem population unable to function adequately without assistance; these people must therefore be helped through social services. These services must be comprehensive, and they must be coordinated. Such coordination is facilitated through technical efficiency. Community decision organizations fulfill this important function of coordination.

Although it cannot be adequately substantiated in this paper, it is pertinent to note the considerable power which lies in the ability of such community decision organizations to:

(1) define the "social problems" which they are addressing;

(2) define the nature of what "must be done" in order to solve them;

(3) control the intervention strategies that are brought to bear on them;

(4) evaluate the results of their interventions; and

(5) "control" the communications media through which these listed aspects become the subject matter for public discussion—in newspapers, professional schools, and professional journals.

Needless to say, each of these power aspects is currently under challenge by various militant groups speaking for ghetto residents as well as by intellectual dissidents. We shall return to this challenge later for analysis from the standpoint of the sociology of knowledge.

SOCIAL RESEARCH AND EVALUATION

Organizational reform, science, and technical efficiency constitute strong related supports for research and evaluation. We refer here to the application of the methods and findings of social science in order both to develop more effective services to help those who need them and to evaluate the effectiveness of the services which are given. The ascendancy of social science and social research in relation to social service agencies in the last two decades hardly needs documenting. Its function in relation to Paradigm I will be considered later.

CHARACTERISTICS OF THE INTERORGANIZATIONAL FIELD

The Brandeis study was directed not only to the class of individual community decision organizations as units of analysis, but also to the field, or network of such organizations in each city, taken as a unit of analysis in its own right. Several characteristics of this interorganizational field in the various cities are pertinent to the present discourse.

First, the field was found to be surprisingly stable in its major dimensions over a period of years during which many impacts were being made both from national programs and from slum resident agitation. An earlier study by Rose documented substantially the same phenomenon for the poverty program as was found for the Model Cities program. Organizational domains remained substantially the same, and taken as a whole the organizations were able to absorb the impact from federal programs and local disadvantaged groups with a minimum of noticeable change either as individual organizations or in relationship to each other.

Surprisingly little interaction of any but the most routine type among these organizations was uncovered by the study. It had been anticipated —mistakenly—that the scramble for federal funds would engender much intense competitive interaction. Very little was found. The reason seems to be that the respective domains have emerged through time and through a process of competitive mutual adjustment, so that only rarely do these agencies struggle intensely over the question of which of them should do a particular thing. Likewise, since their respective technologies and administrative styles are geared to the same basic diagnostic paradigm and intervention strategy, they contest with each other only rarely about the substance of what should be done.

This ecological balance among and within CDOs, like Norton Long's owls and field mice in a five-acre woodlot, is well adapted to the technologies, administrative styles, and institutional positions of the individual CDOs. The ecological balance is based on reciprocal support. Putting this another way, given the existing balance, if any particular CDO did not exist, it would almost "have to be invented"—or at least its function would have to. This may be one reason why such CDOs appear so characteristically across the whole face of the United States, and why in this nine-city study, the entire *dramatis personae* of CDOs was there in each city.

As an interacting system, these CDOs and others like them do not often manifestly or dramatically "resist change." Rather, they manifestly "desire change" and attempt to bring it about on behalf of their clients. But they dominate the definition of where the problem lies, what has to be changed, and by whom, and with what methods. As indicated above, the resulting "changes" constitute mutually compatible adaptive adjustments at the margins within a stable and controllable (even if not wholly predictable) environment.

"MODEL CITIES" AND THE INSTITUTIONALIZED THOUGHT STRUCTURE

The Model Cities program was a program to "improve the quality of urban life" especially in the slum areas of the 150 participating cities. This was to be accomplished through concentrating a comprehensive program in these slum areas. It was recognized that if the effort was to be successful, the agencies, public and private, concerned with these problems and operative in the slum areas would have to become increasingly responsive to the needs and wishes of the residents. An essential means for bringing this about was to be the participation of the residents in the planning of these programs. Final authority must rest with the municipal government. Although not mentioned in the 1966 legislation, the objective of strengthening the city government, particularly the mayor or chief executive, was considered highly desirable and essential for lasting progress. It was also recognized that new types of programs would have to be developed.

A specific list of objectives was given in the 1966 legislation and became the outline for the administrative guidelines to implement the program:

. . . *to plan, develop, and carry out locally prepared and scheduled comprehensive city demonstration programs containing new and imaginative proposals to rebuild or revitalize large slum and blighted areas; to expand housing, job, and income opportunities; to reduce dependence on welfare payments; to improve educational facilities and programs; to combat disease and ill health; to reduce the incidence of crime and delinquency; to enhance recreational and cultural opportunities; to establish better access between homes and jobs; and generally to improve living conditions for the people who live in such areas, and to accomplish these objectives through the most effective and economical concentration and coordination of Federal, State, and local public and private efforts to improve the quality of urban life.*

It should be noted that these objectives are compatible with the prevalent diagnostic paradigm of individual deficiency (Diagnostic Paradigm I) as well as the alternative paradigm of a dysfunctional social structure (Diagnostic Paradigm II).

In the Model Cities activity in the nine cities of the Brandeis study, two observations seem warranted:

1. Although the Model Cities objectives were amenable to either of the two diagnostic paradigms, Diagnostic Paradigm I prevailed in almost all situations. We believe that the explanation for this circumstance is available in the analysis of the operation of the institutionalized thought structure based on this paradigm.

2. A major difference between the two diagnostic paradigms is that Paradigm I is accompanied by other components of an institutionalized thought structure, but Paradigm II is not. The absence of, or severe deficiency in, other components of an institutionalized thought structure corresponding to Paradigm II helps account for the constantly observed "drift" of organizational behavior toward Paradigm I wherever an alternative is presented.

On the basis of the above, we state a third proposition:

3. Purposive change strategies such as the anti-poverty program and the Model Cities program are bound to have extremely little effectiveness in changing social conditions so long as they do not help to create alternative institutionalized thought structures based on different diagnostic paradigms and containing components which are as integrally supportive of the alternative paradigms as are the components of Paradigm I.

These propositions are stated didactically here, so that the reader may keep them in mind as he considers the following analysis of the relation of the response to Model Cities in these nine cities to the existence of an institutionalized thought structure associated with Paradigm I. We shall try to show how the response, even on the part of residents who were hostile to the existing interorganizational structure, was such as to strengthen this existing structure rather than to weaken it or supplant it or modify it in major fashion.

SOME CONSEQUENCES OF THE INSTITUTIONALIZED
THOUGHT STRUCTURE

Consider Diagnostic Paradigm I with its attendant institutionalized thought structure. It accepts the main outlines of the American social structure but sees individual deviants as problematic, the anomalies which still impede the optimal functioning of the system. It defines the intervention problem as treating these anomalies. Ineffectiveness in the application of such therapy is in turn diagnosed in terms of the system as a whole: the essentially therapeutic social services are not coordinated, they are not rationalized. The remedy lies in their being brought into more deliberate and purposive systemic relationship to each other. Hence: comprehensiveness, coordination, planning, and participation. These are all directed at making the system more effective as it controls the anomalies of individual deviance. Note that the remedy is not in changing the major structural aspects of the system, but rather in improving the coordination among those components of the system which treat anomalies. The anomalies, deficient individuals, constitute the fringe problems which supporters of the paradigm work on in system-maintaining activities corresponding to "normal science" in the explanatory mode —marginal "mopping-up" operations. By the same token, attention is upon the "public interest," rather than the interests of such marginal problematic individuals. They must be helped, but it may be in the public interest to put welfare mothers to work, to remove low-income homes for highway construction, to gather data-banks for the more effective operation of agency programs, etc.

Again, participation of the poor in devising programs for improving living conditions (amenable to either Diagnostic Paradigm I or II) is desirable; but it must of course flow through regularized channels, must not become "disruptive," and must somehow blend into the notion of comprehensive planning in the public interest. If not, it is obstructionist, disruptive, irrational, ineffective, and rebellious.

Innovations, in turn, take on a particular meaning when associated with a thought structure which emphasizes system stability, which seeks to "contain" deviancy, and which looks for maximal "coordination" of · parts (whether or not it finds it). Innovation is mightily constrained by such considerations. Innovation which is not so constrained is considered nonprofessional, irrational, unscientific, wasteful, and potentially destructive.

And, indeed, we have been impressed by the finding that innovation in Model Cities programs has been contained almost completely within the components and constraints of the institutionalized thought structure associated with Diagnostic Paradigm I. Further, in those very few instances in which innovation took the form of a program derived from Diagnostic Paradigm II, it was vigorously opposed by the existing organizations.

Likewise, responsiveness—sensitivity to the needs and wishes of the disadvantaged population—was considered an objective to be striven for in the Model Cities program in order that services might be made more effective in helping deficient individuals. Our findings indicated that the moves toward increasing responsiveness were almost all within the constraints of the control of the situation by the agencies, and under such constraints as those of scientific and professional expertise (technical rationale) and of the need for continued convenience and viability of the organizations (administrative rationale) and within the mandate of these community decision organizations to provide needed services to a clientele who in the last analysis are laymen and not in a position to define their own needs, even though they may be highly articulate about their own wishes.

One can go right down the line indicating the manner in which the Model Cities program has been molded to fit the components of the prevalent institutionalized thought structure. The overwhelming preponderance of individual projects, in Model Cities as earlier in the poverty programs, was based on a services strategy rather than a structural change strategy.[10]

We have already indicated, in terms of comprehensiveness, concentration, coordination, participation, and central control (in the form of strengthening City Hall), how the intervention strategy of Model Cities was directed at changing not the social structure which generates poverty and "deviancy" but rather changing (by making more effective through "planning") the organizations directly dealing with poor populations so that their services would be more effective.

We have indicated that a belief-value system which emphasizes the essential soundness of the institutional order, democratic pluralism, science, organizational reform, and the principle of inducements, is admirably suited to a response such as Model Cities to the increasing salience of inner cities problems.

We have also alluded to administrative and technical rationales which, as we shall show, operate to form constraints on change, particularly on change which would institute programs based on a different diagnostic paradigm.

Four developments have appeared frequently in the Model Cities activities in the nine cities and are related especially to the matter of the technologies associated with Paradigm I. We believe they all are accountable for by the apparent rejection of Paradigm I by disadvantaged groups but the ab-

---

[10] This statement is based on Rose's work cited earlier and on an analysis of the supplementary funded Model Cities programs in the nine cities of the present study.

sence of a technology which would implement programs based on an alternative paradigm, such as Paradigm II (dysfunctional social structure).

1. The first is the widely noted dissent behavior, involving protests, boycotts, and other kinds of veto activity. This activity we conceive as a rudimentary and elementary way of reacting against the institutionalized thought structure of Paradigm I in the absence of a technology suited to a different paradigm. The criticism is often made that such resident groups are loud in their protest but have no viable alternatives to present. We believe this is quite true; but it is given an adequate assessment only if the relationship of the dissent to the entire institutionalized thought structure is properly understood. Yes, they only protest; and yes, they have no alternative technology to offer.

2. This being the case, the second development is highly relevant. There has been a growth of "advocacy planning" precisely in order to afford disadvantaged groups the technical competence which they need in order to formulate program proposals of their own. But the important—widely ignored—aspect of this situation is that advocacy planners, themselves, have technical competence only of the type which is applicable to operation within the prevalent institutionalized thought structure. They do not have an articulate technology and expertness regarding alternative strategies designed to change the institutional structure on the basis of Paradigm II. Hence, we come to a development which was seen at first as quite anomalous in terms of the study's original assumptions.

3. The third development has been that to the extent that resident groups have gained power in the program-planning process, they almost without exception have come up with substantially the same type of (Paradigm I) programs as have the more established agencies in cases where resident groups had little power. Decision-making power, often hard-fought and hard-won by resident groups,[11] seems to have made little difference in the actual programs. We had anticipated that since such resident groups were highly critical of the existing programs, and since many of them expressed in one way or another an apparently clear grasp of and identification with Paradigm II (dysfunctional social structure), they would drastically alter the nature of the programs when they had power. Both they and their advocacy planners, where they had them, slipped inadvertently into modes of response based on Paradigm I, the only paradigm which offered explicit technologies for addressing the problems.

4. The fourth development overlaps the other somewhat, but deserves special treatment. Cooptation occurred, both of the usual types and of a

[11] Roland L. Warren, "Model Cities First Round: Politics, Planning and Participation," *Journal of the American Institute of Planners,* 35 (July, 1969). This is also included in the author's *Truth, Love, and Social Change.*

type not yet treated in the literature.[12] We have seen in numerous instances the success which community decision organizations have had in confronting challenges by disadvantaged citizens who were rejecting the placing of the problem at their own door, and who claimed to see it in the institutional structure. The interaction process characteristically worked out in such a manner that the organization could appeal to its administrative and technical constraints—to the exigencies of running an organization, to civil service requirements, to law or regulation, to the "facts of organizational life" —or to a set of professional standards or procedures—whether for curriculum building or for the administration of health care or the proper role of therapist and client—which in effect resulted in the problem's being defined in such a way that no matter how it was resolved, the organization could accommodate the resolution without major difficulty, and often with distinct advantage. This often was accompanied by an incipient redefinition of the problem from that of Paradigm II to that of Paradigm I.

Thus, the absence of a technology to correspond to Paradigm II was a distinct handicap in the citizens' attempt to challenge or repudiate Paradigm I, and eventuated in their inadvertently returning to Paradigm I either of their own accord, or in interaction with an agency, or through the mediation of advocacy planners.

But such cooptation is not the only resource available to existing agencies in encountering challenges to Paradigm I. The analysis by Berger and Luckmann is especially crucial at this point. They note that "the appearance of an alternative symbolic universe poses a threat because its very existence demonstrates empirically that one's own universe is less than inevitable."[13] They indicate that those who question the existing ideology are perceived as deviants, and they then point out that the expected strategy for the deviant is "therapy." They note the important function of such therapy from the standpoint of the sociology of knowledge: "Successful therapy establishes a symmetry between the conceptual machinery and its subjective appropriation in the individual's consciousness; it resocializes the deviant into the objective reality of the symbolic universe of the society."[14] Therapy, they point out, is a means of keeping everyone within the accepted thought structure. Nihilation, on the other hand, is a process used to "liquidate conceptually" everything *outside* the same thought structure.[15] They speculate further: "Whether one then proceeds from nihilation to therapy, or rather goes on to

[12] J. Wayne Newton, "Cooptation in the Interaction of Community Decision Organizations," Mimeographed, Florence Heller Graduate School for Advanced Studies in Social Welfare, Brandeis University, December 1970.

[13] Peter L. Berger and Thomas Luckmann, *The Social Construction of Reality: A Treatise in the Sociology of Knowledge* (Garden City: Anchor Books, 1967), p. 108.

[14] *Ibid.*, p. 114.

[15] *Ibid.*

liquidate physically what one has liquidated conceptually, is a practical question of policy."[16] Such physical liquidation, in the current jargon, is the familiar "repression." The widespread use of the term, one might add, indicates that the possibility of physical liquidation as an alternative to therapy is not only an abstract, conceptual one, but one which plays a role in the struggle of competing ideologies.

But again, on what power base would new, competing ideologies rest? "How many troops do they have?" Many ideas that challenge the prevalent thought structure are entertained and considered with little apparent resistance so long as they are not linked to a power base, to a dynamic movement which threatens to "carry" the ideas in competition with the prevailing ones. It is at such a point of threat that power beyond the ordinary system-maintaining operations of the institutionalized thought structure will likely be employed. But such power is a second line of defense for an existing institutionalized thought structure, the first being its ability to redefine the challenge in its own terms, or, in our language, to translate it into the prevalent paradigm, where what "fits" can be dealt with within the institutionalized thought structure and what cannot be made to fit can be sloughed off as unimportant or as a temporary aberration—an anomaly. Berger and Luckmann's stern words about physical liquidation are therefore pertinent primarily in those situations where therapy and "translation" are ineffective in neutralizing the counter-paradigm, and where that paradigm has acquired the social dynamic of a supporting group with sufficient power to challenge the prevalent institutionalized thought structure.

These statements are didactic; we do not claim to have proved them. Rather, we merely assert that such statements help clarify our own findings, and our findings lend them strong circumstantial support. This is especially the case in regard to the central theme of "therapy" in Diagnostic Paradigm I and to the processes of administrative, technical, and personnel cooptation which were operative.

The power to define the problem, or in our terms, to impose one's own diagnostic paradigm and its attendant institutionalized thought structure, is especially pertinent to the conducting of research. In considering the supportive role of social research, it is important to recognize that most of the prevalent research takes as its point of departure the prevalent diagnostic paradigm.

One can identify five principal types of social science research related to the attack on the problems of the inner city. The first is a general category of social science studies which were not designed specifically for the improvement of services, but which nevertheless describe conditions or circum-

[16] *Ibid.,* p. 115.

stances in findings which have been picked up by the agencies and social scientists doing research for them. An excellent example of this is the work of Oscar Lewis on the culture of poverty, a conception which gives universal credibility to the notion of individual deficiency.[17] Other types of social science analysis, equally relevant, do not get "picked up" in such a manner. One is the Marxian studies, both in this country and abroad, which not only challenge the paradigm but have the most nearly complete set of component parts of an alternative institutionalized thought structure. The other is the writings in this field of the New Left "radical" sociologists who most explicitly challenge the paradigm but, like dissident resident groups in the inner city, do not have a set of component parts for an alternative institutionalized thought structure. Even in connection with their own special field, they tend to veer back toward existing paradigms, unable to establish a bridgehead to an alternative. As Gouldner observes, "Many radical sociologists, however, divorce their radicalism and their sociology and write a conventional sociology which is often scarcely distinguishable from that of their apolitical or conservative brethren."[18]

The second category is research having to do with client populations and their cultural and other resistances to social services.

The third is research on service delivery systems, with a view toward making them more effective.[19]

The fourth is evaluative research on "social action" projects.

A fifth pursuit has to do with evaluating the impact of service programs, a particularly crucial challenge, especially since many such studies have been so negative in their findings. But here again, the remarkable thing is that although such studies often reach conclusions which challenge Diagnostic Paradigm I, the conclusions are seldom picked up and implemented. The reason seems apparent: There is no other place to go with such conclusions than to cast them back against Diagnostic Paradigm I and formulate the new problem as: How to give services in a manner that *will* be effective in its impact. Indeed, the studies which report negative findings on the impact of services usually are strong in their support of the more inclusive intervention strategy of coordination. It is just such studies which provide the intellectual base for the Model Cities program, and which support its strategy of comprehensiveness, coordination, concentration, and the rest.

Viewed from the standpoint of their manifest or latent support of the

---

[17] See for example, Oscar Lewis, the Introduction to *La Vida: A Puerto Rican Family in the Culture of Poverty—San Juan and New York* (New York: Vintage Books, 1966).

[18] Alvin Gouldner, "Toward the Radical Reconstruction of Sociology," *Social Policy*, 1 (May/June, 1970), p. 21.

[19] Edwin J. Thomas, ed., *Behavioral Science for Social Workers* (New York: The Free Press, 1967) contains several examples.

prevalent institutionalized thought structure, the social research and evaluation are reminiscent of Znaniecki's social role of the "sage."

A distinct kind of social role develops which may be called by the old term "sage." . . . It is his duty to "prove" by "scientific" arguments that his party is right and its opponents are wrong. . . . The traditional order is thus normatively criticized, systematized, and perfected. This does not mean that the sage desires to innovate: the essence of the existing order is right; its defects are accidents due to the imperfection of human nature.[20]

The social researcher, in other words, performs the "mopping-up" operations of "normal science" within the assumption of the validity of the prevalent diagnostic paradigm.

[20] Znaniecki, *Social Role of the Man of Knowledge,* pp. 72, 73, 77.

SECTION FIVE

Citizen Action

Introduction

When participation in community activities is mentioned as a salient characteristic of American community life, it is not usually a type of on-the-job vocational activity which is meant. The term is usually confined to participation by citizens in a voluntary, rather than a professional, capacity. Such participation is usually structured through special types of nonprofit associations, including clubs, churches, associations, voluntary agencies, unions, social action groups, and so on. Often, the discussion centers on activity of a relatively disinterested nature, as far as economic self-interest is concerned, thus tending to exclude unions, trade associations, and similar self-interest organizations. Sometimes, the discussion is further confined to activities which do not have a partisan political component, thus excluding political party activity as such. Recently, however, there has been a proliferation of organizations designed to serve the interests of the residents of low-income neighborhoods.

This section merely takes note that such dimensions of participation exist but is highly inclusive in its concept of citizen participation. The selections included all speak in one way or another to the much-proclaimed propensity for Americans to join voluntary organizations, organizations which they encounter preponderantly in their own immediate locality (although certain professional organizations, for example, may not have locally organized groups but may be encountered only on the state or national level).

But how widespread is such participation? Is it characteristic of the entire population, or only of certain segments of it? To what extent does such participation afford individual citizens a channel through which they can relate themselves meaningfully and effectively to the larger forces which influence their lives? Do citizens join organizations in order to represent and further their own "interests," or are other kinds of causal configuration involved? These are some of the questions which are central to the selections in this section.

The emphasis on voluntary associations is hardly new. Over a century and a quarter ago, the great French observer of American life, Alexis de Tocqueville, made some brilliant observations on what was even then a marked characteristic of the new nation which had already developed its own social patterns. The proliferation of what he called "public associations" impressed him greatly as one of the distinguishing features of the new society.

"As soon as several of the inhabitants of the United States have taken

342

up an opinion or a feeling which they wish to promote in the world, they look out for mutual assistance; and as soon as they have found one another out, they combine. From that moment they are no longer isolated men, but a power seen from afar, whose actions serve for an example and whose language is listened to." De Tocqueville not only recognized the large number and great importance of such voluntary formations, he inquired why this should be so, and how it might be related to the democratic political institutions which the country had developed.

In the brilliant analysis included here, de Tocqueville asserted that the proliferation of associations is directly related to the major commitment of American society to equality. In an aristocratic society, new needs can be perceived and confronted by individuals with great power. But with power more widely spread, men must join together to confront their problems. Hence, "If men are to remain civilized or to become so, the art of associating together must grow and improve in the same ratio in which the equality of conditions is increased." Voluntary associations are not simply a luxury provided by an equalitarian society; they are its lifeblood.

Many of the interests on the basis of which local people participate in associational activities are issues on which different groups of people have different points of view about what should or should not be done. One current nationwide program which specifically calls for citizen participation at the local level as a prerequisite for federal support is the urban renewal program. James Q. Wilson points out the frequent polarization of citizen participation in urban renewal programs into two contrary types of activity. On the one hand, city-wide organizations of comparatively active, well-to-do, and well-educated people support various urban renewal activities on the basis of their alleged benefit to the entire community. These people can be described as having a "public-regarding" political ethos. On the other hand, residents of urban renewal areas, and especially of slum clearance areas, are less active, ordinarily, in the public affairs of the community, and are less well to do and less well educated. They are characterized by a "private-regarding" ethos, tending to relate community actions to how these will affect them, rather than to how they affect the "general welfare." But in addition, the people of these areas are likely to be personally disadvantaged by the urban renewal programs. They may be forced to give up their present dwelling, which is marked for destruction. Their whole neighborhood may be literally obliterated, the space to be used for a quite different purpose by quite different people. Small businesses and the self-employed may be especially handicapped by the forced move. The informal associations of the local neighborhood will be largely destroyed as the inhabitants are relocated in various sections of the city. For these people, citizen participation in the question of urban renewal often takes the form of combating the program.

Thus, "the higher the level of indigenous organization in a lower-class neighborhood, the poorer the prospects for renewal in that area." If urban renewal programs are to move forward, they can hardly wait for the willing assent of the inhabitants of the renewal areas. Assent on a city-wide level is much more readily obtainable but is of a somewhat different order. A program which may at the community level be described as arising with the participation and assent of a broad citizen constituency can at a closer level be conceived as "imposed." Meanwhile, in the politics of the process, "the mayor must move cautiously between the twin evils of doing so little as to disappoint community-regarding voters and doing so much as to antagonize private-regarding voters."

An important and growing development has been the emergence of a large number of federal programs which support some type of activity at the local level and which require a citizen participation component in their local implementation. The most widely discussed have probably been the Community Action Programs and the Model Cities Programs, but they also include urban renewal, public housing, metropolitan development and planning, comprehensive health planning, various public education programs, and even highway programs.

There has been much experience accumulated through such programs. Hans B. C. Spiegel attempts a review of that experience in the selection on "Citizen Participation in Federal Programs: A Review." He first states some ideas about the meaning of citizen participation, and then, in a long passage omitted in the present version, describes the provisions for citizen participation in each of the more important federal programs. In the subsequent analysis, he draws an interesting contrast between the roles and conceptions of two principal types of actors in such programs—the program manager and the neighborhood spokesman. He offers several propositions summarizing the experience to date with citizen participation in governmental programs.

Finally, as an aid to further reading as well as a source for the quotations he uses and references he makes, he appends a lengthy and useful bibliography, which is reproduced here in full.

Harry Specht addresses a major contemporary problem in his analysis of "Disruptive Tactics." It is the problem of how to assess, both in terms of effectiveness and in terms of social morality, the various strategies for behavior in situations of major disagreement on social issues. In order to do this, he raises the question of how strategies are to be classified, and on what basis. The basis for such classification is the perception which the participants themselves have of what is going on. If the issue is perceived simply as a rearrangement of resources, the response is likely to be consensus, and the appropriate mode of intervention is collaboration. If the issue is perceived as a redistribution of resources, the response is likely to be difference, and the appropriate mode of intervention is a campaign. If the issue is perceived as a change in status relationships, the response is likely to be dissensus and the appropriate mode of intervention is contest or disruption. In extreme cases, the issue may be perceived as a reconstruction of the entire system, in which case the response may be termed insurrection, with violence the mode of intervention.

Disruptive tactics, then, consist of those tactics utilized in situations involving a perceived change in status relationships. They may be characterized by a clash of position within accepted social norms or by a violation of normative behavior (manners), or by a violation of legal norms. Specht analyzes these alternatives explicitly, and then goes on to consider the tactics of violence. He considers not only the question of the effectiveness of these tactics, but their morality. Unless change is possible within the framework of what existing institutions permit, we all face the dilemma that "we must either continue to act in a drama that has lost its purpose or join in the destruction of society." More than disruption and violence, he says, are required to transform America.

The article on "Maximum Feasible Manipulation" is unique. It is not a scholarly article in the usual sense of the word. Although certain conclusions or "lessons" are drawn, it is principally descriptive, and thus one of the few exceptions in this book to the general intent of emphasizing analysis rather than simply description of what happened here or there.

The North City Area Wide Council, Inc., became the formally prescribed organization for the channeling of citizen participation in the Philadelphia Model Cities program. Philadelphia's program involved a relatively strong component of citizen participation including in its original application for funding the assurance that it would "strive to incorporate within its very core guarantees of citizens' authority to determine basic goals and policies for planning and implementing the program." Those are strong words. The program plans, as they were eventually drawn up, emphasized that the basic problems of the model neighborhood were poverty and powerlessness. Then, unlike many programs in other cities, it turned away from a predominant emphasis on improving and expanding services to people presumably in need of them, and concentrated on economic development, community development, and physical improvements, leaving only 6 percent for social service delivery systems. In several other aspects the plans were rather different from what was being developed in other cities. By their very nature, they were threatening to some of the established institutions and interests within and outside the Philadelphia government. But in addition, these developments were characterized by increasing rancor stemming largely, though not exclusively, from the bitterness left by a violent encounter between police and demonstrating youths and differences of opinion as to whether it was legitimate for the council to support the youths in their demonstration efforts.

The article documents what was perceived by the citizens' organization as continued harassment and dramatizes the widespread complaints of citizens that governmental officials at various levels, through malice or ineptitude, act in such a way as to hamstring the kind of meaningful citizen participation which many citizen groups demand and many officials claim to welcome.

Erasmus Kloman seeks to give an analysis of the development of citizen participation in the Philadelphia Model Cities program from the standpoint of a detached observer, not of a partisan. His account does not challenge the veracity of the preceding article, but it does provide supplementary facts which give a more balanced picture, such as the gradual narrowing of participation within the Area Wide Council and its increasing orientation toward almost exclusive concern with the problems of the blacks and Puerto Ricans in the model neighborhood, as well as some of the rationale supporting city hall's actions at various times.

Three developments stand out in the account given by Erasmus Kloman. One was the growth in intensity of antagonism between city hall and the Area Wide Council. Another was the partially avoidable difference in conception of what citizen participation might be expected to involve— on the one hand from the standpoint of the AWC, and on the other from the standpoint of municipal officials. This misunderstanding was furthered by the ambiguity of the regulations promulgated by the federal Department of Housing and Urban Development.

A second major development was the change in federal administrations which occasioned a strong change in emphasis on what federal officials would support or countenance by way of specific implementation of the "widespread citizen participation" mandate. The change was one which weakened the federal support of strong citizen participation in other than largely consensual matters.

The third major development was the litigation which ensued when the Area Wide Council decided to take its case to court. The delays served not only to constitute another hiatus hindering planning and program development, but constituted an additional component of delay superimposed on the delays occasioned by the federal administration and experienced by other cities across the United States.

Part of the sequence of developments surrounding participation by the poor in community decision-making has been a gradual growth of distrust in the notion of a single "community interest" which is presumably represented and furthered by such large organizations as boards of education, urban renewal agencies, health and welfare councils, and so on. The poor somehow are disregarded in many decisions which affect their lives. When they occasionally protest an urban renewal project or some action by the board of education, they usually have no substitute plans to offer. This is because they may not be sufficiently organized to begin with, may not have developed a consistent unified position on the issue, and may not have the expertness to develop alternatives which would be feasible. Meanwhile, existing planning and program organizations, while professing to serve the whole community, neglect the poor, ethnic minorities, and so on.

Hence, to participate adequately, the poor need experts who are under their own control, rather than under the control of the city-wide agencies. The term advocacy planning has been used to designate this professional role. It implies not only the drawing up of technical plans, but also helping the poor to organize themselves, develop a set of positions, and then represent those positions either through litigation or through other methods.

Frances Fox Piven employs the term advocacy to denote these various activities, and differentiates the specific planning activities from other activities of what are generally called advocate planners. Her critique suggests that the development of technical plans by groups of the poor is essentially a blind alley, distracting them from more important activities and usually resulting in little tangible benefits to them.

In his comments, Rosen alludes to benefits derived by the poor from activities of advocate planners other than planning, and stresses that the poor are handicapped on contested issues if they are not well-informed and do not have the expertise to confront professionals on a professional level.

Piven, however, asserts that the poor influence policy not through expertise but through power. Since their resources are limited, they may exercise such power through effective organization. She states that "the reality is that the poor get responses from government mainly through disruption," and dismisses their activities in technical plan-making as "intellectual exercises."

30. Associations in American Life

BY ALEXIS DE TOCQUEVILLE

I do not propose to speak of those political associations by the aid of which men endeavor to defend themselves against the despotic action of a majority or against the aggressions of regal power. That subject I have already treated. If each citizen did not learn, in proportion as he individually becomes more feeble and consequently more incapable of preserving his freedom singlehanded, to combine with his fellow citizens for the purpose of defending it, it is clear that tyranny would unavoidably increase together with equality.

Only those associations that are formed in civil life without reference to political objects are here referred to. The political associations that exist in the United States are only a single feature in the midst of the immense assemblage of associations in that country. Americans of all ages, all conditions, and all dispositions constantly form associations. They have not only commercial and manufacturing companies, in which all take part, but associations of a thousand other kinds, religious, moral, serious, futile, general or restricted, enormous or diminutive. The Americans make associations to give entertainments, to found seminaries, to build inns, to construct churches, to diffuse books, to send missionaries to the antipodes; in this manner they found hospitals, prisons, and schools. If it is proposed to inculcate some truth or to foster some feeling by the encouragement of a great example, they form a society. Wherever at the head of some new undertaking you see the government in France, or a man of rank in England, in the United States you will be sure to find an association.

I met with several kinds of associations in America of which I confess I had no previous notion; and I have often admired the extreme skill with which the inhabitants of the United States succeed in proposing a common object for the exertions of a great many men and in inducing them voluntarily to pursue it.

I have since traveled over England, from which the Americans have taken some of their laws and many of their customs; and it seemed to me that the principle of association was by no means so constantly or

From *Democracy in America*, II, 106–10, by Alexis de Tocqueville, translated by Phillips Bradley. Copyright 1945 by Alfred A. Knopf, Inc. Reprinted by permission of Alfred A. Knopf, Inc.

adroitly used in that country. The English often perform great things singly, whereas the Americans form associations for the smallest undertakings. It is evident that the former people consider association as a powerful means of action, but the latter seem to regard it as the only means they have of acting.

Thus the most democratic country on the face of the earth is that in which men have, in our time, carried to the highest perfection the art of pursuing in common the object of their common desires and have applied this new science to the greatest number of purposes. Is this the result of accident, or is there in reality any necessary connection between the principle of association and that of equality?

Aristocratic communities always contain, among a multitude of persons who by themselves are powerless, a small number of powerful and wealthy citizens, each of whom can achieve great undertakings single-handed. In aristocratic societies men do not need to combine in order to act, because they are strongly held together. Every wealthy and powerful citizen constitutes the head of a permanent and compulsory association, composed of all those who are dependent upon him or whom he makes subservient to the execution of his designs.

Among democratic nations, on the contrary, all the citizens are independent and feeble; they can do hardly anything by themselves, and none of them can oblige his fellow men to lend him their assistance. They all, therefore, become powerless if they do not learn voluntarily to help one another. If men living in democratic countries had no right and no inclination to associate for political purposes, their independence would be in great jeopardy, but they might long preserve their wealth and their cultivation: whereas if they never acquired the habit of forming associations in ordinary life, civilization itself would be endangered. A people among whom individuals lost the power of achieving great things single-handed, without acquiring the means of producing them by united exertions, would soon relapse into barbarism.

Unhappily, the same social condition that renders associations so necessary to democratic nations renders their formation more difficult among those nations than among all others. When several members of an aristocracy agree to combine, they easily succeed in doing so; as each of them brings great strength to the partnership, the number of its members may be very limited; and when the members of an association are limited in number, they may easily become mutually acquainted, understand each other, and establish fixed regulations. The same opportunities do not occur among democratic nations, where the associated members must always be very numerous for their association to have any power.

I am aware that many of my countrymen are not in the least embarrassed by this difficulty. They contend that the more enfeebled and incompetent the citizens become, the more able and active the government ought to be rendered in order that society at large may execute what individuals can no longer accomplish. They believe this answers the whole difficulty, but I think they are mistaken.

A government might perform the part of some of the largest American companies, and several states, members of the Union, have already attempted it; but what political power could ever carry on the vast multitude of lesser undertakings which the American citizens perform every day, with the assistance of the principle of association? It is easy to foresee that the time is drawing near when man will be less and less able to produce, by himself alone, the commonest necessaries of life. The task of the governing power will therefore perpetually increase, and its very efforts will extend it every day. The more it stands in the place of associations, the more will individuals, losing the notion of combining together, require its assistance: these are causes and effects that unceasingly create each other. Will the administration of the country ultimately assume the management of all the manufactures which no single citizen is able to carry on? And if a time at length arrives when, in consequence of the extreme subdivision of landed property, the soil is split into an infinite number of parcels, so that it can be cultivated only by companies of tillers, will it be necessary that the head of the government should leave the helm of state to follow the plow? The morals and the intelligence of a democratic people would be as much endangered as its business and manufactures if the government ever wholly usurped the place of private companies.

Feelings and opinions are recruited, the heart is enlarged, and the human mind is developed only by the reciprocal influence of men upon one another. I have shown that these influences are almost null in democratic countries; they must therefore be artificially created, and this can only be accomplished by associations.

When the members of an aristocratic community adopt a new opinion or conceive a new sentiment, they give it a station, as it were, beside themselves, upon the lofty platform where they stand; and opinions or sentiments so conspicuous to the eyes of the multitude are easily introduced into the minds or hearts of all around. In democratic countries the governing power alone is naturally in a condition to act in this manner, but it is easy to see that its action is always inadequate, and often dangerous. A government can no more be competent to keep alive and to renew the circulation of opinions and feelings among a great people than to manage all the speculations of productive industry. No sooner does a government attempt to go beyond its political sphere and to enter upon this new track than it exercises, even unintentionally, an insupportable tyranny; for a government can only dictate strict rules, the opinions which it favors are rigidly enforced, and it is never easy to discriminate between its advice and its commands. Worse still will be the case if the government really believes itself interested in preventing all circulation of ideas; it will then stand motionless and oppressed by the heaviness of voluntary torpor. Governments, therefore, should not be the only active powers; associations ought, in democratic nations, to stand in lieu of those powerful private individuals whom the equality of conditions has swept away.

As soon as several of the inhabitants of the United States have taken up an opinion or a feeling which they wish to promote in the world, they look out for mutual assistance; and as soon as they have found one another out, they combine. From that moment they are no longer isolated men, but a power seen from afar, whose actions serve for an example and whose language is listened to. The first time I heard in the United States that a hundred thousand men had bound themselves publicly to abstain from spirituous liquors, it appeared to me more like a joke than a serious engagement, and I did not at once perceive why these temperate citizens could not content themselves with drinking water by their own firesides. I at last understood that these hundred thousand Americans, alarmed by the progress of drunkenness around them, had made up their minds to patronize temperance. They acted in just the same way as a man of high rank who should dress very plainly in order to inspire the humbler orders with a contempt of luxury. It is probable that if these hundred thousand men had lived in France, each of them would singly have memorialized the government to watch the public houses all over the kingdom.

Nothing, in my opinion, is more deserving of our attention than the intellectual and moral associations of America. The political and industrial associations of that country strike us forcibly; but the others elude our observation, or if we discover them, we understand them imperfectly because we have hardly ever seen anything of the kind. It must be acknowledged, however, that they are as necessary to the American people as the former, and perhaps more so. In democratic countries the science of association is the mother of science; the progress of all the rest depends upon the progress it has made.

Among the laws that rule human societies there is one which seems to be more precise and clear than all others. If men are to remain civilized or to become so, the art of associating together must grow and improve in the same ratio in which the equality of conditions is increased.

31. Planning and Politics: Citizen Participation in Urban Renewal

BY JAMES Q. WILSON

Few national programs affecting our cities have begun under such favorable auspices as urban renewal. Although public housing was from the very first a bitterly controversial policy, redevelopment and renewal by contrast were widely accepted by both Democratic and Republican administrations and had the backing of both liberals and conservatives, labor and business, planners and mayors. Yet today, almost fourteen years after urban redevelopment was inaugurated as Title I of the Housing Act of 1949, the program is beset with controversy and, what is even more dismaying to its supporters, lagging far behind its construction goals.

Although there are nearly 944 federally-approved slum clearance and urban renewal projects scheduled for over 520 different communities, only a little more than half have proceeded to the point where the cities are authorized to begin assembling and clearing land. And most important, of all the projects authorized, only 65 have been completed.[1] In New York, the city which has been the most active in renewal programs of all kinds, all the publicly-supported projects undertaken over the last quarter century cover less than one per cent of the city's surface.[2] Further, most of the projects completed can be found in or near the central business districts of cities rather than in residential areas, and they have often involved clearing, not slums, but deteriorating commercial and industrial structures.

Some of the reasons for the relatively slight accomplishments of urban renewal are not hard to find. Federally-sponsored projects such as renewal require dealing successfully with almost endless amounts of red tape; it has taken a long time for city governments and private developers to acquire the knowledge and experience required for this. Furthermore, even though the federal government pays most of the cost of assembling and clearing the

Reprinted with permission of the author and publisher from James Q. Wilson, "Planning and Politics: Citizen Participation in Urban Renewal," *Journal of the American Institute of Planners*, XXIX, No. 4 (November, 1963), 242–49.
    [1] Housing and Home Finance Agency, *Housing Statistics: Annual Data*, April, 1962, p. 76.
    [2] See Raymond Vernon, *The Myth and Reality of Our Urban Problems* (Cambridge, Mass.: Joint Center for Urban Studies of MIT and Harvard, 1962), p. 40.

land on which a project is planned, it is not always easy to find a private developer to whom the land can be sold.

An additional reason for slow progress in urban renewal is racial. Blighted areas are often Negro areas. The political and social problems involved in relocating Negroes in other areas of the city are often sufficiently formidable to make opposition to the renewal program as a whole very powerful.

But the most important reason for controversy and slow progress is the mounting disagreement over the methods and even the objectives of urban renewal. The coalition among liberals, planners, mayors, businessmen, and real estate interests which originally made renewal politically so irresistible has begun to fall apart. Liberals, who still see the rehabilitation of the central city as a prime goal for government, have begun to have doubts, particularly about redevelopment that involves wholesale clearance by bulldozers. They are disturbed by charges from many Negro leaders—whom liberals are accustomed to regarding as their natural allies—that liberals have aided and abetted a program which under the guise of slum clearance is really a program of Negro clearance. They have been disturbed and even angered by the elimination of whole neighborhoods, like the Italian West End of Boston; by the reduction in the supply of low-cost housing to make way for high-cost housing built with federal subsidies; and by what they take to be the inhuman, insensitive, and unrealistic designs of some city planners. Jane Jacob's book, *The Death and Life of the Great American Cities,* is expressive of one powerful segment of opinion in this regard.[3] The liberals are everywhere demanding that redevelopment (that is, wholesale clearance) be abandoned in favor of rehabilitation—conserving as many existing structures as possible.

Mayors and other city officials in some cities (although not yet in all) have seen in these debates a sign that a program which began as "good politics" has turned into something which at best is difficult politics. When it seemed possible that a vigorous and ambitious mayor could place himself at the head of an alliance of liberals, planners, businessmen, and newspapers on behalf of restoring the central city, urban renewal became a top priority civic objective. An initial burst of enthusiasm greeted renewal in almost every city where the idea was broached. But after the first few projects were undertaken, the hidden political costs began to become evident. Voters who did not like being called slum-dwellers and who liked even less being forced out of their old neighborhoods began to complain. As the enthusiasm of the

[3] See also, as an example of liberal objections to renewal, Staughton Lynd, "Urban Renewal—for Whom?" *Commentary,* January, 1961, pp. 34–45. The consequences of urban renewal for the underprivileged in American cities are discussed in Peter Marris, "The Social Implications of Urban Redevelopment," *Journal of the American Institute of Planners,* XXVIII (August, 1962), 180–186.

civic boosters began to wane, many mayors began to wonder whether they were going to be left alone on the firing line to answer for projects which the boosters had pushed them into in the first place.

What in many ways is the most interesting aspect of the controversy surrounding urban renewal is not the breakup of this coalition, however, but the growing resistance of neighborhoods to clearance and renewal programs. The growth of neighborhood resistance to urban renewal has been gradual and cumulative. Many of the earliest redevelopment projects were completed with little organized opposition. Somehow, however, people have learned from the experience of others, and today, in cities which have been engaged in renewal for several years, the planners often find prospective renewal areas ready and waiting for them, organized to the teeth. In Chicago, for example, the Lake Meadows redevelopment project met with relatively little organized indigenous opposition (although considerable opposition from forces outside the area). The Hyde Park-Kenwood project, undertaken a few years later, was greeted with considerably more opposition. Today, plans for the Woodlawn and Near West Side areas have been met with impassioned opposition from many of the residents of the neighborhoods involved. Similarly, the West End project in Boston had relatively little difficulty in dealing with people in the area; the project planned for Charlestown, begun some time later, has been—at least for the time being—stopped dead in its tracks by organized neighborhood opposition. Today, according to Robert C. Weaver, Administrator of the Housing and Home Finance Agency, "in nearly every major city in the country and many small cities there are heated debates over urban renewal projects that are underway or under consideration."[4]

Mr. Weaver might well be concerned over these debates, for federal policy requires local citizen participation in the formulation of local renewal plans before federal money can be spent on them. As he himself stressed on another occasion, "We mean [by citizen participation] not just a passive acceptance of what is being done, but the active utilization of local leadership and organization which can profitably assist in the community's efforts."[5]

Local citizen participation on a city-wide basis is usually not difficult to obtain. "Civic leaders" representing various groups and interests in the community can always be assembled for such purposes. But getting the participation, much less the acquiescence, of citizens in the renewal neighborhood is something else again. Although federal law does not require participation at this level, the increased vigor of neighborhood opposition has made such participation expedient if not essential—particularly with the new emphasis on rehabilitation and self-help.

[4] Quoted in *St. Louis Post-Dispatch,* February 27, 1963.
[5] From an address to the 50th Anniversary of the Family Service Association of America, New York City, November 13, 1961.

THE HYDE PARK-KENWOOD EXPERIENCE

The fullest account we have of such participation is that found in the book, *The Politics of Urban Renewal,* by Peter H. Rossi and Robert A. Dentler. This study dealt with one neighborhood—Hyde Park-Kenwood in Chicago—which in many ways is remarkable if not unique. The site of the University of Chicago, it is heavily populated with University professors and business and professional people, all possessing an inordinate amount of education, experience, and skills, and all having a strong commitment to the community. From 1949 on, these people were organized into the Hyde Park-Kenwood Community Conference, a neighborhood group with a professional staff, dedicated to conserving the area against blight. Actual planning for the area was not, of course, done by this organization—that was beyond its resources—but by the planning staff of the University of Chicago and by various city agencies.

The Community Conference took a deep and continuing interest in the $30,000,000 urban renewal plan for the area and meticulously examined and discussed every part of it. Local and federal authorities judged the Conference to be an excellent example of genuine grass-roots participation in a major renewal effort. After the plan was finally approved by the Chicago City Council, it commanded widespread (although not unanimous) citizen acceptance, even though about 20 per cent of the buildings in the community were to be torn down.

In evaluating the work of this local citizens group, Rossi and Dentler conclude that the Hyde Park-Kenwood Community Conference played two important roles. First, it stimulated public awareness of the necessity and practicability of change and gave people confidence that something could be done to save their neighborhood. Second, the Conference managed to create a climate of opinion in which the actual planning was done, and, although it is impossible to tell exactly what impact this climate had on the planners, it is likely that the general mood of the community as articulated by the neighborhood organization influenced at least the most general goals that were embodied in the final plan.

But it is also important to note what the Conference did not do. According to this study, the organization did not play a crucial part in influencing the specific details of the plan. Instead, it created broad popular acceptance for a plan which was not entirely in keeping with its own objectives. Rossi and Dentler conclude that the "maximum role to be played by a citizen-participation movement in urban renewal is primarily a passive one."[6]

Considering what I have said about the rising opposition of local neighborhoods to urban renewal, the acquiescence of this grass-roots organization

[6] Peter H. Rossi and Robert A. Dentler, *The Politics of Urban Renewal—The Chicago Findings* (New York: Free Press of Glencoe, 1961), p. 287.

seems to require explanation. In the narrowest terms, this support was due to the fact that the Hyde Park-Kenwood Community Conference represented that part of a very heterogeneous community which would ultimately benefit from renewal. The upper-middle-class professors, housewives, and business and professional men (both white and Negro) who made up the bulk of the Conference were mostly people who were going to remain in the community and whose peace, security, cultural life, and property values would probably be enhanced by a successful renewal plan. The persons who were to be moved out of the community and whose apartments and homes were to be torn down were usually lower-income Negroes who, with very few exceptions, were not part of the Community Conference.

But this narrow explanation in terms of self-interest is only partly true, for if low-income Negroes were not directly represented on the Conference they were often represented vicariously—at least in the eyes of the Conference members. Time and again the Conference, or leading members of it, pressed the city to provide middle- and low-income public housing in the renewal area in part to accommodate persons who would be displaced by demolition. The Conference was firmly committed to the idea of a multiracial community; some of its members were committed in addition to the idea of a multiclass community.

I would argue that this broader consideration was equally as important as the narrower one in explaining the positive and constructive role of the Conference. The organization was made up to a large degree of persons who attached a high value to community-wide and neighborhood-wide goals, even (in some cases) when attaining those goals entailed a sacrifice in personal, material satisfactions. They are people who partake to an extraordinary extent of what Edward C. Banfield and I have called in a forthcoming book the "community-regarding" or "public-regarding" political ethos.[7] This ethos, which is most likely to be found among citizens who rank high in income, education, or both, is based on an enlarged view of the community and a sense of obligation toward it. People who display it are likely to have a propensity for looking at and making policy for the community "as a whole" and to have a high sense of personal efficacy, a long time-perspective, a general familiarity with and confidence in city-wide institutions, and a cosmopolitan orientation toward life. In addition, they are likely to possess a disproportionate share of organizational skills and resources.

It is just these attributes, of course, which make such people most likely to participate effectively in organizations whose function—whatever their ostensible purpose—is to create a sense of community and of community confidence and to win consent for community-wide plans. They are, in short,

[7] Edward C. Banfield and James Q. Wilson, *City Politics* (Cambridge, Mass.: Harvard University Press, 1963), esp. chap. xvi.

precisely those attributes which are likely to produce "citizen participation in urban renewal" that planners and community organizers will consider "positive and constructive"—this is, participation which will influence some of the general goals of renewal and modify a few of its details, but allow renewal to proceed.

SOCIAL DIFFERENCES IN CITIZEN PARTICIPATION

Most neighborhoods which planners consider in need of renewal are not, however, like Hyde Park-Kenwood in Chicago and are not heavily populated with citizens like the ones who organized the Hyde Park-Kenwood Community Conference. Most renewal areas are likely to be low-income, often Negro sections, many of whose inhabitants are the opposite in almost every respect from the cosmopolitan elite of Hyde Park-Kenwood. Such people are more likely to have a limited time-perspective, a greater difficulty in abstracting from concrete experience, an unfamiliarity with and lack of confidence in city-wide institutions, a preoccupation with the personal and the immediate, and few (if any) attachments to organizations of any kind, with the possible exception of churches.[8] Lacking experience in and the skills for participation in organized endeavors, they are likely to have a low sense of personal efficacy in organizational situations. By necessity as well as by inclination, such people are likely to have what one might call a "private-regarding" rather than a "public-regarding" political ethos. They are intimately bound up in the day-to-day struggle to sustain themselves and their families.

Such people are usually the objects rather than the subjects of civic action: they are acted upon by others, but rarely do they themselves initiate action. As a result, they often develop a keen sense of the difference between "we" and "they"—"they" being outside, city-wide civic and political forces which seek to police them, vote them, and redevelop them. It is quite natural that the "they" are often regarded with suspicion.

Although such people are not likely spontaneously to form organizations to define and carry out long-range very general civic tasks, it is wrong to assume that they are not likely to organize—or to allow themselves to be organized—for any purpose. The important thing is not that they are un-organizable, but that they can be organized only under special circumstances and for special purposes. Except for organizations which are in some sense extensions of the family and the church, lower-income neighborhoods are

---

[8] Cf. Seymour Martin Lipset, *Political Man* (Garden City, N.Y.: Doubleday & Co., 1960), chap. iv, and Robert Agger, *et al.*, "Political Cynicism: Measurement and Meaning," *Journal of Politics*, XXIII (August, 1961), 477–506. See also the vivid account of the culture of a lower-income Italian section of Boston in Herbert J. Gans, *The Urban Villagers* (New York: Free Press of Glencoe, 1963).

more likely to produce collective action in response to threats (real or imagined) than to create opportunities. Because of the private-regarding nature of their attachment to the community, they are likely to collaborate when each person can see a danger to him or to his family in some proposed change; collective action is a way, not of defining and implementing some broad program for the benefit of all, but of giving force to individual objections by adding them together in a collective protest.

The view which a neighborhood is likely to take of urban renewal, then, is in great part a product of its class composition. Upper- and upper-middle-class people are more likely to think in terms of general plans, the neighborhood or community as a whole, and long-term benefits (even when they might involve immediate costs to themselves); lower- and lower-middle-class people are more likely to see such matters in terms of specific threats and short-term costs. These differences account in great measure for some of the frustrations of the planners, redevelopers, and community organizers who are involved in urban renewal. Whereas it is relatively easy to obtain consent to renewal plans when people are thinking in terms of general goals and community-wide benefits, it is much harder—often impossible—when people see the same set of facts in terms of possible threats and costs.

This interpretation of lower-class behavior applies in its full force only in the extreme case, of course. There are many stable working class neighborhoods where indigenous leadership can be developed and involved in urban renewal programs on a "constructive" basis. The Back of the Yards area of Chicago is an example of one neighborhood of blue-collar families with strong local leadership (although even here, it should be noted, one powerful impetus to community organization was the fear of Negro invasion). But many potential renewal areas, particularly in Negro sections, do not even qualify as "stable working class." Half of all urban Negro families had an income of less than $3,000 a year in 1960. Thus, although the contrast I draw between middle-class and lower-class with respect to their attachment to neighborhood and community is deliberately extreme, it must be remembered that urban renewal is a policy intended in great part to apply to "extreme" areas.

COMMUNITY ORGANIZATION STRATEGIES

Among community organizers, two radically different strategies have been evolved to produce citizen participation under such circumstances. One recognizes the special character of depressed lower-income neighborhoods and seeks to capitalize on it. The most prominent and controversial exponent of this approach is Saul D. Alinsky, executive director of the Industrial

Areas Foundation of Chicago. He has created in a lower-income, heavily Negro area near the University of Chicago an organization ("The Woodlawn Organization") built in large part upon the residents' fears of urban renewal. According to a recent account, "Alinsky eschews the usual appeals to homeowners' interests in conserving property values or to a general neighborhood spirit or civic pride—appeals, in his view, that apply only to middle-class neighborhoods." Instead, he "appeals to the self-interest of the local residents and to their resentment and distrust of the outside world."[9] If residents do not have what I have called a "public-regarding" ethos, Alinsky is perfectly willing to appeal to their "private-regarding" ethos and to capitalize on the fact that collective action among such people is possible only when each person fears some threat to his own interests.

By stimulating and focussing such fears, an organization is created which can then compel other organizations—such as the sponsors of an urban renewal project—to bargain with it. Often the only terms on which such negotiations are acceptable to the neighborhood organization are terms unacceptable to the sponsors of renewal, for they require the drastic modification or even abandonment of the renewal plan. When an organization is built out of accumulated fears and grievances rather than out of community attachments, the cost is usually the tearing up of any plans that call for really fundamental changes in the landscape. On the other hand, such an organization may be very effective in winning special concessions from city hall to remedy specific neighborhood problems.

Many, probably most, planners and community organization specialists reject Alinsky's tactics. To them, his methods produce and even exacerbate conflict rather than prevent it, alienate the neighborhood from the city as a whole rather than bring it into the normal pattern of civic action, and place a premium on power rather than on a co-operative search for the common good.

The alternative strategy of most community organizers is to stimulate the creation of neighborhood organizations which will define "positive" goals for their areas in collaboration with the relevant city agencies and in accord with the time schedule which binds most federal renewal efforts. In Boston, for example, a new quasi-public agency—Action for Boston Community Development, or "ABCD"—has been created with both public and Ford Foundation funds in part for the purpose of stimulating the formation of neighborhood associations which will provide citizen participation in (and citizen consent to) the renewal plans of the Boston Redevelopment

<hr/>

[9] Charles E. Silberman, "The City and the Negro," *Fortune*, LXV (March, 1962), 88–91. See also Saul D. Alinsky, "Citizen Participation and Community Organization in Planning and Urban Renewal," address before the Chicago chapter of the National Association of Housing and Redevelopment Officials, January 29, 1962.

Authority. So far, it has been put to the test in two neighborhoods selected for renewal. In one, Washington Park-Roxbury, where it assisted in creating an organization "from the top down" by gathering together ministers and others prominent in this Negro community, it was able to win from the middle-class Negroes who would benefit from the plan consent "in principle" to a rehabilitation program the details of which are not yet entirely clear. In the other case, Charlestown, an old, lower-middle-income Irish neighborhood, ABCD brought many existing grass-roots organizations together for the purpose of ratifying a renewal plan. The citizens of Charlestown, however, knew their own interests well enough to cripple, at a public hearing, the proposed renewal plan with a flood of objections and conditions which, at least for the time being, the renewal authorities could not meet.

IMPLICATIONS FOR RENEWAL PROGRAMS

If one's goal is urban renewal on any really large scale in our cities, the implications of these observations are disturbing. The higher the level of indigenous organization in a lower-class neighborhood, the poorer the prospects for renewal in that area.

To say that the prospects are poorer does not, of course, mean that renewal will never occur with the consent of strong indigenous organizations in lower-class areas. But the difficulty is substantially increased, and a protracted, subtle, and assiduous wooing of neighborhood sentiment must first take place.[10] Perhaps this explains why, at least until very recently, most local urban renewal directors made no effort to encourage citizen participation except on a city-wide basis—with little or no representation from the affected neighborhood.[11]

In short, while the devotion of some planners today to the concept of "planning with people"—that is, citizen participation in neighborhood rehabilitation—may be an improvement over old-style urban redevelopment which ignored or took little account of neighborhood interests, the enthusiasm with which the new doctrine is being advocated blurs many important problems. The most important of these is that "planning with people" assumes on the part of the people involved a willingness and a

[10] See the account in Alfred G. Rosenberg, "Baltimore's Harlem Park Finds 'Self-Help' Citizen Participation is Successful," *Journal of Housing*, XVIII (May, 1961), 204–209. The initial reaction in the neighborhood to a renewal plan was bitter and got worse for three years. Patient community organization managed to overcome some of this resistance after much effort.

[11] See the survey reported in Gerda Lewis, "Citizen Participation in Urban Renewal Surveyed," *Journal of Housing*, XVI (March, 1959), 80–87. Questionnaires returned by about half the local renewal directors in the 91 cities which had approved "workable programs" as of July 31, 1956, showed that "the residents of project areas . . . seem to be relatively uninvolved in urban renewal"; representation from these areas on citizens' committees dealing with renewal was "almost totally absent."

capacity to engage in a collaborative search for the common good. The willingness is obviously almost never present when the persons involved will be severely penalized by having their homes and neighborhoods destroyed by wholesale clearance. Nor will that willingness be present when "rehabilitation" means, as it usually does, that the residents must at their own expense bring their homes up to standards deemed satisfactory to the renewal agency or have their homes taken from them. But what is less obvious is that it may not be present, even when such clearance is not envisaged, because of important class differences in the capacity to organize for community-wide goals. This means that middle-class persons who are beneficiaries of rehabilitation will be planned with; lower-class persons who are disadvantaged by rehabilitation are likely to be planned *without*.

The fact that some people will be hurt by renewal does not, of course, mean that there should be no renewal. There are scarcely any public policies which do not impose costs on someone. What it does mean is that planners might more frankly take such costs into account, weighing them against the benefits renewal may confer on individuals and the community. There is little except obfuscation to be gained from attempting to maintain, as the slogan "planning with people" implies, that urban renewal and perfect democracy are and always should be compatible; that not only can the city be revitalized, it can be revitalized with the consent of all concerned.

If we decide to try to obtain the consent of those neighborhoods selected for renewal, we had better prepare ourselves for a drastic re-evaluation of the potential impact of that program. Adjusting the goals of renewal to the demands of the lower classes means, among other things, substantially reducing the prospects for assembling sufficiently large tracts of cleared land to make feasible the construction of dwelling units attractive to the middle-class suburbanite whom the city is anxious to woo back into its taxing jurisdiction. This, in turn, means that the central city may have to abandon the goal of recolonizing itself with a tax-paying, culture-loving, free-spending middle class and be content instead with serving as a slightly dilapidated way-station in which lower-income and minority groups find shelter and a minimal level of public services while working toward the day when they, too, can move out to a better life. That, of course, is in great part the function that at least the older central cities of this country have always performed, and until we run out of lower classes (a day unfortunately far in the future), that may be the function they must continue to perform.

POLITICAL EFFECTS

Not only does the question of citizen participation in urban renewal have important implications for the goals of planning and even for one's conception of the function of the central city; it also goes to the heart of a fundamental problem in the urban political process. Resolving this issue is not simply a problem in planning priorities, but in addition a problem in electoral politics.

American mayors today are faced with the problem of governing cities in which to a great extent the traditional sources of political power have been dispersed or eliminated. The old-style political machine is gone except in a very few big cities. Party organization generally is weak. Mayors must still assemble the power to govern but they can rarely do so today by relying on loyal party lieutenants who occupy the lesser city offices and who sit on the council. Instead, the major must try to piece together that power out of the support he can receive from city-wide interests, such as newspapers, civic associations, business organizations, and labor unions. Support from such sources, valuable as it is, does not always carry with it the assurance that the support of the rank-and-file voter will also be forthcoming. Average citizens have a way of not sharing (or sometimes not even knowing about) the enthusiasms of the top civic leadership.

To insure against this possibility, many "new-style" mayors are trying to build up new neighborhood associations and enter into relationships with old ones in order to provide themselves with a way of reaching the average voter and of commanding his support. In Boston, for example, it is an open secret that Mayor John Collins is hoping that the support and attention he has given various neighborhood associations will be reciprocated, on election day, by the support of their members for him.

To the extent that these neighborhood associations are courted by mayors, they attempt to extract in return concessions on matters of city policy (such as street sweeping, garbage collection, or playground maintenance) which affect their areas. They see themselves as instruments for adapting the programs of an impersonal city bureaucracy to the various and often conflicting needs of neighborhoods. In a sense, they perform (for entirely different reasons, of course) the same function which the political machine once performed.

The neighborhood civic association is widely regarded as not only a new mechanism for representing citizen wants to the city bureaucracy, but a means of ending the political "alienation" of those citizens. Much has been written of late to suggest that a large and perhaps growing number of people are "alienated" from the American political process, but particularly from the political process in their communities. In Boston,[12] Cam-

---

[12] Murray B. Levin, *The Alienated Voter* (New York: Holt, Rinehart & Winston, 1960), pp. 58–75. See also Murray B. Levin and Murray Eden, "Political Strategy for the Alienated Voter," *Public Opinion Quarterly,* XXVI (Spring, 1962), 47–63.

bridge,[13] Detroit,[14] Nashville,[15] upstate New York,[16] and various other places where studies have been made, the voters—usually (though not always) those with little income or education—feel, we are told, estranged from and even threatened by the political life of their cities. To the extent that this alienation exists (and the studies are not very precise on this), the neighborhood civic association is seen as an important way of giving the citizen a meaningful and satisfactory relationship with his community— a way, in short, of ending his "alienation."[17]

It is not yet clear, however, whether such neighborhood groups will provide a means whereby citizens overcome their "alienation" or whether they will simply provide a forum in which citizens can give expression to it. These groups, after all, are usually concerned about neighborhood, not city-wide, problems, and the member's attachment is often at most only to his immediate family and neighbors, not to the community as a whole. Neighborhood associations seek many goals in their dealings with city hall. Generally speaking, however, they want higher levels of community services but they oppose extensive physical changes in their areas, as would be caused by highway construction or urban renewal programs.

For city-wide officials, such as mayors and planners, the crucial problem is how to make attention to these neighborhood demands compatible with city-wide programs, almost all of which will, to some extent, impose hardships on some neighborhoods. The old-style political leaders who were bosses of city machines were not faced to the same degree with this problem. Whenever they could, they avoided the conflict between neighborhood and city by not proposing any extensive programs designed to appeal to city-wide interests. When such programs were politically unavoidable, they resolved the inevitable conflict by "buying off" their neighborhood opponents. The bosses used the jobs, favors, and patronage which they con-

[13] See William A. Gamson, "The Fluoridation Dialogue: Is It An Ideological Conflict?" *Public Opinion Quarterly*, XXV (Winter, 1961), 526–37, and Arnold Simmel, "A Signpost for Research on Fluoridation Conflicts: The Concept of Relative Deprivation," *Journal of Social Issues*, XVII (1961), 26–36.

[14] Arthur Kornhauser, *Attitudes of People Toward Detroit* (Detroit: Wayne University Press, 1952), p. 28.

[15] E. L. McDill and J. C. Ridley, "Status, Anomia, Political Alienation and Political Participation," *American Journal of Sociology*, LXVIII (September, 1962), 205–213.

[16] Wayne E. Thompson and John E. Horton, "Political Alienation as a Force in Political Action," *Social Forces*, XXXVIII (March, 1960), 190–5 and Horton and Thompson, "Powerlessness and Political Negativism: A Study of Defeated Local Referendums," *American Journal of Sociology*, LXVII (March, 1962), 485–93.

[17] Cf. William C. Loring, Jr., Frank L. Sweetser, and Charles F. Ernst, *Community Organization for Citizen Participation in Urban Renewal* (Boston: Massachusetts Department of Commerce, 1957), pp. 232–238.

trolled to enforce their wills on neighborhood political leaders and to compensate the neighborhood voters for their distress.

Today's mayor can neither avoid proposing large programs to satisfy city-wide interests nor can he buy off the neighborhood opponents of such projects. Under these circumstances, the mayor must move cautiously between the twin evils of doing so little as to disappoint community-regarding voters and doing so much as to antagonize private-regarding voters.

Citizen participation in urban renewal, then, is not simply (or even most importantly) a way of winning popular consent for controversial programs. It is part and parcel of a more fundamental reorganization of American local politics. It is another illustration—if one more is needed—of how deeply embedded in politics the planning process is.

32. Citizen Participation in Federal Programs: A Review*

BY HANS B. C. SPIEGEL

INTRODUCTION

Citizen participation in governmental programs, though not exactly invented during the past five years, has recently received dramatic attention and visibility. A number of federally sponsored programs have begun to require resident or consumer participation and the resultant effects have caused widely divergent expressions. "Maximum feasible misunderstanding" is the opinion of a well-known urban specialist, who goes on to raise the specter of "private nullification" of the legislative will (Moynihan, 1969, p. 182). "Let's stop all this nonsense," pronounces an exasperated local housing official who has had his fill of rhetoric and requirements about citizen participation. (Louis Danzig, quoted in Campbell, 1969, p. 24.) A husband and wife team of lawyers, well versed in the war on poverty, offer a choice between genuine citizen participation and rebellion, declaring that the former is "probably the only guarantee, frail though it may be, that people will be willing to abide by the terms of today's social contract . . ." (Edgar S. and Jean Camper Cahn, 1968, p. 222.) Another observer likens citizen participation to eating spinach, "no one is against it in principle, because it's good for you," but the principle explodes when the "citizens" are defined as the "have-nots." (Arnstein, 1969, p. 216.) All these observers would probably agree that "citizen participation virtually defies generalization and delights in reducing abtractions to dust." (Spiegel and Mittenthal, 1968 b, p. 3.)

Indeed, the various sets of activities and roles that are subsumed under the rubric of citizen participation create serious definitional problems in the context of volunteerism. "Citizen participation" can be the label applied to relatively powerless advisory committees that gather at the beck and call of a

Reprinted with permission of the author and publisher from Hans B. C. Spiegel, "Citizen Participation in Federal Programs: A Review," *Journal of Voluntary Action Research,* Monograph No. 1 (1971), pp. 4–31.

* The assistance of Sherry Arnstein in gathering crucial data under fierce time pressure is gratefully acknowledged. Mrs. Arnstein is a Washington-based Urban Affairs Consultant who was working under a grant from the Center for a Voluntary Society in investigating current policies and practices of various federal agencies in the realm of citizen participation as background for this paper.

Mayor; it can also be applied to a paid group of area residents exercising veto power over policy decisions about the area's physical development. It can mean the opportunity for groups of citizens to join governmental bodies in a coalition (Mogulof, 1969, pp. 225–226) where "convergent action" (Soysel, 1966, p. 46) is encouraged and where citizens are expected to give opinions while respecting the pro-active role of the professional (Pomeroy, 1953, pp. 31–34). But it can also result in confrontation, divergent action, and political challenge.

Smith and his colleagues (Smith, et al., 1972) define voluntary action at the level of individuals as "behavior that is primarily motivated by the expectation of psychic benefits, rather than being primarily motivated by: (a) expectations of the application of physical force or punishment for noncompliance, (b) expectations of strong social-legal-economic sanctions for failure to act in a certain manner . . ." While this definition is broad enough to cover most aspects of citizen participation in federal programs, I continue to have a nagging sense that even this thoughtful conceptual net is not quite subtle and tightly knotted enough to catch all its squirming and divergent activities. For one thing, citizen participation is a mandated, not a permissive, facet of a number of programs. A given jurisdiction of persons, then, cannot opt *not* to engage in "voluntary" action—unless, of course, the federal program itself is rejected by the intended consumers. Furthermore, I wonder whether psychic *benefits* are the prime motivational force behind individuals engaging in, say, the Tenant Committee of a public housing project (See "Tenant-Management Issues" 1970) rather than the desperate attempt at avoidance of physical *disbenefits*. Many persons who are the object of federal programs appear to be motivated into actual participation, at least initially, for essentially negative psychic reasons, such as avoidance of "maximum feasible manipulation" (Arnstein, 1970). The scope of citizen participation is so vast that examples can be placed in all of the cells describing various forms of voluntary action in Figure 1 of Smith, et al. (1970). That is, citizen participation in federally sponsored activities can be remunerated or not, can take place in formal or informal settings, and can take on autonomous and non-autonomous organizational forms.

Perhaps the basic reason why the elusive concept of "citizen participation in federal programs" tends to sprawl all over—and sometimes beyond—"volunteer action" (even of federally sponsored volunteer action such as VISTA and the Peace Corps) revolves around the term "citizen." A citizen, presumably, not only has responsibilities toward the state, but his will helps to master the state. As will be pointed out later, many federal programs now permit or even require affected citizens to help formulate local policies concerning the program, in addition to discharging program-implementing or assisting functions. In other words, "citizen participation" can go considerably beyond citizens assuming service-supplementary or program-advisory roles; it can also mean that local citizens carry policy and decision-making responsibilities. The current debate about the question of citizen participation revolves exactly around this question of citizen power: how much decision-making power should be maintained by the elected officials and "the essential machinery of conventional democracy" (Soysel, 1966, pp. 23–25) and how much power should be delegated to those directly affected by a given program, be they known as "consumers of services," "citizens," "the poor," or "residents"?

How then can we define citizen participation in federal programs? *As we shall use the term here, "citizen participation" represents the acts of those who are not formally part of the legislative or public administrative hierarchy but who nonetheless intend to influence the efficacy of the program and the behavior of those public officials responsible for ultimate policy and operational decisions.* This definition should accommodate a wide spectrum of activities, including individual and collective citizen acts, that may be convergent with or divergent from the goals of a given governmental unit. Citizen participation thus includes altruistic and machiavellian acts; acts of high and low social change potential; acts that can be focused on all residents of a given area and those focused on a specific target population such as the poor; and remunerated or non-remunerated acts.

It should be noted that all these acts are performed in the context of a given governmental program and thus vis-a-vis certain political structures. Citizen participation in this context involves decisions—and often struggles— over the allocation of scarce resources. It follows that the present essay stresses the political aspect inherent in this form of voluntary action. I have chosen to highlight the fascinating interplay between deliberate citizen acts and a given administrative governmental program. Excluded from the present essay, therefore, are citizen acts that are independent of and have no immediate need for federal program assistance, such as a local church's Clean Block Campaign.

*   *   *

WHERE WE'RE AT

In terms of federal policy on citizen participation, where does this leave us? The above discussion may justify the following observations:

Proposition 1: Administrative regulations concerning citizen participation have permeated Federal domestic programs in several Washington agencies.

Proposition 2: Existing regulations are more cognizant of, more numerous, more developed, and more consequential toward participation than they were a decade ago.

Proposition 3: A single, explicated uniform and consistent Federal policy concerning citizen participation has neither been established legislatively nor administratively.

Proposition 3.1: The Federal administration at its highest levels favors citizen participation that is congruent with and not disruptive of municipal and federal program management.

Proposition 3.2: The Federal administration at its highest levels opposes citizen participation that results in citizen control over, as contrasted with citizen involvement in, any key aspects of programs.

Proposition 4: Administrative regulations concerning the nature, purpose, support, and enforcement of citizen participation activities vary from Federal agency to agency and even from program to program within any given agency.

Proposition 4.1: Administrative regulations concerning citizen participation range from being vague and permissive to being specific and mandatory (e.g., they vary from general encouragement for informing affected citizens to requiring specific involvement of citizens in organizational structures in which they must be able to exercise certain irreducible powers).

Proposition 4.2: There is no correlation between the amount of financial expenditures of a given Federal program and the citizen participation regulations. (E.g., an "expensive" program such as public roads has rather limited regulations, whereas the relatively low budget Head Start program has extensive regulations.)

Proposition 5: The crucial variables determining the stance of a Federal program toward citizen participation appear to be: (a) the statutory language of the legislative enactment; (b) the availability of and willingness to utilize administrative sanctions to enforce administrative regulations; (c) the power that can be generated by the program's citizen clientele (often dependent on the degree to which such citizens are organized); (d) the power generated by those opposing strong citizen participatory regulations (often the program's local managers as detailed below); and (e) the availability and performance of staff in the Federal program (especially at middle and upper management levels) in monitoring and supporting citizen participation activities.

THE LOCAL SCENE

How do the federal regulations unfold themselves locally? Who are some of the key actors? What characterizes some of the emerging institutions in the neighborhoods? How can the evolving participatory processes best be described and categorized?

Hard, empirical findings concerning these questions are still relatively sparse. I shall try to concentrate on those aspects of participation that are directly connected with the Federal policy stance previously described. Generalizations about the participatory or volunteer process *per se* I gladly leave to others.

A PHENOMENOLOGY OF CITIZEN PARTICIPATION

Two crucial local actors step into the foreground as a Federal program finally arrives at the local level: (1) the governmental program manager who is responsible for the program's local administration and (2) the spokesman representing the citizens who are affected by the program (which, in urban-related programs, often means a neighborhood target population). It may be useful to examine quickly the manner in which these two important actors view citizen participation. In short, we want to sketch an abbreviated phenomenology which, hopefully, will illustrate how "citizen participation" generally, and the Federal laws and regulations cited earlier, are perceived differentially. It can be expected, of course, that each actor pursuing an active role in the citizen participation drama will define the term to fit his own function, convenience, and perspective.

1. *The Program Manager.* This person may be the head of a municipal urban renewal program, or a city's anti-poverty or Model Cities program. He is likely to have been appointed by the Mayor or the local governing body and therefore is directly responsible to the Mayor or City Manager. He is often the city's entree to the coffers of a specific program.

It may be superfluous to say that the urban program manager is oriented toward program results and efficiency. He wants program applications to be locally approved and sent to Washington for formal approval there. He wants to deliver a program's goods and services as efficiently and quickly as possible. (His definition of both "efficiency" and "goods and services" may, of course, be at variance with that of the intended recipient.) The Federally-endorsed Planning—Programming—Budgeting System (PPBS) puts a premium on the program manager being able to maximize limited resources and to control some of the essential variables in municipal programming. The powers and responsibilities of an executive character must be clearly lodged in the Mayor and not in two or three bodies, insists New York City's former Budget Director, who warns that, "A return to the divided executive responsibility and accountability and the sheer red tape of the prior system would have severe adverse effects upon the quality of government." (Hayes, 1970, p. 31.)

It is not surprising that a number of program managers declare, "from a bureaucrat's viewpoint, there is always trouble in citizens organizations . . ." (Herman, 1969, p. 602.) Program managers appear to think in terms of "production versus participation" (Ascher, 1970, pp. 9–10), and this polarization may lead to a perceived inverse correlation between the degree and strength of citizen participation and the production of program results.

To be sure, program managers usually endorse a style of citizen participation that is essentially collaborative-integrative in nature. In this context, citizen participation can be seen as a device whereby public officials induce nonpublic individuals in a way the officials desire (Moynihan, 1970, p. 13). It is the oppositional-conflicting style that is perceived as disruptive to the governmental program pipeline that has its fountainhead in Washington and flows through a carefully patched-together and complex system to the eventual consumer. "I share enthusiasm for maximum feasible participation in the process of local governments," states an experienced public administrator, "but I also favor orderly administrative processes and governmental action not unduly impeded by neighborhood power struggles and competing squabbles . . ." (Hamilton, 1969, p. 7.)

The fear of citizen participation resulting in programmatic stalemates and paralysis is repeated often. Roger Starr devotes the better part of his book (Starr, 1967) to the need for public officials to make decisions, even in the face of objections or of conflicting preferences of residents and "that action which is taken imperfectly . . . is ultimately more popular than no action at all." (p. 275.) Otherwise, many program managers would argue, urban programs will never get off the ground and get fouled up in "the mutual stymie," a phrase attributed to Paul Ylvisaker (Campbell, 1969, p. 24). The anguished words of the Director of a local housing authority concerned with the production of badly needed shelter well illustrates this fear:

> *When I think of all the pieces that have to fall together before a public housing unit is constructed, you can see why mankind's first effort at a high-rise as the Tower of Babel never came through . . .*
>
> *We've got people like me and the people who work for me. We've got to listen to board members. One of them says, 'I want big projects.' One of them says, 'I want little projects.' One of them doesn't want anybody to build unless he's a member of the home builders association.*
>
> *We've got the city planning commission; we've got the city council; we've got half a dozen other public agencies.*
>
> *We've got civic associations, pros and cons; we've got neighborhood groups.*
>
> *We've got the Federal Housing Assistance Office . . . and they don't always agree with us.*
>
> *We've got the developer and the matter of whether he's making a bundle or not making a bundle.*
>
> *We might have a non-profit sponsor.*
>
> *We've got the prospective tenants.*
>
> *All of these people have got to agree in some way, shape, or form before anything's done. But don't get exercised. This is democracy in action.*
>
> *For the process to work someone's got to say, 'Okay, Mr. Neighbor-*

hood Group, you can plan with us; but remember, there's a limit as to what you can do. And there sure is a limit on what you can stop us from doing.' (Brignac, 1969, p. 604.)

2. *The Neighborhood Spokesman.* This person may be the head of a neighborhood council, community corporation, or Model Cities citizen organization. He is usually appointed by his organization and sometimes by a special, publicly supervised election. He may be the executive and paid director of an organization or the elected president. He probably is indigenous to the area and, even if he is not, he is accountable to an indigenously-based policy making group. In short, he is the spokesman for the neighborhood or for that element in the neighborhood that has a dominant voice in the respective neighborhood organization.

There is growing evidence (see, for example, the case studies of Oakland, New Haven and the South Bronx in Mittenthal and Spiegel, 1970) that a number of neighborhood spokesmen are viewing Federal citizen participation requirements as political levers which can be utilized to gain advantages for the neighborhood far beyond the boundaries of a specific program. While the program manager looks toward program efficiency and utilizes citizen participation to enhance the flow of program services, so the neighborhood spokesman may be said to regard redistribution of power as his main objective and, likewise, looks to citizen participation to accomplish *his* ends. He may advocate, for example, the delegation of considerable governmental responsibilities to the neighborhood organization and away from City Hall. And, in a number of significant instances, he has accomplished just that (Warren, 1969, p. 248). Though such a shift in power may not have been anticipated or desired by the Congress when it passed recent social legislation (Moynihan, 1969, pp. 88–100), the neighborhood spokesman can utilize the new-found legitimacy of citizen participation for whatever political leverage it may yield.

The theme of redistribution of power appears particularly evident in black neighborhoods. The following statement made by the head of a Model Cities citizen group to a white representative of HUD, who had urged him to consult with City Hall, is revealing. Note how the contempt of white-controlled institutions is utilized to draw political battle-lines over issues that presumably go beyond the limitations of a specific Federally sponsored program.

The time has passed for me that I will be defined by you or others like you and be told what is reasonable by folk like you . . . Whether you wish to agree or not, Congress and City Halls around the country are the enemy of the poor because they control the public institutions which oppress many of the poor. And if the poor happen to be black the oppression seems more acceptable and rational. That kind of polarity existed before my time and will in all probability continue after my time . . . The problem is to recognize a polarity and move toward a bargaining situation in which the interests of parties in conflict can be negotiated. I intend that the representatives of the black community of the poor in West Oakland approach that situation with a strong bargaining position with hat on head and not in hand. (Percy Moore, quoted in Spiegel and Mittenthal, 1968, p. 82.)

The above is probably not the most typical example of neighborhood spokesmen. There are surely numerous citizen group leaders who presently don't have the political skills or motivations to maximize the potential foothold on neighborhood power facilitated by citizen participation regulations. But to others, the foothold has been eagerly grasped and enlarged into a beachhead. As HUD's former chief advisor for citizen participation in the Model Cities program states, ". . . citizen participation is a categorical term for citizen power. It is the redistribution of power that enables the have-not citizens, presently excluded from the political and economic processes, to be deliberately included in the future." (Arnstein, 1969, p. 216.)

As a corollary to the presumed goal of power distribution, the neighborhood spokesman will also enter a Federally sponsored program with a high degree of skepticism. He often perceives government-citizen partnership as, in reality, an arena for power struggles which he enters at a distinct disadvantage. In the words of frustrated Model Cities neighborhood leaders in North Philadelphia:

If only we had known two years ago what we now know about city and Federal politics, it might have been a different story. But we were political novices, and they were experts in political chicanery. We were trying to change things, and they were trying to keep us boxed in . . . They had the upper hand, particularly the money and the sophisticated methods for maximum feasible manipulation. (Arnstein, as told to, 1970, p. 31.)

This same group, the North Philadelphia Area Wide Council, concludes with eight lessons that were reportedly learned in the process of dealing with the city and the Federal government, the first two of which are, "No matter what HUD says, Model Cities is first and foremost a politician's game," and "You can't trust City Hall or HUD." (Ibid, p. 37.)

PARTICIPATION AS POLITICAL PROCESS

From the foregoing it can be surmised that one way of viewing citizen participation in Federal programs as a local phenomenon is in a political and power context. Indeed, my colleague Mittenthal and I (Mittenthal and Spiegel, 1970, pp. 6–9) ventured to make the following statements which I am slightly altering for presentation as propositions.

Proposition 6: Participation of organized local citizen groups in federal programs cannot be considered apart from a context of power. Issues of organizational development and survival, power and control become transcendent themes in consideration of specific issues, especially those issues that deal with the planning and execution of delivery of services to low income areas. (The lexicon of citizen participation has lately been interspersed with repeated references to power not only by neighborhood spokesmen such as the ones cited, nor by social actionists such as Saul Alinsky (see, for example, Spiegel 1968 a, pp. 149–205), but also by students of the subject who find the concept of power a convenient context to help understand the dynamics of participation. Indeed, it might be argued that an exclusion of power in the consideration of participation in governmental programs is something akin to describing free enterprise capitalism without talking about the profit motive.)

Proposition 7: Organized local citizen groups that have gained a measure of power and/or control over aspects of the local allocation of federal program resources tend to trigger a set of socio-political processes that often engender community-wide conflict. (Once the neighborhood organization has resisted or challenged city hall, the issue no longer remains localized to the target area but becomes a city-wide political conflict, as the controversies over Model Cities in West Oakland, South Bronx, and New Haven illustrate (Mittenthal and Spiegel, 1970). While conflict is not predestined, there frequently is struggle over the allocation of scarce resources that plays itself out in confrontation between rival actors—and each actor attempts to involve sympathizers to his cause.)

Proposition 8: Dominance in the frequently protracted struggle between neighborhood groups and city hall over control of program resources is often a function of the ability to sustain a permanent, bureaucratic, and financially viable organization over an extended period of time. (As Austin, 1970, points out, the city can often "wait out" the neighborhood by the simple expedient of inaction over a period of time. The neighborhood organization often is unable to survive a period of time when no funding is forthcoming. Austin stresses the inherent advantage of established and financially viable community agencies over more vulnerable neighborhood organizations as they compete for the federal dollar.)

Proposition 9: Responding to local political contingencies involving city hall and local citizen organization, federal policies appear to permit considerable local option that varies in time and place and to allow the local citizen participation pendulum to swing once toward the city, then toward the neighborhoods, as the body politic requires. (As has been demonstrated, the federal government has no single citizen participation policy that is uniformly enunciated from Washington. But even if it were, the federal program would have to take local political contingencies into consideration and make adaptations, even if only in nuances. Mittenthal (1970), Rosenbaum (1970), and Warren (1969) write about citizen participation practices that are, to a considerable degree, adjusted and sandpapered to meet local political realities.)

Proposition 9.1: When both city and neighborhood are determined and strong, a major stalemate tends to occur with both parties rallying federal policies and regulations to bolster their respective arguments. (In Newark, N. J., for example, the battle between city hall and a neighborhood group over the location of a medical and dental complex forced the high level intervention of a joint memo by both HUD and HEW Under Secretaries explicating specific ground rules. This attempt at *ad hoc* policy interpretation, incidentally, appears to have left both local parties considerably less than satisfied. See Altshuler (1970, pp. 178–180), Williams (1970), and Duhl (1969, pp. 537–572, plus rejoinders pp. 573–588).)

A TYPOLOGY OF PARTICIPATION

There have been a number of writers trying to categorize the styles of action of citizen groups *vis-a-vis* a governmental program. A continuum is frequently drawn from little or no participation to much or full participation. As Marcuse (1970, p. 5) has pointed out, this linear approach to participation frequently begs the question of the *goals* of participation. It also uses concepts such as power, control, involvement, and participation in a unitary sense and places them on a continuum as though they were synonymous when, in reality, important differentiations should be drawn. Despite these shortcomings, the literature is beginning to disect the conceptual umbrella of "citizen participation".

Arnstein (1969, p. 217) speaks of "a ladder of citizen participation", the lower rungs of which are characterized by manipulation, therapy, information-giving, consultation, and placation. The higher rungs represent partnership, delegated power, and resident control. Arnstein acknowledges that her ladder is a homogenizing abstraction, but insists that human perceptions often appear to be shaped more by image than by substance. "In most cases," she says, "the have-nots really do perceive the powerful as a monolithic 'system', and the powerholders actually do view the have-nots as a sea of 'those people'."

Spiegel and Mittenthal talk of "levels of participation . . . . as steps in an evolutionary scale" in the context of Model Cities planning (1968 b, pp. 31–33) which are derived from Arnstein's formulations in an earlier memo: information, consultation, negotiation, shared policy and decision-making, joint planning, delegation of planning responsibility, and neighbor-hood control.

Burke (1968, pp. 287–294) establishes five types of participation: edu-cation-therapy, behavioral change, staff supplement, cooperation, and com-munity power. Again, power in the hands of residents is the ultimate type of participation but not necessarily, as Burke takes pain to underline, the most functional for all planning activities.

Other writers do not describe a linear continuum, but emphasize basic modalities of participation which can be differentiated from one another. Ascher (1970, p. 2) makes the useful distinction of citizen participation as *service* "to supplement the services of paid civil servants. . . ." and as *decision-making*. Mogulof (1969, pp. 225–232) historically traces citizen par-ticipation through an elitist model (as characterized by the juvenile delin-quency program of the early 1960's), to a coalition or broker model (as in the war on poverty), to what he describes as an adversary or confrontation model. Other scholars such as Marris and Rein (1967), Hyman (1969), and Warren (1969) have mentioned different sets of typologies.

As has already been noted in a previous proposition, governmental agen-cies seem to oppose citizen participation that results in their control over a program. There is less empirical evidence that *most* citizen groups desire maximal power, though it is a hypothesis worth testing. Regardless of whether we speak of "rungs" or "steps" or "models" of citizen participation, it is difficult to predict exactly where the governmental unit and/or the citizen organization will finally draw a line of *modus operandi* demarcation. What appears to be emerging from the previously cited literature, however, is that *at the local level* this line is often negotiated.

WHO PARTICIPATES, HOW MUCH, IN WHAT STRUCTURES
AND WITH WHAT RESULTS?

At this time, these vital questions cannot really be answered with any degree of certainty. To the extent that the literature sheds some light on these issues I have so indicated below in abbreviated fashion. The evidence at hand, however, is too skimpy in my estimation even to formulate reason-able propositions.

1. *What local institutional structures for citizen participation have evolved?* They range from advisory councils with relatively few powers to neighborhood boards with *de facto* veto powers. We know of no national survey critically examining the varied structures of community action and model cities agencies. Among the studies touching on this matter are Kramer (1969), Spiegel and Mittenthal (1968), Mittenthal and Spiegel (1970), Mogulof (1969, 1970a, 1970b), MARC (1968), HUD (1969), Austin (1970).

2. *What leadership has evolved from this participatory process with*

what impact on the program, constituency, and political structures? One of the most perceptive analyses is contained in Zurcher (1970), which is limited, however, to one city. See also Mann (1970), Hunter College (1969).

3. *How many participants are really involved—and to what degree— under the banner of "maximum feasible" and "widespread" participation?* We know of no national empirically-based studies on how many "rank and file" residents participate in what program planning and execution tasks. Brandeis University's study of Community Representation in Community Action Agencies, under contract with O.E.O., studied 20 city programs and reports that "Target area residents across all C.A.A.'s had very little impact on the major program strategies." (Austin, 1970, p. 24) The full Brandeis study may shed welcome light on this area. The number of citizens responding to opportunities to vote for their representatives on citizen boards may be another clue as to "widespread participation. Mathews (1968, p. 56) cites election results from five cities for local anti-poverty boards with an average voter turnout of 4% of those eligible to cast a ballot. Hallman (1969, p. 174) writes about an election turn-out of 25% in voting for representatives of a community corporation. Arnstein and Fox (1968) report an even higher level (up to 40%) in some Model Cities elections.

4. *Cross-cutting the above is the basic efficacy question: Does participation work? How are the outputs of a program with high degree of participation different compared with those evidencing little citizen participation?* Observers have taken hold of this question from different vantage points without coming to definitive judgments. Crain and Rosenthal (1967) and Van Til and Van Til (1970) are among the writers who suggest that citizen participation can lead to stalemates where action in any direction may become paralyzed. Mogulof (1969, 1970b) and Spiegel and Mittenthal (1968) point to citizen participation as a political lever for power redistribution, but both authors deliberately leave unanswered the question of improved programmatic outputs. MARC (1968, p. 248) concludes that the required involvement of the poor is "no assurance of effectiveness of these programs" and, "while theoretically and democratically sound, [it] is more illusory than real." Mathews (1968, p. 56) claims that citizen representatives on poverty boards "have shown more interest in personnel and program control than in program content." However, Kaplan, Gans, and Kahn (HUD, 1969a) are rather supportive of the efficacy of citizen participation in their recent evaluation of the Model Cities Program.

WHERE TO NOW?

Crystal-ball gazing concerning the future of citizen participation is an enterprise fraught with more than the usual uncertainties. The variables involved, to the extent that they can be identified, spread across many classifications. At the risk of skating on very thin empirical ice, let me venture the following generalization.

Proposition 10: Among the factors that will influence the future utilization of citizen participation in federal programs are: a) the developing nature and strength of minority and protest movements, particularly the black and consumer movements; b) the establishment of new federal statutes and guidelines and the manner in which old and new regulations are interpreted and enforced; c) the degree to which technical assistance and training can be given to both citizen groups and the bureaucracies that administer programs; d) the availability of federal commitment and resources to urban programs so that there is something about which to participate; and e) the extent to which local participatory structures can be institutionalized.

In attempting to justify the above predictions, let me cite some brief, personal observations about each factor: a) It appears to me that one of the chief pressures upon Washington that resulted in stronger citizen participation regulations came from the civil rights and black power movements. I don't see any other groups in the wings to continue to exercise this pressure, save perhaps a new consumer coalition. Unless such black or consumer pressures are exercised, citizen participation regulations from Washington will likely diminish. The idea of citizen participation as an integral aspect of federal programs just doesn't have enough spokesmen with political muscle to coast on its own momentum.

I previously discussed item b) concerning the importance of enactment and enforcement of new federal policies. As to c), technical assistance and training, I have the strong feeling that governmental agencies continue to expect impressive results from citizens and bureaucrats to whom only the most modest assistance is given. Both parties must have training available to accomplish the often delicate task of negotiating and implementing the social contracts involved. (It would be useful to compare those local programs where training and technical assistance have been maximal with those where this assistance was absent or only present in token form.) Citizen groups, it seems to me, must be able to secure their own technical advice, and local program management staff must likewise receive technical support and training. The university may be one institution to play a significant role in this endeavor (Spiegel, 1968b, pp. 316–318).

Factor d), about federal commitment and resources, seems self-explanatory. Obviously, if there is no federally sponsored program or money, citizens can't participate in them. Thus, if Model Cities should be scuttled, participatory regulations and existing practices will cease. A legacy will continue, but many of the neighborhood participatory structures would be doomed.

The last factor, e), concerning institutionalization of citizen participation, may be less obvious than the others cited above. Let me explain in a few paragraphs.

The vulnerability of the citizens' organizational base concerns me. As it is, such organizations and/or their leadership can be co-opted or derailed with relative ease. Arnstein (1970) tells such a story from the point of view of a model neighborhood resident group. Austin (1970, p. 48) informs us how anti-poverty agencies with their neighborhood participation often fell prey to co-optation by established and traditional public and private agencies. How can such participatory neighborhood structures be strengthened to function with relative staying power and independence? This line of inquiry is particularly pertinent when considering that there will likely come times when federal and/or city support for this role diminishes, or when resident apathy reasserts itself, and when the need for an institutional base will prove to be critical. It must be one that displays the resiliency, staying power, and functional utility that enables it to be placed beyond the fickle moods of the culture. At the end of their own assessment of citizen participation the Van Tils point to the "critical importance of the development of new institutional forms that will represent the interests of the poor and will build those interests into the larger political and social structure . . ." (Van Til and Van Til, 1970, pp.321–322).

As for particular institutions that appear to be most effective in meeting this goal, there are suggestive models that have been developed but that require testing. For example Hallman (1969) describes the community corporation and neighborhood board that carry out a number of private and quasi-governmental functions in the neighborhood. These community corporations and boards present a suggestive organizational pattern, one that could be utilized as the final part of a triple tiered machinery of federal program administration (Washington, city hall, and the neighborhood). They are accountable to the neighborhood electorate, can enjoy considerable independence from arbitrary city hall actions, and can even generate independent income through commercial enterprises. Advocates of neighborhood control and neighborhood government such as Altshuler (1970) and Kotler (1969) have elaborated on this theme.

Another alternative, of course, would have existing governmental structures become dramatically more responsive to the needs of neighborhoods and accessible to their inhabitants (Mann, 1970). Rather than creating new quasi-independent neighborhood units, according to this line of reasoning, a number of existing bureaucracies can be redirected toward serving the public and the neighborhood with greatly intensified effort and sensitivity, but without radical structural changes. Thus, a housing program would hire indigenous housing aides, train its existing staff to better relate to citizens, establish many more field offices, consult with community groups, organize participatory planning charettes, and possibly introduce a housing ombudsman. Measures such as these, it will be argued, will tend to correct the temporary imperfections of what still can be a truly representative and response-able liberal democracy. Publicly funded citizen participation will thus take place around a single governmental network without necessitating pitting a separate neighborhood paragovernmental structure against the city. Many observers would insist that effective decentralization rather than "evading or avoiding the jurisdiction of established local authorities" (Moynihan, 1970, p. 12) will meet the needs of the neighborhood.

Finally, a mixed model, somewhere between community control and enlightened neighborhood-oriented administration of centrally-controlled programs, suggests itself. New York City's recent efforts at the creation of neighborhood governments appear to be such a mixed model. Mayor Lindsay (1970) wants to meld the separate functions of community planning boards, urban action task forces, neighborhood city halls, neighborhood conservation bureaus, and Operation Better Block into 62 districts throughout the city. While the districts would be intimately involved with their respective communities and responsible for the neighborhood administration of various programs, their policy-setting boards would initially be appointed jointly by city governmental officials and resident constituency and only eventually selected totally by direct election. Precisely how this delicate matter of transfer of powers is to be accomplished is not yet clear.

The problem with the institutional forms mentioned above lies in the impetus for their creation, the resources to sustain them, and, once established, their capacity to foster and broaden the popular participatory base. The ultimate irony of course would be to see such institutions become another oligarchical layer that stifles broad-based community dialogue and decision-making. Then citizen participation (the institution) would have helped to kill citizen participation (the process).

One final thought about the future of governmentally sponsored citizen participation deals not so much with participation-as-involvement but with the goals of participation. As Bertram Gross reminds us, participation can become a device for manipulation under the banner of enlarging human welfare. In his disturbing essay on "friendly facism", he perceives the possibility that, "under the combined blessings of HEW, HUD, OEO, and new coordinating agencies, ever new and changing community participation games and carnivals would be staged to allow low-income and low-status leaders—from both white and black ethnic groups—to work off their steam harmlessly without endangering the system" (Gross, 1970, p. 48). Indeed, the 20th century has an abundance of historical evidence that the totalitarian state often seeks to enlist "widespread citizen participation" in its programs.

It is the more subtle and benign forms of such participation that worries Gross and the unnamed French student who penned the poster declaring, "Je participe, tu participes, il participe, nous participons, vous participez, ils profitent" (Arnstein, 1969, p. 216).

Perhaps the best insurance against the dangers of participation-as-manipulation is the assurance that citizen groups will have the power to do more than engage in genteel advice giving but to carry some fundamental decision-making responsibilities about the program's impact on a specific consumer population. The creation of such citizen organizations and the encouragement of truly democratic and productive decision-making processes is an endeavor, to put it mildly, fraught with difficulties. It seems clear that, whichever organizational pattern citizen participation in governmental programs will follow during the next few years, our nation's, states', and cities' administrative capacities and willingness to innovate will be severely tested.

SELECTED BIBLIOGRAPHY

Aleshire, Robert A.
  "Power to the People? An Assessment of the Community Action and Model Cities Experiences", date and source unknown.
Altshuler, Alan A.
  1970 *Community Control: The Black Demand for Participation in Large American Cities,* New York: Pegasus.
Anton, Thomas.
  1963 "Power, Pluralism and Local Politics", *Administrative Science Quarterly,* VII, 448–57.
Arnstein, Sherry R.
  1969 "Ladder of Citizen Participation", *Journal of the American Institute of Planners,* XXV, 216–24.
Arnstein, Sherry R. (as told to).
  1970 "Maximum Feasible Manipulation in Philadelphia: What the Power Structure Did to Us", *City,* v. 4, n. 3.
Arnstein, Sherry R., and Fox, Dan.
  1968 "Developments, Dynamics and Dilemmas", Internal Staff Memorandum on Citizen Participation in the Model Cities Program, HUD, August 1968.
Ascher, Charles S.
  1970 "The Participation of Private Individuals in Administrative Tasks", paper delivered at International Academy of Comparative Law, Pescara, Italy.
Ash, Joan.
  1965 *Planning with People, U.S.A.,* London: Ministry of Housing and Local Government.

Austin, David M.
    1970 "The Black Civic Volunteer Leader: A New Era in Voluntar-
          ism", Harriet Lowenstein Goldstein Series, Issue n. 5; *The Vol-
          unteer in America,* The Florence Heller Graduate School for
          Advanced Studies in Social Welfare, Waltham, Massachusetts:
          Brandeis University.
Babcock, R., and Bosselman, F.
    1967 "Citizen Participation: A Suburban Suggestion for the Central
          City", *Law and Contemporary Problems,* XXXIII, 220–31.
Baida, Robert.
    1970 "Local Control Essential in Model Cities Program", speech re-
          ported in *HUD News,* July 18, 1969.
Bell, Wendell, and Force, Maryanne.
    1965 "Urban Neighborhood Types and Participation in Formal As-
          sociations", *American Sociological Review,* XXI, 25–34.
Bike, E.
    1966 "Citizen Participation in Renewal", *Journal of Housing,* XXIII,
          18–21.
Boone, Richard.
    1970 "Reflections on Citizen Participation and the Economic Oppor-
          tunity Act", paper prepared for the National Academy of Public
          Administration.
Brignac, Ronald L.
    1969 "Public Housing Official Reacts to Citizen Participation Menages
          with One-Man Drama", *Journal of Housing,* XXVI, 604–605.
Buchanan, Jeffrey D.
    1970 "Urban Renewal in DeSoto-Carr: Citizen Participation Comes
          of Age", *Urban Law Annual,* St. Louis, Washington University,
          103–132.
Burke, Edmund M.
    1966 "Citizen Participation in Renewal", *Journal of Housing,*
          XXXIII, 18–25.
    1968 "Citizen Participation Strategies", *Journal of the American In-
          stitute of Planners,* XXXIV, 287–94.
Cahn, Edgar S., and Cahn, Jean C.
    1964 "The War on Poverty: A Civilian Perspective", *Yale Law
          Journal,* 1317–1352.
    1968 "Citizen Participation", in Spiegel, Hans, B. C., *Citizen Partici-
          pation in Urban Development,* 211–224.
Campbell, Louise.
    1969 "Paul Ylvisaker: The Art of the Impossible", *City,* III, no. 2.
"Citizen Participation in Urban Renewal."
    1966 *Columbia Law Review,* 486–607.

Crain, Robert, and Rosenthal, Donald.
　　1967　"Community Status and a Dimension of Social Decision-Making", *American Sociological Review*, XXXII, 132–35.
Cunningham, James.
　　1965　*The Resurgent Neighborhood*, Notre Dame: Fides Publishers, Inc.
Dahl, Robert A.
　　1960　"The Analysis of Influence in Local Communities", in *Social Science and Community Action*, edited by Charles Adrian, East Lansing: Institute for Community Development and Services, Michigan State University.
Davies, J. Clarence, III.
　　1966　*Neighborhood Groups and Urban Renewal*, New York: Columbia University Press.
Davis, James W., and Dolbeare, Kenneth M.
　　1968　*Little Groups of Neighbors*, Chicago: Markham Publishing Co.
Davis, Lloyd.
　　1965　"With Citizen Participation: New Haven Has Neighborhood Rehab Success Story", *Journal of Housing*, XXII, 132–35.
DeHuzar, George B.
　　1945　*Practical Application of Democracy*, New York: Harper and Bros.
Denhardt, Robert.
　　1968　"Organizational Citizenship and Personal Freedom", *Public Administration Review*, XXVIII, 47–53.
Denise, Paul.
　　1969　"Some Participation Innovations", in Spiegel, Hans B. C., *Citizen Participation in Urban Development*.
Donovan, John C.
　　1967　*The Politics of Poverty*, New York: Pegasus.
Duhl, Leonard J.
　　1969　"Community or Chaos—A Case Study of the Medical School Controversy", *Journal of Applied Behavioral Science*, Vol. 5, No. 4.
Edelston, Harold, and Kolodner, Fern.
　　1967　"Are the Poor Capable of Planning for Themselves?", address before the National Association of Social Welfare Conference, Dallas.
Gross, Bertram.
　　1970　"Friendly Facism: A Model for America", *Social Policy*, Vol. 1, No. 4, 44–53.
Hallman, Howard.
　　1969　*Community Control: A Study of Community Corporations and*

Neighborhood Boards, Washington: Washington Center for Metropolitan Studies.

1970 "Federally Financed Citizen Participation", paper prepared for the National Academy of Public Administration.

Hamilton, Randy.

1969 "Citizen Participation: A Mildly Restrained View", *Public Management,* LI, no. 7, 6–8.

Hayes, Frederick.

7/3/70 "Text of Hayes Memorandum on Consultant Contracts", *The New York Times,* p. 3.

Herman, M. Justin.

1969 "Renewal Official Responds to Citizen Participation Statements of Messrs. Burke and Rutledge", *Journal of Housing,* XXVI, no. 11.

Hunter College, Department of Urban Affairs.

1969 *The Citizen Planner Speaks: Citizen Participation in the New York City Model Cities Planning Process,* Hunter College, Department of Urban Affairs, New York.

Hyman, Herbert H.

1969 "Planning With Citizens: Two Styles", *JAIP,* 105–112.

Kaplan, Harold.

1963 *Urban Renewal Politics: Slum Clearance in Newark,* New York: Columbia University Press.

Kaplan, Marshall.

5/68 "The Role of the Planner in Urban Areas: Modest, Intuitive Claims for Advocacy", paper presented at the National Association of Social Welfare Conference, New York City.

1970 "HUD Model Cities—Planning System", paper prepared for the National Academy of Public Administration.

Kaufman, Herbert.

1969 "Administrative Decentralization and Political Power", *Public Administration Review,* XXIX.

Keyes, Langley.

1969 *Rehabilitation Planning Game: A Study in the Diversity of Neighborhood,* Cambridge: M.I.T. Press.

Kohn, Sherwood.

1969 *Experiment in Planning an Urban High School: The Baltimore Cigarette Report,* Educational Facilities Laboratories, New York.

Kotler, Milton.

1969 *Neighborhood Government: Local Foundations of Political Life,* Indianapolis, Indiana: The Bobbs-Merrill Company.

1967 "Two Essays on the Neighborhood Corporation", in *Urban American: Goals and Problems,* edited by Subcommittee on

Urban Affairs, Joint Economic Committee, U.S. Congress, Washington, D.C.: Government Printing Office.

Kramer, Ralph M.
  1969 *Participation of the Poor,* Englewood Cliffs, N.J.: Prentice-Hall, Inc.

Larrabee, Kent R.
  1970 "Highway Project Planning with Local Citizens", remarks at Highway Management Institute, University of Mississippi, March 13, 1970.

Lewis, Gerda.
  1959 "Citizen Participation in Renewal Surveyed", *JAIP,* XVI, 80–87.

Lindsay, John V.
  1970 "A Plan for Neighborhood Government for New York City", City of New York.

Lipsky, Michael.
  9/69 "Toward a Theory of Street-Level Bureaucracy", paper delivered at the American Political Science Association, New York City.

Mann, Seymour Z.
  1969 "Participation in Model Cities Planning", paper presented at the 75th National Conference on Government, National Municipal League, Philadelphia, Pa.
  1970 "Participation of the Poor and Model Cities in New York", paper prepared for the National Academy of Public Administration.

Mann, Seymour Z., ed.
  1970 *Proceedings of National Conference on Advocacy and Pluralistic Planning,* Urban Research Center, Department of Urban Affairs, Hunter College, New York.

Marcuse, Peter.
  1970 *Tenant Participation—For What?,* Working Paper, The Urban Institute, Washington, D.C.

Marris, Peter, and Martin Rein.
  1967 *Dilemma of Social Reform,* London: Atherton.

Mathews, Vincent.
  1968 *Citizen Participation: An Analytical Study of the Literature,* Catholic University, Washington, D.C.

Metropolitan Applied Research Center (MARC).
  1968 *A Relevant War Against Poverty,* New York.
  1968 "The Future of Maximum Feasible Participation", unpublished paper delivered at the Alumni Meeting, Columbia University School of Social Work, New York.

Mittenthal, Stephen D.
1970 "The Power Pendulum: An Examination of Power and Planning in the Low-Income Community", Ph.D. Dissertation, Columbia University, New York.
Mittenthal, Stephen D., and Spiegel, Hans B. C.
1970 *Urban Confrontation: City Versus Neighborhood in Model City Planning Process,* New York: Institute of Urban Environment, Columbia University.
Mogulof, Melvin.
1969 "Coalition to Adversary: Citizen Participation in Three Federal Programs", *JAIP,* XXXV, 225–32.
1970a *Citizen Participation: A Review and Commentary on Federal Policies and Practices,* Part 1, working paper for the Urban Institute, Washington, D.C.
1970b *Citizen Participation: The Local Perspective,* Part II, working paper for the Urban Institute, Washington, D.C.
Moynihan, Daniel P.
1969 *Maximum Feasible Misunderstanding: Community Action in the War Against Poverty,* New York: Free Press.
Moynihan, Daniel P., ed.
1970 *Toward a National Urban Policy,* New York: Basic Books.
Office of Economic Opportunity.
1965 *Community Action Guide,* Washington, D.C.: OEO.
1968a Community Action Memorandum 80—Designation and Recognition of Community Action Agencies Under the 1967 Amendments.
1968b Community Action Memorandum 81—The Organization of Community Action Boards and Committees under the 1967 Amendments.
1968c OEO Instruction #6907-1, Restrictions on Political Activities, Community Action Program, September 6, 1968.
1970 OEO Instruction #6320-1, The Mission of the Community Action Agency, November 16, 1970.
Office of Voluntary Action.
1970 *National Center for Voluntary Action—Office of Voluntary Action,* as of November 1970, Washington, D.C.
Peattie, Lisa R.
1968 "Reflections on Advocacy Planning", *JAIP,* XXXIV, 80–88.
Perloff, Harvey, and Hansen, Royce.
1967 "Inner City and a New Politics", in *Urban America: Goals and Problems,* edited by Subcommittee on Urban Affairs, Joint Economic Committee, U.S. Congress, Washington, D.C.: Government Printing Office.

Piven, Frances.
  1966 "Participation of Residents in Neighborhood Community Action Programs", *Social Work,* v. 1, n. 1.
Pomeroy, Hugh R.
  1953 "The Planning Process and Public Participation", in *An Approach to Urban Planning,* edited by Gerald Breese and Dorothy E. Whiteman, Princeton: Princeton University Press.
Rein, Martin.
  1969 Social Planning: The Search for Legitimacy", *JAIP,* XXXV, 233–44.
Robinson, David Z., ed.
  1968 *Report of HUD/NYU Summer Study on Citizen Involvement in Urban Affairs,* report to the U.S. Department of Housing and Urban Development, Washington, D.C.; New York: NYU.
Rosenbaum, Allen.
  1970 "Participation Programs & Politics—The Federal Impact on the Metropolis", paper presented at the American Political Science Association, Los Angeles, California.
Rossi, Peter.
  1960 "Theory in Community Organization", in *Social Science and Community Action,* edited by Charles Adrian, East Lansing, Michigan: Institute for Community Development & Service.
Rossi, Peter, and Dentler, Robert A.
  1961 *The Politics of Urban Renewal: The Chicago Findings,* New York: Free Press.
Seaver, Robert.
  1966 "The Dilemma of Citizen Participation", *Pratt Planning Papers,* n. 4, 6–10.
Siegal, Roberta.
  1967 "Citizen Committees—Advice vs. Consent", *Trans-Action,* 47–52.
Smith, David Horton; Reddy, Richard D.; and Baldwin, Burt R.
  1972 "Types of Voluntary Action: A Definitional Essay", in *Review of Voluntary Action Theory and Research,* v. 1, edited by Smith, D. H., et al, Beverly Hills, California: Sage Publications.
Soysel, Mumtaz, ed.
  1966 *Public Relations in Administration: The Influence of the Public on the Operation of Public Administration,* Brussels, International Institute of Administrative Science.
Spiegel, Hans B. C.
  1968b "Human Considerations in Urban Renewal", *University of Toronto Law Journal,* XVIII, 308–18.

Spiegel, Hans B. C., ed.

1968a *Citizen Participation in Urban Development: Concepts and Issues,* Washington, D.C.: NTL Institute for Applied Behavioral Science.

1969 *Citizen Participation in Urban Development: Cases and Programs,* Washington, D.C.: NTL Institute for Applied Behavioral Science.

Spiegel, Hans B. C., and Alicea, Victor G.

1969 "The Trade-Off Strategy in Community Research", *Social Science Quarterly,* L, 598–603.

Spiegel, Hans B. C., and Mittenthal, Stephen D.

1968 *Neighborhood Power and Control: Implications for Urban Planning,* report to the U.S. Department of Housing and Urban Development, Washington, D.C.; New York: Institute of Urban Environment, Columbia University.

Starr, Roger.

1967 "An Attack on Poverty: Historical Perspective", in *Urban America: Goals and Problems,* edited by Subcommittee on Urban Affairs, Joint Economic Committee, U.S. Congress, Washington, D.C.: Government Printing Office.

Sundquist, James L., ed.

1969 *On Fighting Poverty,* New York: Basic Books.

"Symposium on Alienation, Decentralization and Participation", January/February 1969, *Public Administrative Review,* XXIX, 2–64.

Taylor, Ralph C.

9/28/68 Speech to the National Association of Housing and Redevelopment Officials, Minneapolis.

"Tenant-Management Issues", *Journal of Housing,* v. 27, n. 10, 534–43.

Unger, Sherman.

1970 "Citizen Participation—A Challenge to HUD and the Community", *Urban Lawyer,* v. 2, 29–39.

U.S. Department of Health, Education and Welfare.

1967 *Head Start Child Development Program: A Manual of Policies and Instructions,* Office of Child Development.

1968 *Parents as Partners in Department Programs for Children and Youth,* report to the Secretary of HEW by the Task Force on Parent Participation.

1970a Memorandum to Chief State School Officers: Advisory Statement on Development of Policy on Parental Involvement in Title 1, ESEA Projects, Washington, D.C.

1970b Transmittal Notice: Head Start Policy Manual 70.2, August 10, 1970.

1970c *Project Guide for Areawide Comprehensive Health Planning,* Public Health Service.

1970d "Joint HUD-OEO Citizen Participation Policy for Model Cities Programs", CDA Letter #10B.

U.S. Department of Housing and Urban Development.

1966 *Program Guide: Model Neighborhoods in Demonstration Cities,* Washington, D.C.

1967a *Citizen Participation,* CDA Letter #3.

1967b "Draft Guidelines for the Social Service Program", Housing Assistance Administration, Washington, D.C.

1968a *Content Analysis of First Round Model Cities Applications,* Washington, D.C.

1968b *Citizen Participation Today,* Proceedings at a Staff Conference, Region IV, Chicago, Ill.

1969a *The Model Cities Program: A History and Analysis of Planning Process in Three Cities,* prepared by Marshall Kaplan, Gans, and Kahn, Washington, D.C.: GPO.

1969b *Urban Renewal Handbook,* LPA Administration, Chapter 5, Washington, D.C.

1969c *Comprehensive Planning Assistance Handbook,* v. 1, MD 6041.1, Chapter 61, Washington, D.C.

1970a *Citizen and Business Participation in Urban Affairs: A Bibliography,* Washington, D.C.

1970b *Workable Program for Community Improvement,* Washington, D.C.

1970c "Circular: Appointment of Tenants as Local Housing Authority Commissioners", Washington, D.C.

1970d "Joint HUD-OEO Citizen Participation Policy for Model Cities Program", CDA Letter #10B.

U.S. Department of Transportation.

1969 Policy and Procedure Memorandum, Transmittal 162, Federal Highway Administration, November 24, 1969.

Van Til, Jon, and Van Til, Sally Bould.

1970 "Citizen Participation in Social Policy: The End of the Cycle?", *Social Problems,* XVII, 313–23.

Verba, Sidney.

1967 "Democratic Participation", *The Annals,* II, 53–78.

Voluntary Action News.

1970 v. 1, n. 2, November 1970, National Center for Voluntary Action, 1735 Eye Street NW, Washington, D.C.

Warren, Roland.

1969 "Model Cities First Round: Politics, Planning and Participation", *JAIP,* XXXV, 242–52.

Watson, Norman V.
  1970 "The Role of Tenants in Public Housing", remarks at the Conference of the National Tenants Organization by HUD Acting Secretary, Winston Salem, N.C., November 21, 1970.
Weaver, Robert C.
  1961 Speech to Family Service Association of America, New York City, November 13, 1961.
White House News Release.
  1969 Executive Order Prescribing Arrangements for the Structure and Conduct of a National Program for Voluntary Action, May 26, 1969.
Williams, Junius W.
  1970 "The Impact of Citizen Participation", paper prepared for the National Academy of Public Administration.
Wilson, James Q.
  1963a "Planning and Politics: Citizen Participation in Urban Renewal", *JAIP*, XXXIX, 242–49.
  1963b "The Citizen in the Renewal Process", *Journal of Housing*, XX, 622–27.
Wood, Robert C.
  10/68 "Science: The Urban Witch", unpublished paper delivered at the Second Annual Symposium of the American Society of Cybernetics, October 1968, Washington, D.C.
  3/28/68 "Citizen Participation in the Administrative Process", address to the National Conference of the American Society of Public Administration, Boston, Massachusetts.
  1969 "A Call for Return to Community", *Public Management,* LI.
Zurcher, Louis A.
  1970 *Poverty Warriors: The Human Experience of Planned Social Intervention,* Austin, Texas: University of Texas Press.

33. Disruptive Tactics

BY HARRY SPECHT

There is both confusion and uncertainty about the use of disruptive tactics to bring about planned change in American communities. The confusion, in part, grows out of a major problem the United States faces today—violence, its causes and resolution. Indeed, it is the major problem throughout the world, which we have succeeded so little in dealing with. In addition, in the social sciences as in social work there is neither extensive knowledge about the dynamics of either disruption or violence nor systematic processes the practitioner can use to deal with them.[1]

The idea of government by and through elected officials is being seriously questioned on all sides. Many have lost confidence in the viability of established democratic political structures—students and other young people, minority groups, and the political left. But today, the ubiquity of violence and illegal behavior in American communities is only a reflection of the violence and lawless behavior supported by many of the country's leaders. Thus, the mayor of a large city castigated his police force for not "shooting to kill or to maim" young arsonists and looters; the governor of a large state called rioters "mad dogs"; and the former President lost his credibility when the deception, corruption, and violence of the country's foreign policy became evident.

It seems that Fanon's belief in the cleansing force of violence and the need to use violence as an agent of change is gaining wide support as many white families buy guns to defend themselves against blacks, black action groups arm to protect themselves against the police, and the police increase their arsenals to defend the cities against black insurgents. It is as though the whole country is caught by Fanon's ideas:

For if the last shall be first, . . . this will only come to pass after a murderous and decisive struggle between the two protagonists. That affirmed

Reprinted with permission of the author and the National Association of Social Workers from Harry Specht, "Disruptive Tactics," *Social Work* 14, no. 2 (April, 1969): 5–15.
[1] Raymond C. Mack, "Components of Social Conflict," *Social Problems,* Vol. 12, No. 4 (Spring 1965), pp. 388–397.

intention . . . can only triumph if we use all means to turn the scales, including, of course, that of violence.[2]

It is only in a climate of unreason that this mixture of "blood and anger," which can lead to insurrection, becomes thoroughly confused with legitimate dissent and political radicalism. We should not talk of crime in the streets or violence on the campus in shocked dismay when the larger part of the nation's resources are being used to fashion this country into the world's greatest instrument of violence.

A discussion of the moral and ethical, as well as the programmatic, consequences of disruptive tactics used in efforts at planned change presupposes the existence of some organized system of available tactical choices. This paper will first distinguish different kinds of tactics that constitute the spectrum of choices and then discuss disruptive tactics in detail. This order is necessary if the use of disruptive tactics is to be understood as a consciously planned choice made on the basis of moral and ethical considerations as well as strategic objectives. The author uses "strategy" to refer to an over-all plan of action and "tactics" to indicate the more specific actions of moving and directing resources to attain goals. Strategy requires a long-term plan of action based on some theory of cause and effect, while tactics are the somewhat more constant methods of action.

WHY DISRUPTION?

What is it about issues that makes them subject to one or another set of tactics? Warren describes the association between different modes of intervention and different responses to issues.[3] (Modes of intervention are categories of tactics.) The range of responses to issues he describes are the following: (1) *issue consensus,* when there is a high possibility of agreement between the action and target system; (2) *issue difference,* when for one reason or another the parties are not in complete agreement but there is a possibility of agreement; and (3) *issue dissensus,* when there is no agreement between the parties. Consensus is associated with collaborative modes of intervention; difference with campaigns of a competitive, persuasive, or bargaining nature; and dissensus with contests in which there is a high degree of conflict between the parties. (Conflict may be considered as an element in all modes of intervention to some degree.) In this paper, disruptive and contest tactics will be associated with dissensus.

[2] Frantz Fanon, *The Wretched of the Earth* (New York: Grove Press, 1963), p. 37.
[3] Roland L. Warren, *Types of Purposive Social Change at the Community Level,* University Papers in Social Welfare, No. 11 (Waltham, Mass.: Florence Heller Graduate School for Advanced Studies in Social Welfare, Brandeis University, 1965).

The question still remains: Why these responses? The response to an issue, whether rational or not, indicates how the issue is *perceived* by the different parties; perception determines response. By extending Warren's typology, the associations among different perceptions of change, responses to the change, and the kinds of intervention these responses command may be suggested. Table 1 combines these elements but adds violence as a fourth mode of intervention based on a perception of change that aims at "reconstruction of the entire system" to which the response is "insurrection."

PERCEPTIONS, RESPONSES, INTERVENTIONS

Collaboration is based on consensual responses to planned changes that are perceived as a rearrangement of resources. For example, the parties to the change are in essential agreement about the co-ordination or reorganization of services. No one thinks they will lose a great deal in the change. Until only recently, there had been a rather narrow concentration on this kind of intervention in social work, based on work with homogeneous and elitist types of community action systems. For the most part, the action system (that undertaking change) and the target system (that being changed) are identical, and the client system (on whose behalf change is sought) is probably not involved at all. The role of the worker is most frequently that of enabler and educator.

Redistribution of resources is a qualitatively different perception of a change. One of the parties expects he will end up with more or less of something (money, facilities, authority) but, because they perceive the need to remain within the rules of the game—the institutionalized system of competition—the contending parties utilize campaign tactics to persuade, negotiate, bargain, and, eventually, compromise and agree. The action, target, and client systems might be expected to appear as separate entities, with the action system serving as mediator or arbitrator between the other two. The role of the professional change agent is most likely to be that of advocate.

Contest or disruption is generated by a challenge to existing status relationships and this view of change creates an entirely different type of discourse than any of the others mentioned. Contest or disruption is rooted in the competition for power in human relations. Status relationships refer to the social arrangements (the institutionalized system) by which promises, expectations, rights, and responsibilities are awarded, and the social arrangements always give more to some than to others. A threat to the system of relationships in which some people have power over others is the basis for this kind of response whether it involves parents and children, welfare workers and clients, students and teachers, or blacks and whites. None surrenders power voluntarily. The ability to perpetuate these patterns of varied and complex relationships long after the historical conditions that gave rise to them cease to exist is a human quality but also creates conflict.

When community issues are perceived by one group as eliminating or diminishing its power over others, the response will be dissensus; contest and disruption, the result. "To carve out a place for itself in the politico-social order, a new group may have to fight for a reorientation of many of the values of the old order" is the way Key states this proposition.[4] In these kinds of change efforts, the action and target systems are distinctly separate and the client system is closely aligned or identical with the action system. The role of the community worker is that of partisan or organizer.

A change perceived as intended to overthrow the sovereign power of the state is responded to as insurrection. The mode of intervention associated with it—violence—is not part of the arsenal of tactics available to professional social workers and, therefore, the author will not comment on the relative positions of the action, target, and client systems or the worker's professional role. However, these tactics do pose serious dilemmas for community change agents, which will be discussed in the final section of the paper.

However, it should be said here that the major overriding objective of community organization is to enable communities to create a strategy of reconciliation, to move from insurrection to contest, to campaign, to collaboration. It is necessary for the professional change agent who utilizes the tactics described in this paper to operate with goals that will, as Cloward puts it "eventually heal, not further disrupt."[5]

EXAMPLES

The following examples will illustrate the interplay of the three elements that comprise Table 1: perceptions, responses, and modes of intervention.

Objectively, fluoridation should present a good case for collaborative modes of intervention. It is said to be sensible, scientific, and not only inex-

TABLE 1. CHANGE: PERCEPTIONS, RESPONSES, AND MODES OF INTERVENTION

Perception of Change	Response	Mode of Intervention
Rearrangement of resources	Consensus	Collaboration
Redistribution of resources	Difference	Campaign
Change in status relationships	Dissensus	Contest or disruption
Reconstruction of the entire system	Insurrection[a]	Violence

[a] Insurrection is used here because the word "revolution" can only be applied to a successful insurrection.

4 V. O. Key, Jr., *Politics, Parties and Pressure Groups* (5th ed.; New York: Thomas Y. Crowell, 1964), p. 48.

5 Richard A. Cloward, "A Strategy of Disruption," *Center Diary: 16* (January-February 1967), p. 34.

pensive, but money-saving. Many health officials and community organizers have approached it with exactly that logical frame of mind because superficially fluoridation would appear to be a rather simple rearrangement of resources that calls for an educational mode of intervention. Yet the issue of fluoridation has been the basis for harsh, vindictive social conflicts in hundreds of communities in the United States.[6]

There appear to be two major sets of reasons for the resistance. First, there are those people who question the effectiveness of the proposed change or who fear that fluoride may be poisonous. This type of resistance does yield to collaborative modes of intervention.[7] But the second basis for resistance does not respond to such methods at all. This is resistance based on the belief that fluoridation infringes on the rights of individuals, that "compulsory medication" usurps the rights of free men. Green supports this contention with concrete findings. His research indicates that indignation over the *presumed* violation of personal freedom is more fundamental than the danger of poisoning. The fear of poisoning symbolizes a disposition to see fluoridation as an insidious attack by a vague constellation of impersonal social forces bent on usurping the powers and prerogatives of the common citizen, and the root cause of this feeling of being victimized experienced by active opponents of fluoridation is the increasing remoteness and impersonality of the sources of power and influence affecting the daily life of the individual.[8] In short, the issue of fluoridation becomes a contest when it is perceived to be a threat to status.

Another example of the delicate balance between perceptions of change as a redistribution of resources and an alteration in status is provided by Marris and Rein in their analysis of community action programs. They pose this question: If community planners had larger grants of money available to them, would it have been easier for them to move the bureaucracies along the lines of the change they desired? This is their answer:

> *If the funding agencies had offered more money, they would . . . have given communities a greater incentive to meet the criteria of concerted action. But they would also have raised the stakes in the competition for control of the project's resources. . . . A marginal addition to the city's resources stood at least a chance of insinuating an influence for change, without intruding a challenge to bureaucratic authority too obvious to overlook.*[9]

[6] "Trigger for Community Conflict," entire issue of the *Journal of Social Issues,* Vol. 17, No. 4 (October 1961).

[7] Benjamin D. Paul, "Fluoridation and the Social Scientist: A Review," in *ibid.,* p. 5.

[8] *Ibid.,* p. 7.

[9] Peter Marris and Martin Rein, *Dilemmas of Social Reform* (New York: Atherton Press, 1967), p. 158.

This suggests that an increase in the amount of resources may convert a perception of change from one of a rearrangement or a redistribution to a change in status.

The civil rights movement seems to have shifted in the last five years from a major focus on the rearrangement and redistribution of resources to a greater concern with change in status. Of course, all along, the demands being made by the movement may have *required* change in status for success, but the movement has increasingly recognized that the power of whites over blacks is the issue, as is pointed out in the following statement by Hamilton:

> *While there are masses of poor, powerless whites, they do not* perceive [*emphasis added*] *their condition as a result of deliberate policy. . . . Many blacks do have such a view.*[10]

Memphis, Tennessee, in the events preceding the assassination of Martin Luther King, was not confronting a simple question of the redistribution of resources as in an ordinary labor dispute. That the striking workers recognized the question of status was quite evident in their signs that read: "I Am a Man!" for indeed it was their manhood they perceived to be at stake. That the mayor of Memphis saw it the same way is clear from his statement that he would be damned if he would be the first southern mayor to bargain collectively with a black union.

TACTICS

Modes of intervention comprise sets of tactics. While the purpose of this paper is to discuss disruptive tactics, the idea that there is a dynamic relationship between tactics used for different modes of intervention is helpful in understanding their use. Table 2 suggests what this relationship may be.

These behaviors constitute a continuum of interventive modes rather than discrete actions. A strategy for change might utilize tactics from one or more modes of intervention simultaneously, depending on the goals of the action system and the organizational context within which it operates.[11] For example, in *A Manual for Direct Action,* a handbook of action for civil rights and other nonviolent protests, the authors instruct organizers in the

[10] Charles Hamilton, "The Meaning of Black Power," reprinted from the *New York Times* in the *San Francisco Chronicle,* "This World," April 21, 1968, p. 25.

[11] For an interesting discussion of the relationship between these variables *see* Martin Rein and Robert Morris, "Goals, Structures, and Strategies for Community Change," in Mayer N. Zald, ed., *Social Welfare Institutions* (New York: John Wiley & Sons, 1965), pp. 367–382.

TABLE 2. THE RELATIONSHIP BETWEEN TACTICS AND MODES OF INTERVENTION

Mode of Intervention	*Tactics*
Collaboration	Joint action
	Co-operation
	Education
Campaign	Compromise
	Arbitration
	Negotiation
	Bargaining
	Mild coercion
Contest or disruption	Clash of position within accepted social norms
	Violation of normative behavior (manners)
	Violation of legal norms
Violence	Deliberate attempts to harm
	Guerilla warfare
	Deliberate attempts to take over government by force

use of bargaining and educational tactics along with disruptive tactics, and sometimes all three are directed at the same system.

> *Poor negotiation . . . can bring a return to open conflict. . . . [In work with the target system] describe the results of change as less threatening than the opponents suppose, and . . . describe the results of not changing . . . as more threatening than . . . change. . . . Bring illustrations of successes in other places.*[12]

What is meant by disruptive tactics? They are used by one or both parties to a contest. Their purpose has been described as preventing an opponent from continuing to operate, to neutralize, injure, or eliminate him.[13] Warren describes tactics as "processes where deliberate harmful activity is directed toward an opposing party."[14] However, in the strategic viewpoint outlined in this paper, disruptive tactics are considered those that aim in different ways to move the other party toward some acceptable reconciliation. The term "disruptive" seems most appropriate for these tactics because their major objective is to *prevent* the target system from continuing to operate as usual, i.e., to disrupt, but *not* to injure, harm, or destroy. The latter are the goals of the tactics of violence.

[12] Martin Oppenheimer and George Lakey, *A Manual for Direct Action* (Chicago: Quadrangle Books, 1964), p. 24. An interesting related question that cannot be considered in this paper is how the structure of an action system is related to these modes of intervention. All action systems expand and contract throughout their history and one might predict the relationship between organizational structure and tactical choices. For example, movement to insurrection would be accompanied by narrowing the action system and movement from campaign to collaboration by its expansion.

[13] Lewis Coser, *The Functions of Social Conflict* (Glencoe, Ill.: Free Press, 1956), p. 8.

[14] Warren, *op. cit.*, p. 29.

DISRUPTIVE TACTICS

Clash of postion. This tactic is used within accepted social norms and essentially involves such actions as debate, legal disputes, written statements of intent, or public speeches. The objective of this tactic is to bring the issue to the attention of the public, usually in such a way as to mobilize sympathy from the larger community as well as to stir discontent among the "oppressed."

The way in which Gandhi's philosophy of nonviolence has been popularized in the United States often causes Americans to overlook many of the subtle meanings of the elaborate system Gandhi developed, which he called *satyagraha* (search for truth). *Satyagraha* is a complicated and difficult term to define because it embraces both a philosophy of life as well as a methodology of social action and, therefore, is certainly a more developed system than the one described in this paper. It is a refined technique for social and political change that transcends the simple concepts of civil disobedience, nonviolence, or disruptive behavior.

In the Gandhian view, clash of position comes at quite an advanced stage in dealing with an issue, and a number of other steps are required before a *satyagrahi* makes use of this tactic, such as negotiation, arbitration, reasoning, and other methods designed to win over the opponent. Civil disobedience is, of course, one of the final stages of this action system.[15]

Oglesby and Shaull, in analyzing the process by which the oppressed become revolutionaries, describe a clash of position as the tactic of "mass-based secular prayer." This appeal to a higher power, they say, sometimes results in change. More often, it shows the victim-petitioner that change is more difficult to achieve than he imagined, and this may become "the spiritual low point of the emergent revolutionary's education," for he learns that "the enemy is not a few men, but a whole system."[16]

Violation of normative behavior. This tactic refers to actions that might be viewed as a moving away from what may be deemed good manners and involves activities like marches, demonstrations, boycotts, protests, vigils (extended demonstrations), rent strikes, dropping out, haunting (following one's opponent for long periods), renouncing honors, *hartals* (having large masses of people stay at home, a sort of spiritual variation of a general strike), fasts, and interjection (having large masses of people congregate in an area, as, for example, 10,000 Japanese did in 1956 to prevent successfully the use of the site for a U.S. Air Force base). The objectives of these actions are the same as those listed under the heading "clash of position" as well as

[15] Joan V. Bondurant, *Conquest of Violence* (Berkeley: University of California Press, 1965), pp. 40–41.
[16] Carl Oglesby and Richard Shaull, *Containment and Change* (New York: Macmillan Co., 1967), p. 145.

to generate conscience, discomfort, and guilt in the oppressors and an *esprit de corps* among the oppressed.

This tactic, more than any others, demonstrates the effects of changing social and legal definitions of behavior. Rent strikes and boycotts, for example, lie in a gray area between violation of normative behavior and violation of law. The increased number of protests by citizens over the last decade has elevated demonstrations and marches to a tactic that is more like a clash of position than anything else. One can hardly announce a grievance today without a public demonstration of some sort. Furthermore, the tactic of choice is, to some degree, specific to the group. For example, only those who have been included in society can drop out; that tactic is available to middle-class college students, not to the hard-core unemployed of the ghetto. Fasting, a technique used with enormous success by Gandhi, is reserved for situations in which there is a rather special relationship of mutual respect between the opposing parties.

Moreover, tactics are *patterned* group behaviors. Whether used consciously or not, the styles of action in different action systems are based on numerous group and organizational variables, such as social class, ideology, resources, and values.

Violation of legal norms. This tactic includes techniques like civil disobedience and nonco-operation, tax refusal, sit-ins, draft resistance, and other violations of law. Carried to its final stages in *satyagraha*, this tactic includes usurping the functions of government and setting up a parallel government. The objectives of this tactic include all those listed for the other types of disruptive tactics and, in addition, they aim to demonstrate that people feel strongly enough about an issue to expose themselves to the danger of punishment by legal authorities for violating the law.

Civil disobedience presupposes an absence of, or inadequacy in, established law that morally justifies violation of it. The difficult moral question with which action systems must deal is whether they can find it morally correct to disobey an unjust law to protest its injustice or a morally just law to protest another injustice. Based on a philosophical anarchism and the concept of "natural rights," these acts have quite an honorable tradition in American life—a tradition that recognizes that the legal system is and always will be imperfect; the majority, whose wishes the laws (at least theoretically) are supposed to reflect, is itself imperfect; and all moral values have not been and never will be enacted into law.[17]

There are specific requirements of actions classified as nonviolent civil disobedience. They are only utilized after all other remedies have been exhausted and are used openly and selflessly. (That is, the actions have a public

[17] Vernon Louis Parrington, *Romantic Revolution in America, 1800–1860,* "Main Currents in American Thought" (New York: Harcourt, Brace & Co., 1930), pp. 271–460.

character and are carried out with public explanations of the reasons for the action in the name of some higher morality.) Furthermore, they are utilized with an awareness of the consequences for the participants.[18] These tactics are exemplified by the nonviolent resistance to police enforcement of laws. Indeed, the major tenet of those who have committed themselves to these actions expresses a profound faith in the value of the existing legal-political system and it is the absence of this faith that characterizes changes perceived as insurrection. While rebellion may claim moral justification, un-like civil disobedience its aim is to overthrow the social order, not to change and reconcile. This separation between the legality and the morality of the social order was precisely the distinction Socrates made in recognizing the right of his judges to condemn him to death.

OBJECTIVES AND EFFECTIVENESS

It should be noted that the direction of issues can be from consensus to vio-lence or the reverse, but, as Simmel pointed out in his still relevant seminal work on conflict written in the early 1900's, "the transitions from war to peace constitute a more serious problem than does the reverse."[19] Certainly, the use of disruptive tactics has the potential for great harm to the group in whose interests they are used. It allows the oppressor to put increasingly fewer limits on himself, freeing him to act disruptively or violently when he might otherwise have been constrained to avoid such behavior. For example, the police in many cities have attacked demonstrators with obvious relish when they used what the police perceived to be tactics of violence, as was the case in the antidraft demonstrations of October 1967 when some student groups attempted to shut down draft centers by violent means. In just this way, Mayor Daley attempted to justify the attacks on demonstrators by the Chicago police during the 1968 Democratic Convention.

Violent tactics can provide the other party with the opportunity to "change the subject," so that the public's concern switches from the issue to the illegal behavior of the demonstrators. Both King and Gandhi always consciously sought to use nonviolent techniques as a rein on the violence of the established ruling class—"to keep the conversation open and the switch-blade closed"[20]—and the correctness of their views is borne out by the fact that there were fewer deaths in ten years of nonviolent direct action in the South than in ten days of northern riots.

Stinchcombe asserts that the resort to violent tactics is related to the

[18] John de J. Pemberton, Jr., "Is There a Moral Right to Violate the Law?" *Social Welfare Forum, 1965* (New York: Columbia University Press, 1965), pp. 194–195.

[19] Georg Simmel, "On Conflict," in Talcott Parsons, ed., *Theories of Society* (New York: Free Press of Glencoe, 1961), p. 1325.

[20] Oglesby and Shaull, *op. cit.,* p. 149.

strengths of social norms governing the use of violence in society. In particular, his comments point up that nonviolent methods are viable only as long as civil authorities continue to accept the responsibility for carefully controlling their own use of violence in dealing with civil disputes. He says:

> *The crucial question . . . about the violent organizations of a society [i.e., the police and the army] is how far their entry into politics is governed by an understood set of limiting norms. For if the army and police enter the conflict unconditionally on one or another side of the conflict, supplying a ruling group or a revolutionary group with unlimited power to dispose of its enemies, then competition for place among organizations tends to become unlimited. Because the opposition to currently ruling powers is equally punished, whether it uses speech or riot, opponents are likely to choose the most effective means . . . of combatting government terror [which] are not always peaceful. And a government or revolutionary group supported by the army and police in an unlimited fashion is likely to undertake to root out its opposition, rather than to limit the opposition to approved means of conflict.[21]*

To use disruptive tactics, several questions must be considered by the action system: Is the stress that stimulated the use of these tactics recognizable to the opponent? Is there support and reassurance to the opponent whose change is desired that the extent of change is not unlimited? Have encounters opened or closed communication between contending parties? Has there been an adequate process of inquiry and exploration prior to the disruption? In the Gandhian use of disruptive techniques, the major question asked of the *satyagrahi* is whether he has engaged the opponent in a manner designed to transform the complexity of relationships so that new patterns may emerge.[22] When all these attempts fail, violent tactics become a likely alternative.

TACTICS OF VIOLENCE

Insurrection differs from disruption both in the tactics used and the ends sought. It is not a call to resist the immoral acts of legitimate authority, but the withdrawal of legitimacy from the the sovereign authority. It ties up the conflict over status relationships with something much larger, whereby the entire system is viewed as impossible to reform.

[21] Arthur L. Stinchcombe, "Social Structures and Organizations," in James G. March, ed., *Handbook of Organizations* (Chicago: Rand McNally & Co., 1965), p. 97.
[22] Bondurant, *op. cit.,* p. viii.

> *The leap into revolution leaves "solutions" behind because it has collapsed and wholly redefined the "problems" to which they referred. The rebel is an incorrigible absolutist who makes the one grand claim that the entire system is in error.*[23]

The tactics of violence are not available for use by the professional social reformer for several reasons. Quite practically, he cannot practice social work if he is a fugitive from justice, in jail, or dead. But, more important, a professional receives his sanction for practice from the larger society he serves and its legal and political systems. Morally, he may reach the conclusion that the framework is no longer worthy of legitimacy, and it is certainly difficult to argue that the moral basis for that choice does not exist in today's society. But it should be clear that this is the choice that must be made, and the professional should not be confused about what he is undertaking when he commits himself to violence.

This confusion is often encountered among students who think their protest actions should lead to a reversal of policy even if their behavior is violent. But to be a revolutionary requires that one believe that policy *cannot* be changed without replacing the government by force.

The social worker's authority stems from his knowledge, values, skills, and sanction to deal with social welfare institutions and to use social work methods. Although he may give his personal commitment to rebellion, it is improper to use his authority to give legitimacy to the destruction of institutions. This is when the larger strategy that directs a professional's work is especially important because it forces him to test his choice of a specific tactic in relation to its historical perspective. Is the choice of tactics dictated by his view of the long-range struggle and within a professed area of competence? Disruption used without some strategy for change is unlikely to achieve anything but escalation to violence; it certainly will not provide a means for changing the structure of American society.

The task of the intellectual leaders of any community undertaking is to help community action systems maintain freshness and vigor in moving toward goals by elucidating the legal, political, and historical relationships that underlie their efforts.[24] Invariably, revolutionary movements develop with strong, narrow ideologies that monopolize the conduct of the struggle over issues and bind the rebels in a united contempt for all other solutions. Social workers should expect neither support nor quarter from revolutionary groups because, as a rule, they consider others who are struggling on the same side to be more dangerous than the oppressor since they must disallow

---

[23] Oglesby and Shaull, *op. cit.*, p. 146.

[24] Harry Specht, *Urban Community Development*, Publication No. 111 (Walnut Creek, Calif.: Council of Community Services, 1966), p. 44.

any who would offer an appealing alternative. They represent the other side of oppression, "killing their way to power."[25] They believe, with Fanon, that "no gentleness can efface the marks of violence; only violence itself can destroy them."[26]

The question for the professional is whether his objective is to enable people to make choices or to assert *his* choice and cast his lot with those who have arrived at *the* solution. Social work operates in a framework of democratic decision-making, and if one decides that the framework is no longer viable, then there is no profession of social work to be practiced.

DILEMMA

As long as this country participates in unjust wars of conquest and does not provide the resources needed to deal with domestic crises of racism, poverty, and other social injustices, all professionals will face the dilemma of either working through institutions they believe may be unable to overcome social rot or participating in their destruction. But that awful choice should be made with clarity about the consequences for professional status as well as the objectives to be served.

Guevara was extremely clear about the preconditions for choosing revolutionary tactics:

> *It must always be kept in mind that there is a necessary minimum without which the establishment and consolidation of the first center . . . [of guerilla warfare] is not practicable. People must see clearly the futility of maintaining the fight for social goals within the framework of civil debate . . . Where a government has come into power through some form of popular vote, fraudulent or not, and maintains at least an appearance of constitutional legality, the guerrilla outbreak cannot be promoted, since the possibilities of peaceful struggle have not yet been exhausted.*[27]

These clear guides notwithstanding, many young people attempt to impose the strategies of Fanon, Debray, and Guevara on the American society. Given Guevara's preconditions for revolution, these philosophies of social change in the "Third World" can provide vicarious pleasures for American radicals but not realistic action strategies. Moreover, as Lasch warns:

[25] Robert Pickus, "Civil Disobedience But Not Violence," *Dissent,* Vol. 15, No. 1 (January-February 1968), p. 21.

[26] Fanon, *op. cit.,* p. 21.

[27] Ernesto Ché Guevara, *Guerrilla Warfare* (New York: Monthly Review Press, 1961), pp. 15–16.

While violence as a meaningful strategy is tactically premature in the United States, without other strategic perspectives militancy will carry the day by default and is dangerous because it may support the development of an American fascism.[28]

The New Left and student politics should not be dismissed out of hand. Surely they have created a valuable training ground in which a new generation can test its solutions to social and political problems. However, other persons who are committed to radical social change are often caught between two worlds. They have spent much of their lives working to reform the established order and find their perspective inadequate and their strategy ineffective—or at least they are viewed that way by young people. It is like the dialogue between mother and son in a poem by Aimé Césaire:

The Mother:

My race—the human race. My religion—brotherhood.

The Rebel:

My race: that of the fallen. My religion . . . but it's not you that will show it to me with your disarmament. . . . 'tis I myself, with my rebellion and my poor fists clenched and my wooly head. . . .[29]

CONCLUSION

Perhaps, though, new ways may be found to define the roles of reformer and revolutionary despite their seemingly irreconcilable divergence. For example, Shaull, in coming to grips with this dilemma, suggests that it may be oversimplified. He proposes a "political equivalent" of guerrilla warfare and suggests that greater attention be given to the question of the relationship of those working for radical change and the institutions of the established order. He says: "Service in the framework of a particular institution does not necessarily demand complete subservience to it."[30] In Shaull's view, revolutionaries can contribute to the renewal of institutions by being in but not of these structures, by living as exiles within their own society. Whether this alternative is a viable one or simply Utopian cannot be decided without some exploration but, given the size of this society's institutions and the enormous concentration of power within them, it is certainly an important alternative to consider.

[28] Christopher Lasch, "The Trouble With Black Power," *New York Review of Books*, Vol. 10, No. 4 (February 29, 1968).
[29] Quoted in Fanon, *op. cit.*, p. 86.
[30] Oglesby and Shaull, *op. cit.*, pp. 196–197.

Ultimately, choice of tactics must rest on our beliefs about this society. If we believe it is possible to move the community, we can continue to work for change through its institutions. If it is not possible, then God help us all, for then we must either continue to act in a drama that has lost its purpose or join in the destruction of society. Disruption and violence can contribute to change, but more than that will be required for reconciliation—more than that is required to transform America.

34. Maximum Feasible Manipulation

AS TOLD TO SHERRY R. ARNSTEIN

Introduction: We, the North City Area Wide Council Inc., believe this is a unique case study. It has been put together by community people for the benefit of other commnuity people. Although it will be widely read by policy-makers and politicians, it is addressed only to people like ourselves who are struggling against impossible odds to make public programs relevant to poor and powerless people.

Most case studies are written by social scientists whose biases are just like those of the traditional power structure. For years they have been in-vading our communities and diagnosing what ails us blacks, Puerto Ricans, Chicanos, Indians, and bypassed whites. For years they have been analyzing us as apathetic, stupid, and lazy. Until now, action-oriented community groups like the Area Wide Council (AWC) have been unable to fight back. We have had neither the journals, the dollars, nor the luxury of time to put together the six-syllable words and the technical jargon to tell our side of the story.

This community case study is different! It is our analysis of what happened here in North Philadelphia as we struggled to use our model cities program to create a new balance of power between ourselves and City Hall.

This study was made possible by the National Academy of Public Ad-ministration (NAPA). Mrs. Sherry Arnstein* was asked to write it with the clear understanding that she would write *only what we told her to write!*

We gave her access to all our records, including newspaper clippings, minutes of meetings, and correspondence—even a daily personal diary kept by one of our staff technicians. We talked to her for many days and many nights, individually and in groups. We made appointments for her to inter-view other community people in Philadelphia, and established her credibility so that people would share sensitive information with her.

We did this because she and NAPA guaranteed that every word of this case study could be edited in or out by us. In putting her technical skills

Reprinted with permission of Sherry R. Arnstein, North City Area Wide Council Inc., and the publisher from "Maximum Feasible Manipulation," as told to Sherry R. Arnstein, *Public Administration Review* 32, Special Issue (September, 1972).

* Mrs. Arnstein is a consultant to several research and consulting firms and com-munity groups, and former chief adviser on citizen participation for the Model Cities Administration.—Ed.

at our disposal, she had the right to read everything available and to argue with any of us. But we retained full veto power over every comma, word, and phrase. What Mrs. Arnstein agrees or disagrees with in this document is completely irrelevant *to us and to her* since her objective was to *help us do our thing*—not hers, not HUD's, and not the Academy's!

When we started on this unique assignment, we intended to tell what the courts call the truth, the whole truth, and nothing but the truth. As we traveled down that road, however, we discovered that it would be better to deliberately leave out some of the hangups that are internal to our community.

Such hangups are pretty well known to most community leaders. They are not so well known to the establishment types who will also be reading this document. It would be foolish to let them in on such information, because they would use it to hurt the poor and the powerless.

Our case study, therefore, emphasizes what the power structure did to us, and excludes some of those things that we now realize we did to ourselves. . . .

Month-by-month frustration: We want to tell you right off that the AWC is no longer recognized by the power structure as being in the model cities business. HUD and the city foreclosed on us in May, 1969, because they got uptight about the degree of power we managed to achieve over the program.

If only we had known two years ago what we now know about city and federal politics, it might have been a different story. But we were political novices, and they** were experts in political chicanery. We were trying to change things, and they were trying to keep us boxed in. It's so much harder to bring about change than it is to sit there and resist it. They had the upper hand, particularly the money and the sophisticated methods for maximum feasible manipulation.

As long as we were able to centralize the community's demands for change, the city feared us, and we were able to achieve stunning victories. When they finally managed to splinter us, we lost the only real power we had—people power. Here's how it happened day-by-day, month-by-month:

Fall, 1966—Knowing nothing about the possibility of a model cities program, four professional people who worked for different agencies in the community were meeting quietly to talk about the dire need for creating a new community coalition in North Philadelphia. Representing a community group, a settlement house, and a church group, these four staffers discussed how their agencies might support such a new coalition to do three things:

** "They" is the establishment, the manipulators of the status quo. "They" is a shifting collection whose changing identity will become clear in the next pages.

(1) to identify issues, (2) to mobilize the community, and (3) to articulate community-defined plans.

November-December, 1966—Philadelphia officials knew about the model cities program long before most other cities. Inside information from Washington, D.C., was that Philadelphia would be awarded a planning grant of $750,000. Like every city in the country we know about, Philadelphia was planning to submit its application to HUD with no input from the residents of the neighborhood, or with some last-minute public hearings engineered to result in a rubber-stamp approval from the residents.

The mayor appointed a task force to prepare the required bulky application and a policy committee to review it before it was sent to Washington in March. Sitting on that policy committee, the task force, and its several subcommittees were officials from city agencies and a few silk-stocking civic leaders. No grass roots people from the model cities neighborhood even knew about their meetings in November and December.

January, 1967—The mayor announced to his policy committee that he had named his Washington, D.C., lobbyist as development coordinator and head of the model cities program. One of the first products of the new director was an administrative structure chart for the model cities program. The chart confirmed that all policy decisions would be made by him, and that city officials and establishment leaders would be advisory to him. Residents like us were to have no role at all except as the passive dumping ground for the program.

At this same meeting, a few members of the policy committee persuaded the mayor to invite at least one community leader from the model cities neighborhood to sit with them during the remaining weeks before the application was sent to Washington. Little did most of them realize that the token representative they had invited was no token man; that he really knew the historic games being run down on the community under urban renewal and the antipoverty program; that he was one of the four staff people who were already planning to create a community coalition to speak up and speak out for the people's interests. When he heard that the city's Human Relations Commission was trying to open the door for community input by holding an open meeting on those parts of the application that fell in its bailiwick, he put the word out for community volunteers to attend the meeting.

January 20, 1967—Representatives from approximately 30 community groups took time off from work to go to that afternoon meeting. At first, we listened quietly as city officials described three parts of the application: citizen participation, administrative structure, and equal opportunity in employment and housing. Then, having done our homework, we zeroed in with hard-hitting questions. Like, how come they were describing our community organizations and churches as historically ineffectual? Like, what proportion of the policy committee would be neighborhood residents? We argued that the first failure had already occurred because proposals were coming down the pipe from them with no grass roots participation.

Our temporary spokesman stated that his organization was preparing an alternate proposal for citizen participation which would see to it that policy would come up the pipe from citizens instead of down. We demanded that several mass meetings be held in the community at night so that the grass roots people could find out what was in the works and have an opportunity to suggest alternatives. It was futile because the Human Relations Commission did not have the power to agree or disagree with us. All we got was a promise to circulate minutes of the meeting around City Hall. We knew then that it was up to us to mobilize the community and get our views directly to the mayor.

January 25, 1967—When the mayor's policy committee met again, a couple of its members supported our demands for real representation on their committee. Most of them, including the mayor, put the idea down. Instead, two new task force subcommittees were created—a subcommittee on citizen participation and a subcommittee on administrative machinery. The administrative machinery group had only one community representative, but the citizen participation group had 14 of our people including the four community staff people who had been meeting in the fall to talk about the community's powerlessness before they even knew about the model cities program.

January 30, 1967—At the first meeting of the subcommittee on citizen participation, the development coordinator apologized for the lack of citizen involvement in drawing up the application. He invited us to send representatives to sit in on the remaining meetings of all the task force subcommittees. We told him that we probably could get a few people to volunteer to join these task forces. But on such short notice and at such a late date, we wanted to put our real efforts into developing a community-defined approach to citizen participation. We told him that we had called a meeting in the community for January 31, to discuss our tentative definition and mechanism.

January 31, 1967—More than 70 people attended the first meeting as representatives of block clubs, settlement house groups, civil rights groups, and church groups. We laid out our sketchy proposal for what we called an "equal partnership" with the city and talked late into the night about what structure, what ground rules, and what resources could be put together to achieve a real community definition of citizen participation. We appointed a temporary steering committee to put our ideas on paper and to present them to a still larger mass meeting of community leaders.

February 2, 1967—When the city's citizen participation subcommittee met again, we told them about our plans for a second mass meeting. Again the city invited us to send representatives to the remaining meetings of the other task force subcommittees. Again we reminded the city that while about 12 people had volunteered to attend those meetings, our real concern at this late date was not to argue over the details of 350 pages that they had already written. Instead, we wanted to focus on our partnership model for citizen participation plus a complete rewrite of their first chapter, which outlined the city's warped and paternalistic view of our neighborhood.

Late February, 1967—By late February, our temporary steering committee had worked out the details of the partnership proposal. It called for the creation of a broad-based coalition of all active community organizations that would call itself the Area Wide Council (AWC). The AWC would have partnership status at City Hall to represent the community's interests in the model cities program. To make the partnership real, the city would contract $117,000 of the HUD planning grant to the AWC. The funds would be used by the AWC to hire its own community planners, organizers, lawyers, etc., to help the community react to plans prepared by the city and to enable the community to develop plans of its own for the city's reaction. The proposal spelled out guarantees that whenever there were disagreements over plans or policies between the city and the AWC, those disagreements would be negotiated until a solution acceptable to both parties was reached. It asked for six out of 15 seats on the policy committee of the model cities program and for AWC representation on all of the city's task forces. In short, the AWC would be the legally constituted citizen structure for the program. It would have the authority, the financial resources, and the independence to bargain with the city on behalf of the community.

More than 140 representatives from the community groups helped work out the details of that proposal. It was the first time that so many groups with such diverse and competing interests had gotten together. We were black, Puerto Rican, and white organizations. We were conservatives and militants. We were from both sides of Broad Street, which had always been an organizational dividing line in the community. It was beautiful!

March, 1967—The mayor knew that we were prepared to send a delegation to Washington to protest his application, and since he desperately needed the votes from our neighborhood to get reelected, he agreed to our partnership proposal. The application that went to Washington included our proposal almost word for word and said in plain English:

"Recognizing that the quality of citizen participation in government programs has often fallen short of the mark, even when it was sincerely sought, the MCP in Philadelphia will strive to incorporate *within its very core guarantees of citizens' authority to determine basic goals and policies for planning and implementing the program.*" (Emphasis added.)

April, 1967—Since insiders knew that Philadelphia was definitely going to be named a model city, we moved ahead without HUD funds to develop the internal structure of the AWC. After many evening meetings, we came up with a structure which would assure that the AWC remained accountable and responsive to the total community. On April 20, more than 500 people showed up at a mass meeting and voted unanimously to "formally establish the AWC" and to adopt the recommendations of our hard working temporary committee on structure.

The AWC structure was designed to strengthen existing community organizations and interest groups in the community. It called for the creation of 16 "Hubs" located throughout the model neighborhood. Each Hub would build itself on whatever community groups already existed and would locate itself in offices volunteered by friendly neighborhood settlement houses, churches, or community agencies.

The AWC Board would have 92 members: 12 of the 14 original organizers who had negotiated the partnership arrangement with the city, plus the elected chairman of each of the 16 Hubs, plus the four representatives selected by each Hub to serve on the four AWC standing committees. (These committees were created to correspond to the city's four task forces on physical environment, human resources, employment and manpower, and education.) The AWC structure also called for a 27-man staff which would be responsible to the AWC board. Sixteen of the AWC staff would be field workers assigned to work with the 16 Hubs.

May-July, 1967—By June, when HUD was supposed to have awarded the planning grants to the winning model cities, we had already begun to organize the 16 neighborhood Hubs, and had started working within each of our newly created standing committees.

In July, when HUD still had not announced the winning cities and we heard that Congress might cut some of the model cities appropriation, various community leaders were urged to write their Congressmen and Senators to demand full support for the program.

We also used the waiting period to support various happenings in the community. In July, for example, we organized a mass meeting to introduce the new school superintendent to the community. We begged poster paper, borrowed sound trucks, and did everything we could to get a mass turnout for him.

During that waiting period, we learned that if we were going to organize the community, we would have to respond to all kinds of community demands to deal with existing problems. We could not tell the woman whose child had just been bitten by a rat that she should join us in a year-long model cities planning process. We would have to begin to help people with today's problems today, or they would not believe that the model cities planning process would affect their lives tomorrow.

We began to digest thick reports and evaluations written by various public and private agencies—in short, to educate ourselves on what was happening and who was doing what to whom.

August, 1967—We held an emergency session to discuss the governor's announcement that the state might get the model cities program rolling by making state funds available immediately to each of the Pennsylvania cities waiting for federal funds. On the one hand, we were delighted. On the other, we were worried that the state might not respect the partnership we had worked out with the city. We talked about sending a delegation to Washington to find out why HUD was still holding back on its promised announcement.

Finally, we were advised that the mayor would advance the AWC $57,000 of city funds so that we would not lose the model cities momentum built up in the community. Finally, we could hire staff, rent office space, install telephones, and buy typewriters. Finally, we could hire an executive director. Our first move was to call a mass meeting to let the community know we were really in business. Someone figured out by then that we had already put in more than 100,000 hours of volunteer work. Calculated at the rate of $2.50 per hour, the community had already contributed the equivalent of $250,000 to get the model cities program rolling.

In August, more residents started attending AWC board meetings and raising new issues that needed immediate responses. For example, one of our Hubs pointed out that Temple University had held a hearing to expand its campus into the community, but residents had not attended because they didn't know about it and didn't understand its importance. It was agreed that the AWC would be ineffective if it limited itself to future planning and ignored immediate issues like informing and mobilizing the community to protect itself at such hearings.

Again we voted to write to our Congressmen to protest the continuing delay in launching the model cities program.

November 16, 1967—HUD finally announced that out of 194 contestants, Philadelphia was indeed one of the 63 winners. However, instead of the expected $750,000 planning grant, HUD gave the city only $278,000.

November 17, 1967—More than 3,500 black students turned out for a demonstration at the school administration building downtown. They were demanding 14 major changes in the high schools, including recognition of the black student movement and the right to have black studies, black values, and black principals. Inside the school superintendent's office, adults from the community were discussing the legitimacy of the students' demands. All of a sudden, without provocation, police attacked the youths and turned a street demonstration into a scene of violence in which 57 people were injured and 29 arrested.

This incident became a major turning point in the life of the AWC when police jailed two black community leaders who had helped the students organize the demonstration. One of the jailed organizers was an AWC community organizer! From this point on, the city was bent on destroying the power of the AWC.

November 18, 1967—News headlines the following day were mixed—some blamed the police, others blamed the students. News accounts revealed that the leaflets for the demonstration had been mimeographed at AWC offices. Our executive director immediately acknowledged that the students had asked to use the AWC mimeographs. He felt it was a legitimate request from a community group (and he later argued in court that AWC's first responsibility had to be the community).

The two black community leaders were released from jail; their bail, which had been set at $50,000, was reduced to $5,000. This action was prompted by a five-man interdenominational clergy group which petitioned the judge on the grounds that the two men weren't even present when "the police began their brutal attack on the students, nor did the defendants do anything whatsoever to incite a riot." The clergymen stated that they considered the high bail a "ransom," and one of their group wryly pointed out, "It's a strange system of justice indeed that Father _____ who is white and wears a collar is released on $1 bail, while _____ who is black and wears a beard is held on $50,000 bail."

November 21, 1967—The city development coordinator demanded that the AWC redefine its role and stick "simply and solely to planning." Trying to intimidate us, he sent an auditor to review our books for improper use of the $39,000 advanced to us by the city. At least two federal agencies, including the FBI, did character investigations on several AWC staff to determine what should be done about the "troublemakers."

November 24, 1967—We refused to be intimidated and behave like a bunch of apologetic children caught stealing from the cookie jar. Instead, we reaffirmed our rights by issuing a policy statement that outlined the AWC's view of self-dignity, self-expression, and self-determination. The statement underscored the basic principle of community organization by pointing out that AWC's "acceptance in the community hinges on meaningful involvement in dealing with immediate problems while planning for longer-range solutions."

Some of our members at first objected to the proposed policy statement. There was lengthy debate on the issue. Finally, there was rousing support for the students' demonstration and the AWC's support for their demands.

December 7, 1967—Close to 600 people turned out for a special meeting called by the AWC to explain the role it had played in the students' street demonstration.

Also at the meeting was the city development coordinator. He made it clear that City Hall and HUD were planning to punish the AWC by cutting back on the city's firm commitment to fund AWC operations at a level of $21,000 a month. He refused to see our point that when constituents who had helped to build the AWC demanded legitimate help in expressing their discontent, the AWC could not turn its back on that demand. To do so would reduce the AWC to nothing more than a tool of the power structure.

It was a noisy meeting with heated debate among community people who ranged all the way from conservative citizens to militant youth. Though some objected to the AWC's position, the overwhelming number backed us all the way. They approved an AWC policy statement that residents of North Philadelphia would "determine their own capacity for participation" and endorsed a resolution "extending our support to all students who participated in the demonstration, in their struggle to get a better education."

December 10, 1967—Later in the week, the AWC's "punishment" was announced. The city used the cutback in HUD planning funds as an excuse to cut us back to $13,000 a month to force us to fire several AWC staff. Though the city was planning to accept state funds and add $187,000 from its own coffers to make up for some of the reduced HUD grant, it would not give us any of that money. The development coordinator announced that unless we agreed to the cutback, he would not sign any contract with us— even though he knew that we didn't have enough money left to meet the next AWC payroll.

December 12, 1967—We demanded a meeting with the mayor, who refused to see us. The development coordinator threatened to find another community organization in North Philadelphia to unseat the AWC if we didn't agree to a $13,000 contract. Still we insisted that we had done nothing wrong in supporting a request from the community and would not be demeaned by accepting the cutback. The city admitted that the auditors had found no discrepancies in our books and nothing which indicated dishonesty in our use of the $39,000 advanced to us by the city.

December 14, 1967—Our board announced formally that it would reject the $13,000 and try to meet our payroll by raising funds in the community. The Philadelphia Crisis Committee supported our appeal to the mayor.

January 15, 1968—The mayor appointed a new development coordinator to head the model cities program. Still we were without funds!

Late January, 1968—To dramatize our stalemate with the city, and to help some of our employees get money to meet emergency food and rent problems, 10 of our staff were escorted to the Welfare Department by the Welfare Rights Organization to apply for public assistance grants. By then, some of the staff had not received paychecks for more than seven weeks even though the community came to our rescue with contributions of $7,500! (Contributions the city has never repaid despite its public promise to reimburse us so that we, in turn, could offer to give the money back to the donors.)

January 22, 1968—Finally our determined campaign paid off. The city signed a contract with us for $18,000 a month. We remained committed to our position that planning and action go hand-in-hand or neither are meaningful.

February 22, 1968—One of our Hubs reported that residents in the Simon Gratz High School neighborhood were furious because the planned expansion of the overcrowded school had been stalemated by the city's refusal to condemn 14 homes occupied by white families. The Hub asked the AWC to support a neighborhood demonstration at the Board of Education.

Keeping with our commitment to combine planning with social action, we, of course, supported their request. We felt it was both an educational and moral crisis. More than 40,000 black people had been kicked out of their homes in North Philadelphia for the benefit of urban renewal and Temple University. But now that 14 white families were objecting, it looked as if the desperately needed expansion of the Gratz School might go down the drain. (The issue was ultimately settled, but unlike the thousands of dislocated black families, the white people got paid off handsomely for their homes.)

February 26, 1968—We objected to the city's unilateral deadline of March 15 for developing a Joint Work Program for HUD. We pointed out that our AWC standing committees had to take their proposals back to the Hubs for approval before the AWC could commit itself as an organization. We proposed an alternate schedule which showed how the community's voice could be built in by adding two weeks to the schedule. Finally they agreed, but it was typical of the many incidents between us when we emphasized the AWC's interest in honest involvement as opposed to the development coordinator's interest in using the community as a rubber stamp.

March-May, 1968—Though we won our battle with the city and HUD over the November 17 incident, the battle had significant side effects. Some white liberal and conservative Negro leaders dropped away from the AWC. On the other hand, the more militant sectors of the community became more active in AWC affairs. It was a turning point: AWC became more militant, more angry, and more determined.

Meanwhile, back at City Hall, the development coordinator was violating our partnership agreement left and right. He didn't even send us copies of correspondence on his wheeling and dealing. His task forces were meeting regularly, but only the Welfare Task Force notified us of its meetings so that we could attend. He hired a man to work directly with the Hubs to try to divide and conquer the Hub structure. His Physical Planning Task Force was emphasizing lots of new public housing, while our committee endorsed strategies of subsidized homeownership for poor people. He was ramrodding plans through that would improve the city's image with HUD, while we were struggling for major constructive change in our neighborhood's quality of life.

The final blow came when we learned that instead of submitting to HUD the Joint Work Program that we had so carefully negotiated with him, he had sent in three different Work Programs: ours, his, and the individual city agencies'. We considered the pros and cons of demanding his resignation on the grounds that he couldn't relate to the community in even an elementary way to say nothing of an honest partnership.

May 9, 1968—Instead we asked for a meeting with HUD officials. That's how we learned that while HUD was requiring the city to submit the finished Comprehensive Demonstration Plan by January, 1969, he was pushing to finish a plan within *one month* (so that Philadelphia could get model cities action money for pacification programs to "cool the hot summer"). That's when we realized that after all the meetings we had gone to, and all the listening we had done, and all the negotiating we had engaged in, *he was quietly moving ahead on his own to violate every one of those agreements!* How's that for a guaranteed partnership between community and City Hall!

Late May, 1968—Another major clash between the city and the community arose over the use of open space money which HUD was making available to model cities in order to get some quick visible results. We looked at the program and saw in it all kinds of opportunities for construction jobs for community people, planning and architectural jobs for black and Puerto Rican professionals, plus linkages with new and exciting recreation programs planned by the youth themselves. The city, on the other hand, wanted us to concentrate solely on site selection and leave all those "minor details" to the Recreation Department.

June, 1968—Having uncovered just how dishonest our second model cities director was, we called a mass meeting to demand that he be replaced by a black director screened by the black community. But we knew by then that his dishonest dealings with us were really a reflection of the city's callousness toward the community. Our distrust of the mayor had zoomed sky-high.

Though we knew the development coordinator was on his way out of his job, he did not. His next move, therefore, was to throw still another ball down the street for us to go chasing after. He gleefully reminded us that our contract with the city was again expiring on June 30, and he imposed a whole set of unreasonable conditions on its renewal. He wanted a copy of our bylaws, which he knew well that we had not yet managed to put together because of all the other balls we had been chasing. He wanted copies of

all our minutes, which he knew we wouldn't entrust to him since those carefully kept minutes revealed our strategies for dealing with him. He wanted
the names and addresses of our leaders, which we knew he would use to
harass them since many of them held jobs in government agencies. Though
he sent us late notices of official task force meetings, he demanded advance
notice of all Hub meetings. This he wanted so that he could try to drive
wedges between us and the Hubs by manipulating them.

We set up a contract negotiating committee. We instructed it to take
a hard line to be sure that the community's interests were not sold down
the river. We also voted to negotiate for a larger contract. We wanted more
money to strengthen the Hubs—to pay for their office expenses and to pay
stipends of $7 per meeting to Hub chairmen and other community leaders
who were by then sacrificing three or four evenings almost every week for
the program.

In late June, our efforts to oust the second development coordinator
paid off. Though the mayor did not allow us to join him in selecting a new
man, he did at least appoint a black man as the model cities administrator.

July-August, 1968—This move created a temporary truce between us
and the city. First we resolved the contract dispute. We came out of those
negotiations with an AWC contract for $46,000 per month! Next we worked
out a new structure for joint city-community planning.

We all agreed that the model cities executive committee which had
formerly been like a secret society would now include the city's task force
chairman and city-staff, the AWC's standing committee chairmen and AWC
staff, the model cities and the AWC directors. We also agreed that the
executive committee would meet every two weeks to review the work of
the city's task forces and the AWC standing committees.

We further agreed on the composition of a policy committee to mediate
disputes which might arise between the city and AWC; and if that mediation
failed, the disputes would be referred to the mayor who would decide the
issue. Finally, we agreed to a new work program under which an interim
report would be sent HUD by September 15 and the first-year action proposal would be ready by January 15, 1970.

September-December, 1968—What a wild report! To meet that January
deadline for getting a plan to HUD, both the AWC and the city had to hire
many new people, orient them to what it was all about, and let them sink
or swim! By November (when the Republicans got elected) we were advised
to get the plan in by December 31, because once the Republicans took over,
they might hold up funding of all first-year action programs from all cities.

We worked night and day, weekends, and holidays to put together our
ideas and the city's ideas. We had many differences in approach, but with
our partnership arrangement, we were able to trade off so that they got
some of their priorities, but so did we. At the end, it was literally a last

minute cut-and-paste job which reflected our agreements on how Philadelphia would move ahead with $49 million for the first year of action.

The significance of our struggle for partnership status is best seen in the model cities administrator's page of acknowledgements: "Most rewarding was the destruction of the myth that a model cities community and a governmental body politic cannot enjoy a successful partnership." In addition the application said:

"This joint planning relationship between the city and the community, as could have been anticipated, has not been without its share of conflict. . . . There is every indication that with time, Philadelphia will become a model for the country of what form joint planning with citizens should assume. It must be understood, however, that this relationship will never be static or conflict-free. Rather, the basic realities of life in America today insure that some conflict will be inevitable. It is the opinion here, however, that this residual conflict may provide the kind of dynamism that is necessary to make government truly responsive to the needs of its citizens and to further the realization of an ever-elusive democratic society."

January-February, 1969—Can you believe that after having managed to achieve this level of interaction, that right after the application went to Washington, we were again betrayed by City Hall?

What happened was that HUD decided that the $49-million plan had to be revised and scaled down to projects totaling $25 million. HUD said that the revisions and paring process should be done during what is called a hiatus period. HUD offered the city a Letter to Proceed which meant that if HUD accepted the revised plan for $25 million, the city would be reimbursed for its operating expenses during the hiatus period.

We had known about this hiatus thing back in December, and had been .assured verbally by the city and by HUD that the promised Letter to Proceed would include the AWC at its $46,000-per-month level of operations. But because our legal guard was down, we did not ask for this in writing. Well, the city arbitrarily decided in January not to renew our contract unless we would agree to slash our 52-man staff down to 22.

We were outraged! All of our "partners" were drawing their full pay during this damned hiatus period, but *we* were expected to fend for ourselves unless we were willing to fire more than half of our staff. It took nine weeks, a mass meeting, and two marches down to the mayor's office to turn him around.

During the nine nasty weeks, the city played real dirty pool. Trying to split the AWC staff, it offered city paychecks to the 22 AWC staff people whose jobs were not at stake. It even tried to buy some of them off with offers of permanent city jobs. Nevertheless, the staff stayed together. Again, the Welfare Rights Organization helped them get emergency welfare checks, and somehow they managed to survive. Finally, the mayor asked the City

Council to approve city funds being advanced, and finally our whole staff got retroactive paychecks. But it was hell, and during the controversy some community factions and staff factions began to turn on each other.

March, 1969—In early March, we got our fourth model cities administrator, because the third one decided to seek election as a judge. Once again, the community was not consulted. We all learned about the changeover by reading the morning newspaper. This time the mayor picked a black woman from the community who knew the AWC from her personal experience with a Hub.

Despite the unexpected changeover, we and the city managed to continue to work together to complete the revised $25-million plan. Strangely enough, despite all the double-dealing, our partnership was really beginning to make an impression. Some of the city and private power structure had actually learned to swing with us. Some of them really were able to appreciate what we were fighting for and to agree that our demands for drastic changes in the system were more than legitimate.

The revised Comprehensive Plan is a testimonial to that learning. It stated boldly on page one that the two basic problems in the model neighborhood were poverty and powerlessness. It therefore promised that Philadelphia would use the $25 million to deal with those twin problems by: "1. assisting model cities residents to assume some control over their own economic resources and providing effective mechanisms for participating in the policy-making system of the city, and 2. providing programs and services which are developed by, and [are] therefore more capable of meeting the needs of the . . . residents."

Page three showed the agreed-upon priorities: 50 per cent for economic development, 23 per cent for comprehensive community education, 21 per cent for physical environment, and only 6 per cent for social service delivery systems.

Later pages showed how some of these priorities would be realized by creating seven new corporations, four of which were to be community controlled in that the majority of their Board of Directors would be chosen by the AWC.

There it was, right out in the open for everyone to see that this was a radically different proposal from any that the politicians would have come up with if they had not been forced to bargain with the community. Among the many innovative projects proposed were:
• an economic development corporation with the power to buy land, machinery, buildings, borrow and lend money;
• a land utilization corporation or land bank to acquire needed land for community purposes;
• a housing development corporation to construct new housing and rehabilitate old houses;

- an urban education institute to retrain and retread insensitive teachers;
- a career institute to train residents for the hundreds of model cities jobs that would be created;
- six communications centers where residents would have new educational avenues for developing communications skills, and learn how to use films, videotapes, to present their points of view and to increase their ability to make sounder decisions about public programs;
- incubator plants in which businessmen could be taught managerial skills on the job.

April, 1969—Two days before the revised plan was sent to HUD, the Nixon Administration announced new guidelines for model cities and stated that all applications from all cities would be completely scrutinized to weed out "unwise and unnecessary proposals." Little did we realize that Philadelphia would be the first victim of those vague words!

May, 1969—In late May, HUD wrote to the mayor that the city's plan had "unusually heavy reliance on new corporations," had "too heavy involvement [of the AWC] in these operating corporations," and had "insufficient involvement of the city . . . and established institutions." In other words, HUD objected to the plan's fundamental strategy of power redistribution as projected in the creation of new community corporations. HUD was placing its confidence in the same old-line institutions that have traditionally betrayed the community.

June 9, 1969—Completely negating our partnership, the model cities administrator responded to HUD's qualms about the AWC's power by chopping us right down to a strictly advisory role in all seven of the proposed corporations. Without consulting us, she unilaterally sent HUD a Supplementary Statement, which promised that the AWC would only be allowed to nominate one-third of the board of the new corporations; the remaining two-thirds would be chosen personally by her or by some other citizen groups chosen by her.

Late June, 1969—HUD and the city must have assumed that we would accept their outrageous conditions because they were still quite willing to sign off on the AWC's new $540,000 contract for its next year of operating expenses. In their minds, one-half million dollars must have seemed like a pretty good price for selling out a community.

As you can see, the model cities administrator carried out the bidding of the power structure against her own people. As we got down to the June 30 deadline when our contract would run out once again, she ignored our appeals to restore our partnership agreements (and other contract issues she was trying to force on us). Using a "take it or leave it" attitude, she insisted that if we didn't cave in by June 30, then any contract we might agree to at a later date would not be made retroactive.

We searched our souls. A few of us *were* ready to be bought off for that dollar figure. Some of us argued sincerely that it was better to accept a drastically reduced role in the program than to chuck it all after two years of blood, sweat, and tears. After much discussion, we voted overwhelmingly to refuse the unilateral contract terms. Instead, we decided to take both the city and HUD to court to demand that our right to participate meaningfully be restored.

July-August, 1969—Completely ignoring our objections, HUD announced that it would award the city $25 million for the first action year. It promised $3.3 million for immediate use to mount those few proposed projects that HUD liked. It told the city to go back to the drawing boards for the remaining $21.5 million because HUD wanted the whole community corporation strategy knocked out.

HUD allowed as how it might approve one corporation for the first year if the city could "justify not using existing institutions." But, in that event, HUD demanded two more blows against the AWC's power: that it not be allowed to nominate *any* of its own members to serve on the corporation's board, and that it not be allowed to nominate *any* of the board members after the first year of operation. In other words, even the city's drastic cut in the AWC's powers did not satisfy HUD. Incredible as it may seem, HUD demanded that the AWC be stripped of every shred of influence over any corporation that might be created.

To keep ourselves going, we again turned to the community. We launched a $10,000 drive and arranged to have our rent and telephone expenses drastically reduced. By August 15, we filed our court suit charging HUD and the city with illegally limiting our right to participate.

November, 1969—The rest of our bitter story is also a matter of history. In November, the Eastern District Court of Pennsylvania dismissed our court suit on the incredible grounds that we lacked "standing to sue." Our lawyers were just as outraged as we by the injustice of the court's decision. They and other lawyers, from as far away as California, volunteered their services to help us file a legal appeal.

Until we lost our first round with the courts, the AWC was together, and the city was restrained from organizing its own co-opted citizens group to act as representatives of the Model Neighborhood. When the district court handed down its negative decision, we were torn apart.

The five-month holdup had taken its toll and split the community into many factions. Our unpaid staff had, of course, taken other jobs. Even some of our faithful AWC supporters had given up, or they were saying that it was better to have a minor AWC role than no role at all.

December, 1969, to the present—The strongest of us refused to be beaten down. We decided to keep the AWC alive and to fight for our rights. By February, we and our lawyers had worked out the details of a legal appeal.

We are now waiting for the decision of the U.S. Court of Appeals and hoping against hope that it will make several findings on our lawsuit: (1) that the AWC, the official citizens structure of the model cities program, does indeed have the right to sue HUD and the city to protect our basic rights; (2) that the Secretary of HUD had no right to require the city to change the basic strategy of its model cities plan just because that strategy didn't fit in with his limited wisdom about power and powerlessness; (3) that the city had no right to agree to HUD's appalling requirement without even consulting the AWC which was the legally constituted citizen structure for the model cities program.

By January, 1970, the model cities administrator appointed a Citizens Advisory Committee, and we are sorry to say that even some of the AWC's top leaders agreed to serve on that plantation-type structure which (like the old days of urban renewal) can only advise, while the politicians decide. They are just names on a letterhead with no accountability to the community.

The city is now trying to turn each of the AWC Hubs into Neighborhood Councils. It hopes to buy off each council with a lousy $10,000 or $12,000 contract if it will "participate in an advisory capacity." You won't believe us, but those stranglehold contracts actually say: that if HUD reduces or terminates its funds to the city, the councils' funds may be reduced or terminated by the city *"at its sole discretion"*; that the "city may suspend or terminate payments" if the councils' required monthly reports "are incorrect or incomplete in *any* material respect"; that the city may withhold payment if the council "is *unable* or unwilling to accept *any additional* conditions that may be provided by law, by executive order, by regulations, or *by other policy* announced by HUD or [the] city"; and finally that "notwithstanding anything to the contrary contained herein, either party will have the right to terminate this contract upon 30 days written notice." (Emphasis added.)

So, temporarily, the shortsighted politicians have won. The innovative citizen-City Hall balance of power is dead here, and we have returned to an insulting plantation model under which the masters are assumed to know best and the slaves are expected to obey meekly.

They think they have beaten us down, and maybe they have cut the ground out from under what was called the Area Wide Council, but fools that they are, they forgot what President John F. Kennedy once said about those who crush efforts at self-determination: "Those who make peaceful revolutions impossible make violent revolutions inevitable."

Lessons We've Learned: Now! Having told you what happened to us, you might ask what that means for other community groups in the country, who like the AWC, are struggling to turn things around in their community. You might even want us to give you a list of dos and don'ts based on what we have learned.

The truth is that such a list would really not help you. It might in fact be harmful because each city is different; each state is different. Even the regional offices of each of the federal agencies are very different. What works best in Philadelphia might be disastrous strategy in Nashville.

So, instead of giving you advice, we will tell the major lessons *we* have learned here in North Philadelphia, and you can use them for your own purposes. Not as dos and don'ts but as checkpoints for analyzing your own political scene and for finding your own solutions.

Lesson Number One: No matter what HUD says, model cities is first and foremost a politician's game. Although the mountains of HUD guidelines and technical bulletins insist that model cities is a technical planning process, everyone but community people seem to know by now that it's really a political process.

Each of the federal agencies involved, like HEW, Labor, and OEO, has its political motives for either cooperating with or fighting against HUD. Each of the city officials has his own vested interests and political agendas. Similarly, the private agencies and businessmen are looking for their piece of the action to fatten their agency budgets or personal wallets.

HUD, the White House, City Hall, and the Congress are constantly bickering over their conflicting political agendas for model cities. On paper, however, they carefully maintain the fairy tale that if all the right local and federal holders jump into the model cities bed together, they will live happily ever after doing good for the poor.

In reality, HUD has created a game called model cities. HUD's rules for the game give each of the traditional power holders a certain number of playing chips depending on their political clout. But the community is told to play the game with no chips at all. It is told to beg while everyone else bargains.

HUD knows that the power holders will bicker and barter over the division of the model cities pie. But the community is told to cool all conflict and confrontation. It should achieve its goals by advising the power holders and watching the results.

Nuts! It's certainly true that the power structure is not monolithic, and that there are different sets of power holders with different sets of agendas. But it simply isn't possible for the powerless to change these agendas from a nonpolitical begging position. We must have bargaining power!

Though the model cities legislation gave the City Hall politicians final decision-making power, we managed to get them to agree to share some of that power with the community. We all knew that City Hall was the senior member of our "partnership." The important thing about the partnership was that it enabled the community to enter the model cities game with its own stack of chips. Those chips made it possible for us to bargain instead of beg.

Philadelphia's Comprehensive Plan testifies to just how different a model cities plan did emerge when the politicians were required to negotiate with the community instead of just trampling all over it.

Lesson Number Two: You can't trust City Hall or HUD. That's what the Nixon Administration ignores when it pronounces from on high that the goal of citizen participation is to "build trust" between City Hall and the community.

It might be beautiful if City Hall and HUD were trustworthy. But our history testifies to the fact that we'd be fools to trust the politicians. We were cheated each time we let our legal guard down. We only succeeded when we insisted that the politicians live up to their promises, and when we demonstrated that we had some power.

All four model city directors used us to achieve their own ends. Each was willing to negotiate with us when he assumed the job and had some important HUD deadline to meet. Right after that goal had been achieved, each tried to renege on the partnership arrangement by creating an outrageous crisis around the renewal of our contract. Though some of the staff of the city and federal agencies were clearly honest and helpful, most of them lied, equivocated, cheated, and distorted.

HUD itself has demonstrated that it can't be trusted. Its official guidelines admitted that existing institutions have historically failed the community. It said that the cities had to demonstrate willingness to innovate if they wanted the model cities money. It promised that Washington would not dictate the methods to be used because it wanted the cities to create their own strategies for social change. Though HUD never advocated community control as a strategy for institutional change, it officially endorsed power sharing with the citizens as an experimental strategy.

So what happens? We took those guidelines at face value and struggled to achieve power sharing with our city. We were one of the few communities in the country with a community power base sufficient to get the city to agree to our demands. HUD put its seal of approval on our agreement. Despite many attempts by the city to subvert it, we managed to hang in. Through thousands of hours of blood, sweat, and tears, we managed to negotiate a plan which had some genuine promise for community renewal. The plan clearly articulated that the basic strategy for achieving lasting social change is to shift the balance of power between exploiter and exploited. The mayor approved and sent the plan to Washington. Then HUD, the Big White Father, violated that agreement by announcing that the new Administration (with its limited wisdom about inner-city communities) thought it was too risky for the mayor and wanted it changed! The mayor happily agreed and submitted a different strategy without even consulting us! And HUD claims not to understand why people like us don't trust them! Why people like us feel they use Maximum Feasible Manipulation.

Lesson Number Three: Community coalitions need to develop their own agendas instead of constantly reacting to the agendas of outside forces. If you allow yourself to be kept busy reacting to the *government's* short-term contract negotiations, unrealistic deadlines, and mountains of bureaucratic paper requirements, you get diverted from the really important task of initiating, refining, and acting on your *community's agenda.* You also can get diverted from keeping your own house in order.

The Hubs, for example, in responding to all the real tasks of the AWC and the phony crises created by the city, got sidetracked from the job of expanding their power base in the neighborhood and representing that base. Since there are a limited number of hours in the week, community people need to guard those hours like dollars in the bank to make sure that the community's agenda is not shortchanged in the thousands of transactions.

Some of us believe that if we managed to stay closer to the ground, we could have mobilized enough community support to march by the thousands on City Hall and forced the mayor to tell HUD to keep its hands off a local plan that met all of HUD's legal requirements. (Some community groups have managed to pull this off.)

Maybe it's not possible, under a federal program, to keep such a community coalition of the most activist to the most conservative continually expanding and continually increasing its level of sophistication. Some of us still believe it is. But we'll never know what would have happened if we could have developed at our own pace with the support of the city and the federal government instead of their harassment.

Lesson Number Four: Community organizations must have the dollars to hire their own staff technicians, and must be able to direct that staff and to hold it accountable. We knew when we started that without our own staff of technicians, we couldn't possibly keep up with all the legitimate and illegitimate agendas that they would be running on us. One of the surprising lessons we learned was that some of our own community staff could be coopted by the power holders or be moving without us on their own agendas.

We discovered that if we were not equipped to do our own thinking, we could easily become patsies for some of our own pros. Today, we would place more emphasis on training for ourselves as community leaders and for our staff as technicians. In saying that, however, we want to emphasize that we don't mean the kind of patronizing gobbledygook that is usually passed out by the old-line educationists. We mean honest training that is designed with us and not for us. We mean trainers selected by us for their technical knowledge, their integrity, and their ability to relate to the community.

Lesson Number Five: You can't organize a community without "deliver-

ables." By this we mean that community people are daily struggling with basic bread-and-butter survival issues for themselves and their families. Attempts to organize them around their mutual problems for their mutual gain are doomed unless they can see tangible results of their efforts.

The model cities planning process, which required great personal sacrifices in hopes of uncertain payoff 12 months later, was a poor vehicle for building and maintaining a representative community coalition. For a group like the AWC to successfully organize a community, we needed to be able to deliver concrete benefits that could demonstrate the value of sticking together, struggling together, and holding each other accountable, e.g., an AWC Ombudsman who could have arranged immediate help to individuals with personal problems like evictions, lack of bail money, or a child's expulsion from school.

Some of us are ready to say that it is impossible to organize a community today under any federal program in light of their pacification motives, unrealistic deadlines, insensitive requirements, and phony guidelines. On the other hand, if a community group has to work with pennies, while the establishment manipulates our lives with millions, the community gets nowhere in terms of tangible benefits. So it would be senseless for community groups to adopt a hands-off position on all federal dollars. Frankly, we haven't got a solid answer to this problem of heads-they-win, tails-we-lose. We include it among our lessons, because we now know that it is a fundamental question to which all community people must try to find an answer.

Lesson Number Six: Don't underestimate the potential support for the community's agenda from sympathetic people outside the community. During AWC's four contract crises, we learned that our struggle had considerable meaning to some people outside the community.

For example, some of the staff of the city agencies and some of the HUD and OEO people were real swingers who helped us time after time. Some of them told us inside information that gave us the upper hand in negotiating with their agencies. Some of them worked with us at night and on weekends giving us great technical help on our program ideas and showing us how to use some of the laws already on the books to achieve our priority agendas.

During the first crises, some of the professionals working for the City Planning Commission were so outraged by the mayor's position that they actually contributed money from their own pockets to help us keep the AWC alive.

Some of our own AWC staff wrote checks as big as $100, $250, or $500 to help other staff deal with the payless paydays. Contributions were given by university people, black churches, white churches, denominational offices, and the local chapter of the National Association of Intergroup Relations Officials.

Similarly, some of the press and elected officials turned out to be powerful allies. Community groups should systematically identify and encourage these political, technical, and financial allies.

Lesson Number Seven: Be prepared to fight each frustrating step of the way when you're trying to break new ground. Here again, the establishment refuses to see what dehumanizing hoops we have to jump through every time we agree to play in their ballpark. Look what happened on just one simple AWC project.

After a meeting with our school superintendent (who is one of the most approachable officials in our city) he agreed that an AWC pupil-parent attitude survey would be valuable to him in developing quality education. As soon as we left him and his close circle of associates who claimed to understand what AWC and the black students were striving for, we ran into one roadblock after another. The survey was doomed before it began.

Our first step was to visit his research department because its input was essential. Talking to the top research man, we got a lot of stuff like, "I don't have the authority to let my staff help you." We had to trot back to the superintendent's office to get official clearance. Then we had to play tag with the research people. They took the position that we had developed our ideas about the survey too far to suit them. Once again, we had to go to the superintendent's office to force a decision that several research staff members were to spend at least two hours each week to help us do our thing and not theirs.

When the survey was finally ready for the neighborhood, the district superintendent objected because she had not been informed. So we lost several more weeks until we realized what her hangup was about and went back to the superintendent again. After she received his clearance letter, she agreed to cooperate.

Our next problem was that the school-community coordinators had not been informed and involved in the project. So some of them felt they shouldn't "be used this way." They were instructed by the local superintendent to cooperate with us. But some remained adamantly opposed to our efforts, and this affected the way they assisted in administering the survey.

When the survey was completed, we again had to return to the superintendent's office to negotiate for staff time to analyze the results because this had not been specified earlier and had to be agreed to in writing. Here we ran into the ultimate absurdity—the question of who was going to pay for the computer cards since there was allegedly no money in the school budget for this. Lord knows what would have happened if a community person hadn't solved this hangup by getting his employer to donate the damned computer cards.

We had to spend all this energy just to find out how many of our children and parents felt the way the black students did when they complained about teachers who looked down their noses at them, and acted as if their culture was crude, their speech wrong, their dancing sensual, and their families unacceptable.

Frustrating experiences like these with "sympathetic" agencies reinforced our thinking about community-controlled institutions as the most hopeful strategy for dealing with our daily victimization.

Our experiences with unsympathetic and antagonistic officials were even worse. They have convinced us that model cities is designed to deceive the community by pacifying our minds, our spirit, and our ambition.

Lesson Number Eight: Community people all over the country need to get together to create our own national power base to force "our" government to deal with us directly. We need to be able to communicate with each other, to teach each other, and to jointly pressure the government into creating honest community programs with straightforward guidelines.

We have already been in touch with community people from more than 20 other model neighborhoods and have been struggling for some time to get funds from the foundations and churches to create a National Citizens' Institute on Model Cities. Our struggles for money without strings have yet to pay off, but we'll get it somehow. In carrying out that struggle, we are mindful of what the black abolitionist-scholar Frederick Douglass said more than 100 years ago:

"The whole history of progress of human liberty shows that all concessions yet made to her august claims have been born of earnest struggle . . . if there is no struggle, there is no progress."

35. Citizen Participation in the Philadelphia Model Cities Program: Retrospect and Prospect

BY ERASMUS KLOMAN

The following discussion presents a retrospective evaluation of the issues and an appraisal of the future prospects for citizen participation in the Philadelphia Model Cities Program. The main purpose of this discussion is not to assess or make judgments on the validity of one or another version. What matters far more than disputes over past history is the ability to learn from the past and to transfer that learning experience to the future. Only if the lessons of the past can be applied to directing the program in the future will programs such as Model Cities begin to achieve their objectives and provide social benefits for the citizenry they seek to reach. Out of a difficult and frustrating experience have come some gains and some losses for the residents of the Model Cities community of North Philadelphia. How can they build on the gains while minimizing the losses in the work to which they have already devoted considerable effort?

PHILADELPHIA'S APPROACH TO CITIZEN PARTICIPATION

Philadelphia entered into the planning for the Model Cities Program six years ago with a belief shared by both officials of City Hall and citizens of the model neighborhood that citizen participation would be critical to the success of the experiment. The program was heralded as a significant breakthrough offering the residents of inner-city poverty areas a new opportunity to help them improve their futures. While officialdom and the new spokesmen for the citizenry may not have seen eye to eye on what participation meant in practice, each began with the belief that community involvement was essential to the program's success and each recognized that the program would be a failure unless it produced significant institutional change. In Washington and in other communities the Philadelphia model was widely cited as an example of the fulfillment of the intent of the United States Congress and HUD to establish inner-city programs in which citizens

Reprinted with permission of the author and publisher from Erasmus Kloman, "Citizen Participation in the Philadelphia Model Cities Program: Retrospect and Prospect," *Public Administration Review* 32, Special Issue (September, 1972): 402–408.

would participate in the reordering of local community political and economic systems no longer serving the interests of inner-city inhabitants.

As in other cities receiving Model Cities planning grants, so in Philadelphia the citizen participation concept aroused considerable interest and anticipation in deep poverty communities which had all but abandoned hope of anything more than handouts from the establishment. Signals from top levels of HUD in Washington seemed to indicate that this was to be a program aimed at treating causes rather than symptoms and that it would help the urban poor and disadvantaged to help themselves. It appeared that HUD sought to create at the grass-roots levels new institutional forms engaging the loyalties of the residents of poverty areas and helping them pull together. Washington, it seemed, was prepared to sanction the setting up of community associations with quasi-governmental authority. The people were to be involved in the decision-making process. Citizens were to have the "right to negotiate" with city administrations. In the words of one of the basic HUD instructions setting out requirements for a Model Cities Program, "citizen participation called for . . . some form of organizational structure, existing or newly established, which embodies neighborhood residents in the process of policy and program planning and program implementation and operation."

These were bold and heady ideas. They intrigued not only certain leadership elements representing the poor but also those in both public and private social agencies who wanted to take meaningful action to deal with the critical problems of urban poverty. Out of this enthusiasm grew the Philadelphia approach to Model Cities. Whatever may have been the flaws in the early plans, they entailed full commitment to citizen participation and to innovation. The idea that there could be an effective working partnership between elected officials and representatives of local communities took hold on both sides.

The implementation of the basic concept suffered gravely from confusion at HUD concerning the meaning of citizen participation. HUD and the Administration in Washington had very real problems in providing definitive language to spell out exactly how much authority and power should rest in the hands of citizen groups. Within the Office of Economic Opportunity, citizen participation had already sparked heated controversy over where the line should be drawn between participation and control. Different factions within HUD espoused different views, and neither faction was prepared to yield to the other. To avoid confronting the basic issue head-on, some HUD spokesmen offered the argument that rigid federal guidelines be avoided for fear they would stymie innovation at the community level. Compromising left citizen participation as a matter for local interpretation. HUD did specify that ultimate program control rested with elected officials, but there were no clear guidelines on how far citizen participation could go up to this point. Until the spring of 1969, City Hall in Philadelphia did nothing to clear the air. It was running scared. It feared to tell the citizen groups that the city had no intention of surrendering ultimate control and decision-making power to the people.

At the community level, people tended to hear whatever interpretation of citizen participation most suited their own outlook. The regional HUD office, headquartered in Philadelphia, favored a liberal interpretation of citizen participation and encouraged the city to provide funds for the Area Wide Council to permit recruiting and training professional staff to organize and train area residents. Philadelphia HUD staff, in effect, allied themselves with the Area Wide Council as adversaries vs. City Hall.

RACIAL DIVISIONS COME TO THE FORE

The Area Wide Council had begun to take form in the North City area before Philadelphia started planning for the Model Cities Program. AWC had deep roots in the North City and many of its board and officers were area residents. It began as an organization widely representative of the many different ethnic groups living in the North City area. Blacks and Puerto Ricans played leading roles from the beginning, but many white residents were active in the planning activities of the hubs representing their local neighborhoods and in the board for the overall organization. The crossover of racial lines in a communitywide citizens self-improvement endeavor was certainly one of the more hopeful aspects of the Area Wide Council in its early stages. A color-blind approach to community development appealed to wide segments of the greater Philadelphia area, particularly white liberals and the leadership of social welfare and civic groups. The history of the AWC, however, revolves in large part around racial polarization and the increasing influence of minority militants.

The question of what is cause and what is effect can be legitimately raised at this point. Was the increasing influence of minority militants a result of environmental change, or did the militants take hold of a situation and create their own environment? The truth probably lies somewhere in between. The facts are that an organization originating as a multiracial representative group with wide involvement of community leaders came to be dominated by its professional staff and particularly its executive director. In accordance with specific instructions from City Hall, the AWC leaders recruited many staff members from outside the model neighborhood. In comparison with a zealous and highly partisan professional staff, the large and unwieldly AWC board of 96 came to have a role of diminishing significance. Despite a standing rule that decisions affecting the organization were to be taken only by the board or its subcommittees, power gravitated to the staff. From then on, the board role appreciably diminished. Within the staff, moreover, there was very little delegation or decentralization. At the same time, the organization came to focus almost exclusively on the problems of black and Puerto Rican minorities in the model neighborhood. This basic change in orientation was partly a reflection of the polarization process occurring in Philadelphia at the time and partly a function of the outlook and views of AWC professional staff as supported by the HUD regional office in Philadelphia.

Gradually emerging under these auspices was a three-part set of goals which came to govern all AWC efforts. These goals were to: (1) redistribute the balance of power between government and community; (2) reorganize institutions, in both the public and private sector, which had failed to serve the community; and (3) reorient the values of citizens in the model neighborhoods as a means of reinforcing and sustaining the total effort.

Although these goals were never formally publicized outside of AWC circles, they were openly announced in AWC meetings with Philadelphia Model City administration staff. While some Model Cities professionals found themselves in sympathy with these objectives, others undoubtedly considered them threatening and beyond the scope and intent of Model Cities legislation. A city administration dependent on political support cannot afford to ignore any community movement which seeks to organize large numbers of people to effect basic change in the power structure. The AWC tried to avoid becoming involved in party political struggles, but the mayor and his advisors could readily see that, if the Area Wide Council were to become a rallying point for North City residents, it would pose a real threat to the Democratic Party of Philadelphia. Fearing the challenge to its power, the city administration employed high-handed tactics, such as holding up on funding and the cancellation of contracts, which caused the citizens groups to question the sincerity and good faith of municipal government.

THE MAYOR AND CITY HALL

On the other hand, as much as any political leader can do so, the mayor tried to avoid the injection of partisan politics into the administration of the program. He consciously maintained a distance between himself and the program's administrators. In the early phases of the program, in fact, he took little or no personal interest in it. Even later, he tended to become personally involved only when its troubles reached the crisis point, as when a change in administrator had to be made. Almost instinctively, however, the mayor, as the leader of a political party, viewed Model Cities Programs in terms of what they could accomplish politically more than in terms of their intrinsic merit. He demonstrated the slant in his perception of the program in his first two appointments of program administrators. Whatever their strengths and capabilities, neither of these appointees had the kinds of background, orientation, and personality which would assure good communications with their constituents in the Model Cities neighborhoods. Both, it should be noted also, were white.

The mayor's persistence in designating new administrators without consulting AWC leadership was another indication of a certain aloofness and unawareness of the true spirit of the program. Finally, the image of the mayor and his administration that began to emerge in an increasingly hostile racial environment was hardly likely to arouse sympathetic understanding among blacks and other minorities who represented a major portion of the city's poor. This image was a decidedly negative factor in City Hall-AWC relationships. Any appointee of the mayor was almost automatically suspect in the eyes of minority groups in North Philadelphia, particularly when AWC had been denied any role in his selection.

The Model Cities administration of Philadelphia found itself in a difficult middleman position. Washington insisted that, in order to qualify for Model Cities grants, applications had to be prepared in consultation with, and have the full support of, the citizens groups. Relatively few other cities in the United States had citizens which had organized as highly and formulated goals as precisely as the AWC. Moreover, as previously noted, the HUD regional office in Philadelphia had become closely involved in a partisan relationship with the AWC, counselling the staff on how to out-maneuver City Hall.

NOVEMBER 1967 SCHOOL DEMONSTRATION

The incident of the school demonstration of November 1967 probably marks the point at which City Hall doubts about the feasibility of working with the Area Wide Council culminated in the firm conviction that the AWC could not be trusted. An AWC staff member, who served as an assistant field work director, was primarily responsible for the AWC involvement in the incident. He made AWC mimeograph equipment available for duplicating protest leaflets. Having done so, he was fully supported by the AWC executive director. For the two years in which he served on the AWC staff, this AWC staff member continued to engage in such non-AWC organizational activities seeking to help people of the community organize effectively on important civil rights issues. He and his followers represented a relatively small, but highly visible, element of the Area Wide Council. It was the leadership of this element that City Hall feared most and sought unsuccessfully to secure their dismissal from the organization. The executive director and his associates would not yield to City Hall pressure.

After the November 1967 incident, City Hall came increasingly to suspect that the Area Wide Council wanted a good deal more than "equality" in a partnership, that "irresponsible" elements were taking over the organization, and that the partnership principle was too much of a threat to city control. Whether consciously or unconsciously, City Hall policy became a matter of alternating between compliance with HUD grant requirements to meet each new Model Cities deadline and, once a new grant had been awarded, maintaining pressure on the AWC. The pressure took the form of cutting back on the contract, calling for a reduction in staff or making demands for redirection of AWC activities.

CHANGING SIGNALS FROM WASHINGTON

Only in the spring of 1969, after it was apparent that the new Republican Administration in Washington was changing signals and that the Philadelphia grant would be secure, did City Hall make a clear declaration of its intent regarding the limits of citizen participation. In fact, the difficulties City Hall was having with the Area Wide Council were one of the factors taken into account in HUD's redefining of citizen participation. But this redefinition process took place *after* HUD had already specified in written instructions that involvement of citizens in the planning and implementation of programs was a requirement of all Model Cities Programs.

If Philadelphia's city administration was not an example of enlightened democracy at work in the service of its citizens, it was in the company of many other large metropolitan governments. All faced daily crises in their efforts to survive. The problems of urban government had figured significantly in the 1968 elections, and the new Administration in Washington was not without its own ideas on the nature and cause of urban problems and how to administer the programs seeking to deal with them.

Not long after the changeover in Washington, it became clear that the Republicans were not going to permit citizen participation the same latitude or the same extent of control as the previous Administration. The new HUD leadership was receiving too many reports of trouble from "overzealous" citizen groups threatening the position of city government to allow the policy direction of the past to go unchanged. As a creature of a Democratic Administration, the Model Cities Program was not one of the most welcome members of the new Republican household. Serious consideration was given to discontinuing the program, but that suggestion was dropped, partly because of the political liabilities it would have entailed. The program was to be continued, but on sufferance, and without the highly controversial and potentially "dangerous" turnover of government powers to other citizen representation which had not been duly elected. Philadelphia's City Hall welcomed the signs of change at the national level.

HUD decided to limit the extent of citizen participation in all Model Cities Programs to advisory roles, while specifying that control would remain in the hands of elected officials. The application of this guideline to Philadelphia resulted in the rejection of the proposal for Area Wide Council-controlled corporations to serve as the principal vehicles for carrying out the Model Cities Program. City Hall used this as a means of reasserting its control of the program. It was now in a position to be able to dictate terms to the Area Wide Council in the expectation that they would accept the new conditions rather than risking the loss of further contract funding.

AWC TAKES ITS CASE TO COURT

The AWC, however, felt that too much principle was at stake to accept the new terms. It was convinced of the rightness of its cause, and took its case to the courts. The first decision, at the District Court level, went against the Area Wide Council. On appeal to the Circuit Court, however, AWC won a significant legal battle against both the city and HUD. The Circuit Court opinion ruled that the city had not adequately consulted with the AWC in preparing the June 1969 submission to HUD and that HUD had violated the Model Cities Act in accepting that proposal. After thus reversing the lower court, the Circuit Court remanded the case back to the District judge for further hearings and court action.

At the District level the case went back to the judge issuing the original decision. The AWC had never expected that its case would obtain favorable opinion at this level, believing that the judge was too closely associated with City Hall. Members were therefore not surprised when, in July 1971, the District Court for the second time ruled against the AWC and in favor of the city. Again, the AWC appealed to the Circuit Court.

The issues raised in the appeal, like those asserted when the suit was initiated, were that citizen participation is an important requirement of the law establishing the Model Cities Program, and that HUD and the City of Philadelphia violated this requirement when they amended the basic strategy of the Philadelphia Model Cities Program without the participation of the citizens of the target area. The suit contended that the District Court failed to deal with the basic questions with which it had been charged by the Circuit Court. It requested reinstatement of the Area Wide Council as the citizen participation organization, and agreement by the city to enter into a new contract with the new AWC which would be reconstituted to incorporate the existing citizens organization.

The suit held major implications for the entire issue of citizen participation in the national Model Cities Program. It addressed the basic questions of the real meaning of citizen participation and whether the apparent shift in interpretation on the part of HUD could be defended on legal grounds.

COURT UPHOLDS AWC

In what may become a landmark decision, delivered in February 1972, the Third Circuit Court of Appeals for the second time reversed the District Court, upholding the Area Wide Council and calling for its reinstatement as the citizen participation organization for the Philadelphia Model Cities Program. The AWC was instructed to negotiate in good faith with the existing citizen structure in order to integrate the structure into the AWC. Although HUD and the city sought to take the case before the Supreme Court, the latter refused the appeal and the Circuit Court opinion stands.

After the lapse of two and a half years since the termination of the AWC contract with the city administration, AWC had survived only as a skeletal organization. In fact, its main purpose had been to remain in existence to pursue its case in the courts and be revived in the event of victory. The task of reforming the organization and breathing new life into it remains formidable. Still another change of Philadelphia's Model Cities horses in mid-stream will not be easy, and it is too soon to predict the practical consequences of the Philadelphia decision in terms of impact on the content of the Model Cities Program. Although the Area Wide Council can take satisfaction in being upheld by the American judicial system, it also recognizes that it has lost valuable time in the critical years of a new program. City Hall's Model Cities administration, which had totally severed connections with the remnants of the Area Wide Council, will find it difficult at best to resume a relationship. The Circuit Court judges, in their opinion, expressed the hope that "the passage of time may have sweetened the minds of the parties to this suit." That remains to be seen.

From a juridical viewpoint, the initial concept of citizen participation as incorporated in the Philadelphia Model Cities Program has been sustained, at least for the area in the jurisdiction of the Third Circuit Courts. The opportunity to test this important finding on a wider basis was denied when the Supreme Court refused to hear an appeal which the City of Philadelphia sought to present. HUD has as yet to issue a public statement on the implications of the Philadelphia decision for the national programs. Other similar cases, however, are pending at lower court levels.

ASSESSING THE IMPACT

In comparison with the dimensions of the national task of rehabilitating the inner cities of the nation's major metropolitan areas, the levels of total

Model Cities expenditures are modest. Moreover the programs instituted under Model Cities auspices have been running for only brief periods of time. Finally, the system for evaluation of program effectiveness has as yet to be fully applied. Nonetheless, it is reasonable to ask in what way have the people of a model neighborhood, such as North Philadelphia, gained, and how can those gains be measured in relation to the human resources invested?

The significant measures of gains and losses of Philadelphia's North City residents are not to be found in looking at individual programs or statistics on people receiving help, but rather on the broader issue of the meaning of citizen participation. For a brief period, while the Model Cities Program was in its preliminary phases, the officials of City Hall and the Area Wide Council were working together with an apparent understanding of what was meant by citizen participation. Whether the idea ever could have worked in practice may have to remain forever a matter of speculation. If there were other more conclusive examples in other cities of successful experiments, there might be sounder grounds for a conjecture on the possibility of a success story in Philadelphia. What seems so unfortunate in this instance is that the chance for a very worthwhile experiment in citizen participation was abandoned, partly because of the basic insecurity and the tendency to temporize within City Hall and partly because the leadership of the citizens organization was unwilling to continue to work within the system.

The neighborhood councils which displaced the hubs of the AWC were based on a concept which limited citizen participation to an advisory role. That meant taking part in the planning of community programs, and, when those programs were funded through their organization, monitoring the programs to see that they were accomplishing what was intended. Although this role represented a great deal less in the way of operational authority and management control than was first envisaged by the Area Wide Council, it still put more potential power at the grassroots level than was there before the Model Cities Program was initiated.

At first, there seemed to have been little community opposition to the modified concept of citizen participation. Several reasons explain why it was not too difficult to make a transition from one to another concept. The Area Wide Council, though it had started out with wide community support, had stirred up so much controversy and internal friction that some North City residents had no regrets in seeing its departure from the scene. Secondly, the current Model Cities administrator has proven an extremely competent organizer and has won wide respect for the firmness of her conviction and her ability to remain on top of the situation. The people of the North City area may have needed the kind of success symbol she provided. In any event, many seemed to accept what she represents, and the North City area was reorganized into 16 neighborhood councils with a minimum of excitement and turbulence.

Eventually, however, a number of the new councils came into conflict with City Hall's direction of the program. In several instances representatives of the Black Panthers or other militant groups were elected to chairmen or other positions. Where strong anti-white attitudes prevail in various neighborhoods, there is hostility and resentment against City Hall and a Model Cities administrator who is regarded as autocratic and dictatorial. Two councils filed suits against the city alleging that there has been inadequate citizen participation in development of their programs.

The actual programs initiated under Model Cities have had very little tangible or physical impact. A walk through the model neighborhood reveals slight visible evidence of rehabilitation. Most of the Model Cities Programs under way are institutional and social, not physical. Philadelphia is sometimes compared favorably with most other Model Cities Programs around the nation. Perhaps it could be argued that, out of the crisis and conflict of the early Model Cities years, has come a certain creativity. However, some elements of the model community would contend that the Model Cities Program as it has been administered to date represents nothing innovative, but simply more game playing by City Hall.

While the city was the first to renege on its partnership with the citizens, HUD in Washington undermined the chance for significant citizen participation with the changes it initiated early in 1969. Neither HUD nor the city displayed much concern for the impact of their actions on the motivation of their former citizen partners. It was as if people could be turned on and off like water from a tap. But people, unlike water, have memories. They do not forget unfulfilled promises. The effort to change signals on the meaning of citizen participation gave Model Cities residents one more reason to add to their already lengthy list of doubts concerning the commitment of government of whatever level to help them improve their condition. Many of the minority group representatives who worked in the Model Cities Program in Philadelphia remain skeptical as to whether HUD has ever viewed the program as anything but a diversionary tactic or a public relations effort.

TRANSFERRING THE LEARNING EXPERIENCE

The experiment, however, was certainly not without some very significant benefits. Perhaps the most important objective which any citizen participation program can hope to achieve is the education and training of citizens to work in community action programs and to deal effectively with their local government. The people who worked for the Area Wide Council, whether as staff, board members, field workers, or members of the hub organizations, all learned a great deal in the way of very practical lessons. Most of the AWC personnel were members of minority groups either black or Puerto Rican, and they gained a knowledge of the politics of bureaucracy which could serve them well in the future. Many have gone on to use that experience in the political arena. The notable stepping up of black community political activity must be regarded as one of the more hopeful signs on Philadelphia's political horizons.

An outsider looking back at the Philadelphia Model Cities experience might be inclined to think that the AWC personnel would have emerged with such bitter memories that they would no longer be able to work effectively within the system. But that is not the way it worked in Philadelphia. Of course, there is a serious residue of bitterness and racial mistrust, but the bitterness has not prevented many former AWC personnel from continuing to work in constructive ways for their cause. While the AWC professional staff has largely dispersed to other areas than Philadelphia, many of the AWC community-level personnel have continued to work in the ongoing Model Cities Program. Some of the former board members have joined the new neighborhood councils. They provided much-needed continuity to the program. The former executive director of the AWC now serves on the faculty of the University of Pennsylvania School of Social Work and on the technical staff of the City Planning Commission, while also being actively engaged in a number of important civic organizations.

Overshadowing the entire issue of the future of the Philadelphia program is a cloud of uncertainty about the future of the national Model Cities Program. Unless the national program receives vigorous leadership and real commitment from both federal and city governments, it has little chance of realizing the potential for which it was once heralded. It is unfortunate that neither Philadelphia nor any other Model Cities Program stands out as show-window example of the success of the program. But the federal government should look to its own record of policy making and implementation for some causes of failure.

Whatever chance the program had to succeed, it depended on creating a basis for hope among the residents of the model neighborhoods that through citizen participation they would become an effective part of the process by which the quality of life in the inner cities was to be improved. Equivocation and backtracking on the part of HUD and the Administration in Washington have done little to nourish hope among the men, women, and children whom the program was designed to help.

The Third Circuit Court decision provides a clear signal that the "very essence of the [Model Cities] Act is participation by the inhabitants of the affected community." Citizen participation is being given another direction but also a new chance in Philadelphia. Is it too late to make the program take hold? What will the Philadelphia revision of citizen participation mean for the national program?

36. Whom Does the Advocate Planner Serve?

BY FRANCES FOX PIVEN

A new kind of practice, advocacy for the poor, is growing in the professions. The new advocacy has thus far been most vigorous in the legal profession, where the term originates. Traditional legal-defense organizations are challenging in test cases regulations and practices of agencies serving the poor, and new legal agencies offering direct legal services have mushroomed in the slums. Social workers are also stationed in neighborhood storefronts where they act as the advocates of a "walk-in" clientele by badgering public agencies for services. Now planners and architects are offering their services to local groups confronted with neighborhood development proposals.

To account for this new practice, lawyers would probably trace their inspiration to Jacobus Tenbroeck and Charles Reich, two legal scholars who exposed injustices perpetrated on the poor by agencies of the welfare state. Social workers might see their advocacy as a reaction against a "mental hygiene movement" which had come to dominate social agencies, orienting practitioners toward a psychiatrically based therapy and a middle-class clientele amenable to such therapy. And planners and architects would probably say that advocacy reflects their growing unease at the devastations visited on the uprooted poor by a decade and a half of urban redevelopment. In other words, each profession sees the emergence of advocacy as the expression of an enlightened professional conscience.

No doubt early volunteer advocates were stirred by the civil rights movement and troubled by the growing concentration of black poverty in the cities. But the efforts of early volunteer advocates were scattershot and ineffective. Nor were their ideas earthshaking. There are always many currents in professional thought.

Advocacy now, however, has become popular and may even become widespread as a form of professional practice because opportunities for advocate practice have been created by the array of federal programs for the inner city launched during the Sixties. Social workers and lawyers were hired by federally funded projects in delinquency, mental health, education, and poverty. Now advocate planning also is becoming both feasible and

Reprinted with permission of the authors and publisher from Frances Fox Piven, "Whom Does the Advocate Planner Serve?," (with comments by Sumner M. Rosen and a reply by Frances Fox Piven), *Social Policy* (May/ June, 1970): 32–37.

popular with funds provided by the Model Cities program. In our enthusiasm for the idea, we have tended to see professional advocates as free agents because they are independent of local government, and we ignore the federal dollars which support them and the federal interests they serve.

These federal programs were prompted, as was much else that happened in this nation in the last decade, by the massive migration of blacks into cities. Having been liberated from southern feudal controls without being absorbed into the regulating political and economic institutions of the cities, blacks were becoming volatile. The new Democratic Administration in 1960 was keenly alert to the key role of this swelling urban black population which had turned increasingly independent at the polls, even as it became a major force in national Democratic politics.

Accordingly, Administration analysts began to explore new programs for the cities that might cement the allegiance of the urban black vote to the national party and stimulate local Democratic organizations to be more responsive to the new voters. What followed was a series of federal programs directed to the "inner city," beginning with the Juvenile Delinquency and Youth Offenses Control Act of 1961 and continuing through the legislation for Model Cities in 1966. However worthy one thinks the social goals attributed to these programs, and whatever their actual social benefits, they also met the political needs of the Democratic Administration in adjusting to population changes in the cities.

Nor should it be surprising that these services were presented as programs to solve such social problems as delinquency and welfare dependency. This, after all, was what urban whites thought the "Negro problem" was all about. By minimizing the resentment of the white working class, who were still the major Democratic constituents in the cities, such definitions helped to lessen opposition—both in Congress and among the general urban population—to new service programs for blacks.

Despite the presumably different social problems to be attacked, the various programs were remarkably similar. Under the broad umbrella of "comprehensive community development," each provided a battery of services not unlike those of old-time political clubs. Equally important, each called for "citizen participation," to be promoted by federal funds under federal guidelines. Whatever the stated goals, these efforts can be understood as a strategy to integrate the new migrants into the political structure of the city by offering them various forms of patronage distributed by local "citizen participants" whom the projects selected and cultivated. To execute the strategy, the projects brought to the ghetto a variety of professionals, many of whom were called "advocates."

There is a minor irony in this, for whatever the variants of the advocacy idea, two elements are essential to it: professional services must be made available to the poor, and these services should be so structured as to assure that profesionals are responsive to the interests of the poor as the poor themselves see them. In other words, it is not so much that professionals have been strangers to the slum; rather, it is that those professionals who work with slum people and slum problems are traditionally under hire by, and therefore responsive to, public and private agencies which represent interests other than those of the poor. There is, of course, a dilemma in the ideal, for if professional services are in the end responsive to whoever finances them, where can the poor find the money to pay their advocates? The dilemma, however, concerns the ideal of advocacy, not the realities of advocate practice on the federal payroll.

To point out that advocacy was promoted by national Democratic political interests is not to deny that the poor have benefited from professional advocacy or, put another way, that the poor have gained from federal efforts to integrate them into local and national politics. Overall, it is difficult to dismiss the results. Social workers who pried loose delayed welfare checks, or harassed housing inspectors into taking action, were in a small way easing oppressive conditions, as were lawyers who prevented an eviction or defended a youngster from police harassment. To argue that these small gains diverted the black poor from making greater demands is to set a dubious possibility against a gain that is real, however limited. Furthermore, small material advances, by raising the expectations of blacks, may actually have spurred them to greater demands. In this sense, the federal strategy for the cities, and especially the poverty program, may have contributed to a growing discontent and turbulence in the ghetto, at least in the short run.

But whatever may be said for the tangible accomplishments of social workers and lawyers stationed in the ghettos, the same cannot be said for planning advocates. Planners offer no concrete service or benefit. Rather, they offer their skill in the planning process. The object, planning advocates would say, is to overcome the vast discrepancy in technical capability between local communities and the city bureaucracy, because it is with the bureaucracy that local groups must contend to protect and improve their neighborhoods.

Implicit in this view is the recognition that planning decisions are decisions about who gets what in the city. That is, to determine what kinds of schools, or hospitals, or housing, or recreational facilities will be built, and where they will be located, is to determine who will benefit from the facilities. And to determine which neighborhoods will be demolished to provide space for new facilities or housing is to determine who will lose out. Planning decisions, in other words, are political decisions.

Implicit in the advocate planner's view also is the notion that the urban poor can influence these decisions once they are given the technical help of a planner—or better still, once they actually learn the technical skills of planning. And this is exactly what many neighborhood groups have been trying to do, sometimes with volunteer planners, more often with the help of eager young professionals hired with Model Cities or poverty program funds. The results are worth pondering.

One of the earliest and most dedicated of such efforts began in 1959, in a neighborhood called Cooper Square, on the Lower East Side of New York City. Various neighborhood groups had rallied to fight an urban renewal designation which, familiarly enough, called for demolition of 2,150 existing housing units, half of which were renting for under $40 a month. They secured the services of Walter Thabit, a dedicated New York planner, who set to work in consultation with neighborhood representatives on an "Alternate Plan for Cooper Square." By 1961 the Alternate Plan was presented to the public with much fanfare and the chairman of the city's Planning Commission pronounced it commendable. Then, from 1961 until 1963, the Cooper Square Committee and its advocate planner negotiated with city officials. In 1963 the city prepared once more to move on its own renewal plan. Again the neighborhood rallied, with mass meetings of site tenants. The city withdrew, and new conferences were scheduled to discuss the Alternate Plan. In 1966, however, a new mayor announced indefinite postponement. Then, in January 1968, Walter Thabit was asked to prepare a new, smaller plan, and in 1969 new meetings were conducted between city officials and the Cooper Square Committee.

Early in 1970, the Board of Estimate approved "an early action plan." After ten years of arduous effort on the part of an extraordinary neighborhood group, a small portion of the Alternate Plan had been given formal sanction even though that portion was still far from implementation. The chief accomplishment was that the neighborhood had stopped the early threat of renewal. As Walter Thabit said sourly when it was all over, "Protest without planning could have done as much."'

Most advocacy efforts are not yet old enough to provide such overwhelming discouragement. But the signs so far are bleak. In one city after another, local groups in Model Cities neighborhoods are involved in the technical dazzlements of planning, some to prepare plans, others to compete with counterplans. But there is little being built in these neighborhoods. Nor are locally prepared plans likely to change the pattern. A plan, of itself, is not force; it is not capable of releasing the necessary federal subsidies or of overcoming the inertia of the city agencies. Quite the contrary, for those people who might otherwise have become a force by the trouble they made are now too busy. As one advocate planner for a Harlem neighborhood that is still without construction funds proudly said, "They are learning how to plan."

What all of this suggests is that involving local groups in elaborate planning procedures is to guide them into a narrowly circumscribed form of political action, and precisely that form for which they are least equipped. What is laid out for the poor when their advocate arrives is a strategy of political participation which, to be effective, requires powerful group support, stable organization, professional staff, and money—precisely those resources which the poor do not have. Technical skill is only one small aspect of the power discrepancy between the poor and the city bureaucracies.

Not only are low-income groups handicapped when politics becomes planning, but they are diverted from the types of political action by which the poor are most likely to be effective. For all the talk of their powerlessness, the masses of newly urbanized black poor did prompt some federal action long before advocates came to their aid. The threat of their growing and volatile numbers in the voting booth and in the streets exacted some responses from national and local political leaders: the curtailment of slum clearance; the expansion and liberalization of some existing services, such as public welfare; and the new federal programs for the ghetto. But the planning advocates who came with the new programs have not added to the political force of the ghetto. Quite the contrary, for the advocates are coaxing ghetto leaders off the streets, where they might make trouble. The absorbing and elaborate planning procedures which follow are ineffective in compelling concessions, but may be very effective indeed in dampening any impulse toward disruptive action which has always been the main political recourse of the very poor.

To be sure, a few neighborhood leaders do gain something from these planning activities. The lucky members of the local "planning committee" become involved in overwhelming and prestigious rites and mysteries, which often absorb them even while action for their neighborhood is going forward without them. In effect, those few selected leaders are drawn away from their base in the community into a lengthy educational program, the end product of which, if all goes well, may be a neighborhood plan. Once produced, that plan is easily stalled by the city, negotiated beyond recognition, or accepted only to be undermined in implementation. In the meantime, the local "planning process" has diverted and confused, and perhaps divided, the community, and surely has not advanced it toward effective political mobilization.

Although the language is new, this kind of advocacy follows a long tradition of neighborhood councils in the slums, through which local residents were encouraged to "participate" in the elaborate rituals of parliamentary procedure as if that were the path of political influence for the very poor. In the past such participation absorbed slum leadership and rendered it ineffective. That may well be the chief result of current planning advocacy. It deflects conflict by preoccupying newcomers to city politics with procedures that pose little threat to entrenched interests. It is a strategy which thus promotes political stability in the city. But if the force of the poor depends on the threat of instability, planning advocacy does little to promote equity.

SUMNER M. ROSEN COMMENTS

Frances Piven's critique of advocacy planning is consistent with her distrust of politically integrating techniques as co-optative as well as her preference for direct group action as a route to political effectiveness. She grudgingly concedes that some efforts—by lawyers, social workers, etc.—have gained limited benefits for individual clients, but nothing more. She ignores the recent extension of legal advocacy to the level of class actions, directly challenging fundamental patterns of injustice and discrimination in the law. This new level of action is the further development of a practice of social intervention which logically began with the individual client and moved beyond the individual to the group or class as experience taught the advocates the necessary political lessons. The advocates' maturity and growing effectiveness are attested to by recent efforts in California to kill the OEO-funded system of legal services to the poor. In short, the Establishment has been hurt, and the judicial system moved, by advocacy.

More important is the question of where, in Piven's scheme of things, substantive issues ought to be discussed and programmatic choices clarified. Health advocacy is fairly new. Its practitioners believe that community-based groups need to know the implications of the choices to be made in the use of resources, as between, for example, new hospital facilities, more ambulatory-care facilities, more group-practice centers, more public health expenditures, etc. The answers are not self-evident, but each plausible pattern of response, besides exerting important influence on the quality, cost, and accessibility of health care, will benefit one group of providers, increase the influence and power of one point of view, advance or retard the achievement of a decent, humane and effective health care system. Community groups need to participate in these decisions, to understand the stakes, and to decide what is in their own best interest. Good advocacy will help them to the necessary understanding.

New York's Health Policy Advisory Center exemplifies this approach. Health-PAC's experience to date indicates that this infusion of expertise is not politically debilitating; on the contrary, by de-mythologizing the planning process it serves to energize local groups by showing them the direct connection between the planning process and the quality of their own lives. It also connects local insurgency with other levels of decision-making and overall resource allocation. Neither Health-PAC nor ARCH (Architects

Renewal Committee for Harlem) was founded with federal funds, nor does Health-PAC receive any today. No one who has followed health-planning controversies in New York City in recent years can seriously question either Health-PAC's independence or its ability to increase the pressure of the community on the political establishment without reducing the level of militance. Sophistication is no enemy of effective political action, provided always that the experts are kept "on tap, not on top."

Piven apparently believes that programs which governments adopt in response to political needs are thereby tarnished and rendered suspect. But any political system survives because those who run it understand and respond to the expression of needs, whether these take organized or disorganized form, whether they are made manifest through normal channels or through the mobilization of people in the street. There is a difference between response and co-optation.

The political task of the insurgent, and the advocate who seeks to serve insurgency, is to preserve the independence and freedom of action of those who are demanding change. The secret of success is not perpetual militance, but earning and keeping the support of one's primary constituency. Integrating new groups into the social and political structure is not inherently bad; what matters is the terms on which such integration occurs. Groups that acquire more power, and thus can more effectively serve the needs of their members, gain from the process of political integration. To bring new groups into the "mainstream" does not automatically mean that the older mainstream elements will control, dominate or manipulate them. Good advocacy will help people to move with maximum effectiveness and minimum loss of freedom of action, option, or ally. An alternative plan may, in the short run, move leaders off the streets, as Piven says (does she want them always there?); the real issue is what they bring with them when they return to the streets.

To learn the methods by which the established planning forces use technique and "objectivity" as smoke screens is important in the struggle to move the issue to the political plane, where—as Piven correctly says—it belongs. But how will the militants bring their constituents to wage an effective long-run struggle unless they can show what the stakes are, who and where the real allies and opponents are, what steps are involved in an effective struggle? And how will they go outside the base of their own direct support, when it is too narrow to win unaided, to get the allies they need over the long haul, unless the decisions at issue are politically linked to the interests and welfare of those who may not appear to be directly involved?

Uninstructed militance can be self-defeating. At the 1969 Health Forum, Piven's and my own favorite example of organized militance, the National Welfare Rights Organization, seized the microphone at the closing session to demand that every welfare family be provided *access to a family doctor!* At this level of sophistication, the Establishment need have no fears. Such slogans leave wholly untouched all of the basic problems of the American health system, particularly its domination by the organized free-standing practitioners. In this as in many other cases, a little advocacy would have gone a long way.

FRANCES FOX PIVEN REPLIES

I am puzzled by Sumner Rosen's response. He fails to deal with the main issue I raised: Do the poor benefit from planning advocacy?

Let me first clear away a few of Rosen's assertions which answer points I did not make. Since I regard political integration as inevitable, I do not worry whether to be for it or against it. I also regard integration as necessarily co-optative, as I understand the meaning of that word. The questions I addressed follow from my assumption that the process of integration is natural to government: First, what kind of force will precipitate governmental efforts to integrate the poor, and do planning advocates escalate or curb that force? Second, what are the terms of integration—that is, do the poor get anything from the process—and do planning advocates help them get more?

Rosen does not discuss planning advocacy (except to assert, incorrectly, that ARCH did not receive federal funds). Instead he discusses legal advocates, whom I also commented upon favorably, though with a less sweeping enthusiasm. The poor got those legal advocates through OEO, a government program launched in response to the increasing volatility of urban blacks at the ballot box and in the streets. In other words, it was the turbulence of the poor, not their sophistication about legal inequities, that produced the legal gains—the integrative concessions—that Rosen and I agree upon. It is precisely because such concessions make some difference in the life conditions of the poor that I am for "direct group action as a route to political effectiveness."

As for Health-PAC, it is a group I admire. It generates a steady stream of information and critical analysis of health systems, and sometimes manages to draw some public attention to health issues. But that said, why is Health-PAC being raised up as an example to defend advocate planners?

Health-PAC's kind of radical analysis of public programs is all to the good (and writing analyses is usually all we can think to do). But that is not to say that information and analysis will turn the world around; it is not the correctness of the slogans which makes the Establishment tremble. When the National Welfare Rights Organization seizes the mike, their militancy over health issues may be more important than whether they demand "More

Ambulatory Care Facilities" or "A Family Doctor for Every Welfare Family." The slogan will not determine government's health care responses any more than NWRO's "demands" for a $5,500 guaranteed income determined government's welfare responses. It was not NWRO's "demands" which led to rising welfare expenditures and proposals for welfare reform. But trouble in the cities did, and the turmoil NWRO created in welfare centers compounded that trouble.

No one would quarrel with Rosen's ideal that "community groups need to participate in these decisions, to understand the stakes, and to decide what is in their own best interest." But ideals aside, the reality is that the poor get responses from government mainly through disruption, and the question to ask about any radical analysis we contribute is whether it stimulates action or mutes it. If instead of agitating in welfare centers NWRO groups had devoted the last few years to studying guaranteed income plans to decide "their own best interest," they still would not have gotten a guaranteed income, or the welfare dollars they did get.

But it is into such intellectual exercises that advocate planners are leading community groups who are aroused by bad housing or the threat of redevelopment, and the planners generally lack even the virtue of a radical outlook. Study and analysis, of course, are only the first step, a step to be followed by endless meetings and lengthy negotiations with innumerable bureaucrats. Years later, there may be a plan but, as sad experience shows, one that will probably never be implemented. Meanwhile, no housing is built and no mass transit facilities are added, and with leaders absorbed in bureaucratic minuets there may be no force left in the community to press for them. That is my argument, and Sumner Rosen did not answer it.

SECTION SIX

Alternative Communities

Introduction

What can be done with American communities? Or perhaps the question should be: What can be done *instead of* American communities? In one form or another, both questions are being raised these days, as public concern mounts for a series of problems manifested not only in large cities, where they are perhaps more dramatic, but also in smaller cities, suburban communities, and rural villages.

There are many ways of summing up the current disenchantment with conditions at the locality level, and the problems which occasion it. Two strains stand out among these. One is the old, familiar concern that the face-to-face community is dying out as people come to live in larger and more impersonal population aggregates. The "glue" which held together the rural communities of previous centuries was compounded of such components as shared values, face-to-face relationships among those who know each other, shared facilities, and comparative isolation and self-sufficiency. As such characteristics become progressively less relevant to local community living, the more formal organizations and less personal relationships and great discrepancy in values, points of view, and life styles apparently do not provide for the same kind of solidarity and coherence which presumably characterized earlier times.

A related concern is the spectrum of social problems such as delinquency, crime, drug addiction, dependency, rising costs of health care, and on through a long list, which leads some public leaders to state that cities are rapidly becoming virtually ungovernable.

What are the alternatives to the troubled perplexities of contemporary American communities? Under current circumstances there is an extraordinary amount of casting about for such alternatives. The selections in this final section all relate in direct fashion to the alternatives to the existing configuration of most American communities. They are far from a complete "sampling," but they do illustrate three important directions of thought. First, one may simply dismiss the conception of community as a locality group, acknowledging and emphasizing that especially under modern circumstances, people derive their sense of belonging and participation and social affiliation not so much on the basis of locality as on the basis of interests, ethnic identification, and so on.

Or, if locality is to remain an important focus as people persist in aggregating into geographic clusters, there are two additional broad options.

450

The first is to take the "natural" or "crescive" communities—large and small —which have grown up over time, and consider how they can be modified in their institutional configuration to be made more meaningful and satisfactory social forms. The second is to seek to replace them, either by new towns which make certain presumed improvements within the existing institutional structure, or by experimental communities which seek to offer substantially different modes of community living, based typically on a substantially different set of social values.

But regardless of what option is taken, it is important to be clear about what alternatives are at least internally consistent and theoretically possible, and to have some conceptual basis for examining these possibilities and their different sets of implications.

Israel Rubin asks for a thorough reexamination of the concept of community. He takes as his point of departure a widely recognized historical trend in the Western world generally and in American communities specifically. This trend has been for the element of residence and locality to become progressively less important as the determinant of significant social ties. Division of labor, increased transportation and communication facilities, and consequent exchange of ideas and material goods lessen the dependence of people on their immediate surroundings and bring them into social contacts and relationships extending far beyond their immediate geographic localities. Social ties spring up around other foci than common residence, such as occupational role, ethnic identification, political or religious persuasion, and so on. These affiliations serve as links between individuals and the larger society, thus performing functions which in times past were to a much larger extent performed by the local community.

Israel Rubin seizes on this widely acknowledged circumstance and draws from it the conclusion that the concept of community must consequently be redefined without any necessary reference to locality. Rather, community must be conceived and defined in terms of those ties which link the individual meaningfully to the larger society, a set of ties which may or may not involve his residential locality, and a set of ties which need not reproduce in miniature the larger social macrocosm. Such ties are to be found in concrete organizations, situated in important institutional areas, and characterized by primary and secondary interaction of the members.

Although Rubin prefers to restrict the concept of community primarily to those social ties which bind the individual meaningfully to the larger society rather than to denote the social organization of localities, there is still the persistent fact that people cluster physically in space and the problem of the social organization which sustains this spatial clustering and may or may not result in a type of collective social experience which is deemed satisfactory. Hence, most of the concern in the community field involves locality groups and how they might be structured differently. The developments include not only the theoretical work of social scientists, but the growth of numerous actual experiments in alternative forms of community living conducted not by social scientists but by people who are committed to devise a more acceptable mode of community living, or people who seek to establish new towns, more carefully planned, or to improve existing communities.

The selection entitled "The Good Community—What Would It Be?" addresses all these alternatives. It challenges the assumption that people are largely in agreement on what a good community would be like. Indeed, it asserts that sometimes quite contradictory characteristics are sought for in a new or improved community, either by people with different preferences or even by the same people who express preferences which are inherently self-contradictory but do not realize it because they have not examined the possible interplay of different objectives. Sometimes in this interplay, two objectives may actually be mutually antagonistic, in the sense that progress towards one jeopardizes the other. Hence, "the good community is not a 'grab-bag of goodies' to satisfy every conceivable desire. It involves choices and rejections which we make either deliberately or by default."

With the resurgence of interest in community living and community problems, a basic question is the manner in which economic institutions are related to local communities. What kind of institutional arrangement might assure that decisions concerning business and industry in a community would be made with adequate regard for the well-being of that community and the people in it, including the employees of the firms involved?

Barry Stein has made an extensive study of the impact on communities of absentee-owned corporations and of corporations that are locally owned. He concludes that locally-owned corporations are more likely to be responsive to local needs than are absentee-owned corporations. Even locally-owned firms, however, must put their own survival and prosperity ahead of community interests when it comes to decisions about expansion, contraction, or closing down or moving away. The excerpt included here proposes community-owned corporations as one possible solution to this problem. Although shifts in ownership patterns are of great importance, Stein's article is essentially conservative in two important respects: It emphasizes the conception of community as a locality; and it seeks to place greater stress on the importance of the local community as a basic institution of American society. Rather than looking for substitutes for the American community, it accepts the existing community structure, and asks how this structure might be improved.

One practical alternative seized upon by private industrial developers and subsidized by the Department of Housing and Urban Development is the planning of entire new cities as an alternative to the crescive communities which simply grow and expand without deliberate direction. The idea of "new towns" (the term has been borrowed from the English, who have had considerable experience with them) has great appeal perhaps for two principal reasons. The obvious one is that new towns provide an opportunity to get out from under the existing bundle of problems which are the historical accumulation from previous decades and centuries, and to start anew, with what we now know, and "closer to the heart's desire." The second important reason for their appeal is that they incorporate the idea of comprehensive planning. Deliberate attention can be given to the kind of community that is desired, and its various aspects can be planned with this set of objectives in mind.

The new town which, because of the thought which went into it and because of the high social purposes announced by its developer, has attracted the greatest attention is Columbia, Maryland. Richard Brooks, an attorney and social planner who was employed as a consultant in one aspect of Columbia, has made an extensive study of the actual unfolding of events and developments in Columbia as these relate to the original intent or objectives which had been planned. In the present article, he describes a number of aspects of the gradual transformation of Columbia from a new town plan controlled by the developer into a community inhabited by thousands of people. It is an important assessment of one kind of alternative to existing American communities. Brooks' analysis is particularly interesting in addressing the manner in which the social realities of the surrounding society, including the preferences and activities of the new inhabitants, begin to exercise an attrition on the new town's original objectives in the transition from new town to crescive community.

New towns, company towns, utopian communities—there is an abundance of alternatives to the crescive community. How can these alternatives be classified? What are the important dimensions according to which alternative communities can be sorted out and characterized, for purposes of understanding and assessment?

Following in the theoretical approach of George Hillery, Jr., Shimon Gottschalk has developed an important theoretical framework for the classification of different types of communities, some of them extremely different from the crescive communities we know. An important dimension of his analysis is that of three levels of possible emphasis in any community form. First, there is the most inclusive, or societal level. Second is the community level itself. Third is the intra-community level of individuals and families. Each level may be high or low in the extent to which it is emphasized in the particular community form. Crescive communities are low in goal orientation on all three levels. This important point derives from Hillery's thesis that communal organizations are low in goal orientation, as opposed to formal organizations, which are specifically oriented toward the attainment of a goal. Following this model of the crescive community, Gottschalk characterizes deviant communities as those in which two of the levels are high in goal orientation and one is low. According to which combination constitutes the high goal orientation levels, the communities are "administered," "designed," or "intentional." Another type of community form may be called the "anti-community," which strictly speaking is not a community at all. There are four possible types, three of which involve low goal orientation on two levels and high on one level, and the fourth, totalitarianism, which involves high goal orientation on all levels.

Communes comprise one of the interesting alternatives to crescive communities. (They come under Gottschalk's "intentional" category.) In recent years there have been—and continue to be—numerous experiments with communes as drastic alternatives to the usual crescive communities. In his article on "Families, Communes, and Communities," George Hillery, Jr., reports on an exploratory analytical study of eleven communes of the most varied types. He gives a brief recapitulation of his theory of communal organizations, and describes communes as communal organizations which are more purposive than crescive communities (vills), and whose purposiveness is found in their ideology.

But if a community is purposive, must it not also be goal-oriented, and thus a formal organization rather than a community? Hillery treats the difference between purposiveness in communes and the goal orientation of formal organizations. Communes, he avers, require and are characterized by high ideological orientation, an orientation which "usually stands for some alternative to the behavior patterns of the larger society." This constitutes both their strength and their weakness. They require a high degree of commitment, because their departure from the norms of the crescive community places strains on their existence—not only external strains from the larger society which may reject them just as they reject it, but also inherent strains, particularly in connection with their patterns of family or non-family behavior. Communes thus pose interesting versions of both freedom and conflict.

In this selection, as in all Hillery's writings, there is a remarkable ability to move back and forth between empirical data and theoretical conceptualization. Hillery's overall investigative strategy is to test his key concepts and hypotheses against limiting cases, thus to see just where they apply and where they don't apply, and to ascertain the why in each case.

Rosabeth Moss Kanter has concerned herself over a period of years with both the utopian communities of the nineteenth century and contemporary communes. For both, in her estimation, the greatest problem is that of securing commitment to the ideals and behavior patterns of the group. As Hillery also noted, this task is made particularly crucial by the fact that these communities reject the behavior patterns of the surrounding society and in some ways, at least, go about striving to forge new, alternative ways of relating to each other.

Commitment arises at that point where the community's needs and the individual's desires converge. Full commitment is present when people voluntarily do the things which the community needs to get done in order to survive and prosper, and when they do them because they find them approvable and personally satisfying. There are three points at which this correspondence between community needs and individual wishes are especially important. These have to do with the retention of members, the cohesiveness of the communal group, and social control over member behavior. Kanter points out that these three major aspects are analytically distinct from each other, in that one may be present without the others.

On the personal side, there are likewise three aspects of commitment: instrumental, affective, and moral. They correspond to the communal needs for retention of members, for cohesiveness, and for social control.

It can therefore be asked of any intentional community, whether commune or utopian community, how it is organized to achieve sufficient commitment to provide that the necessary work get done and that individuals have the motivation to remain within it. A number of commitment mechanisms can be developed to generate strong commitment and thus ensure the viability of the group and the satisfaction of its members.

37. Function and Structure of Community: Conceptual and Theoretical Analysis*

BY ISRAEL RUBIN

INTRODUCTION

If we begin with the truism that a scientific concept is useful to the degree that it enables the isolation of a distinct phenomenon or unit worthy of study and analysis, we are led to serious doubt concerning the continued utility of the concept of "community" in social science. The difficulty clearly emerges when it comes to assessing the modern scene in developed societies, especially the United States. A cursory examination of the mainstream of community literature reveals three general tendencies, occasionally overlapping with each other, all of which are, in my view, unsatisfactory. First, we detect the Toenniesian tendency to link community with the small town or village of traditional society, a tendency that leads into the futile path of romantic revery and the bewailing of the fate of modern man, who has "lost his community."[1] Then, we find application of the concept to almost any form of social organization that is territorially bounded, especially if the size of the unit renders it accessible on a daily basis to its members.[2]

With this loose perspective, it becomes virtually impossible to even ap-

Reprinted with the permission of the author and publisher from Israel Rubin, "Function and Structure of Community: Conceptual and Theoretical Analysis," *International Review of Community Development*, No. 21–22 (1969): 111–119.

* This is a revised version of a paper entitled "A Revision of the Concept of Community" that I read at the annual meetings of the American Sociological Association, August, 1968, Boston, Massachusetts. I am grateful to my colleague of the History Department at Cleveland State University, Professor Julius Weinberg, who read an earlier version of the paper and offered valuable comments. I am equally indebted to all participants in the round table discussion at Boston. They have been of considerable assistance in clarifying my ideas.

[1] See Ferdinand Toennies, *Community and Society (Gemeinschaft and Gesellschaft)*. Trans. and Ed. by C. P. Loomis (Ann Arbor, Michigan, 1957). R. A. Nisbet, *Community and Power* (New York, 1962). A somewhat modified approach, but within the same basic tradition, is offered by J. S. Coleman under the title "Community Disorganization" in R. K. Merton and R. A. Nisbet, eds., *Contemporary Social Problems,* Second Edition (New York, 1966), pp. 670–722.

[2] Cf., for example, C. M. Arensberg and S. T. Kimball, *Culture and Community* (New York, 1965), esp. pp. 15–16, 102; B. M. Mercer, *The American Community* (New York, 1956); I. T. Sanders, *The Community, an Introduction to a Social System* (New York, 1958); and L. F. Schnore, "Community" in N. F. Smelser, eds., *Sociology, an Introduction* (New York, 1967), pp. 79–150, esp. p. 95.

proach a realistic evaluation of how modern industrial man is faring com-munity-wise.[3] And finally, we notice a degree of restlessness on the part of some students who feel unhappy with either of the two aforementioned views and are, hence, inclined to cease insisting on geographic boundaries as neces-sary for community.[4] However, while this negation, as we shall later see, is a welcome departure from orthodoxy, the alternatives offered are equally lack-ing in rigor, often leaving us with such intangible framework as "community of interest" thus searching for community anywhere from the psychiatrist's couch to the state.[5] It is, hence, no wonder to find that a leading student of the subject has, after long years of research in this area, recently appealed for discontinued use of the term because it "has become an omnibus word."[6]

In this paper I shall endeavor to argue that the mess contains a healthy residue worthy of retrieval; that careful scrutiny points to an area of reality appropriately termed community. I shall then argue that if carefully used, the concept of community may direct our attention to a highly important aspect of social life and, especially, to the way this aspect has been affected by modern conditions.

SEARCH FOR STRUCTURE VIA FUNCTION

It seems appropriate, for our purpose, to approach the problem of com-munity structure through the back door, i.e., by first clarifying the function of the structure we are seeking. Without such clarification, discussion of whether or not modern man's community has been going through disorgani-zation or reorganization is bound to remain academic in the worst sense of the term. A sampling of the literature on community function at once reveals

---

[3] For an admission of this problem see J. Bernard, "Community Disorganization" in *International Encyclopedia of the Social Sciences,* 1968, vol. 3, pp. 163–169.

[4] Most outspoken along this line has been D. Martindale. See Chapter 5 "The Community" in his *American Social Structure* (New York, 1960), pp. 131–150. Also, A. K. Basu, "The Concept of Community in Developing Nations" in *Sociology and Social Research,* 1968, pp. 193–202. As noted, these trends overlap. Many continue to insist on territoriality and, at the same time, search for new dimensions. See Arens-berg and Kimball, *op. cit.;* M. R. Stein, *The Eclipse of Community: an Interpretation of American Studies* (Princeton, 1960); M. Freilich, "Toward an Operational Defini-tion of Community" in *Rural Sociology,* 1964, pp. 117–127; and W. A. Sutton and J. Kolaja, "The Concept of Community" in *Rural Sociology,* 1960, pp. 197–203. Others merely note difficulties without indicating new approaches. See N. Anderson, "Rethinking our Ideas about Community" in *International Review of Community De-velopment,* 1962, pp. 143–153 and R. L. Simpson, "Sociology of Community" in *Rural Sociology,* 1965, pp. 127–149.

[5] See especially Basu, *op. cit.,* Stein, *op. cit.,* p. 130 and ff. and H. Zentner, "The State and the Community: A Conceptual Clarification" in *Sociology and Social Re-search,* 1964, pp. 414–427.

[6] G. A. Hillery, Jr., "Villages, Cities, and Total Institutions" in *American Socio-logical Review,* 1963, pp. 779–791.

the confusion that beclouds the entire community literature. For example, we are told by leading students that the function of community is to provide for the daily needs of the individual,[7] help preserve culture and society,[8] or provide specialized services.[9] The obvious difficulty with these general and diffuse claims is that they lack not only data to substantiate that these functions cannot be performed by any structure other than that termed "community" by the respective authors, but they actually lack any sound theoretical basis that would at least lend logical support for these theses. Why should one assume that the satisfaction of daily needs must take place within a community? Unless, of course, one chooses, as some do, to define the term as the territory within convenient daily reach of the individual. But then we fall into tautological reasoning, for, each individual who manages to survive has, by definition, access to sources that provide for his daily necessities. Hence, what purpose does it serve to search for the nature of modern man's community beyond the obvious observation that unlike his predecessor, urban-industrial man has daily access to a larger chunk of territory and greater variety of goods and services that came, by virtue of their availability, to be included in the list of one's "daily needs?" With minor variations the argument could be repeated with regard to the claimed function of providing "specialized services" or the preservation of culture and society.[10]

It seems, therefore, justifiable to first search for a need or a set of needs the satisfaction of which is more specifically linked to a structure reasonably termed "community" and then proceed to examine the necessary (from the point of view of the claimed need-satisfaction) parameters of such a structure. Such an examination will have to be characterized by open-mindedness with regard to the exact form of the structure. We shall assume that the necessary elements may be found in a variety of structural forms, as the latter may be a function of the sociocultural context. Only then shall we be ready to attempt an assessment of the modern scene; whether or not (or to what degree) modern man has managed to satisfy his need for community.

Over a half century ago, Durkheim provided the theoretical nucleus for the present approach. He stated:

A society composed of an infinite number of unorganized individuals that a hypertrophied State is forced to oppress and contain, constitutes a

[7] Mercer, *op. cit.;* Sanders, *op. cit.;* Also implied in Schnore, *op. cit.* and in R. Warren, *The Community in America* (Chicago, 1963), esp. pp. 9–10.

[8] Most explicit on this point are Arensberg and Kimball, *op. cit.* The view is partially echoed in Mercer, *op. cit.,* Schnore, *op. cit.,* and Zentner, *op. cit.*

[9] Mercer, *op. cit.* and Schnore, *op. cit.*

[10] Many writers on the subject (e.g., Bernard, Coleman, Freilich, Martindale) avoid the problem of function altogether.

veritable sociological monstrosity. For collective activity is always too complex to be able to be expressed through the single and unique organ of the State. Moreover, the State is too remote from the individuals; its relations with them too external and intermittent to penetrate deeply into individual consciences and socialize them within. Where the state is the only environment in which we can live communal lives, they inevitably lose contact, become detached, and thus society disintegrates. A nation can be maintained only if, between the State and the individual, there is intercalated a whole series of secondary groups near enough to the individuals to attract them strongly in their sphere of action and drag them in this way, into the general torrent of social life.[11]

Thus, it is this need for intermediary structures through which individuals feel meaningfully related to the larger society of which they are members, the need not to feel alienated, that gives rise to what Nisbet has called "the quest for community."[12]

Let us now examine socio-logically what properties such a structure would need to possess if it is to fulfill this mediating function between individual and society. Five structural characteristics readily come to mind.

1. *Intermediate size.* We are, obviously, searching for structures that are, on the one hand, small enough to enable individuals to experience what is commonly called a "sense of community" and are, on the other hand, large enough to give members a feeling of meaningful incorporation into the larger societal structure, a feeling that the small friendship group cannot provide.

2. *Presence of Significant Primary and Secondary Interaction.* Although we are aware of the fact that virtually every real human group or organization is characterized by some measure of both primary and secondary interaction,[13] we also recognize that in some structure one or the other tends to dominate. However, in order to fulfill the community function, an organization must be the scene of both varieties of interaction that are, furthermore, inextricably intertwined. For, a "sense of community" implies a feeling that the organization provides simultaneously both a sphere of congeniality and

[11] E. Durkheim, *Division of Labor in Society,* Transl. by George Simpson (Glencoe, Illinois, 1964), "Preface to the Second Edition: Some Notes on Occupational Groups," p. 28.

[12] *The Quest for Community* was the earlier title of the above-cited *Community and Power.* It is interesting that Nisbet, who uses the mediating function of community as the central theme of this book and cites Durkheim frequently on the nature of anomie, fails to credit Durkheim with the basic idea of community function. It is also ironic that despite its basically romantic view, Nisbet's book is, as far as I could establish, the only contemporary explicit statement that accepts that Durkheimian view, which, as we shall see, militates heavily against the romantics' gloominess.

[13] Cf. S. Greer, *Social Organization* (New York, 1962), p. 33 and ff.

an opportunity to partake in social processes that affect some vital area (or areas) of existence.[14]

3. *Key Institutional Setting.* Unless an organization focuses around an area of behavior considered to be of central importance within the culture, it cannot possibly convey to its members a sense of significant incorporation in society via membership in the organization. It follows that we may expect community organizations to vary in their institutional setting from culture to culture, as well as from one sub-culture to another.

4. *Relative Stability.* There are two aspects of stability and both seem necessary for a community. First, we barely need to belabor the point that the organization must endure for a considerable stretch of time; that an ad hoc structure cannot function as a community. Then, the individual must belong to the organization for a significant portion of his adult life. Organizations (e.g., a typical modern urban neighborhood) with a high rate of membership turnover cannot be expected to assume a high level of significance for the individual.[15]

5. *Concreteness.* Finally, it should by now be clear that we are speaking of concrete social structures within which individuals recognize at least a significant number of fellow members with whom they interact and identify. A mere aggregate of people who constitute some "community of interest" will, obviously, not serve our purpose.

Equally important for the purpose of enabling identification of communities is the isolation of unnecessary characteristics. Since we have settled on mediation between individual and society as the core function of community and rejected the necessity of such functions as provision of daily needs or preservation of culture, we should be able, as a concomitant, to strike from our required list those structural features that are frequently associated with community, but which are tied to the functions that we have judged as nonessential. Of central importance here are two items, institutional microcosm and territorial focus.

There is no apparent reason why a community should contain a cross-section of all major institutions, why the community ought to encompass family or religious behavior. Such a claim would especially be difficult to defend with regard to western-style developed societies with highly developed institutional division of labor. If such functions as economic production or education have proven to be feasibly (in fact, necessarily) accomplished in functionally specific structures, why insist that the community function require a diffuse setting?

[14] Obviously, many organizations are the scene of such dual interaction for some members and not for others. The implications will be noted later.

[15] What was said in n. 14 also applies with regard to stability.

Even more important is the issue of territorial boundaries, a character-istic on which most community students insist.[16] This insistence is clearly associated with the assumed function of daily-need-provision, which, by its very nature, takes place within a geographic unit or a set of units (neighbor-hood, township, metropolitan area). The territorial view of community is probably responsible for most of the fuzzy theorization that we have dis-cussed above. For example, the romantic theme that modern man has "lost" his community is fed by the common observation that the neighborhoods, towns, and cities have ceased to serve as significant foci of identification for the mobile man of industrial society. However, from our vantage point we see no reason for saddling the concept with the territorial element. In-dividuals may meaningfully relate to their respective societies through non-territorial as well as through territorial sub-structures. In fact, this is the very heart of the present thesis and there is ample support for this view in both theory and research.

BACKGROUND OF THE PRESENT APPROACH

Durkheim has not only provided the theoretical foundation for understand-ing the function of community, but he also laid the groundwork for the analysis of community structure in modern conditions, indicating that "as advances are made in history, the organization which has the territorial groups as its base (village or city, district province, etc.) steadily becomes effaced." We are further cautioned against confusing persistence with ade-quate function. "To be sure, each of us belongs to a commune or department, but the bonds attaching us there become daily more fragile and more slack. *These geographical divisions are, for the most part, artificial and no longer awaken in us profound sentiments. The provincial spirit has disappeared never to return; the patriotism of the parish has become an archaism that cannot be restored at will"*[17] (italics mine).

And finally, avoiding the romantic despondence, Durkheim visualized not only the possibility but the probability of substitute structures that would emerge to replace the outdated territorial units.

This early statement, which contains most of the theoretical elements of

---

[16] In an early article entitled "Definition of Community: Some Areas of Agree-ment" (*Rural Sociology*, 1955, pp. 111–123), Hillery analyzed over ninety definitions of community and found that with few exceptions there is agreement on inclusion of territory in the definition. Of the more recent statements that I have examined, the territorial element is either explicitly or implicitly included in the above-cited writings of Anderson, Arensberg and Kimball, Bernard, Coleman, Freilich, Sanders, Schnore, Simpson, Stein, Sutton and Kolaja, and Warren.

[17] *Op. cit.*, pp. 27–28.

the present proposition, has, curiously, gone unnoticed by most students of the subject. The few exceptions, especially Martindale, have not been specific enough in their suggestions of alternative approaches and have occasionally even reinforced views of those who remained in the mainstream of community study.[18]

In 1957, Goode drew our attention to the possibility of regarding professions as "communities within communities," indicating that a profession may be a community despite its lack of a "physical locus."[19] Thus, Goode, after a half-century lapse, attempted to renew Durkheim's erstwhile plea (though, like Nisbet, not specifically acknowledging the ancestry) for the abolition of the territorial crutches, and even looking in the direction indicated by Durkheim, the occupational sphere, for the emergence of nonterritorial communities. Although Goode's effort goes beyond Durkheim's general and abstract statement, the plea being more specifically directed at community theorists, his statement has also been largely ignored.

Fortunately, assistance has been forthcoming from the world of empirical research. Data, though widely scattered, have been accumulating that do not allow us to ignore the subject for another half-century.

Several types of data are relevant to our theme.

First, research has consistently substantiated the common observation that in the modern setting territorial units have been strained by the emergence of structures that cut across town, city, or state boundaries. This has become clear from the early investigations by Warner et al.,[20] to subsequent studies such as the ones by Vidich and Bensman,[21] or Lois Dean.[22] Aside from bolstering our impressions with facts, these studies have two additional advantages over our casual observations: they extend the view to the small town and they point not only to strain experienced by the "local," but also the concurrent adaptive advantage of the "cosmopolitan."

Reinforcement for this view comes from studies that focus on various aspects of elite and leadership structure. For example, Photiades found small-town businessmen to feel more alienated than those of larger cities.[23] And in

[18] For example, Schnore uses the intangible nature of the "community of interest" alternative in his argument for viewing community in terms of geographic boundaries. *Op. cit.,* pp. 90–92. We shall soon see that this is not necessarily the case.

[19] W. J. Goode, "Community Within a Community: The Professions." *American Sociological Review,* 1957, pp. 195–200.

[20] W. L. Warner and J. O. Low, "The Factory in the Community" in W. F. Whyte, ed., *Industry and Society* (New York, 1946), pp. 21–45.

[21] A. J. Vidich and J. Bensman, *Small Town in Mass Society* (Garden City, New York, 1960).

[22] L. Dean, *Five Towns: A Comparative Community Study* (New York, 1967).

[23] J. D. Photiades, "Social Integration in Varied Size Communities" in *Social Forces,* 1967, pp. 229–236.

a pair of articles Young and Larson report findings that show (a) the importance of membership in large voluntary organizations, (b) furthermore, the high prestige organizations are those that transcend local boundaries, and finally (c) significant primary interaction occurs within the confines of large-scale organizations.[24] The latter finding, particularly important on account of its indication of the large organization's potential for community function, ties in to still another series of studies that concentrated on primary interaction and/or political function of associations traditionally dubbed "secondary."

In a pioneering study over a decade ago, Bell and Boat[25] attempted to pierce the stereotype image of the impersonal nature of urban life. Their data not only showed the existence of widespread informal interaction within the city, but also that some of the so-called secondary associations often provide the framework of such interaction. Inching a bit closer to our mark, Greer and Orleans found in St. Louis that certain associations serve as "parapolitical structures," i.e., they contain cells of important political activity.[26] Even more important for our purpose is their finding that these parapolitical structures serve mainly the "cosmopolites" who are "unengaged in the local area as a community" and are, instead, politically active "through organizations based upon occupational, class and ethnic interests."[27] Hall and Schwirian, confirming these observations in a recent study, consequently conclude that in mass society occupational situs is a more significant determinant of political behavior than locality of residence.[28]

Finally, turning our attention to a different cultural setting, Rubin,[29] analyzing the pietist Chassidic movement among Jews, suggests that the apparent tenacity of the Chassidic community may, at least in part, be attributed to the nongeographic structure of that community type which rendered it less vulnerable to the frequent uprootings experienced by Jews. The implication is offered that wherever residential continuity is strained, a successful adaptation to the strain may involve transition to a community type with a focus other than residence.

[24] R. C. Young and O. L. Larson, "A New Approach to Community Structure" in *American Sociological Review*, 1965, pp. 926–934 and "The Contribution of Voluntary Organizations to Community Structure" in *American Journal of Sociology*, 1965, pp. 178–186.

[25] W. Bell and M. D. Boat, "Urban Neighborhood and Informal Social Relations" in *American Journal of Sociology*, 1957, pp. 391–398.

[26] S. Greer and P. Orleans, "Mass Society and Parapolitical Structures" in *American Sociological Review*, 1962, pp. 634–646.

[27] *Ibid.*, p. 646.

[28] N. E. Hall and K. P. Schwirian, "Occupational Situs, Community Structure, and Local Political Participation" in *Sociological Focus*, 1968, pp. 17–30.

[29] I. Rubin, "Chassidic Community Behavior" in *Anthropological Quarterly*, 1964, pp. 138–148.

It is now time to integrate these bits and pieces into a comprehensive set of propositions.

THE PRESENT FORMULA

Proposition 1. There is a need for intermediate size structures—communities— to serve as buffers between the individual and the larger society. It is understood that the assumption of this need is made with respect to virtually every society, excepting only some simple societies that are not larger in size than we would consider to be the optimal size of a community. It is not important for our purpose to establish the exact nature of this need. It may be an objective need, as Durkheim claims. It may also be that the claim that such a need exists constitutes a value judgement, as Nisbet would have it. The main point to be kept in mind is that if alienation is to be prevented, community needs to exist.

Proposition 2. In order to fulfill its function, a community must be a concrete organization, that is relatively stable, situated in a central institutional area, and within which members of the organization interact significantly both on the primary and secondary level.

Conversely, there is no need that the community provide for the daily needs of its members and, hence, there is no reason that it constitute a microcosm of the larger sociocultural system.

There is no need to further belabor these points that have been discussed in detail.

Proposition 3. Communities may be organized either along residential lines or along other, non-residential boundaries, as the necessary functional and structural elements do not appear to require territorial focus.

Proposition 4. While limited communication technology of pre-industrial societies may favor territorial communities, modern conditions appear to encourage the formation of communities that, though occasionally located within a geographic boundary, are focused on other than territorial or residential factors.

This is, of course, not suggesting that non-territorial communities are confined to modern societies, or that modern conditions absolutely preclude the possibility that some territorial units will continue to serve as communities, at least to some individuals. And certainly we do not overlook the fact that territorially based structures continue to exist and perform a category of important functions (in the general area of "daily needs" that we discussed). I merely suggest that due to increased mobility in modern societies, we should expect a relative shift in importance away from the neighborhood or town community; that, as Durkheim pointed out, the mere existence of, say, a town, does not automatically mean that it continues to elicit from its inhabitants the strong sense of identification required for a community. The assumption seems warranted in the light of studies such as the ones by Goode, Greer and Orleans, Hall and Schwirian, Rubin, or Young and Larson, that were cited previously.

QUESTIONS AND PROBLEMS

Obviously, the above outline constitutes, at best, no more, than a series of guesses, albeit warranted by available scant knowledge. We are in need of systematically focused and far more extensive validating data before we accept this as a realistic view. Furthermore, the model has serious gaps that need to be filled with further empirical research.

Thus, we do not know what proportion of the population in our society, and in equally developed societies, have either made the transition to non-territorial communities or are in the process of doing so. Nor do we have an idea as to which segments of society are involved; whether the selective process follows along class, ethnic, religious, or any other lines. Similarly, we are in dire need of comparable data with regard to societies in various stages of development. Another uncharted area concerns the complexity of modern community life. The view presented here points to the probability of partial as well as multiple community. In other words, we have some reason to believe that, on the one hand, some organizations may serve as communities to some but not all members[30] and, on the other hand, some individuals probably relate to their society through several rather than a single community. Which organizations and what category of individuals are respectively involved and what patterns the processes follow are currently open questions.

Paralleling our lack of data, present theory shows considerable lag in most of these areas and will probably not advance significantly before fresh data are in. For example, should we find that working-class individuals have been lagging behind their middle-class contemporaries in adapting to the mobile conditions of modern life, we would be capable of no more than guessing concerning the aspect of working-class existence to which we ought to attribute the lag. We would be at a similar loss with respect to ethnic or religious variables should the latter appear to be significant factors in the process.

SUMMARY AND CONCLUSION

In this paper I have argued for a view of community in terms of its mediating function between individual and society and suggested an open-minded

[30] See ns. 14 and 15.

approach regarding structure, with particular emphasis on the necessity to discard the territorial crutches. I have, further, stressed the desirability of research for testing the validity of the presented view as well as for reducing our current gaps in both empirical data and theory. It seems to me that the approach has significant potential for the human sciences. As far as modern man is concerned, we might be able to pinpoint realistically the extent and locus of alienation, isolate the variables involved, and, perhaps, indicate avenues toward solution of alienation problems that may be found to exist in our midst. We may even be able to shed new light on some specific problems such as union behavior (are some problems of unions associated with their local focus?) or the current controversy about "community control" (to what extent and for whom do the black and other ethnic ghettos serve as real communities?). As for developing societies, a clear view of the changing nature of community and an understanding of correlates of adaptation should enable anticipation of emerging alienation problems and, hence, preventive planning. However, as a first step, we need to exchange loose theory and romantic daydreaming for rigorous open-minded research on community structure and process.

38. The Good Community—What Would It Be?

BY ROLAND L. WARREN

Although social scientists have been active in addressing themselves to community problems and in engaging in community development efforts, they have produced little systematic thinking regarding the characteristics of a "good" community. Nine issues confront anyone who seeks to formulate a model of a good community under today's circumstances. These are: primary group relationships, autonomy, viability, power distribution, participation, degree of commitment, degree of heterogeneity, extent of neighborhood control, and the extent of conflict.

Not only is there extensive disagreement on what resolution of these individual issues a "good" community would embody, but some research findings indicate that certain commonly-accepted characteristics of a good community—autonomy, viability, and broad distribution of power—may be incompatible. Research regarding such interrelationships can illuminate political decision-making, though it cannot replace it.

When I was writing *Studying Your Community* about 15 years ago, I came across a passage from Josiah Royce which had a great deal of meaning for me so I included it on a separate page at the beginning of the book. It read: "I believe in the beloved community and in the spirit which makes it beloved, and in the communion of all who are, in will and in deed, its members. I see no such community as yet, but nonetheless my rule of life is: Act so as to hasten its coming."

The statement was appealing in its suggestion that there is a good way for us to live together; there is a regard for the whole and a compassion for the individual, a way in which we can treat each other as brothers, a sense of caring and being cared about. I found the image very moving; and I still do. I suppose it is another way of getting at what some of our young people are also seeking to express: that there must be a way to love and to care, but our local communities today fail miserably in measuring up to this simple image of what human life really might be, if we took it—and some of our other professed aspirations—seriously.

Reprinted with permission of the publisher from Roland L. Warren, "The Good Community—What Would It Be?," *Journal of the Community Development Society* 1, no. 1 (Spring, 1970): 14–23.

In these days when riots break out in our cities, when parents find it difficult to maintain a meaningful relationship with their children, when fluoridation creates violent controversy, when part of the people think that the local community is too conservative and another part think that the old values are being undermined by liberalism and the welfare state, when neither whites nor blacks can agree among themselves or with each other on desegregation or separatism, when the call is for greater federal involvement at the same time as more neighborhood control, and greater rationality and systems analysis for efficiency are demanded at the same time as increased citizen participation in policy-making—few people are thinking in any systematic fashion about what a good community would be if we had one.

How is it possible for citizens working to improve their own communities, or for professional community development workers, to operate effectively? How can they set realistic goals, and measure progress toward them, unless they have, even in general terms, a clear conception of what the community would be like that they are striving for? Let us examine the nine issues mentioned earlier.

1. PRIMARY GROUP RELATIONSHIPS

By way of illustrating the problems involved, let us take the question of the extent to which people may or should really know each other in the community, and should interact with each other on a personal basis. The very ambiguity of the term "community" allows us to sustain some extremely implausible images of what communities should be. For example, when we read in Baker Brownell's *The Human Community* that "A community is a group of people who know one another well," we nod our heads in agreement (1). He goes on to point out that "knowing well" must mean "the full pattern of functional social relationships which people may have with one another." To put this another way, we must know the grocer or lawyer not only as such, but also as persons—whether or not they go to church, how they feel about politics, where they live, how they get along with their family, what they think about the local school, and so on.

At the same time we nod our heads in assent, however, we realize, when reminded, that such *personal acquaintance* among all community people is impossible in all but the very smallest communities. And since more than 70 per cent of our people in this country live in large metropolitan areas, this component of the community—so important that Brownell makes it a criterion of community—becomes largely irrelevant. Brownell acknowledges this situation—but he doesn't have to like it. He writes:

The great city rises; the human community declines. The stability of little places and the ordered rhythm of rural life are lost. The intimate faith that this man belongs here in the little group of people known well calls only for a "wisecrack" or contemptuous indifference (2).

Three questions may be useful as we examine Brownell's prescription, or prescriptions by others regarding desirable characteristics of a community.

To what extent is the desired characteristic possible under the circumstances of 20th century living?

How much of any particular good thing do we want?

What is its price in terms of other values?

Brownell's conception of a desirable community does not do well in answering our first criterion: To what extent is it possible under circumstances of 20th century living? But even if it did, there are those who question whether this small community, where everyone knows his own and everyone else's place, actually is or ever was quite so desirable as many people assume.

Yet the issue is more complex. If both advantages and disadvantages exist in the primary relationships of a tightly-knit neighborhood, this can be extremely important. For example, Zorbaugh pointed out four decades ago that in Chicago it was in the "World of Furnished Rooms," a neighborhood characterized by little primary group contact, where neighbor did not know neighbor, where one was truly anonymous, that there was the greatest freedom from the prying eyes of neighbors, the greatest liberation from small town gossip and back-biting, the freedom to be oneself. At the same time, there was the highest suicide rate of any area in the city, and other social indicators suggested that a price was paid for this freedom. There was little gossip because people didn't care enough to gossip about each other. They also didn't care enough to help out a person if he got sick, or even to know who the neighbor was, let alone knowing or caring if he was sick (11).

The question of how well people should be expected to know each other has relevance today to what may be called the revival of the neighborhood movement, and increased emphasis on neighborhood self-determination. These neighborhoods are each comprised of many components, including the movement toward decentralization, emphasized by the present federal administration, the movement for participatory democracy, and the Black Power movement. The question of how well people should know each other not only illustrates the complexity of the problem of what sort of communities we want, but it illustrates the relevance of the three questions raised concerning any proposed characteristic of the good community.

2. AUTONOMY

The next issue to be considered is autonomy. It is often said that a community should, insofar as possible, be "master of its own fate." Decisions as to what goes on in the community should be made by local people. They should not be made by federal officials, or in the state house, or in the headquarters offices of a national corporation or voluntary association. Rather, local people should have the principal say about business, governmental, and voluntary associations operating in the local community.

Unless the talk about *local community autonomy* is to be empty rhetoric, we must be willing to follow some of its implications. A community which was serious about its own local autonomy would tend to be rather resistant to things which made definite encroachments on local autonomy. Since federal and state grant-in-aid programs often place considerable limitations on such local freedom of choice, a community that was serious about its autonomy would turn them down—at great financial expense to itself, incidentally.

It would also shy away from voluntary organizations such as some of the national health associations, whose local units are merely branches whose policies are determined at state or national headquarters. Likewise, it would hesitate to attract branch plants of national industrial firms, since decisions as to whether the local plant is to be expanded or not, whether local workers will be hired or laid off, would likewise be made by absentee owners, not local people.

These may seem like extreme examples. But if we mean anything at all when we say that local communities should insofar as possible direct their own affairs, what do we mean? We may mean these things, and we may mean other things. My point is not which ones we should mean, but rather that we are not at all clear about this business of local autonomy, and if we want to be clear about what kind of community we really want, we have to think it through.

3. VIABILITY

A third important issue with which we have to grapple in conceiving of the good community is that of *viability*. By viability I refer to the capacity of local people to confront their problems effectively through some type of concerted action. Much of the community development movement, much of voluntary community work and professional community organization has been devoted to this goal of helping communities to assess their problems and take action with respect to them. I shall return to this matter of viability later.

4. POWER DISTRIBUTION

Another issue with which we must come to grips if we are serious about our communities is the issue of *power*. Although numerous studies of community power structure have followed upon Floyd Hunter's ground-breaking book published in 1953, (7) not a single study finds power over decision-making to be equally distributed throughout the population. To the contrary, although differing in degree, all the studies find that the power over community decisions is unevenly distributed, with a relatively small minority of people exercising inordinate power in decision-making.

The numerous studies of community power distribution have been conducted by sociologists and political scientists. They have directed themselves at how power is actually distributed, rather than at how it should be distributed. Yet, in many of the study reports it is quite clear that the author has a frankly "democratic" bias in the sense of believing that community power should actually be distributed more broadly than it is. The concentration of power, in other words, is looked upon with diffidence—sometimes, as in Hunter, to the point of alleging that it constitutes a conspiracy to subvert democracy. The relative "powerlessness" of poor and Black groups constitutes an important current issue. But I do not know of a study which attempts to answer the question of how power should be distributed in the good community, beyond the simple and unexamined admonition: "More broadly than now."

Should all people have equal power? Can they? And if they can, at what price in terms of other desirable values?

5. PARTICIPATION

The fifth issue raised is *participation*. Most people who concern themselves with the community believe that it would be better if more people participated in community affairs. This has been especially true of community development workers.

Two interrelated circumstances are pertinent. On the one hand, as indicated by various power structure studies, large groups of citizens are systematically excluded from the decision-making process governing some of the most important community decisions. On the other hand, there is often widespread apathy, and many citizens do not participate, even where the opportunity is there for them.

But how widespread should participation be? Should all community people actively pursue all the important decisions that are made in the community? This would be mathematically impossible, for there is not time enough in the day for citizens to keep themselves well informed and fully participating on all issues. Some of them they must leave to others. Where are the limits, here? And if not everyone can participate in everything, what would be a suitable arrangement?

6. DEGREE OF COMMITMENT

A sixth issue closely related to participation, is the matter of *commitment*. How important should my local community be to me? Should it be an over-riding preoccupation, or is it purely secondary? Many community workers assume that the community should be an important focus for the individual's life. Lawrence Haworth, a philosopher who has come as close as anyone I know of to writing a systematic work on the good community, writes:

If the city is to become a community, then, the inhabitants must identify the settlement itself as the focal point of their individual lives (6).

But in today's differentiated world of continental and intercontinental communications and transportation, and of changes of residence as people move from place to place, how realistic is it to presume that the local community will be the identification of overriding importance? And should it be? Should we all be localites, rather than cosmopolitans, in Merton's terminology (8)? And what of the many people who are very happy being cosmopolitans, equally at home in any community? Is there something deficient about them? Clearly, many people would not want to live in a community where people expected them to make the community the most important focus of their lives. Yet, obviously, there must be some people who consider the local community most important. How many? What proportion? And, how much is too much?

7. DEGREE OF HETEROGENEITY

Let us turn now to a matter which is even more perplexing: the matter of *homogeneity or heterogeneity*. How much difference would you have among people in your good community—and how much likeness?

Consider just a few random aspects of this controversial question. In the city planning field, as well as in many other fields, the idea of heterogeneity has long held moral sway. It has simply been accepted as a value that it is better for people to live in communities which are more or less a cross-section of the population than to live in economically or racially or ethnically segregated communities. Yet, interestingly, many of these same city planners show through their behavior that they themselves prefer to live in communities which are segregated, in the sense of being economically, racially, and ethnically homogeneous. They choose to live, according to the standard joke, where the man gets off the commuter train, gets into the wrong station wagon, goes home, spends the night, and gets back onto the train the next morning never having noticed the difference.

Note also the gradual breakdown in the constitutionality of ordinances or covenants which exclude poor people by acreage zoning, and exclude Blacks and other minorities by collusion or covenant. At the same time, note the rise in separatism on the part of Black and Chicano militants, as well as the more long-standing separatism practiced by whites in the form of segregation. Note the different decisions made in various cities in determining the borders of the Model Neighborhood in the Model Cities program, with some deliberately opting for a mixed neighborhood, others for a homogeneous neighborhood—in most instances, all Black.

It is one thing to talk of the values of different life styles, the greater variety caused by a plurality of sub-cultures. But how much heterogeneity can a community stand and still retain some degree of coherence. If we really want a heterogeneous community, if we really want all kinds of people, from John Birchers to socialists, can we expect not to see the sparks fly once in a while? And, in a different vein, how acceptable is the notion, often voiced today in one form or another, of homogeneous neighborhoods within heterogeneous communities?

8. EXTENT OF NEIGHBORHOOD CONTROL

This brings us to the matter of *neighborhoods,* and their relation to the larger local community. Here we have an issue around which there is great controversy today. How much shall we invest in the neighborhood, as an important social unit, as distinguished from investing in the community as a whole. Haworth concludes:

> *We would not want to decentralize urban institutions to such an extent that the city becomes a mere confederation of neighborhoods. But this danger appears so remote, at least in American cities, that it seems insignificant (9).*

In recent years, however, there has been a tremendous acceleration in the movement toward decentralization and neighborhood control. There are many reasons for this, one being the simple one that the complex larger cities are proving themselves more and more difficult to manage from centralized offices. Another is the increasingly recognized need, in many fields, to have services distributed closer to the recipient in his own neighborhood. Still another is a growing sense, both within racial ghettos and outside them, that control centers are too remote and insensitive, that neighborhood institutions have too long been run by outsiders in the larger community, that neighborhood people must have a larger say in the decisions that govern their lives. In short: "community autonomy," but in this case at the neighborhood level.

An additional underlying reality is that many so-called city neighborhoods are larger than many entire cities, so that in one sense the autonomy that some people demand in the name of an entire community may be demanded with equal logic by the inhabitants of a neighborhood of similar size. If 60 thousand people in a small city can control their own schools through their own board of education, why shouldn't 60 thousand people in one of the many large neighborhoods of a metropolis have the same right? In any case, the question of the relative strength of the neighborhood versus that of the city has to be faced by anyone presuming to become specific about what he means by a good community.

9. EXTENT OF CONFLICT

Only one more knotty issue, last but not least: How much *conflict* will there be in your good community? Up until 10 years or so ago, the answer by most interested Americans would have been virtually: "None." For conflict was simply a dirty word. Conflict was something whose effect can only be destructive. Now, all that has changed, and each of these statements is questioned.

Probably the most identifiable intellectual influence in this change in viewpoint has been Coser's book on *The Functions of Social Conflict* (4). Although this book has a deservedly high reputation, its great impact may be based in part upon a misunderstanding of its contents. Most of the book is devoted to the ways in which conflict is functional for a unit taken as one of the parties to a larger conflict, rather than a unit which is itself torn by conflict. Thus, conflict in Belfast between Catholics and Protestants may be functional for the solidarity of each conflicting group, but I don't think Coser would argue that it promotes solidarity in the city as such.

Another reason for the growing acceptance of conflict is the growing conviction in many quarters that strategies based on consensus play into the hands of the status quo, and permit the continuation of gross injustices. Hence, though conflict may be less desirable as a method of change than collaborative change strategies based on consensus, it is considered by many to be preferable to its alternative, the seeking of consensus and hence the preservation of social injustices in substantially their current form.

It is no longer generally agreed that the good community is a community without conflict—which places conflict on the agenda as one of the issues we must face if we are to speak meaningfully about what a good community would be like.

One possible implication of this list of issues which must be addressed in considering the character of a good community is that there is no such thing as *the* good community. There are *many* good communities, all according to the specific combination of preferences which may be held regarding each of these issues, in an almost infinite variety of combinations. On so many of these issues, there is simply no way to demonstrate that one viewpoint is more valid or more moral than another.

It is perhaps for this reason that social scientists have avoided the pursuit of definitions of the good community. Nevertheless, a review of the issues raised here does substantiate their importance. Such issues must be faced, and unless we face them, we are working in the dark when we seek to build better communities.

Perhaps the most we can aspire to is to give sustained attention to such considerations as have been raised in this paper, especially in connection with the three questions raised:

How much of what we want is actually possible?

How much of what seems desirable do we actually want?

How much of a price are we willing to pay for it when other values are jeopardized by it?

In closing, this last question can be illustrated by examining the relation between the first three values mentioned: Community autonomy, community viability, and a broad distribution of community power. There is some research which indicates that these three values, as desirable as they may be, do not always support each other. In a sense, what you gain in trying to pursue one of them may be paid for in a loss to the others. For example, a considerable number of studies are beginning to show that the broader the distribution of power and the more vigorous the public participation in a city, the less likely is a school integration campaign or a fluoridation campaign or an urban renewal proposal or other types of community improvement venture to be successful (5).

Hence, those who accept such measures as indications of a community's viability and its ability to confront and resolve its own problems must recognize that in such cases, viability and broad power distribution are likely to work at cross purposes.

Although other research findings offer almost contradictory conclusions (3), the important point is that one is not justified in simply assuming that such values as these can be maximized simultaneously.

Likewise, there is much theory and research to support the statement that community autonomy and a broad distribution of power are mutually incompatible. In a review of the power structure literature, John Walton found that it was the cities which were the least autonomous which had the broadest distribution of power. Dependence on governmental, business, and political networks extending beyond the community tends to diffuse power, rather than concentrate it (10).

By the same token, community autonomy, if pressed too far, apparently threatens viability, the ability of community people to confront their own problems. Obviously, to the extent that a community deliberately cuts itself off from sources of grant-in-aid programs, whether from state or federal government or from national foundations, it foregoes the access to important financial resources which might help to solve its problems. Likewise, to the extent that it discourages branch plants and other types of absentee-owned industrial activity, it takes on a self-imposed threat to its economic base.

How much of what kind of autonomy do communities want, and how much are they willing to sacrifice for this autonomy in terms of other things they want—like problem-solving ability and a broad distribution of power, rather than a concentrated power structure? These are the kinds of questions that seem relevant when we begin to dig underneath the surface of our conception of what a good community would be like.

I want to return to my earlier quotation from Royce. I believe in the beloved community. But unless this concept is to be a mere poetic expression, a sort of sentimental catharsis, we have to become serious with it and make some difficult choices.

Hence, the question: Do we really agree on what a good community would be like? When we become specific about its qualities, a number of crucial questions arise, about which there is much disagreement. The good community is not a "grab-bag of goodies" to satisfy every conceivable desire. It involves choices and rejections which we make either deliberately or by default.

These choices are worked out in the interplay of political forces, as different groups bring their different combinations of preferences to the arena of community decision-making. A careful analysis of the implications of such choices can help illuminate the political decision-making process, though it cannot replace it.

REFERENCES

1. Brownell, Baker, *The Human Community: Its Philosophy and Practice for a Time of Crisis* (New York: Harper & Brothers, 1950) p. 198.
2. *Ibid.*, p. 289–290.
3. Clark, Terry N., "Community Structure, Decision-Making, Budget Expenditures, and Urban Renewal in 51 American Communities," *American Sociological Review,* Vol. 33 No. 4, August, 1968; Michael Aiken

and Robert R. Alford, "Community Structure and Innovation: The Case of Urban Renewal," Institute for Research on Poverty, University of Wisconsin, June, 1969, mimeographed, paper presented at the September, 1969, annual meeting of the American Sociological Society; and Wayne Paulson, Edgar W. Butler, and Hallowell Pope, "Community Power and Public Welfare," *American Journal of Economics and Sociology,* Vol. 28 No. 1, January, 1969.

4. Coser, Lewis, *The Functions of Social Conflict* (New York: The Free Press of Glencoe, 1956).

5. Hawley, Amos H., "Community Power and Urban Renewal Success," in Terry N. Clark, *op. cit.,* p. 405; Donald B. Rosenthal and Robert L. Crain, "Structure and Values in Local Political Systems: The Case of Fluoridation Decisions," in Terry N. Clark, *op. cit.,* pp. 241–242 *et passim.* See also Robert L. Crain, Elihu Katz, and Donald B. Rosenthal, *The Politics of Community Conflict: The Fluoridation Decision* (New York: The Bobbs-Merrill Company, 1969); and Herman Turk, *A Method of Predicting Certain Federal Program Potentials of Large American Cities* (Los Angeles: Laboratory for Organizational Research, University of Southern California, 1967).

6. Haworth, Lawrence, *The Good City* (Bloomington: Indiana University Press, 1963), p. 87.

7. Hunter, Floyd, *Community Power Structure: A Study of Decision Makers* (Chapel Hill: University of North Carolina Press, 1953).

8. Merton, Robert, "Patterns of Influence: A Study of Interpersonal Influence and of Communications Behavior in a Local Community," in Paul F. Lazarsfeld and Frank N. Stanton, eds., *Communications Research 1948–1949* (New York: Harper & Brothers, 1949).

9. Haworth, *op. cit.,* p. 72.

10. Walton, John, "The Vertical Axis of Community Organization and the Structure of Power," *Southwestern Social Science Quarterly,* Vol. 48 No. 3, December, 1967.

11. Zorbaugh, Harvey W. *The Gold Coast and the Slum* (Chicago: University of Chicago Press, 1929).

39. A Step Toward Community Autonomy

BY BARRY A. STEIN

One of the critical issues facing most communities—and the smaller they are, the more generally true it is—is the lack of significant control over their own future. They are subject to decisions made in other places, by other people, on the basis of criteria not strongly tied to the community. Roland Warren identified this trend as the most significant modern change in American communities:

> . . . the "great change" in community living includes the increasing orientation of local community units toward extra-community systems of which they are a part with a corresponding decline in community cohesion and autonomy.[1]

This change has not simply been forced on communities and their citizens. As power increasingly becomes exercised elsewhere, local agencies tend to abdicate even from what potential for local control still exists. Vidich and Bensman have described this process in detail in their study of a small town in upstate New York. "Instead, [the community] orients its actions to the facilities and subsidies controlled and dispensed by other agencies and by virtue of this, forfeits its own political power."[2] To reverse this trend, or even to restrain it from further extension, there must *be* real options.

Three options come to mind, by which communities might recapture a degree of local stability. They are (1) private (non-absentee owned) businesses rooted in the community, (2) larger multi-facilitied corporations with more concern for their local setting, and (3) broadly community-owned enterprises. But in fact, the first two alternatives, while seductive and relatively straightforward, are inadequate long-term solutions even though they may ameliorate immediate economic problems. A closer look at each of these options is relevant here.

Reprinted with permission of the author from Barry A. Stein, *The Community Context of Economic Conversion* (Cambridge: Center for Community Economic Development, 1971), pp. 29–42.
[1] Roland L. Warren, *The Community in America* (Chicago: Rand McNally, 1963), p. 53.
[2] Arthur J. Vidich and Joseph Bensman, *Small Town in Mass Society* (Princeton: University of Princeton Press, 1958), p. 101.

LIMITS OF PRIVATE CONTROL

The principle of local control—locally owned business—is part of the American experience. It involved the prosperous community whose economy (and the autonomy it conferred) was determined by a few *local* people or families. In some cases, the benefits were substantial. Where such people took seriously their "civic" responsibility, the towns often had unusual stability, attractive and expensive amenities and facilities, and essentially full employment.

In St. Johnsbury, Vt., the Fairbanks family, which owned the only significant local industry, was responsible for the town's railroad, its first bank, a private secondary school, free gas for public buildings, a library, a YMCA, and a museum of natural history—all built before 1900. According to *Vermont Life*, "As the Fairbanks' wealth increased, so did the mutual esteem between them and the townspeople. . . ."[3] W. Lloyd Warner, in his classic study of "Yankee City" (Newburyport, Mass.), describes the same process in detail.

Prior to bureaucratization there was a community consciousness in Newburyport that allowed the old families to provide leadership that symbolized the aspirations of the whole community in a fashion rarely approximated in American life.[4]

These situations developed out of an historical experience in which the onset of industrial economies permitted new options, albeit options based on traditional social patterns. But Yankee City must now fend for itself, partly because ownership of local industry was transferred to New York interests. In St. Johnsbury, the Fairbanks family sold its mill to Fairbanks-Morse, a Chicago-based corporation, which decided in the early 1960s to move it elsewhere but was convinced to do otherwise at the last minute by an heroic —and financially draining—effort on the part of the townspeople.[5]

---

[3] Louis A. Lamoureux, "Victory in St. Johnsbury," *Vermont Life*, Summer 1968, p. 51ff.

[4] Four volumes have been published on this study. For present purposes, Warner and Low, *The Social System of the Modern Factory* (New Haven: Yale University Press, 1947) (the fourth volume of the series) is the most germane. The quote is from Maurice R. Stein, *The Eclipse of Community* (Princeton: Princeton University Press, 1960), p. 281.

[5] *Vermont Life, op. cit.* The community financial effort apparently included children going door-to-door seeking contributions, much as they do for UNESCO at Halloween! Carl Sussman of the Cambridge Institute has pointed out in a private memo that the earlier situation could be viewed as paternalism on the part of the local company (and its owners), but the financial effort by the community constituted a kind of reversal in which the community assumed responsibility for the company (although the profits remain strictly with the latter). Obviously, this is an excellent deal for the company!

Such situations are not uniquely American. In England, for example, A. H. Birch has described the extent to which the town of Glossop, seat of the Dukes of Norfolk,

Although such communities still exist (Columbus, Indiana, headquarters of the Cummins Engine Co., is one), they are increasingly rare.[6] The nearest modern equivalent is the "company town" built around a branch plant of a larger industry. These, of course, are prey to all the problems described earlier. And the attempt to resolve community economic problems by enticing another company to replace the one just lost simply recreates the same potential problem, although the short-term result may be beneficial.

Clearly, if communities are to sustain the autonomy they achieve through locally-controlled businesses, they must go beyond the pattern of ownership by local elites as in St. Johnsbury, Newburyport, or Columbus, for the simple reason that an individual owner or small group may tend to see his or their interests as diverging from those of the community. As these businesses prosper, and as their owners or their owners' families see the prospect of substantial wealth without risk of loss or need for continued effort, such firms become all too susceptible to acquisition by others. To make the point more sharply, some 8,152 significant manufacturing and mining firms disappeared as independent entities in the five years from 1964 to 1969, *not including* a large number of smaller ones. Size alone is no deterrent; 698 of these had assets of more than $10 million.[7] Richard J. Barber, in a recent study of the American corporation, commented as follows:

Closely held, narrowly specialized, and local-regional firms have disappeared in great numbers in recent years, leaving more and more industries dominated by big, broadly diffused, and nationally—even internationally—based companies.[8]

In any case, decisions (such as to sell) are made by individual owners on the basis of *their* priorities and interests, rather than those of the community.

Above and beyond that, many Americans today are no longer willing to settle for "security" in exchange for continuing dominance by social and economic elites composed of mill owners and their families. Increasingly, the federal government provides this security, and work alone rarely offers sufficient personal fulfillment. The American economic machine has shown itself to be capable of immense—even profligate—productivity, and most

---

benefited from their presence. One Duke built at his own expense both a railroad station and the entire line of track needed to connect it to the nearest junction. See A. H. Birch, *Small Town Politics: A Study of Political Life in Glossop* (London: Oxford University Press, 1959).

[6] See "Company Town," *Wall Street Journal,* 29 June 1970.

[7] Figures are taken from the *American Almanac, 1971* (New York: Grosset & Dunlap, Inc., 1971), pp. 465ff. By way of comparison, it should be noted that the *total* number of manufacturing and mining corporations in the U.S. in 1967 was 197,000 for manufacturing, and 16,000 for mining—213,000 in all.

[8] Richard J. Barber, *The American Corporation* (New York: E. P. Dutton & Co., Inc., 1970), p. 30.

people have definite—and rising—expectations about sharing more fully in its potential. All in all, it is difficult to imagine that many people, or communities, will put those expectations aside for long.

LIMITED CORPORATE CONTROL IN COMMUNITIES

In defense-related contracts, absentee owners, and industrial trends, the corporation plays a major, and often pivotal, role. When federal contracting patterns change, it is "private" corporate contractors that are most immediately affected, and that make the critical local decisions. Problems of absentee ownership and of branch plants are, by definition, corporate concerns. And industrial trends, though a problem of different dimension, make their presence felt most keenly by the action of major firms responding to, or attempting to offset, those trends. It is therefore of special importance to look briefly at the nature of modern corporations, and the potential for communities to change the nature of their interaction with business enterprises so as to minimize unhealthy dependence.

The concept of the corporation in its present form derives from much earlier times, when the mechanisms for control were consistent with the social and economic order. But widespread and intermediary capital markets, the shift from owner management to professional management, and the enormous scope and power of the modern corporation raise serious questions about its governance in light of the constituencies served.[9] Stockholders, of course, are supposedly in the controlling position, but both the extent of their control, and its appropriateness, are open to serious question. To quote Abram Chayes:

Of all those standing in relation to the large corporation, the shareholder is least subject to its power. . . . He can sell his stock and remove himself, as a shareholder. . . . A concept of the corporation which draws

[9] Since Adolf A. Berle and Gardiner C. Means published *The Modern Corporation and Private Property* in 1932, an enormous literature has developed around these issues. One could well start with the revised edition of Berle and Means (New York: Harcourt, Brace & World, Inc., 1968), and indeed include more by Berle: *The American Economic Republic* (New York: Harcourt, Brace & World, Inc., 1964); and *Power Without Property* (New York: Harcourt, Brace & World, Inc., 1959).

In addition, the following list is further representative: John Kenneth Galbraith, *American Capitalism: The Concepts of Countervailing Power* (Boston: Houghton Mifflin Co., 1956), and *The New Industrial State* (Boston: Houghton Mifflin Co., 1967); Edward S. Mason, ed., *The Corporation in Modern Society* (Cambridge: Harvard University Press, 1960); Harry M. Trebing, ed., *The Corporation in the American Economy* (Chicago: Quadrangle Books, Inc., 1970); Andrew Hacker, ed., *The Corporation Takeover* (New York: Harper & Row, 1964); Daniel Bell and Irving Kristol, eds., *Capitalism Today* (New York: Basic Books, Inc., 1970); Peter F. Drucker, *The Concept of the Corporation* (New York: Day, 1946); and Robert L. Heilbroner, *The Limits of American Capitalism* (New York: Harper & Row, 1966).

the boundary of "membership" this narrowly is seriously inadequate. . . . A more spacious conception, and one closer to the facts of corporate life, would include all those having a relation of sufficient intimacy with the corporation or subject to its power in a sufficiently specialized way.[10]

In the general case, this has been accepted as a practical matter. Indeed, the presence of a large corpus of law attests to the attempt to force attention to these and other related issues of corporate control. Anti-trust legislation, trade policies, protection for stockholders, regulation of financial markets, and a legal framework for union representation and negotiation can be viewed as protective devices for the benefit of one or more corporate constituent groups, including the public at large. As a class, however, dependent communities have less protection, and are more exposed to risk than any other significant constituency. Workers can organize (in principle) and strike; customers can buy from other sources (even in oligopolistic industries, there is generally that degree of competition); competitors can force equivalent access to needed resources; and stockholders can bring suit (or for that matter, sell out). However, save for those rare cases in which residents of the community in question form an important subset of those classes, they have little legal protection against external decisions of great importance to their economy.

In other words, there is no market place within which the *community* and the producers of goods or services routinely interact. They may share space for a while, but largely as independent rather than interdependent entities. If local communities need to become self-controlling there is thus a need for the development of new mechanisms, whether they derive from the bringing together of the community with more conventional parties in the marketplace (as in the case where the enterprise largely *serves* local needs, thus bringing its customers into closer registration with the community) or by devising new strategies or structures (for example, by means of community organizations negotiating more influence and participation as a condition of entry or growth for corporations).[11]

[10] Abram Chayes, "The Modern Corporation and the Rule of Law," in Mason, *op. cit.,* pp. 40–41.

[11] Merely because the enterprise is strictly of local character does not, of course, assure that it will be subjected to any degree of community influence, much less control. If consumers behave as individuals responding to their private interests only, and/or if the firm is large enough to have a degree of market control, the situation will be no different than in the usual case. However, under the circumstances, it is possible for the community to *organize* and therefore to exert substantial—even pivotal—control. One more or less accepted means, for example, is a boycott. In any case, what is needed to deal with such organizations is some form of community organization.

Such changes cannot be made overnight. It will take time and resources to begin to focus communities and community organizations in these new directions. However, even in the short run, alternatives exist. Many branch plants or enterprises owned by larger corporations are closed because of reasons not directly related to the community. Such facilities could be acquired by a community and operated for its benefit.[12] Because of differences in goals, and in criteria applied to such a decision, a facility which is not seen as desirable property by a large corporate entity may be eminently so as an independent community venture.

Another problem related to large corporate structures, which exacerbates the situation in communities suffering from "economic conversion," is that management and professional personnel attached to local branch plants have no particular allegiance to that community. As Norton Long has said, "It would scarcely be saying too much and perhaps is tritely apparent that people may be more citizens of the corporations for whom they work than of the local communities in which they reside."[13] In fact, John R. Seeley suggested that the only realistic option might be to develop more communitarian corporations, even at the loss of some economic efficiency.[14] When a plant closes, the key staff often move, thus depleting the community of some of its critical resources. It is a sort of social distillation, whereby the more valuable and volatile people are driven off to condense elsewhere, leaving behind an increasingly concentrated residue of poverty and need. If alternatives were available which offered them a stake in staying, and a basis for greater commitment to the community, they would just as (or more) readily stay.

In the end, a community might seek to force outside corporations (or other agencies, for that matter) to put a higher premium on community needs. But, even if that approach was legislated (for example, by setting taxes or changing accounting principles so that a firm had need to bring into its calculations otherwise unrecognized costs), it would fall short of full effectiveness because of the unavoidable disparity between a corporation's and a community's ultimate priorities.

[12] These events, as noted earlier, are not infrequent, although detailed information on the overall problem is scarce. It should also be noted that antitrust and monopoly controlling agencies of the government, such as the Federal Trade Commission and the Justice Department, often require a company to divest itself of a branch or subsidiary under conditions which require that it be left as a self-sustaining competitive enterprise. These actions provide a major opportunity for community-based groups that are ready to accept it.

[13] Norton E. Long, "The Corporation, Its Satellites, and the Local Community," in Edward E. Mason, ed., *op. cit.*, p. 202.

[14] John R. Seeley, "The Corporation and Youth," *The Center Magazine* II, Center for the Study of Democratic Institutions (July 1969), p. 89.

ACCOUNTING FOR COMMUNITY PRIORITIES

Communities need some assurance that their economies are not likely to collapse or become critically ill. That means reducing the extent of external control to assure that the *community's* goals are given the highest priority. The greater the extent of local autonomy, the greater the control exercised within the community, the more opportunity for it to survive, to develop, and to grow in its own fashion. Only this process will permit increased investment in the community's future, and the corresponding increase of personal commitment on the part of its citizens.

To the extent that an absentee owner, a national firm, or a governmental agency can legitimately take the local situation more carefully into account, they certainly *should*. However, this desirable strategy becomes positively mercurial on closer inspection. As soon as it is pushed slightly, it dissolves into fragments. Whatever charge is placed on those outside agencies, so long as they have the authority to make the decisions, then their estimate of the situation is the one that counts. Their priorities, their tradeoffs, most likely will not coincide with the *community's*. They may well believe in a "best" course of action that is in fact least useful (or most harmful) to any specific community.

And, in fact, they may well be right, from their own point of view. *Any* organization, whether governmental or private, has the ultimate obligation to frame its actions in terms of the *whole* system over which it operates. It must (at least should) consider the special needs of its constituent elements, but in and of itself, it must balance those special needs to arrive at an overall decision. By definition, an organization's function is to attempt to optimize the benefits or values for the whole. To do otherwise is to invite legitimate complaints from its other constituents, as well as to risk failure to provide such *real benefits* as should result from its larger scale and scope.[15]

The conceptual basis—the reason—for the formation and utility of organizations lies in their ability to achieve things that are difficult or impossible otherwise. Thus, if those things would be more easily or effectively achieved by an organization of different size or scope, the indicated changes should be made. Scale, in other words, should be a function of the goals to be pursued.

[15] It should be noted that the "real benefits" may or may not be dignified by formal identification as organizational goals. Invariably, organizations serve several purposes at once, and the original basis for their establishment may or may not remain the publicly identified purpose. Often, therefore, entities which do not seem to be fulfilling very well their *stated* function should be examined in a different light to see whether they are in fact fulfilling some other (unstated) purpose for one or more constituent elements. The importance of this distinction lies in the fact that the people who manage the organization may well perceive it as carrying out some purpose important to them, and in the process *marginally* pursuing the public purpose!

What is needed, therefore, is an overall structure by which larger units —corporate or governmental—can provide the *overall* benefits and opportunities which only their size can offer, but within which smaller entities have the control and legitimacy appropriate to their more specialized purposes and needs. There is, in short, a need for some basis by which the *community* can act in *its* own unique interest within the broad spectrum of overlapping institutions which—often by default—now determine the community's future.

The possibility of action within a community is illustrated by events following Westvaco's closing of its Mechanicville mill.

After the closing of the paper mill was announced, seven middle managers offered to purchase the plant from Westvaco, with the goal of worker and/or community ownership. The local union chapter agreed to take a 10 percent pay cut, and a local bank agreed to put up the needed working capital of nearly 3 million dollars. After extensive negotiation (and an initial turndown from the company), Westvaco agreed to sell the property.

The arrangement is highly plausible in principle. Westvaco recently invested over 60 million dollars in a new and automated facility, as part of a corporate strategy to mechanize as much production as possible. As a consequence, their market orientation is towards large volume users of paper which can be economically produced on such equipment. The Mechanicville plant is not able to produce effectively for those markets, since its capability lies in the production of small quantities of paper tailored to customer requirements.

From the viewpoint of the new group, however, such a facility is an ideal base for independent production. It provides opportunity for specific service-oriented relationships with customers, it is not subject to strong competition from highly automated plants, and it requires the craft skills of local trained paper-makers. Final results await the test of time, but it can work.[16]

This example is obviously unique, but it demonstrates the different criteria that different groups apply. It suggests, moreover, that opportunities do exist, and exist routinely, though they are not usually recognized. The experience of a plant or a defense installation closing, or the loss of any significant part of a community's economic base can be of critical service in galvanizing the community into action.

[16] Personal communication from Mr. Carl Fagins, formerly of Westvaco Corporation, Mechanicville, and one of the prime movers in the transaction described here.

COMMUNITY OPTIONS

In order to maximize the benefits that the *community* might derive from conversion, what is required is an agency, organization, or informal group whose constituency *is* related to the community. Furthermore, whatever the specific structure, community control requires more or less formal organizations, able to focus citizens' energies towards particular ends, and to provide the means for action. To meet both social and economic needs, several criteria suggest themselves.

First, the organization should allow for the *meaningful* involvement of community members. Second, the priorities that determine the focus and tasks of the organization must be set by community residents themselves. No other arrangement can build commitment to the organization or accurately respond to the wishes of community members, no matter how "reasonable" or "appropriate" it might seem to an outside agency, and regardless of the apparent similarity of the end result. It is the *process* that builds commitment.[17] Third, all members of the community in question should be enabled to participate equally, independent of their social, educational, or economic position. Otherwise, fragmentation will continue, even if along different lines, expectations will be further frustrated, and distinctions that sever rather than bind will be created among the community's citizens.[18]

One structure that meets these criteria is the community development corporation (CDC).[19] CDCs can operate businesses, perform social and community services, and negotiate with other agencies. Moreover, *every* community member can participate on an equal basis (one man, one vote) with others, and the cost of entry (one share) is set at a level which excludes no one. Local government, too, can own commercial properties (as in Deming, N.M.) or hold a profitable lease on industrial parks (as in Rock-

[17] For example, see Rosabeth Moss Kanter, "Some Social Issues in the Community Development Corporation Proposal," in C. G. Benello and D. Roussopolis, eds., *The Case for Participatory Democracy* (New York: Grossman Publishers, Inc., 1971), p. 65ff.

[18] See, for example, Elliott D. Sclar, *The Community Basis for Economic Development* (Cambridge, Mass.: Center for Community Economic Development, 1970).

It is interesting to note that Arnold Toynbee, in searching for the historical roots of the rise and fall of societies, concluded that the growth of civilization was intimately interlinked with progress towards self-determination. See Arnold J. Toynbee, *A Study of History*, in the abridgment by D. C. Somervell of volumes I–VI (New York: Oxford University Press, 1947), p. 198ff.

[19] Most of the material written on CDCs is specifically related to ghettos or poor ethnic enclaves. However, the same notions and the structure are fully applicable in broader community settings and with other groups. See, for example, Michael Brower, *Why Do We Need Community Development Corporations for Ghetto Development* (Cambridge, Mass.: Center for Community Economic Development, 1970); Geoffrey Faux, *CDCs: New Hope for the Inner City* (New York: Twentieth Century Fund, 1971).

ville, Md.) for the benefit of the community;[20] so also can the local development corporations, operating as quasi-independent entities (like authorities) to channel resources and provide the foundation for other enterprises.

It has been argued that an increase in community autonomy works a dis-economy on the larger society. On the contrary: it can be beneficial at both levels. Certainly what is proposed here would have social value by increasing the economic health of towns and cities, providing meaningful opportunities for them to invest in their own future, and enabling their citizens to regain both a sense of influence or power and of shared community. Further, these options would minimize the increasing dependence of individuals and communities on larger, ever-more-burdensome bureaucracies; they would offer a much broader set of alternatives for growth and development (since they would be more uniquely tailored to reflect local diversity), and they would reduce such present problems as are due to out-migration from poorer areas into urban centers.

These potential gains alone would justify the strategies proposed. However, even in the narrower sense of economic efficiency, the decentralized industrial system that would result from greater community economic autonomy based on independent enterprises would probably be less wasteful of resources. Highly efficient enterprises, even in manufacturing industry, are increasingly possible on the modest scale appropriate to community-based economic development.[21]

Conversion to greater community economic autonomy is both important and possible, although the specific means for so doing will vary with the situation. What is needed is both the real means to make such a strategy feasible, and attitudes and structures that can capture the imagination and will of community members; that can be forged into instruments of community power; and that increase the community's capacity to improve the options for its poorer as well as its more affluent, members.

[20] The Deming situation was described in a personal communication from John McClaughry, McClaughry Associates, Washington, D.C. Rockville is the subject of an article by Fred Jordan, "Land Speculation in the Public Interest," *City* (January/February, 1971), p. 85.

[21] This assertion will not easily be accepted by most readers. For interesting and relevant data, see "Concentration and Efficiency," in *Economic Concentration,* Hearings before the Senate Subcommittee on Antitrust and Monopoly, Part 4 (Washington, D.C.: Government Printing Office, 1964). See also *Investigation of Conglomerate Corporations,* Report by the Staff of the House Antitrust Subcommittee (Washington, D.C.: Government Printing Office, 1971), and Barry Stein, "Economics of Community Enterprise Scale" (Cambridge, Mass.: Center for Community Economic Development, forthcoming 1972).

40. Social Planning in Columbia

BY RICHARD BROOKS

The Rouse Company and its planners have won considerable praise in planning circles for their efforts to guide the development of the new town of Columbia. Twelve thousand residents are now living there in a series of neighborhoods grouped around village centers. A downtown, dominated by the tall gleaming white American City Building, rises on the shores of man-made Lake Kittimuqundi. A variety of prestigious institutions ranging from the unpredictable Antioch College, with its long-haired denizens, to respectable Johns Hopkins Clinic have established branches in "The Next America" (the term modestly used by the Columbia Exhibit Building), and work is underway on a 1,100 acre General Electric Appliance Park.

My observations of the development process of Columbia suggest that it can be viewed as a series of social dilemmas. The residents and developers of Columbia are seeking to define the goals of a post-industrial city,[1] but the goals are elusive. Subtle day-to-day pressures force the developer to meet the suburban ideals of early residents, threatening to transform the proposed urban community into a gilded suburb. The massive General Electric Appliance Park, while promising economic rewards to Rouse Company, threatens to engulf "The Next America" with the social problems of the old industrial America. The developer finds himself gradually losing control of the development process, while both he and the residents anguish over whether his continued control promises the beneficial products of planning or an enervating benevolent despotism.

Such a scenario undoubtedly overdramatizes the sense of crisis. Certainly Columbia has escaped some of the more unsettling events, such as drastic management turnover, which may characterize a new town development. But some deep and troubling questions remain.

How does a developer make the transition in a new town from the "company town"—totally owned and managed—to a thriving pluralistic

Reprinted with permission of the author and publisher from Richard Brooks, "Social Planning in Columbia," *Journal of the American Institute of Planners* 37, no. 6 (November, 1971): 373–379.
[1] One account of the early planning is given by Hoppenfeld (1967). The working papers of the early planning process, to the extent that they are available, suggest a tremendous early planning effort to recommend a variety of institutions for Columbia.

democratic polity?[2] Can a new suburban satellite city effectively compete with the flexible living arrangements offered by the existing metropolis? What are the goals of a "post-industrial" city, and are these goals compatible with the free enterprise industrial context out of which they arise?

COMPANY TOWN TO POLITY

Columbia's development should not be viewed as a process of organic growth, but rather the movement from company town through a process of diffusion of power and participation to the unstable pluralistic polity we call a "city."

A new town begins as the product of a corporation. Large-scale community building as a business demands complex specialization.[3] The tasks of new community development are delegated to several special corporate divisions—shopping centers, mortgage financing, legal, residential development, industrial development, site planning.[4] Such a specialization of labor is necessary for any large-scale venture. As a consequence, there is a tendency within the development company to treat the new town as a "machine," no matter what ideology individual staff members may have. From the viewpoint of the development company the new town is made of parts, each the responsibility of a particular division.

From the point of view of existing residents of the surrounding area and early new town settlers, the new town is more like Goffman's (1961) concept of a "total institution." "Total institutions" attempt to establish barriers to social intercourse with the outside in order to care for persons felt to be incapable of caring for themselves or persons considered a threat to the outside community, or in order to protect the community against outside dangers. New communities are often established on the premise that the ordinary community has been incapable of planning for itself. Hence the new, unified control of the developer is needed. The developer assures the existing residents that his new town will "protect" them from unplanned incursions of undesirable urbanization and its attendant costs.[5] New town residents are similarly soothed with the promise of protection from rule by unenlightened local government.

[2] This question was first posed to me by Dr. Roland Warren of Brandeis University. A review of the history of new town development, communes, and utopian communities suggests that this question is crucial. See, Conkin (1969); Banfield (1951); and Bestor (1950).

[3] Eichler and Kaplan (1967) describe some of the business aspects of community building.

[4] See *The Community Builder's Handbook* which outlines this process. Rouse Company has tried to develop cross-functional lines of decision-making as well.

[5] These promises are set forth in a document which was provided Howard County when the Rouse Company was presenting the Columbia concept to the county.

The new town as a "total institution" has several unique social characteristics. First, there is initially a sharp separation between staff and those who are "planned for."[6] Second, the development staff and its consultants attempt to specify the goals for the community. Third, there is an attempt to establish barriers between the residents and outsiders, including a separate physical plan prepared under a new town or planned unit ordinance, separate fiscal arrangements, and a distinct "proto-government."[7]

Soon, however, participants in the planning and political process multiply.[8] New institutions, such as the Johns Hopkins Columbia clinic, become independent sources of power and action. New residents arrive and demand participation. Old institutions, such as the county school system, begin to assert their influence.

Since a developer cannot absolutely screen out participants, choosing only those with ideas compatible to his (although he can encourage some and discourage others), new participants bring new goals and values. As these residents and institutions demand participation in the planning process, the early distinction between staff-planners and resident-consumers breaks down. Since many new participants have ties outside the community, barriers between the new community and the society around it begin to erode.

What results is a community with permeable boundaries, a variety of different and conflicting goals, and a loose coordination of parts. At this stage the development moves from the "total institution" phase to the "community" phase.

For some, the old image retains its appeal. The president of the development company still talks longingly about work groups setting goals for the community;[9] and at least some of the residents express the hope that the developer will take charge and give direction to the community. Yet, setting such goals becomes an increasingly academic exercise as participant institutions and residents of the new town increase. This is clear in Columbia's social planning history.

SOCIAL PLANNING IN COLUMBIA

James Rouse, as developer but also as a man of vision and tremendous idealism, tried to avoid taking a narrow real estate approach to building

---

[6] Various recommendations regarding citizen participation in beginning new towns have been made but few implemented.

[7] Examples of barriers between the county and Columbia include: (1) the secret acquisition of land by Rouse without involving Howard County; (2) the new town ordinance which initially excludes the county from the planning process; (3) recommendations by Bain, a member of the initial work group, for governmental arrangements to insure autonomy; and (4) actual arrangements such as covenants running with the land.

[8] The invasion of "outside" institutions into local communities was best documented by Warren (1963). The conclusion that "communities" may not have goals as such is set forth in Hillery (1968).

[9] In personal discussions with the author.

Columbia. He commissioned a work group of behavioral scientists to sketch out ideals in education, social services, government, recreation, and the like. Unfortunately, there was no large-scale systematic followup on the developer's part to insure that these social planning notions were institutionalized.[10]

Instead of marshalling a large social development staff, Rouse designated Wallace Hamilton as Director of Institutional Planning. Hamilton, a talented playwright, viewed his role as one of institutional entrepreneurship, attracting prestigious institutions to Columbia. His criteria for selection included reputation for excellence, an emphasis on high culture, and counter-institutions such as Antioch-Columbia to "stir the city up." Johns Hopkins Columbia Clinic, a branch of Corcoran School of Art, and the Washington Symphony were some of the prizes.

Increasing concern about interorganizational problems led to the hiring of a Director of Institutional Relations, John Levering, who was primarily concerned with smoothing the relationships between the developer and the citizens; Columbia and the county; and among the institutions of Columbia. An early futile attempt to coordinate the many institutions within Columbia and the Rouse Company through a Community Resources Council failed. As Columbia developed, planning became diffused into a variety of centers including the County Planning Commission, Department of Education, Columbia Association, Rouse Company Planning Division, Antioch-Columbia, the Columbia Development Corporation, and others. The Community Resources Council received seed-funds from the developer but was not able to establish the authority nor the long-term financing to coordinate these efforts.[11]

PROBLEMS OF PASSAGE

The transition of the new town from a total institution to a community creates at least four serious problems: (1) the problem of defining the scope of planning in the "total-institutional" stage; (2) the problem of screening new community entrants; (3) the problem of retaining developer legitimacy during the transition; and (4) the problem of the constitutional crisis.

The problem of defining the scope of planning in the early stages stems from the difficulty of anticipating the form of future social programs. Early planning of health, employment, law and correction, social and other

[10] This omission stemmed, in part, from Rouse's belief that such social planning recommendations might better emerge with the new residents present, but less noble motives, including avoidance of full partnership with the existing residents and government of Howard County and pressures of the immediate business of city building, cannot be ignored.

[11] When Columbia residents questioned the wisdom of such a council and many of the institutions showed a lack of interest, the idea was dropped. The author will candidly admit that his lack of enthusiasm for the council as conceived by the Rouse Company and his part-time consultant status contributed to a "lack of leadership" in establishing the project.

services makes sense from a preventive point of view, but such planning is necessarily limited by the perspective of the developer's corporation, staff, and consultants. Columbia proceeded with detailed social pre-planning in the total institution stage, but a considerable gap resulted between this early planning and later efforts. Many of the early plans were not implemented or even considered, while a series of new programs, supported by outside institutions at a later stage in Columbia's development, were implemented.[12]

How open should a new community be in a democratic society? How legitimate is the developer practice of encouraging some institutions through writedown land costs while discouraging other institutions? Rouse Company has operated both to screen out and to recruit institutions. Regardless of the legitimacy of the selection process, Columbia may be engaged in an institutional "creaming" process, while the other America outside Columbia will have to deal with the leftover institutions.

A third problem of the transition arises from the changing role of the development company as it becomes simply one organization among many, influential within the community but competing with and coordinating others. As the development company's influence and legitimacy for intervention shrink, expectations about responsibilities become uncertain. This confusion has manifested itself in the Rouse Company's struggle to define its responsibility for the support of institutions and the solution of social problems.[13] The transition highlights the unsuitability of a corporate structure, which makes its planners responsible to a chain of command while at the same time they are expected to be immediately responsive to resident needs.[14] Since decisions of the development company concerning Columbia are influenced by extra-community financing and market factors, the relationship between the community and the developer is not one of simple local partnership. Yet, this is precisely how many residents and institutions within the new town view the relationship between Columbia and the Rouse Company.[15]

[12] The early working papers were not readily available to many of the developer's staff and the staff of related organizations. Many of the developer's decision-makers have never read the early planning papers.

[13] Rouse Company has continually discussed its role in supporting programs for youth, drug prevention, mental health, counselling, and a variety of other programs. The Community Resource Council was set up by the developer to screen demands from institutions for help and to seek other sources of revenue.

[14] To the credit of many of Columbia's planners, they have settled in Columbia, thus putting their own lives on the line to test the results of their new town planning.

[15] As a result of the changing role of the developer, the "developer entry" problem results. One example of this entry problem is the Columbia Foundation. Henry Bain (1964) recommended that the Rouse Company establish a foundation which would secure some of the "monopoly" profits resulting from limits on competition which are established in the new town planning of village centers and the downtown mall. These profits could be used for social welfare benefits in the community. Each

The "constitutional crisis" of Columbia results not only from the changing role of the developer but also the different perceptions of what makes up a new community. Current participant residents tend to view the new town in Lockean terms, as composed of individuals who should be represented by an elective body. The development company still sees the city as a machine with various parts—shopping centers, housing infrastructure, institutions—to be pieced together. New institutions tend to view the town as a staging area for demonstrating their excellence to the nation.

These differing views of the city contribute to a lack of social compact between the differing governing structures, which have included the development company, the homes association, the county council, the village associations, and the (now defunct) council of community institutions.[16]

Lacking a set of stable, agreed-upon expectations, there tends to be an

---

store, as part of its lease or deed, would pay a certain amount into the foundation. The developer has been careful to retain control over the foundation and the negotiation of leases, to avoid having third party foundation personnel interfering with lease negotiations, hence protecting the development company's profits. The developer now faces the problem of how to bring the foundation into full community view without losing control of the leasing process and without appearing to impose a new institution upon the community.

[16] This governance structure consisted of:

1. *The General Manager* An employee of a fully controlled and owned subsidiary, the development company of the Rouse Company and Columbia's financiers, with broad but publicly undefined duties relevant to the general development of Columbia.

2. *The Columbia Park and Recreation Association, Inc.* A non-profit corporation with broad corporate purposes "to promote the general welfare of its people with regard to health, safety, education, culture, recreation, comfort or convenience." The association operates and maintains the existing neighborhood and village facilities, assists in the development of new facilities, and is responsible for other park and recreation lands in Columbia. The "front end" financing of the association is from the developer, with revenues from the imposition of charge on deed properties. Present control of the association rests with the developer, although a representative of a popularly elected council is eligible for membership "for each 4,000 dwelling units," with a maximum of seven, equal to the number of developer directors.

3. *Howard County Council and Council Executive* Under a recently adopted charter, Howard County has an elected five-member council and an elected executive. It is financed by state revenues and local property taxes. Its departments include police, fire, recreation and parks, and public works as well as departments under state law—libraries, education, welfare, health, civil defense, and assessments.

4. *Village Community Associations* A board of directors is elected annually by eligible property owners and tenants. A manager is selected by the board. The village boards are presently demanding a share of the Columbia Association revenues. The purposes of the associations are broadly stated although their jurisdiction presumably relates to their village.

5. *Community Resource Council* This non-profit corporation was a council of "institutions" of Columbia and Howard County, consumer participants, and representatives of elective institutions and civic groups. Its broad purpose included coordination, program development, and coordination between institutions and citizens in Columbia and Howard County. (It is now defunct, but is listed as part of the intended "governance structure.")

"after-you-Alphonse" phenomenon, in which institutions limit themselves to clearly agreed upon functions while leaving many community problems unsolved.

CONSUMERS AND PARTICIPANTS

Meanwhile, two styles of planning appear to be emerging in Columbia —styles which may ultimately be on a collision course. One style is "consumer oriented," the other "participation oriented."

The Rouse Company approach to institutional development appears to be consumer oriented, "free enterprise" social planning. The market determines the public interest. The planner's task is basically product design, cost cutting, and market analysis. Institutions are developed and sold as part of the new town product. The costs of this approach to institutional development in a community are obvious. The developer controls selection and tends to borrow institutions from outside, as an economical alternative to innovation of institutional arrangements.[17] Just as some residents of Columbia purchase Levitt homes, they also buy institutions which are cut and designed for a national market.

This approach works for those residents who see themselves as *consumers* of a developer packaged community.[18] These residents have bought into the new town as a total planned product as opposed to helter-skelter urbanized spread. Many residents believe they have, in a sense, chosen to sacrifice, to some undetermined extent, their political liberty, or right of participation, for the rewards of enlightened despotism. They are quite

[17] There are some exceptions to this generalization. The Rouse Company has attempted to innovate such institutions as the Urban Life Center, the Columbia Cooperative Ministry, and the Community Resources Council. But these institutions, if not supported by continuous outside funding sources or through the sale of services, can expect limited support from a profitmaking developer. The other institutions which Rouse Company proudly advertises—Interfaith Housing, Religious Facilities Corporation, Howard Community College, and National Training Laboratory are all branches of extra community institutions using Columbia as a showcase or experimental base.

[18] In personal interviews with many residents I have heard expressed the consumer oriented approach to new town living. These residents did not want other activist residents interfering with the developer's plans. Gans, in *The Levittowners,* finds that the new residents were primarily attracted by the home and immediate surroundings—not community facilities or opportunities for community participation. However, the early settlers in Columbia were undoubtably of a higher socio-economic category than the Levittowners. In a recent unpublished study of packaged communities in California, the authors found the demand for "planning" and community facilities intimately related to the person's "class image" of the community. Good planning was identified with a social aesthetic and concern for street layouts, preservation of land, utilities, and the general plan related to the class image of the potential buyer. Secondly, the buyer saw planning as a protection of his investment. Thirdly, faith in the developer appears to be an important component in the purchase decision. These factors all strengthen the desire for a pre-packaged product from the developer (Mandel *et al.* 1965).

critical of the activists who attempt to criticize the developer and thrust themselves between the developer and his consumers.

The participant oriented residents argue that they purchased the right to *participate* in the decisions of the new town through the village boards— elective bodies established by covenants included in their deeds. Moreover, they argue, like Rousseau, that man cannot give up his political liberty and that, in fact, through the mechanisms of county government and planning commission review of the new town plan, they are entitled to participate.

The citizen participation approach to planning has been spearheaded by Antioch-Columbia faculty and students and activist members of the community. Through the vehicle of the HEW charette, planning with the commission on the elderly, and a variety of other planning programs, the college has involved the citizens (including the development staff) in planning efforts that use students and citizens for interviewing, report writing, and discussion of policy. The effectiveness of the Antioch program is marred somewhat by its lack of staff, naive radicalism, and tension between students and community due to differing life-styles. To some extent, neighborhood associations of Columbia have also sought to promote citizen planning although their lack of staff, until recently, has seriously hampered their efforts.

SUBURBIA VERSUS THE GOOD CITY

New towns struggle against the destiny of becoming merely other suburbs. Several of the old Greenbelt towns lost their struggle and settled down into happy suburbs (Mayer, 1968). But it is important for new towns to avoid that fate since they were, in part, an attempt to meet the critique of suburbia of the 1930's.[19] That critique characterized the suburb as a transit center for middle class organization men on their way up. Tremendous pressures for conformity and intense organizational life were said to exist. This life was labelled essentially meaningless since it was separated from the central city and the national problems of race, unemployment, and urban decay. By day, societies of women were separated from their husbands by commuting; suburbia was characterized by deadening and boring homogeneity of people and outlook. Underneath the brittle surface, unhappiness was found to lurk in the "split-level trap." New towns were going to meet these problems by developing a heterogeneous population, eliminating commuting, and importing industry and other city institutions.

Several forces conspire to turn the new town into suburbia. First, people enter new towns looking for suburban features, such as a better and roomier

---

[19] The new town, insofar as it finds its rationale in the critique of suburbia, may have to find a new rationale since recent studies such as Donaldson's *The Suburban Myth* and Berger's *Working Class Suburbs,* have exploded the older critiques of suburbia.

home along with a safe environment for raising a family.[20] At the same time uncontrolled rising land costs have tended to price certain "urban" people out of the market. The private developer makes part of his profits from sales of land to large-scale builders, and they make money from selling relatively expensive homes. In Columbia, the prices of homes range from approximately $15,000 to $100,000, although there are some rental apartments and 300 units of 221(d)(3) federally subsidized apartments.[21] Columbia's population profile illustrates this family oriented pattern with 2 percent elderly and 14 percent single people.

Second, many people do not mind separation of their home and workplace. In Columbia, there is little evidence that the middle class population minds commuting to Baltimore and Washington. These residents are happy in Columbia, focusing on their homes and families. Most Columbia residents have been concerned with inadequate construction of homes, design standards, and cutting trees rather than development of support for urban amenities and a city culture.[22]

As a consequence of the suburban pressures, many of Columbia's urban institutions, in their early stages at least, are "ornamental," servicing the developer's need to create the appearance of a city in the difficult transitional time when only small suburban oriented populations have moved in. The development of ornamental institutions may be viewed as simply an exercise in super-salesmanship, or as the genuine attempt of an enlightened development company. The extent to which a private developer is bound to continue to support such institutions remains undefined. However, the pace of early new town development does not provide the population base for viable urban institutions; those that appear "urban" serve populations outside Columbia.

Authentic urban amenities must be supported by a variety of residents; cosmopolites, the unmarried, and perhaps the ethnic villagers may be neces-

---

[20] In terms of the values of the residents, the Zehner findings cast some doubt on my assertions. For example, he finds that 51 percent of Columbia's residents were motivated to settle because they "liked the town concept (plan idea, image, philosophy). Although this finding appears to separate the "Columbian" from the "Levittowner" ("who seeks a good home for the price"), the explanation may lie in the high educational level of the early Columbia resident (41 percent of man and spouse have at least a B.A. degree). Moreover, the work of Dientsfrey suggests that "plan" may have a class related meaning to planned community residents. It is worth noting that 31 percent of Columbia residents believed "the raising of one's social position is one of the most important goals in life" and 41 percent believe that "it is worth considerable effort to assure one's self a good name with important people" (Lansing, *et al.,* 1970).

[21] At this time approximately 100 homes to be subsidized by Section 235 of the 1968 Housing Act are under construction.

[22] There is expressed desire for a movie theatre. But my attending of citizens' meetings over a period of a year suggests that most residents were occupied with the problems of moving in and getting settled in their homes. This home oriented preoccupation may change over time.

sary to give Columbia a total urban ambience. Unfortunately, Columbia is attracting few, if any, of those people at the present time, and it remains to be seen whether it will be able to attract them in the future.

Thus, several obstacles face new town planners who desire that a specific territory enclose a full set of urban amenities. The suburban man may already be the "metropolitan man" willing to take his culture, professional work, and civic activities in different parts of the metropolis. The institutions may also adopt a metropolitan approach. Antioch-Columbia has developed links to centers in Baltimore and Washington providing educational and teaching opportunities to its staff and students outside Columbia as well as inside. The Columbia clinic is linked to Johns Hopkins in Baltimore. This approach avoids competition with nearby metropolitan institutions while using their facilities and prestige to good advantage.

GOALS OF NEW TOWN DEVELOPMENT

The traditional planner's method of understanding and evaluating new town development is to posit a series of goals for new towns and measure the extent to which these goals are met. The history of Columbia suggests that such an approach may not fit the reality of the development process. The growth of Columbia from a total institution to a pluralistic community implies that many goals, various and conflicting, develop over time. Secondly, the history of Columbia suggests that no matter what the original goals might be, these goals fall far short of attainment as the society around the new towns reasserts its claims. Thirdly, the resulting pluralistic mix of participants in the new town process is not a happy pond of equal sized fish but a turbulent sea of shark and minnow-sized fish. An oligopoly of power results with indeterminate results on the value mix of the new community.

The original statement of goals for Columbia was:

One—to build a complete city with the full range of houses, apartments, stores, offices, businesses and industry as well as the social, cultural, educational an other institutions which serve man's needs.

Two—to respect the land, preserving where possible the natural beauties of the stream valleys, hills, and trees in a system of open spaces.

Three—to create, by superior planning, a higher quality of life for man and his family.

Four—to make a substantial profit.[23]

The ideals of James Rouse combined the city beautiful tradition, a deeply religious communitarian ideology, and a firm faith in the free enter-

---

[23] See, "Financial Planning for the New Town–Columbia, Maryland," pp. 1, 2.

prise system. When Rouse brought together a work group of behavioral scientists, the ideals of Columbia assumed a more secular expression with an emphasis on individual self-development.[24] Meanwhile, the exhibit center for the selling of Columbia emphasizes the attractiveness of the setting and the availability of commercial and leisure time amenities.

INDUSTRIALISM LIVES

The advent of the General Electric Appliance Park reintroduced industrial America into Columbia. Originally, Rouse had been fond of saying that anyone who worked in Columbia should have an opportunity to live there. But the appliance park with its many unskilled and semiskilled workers makes the meeting of this promise difficult, if not impossible, and even with the provision of some lower priced housing, some Rouse officials have become concerned over the possible emergence of "the other side of the tracks" (in this case Route 29).

The massive building of the park and other facilities forced upon Columbia many other problems of our industrial civilization. The integration of construction workers in Columbia and provision of work training and transportation for Baltimore workers began to occupy the development company. At the same time, the contrast between Columbia and the problems of the surrounding county—problems of poverty, inadequate county services, discrimination—began to seep into the consciousness of liberal residents and activist college students. Housing, manpower training, anti-discrimination, better community services for the entire county have begun to occupy the attention of some of the most politically active Columbians.[25] At the same time, the old-time Howard Countians[26] have begun to feel the urban pressures which Columbia brings in its wake. The Howard County Council has threatened to repeal the new town zoning ordinance and has repealed the county's planned unit ordinance.

The combination of free enterprise ideology, communitarian sentiments, a secular self-development ethic, leisure world advertising, social welfare

[24] The work paper completed by Donald Michaels sets forth goals such as planning for the growth of people and the lifelong enrichment of their lives; individual freedom and the maximum of choice within a competitive free market; an environment in which people feel free to express, in work or action, their highest spiritual aspirations; education as a lifelong process—not limited to classroom or to the years of youth; and leisure activities not as a means to other ends, but as a sign and substance of the good life.

[25] This list of concerns animated the attention of the recently held Antioch-Columbia County Charette.

[26] An unpublished study of Howard Countians was conducted on contract with the Rouse Company in 1966. This study reveals county concern about the price and quality of housing, but general approval of the Columbia project. A series of recent public events suggest that at least some members of Howard County Council are less enamoured with Columbia.

concern, and conservative reaction determines the value mix of the next America. The original communitarian ideals of Rouse himself and the ethic espoused by his behavioral scientist planners are merely two themes in the cacophony of values in this new city.

The reasons for the failure to develop a consensus on any new set of values are obvious in retrospect. Rouse and his behavioral scientist consultants built their statements of goals largely on the assumption of a "post-industrial" society which has not yet arrived in America.

POST-INDUSTRIAL GOALS

A post-industrial society is characterized by a service, professional, and technically oriented occupational structure, affluence, high education, and abundant leisure. The early Columbia easily fitted this picture. Many of the firms in and around Columbia are research and development corporations. Educational level of the residents is fairly high. Given the high housing prices, Columbia itself is settled by relatively affluent residents. The exurbanite county surrounding Columbia is also affluent. Free time for the women and children results from this cultural pattern. To be sure, a large industrial complex was planned for Columbia, but the early lives of the present planning staff and residents were not affected by that industrial complex, and for the time being, they could ignore its social consequences.

Assuming a post-industrial society as a basis for planning provides an escape from the knotty problems of inequality, scarcity, and competition, but Columbia will not escape these problems. The development company, by open admission of its planners and president, were in the city building business to make money. This meant the sale of houses and land for industry, and it opened up Columbia to the values of its new residents and to the problems of new industry. Thus, a basic contradiction developed between Columbia's early post-industrial goals and the forces of the open economic market.

Even if Rouse Company could have carefully selected its residents, (as attempted by the early New Deal towns), its commitment to the development of a complete city foreclosed any possibility of preventing the variety of institutions and people which make for a potpourri of values and life-styles. To develop a city and seek a rich variety of institutions, Columbia had to reach beyond its community boundaries to forge links with a variety of national and metropolitan institutions. The goal of the new complete city implied an open city which allowed not only the institutions, but the values of the county, metropolis, and nation to enter its portals.

Although Columbia has become a pluralistic community beginning to confront the problems of an industrial society, one should not conclude that the result is a happy democratic pluralism of equals. General Electric, the

Rouse Company, and the state and county governments are still the giants, while a multiplicity of small institutions and groups have a lesser impact. The oligopoly of power suggests that the ultimate values shaping Columbia's development will be the result of encounters between General Electric, Howard County, and the Rouse Company.

The changing goals of Columbia, the reentry of industrialism, and the developing oligopolic pluralism place serious impediments in the way of the new town as an appropriate means to promoting "the good life" (Adler, 1970).

SEARCH FOR THE GOOD LIFE

As one reviews the list of secular goods believed to provide for the good life, it becomes forcefully evident that the realization of many of these goods is dependent on organizations, cultures, and conditions which extend far beyond the territorial community of Columbia. The limits of the new town are the limits of any local community as an institutional means to the good life. Perhaps this is the lesson most often lost by the utopians of the new town movement. But it may also be that any social structure cannot deliver all the values which modern man believes he should have.

Columbia's developer, after all, is the salesman of a new product—the packaged community. The development company must protect the investment of its financers. It must cope with enormous administrative burdens through division of labor and bureaucratic organization. It must compete in the open market with suburbs and central cities. And, it must make its peace with an American materialistic culture which undercuts institutional commitment to many of the professed values of our civilization. The failure in Columbia may be the heroic failure of its developer and the bulk of its residents to question the basic compatibility between a desirable participant oriented, post-industrial urban community which seeks to realize the good life, and a packaged product designed by a development bureaucracy and sold in the market place, subject to a national culture and a set of national institutions.

REFERENCES

Adler, M. (1970) *The Time of Our Lives* (New York: Holt, Rinehart, Winston).

American Institute of Planners. (1968) "New Communities," Background Paper #2.

Banfield, E. (1951) *Government Project* (New York: Free Press).

Berger, B. M. (1960) *Working Class Suburb: A Study of Auto Workers in Suburbia* (Berkeley: University of California Press).

Bestor, A. (1950) *Backwoods Utopias; the Sectarian and Owenite Phases of Communitarian Socialism in America 1663–1839.* (Philadelphia: University of Pennsylvania Press).

Conkin, P. (1959) *Tomorrow a New World: The New Deal Community Program* (Ithaca, N.Y.: Cornell University Press).

Donaldson, S. (1969) *The Suburban Myth* (New York: Columbia University Press).

Eichler, E. P. and M. Kaplan. (1967) *The Community Builders* (Berkeley: University of California Press).

Goffman, I. (1961) *Asylums* (Garden City, N.Y.: Anchor Books).

Hillery, George. (1968) *Communal Organizations* (Chicago: University of Chicago).

Hoppenfeld, M. (1967) "A Sketch of the Planning-Building Process for Columbia, Maryland," *Journal of the American Institute of Planners,* 33 (November): 398–409.

Lansing, J. B. *et al.* (1970) *Planned Residential Development* (Ann Arbor, Mich.: Institute for Social Research).

Mayer, Albert. (1968) *Greenbelt Towns Revisited* (Washington, D.C.: HUD).

Mandel, Werthman and Dienstfrey. (1965) *Planning and the Purchase Decision: Why People Buy in Planned Communities* (Berkeley: University of California).

Urban Land Institute. (1968) *The Community Builder's Handbook* (Washington, D.C.: Urban Land Institute).

Warren, R. (1963) *The Community in America* (Chicago: Rand McNally).

41. A Classification of Alternative Community Types

BY SHIMON GOTTSCHALK

The eight classifications of community types which follow are deductively derived from our previously stated propositions and definitions. They are to be understood as specifications of ideal types, in the tradition of Max Weber.[1] Like Platonic ideals, these types do not exist in reality; they are prototypes against which reality may be measured.

THE BASIC CONCEPTS

George A. Hillery laid the basis for this classificatory system by calling attention to the distinction between *formal organizations* and *communal organizations*.[2] Whereas formal organizations are oriented toward a specific, defining goal, communal organizations are not similarly oriented. Our analysis has shown that there are additional important differences between the two types of organizations, such as the tendency of communal organizations to be non-hierarchical. Communal organizations tend to be linked (internally and externally) by generalized cooperation, rather than by contract. Within communal organizations the exercise of coercive or utilitarian power lacks legitimacy.

These are among the most significant differences between the two types of organization. Families, tribes, neighborhoods, communities, and nations (not states) are examples of communal organizations. Such organizations are to be systematically differentiated from, e.g., associations, corporations, and governments.

Whereas Hillery has insisted that the distinction between formal and communal organizations is dichotomous, that there is no middle ground, in our view, it is better to think in terms of a continuum. The distribution along

Reprinted with permission of the author from Shimon Gottschalk, "Deviant Communities: A Systematic Analysis of Community Types and of Structural Change on the Community Level." Doctoral dissertation presented at Brandeis University, Waltham, Mass., 1972. Adapted from pp. 61–73. To be published with the title *Communities and Alternatives* by Schenkman Publishing Company in 1973.

[1] Hans Gerth and C. Wright Mills, *From Max Weber: Essays in Sociology* (New York: Galaxy, 1958), pp. 59–60.

[2] George A. Hillery, Jr., *Communal Organizations* (Chicago: University of Chicago Press, 1968).

the continuum is bimodal: most organizations are clustered at either one end or the other. Nearly all organizations exhibit some characteristics of their opposite types, but they are readily classified as either formal, or communal. In order to give expression to the relative nature of this distinction, and for simplicity, we speak of *high goal oriented systems* (formal organizations) as contrasted with *low goal oriented systems* (communal organizations).

A community is a local society, a communal organization including both formal and communal subsystems. The most universal and numerous communal organizational subsystems of communities are families. Formal organizational subsystems of communities are more varied. They include associations, corporations, agencies, governmental units, political organizations, and the like. When we speak of the *family level* the reference is to both the formal and the communal subsystems of the community.

Organizations on the family level are vertically linked to the *community level*. Similarly, the community level is vertically linked to elements of the *external level*. In addition to these linkages, elements of the community level are frequently linked externally, directly to systems that exist beyond the boundaries of the community. This is the case of the subsidiary of the national corporation, or a family with ties to a clan or to an ethnic group.

The external level is not the entire nation, but rather, it consists of all of those elements of the nation which have community relevance. Thus, the external level of a specific community is likely to differ from the external level of another community.

For purposes of convenience and brevity we shall call the external level, level I; the community level, level II; and the family level, level III. Our classificatory system results from the varieties of combinations that are possible when the individual levels are either high or low goal oriented.

In the discussion which follows it will be helpful to the reader to keep an eye on Plate I. We will first discuss the three *Deviant Communities:* the *Administered Community*, the *Intentional Community*, and the *Designed Community*. These three will be contrasted with the *Crescive Community* on the one hand, and with the four types of *Anti-Communities* on the other: the *Total Community, Orwell 1984*, the *Solipsistic Community*, and *Totalitarianism*.

DEVIANT COMMUNITIES

In *Deviant Communities* two levels are high goal oriented and the third level is low goal oriented. The two high goal oriented levels are linked to each other by means of a *partnership*.

A partnership is a contract between two high goal oriented levels of

PLATE I. A CLASSIFICATION OF COMMUNITY AND ANTI-COMMUNITY TYPES

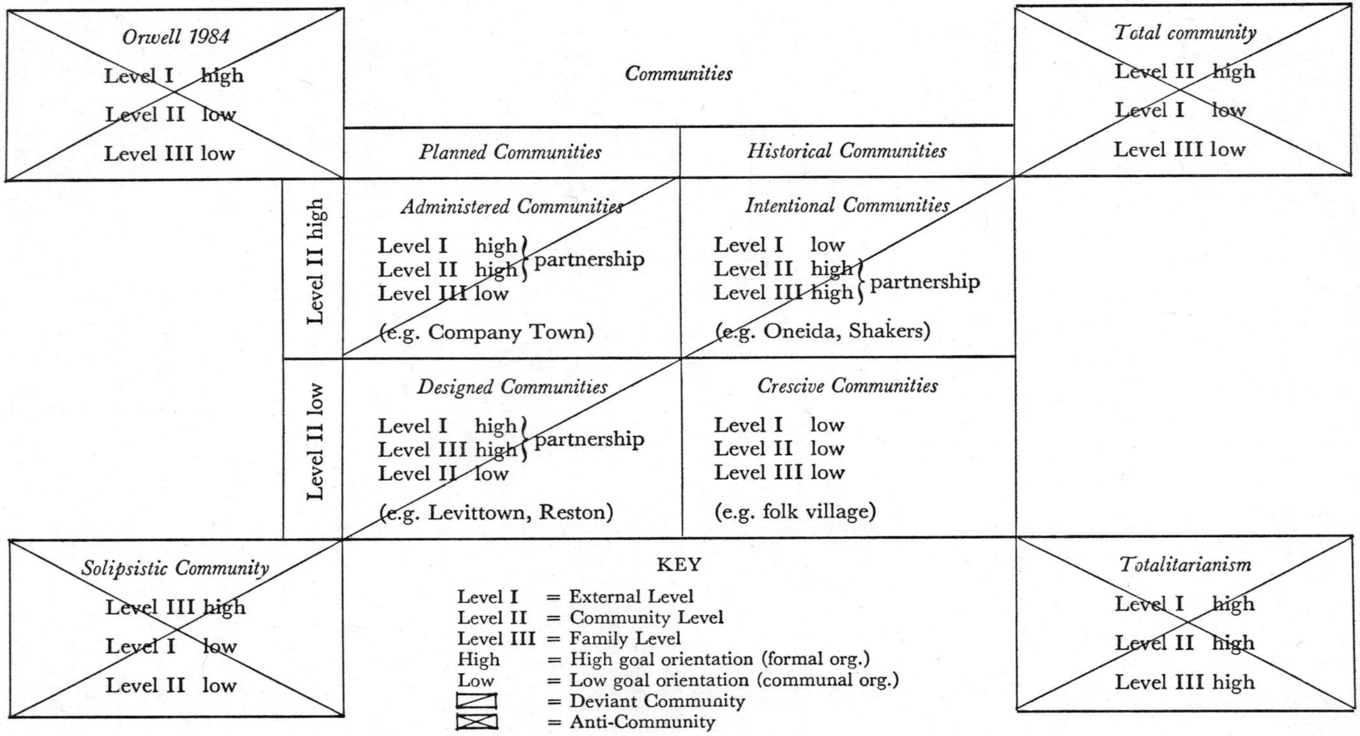

Total community
Level II high
Level I low
Level III low

Totalitarianism
Level I high
Level II high
Level III high

Communities

Historical Communities

Intentional Communities
Level I low
Level II high
Level III high } partnership
(e.g. Oneida, Shakers)

Crescive Communities
Level I low
Level II low
Level III low
(e.g. folk village)

Planned Communities

Administered Communities
Level I high
Level II high } partnership
Level III low
(e.g. Company Town)

Designed Communities
Level I high
Level III high } partnership
Level II low
(e.g. Levittown, Reston)

Level II high

Level II low

Orwell 1984
Level I high
Level II low
Level III low

Solipsistic Community
Level III high
Level I low
Level II low

KEY

Level I = External Level
Level II = Community Level
Level III = Family Level
High = High goal orientation (formal org.)
Low = Low goal orientation (communal org.)
▨ = Deviant Community
▨ = Anti-Community

a community. There are two types of partnership: solidary and reciprocal. In a solidary partnership the two high goal oriented levels are merged into one system, oriented toward a single, specific goal. In a reciprocal partnership the two high goal oriented levels are contractually linked into a market-type system.[3] In a market-type system the major elements (in this case, the two levels) are oriented toward reciprocal goals, as in a commercial exchange where one buys and the other sells.

In the first type of deviant community, the *Administered Community*, the external level and the community level, in solidary partnership, are high goal oriented. A church-sponsored retirement community, a nineteenth-century company town, a frontier stockade, an Israeli development town, are examples of administered communities. In these cases, level II, the community level, has a goal for which it has contracted with the external level, e.g., the social isolation and care of deviant individuals, the conquest and exploitation of new territory, the acculturation of new immigrants. The external and the community level relate to each other as inclusive and included formal organizations (that is why the community is called deviant). Level III, the families, suffer the fate of communal organizations which are included within a formal organization; they are limited and controlled by the inclusive system as suggested by Proposition 8.[4]

The second type of deviant community is the *Intentional Community*. In these communities, the community and the family level, in solidary partnership, are highly goal oriented, and the external level is low goal oriented. Many nineteenth-century utopian communities, and contemporary autonomous religious societies might fit into this category. The goal in these cases usually has an ideological base, a specific social doctrine or a special concept of salvation.[5] Intentional Communities tend to deviate from the norms of the national society. In their ideology, as well as their day-to-day life, such communities set themselves apart from level I. The external level, i.e., the nation's community relevant elements, is here low goal oriented. The best proof of this is the fact that the nation tolerates and does not

---

[3] The idea of market-type systems as contrasted with solidary systems was suggested by Odd Ramsoy, *Social Groups as System and Subsystem* (Glencoe, Free Press, 1962), p. 173.

[4] (Proposition 8: Inclusive level formal organizations attempt to maximize their control over their formal, as well as their communal, subsystems, in the service of their specific goal.) A recent publication has proposed the following hypothesis which is in consonance with our analysis: "If a human group is primarily oriented to the attainment of a specific goal, then it excludes familial behavior." George A. Hillery, Jr., "Freedom and Social Organization: A Comparative Analysis," *American Sociological Review* 36 (1971):52.

[5] The presence of an explicit ideology is not to be construed as a defining characteristic of Intentional Communities, but it is a probable, frequent, if not invariable concomitant.

overtly attempt to control these deviant communities. Thus, the relationship is one of passive generalized cooperation. When and if the national society becomes less tolerant, i.e., more goal oriented with respect to the Intentional Communities, then the community is easily destroyed. This, as we shall see, is what happened to the Bruderhof when it was forced to flee Germany.

In the *Designed Community,* the third type of deviant community, the external and the family level, in reciprocal partnership, are highly goal oriented and the community level is low goal oriented. Private suburban housing developments, Levittown, and Columbia, Maryland, may be classified here. Whereas in the first two types of deviant communities, the partners share a solidary goal, in this case, the two levels have reciprocal goals, as in a market system. The external level in this case may be represented by a government agency, or by a real estate developer. The goal of redistribution of population may apply in the case of the government agency, and financial profits is the goal of the private developer. On the family level, the reciprocal goals are: e.g., a suburban house, a socially and culturally homogenous neighborhood, a high status environment, etc. Level II is low goal oriented and is largely unrelated to the goals of level I or level III.

A government agency which effects population redistribution, it will be quickly agreed, is a high goal oriented community relevant element of the nation. It is a bit more difficult to recognize that private contractors whose goals are financial profits, have a similar systemic role. There is no need to pursue here the essential relationship between developers and the national investment and banking system. The important point for our analysis is that the goals of the developers are viewed from levels II and III as an expression of the external system, and therefore, of level I. The community level, which is in this case low goal oriented, suffers the fate of a communal organization included within a formal organization (Propositions 8, 10, and 11).[6]

The idea of high goal orientation on level III requires additional comment. Is not the family inevitably a communal organization, rather than a high goal oriented formal system? This is a speculative point. Might it not be said, however, that when families are viewed primarily as production units for children, as among black slaves in colonial America, that they

[6] (Proposition 8: Inclusive level formal organizations attempt to maximize their control over their formal, as well as their communal, subsystems in the service of their specific goal.

Proposition 10: If the control of inclusive level formal organizations is contested by included communal organizations attempting to exercise coercive or utilitarian power, they risk being converted into formal organizations.

Proposition 11: If inclusive level formal organizational leaders feel threatened by their included communal organizations they are likely to increase their exercise of coercive power.)

become high goal oriented? The families in rural southern Italy studied by Banfield may be a case in point.[7] For them survival has become the one goal in terms of which all actions must be judged. Similarly, some modern American families which are excessively production-consumption oriented may be approaching this theoretical ideal type, i.e., the noncommunal family.[8] The stress between the economic and social aspirations of middle class American families, and the demands of parenthood and conjugal love is too familiar to require elaboration here. Our point is that they may be viewed systematically, as an example of intra-systemic strain, and perhaps more importantly, as an expression of the contract between the family level and the external level.

Before we leave our discussion of Designed Communities, because of its topical interest, we may mention in passing that urban ghettos appear to fit into this same classification. For the moment, let us make a methodological shift. In the case of the ghetto and the landlords, city hall, the externally controlled social agencies, are viewed by the residents as level I. The residents of the neighborhood are level III. In their effort to survive, they seek to meet the expectations and demands of level I. When survival becomes a day to day struggle, as in the ghetto, then it turns into a highly goal oriented activity. There are reciprocal goals between level I and III: level I exploits level III for profit and level III tries to survive. Level II has been low goal oriented in the ghetto until recent years. With the reassertion of level II, the question is, will it become high goal oriented, i.e., politicized *within* the national society, or will it move in some other direction? The Intentional Community discussed above is one alternative, haltingly being attempted by Floyd McKissick in Soul City.[9]

CRESCIVE COMMUNITIES

Crescive communities are not deviant communities; they differ from them in that they do not contain a partnership between two high goal oriented levels. In this category all three levels are low goal oriented. A Crescive

---

[7] Edward C. Banfield, *The Moral Basis of a Backward Society* (New York: Free Press, 1958).

[8] The highly goal oriented family or individual is much like Etzioni's "inauthentic individual." Such persons are not to be confused with those who are alienated, persons who reject the norms and values of society. Rather, they are true believers, plagued by doubt. They are persons who battle windmills, half aware of the fact that that is exactly what they are doing. The alienated man feels manipulated, the inauthentic man is aware that he is in part participating in his own manipulation. *Vide,* Amitai Etzioni, *The Active Society: A Theory of Societal and Political Processes* (New York: Free Press, 1968), pp. 633–634.

[9] *A Proposal for Planning Funds to Develop Soul City* (New York: Floyd McKissick Enterprises, August, 1969), mimeographed.

Community is a communal organization, within a communal organization, containing communal organizations. Thus, the Crescive Community comes closest to meeting all the criteria of community. The traditional village, town, or city may serve as examples of this kind of community. The question, to what degree can various American communities be classified under this rubric is not addressed here.

ANTI-COMMUNITIES

There are four anti-communities. In three of the four types, *Orwell 1984,* the *Total Community,* and the *Solipsistic Community,* one of the three levels is highly goal oriented, and the other two levels are low goal oriented. In the fourth anti-community, *Totalitarianism,* all three levels are highly goal oriented. In the first three anti-communities there are no partnerships between levels. The fourth case differs in that it constitutes total cooperation, i.e., contracted and unlimited cooperation, among all three levels. Contracted and unlimited cooperation implies the absence of all opportunity *not* to cooperate.

The absence of partnerships between levels among anti-communities highlights a curious phenomenon. The anti-communities, as will quickly become evident from the discussion which follows, are functionally more deviant than the deviant communities. Indeed, the anti-communities are not really communities at all. Yet, structurally, the deviant communities appear to be more deviant than the anti-communities. Whereas three of the four anti-communities are high goal oriented on only *one* level, the deviant communities all are high goal oriented on *two* levels.

The most plausible explanation for this phenomenon derives from the fact that, in the deviant communities, the two high goal oriented levels must reconcile many of their differences before they can be joined in partnership. As a consequence of this reconciliation, the effect of the high goal orientation of the partnership upon the third, low goal oriented level is somewhat muted. In the anti-communities, by contrast, no such reconciliation is required and the single, high goal oriented level becomes exceedingly powerful and dominant.

When level I is highly goal oriented and the other two levels are low goal oriented, then a social system results which finds its most accurate description in George Orwell's novel, *1984.* In this case the community and the family level are likely to have such a low profile that it might best be said that they are excluded. In this anti-community, local societies as well as local subsystems, i.e., families and friendship groups, disappear. Everything is controlled by the nation (i.e., the national government) in the service of its goal.

The *Total Community* results from high goal orientation on the community level and low goal orientation on the family and the external level. Again in this case, levels I and III may be said to have been excluded. This anti-community is much like a total institution that prohibits the development of all subsystems, and that has lost its functional basis within the national society. Its goal is no longer related with level I purposes, e.g., the control of deviant individuals. Rather, it establishes its own goal, its own world within itself. The French prison colonies off the coast of Latin America about which Papillion has written may be a case in point.[10] Aldous Huxley's *Brave New World* is another, but different example of the Total Community.[11]

The anti-community in which the family level is highly goal oriented to the exclusion of the community level and the external level we will call the *Solipsist Community*. In this case there is a total fragmentation of society. Only individual, and perhaps family goals have salience. In such a society cooperation among men is not possible, except perhaps within small groups, as within families. The external level and the community level are excluded because, in the absence of all forms of cooperation they cannot exist.

The fourth and last anti-community that is logically possible according to the model, is the case in which all three levels are high goal oriented. We have chosen to call this anti-community *Totalitarianism*. This is a society —if indeed the word applies at all—which is totally, as if mechanically, integrated from level I, to level II, to level III, in the pursuit of a consistent set of goals. All actions on all levels are directed toward goal attainment and there is no room for included communal organizations.

In reviewing this catalogue of anti-communities it becomes evident that, as mentioned earlier, these are not communities at all. They are marginal, hypothesized states of human existence. All except the Solipsistic Community postulate a strictly ordered, coercive society. For the individual, it probably makes little difference which systemic level exercises the coercive power that controls him. All four anti-communities have in common the fact that at the family level there is no possibility for horizontal linkage by generalized cooperation. This is another way of saying that in each case man has been substantially dehumanized.

PLANNED VERSUS HISTORICAL COMMUNITIES

The model is now complete. In its summarization in Plate I the historical and the deviant communities are located at the center, and the anti-communities at the corners. Administered and Designed Communities have

[10] Henri Charriere, *Papillion* (New York: Morrow, 1970).
[11] Aldous L. Huxley, *Brave New World* (New York: Harper, 1946).

in common the fact that level I is highly goal oriented, i.e., the external level imposes its control upon the community level or the family level. This end is generally accomplished by the inclusion of a team of non-residents, advocates of the external level, within the community. The reference here is to individuals variously called planners, developers, administrators, or in short, staff. They perform a linking function between the local society and its subsystems, and the national society. They implement the contract between the two high goal oriented levels. In other words, *Planned Communities,* as these two deviant types of communities shall be called, are characterized by the fact that there is a staff-resident split.

The staff is a part of a high goal oriented, hierarchical external system exercising coercive, utilitarian and/or normative power. The residents of planned communities are usually in agreement or in compliance with the goals of the staff. In the case of the Administered Community they comply because they have a low goal orientation. In the case of the Designed Community they agree because they are a part of the contract and have reciprocal goals.

Intentional Communities and Crescive Communities have in common the fact that they both function within a national environment whose community relevant elements are low goal oriented. There is no staff-resident split. These two types will be called *Historical Communities.* Leadership at the community level, to the extent that it is identifiable in the Crescive Community, is likely to be informal or charismatic rather than formal and official. In Intentional Communities leadership is official, but local, i.e., not an advocate of the external level. In this sense, the Historical Communities are more democratic in their structure than the Planned Communities.

The difference between Administered Communities and Intentional Communities on the one hand, and Designed Communities and Crescive Communities on the other, is, as Plate I clearly indicates, that the first pair has high community level goals, and that the second pair has low community level goals.

42. Families, Communes, and Communities*

BY GEORGE A. HILLERY, JR.

Communes are experimental communities, and thus they offer a living laboratory wherein can be observed various trial-and-error efforts to achieve the "good life." These efforts, if they continue beyond a few years, also must come to terms with more routine practices that are common to communities the world over. Thus, the sociologist is able to observe behavior that he could never himself hope to induce in a clinical situation. The possibility of making such observations is one of the major justifications for a sociological analysis of communes.

DEFINITIONS AND PROPOSITIONS[1]

One of the problems in using the community as a frame of reference in which to study communes is that the term "community" has many meanings (Hillery, 1955).

As used here, *communal organizations* are those human groups which are heavily institutionalized and are not *primarily* oriented to the attainment of a specific goal. Most simply, by "communal organizations" is meant such things as nations, cities, villages, neighborhoods, and families. They are heavily institutionalized because they are grounded in systems of numerous interlocking rules. In reference to goals, communal organizations are *not* groups in which the existence of the members depends solely or primarily on producing some quantifiable product or task. Thus communal organizations stand in contrast to formal organizations such as business, hospitals, and schools.

There is a special type of communal organization that is central to community theory, if only because practically all of humanity lives in it. The type is represented by cities and villages, and it can be described by

---

* Revised and condensed version of an address delivered at Mississippi State University, February 25, 1971. The complete version is to appear in a forthcoming book, *Search for Group Identity: Concern for Community and Region in the South,* edited by Harold F. Kaufman, J. Kenneth Morland, and Herbert Fockler. Appreciation is expressed to the editors for permission to publish in this form.

[1] The concern of this paper is essentially theoretical. Nevertheless, technical considerations are kept to a minimum. The interested reader may examine other sources (especially Hillery, 1968, 1971a) if he wishes more detailed exposition.

means of one general model, which is called the model of the "vill" (Hillery, 1963, 1968). The term "vill" is used because the model is a rather precise one and because no other term is available (the term "community" has too many meanings to permit its use in any reasonably precise manner).

Each vill, whether it is a folk village or a city, is composed of a multitude of components. Some components are more important than others, in the sense that the other components tend to cluster around them and to change as they change.[2] Shevky and Bell (1955), their associates (see Theodorson, 1961), and numerous other workers have shown that in cities these components are three in number (though the same terms are not always used): the family, the contractual system, and spatial relationships. Since both mutual aid and the contract can be considered a special type of cooperation, it may be said that the vill, whether it is a folk village or a city, revolves around three *focal components:* family, cooperation, and spatial use.

The central premise of this paper is that the commune is a communal organization and that it can be understood best by comparing it to the vill and by contrasting it with formal organizations. But the commune can also contribute to the study of communal organizations, especially in that communes are more purposive, and thus they can give some insight into the meaning of goal orientation (and its lack) in communal organizations. (These distinctions will be developed further in the paper, but for the moment, note that one can be purposive [such as trying to achieve a happy marriage] without attempting to attain a specific goal, which necessarily involves achieving quantifiable objectives.) This purposiveness is found particularly in the ideology,[3] which usually stands for some alternative to the behavior patterns of the larger society. Because of their efforts to realize their ideology, commune members have often encountered persecution and thus have been forced to realize with intensity two critical problems of communal organization: freedom and conflict.

THE DATA

The eleven communes chosen for this study were selected such that they represented as wide a range of variation as possible. In terms of longevity and of achieving their own purpose, some of the communes are successful (such as Palisades Abbey and the Hutterites), some are unsuccessful (such as HIP and St. Samuel), and some are of questionable success (such as the Shakers). The selection includes communes that are rural and urban, large

[2] Change in one cluster, however, is not necessarily integrated with change in another cluster. See Hillery, 1968, and the concept of "structural freewheeling." See also Kaufman's concept of the local agglomerate (1959).

[3] For the use of "ideology," as employed here, see Gould and Kolb, 1964.

and small, religious and atheistic, and celibate, familial, and sexually experimental. All of them are not usually considered to be communes (the monasteries, for example), but in one way or another all are *intentionally founded in order to achieve a fuller realization of some ideology.* At times the ideology is so insubstantial (or perhaps negative) that it has contributed to the demise of the commune, as was apparent in the case of one commune to be studied here (HIP) ; more often the ideology is very carefully developed.

The data for the communes are summarized in Tables 1 and 2.

THE FOCAL COMPONENTS OF COMMUNES

Since communal organizations, and specifically vills, provide the basic framework, relations among the focal components are here considered in some detail.

SPATIAL INTEGRATION AND FAMILY

The way in which the space of the communes is organized seems to have little to with the presence or absence of the family. The more important variable influencing the family is the ideology of the group as a whole: there must be a stable system of sexual norms if the commune is to continue. Any violation of this condition has failed historically. There seems to be no middle ground: either the commune has families, or sexual relations are prohibited. Since the system of sexual norms is embodied in the ideology, the emphasis in this discussion necessarily shifts to the relation between family and ideology.

The HIP commune is the best example of a case in which sexual regulations were relatively absent and the commune failed. The only rule in HIP was "to have no rules." As the members attempted to form the commune, sexual experimentation developed, and concomitantly tensions increased. After two or three months, the commune was in a noticeable disintegration; at the end of the first semester it had broken up. Of course, one cannot "blame" the disintegration on sexual experimentation. More appropriate would be the general lack of norms, of which sexual experimentation was only a part. For example, the students were asked to comment on the statement, "Freedom is closely linked with the idea of sharing and sacrificing." It is significant that of all the groups studied, and even non-communes and prisons, HIP had one of the lowest percentages to agree to this question: 35.3. Only a men's dormitory (at the same university) had a lower percentage: 27.0.

The students were also asked to respond to another statement: "I am threatened by a pressure to be 'cool' and 'in'—and a feeling of playing games with everyone." The proportion agreeing was the highest ever recorded, and

TABLE 1. SUMMARY DESCRIPTION OF THE COMMUNES FOR WHICH PRIMARY DATA ARE AVAILABLE.

Name	Religious Affiliation	Purpose	Rural-Urban Position	Year Organized	Population Total Adult		Population Having Questionnaire Data[2]	Social Units
Palisades	Roman Catholic Trappist monks	Prayer	Rural	Mid 19th Century	70	70	49	Adult males
Caphas	Protestant	Christian witness, community & racial involvement	Rural	1942	25	15	14	Families and single adults, children
Lisa Place	Mennonite and other Protestant	Christian witness	Urban	1956	92	36	none	Families and single adults, children
St. Samuel	Episcopalian	Community involvement & Christian witness	Urban	1970	14	11	11	Families (adults and college students), children
Martin House I &	Lutheran and other	Alternative to dormitory living. Christian witness; to "experience community"	Urban	1969[1]	38	38	33	College students
Martin House II	Protestant			1970[1]	33	33	29	College students
HIP	None	Alternative to dormitory living; to "experience community"	Urban	1969	28	27	18	College students, one child

[1] Structure first organized in 1961; a new community is started each year.
[2] All data gathered by the author. The author has also been involved in participant observation of all communities, ranging in time from four days to one month.

TABLE 2. SUMMARY DESCRIPTION OF THE COMMUNES FOR WHICH SECONDARY DATA ARE USED.

Name	Religious Affiliation	Purpose	Rural-Urban Position	Time in Existence	Population	Social Units
Kiryat Yedidim Kibbutz	Atheist (Jewish)	Marxian Communism	Rural with urban features	1920 to present	500	Families
Oneida	Perfectionist (Christian)	Individual perfection and communal good	Rural with urban features	1844–1880	253, maximum	One "family" —group marriage
Hutterites	Anabaptists	To be obedient to the divine order of God	Rural	1528 to present (in U.S. since 1874)	Varies: often ranges between 70 and 130	Families
Shakers	Believers (Originated as Christian sect)	To obtain salvation, especially by abstinence, celibacy, and withdrawal from the world	Rural	1787 to present, drastic decline after 1860; 2 communities remaining	Varied: usually ranged from 100–350; some had 600 persons	"Families"—both sexes and all ages included, celibacy maintained.

Basic Sources: Kibbutz: Spiro (1956, 1958); Oneida: Carden (1969); Hutterites: Hostetler and Huntington (1967); Shakers: Andrews (1963), Neal (1963).

more than twice as high as any other commune: 61.1 percent. The HIP students were caught in an ancient dilemma of freedom. To be without restriction is to be in a state of chaos, to be normless. As the French sociologist Emile Durkheim pointed out approximately three-quarters of a century ago, humans find such conditions difficult and at times impossible to bear.

Oneida is even more revealing, because it suggests the degree to which sexual norms must be controlled. The community is widely known for its system of group marriage. There was no promiscuity: a well-developed system of norms prevailed. For example, arrangements for sexual relations were made through a third party; incest was not permitted; only certain persons could have children (a form of birth control was practiced); and of course relationships could be refused. Even more interesting, the members were not allowed to develop a relationship of "exclusive love" (Carden, 1969: 52–54). Thus, Oneida fulfills the principle in that it controlled its sexual norms.

Finally, the Israeli kibbutz (in its initial stage) represents an open attempt not at group marriage but at experimentation.

They were convinced that it was possible to create a relationship between the sexes on a sounder and more natural foundation than that which characterized 'bourgeoise' marriage, and they experimented with many substitutes including informal polygyny and polyandry. They attempted to break down the traditional attitude of sexual shame in which they had been reared by instituting a mixed shower, but that was abandoned. (Spiro, 1956:112.)

Then children came, and not unexpectedly, the parents grew to love them. This relationship itself developed into a solidifying factor. Divorce in the early years was frequent. Now it is rare, and the children seem to have had a crucial role in the change (Spiro, 1956:117; 1958:90–91). What appears to have happened in the kibbutz is that familial functions were sharply pared away until only two were left: sanctioned sexual relations among the spouses and emotional nurturance of both spouses and young (see Hillery, 1968:117 *et passim*). The family has emerged in a sturdier form than ever, even if drastically simplified.

The other communes differ from each other in radically opposite ways. The Hutterites, Caphas, St. Samuel, and Lisa Place have very stable familial systems; Palisades, the Shakers, and Martin House officially rule out sexual relations entirely. The monks and the Shakers are much stricter than is Martin House, to be certain. There have been pre-marital sexual experiences in the Martin House communities, but these are sub rosa and at best appear to involve a minority.

One may probably argue that it is the very fact of spatial integration that has prompted the careful control of sexual relations in the first place. Martin House can probably exist as it does because the sexes are segregated at certain times and because they are away from the community frequently. Relations can be more informal, superficial, and casual. At Caphas, where the spatial relations are closer, the sexual tensions seem higher. Sex is also more carefully controlled. Caphas claims to have two strict rules: no drugs and persons who are not married cannot sleep together. The only tensions which the author noticed were in connection with the second of these rules. The tensions were manageable and the relationships between the sexes were controlled, but the control was stricter at Caphas than at Martin House.

COOPERATION AND SPACE

Cooperation is used in the broadest sense to mean the joint effort by two or more persons or groups to attain a common goal. Two opposite types may be conceived. At one pole is mutual aid, where each helps the other as need arises, with no recognized restrictions. At the other pole, cooperation is contractual, and its chief feature is the limitations placed upon it: The *way* in which cooperation takes place is limited (as when one inserts a coin in a soft-drink machine), the *objects* that are being cooperated for are limited (a coin on the one hand, a soft drink on the other—no more and no less), and the amount of *risk* is limited (one cannot sue because the soft drink increased one's weight). Finally, society must protect the entire relationship if it is to be viable (the rules are relatively unenforceable, for example, if the machine is placed untended in a desert) (See Parsons, 1960: 144–45).

Mutual aid was an integral part of all the communes and in all cases contracts were essential, if only in the sense that the occupations of the members should be viewed as contractual relationships. Where the ideology was more developed, mutual aid was more pervasive. The extremes here are HIP and Martin House, but in both cases, there was much "feeling each other out" in efforts to establish expectations. Patterns of mutual aid eventually emerge in the communities of Martin House. HIP, of course, did not last long enough.

Spatial integration may be measured by observing the time members spend within the boundaries of the commune. "Full" communes are those in which most of the activities take place inside the commune. In "partial" communes, members usually sleep and eat within the boundaries but spend significant amounts of time elsewhere. The generalization may be offered that the ideology of full communes is more determinative of occupational choice than is the ideology of partial communes. Among the Hutterites, the Shakers, the kibbutzim, and at Caphas, Oneida, and Palisades, all of which were full communes, one's job was determined essentially by the community. On the other hand, where spatial integration is weaker, as in partial communes, occupation strongly influences membership; that is, the contractual relationship has a significant influence on ideology. This is especially true in St. Samuel, in HIP, and in Martin House. Martin House is composed completely of students; HIP was mostly so. Admission requirements in both were rather open. No formal statements of belief were required; membership merely depended on one's willingness to join and on approval by the commune. St. Samuel had more stringent regulations since members had to agree to participate in the Episcopal liturgy. However, most of the members of St. Samuel are also students at the local university. Thus, the occupation of student dominates the life of all three of these communes.

Lisa Place is intermediate. Most of those who are employed are professionals (or students), and occupational change has had an influence on the membership in at least two cases. For example, one person obtained a job as a professor in another town; this move caused a change in his membership status. The professor did not give up his membership in the commune, but he did go "on leave."

Nevertheless, Lisa Place reacts otherwise as a full commune, in that one joins Lisa Place not because of an occupation but because of religious or ideological commitment. In fact, occupations which conflict with prayer meetings and other community functions at Lisa Place are not chosen by the members. This means that no one selects Sunday and night-time occupations.

There is often a close relation between ideology and occupation, such that one extends into the other, particularly in the full communes. There was, for example, no separation of ideology and occupation in the kibbutz, since agriculture was high on the list of values of the original founders. The monks began as agricultural laborers and still place heavy emphasis on this area, but most do not list agricultural jobs as their main monastic occupation. Ideology is still more important, however, because the occupation is directly assigned by the monastery (through the abbot), even if in consultation with the monk.

Occupation is stressed because it is one of the most contractual forms of cooperation that has yet been developed. But especially in the full communes, cooperation goes much further than occupation. Lisa Place, again, is a good example. When one joins, his earnings are turned over to a central treasurer who allocates an allowance for each person or family, based on experience and individual circumstances. The central treasury pays house payments, fire insurance, liability insurances, automobile costs, utilities, medical, dental and educational expenses, etc. (Redekop, 1970:21). In this example, the *mechanisms* for cooperation are heavily contractual, but the *purpose* of cooperation is closer to mutual aid: assistance is given as required, with no limitations.

Even in communes such as HIP and Martin House, where occupation is dominant, ideology is still important for understanding the basic life of the commune. The ideology determines whether the commune is composed only or mainly of students (as in St. Samuel, HIP, and Martin House), whether the members may or may not be married (as is true of most of the communes studied here), whether there is to be sexual experimentation (as in HIP, in Oneida, and in the early days of the kibbutz). One may argue that HIP is an exception, since its ideology was never formed. But the early dissolution of HIP may be traced directly to this lack of ideology, and the experimentations—sexually as well as otherwise—were because of and perhaps even in search of an ideology.[4]

COOPERATION AND FAMILY

The commune members must cooperate, but whether cooperation is with the family or without it depends on the ideology. The Hutterites, Caphas, Lisa Place, St. Samuel, and (we must add) the kibbutz all have a system of cooperation in which the family has a place. The kibbutz, although initially experimental, eventually made room for families. Oneida and HIP never progressed past the experimental stage. And, finally, the monks, the Shakers, and the students of Martin House have essentially ruled out familial relationships.

Even more interesting, although the ideology may dictate whether the family will be allowed to exist in the group, the ideology can apparently do little to change the core functions of sexual and emotional nurturance, or at least not for long. Oneida attempted a radical change and is no more. HIP attempted to ignore the rules and is no more. The kibbutz attempted to experiment and ended by reinstituting the family, even though in a radically streamlined form. Of the three experiments considered so far, the kibbutz has been the most successful. It also has not reached the point where the third generation is in positions of responsibility.

In most of the communes studied here, cooperation appears to be as much (if not more) a matter between individuals than between families. Obviously this is so in communes where the family is absent, and it was true of HIP (where the "family" was incidental—married members were not living with each other). Oneida was one "family," in a sense, and thus cooperation within the group again was with individuals. And although

---

[4] There was no ideology in HIP in the sense that the students did not commit themselves to a clearly stated purpose.

cooperation between families was not ruled out in the kibbutz, cooperation took place to a large degree among individuals.

An interesting question is whether the commune takes the place of the family, but in reality, any attempt to equate these groups is at best meta-phorical, except in the case of Oneida. In any specific sense, they are different systems. Two types of roles are basic to the family as it is being discussed here: spouses and parent-children. One should not forget the obvious fact that unless sexual relations have occurred, one is not engaging in a spouse role, and unless there is a biological immaturity on the part of one of the members of the role system, there is no parent-child role. Thus, although the abbot of a monastery is called "Father" and the other monks are "brothers," the relationships are not the same as in the bisocial family. It is in this sense that we can call the other relationships "pseudofamilial" (as is true also of the homosexual systems described by Giallombardo, 1966).

Again, the exception is Oneida. In this system of group marriage, all adults were potential spouses, all children were potential siblings. One wonders how far the system could have gone. Everyone could not have been married to everyone without eventually violating incest rules, in every conceivable manner. The problem of incest did arise, but we are not told how it was treated, probably because it did not become statistically important (see Carden, 1969:21n), and the community dispersed before the problem could appreciably grow.

In view of the conceptual difficulties, the more appropriate course is to forego any attempt at equating the commune and the family, simply noting that the ideology of the commune, not the family, is the more important. This is the case in every instance in which the family appears.

If communes differ from other vills in their emphasis on ideology, they differ in another feature, and one that is closely bound with both the ideology and the family: their system of recruitment. Although five of the communes had families of some sort, in only two of these were members born into the system.[5] But in all of the communes that were studied here, each member must decide for himself whether he will join the commune. In practical terms, this means that the adolescent kibbutznik must formally petition the kibbutz for membership; the young Hutterite must ask for baptism (which is essentially equivalent to requesting membership).

This requirement is central, for it will be recalled that communes were defined as systems that were intentionally founded. The requirement presents formidable problems—even paradoxical ones. The first problem concerns the children. The commune may attempt to enforce a system of rigorous indoctrination on the children. If this is done, two risks are encountered:

[5] Members were also born into Oneida, but it represents a special case in the present consideration.

(1) the child may be misinformed about the outside world (or otherwise given limited information); or (2) the intensity of the commitment of the new members may be dampened. The first risk is a serious impairment to the freedom of the members, for it can be argued that the existence of communes depends on maximizing freedom in a very real way. To provide limited information may well mean providing important limitations on choices.

The second risk is more subtle. By attempting to bring all of the children into the commune, the commune thus introduces a greater variety of intensity of commitment than it had when it was founded, because on its founding, commitment was intense. For the Hutterites, the risk of loss in commitment has been lessened in an interesting way through the serious persecutions they have suffered through the centuries. (The question may be asked in the case of the Hutterites whether there is any necessary relationship between commitment and persecution.)

But if the commune does not indoctrinate the young, then it must have resources for recruitment or it will die. This is one of the reasons for the decline of the Shakers. The Trappists avoid the problem to some degree by leaving recruitment to the Mother Church. Caphas and Lisa Place (as well as St. Samuel and the monks) have sizeable streams of visitors who form a potential pool for recruits, but they do not attempt to pressure the children into staying.

Thus, unlike other vills, recruitment is a problem faced by the communes, and it is a problem because of their ideology. They have chosen one extreme of what may be a normal curve of commitment. To continue, they must somehow maintain the intensity of belief among old members and find it in equal vigor among new ones.

IDEOLOGIES AND GOALS

The importance of ideology to communes has been repeatedly encountered. We may say accordingly that communes are established with some sort of goal more or less clearly in view. Findings from the HIP commune would suggest that without such a goal, the commune will not stay in existence, as such. In other words, the HIP's "rule to have no rules" seemed to have in itself disintegrative consequences.

However, communal organizations have been defined as "heavily institutionalized and . . . not primarily oriented to the attainment of a specific goal." If communes are communal organizations (and they are so considered here), then clearly attention must now be given to a discussion of the nature and types of goals.

For the needs of the present discussion, two types of goals are distinguished: specific goals and purposes.[6] (1) Specific goals are in themselves a distinctive type. Above all, progress in reaching the goal must be clearly measurable. Record-keeping systems in such institutions as hospitals and prisons are examples. Parsons (1960:17–18) adds other criteria which are in keeping with this one of measurability. Specific goals must be able to be clearly identified, they must be able to be treated as an out-put that can be an in-put into another group, and they must be such that contracts can be made concerning them. Examples of specific goals would be making a profit, producing automobiles, attaining a college degree, and feeding customers at a restaurant. Some organizations give primacy to the attainment of specific goals. These are called "formal" organizations.

(2) Purposes are not easily defined, but they refer generally to values, standards or conditions, the attainment of which is believed to be desirable by the members of a group (whether the values, standards, or conditions are ever attained or even attainable). Purposes also may be divided into two types: Those that put people first and those that put some ideology first. In either case, *as used here,* purposes are not specific goals. Communes are consequences of purposes.

One peculiarity of purposes is that it is difficult to know whether they are being achieved (an important distinction from specific goals). Thus, it usually takes several generations before one can know if a commune is successful. Total collapse of the commune may be of course a sign of failure.[7] However, even if a commune is able to continue to exist for a considerable period of time, we do not know that thereby it is fulfilling its purpose. For example, a religious organization may last for centuries and then give rise to a reformation movement. The reformation movement will accuse the mother church of having lost its purpose, but quite often, the mother church and its rebellious daughter will both continue to exist, even again for centuries.

This distinction between purposes and goals has important consequences in social behavior, particularly with respect to freedom. In fact, the hypothesis has been offered (Hillery, 1971a): *If a group is primarily oriented to the attainment of a specific goal, then it will not maximize freedom.* Whatever else freedom may be, as used in this discussion, it refers to the ability of an individual to do what he desires, what he wants or wills to do. If a group is primarily oriented to attaining a specific goal, then it follows that the group will not be oriented to individuals. The individuals

[6] See the analysis of "Goals," in the *Dictionary of the Social Sciences,* Gould and Kolb, 1964.

[7] However, note the case of HIP. Although it would be difficult to say that HIP had attained its purpose, and though one of the founders readily admitted this, this same person also claimed that in certain ways, HIP had been successful. See also the discussion of the commune "Strawberry Point" in Yablonsky, 1968:46–51.

must conform to the specific goal. Thus, formal organizations cannot maximize freedom.[8]

Dedication to an ideology (or purpose) has a different impact on freedom than is true of orientation to a specific goal, in at least two ways. First, there is the difficulty in knowing whether the organization is attaining its purpose (i.e., in the light of the ideology). Accordingly, the organization may permit considerable freedom to its members simply because there is often no way to know whether the individual's behavior really threatens the ideology. Second, ideologies vary in the degree to which they put people first. Some have specifically denied freedom to certain people: The Nazis had their Jews, the Communists have their Bourgeoisie. But movements with repressive ideologies, no less than other movements, select people who *want* to join, who are free to join. These are the party members. Freedom is then denied the non-member. The communes studied here differ from repressive movements in that the communes do not limit the freedom of non-members.

The proposition does not say that communal organizations maximize freedom. There are many cases that one could cite to the contrary. However, the hypothesis may be offered that *only* in communal organizations is freedom maximized. A comparison of freedom in communes with that in other vills will not test the hypothesis, but it does suggest ways of maximizing freedom. The difference is found mainly in that the members of the communes have committed themselves *to something*, i.e., to an ideology. This is one dimension of freedom, and it may be called "freedom of discipline." The monks of Palisades Abbey are an especially revealing case. In spite of the fact that they are deprived of numerous things (including, of course, sex and food), they register very few outward expressions of frustration or deprivation. The explanation is simple, but its importance requires that it be clearly spelled out: the monks have chosen their deprivation, and although they certainly feel deprived, they accept their condition (and are free to leave whenever they wish). Though deprived, they are still free, because the deprivation is of their own choosing.

The normal vill member, on the other hand, drifts from job to job, into (or out of) marriage, from vill to vill, as circumstances determine, and the circumstances are generally not selected by him. In contrast, by choosing

[8] This reasoning does not mean that formal organizations have no freedom whatever. Deprivation of freedom in formal organizations is minimized in several ways: (1) If formal organizations require only part-time attendance (such as an eight-hour day), then the person can be free outside of the system (as is true of the staff in a prison, for example). (2) If the person is free to choose his job and leave it, then he is to that extent free. Persons who would be bound to a specific job because of monetary or other circumstances are thus less free. (3) The wider the choice of jobs, the more free the individual becomes. It is recognized, of course, that some members—the rulers (or the administration)—may be more free than others.

an ideology, the commune member selects a discipline, a "circumstance" that determines many other choices. The commune member thus chooses the source of his choices; the vill member chooses mainly the effects.

CONCLUSION

What has been learned by treating communes as experimental communal organizations? Most apparent is the role of the family. We may suggest that the family may not be indispensable to communal organizations but that if it is removed, then the system must make certain major and even radical adjustments. As a minimum, it must have some system of recruitment. But the heavy emphasis on ideology among the communes that have been studied here (including the negative case of HIP) shows that only an intense commitment to some ideology can permit such an exclusion in the first place, and that in many cases the commune itself will do things to strengthen the function of the family, if the family is going to exist at all.

But the importance of the family is shown also in another way: There seems to be no middle ground: either the family is present or it is totally excluded, with heavy sanctions on the exclusion (as in celibacy). Thus, in whatever way, the family is a force to be reckoned with.

However, it was also seen that the family becomes subject to the commune in ways in which it is not subject to more normal communal organizations. Again, the importance of the ideology is evident: For a commune to be successful, the family must conform to the ideology no less than the individual—or at least so it would appear from these limited data (See Kanter 1971, 1972).

The cooperative norms in communes seem to be emphasized to a degree greater than occurs in more normal communities, such as vills. The spatial influence, however, seems less important. Perhaps in both cases, we can turn to the ideology as an explanation. The very existence of an ideology presumes that people have agreed to cooperate, if in no other way than to follow the ideology. And the ideology must be strong enough to override the usual dictates of space—or at least it has been so strong. (The size of communes may be a partial explanation—they have been small enough to control their space; perhaps they must be small enough or they will not last.) We may find here a clue that could help explain the rarity of communes. They require a commitment far beyond that required in other communal organizations (see Kanter, 1968, 1972). Such intensity means that, by definition, only a few will succeed. But this condition raises another question: why must the commitment be so intense? The answer is suggested that the usual pattern of communal organizations, as found in vills, becomes so closely attuned to the human condition that only a massive effort can succeed in breaking from it.

This conclusion should not be interpreted to mean that vills are more "natural" than communes, or that they are somehow more "right." It should be interpreted as a testimony to the strength of the patterns that vills have universally developed and the strength of the effort needed to achieve any significant alternative.

REFERENCES

Andrews, Edward Deming.
    1963   The People Called Shakers. New York: Dover.
Carden, Maren Lockwood.
    1969   Oneida: Utopian Community to Modern Corporation. Baltimore: The Johns Hopkins Press.
Giallombardo, Rose.
    1966   Society of Women: A Study of a Women's Prison. New York: John Wiley and Sons.
Gould, Julius and William L. Kolb, eds.
    1964   A Dictionary of the Social Sciences. New York: The Free Press.
Hillery, George A., Jr.
    1955   "Definitions of community: areas of agreement." Rural Sociology 20 (June):111–123.
    1963   "Villages, cities, and total institutions." American Sociological Review 28 (October):779–791.
    1968   Communal Organizations: A Study of Local Societies. Chicago: University of Chicago Press.
    1971a   "Freedom and social organization: a comparative analysis." American Sociological Review 36 (February):51–65.
Hostetler, John A. and Gertrude Enders Huntington.
    1967   The Hutterites in North America. New York: Holt, Rinehart and Winston.
Kanter, Rosabeth Moss.
    1968   "Commitment and social organization: A study of commitment mechanisms in utopian communities." American Sociological Review 33 (August):499–517.
    1971   "Women, men, and the family in communal orders." Unpublished manuscript (April).
    1972   Commitment and Community: Communes and Utopias in Sociological Perspective. Cambridge: Harvard University Press.
Kaufman, Harold F.
    1959   "Toward an interactional conception of community." Social Forces 38 (October):8–17.

Neal, Mary Julia, ed.
  1963   The Journal of Eldress Nancy. Nashville: Parthenon.
Parsons, Talcott.
  1960   Structure and Process in Modern Societies. Glencoe, Ill: The
         Free Press.
Redekop, Calvin.
  1970   "Lisa Place Fellowship: the gathering of a people." Unpublished
         manuscript.
Shevky, Eshref, and Wendell, Bell.
  1955   Social Area Analysis, Stanford: Stanford University Press.
Spiro, Melford E.
  1956   Kibbutz: Venture in Utopia. Cambridge: Harvard University
         Press.
  1958   Children of the Kibbutz. Cambridge: Harvard University Press.
Theodorson, George A., ed.
  1961   Studies in Human Ecology. Evanston, Ill.: Row, Peterson and
         Co.
Yablonsky, Lewis.
  1968   The Hippie Trip. New York: Pegasus.

43. Communes and Commitment

BY ROSABETH MOSS KANTER

The primary issue with which a utopian community must cope in order to have the strength and solidarity to endure is its human organization: how people arrange to do the work that the community needs to survive as a group, and how the group in turn manages to satisfy and involve its members over a long period of time. The idealized version of communal life must be meshed with the reality of the work to be done in a community, involving difficult problems of social organization. In utopia, for instance, who takes out the garbage?

The organizational problems with which utopian communities must grapple break down into several categories:

How to get the work done, but without coercion;

How to ensure that decisions are made, but to everyone's satisfaction;

How to build close, fulfilling relationships, but without exclusiveness;

How to choose and socialize new members;

How to include a degree of autonomy, individual uniqueness, and even deviance;

How to ensure agreement and shared perception around community functioning and values.

These issues can be summarized as one of commitment; that is, they reflect how members become committed to the community's work, to its values, and to each other, and how much of their former independence they are willing to suspend in the interests of the group. Committed members work hard, participate actively, derive love and affection from the communal group, and believe strongly in what the group stands for.

For communes, the problem of commitment is crucial. Since the community represents an attempt to establish an ideal social order within the larger society, it must vie with the outside for the members' loyalties. It must ensure high member involvement despite external competition without sacrificing its distinctiveness or ideals. It must often contravene the earlier socialization of its members in securing obedience to new demands. It must calm

Reprinted with permission of the author and publisher from pp. 64–74 of Rosabeth Moss Kanter, *Commitment and Community: Communes and Utopias in Sociological Perspective*, Cambridge, Mass.: Harvard University Press, Copyright 1972 by the President and Fellows of Harvard College. Footnotes have been renumbered.

internal dissension in order to present a united front to the world. The problem of securing total and complete commitment is central.

Because communes consciously separate from the established order, their needs for the concentration of members' loyalty and devotion are stronger than are those of groups operating with the support of society and leaving members free to participate in the larger system. The commitment problems of utopian communities resemble those of secret societies, as described by Georg Simmel: "The secret society claims the whole individual to a greater extent, connects its members in more of their totality, and mutually obligates them more closely than does an open society of identical content."[1] The essence of such a community is in strong connections and mutual obligations. Communal life depends on a continual flow of energy and support among members, on their depth of shared relationships, and on their continued attachment to each other and to the joint endeavor.

DEFINITIONS

For communal relations to be maintained, what the person is willing to give to the group, behaviorally and emotionally, and what it in turn expects of him, must be coordinated and mutually reinforcing. This reciprocal relationship, in which both what is given to the group and what is received from it are seen by the person as expressing his true nature and as supporting his concept of self, is the core of commitment to a community. A person is committed to a group or to a relationship when he himself is fully invested in it, so that the maintenance of his own internal being requires behavior that supports the social order. A committed person is loyal and involved; he has a sense of belonging, a feeling that the group is an extension of himself and he is an extension of the group. Through commitment, person and group are inextricably linked.

Commitment arises as a consideration at the intersection between the organizational requisites of groups and the personal orientations and preferences of their members. On the one hand, social systems must organize to meet their systemic "needs"; on the other hand, people must orient themselves positively and negatively, emotionally and intellectually, to situations. While the system is making specific demands for participation, group relatedness, and control, the people in it are investing more or less of themselves, are deciding to stay or to leave, are concentrating varying degrees of their emotional lives in the group, and are fervently obeying or finding ways to sabotage basic principles and rules of the system. For the group to get

[1] Georg Simmel, "The Secret Society," in *The Sociology of Georg Simmel,* ed. Kurt H. Wolff (New York, 1964), p. 366.

what it needs for existence and growth at the same time that people become positively involved requires organizational solutions that are simultaneously mechanisms to ensure commitment by affecting people's orientations to the group.

Commitment thus refers to the willingness of people to do what will help maintain the group because it provides what they need. In sociological terms, commitment means the attachment of the self to the requirements of social relations that are seen as self-expressive.[2] Commitment links self-interest to social requirements. A person is committed to a relationship or to a group to the extent that he sees it as expressing or fulfilling some fundamental part of himself; he is committed to the degree that he perceives no conflict between its requirements and his own needs; he is committed to the degree that he can no longer meet his needs elsewhere. When a person is committed, what he wants to do (through internal feeling) is the same as what he has to do (according to external demands), and thus he gives to the group what it needs to maintain itself at the same time that he gets what he needs to nourish his own sense of self. To a great extent, therefore, commitment is not only important for the survival of a community, but also is part of the essence of community. It forms the connection between self-interest and group interest. It is that identification of the self with a group which Charles Horton Cooley considered essential for self-realization.

To determine the links between person and system that forge the bonds of commitment, one must first distinguish the three major aspects of a social system that involve commitment: retention of members, group cohesiveness, and social control.[3] Retention refers to people's willingness to stay in the system, to continue to staff it and carry out their roles. Group cohesiveness denotes the ability of people to "stick together," to develop the mutual attraction and collective strength to withstand threats to the group's existence.

[2] This definition bears some similarity to Talcott Parson's notion of "institutionalization."

[3] Although recruitment would seem at first glance to be as important as retention of people for continuation of a system, the two problems are distinct, requiring for solution different kinds of organization strategies. Recruitment does not necessarily require commitment but may be accomplished in many other ways with noncommitted actors (for example, birth, accident, and external organizational phenomena may serve to recruit uncommitted individuals). However, once a person has performed any single act within a system, the problem arises of committing him to further and future participation. Thus, the commitment necessary for continuation involves retaining participants, and recruiting them is not a commitment problem (though of course the ways in which they are recruited have implications for commitment). In very complex systems, it might also seem likely that group cohesiveness would be limited to peer groups. However, if cohesiveness is defined not in terms of sociability and mutual attraction but rather in terms of the ability to withstand disruptive forces and threats from outside the group ("sticking together"), it applies to systems of any degree of complexity. See Neal Gross and William Martin, "On Group Cohesiveness," *American Journal of Sociology,* 57 (December 1952), 533–546.

And social control involves the readiness of people to obey the demands of the system, to conform to its values and beliefs and take seriously its dictates.

Continuance, cohesion, and control are three analytically distinct problems, with potentially independent solutions. A person may be committed to continuing his membership but be continually deviant within the group, disloyal and disobedient—that is, *un*committed to its control and unwilling to carry out the norms and values that represent system policy. A rebellious child may reject parental control but be unwilling or unable to withdraw from the family system; he may subvert the values of the system yet be committed to remain within it. Furthermore, a person may be highly attracted to a group within a social system but be uncommitted to continued participation in the system because of other circumstances. An office worker, for example, may take a better job even though his best friends work in his former office. The inmate of a prison may form close ties with fellow prisoners and even with guards, yet certainly wish to leave the system at the earliest opportunity. In specific social systems, one or another of these commitment problems may be of paramount importance. A business organization may concentrate on solving problems of continuance rather than cohesion; a T-group or encounter group may be concerned solely about cohesion; a religious organization may stress control. In other cases the three may be causally related, with solutions to all three problems mutually reinforcing and multiply determined. In a utopian community, for instance, which emphasizes all three aspects of commitment, the more the members are attracted to one another, the more they also wish to continue their membership, and the more they are able to support wholeheartedly its values. Despite this possible overlap, however, for purposes of understanding the roots of commitment, continuance, cohesion, and control must be separated.

At the same time, a person orients himself to a social system instrumentally, affectively, and morally. That is, he orients himself with respect to the rewards and costs that are involved in participating in the system, with respect to his emotional attachment to the people in the system, and with respect to the moral compellingness of the norms and beliefs of the system. In the language of social action theory, he cognizes, cathects, and evaluates.[4] Cognitive orientations discriminate among objects, describing their possibilities for gratification or deprivation, and distinguishing their location and charactertistics. Cathectic orientations represent an emotional state with respect to objects, the kind and amount of feeling they generate. Evaluative orientations refer to standards of judgment: good or bad, right or wrong. As a person relates to the world around him, he gives each element a "rating"

[4] Talcott Parsons and Edward A. Shils, eds., *Toward a General Theory of Action* (New York, 1962), pp. 4–6, 11.

on these three dimensions, and he chooses to behave toward it in accordance with his rating, the degree of its positive or negative value for him.

People orient themselves to social systems in the same way, and the value of a system in each of the three dimensions defines a person's behavior toward it. The system can organize in such a way as to ensure its positive value for the person around each orientation, and if it does, it gains commitment in the three areas that are essential to maintain the system. Each of the personal orientations has the potential to support one particular concern of the social system. Positive cognition can support continuance, positive cathexis can support group cohesion, and positive evaluation can support social control.

Commitment to continued participation in a system involves primarily a person's cognitive or instrumental orientations. When profits and costs are considered, participants find that the cost of leaving the system would be greater than the cost of remaining; "profit," in a net psychic sense, compels continued participation. In a more general sense, this kind of commitment can be conceptualized as commitment to a social system role. It may be called instrumental commitment. Commitment to relationships, to group solidarity, involves primarily a person's cathectic orientations; ties of emotion bind members to each other and to the community they form, and gratifications stem from involvement with all members of the group. Solidarity should be high; infighting and jealousy low. A cohesive group has strong emotional bonds and can withstand threats to its existence; members "stick together." This quality may be called affective commitment. Commitment to uphold norms, obey the authority of the group, and support its values, involves primarily a person's evaluative orientations. When demands made by the system are evaluated as right, moral, just, or expressing one's own values, obedience to these demands becomes a normative necessity, and sanctioning by the system is regarded as appropriate.[5] This quality is here designated moral commitment. In some respects, commitment to norms and values resembles the concept of a superego, which binds the evaluative components of the self to the norms of a system through an internalized authority.

Each of the three kinds of commitment has different consequences for the system and for the individual. Ignoring for the moment all the other diverse sources of influence on group life, groups in which people have formed instrumental commitments should manage to hold their members. Groups in which people have formed affective commitments should report more mutual attraction and interpersonal satisfaction and should be able to withstand threats to their existence. Groups in which members have formed

[5] Social control is possible without moral commitments, of course, but it should not be as efficient or effective.

moral commitments should have less deviance, challenge to authority, or ideological controversy. Groups with all three kinds of commitment, that is, with total commitment, should be more successful in their maintenance than those without it.

At the same time, there are consequences for the person in making these commitments. If the group is such that a person feels he can make an instrumental commitment, he becomes invested in it and finds his membership rewarding. If the group is such that he can make an affective commitment, he gains strong social ties, relatedness, and a sense of belonging. If the group is such that he can make a moral commitment, he gains purpose, direction, and meaning, a sense that his acts stem from essential values. To some extent, a person's identity is composed of his commitments.

COMMITMENT-BUILDING PROCESSES

A group has a number of ways in which to organize so as to promote and sustain the three kinds of commitment. For each commitment, it needs to set in motion processes that reduce the value of other possible commitments and increase the value of commitment to the communal group—that is, processes both detaching the person from other options and attaching him to the community. The person must give up something as well as get something in order to be committed to a community; communes, like all other social systems, have their costs of membership. The person must invest himself in the community rather than elsewhere and commit his resources and energy there, removing them from wherever else they may be invested, or from whatever alternatives exist for commitment. Commitment thus involves choice—discrimination and selection of possible courses of action. It rests on a person's awareness of excluded options, on the knowledge of the virtues of his choice over others. A person becomes increasingly committed both as more of his own internal satisfaction becomes dependent on the group, and as his chance to make other choices or pursue other options declines. This is commitment in Howard Becker's sense.[6] A course of action may involve more of a person's resources, reputation, or choices than he consciously chose to commit, with the result that the line of action simultaneously cuts him off from the chance to commit himself elsewhere. This process is similar, according to Becker, to the making of side bets, gambling on the fact that each step toward complete commitment will pay off. If the commitment is not sustained, and the line of action is not continued, the person then loses more than his original investment. Side bets, therefore, deriving from the fact that any choice may re-

[6] Howard S. Becker, "Notes on the Concept of Commitment," *American Journal of Sociology*, 66 (July 1960), 32–40.

duce the chances of ever taking up excluded choices, help to bring about commitment. These processes of giving up and getting make the group a clearly focused object for commitment. The clearer and more defined a group becomes to a person, the easier it is for him to concentrate his commitment there. This process contains the first principles of a "gestalt sociology": to develop maximum commitment in its members, a group must form a unity or a whole, coherent and sharply differentiated from its environment —a figure clearly distinguished from the ground, whether the ground is the outside society or excluded options for behavior. Commitment to social systems, concentrating the psychic energy in a group, may operate according to the same gestalt principles as object perception. According to these principles, the issue of commitment would occur primarily around the boundaries of a group. The group builds commitment to the extent that it clearly cuts off other possible objects of commitment, becomes an integrated unity tying together all aspects of life within its borders, develops its own uniqueness and specialness, and becomes capable, by itself, of continuing the person's gratification. The strength of commitment, then, depends on the extent to which groups institute processes that increase the unity, coherence, and possible gratification of the group itself, at the same time that they reduce the value of other possibilities. The six commitment-building processes proposed do just that.

Commitment to continued participation involves securing a person's positive instrumental orientations, inducing the individual to cognize participation in the organization as profitable when considered in terms of rewards and costs. Cognitive orientations are those that rationally determine the positive or negative valences of relationships, perceiving their worth in energy and resources. In a purely cognitive judgment, no notion of emotional gratification (cathexis) or of morality (evaluation) is attached to the group. For positive cognition to be acquired by a community, the system must organize so that participation is viewed as rewarding. The individual who makes an instrumental commitment finds that what is profitable to him is bound up with his position in the organization and is contingent on his participating in the system; he commits himself to a role. For the person there is a "profit" associated with continued participation and a "cost" connected with leaving. Thus, sacrifice (detaching) and investment (attaching) are among the components of instrumental commitments. Sacrifice involves the giving up of something considered valuable or pleasurable in order to belong to the organization; it stresses the importance of the role of member to the individual. Sacrifice means that membership becomes more costly and is therefore not lightly regarded nor likely to be given up easily. Investment is a process whereby the individual gains a stake in the group, commits current and future profits to it, so that he must continue to participate if he is going to realize those profits. Investment generally involves the giving up of control over some of the person's resources to the community.

Community is based in part on the desire for strong relations within a collectivity, for intense emotional feeling among all members, for brotherhood and sharing. Utopia is the place where a person's fundamental emotional needs can be expressed and met through the communal group. The community seeks to become a family in itself, replacing or subsuming all other family loyalties. It is this kind of relating, involving commitment to group cohesion, that enables the community to withstand threats to its existence, both as pressure from the outside and as tension and dissent from inside.

Commitment to group cohesion and solidarity requires the attachment of a person's entire fund of emotion and affectivity to the group; emotional gratification stems from participation in and identification with a collective whole. Emotional commitment becomes commitment to a set of social relationships. The individual commits himself to the group as his primary set of relations; his loyalty and allegiance are offered to all the members of the group, who together comprise a community. The group thus has tight social bonds cementing it together. In cases where strong ingroup loyalty is present, a community can stick together even though it is forcibly removed from its home, loses its crop, or is threatened with a lawsuit. Such intense family-like involvement also makes members more willing to work out whatever conflicts and tensions may arise among them. This kind of commitment is aided by renunciation (a detaching process) and communion (an attaching process). Renunciation involves giving up competing relationships outside the communal group and individualistic, exclusive attachments within. Whatever fund of emotion the individuals possess becomes concentrated in the group itself, glueing all members together, creating a cohesive unit. It is to this unit alone that members look for emotional satisfaction and to which they give their loyalty and commitment. Communion involves bringing members into meaningful contact with the collective whole, so that they experience the fact of oneness with the group and develop a "we-feeling."

The search for community is also a quest for direction and purpose in a collective anchoring of the individual life. Investment of self in a community, acceptance of its authority and willingness to support its values, is dependent in part on the extent to which group life can offer identity, personal meaning, and the opportunity to grow in terms of standards and guiding principles that the member feels are expressive of his own inner being. Commitment to community norms and values, or moral commitment, involves securing a person's positive evaluative orientations, redefining his sense of values and priorities so that he considers the system's demands right and just in terms of his self-identity and supporting the group's authority becomes a moral necessity. The person making a moral commitment to his community should see himself as carrying out the dictates of a higher system, which orders and gives meaning to his life. He internalizes community standards and values and accepts its control, because it provides him with something transcendent. This commitment requires, first, that the person reformulate and re-evaluate his identity in terms of meeting the ideals set by the community. For this to occur, the group must first provide ways for an individual to reassess his previous life, to undo those parts of himself he wishes to change, and to perceive that identity and meaning for him lie not in an individualistic, private existence but in acceptance of the stronger influence of the utopian group. At the same time, the person must experience the greater power and meaning represented by the community, so that he will attach his sense of identity and worth to carrying out its demands and requirements. Thus, mortification (a detaching process) and transcendence (an attaching process) promote evaluative, moral commitments. Mortification involves the submission of private states to social control, the exchanging of a former identity for one defined and formulated by the community. Transcendence is a process whereby an individual attaches his decision-making prerogative to a power greater than himself, surrendering to the higher meaning contained by the group and submitting to something beyond himself. Mortification opens the person to new directions and new growth; transcendence defines those directions. Mortification causes the person to "lose himself"; transcendence permits him to find himself anew in something larger and greater.

Six processes are thus available to build commitment to communal groups. To the extent that groups develop concrete organizational strategies around these processes—commitment mechanisms—they should generate a stronger commitment than can those without such strategies. The number and kind of commitment mechanisms instituted should contribute to a community's success—its ability to endure and continue to satisfy its members.

Index

A

Abel, Theodore, 272
Adler, Kenneth, P., 188
Adler, M., 500
Administered community, 505
Adrian, Charles R., 186, 235, 244
Advocate planners, 440ff.
Agger, Robert E., 176, 185, 235, 242, 318
Aginsky, Burt W., 77
Agrarianism, 124
Aiken, Michael T., 174, 177, 235ff., 238, 239, 241, 242, 476
Aleshire, Robert A., 380
Alexander, Frank D., 64
Alford, Robert R., 174, 235ff., 238, 242
Alicia, Victor G., 309, 387
Alinsky, Saul D., 76, 359
Alternative communities, 449ff.:
    types, 502ff.
Altshuler, Alan A., 374, 378, 380
Anderson, C. Arnold, 72, 457, 461
Andrews, Edward Deming, 525
Anti-communities, 508
Anton, Thomas, 380
Arensberg, C. M., 456, 457, 458, 461
Arnstein, Sherry R., 310, 365, 366, 372, 374, 376, 378, 380, 405ff.
Ascher, Charles S., 369, 375, 380
Ash, Joan, 380
Associations, 348ff.
Austin, David M., 373, 375, 376, 378, 381

B

Babcock, R., 381
Bahrdt, Hans Paul, 3, 12ff.
Baida, Robert, 381
Bain, Henry, 490, 492
Balcer, Elizabeth, 235
Baldwin, Burt R., 386
Balzell, E. D., 220, 224, 228
Banfield, Edward C., 103, 131ff., 143, 237, 242, 244, 278, 280, 291, 298, 317, 356, 500, 507
Barber, Bernard, 76, 173, 195, 216ff.
Barber, Richard J., 480

Barrows, H. H., 41
Barth, Ernest A. T., 235, 242
Basu, A. K., 457
Becker, Howard S., 75, 188, 256, 532
Beegle, J. Allan, 74
Belknap, Ivan, 175
Bell, Daniel, 278, 481
Bell, Wendell, 381, 463, 512, 526
Bellah, R. N., 227
Benello, C. G., 486
Bensman, Joseph, 172, 203ff., 220, 224, 253, 462, 478
Bentley, Arthur, 49
Berelson, Bernard, 261, 271
Berger, Bennett M., 105, 152ff., 163, 495, 501
Berger, Monroe, 272
Berger, Peter L., 336
Berle, Adolf A., 481
Bernard, Jessie, 64, 457, 458, 461
Bestor, A., 501
Bike, E., 381
Birch, A. H., 480
Blackwell, Gordon W., 76
Blankenship, L. Vaughn, 175
Blasé attitude, 24
Blau, Peter, 98, 282, 283, 287ff., 297, 298
Blauner, Robert, 139
Bloomberg, Warner, 175
Blumberg, Leonard, 229
Boat, M. D., 463
Bobrow, Davis, 188
Bondurant, Joan V., 397, 400
Boone, Richard, 381
Booth, David A., 186
Bosselman, F., 381
Bradley, Phillips, 348
Brignac, Ronald L., 371, 381
Broek, Johannes Hase, 10
Brooks, Richard, 453, 488ff.
Brower, Michael, 486
Brown, J. F., 65
Brownell, Baker, 62, 83, 468, 476
Buchanan, Jeffrey D., 381
Burgess, Ernest W., 42, 254
Burke, Edmund M., 375, 381
Butler, Edgar W., 180, 477

536

PRINTED IN U.S.A.